*The Friars in Ireland, 1224–1540*

# The Friars in Ireland
## 1224–1540

Colmán Ó Clabaigh OSB

FOUR COURTS PRESS

Typeset in 10.5 pt on 13.5 pt AGaramond by
Carrigboy Typesetting Services for
FOUR COURTS PRESS LTD
7 Malpas Street, Dublin 8, Ireland
www.fourcourtspress.ie
and in North America for
FOUR COURTS PRESS
c/o ISBS, 920 NE 58th Avenue, Suite 300, Portland, OR 97213.

A catalogue record for this title is available
from the British Library.

ISBN 978–1–84682–224–7 hbk
978–1–84682–225–4 pbk

Printed in England
by Antony Rowe, Chippenham, Wilts.

# Contents

# Abbreviations

| | |
|---|---|
| *AFH* | *Archivum Franciscanum Historicum.* |
| *AFM* | *Annála ríoghachta Éireann: Annals of the Four Masters from the earliest period to the year 1616*, ed. John O'Donovan (7 vols, Dublin, 1851). |
| *AH* | *Archivium Hibernicum.* |
| *ALC* | *The Annals of Loch Cé: a chronicle of Irish affairs, 1014–1590*, ed. W.M. Hennessy (2 vols, London, 1871). |
| *AM* | *Annales Minorum seu trium ordinum a S. Francisco institutorum*, L. Wadding OFM (Quaracchi, 1931–). |
| *Anal. Hib.* | *Analecta Hibernica.* |
| *Ann. Conn.* | *Annála Connacht (AD1224–1544)*, ed. A.M. Freeman (Dublin, 1951). |
| *AS* | 'Abbreviatio statutorum tam papalium quam generalium edita apud Barchinonam in conventu Beatae Mariae de Iesu Familiae Cismontanae de Observantia [1451]', ed. M. Bihl, *AFH*, 37 (1942), 106–97; also ed. R. Howlett, *Monumenta Franciscana* (2 vols, London, 1882), ii, pp 81–119. |
| *AU* | *Annála Uladh, Annals of Ulster; otherwise Annála Senait: a chronicle of Irish affairs, 431–1131, 1155–1541*, ed. W.M. Hennessy & B. MacCarthy (4 vols, Dublin, 1887–1901). |
| BAR | British Archaeological Reports. |
| *BF* | *Bullarium Franciscanum Romanorum Pontificum constitutiones, epistolae, ac diplomata continens tribus ordinibus minorum clarissarum et poenitentium a seraphica sancto Francisco institutis concessa ab illorum exordio ad nostra usque tempora*, ed. J.H. Sbaralea et al. (7 vols, Rome, 1759–1904). |
| *BFNS* | *Bullarium Franciscanum continens constitutiones epistolas diplomata Romanorum pontificum, nova series*, ed. U. Hüntemann & C. Schmitt (4 vols, Quarrachi, 1929–). |
| BL | British Library, London. |
| BL Add. MSS | British Library, Additional MSS. |
| BL Harl. MSS | British Library, Harleian MSS. |
| Bodl. | Bodleian Library, Oxford. |
| 'Brevis synopsis' | 'F. O'Mahony: Brevis synopsis provinciae Hiberniae fratrum minorum', ed. B. Jennings, *Anal. Hib.*, 6 (1934), 139–91. |
| 'Brussels MS 3410' | 'Micheál Ó Cléirigh: A chronological list of the foundations of the Irish Franciscan province', ed. J. Moloney, *Anal. Hib.*, 6 (1934), 192–202. |

'Brussels MS 3947'   'Donatus Moneyus: De Provincia Hiberniae S. Francisci', ed.
                     B. Jennings, *Anal. Hib.*, 6 (1934), 12–138; trans. in *Franciscan*
                     *Tertiary*, 4 (Feb. 1894) –6 (Dec. 1896).
*BRUO*               *A biographical register of the University of Oxford to 1500*, ed. A.B.
                     Emden (3 vols, Oxford, 1957–9).
*Bull. Carm.*        *Bullarium Carmelitanum*, ed. E. Monsignano (2 vols, Rome, 1715).
*Bull. OP*           *Bullarium ordinis fratrum Praedicatorum*, ed. T. Ripoll & A.
                     Bremond (8 vols, Rome, 1729–40).
*CLAHJ*              *County Louth Archaeological and Historical Journal.*
Clyn, *Annals*       *The annals of Ireland by Friar John Clyn*, ed. B. Williams (Dublin,
                     2007).
Coleman, 'Regestum'  Ambrose Coleman (ed.), 'Regestum Monasterii Fratrum
                     Praedicatorum de Athenry', *Archivium Hibernicum*, 1 (1912),
                     201–21.
Colker, *Latin MSS*  M.L. Colker, *Trinity College Library Dublin: descriptive catalogue*
                     *of the medieval and Renaissance Latin manuscripts* (2 vols, Dublin,
                     1991).
Cotter, *Friars Minor*  F.J. Cotter, *The Friars Minor in Ireland from their arrival to 1400*
                     (New York, 1994).
*CDI*                *Calendar of documents relating to Ireland, 1171–1251* [etc.], ed.
                     H.S. Sweetman (5 vols, London, 1875–86).
*CPL*                *Calendar of entries in the papal registers relating to Great Britain and*
                     *Ireland: papal letters* (London & Dublin, 1893–).
*DHR*                *Dublin Historical Record.*
*DIB*                *Dictionary of Irish Biography.*
ed./eds              editor(s); edition; edited by.
Fenning, 'Irish      H. Fenning (ed.), 'Irish material in the registers of the
   material'          Dominican masters general (1360–1649)', *Archivium Fratrum*
                     *Praedicatorum*, 39 (1969), 249–336.
*FL*                 *Materials for the history of the Franciscan province of Ireland*, ed.
                     E.B. Fitzmaurice & A.G. Little (Manchester, 1920).
Glassberger,         *Chronica Fratris Nicolai Glassberger* (*Analecta Franciscana*, 2,
   *Chronicle*        Quarrachi, 1887).
Huber, *History*     R.M. Huber, *A documented history of the Franciscan order*
                     (Washington, DC, 1944).
*IHS*                *Irish Historical Studies: the Joint Journal of the Irish Historical*
                     *Society and the Ulster Society for Irish Historical Studies.*
*JCHAS*              *Journal of the Cork Historical and Archaeological Society.*
*JCKAHS*             *Journal of the County Kildare Archaeological and Historical Society.*
*JGAHS*              *Journal of the Galway Archaeological and Historical Society.*
Jones, *Friars' tales*  D. Jones, *Friars' tales: thirteenth-century exempla from the British*
                     *Isles* (Manchester, 2011).

| | |
|---|---|
| *JRSAI* | *Journal of the Royal Society of Antiquaries of Ireland.* |
| *Lib. ex.* | *Liber exemplorum ad usum praedicantium saeculo xiii compositus a quondam fratre minore Anglico de provincia Hiberniae*, ed. A.G. Little (Aberdeen, 1918). |
| Lynch, 'Franciscan docs' | A. Lynch (ed.), 'Documents of Franciscan interest from the episcopal archives of Armagh, 1265–1508', *Collectanea Hibernica*, 31 & 32 (1989–90), 9–102. |
| Martin, 'Augustinian friaries' | F.X. Martin OSA, 'The Augustinian friaries in pre-Reformation Ireland (1280–1500)', *Augustiniana*, 6 (1956), 346–84. |
| Martin & de Meijer, 'Irish material' | F.X. Martin OSA & Alberic de Meijer OSA (eds), 'Irish material in the Augustinian general archives, Rome, 1354–1624', *AH*, 19 (1956), 61–134. |
| McKenna, *Ó Huiginn* | L. McKenna (ed.), *Philip bocht Ó Huiginn* (Dublin, 1931). |
| Moorman, *History* | J.R.H. Moorman, *A history of the Franciscan order from its origins to the year 1517* (Oxford, 1968 [repr. Chicago, 1988]). |
| *MOPH* | *Monumenta Ordinis Fratrum Praedicatorum.* |
| *MRH* | A. Gwynn and R.N. Hadcock, *Medieval religious houses: Ireland* (Dublin, 1970 [repr. Dublin, 1988]). |
| NLI | National Library of Ireland, Dublin. |
| NUI | National University of Ireland. |
| NUIM | National University of Ireland, Maynooth. |
| Ó Clabaigh, *Franciscans* | Colmán Ó Clabaigh, *The Franciscans in Ireland, 1400–1534: from reform to Reformation* (Dublin, 2002). |
| *ODNB* | *Oxford dictionary of national biography* (Oxford, 2004). |
| *Ormond deeds* | E. Curtis (ed.), *Calendar of Ormond deeds* (6 vols, Dublin, 1932–43). |
| O'Sullivan, *MIDS* | Benedict O'Sullivan OP, *Medieval Irish Dominican studies*, ed. Hugh Fenning OP (Dublin, 2009). |
| Pembridge, *Chronicle* | [Chronicle of Friar John Pembridge OP] in J.T. Gilbert (ed.), *Chartularies of St Mary's Abbey, Dublin, with the register of its house at Dunbrody and Annals of Ireland* (2 vols, 1884), ii, pp 303–98. |
| *PRIA* | *Proceedings of the Royal Irish Academy.* |
| TCD | Trinity College Dublin. |
| trans. | translation/translated by. |
| UCC | University College Cork. |
| UCD | University College Dublin. |
| *YLC* | Youghal Library Catalogue in Ó Clabaigh, *Franciscans*, pp 158–80. |

# Acknowledgments

During the long period that it has taken me to research and write this book, I have incurred many debts of gratitude that it is both my duty and my pleasure to acknowledge. In the first instance, I thank my abbot, Fr Mark Patrick Hederman OSB, his predecessor, Fr Christopher Dillon, OSB, and my *confrères* at Glenstal Abbey, for their support and encouragement which, along with that of my father, Mossey Clabby, enabled me to bring this work to completion.

My greatest debt is to those mentors whose passion for the past proved contagious: Thomas Bartlett; Nicholas Canny; Sr M. De Lourdes Fahy RSM; Bridie Clabby NT†; Maura Donoghue†; Fr Colman Cooke; George Cunningham; Caitriona Clear; Seán Devlin; Steven Ellis; Peter Harbison; Colm Lennon; James Lydon; Alexander Murray; Bishop Breandán Ó Ceallaigh; Peadar Ó Conaire NT; Dáibhí Ó Cróinín; Gearóid Ó Tuathaigh; Leslie Smith; Fr Norman Tanner SJ; and, above all, an tOllamh Gearóid Mac Niocaill†.

This book was one of a number of projects undertaken while holding fellowships from the Irish Research Council for the Humanities and Social Sciences. I am most grateful to that body for funding my research between 2003 and 2008 and for the opportunities that this support afforded me. I also acknowledge Dr John McCafferty and the UCD Mícheál Ó Cléirigh Institute for the Study of Irish History and Civilization under whose auspices much of this research was conducted.

I am grateful to the library staffs of the National Library of Ireland; Trinity College, Dublin; the James Joyce Library, UCD; the Boole Library, UCC; the James Hardiman library, NUI Galway; the Bodleian Library, Oxford; Lambeth Palace Library, London; the *Biblioteca del Sacro Convento*, Assisi; the *Biblioteca Apostolica Vaticana* and the *Antonianum*, *Angelicum* and *Augustinianum* libaries in Rome. Particular kindness was shown me by Fr Philip Gleeson OP, St Mary's priory, Tallaght; Fr Ignatius Fennessey OFM, Dún Mhuire, Killiney; Siobhan Fitzpatrick and the staff of the Royal Irish Academy; Ruth Long, Carmelite library, Gort Mhuire, Ballinteer; Fr Patrick McMahon OCarm., *Institutum Carmelitanum*, Rome and by Bernard Meehan and the staff of the Department of Manuscripts, TCD.

I thank Tom Brett; Christy Cunniffe; Cathal Duddy OFM; Dundalgan Press, Dundalk; Susan Saul Gibson; Fr Louis Hughes OP; Maurice Hurley; Yvonne McDermott; Fr Fergal MacEoinín OP; Fr Joseph McGilloway OSB; Josephine Moran; Karena Morton; Michael Potterton and Tony Roche for allowing me to produce images from their collections. Particular thanks are due to my *confrère*

Br Emmaus O'Herlihy OSB, who designed the book cover, to Robert Shaw who produced the maps, and to Jimmy Backes and Jack Dwyer who laboured on the index.

I am deeply indebted to the *periti* who kindly read drafts of this book in whole or in part: Bernadette Cunningham; Terry Dolan; Fr Hugh Fenning OP; Alan Fletcher; Raymond Gillespie; Arlene Hogan; Fr David Kelly OSA; Pádraig Lenihan; Marian Lyons; John McCafferty; Clare McCutcheon; Kevin McDonald; Conleth Manning; Karena Morton; Rachel Moss; Kieran O'Conor; Bert Roest; Salvador Ryan and Brendan Smith. I have also gained much from the expertise of the learned members of the Medieval Religion Internet discussion group and the UCD Mícheál Ó Cléirigh Institute seminar. Their comments and corrections have been of immense benefit. The remaining errors are my own.

I owe much to the scholarship of a number of distinguished friar-historians, some deceased, others happily still with us: Thomas Butler OSA; Patrick Conlan OFM; Francis Cotter OFM; Ignatius Fennessy OFM; Hugh Fenning OP; Urban Flanagan OP; Thomas Flynn OP; F.X. Martin OSA; Benignus Millett OFM; Canice Mooney OFM; Fintan O'Brien ODC; Peter O'Dwyer OCarm. and Michael Robson OFM Conv. Likewise, Edel Bhreathnach and Richard Copsey OCarm. generously shared their unpublished research findings with me and spared me an immense amount of labour. However, my greatest debt in this respect is to Bernadette Williams for sharing her friendship, her culinary skills and her encyclopaedic knowledge of medieval mendicants with me for nearly a quarter of a century

I thank those friends who, in various ways, supported me as I pursued this project: Abbot Aidan Bellenger and the monks of Downside Abbey; Derek and Helen Bennett; Damian and Jacaintha Bracken; Kevin Campion and Eva Hughes; the Carmelite communities at St Teresa's priory, Clarendon St. and Avila, Dublin; Tracy Collins and Frank Coyne; Fr Paul Connell; Fr Eamonn Conway; Fr Enda Cunningham; Maurice Deasy; Fr Luke Dempsey OP; Fr Eugene Duffy; Thomas and Marti Finan; Stephen Fuller; James Gleeson; Siobhán Grimes and Paul Reynolds; Herr Anton Höslinger, Can.Reg.; Seamus and Margaret Kelly; the Keating family; Mena and Artie Kenny; Simon and Victoria Kingston; Ben Kitchin; Fr Dick Lyng OSA; Barry Lysaght; Liz McConnell; John and Elizabeth Martin; Brian and Timmie Maurer; Fr Paul Murray OP; Fr James Noonan ODC; Paul Noyes; Donncha O'Connell; Peter O'Donnell; Terence and Jennifer O'Reilly; Pádraig Ó Riain and Dagmar Ó Riain Raedel; Dom Richard Purcell and the monks of Mt St Joseph Abbey, Roscrea; Diarmuid Scully and John Wright.

Amongst my colleagues and students in Glenstal I gratefully acknowledge the assistance and expertise of Greg Ashe; Martin Browne OSB; Maeve Casey; Abbot

Gregory Collins OSB; Matthew Corkery OSB; Peter Hamilton; Ruth Healy; Anthony Keane OSB; Cyprian Love OSB; Columba McCann OSB; Placid Murray OSB; Maree McCarthy; Cillian Ó Sé OSB and Thomas Williams.

Michael Potterton, Martin Fanning and the team at Four Courts Press showed great patience with a tardy author and produced this volume to their house's usual high standard. Its appearance in paperback and the inclusion of colour illustrations was facilitated by generous subventions from Dr Tiarnan Keenan, Fr Martin Kilmurray OCarm., Mrs Brigid O'Higgins-O'Malley and an anonymous bene-factor. To them, my sincere thanks.

This project, like so much else in my life, would have come to nothing without the mild bemusement, robust criticism and unfailing support of Áine, Aoife and Noel Clabby; Máirtín Ó Conaire; Senan Furlong; Joseph McGilloway; James McMahon; William Fennelly and Luke Beckett. In the Testament he composed shortly before his death in 1226, Francis of Assisi gave thanks for the fact that 'the Lord gave me brothers'. In my siblings, brethren and friends I have been likewise blessed and for this blessing I am grateful beyond expression. This book is for you.

Glenstal Abbey
All Saints' Day, 2011

*Ut in omnibus glorificetur Deus*

# Introduction: sources and historiography

This work surveys the history, lifestyle and impact of the orders of mendicant or begging friars in Ireland from the coming of the Dominicans in 1224 to the Henrician campaign to dissolve the monasteries in 1540. It represents an expansion of an earlier work on the late medieval Irish Franciscans and constitutes the first attempt to examine the Irish mendicant phenomenon as a whole, rather than focusing on individual orders and houses.[1]

The first three chapters provide a chronological overview of the expansion and constitutional arrangements of the friars in Ireland from their arrival to the emergence of a second flowering of the movement in the fifteenth and early sixteenth centuries. This is followed by seven thematic chapters that explore discrete aspects of mendicant life and ministry, namely the friars' relations with their patrons and critics; their lifestyle, liturgy and devotional practices; the art and architecture of their houses; their formation structures and the impact that they had as pastoral agents. The volume concludes with an epilogue summarizing developments in the tumultuous decade between 1530 and 1540.

## SOURCES

Very few contemporary sources survive for the individual orders or their foundations in Ireland. Despite this, when viewed synoptically, the surviving material provides a relatively comprehensive picture of mendicant life in late medieval Ireland, particularly when viewed in its broader European context. In addition, the Irish friars and their activities have increasingly attracted the attention of scholars in other disciplines, and the present work has benefitted greatly from the research of archaeologists, architectural and art historians, folklorists, hagiologists, liturgists, musicologists, philosophers and theologians.

## MENDICANT SOURCES

Each mendicant order was a highly centralized international organization whose rules and constitutions governed the experience of its Irish members. In an attempt to regulate the remarkable flowering of religious life that occurred in the late twelfth and early thirteenth centuries, the Fourth Lateran Council (1215)

---

1 C.N. Ó Clabaigh, *The Franciscans in Ireland, 1400–1534* (2002).

decreed that new religious orders had to adopt a rule of life already approved by the church.[2] For the mendicants, these rules enshrined their core values and articulated the fundamental elements of their vocation. Specific details of observance and organization were addressed in the constitutions enacted by the general or provincial chapters or meetings held by each body.[3]

St Dominic Guzman (d. 1221) began his religious life as an Augustinian canon regular and the rule of St Augustine was therefore a natural choice for the nascent Order of Preachers (OP) or Dominicans.[4] (Curiously, the earliest Irish copy of St Augustine's rule survives in a Franciscan volume, TCD MS 347, a late thirteenth-century *vademecum* book associated with the Anglo-Irish friar, Stephen Dexter, where it is accompanied by an extensive commentary.)[5] The rule's flexibility made it eminently suitable for the new endeavour, and from 1216 onwards the Dominicans enacted constitutions to regulate the practical aspects of their lives, initially drawing on those of the Premonstratensian canons. The order's general chapters held in 1220, 1221 and 1228 enacted further legislation and these early constitutions were revised in 1241 by the order's master general, Friar Raymond of Peñafort (d. 1275), a distinguished canon lawyer. His successor, Friar Humbert of Romans (d. 1277), consolidated the friars' identity by producing commentaries on the rule and constitutions as well as on the duties of officials of the order.[6] Subsequent general chapters promulgated additional legislation, but one of the distinctive features of Dominican government was that definitive changes to the constitutions required the approval of three successive general chapters.

St Francis of Assisi (d. 1226) conceived the life of the Friars Minor (OFM) or Franciscans as a perfect imitation of the example of Christ requiring no more than the gospel for guidance. When this proved impractical, he reluctantly made various attempts to draw up a rule for his followers.[7] This took its definitive form in the bull *Solet annuere* issued by Honorius III on 29 November 1223 and subsequently known as the *Regula bullata*.[8] This short document of twelve chapters gave relatively little guidance on practicalities and placed great emphasis on observance of the vow of poverty. The internal divisions that arose over the legal status of the Testament composed by Francis shortly before his death

**2** N.P. Tanner (ed.), *Decrees of the ecumenical councils*, i (1990), 'Ne nimia religionum', p. 242.   **3** For an overview of mendicant legislation, see A. Vauchez & C. Caby (eds), *L'histoire des moines, chanoines et religieux au moyen âge* (2003), pp 133–78.   **4** L. Verheijen (ed.), *La regle de saint Augustin* (1961), pp 417–37.   **5** TCD MS 347, fos 369–71; commentary, fos 371–4.   **6** Humbert of Romans, 'Expositio super constitutions FF Predicatorum' (1888–9), ii, pp 1–178; G.R. Galbraith, *The constitution of the Dominican order, 1216–1360* (1925), pp 175–91; S. Tugwell OP, *Early Dominicans: selected writings* (1982), p. 455; Vauchez & Caby (eds), *L'histoire des moines*, pp 142–6; R. Ombres OP, 'L'autorità religiosa nei Frati Predicatori come Ordine Mendicante' (2008). I am grateful to Dr Ombres for advice on this point.   **7** For an excellent summary of the development of early Franciscan legislation, see P. Etzi, *Iuridica Franciscana* (2005), pp 13–74.   **8** *BF*, i, pp 15–19; C. Esser, *Opuscula* (1978), pp 225–38; R. Armstrong & I. Brady, *Francis and Clare* (1982), pp 136–45.

bedevilled the Franciscan movement for the rest of the Middle Ages. Interestingly, one of the earliest surviving copies of the Testament is also contained in TCD MS 347.[9] Of particular significance was the Testament's moratorium on any attempt to mitigate the *Regula bullata* and its ban on friars appealing for papal dispensations from the rule's precepts.[10] Despite these injunctions, Pope Gregory IX issued the bull *Quo elongati* in September 1230, which stated that the friars were not bound by the Testament and could request authoritative interpretations of the rule from the papacy.[11] This was the first in a series of papal interventions in Franciscan affairs, of which the bulls *Exiit qui seminat* of Nicholas III (1279) and *Exivi de paradiso* of Clement V (1312) were particularly significant.[12] Combined, the three bulls and the *Regula bullata* constituted the normative texts for Franciscan observance throughout the rest of the Middle Ages.

The oldest surviving Irish copy of the *Regula bullata* is contained in TCD MS 97, a late thirteenth-/fourteenth-century manuscript from St Thomas' Abbey in Dublin, a wealthy house of Victorine canons, where it is found in conjunction with *Quo elongati* and *Exiit qui seminat*.[13] Copies of the *Regula bullata*, the Testament and the three definitive papal declarations are included with other Franciscan legislation in Bodleian Library Oxford MS Rawl. C 320, a copy of the *Scripta ordinis* or normative legislation for the Irish Observant friars compiled for the Adare Franciscan community in 1482. The library catalogue of the friars in Youghal indicates that by 1526 the community there possessed two copies of the same volume.[14]

As with the other friars, legislation on practical matters took the form of constitutions, which assumed definitive shape at the 1260 general chapter meeting in Narbonne. These were divided into a prologue and twelve chapters based on the precepts of the *Regula bullata* and summarized much of the legislation enacted since the foundation of the order. Subsequent general chapters made additions and amendments to the text of the Narbonne constitutions.[15] With the emergence of the Observant movement, the constitutions were revised to accommodate the reformers. Of these revisions, the most important in an Irish context was the *Abbreviatio statutorum tam generalium quam papalium* adopted by the Observant Franciscan chapter meeting in Barcelona in 1451. This became the normative legislation for Observant friars north of the Alps and was included in Irish copies of the *Scripta ordinis*.[16]

**9** TCD MS 347, fos 387v–388v.   **10** Esser, *Opuscula*, pp 315–16; Armstrong & Brady, *Francis and Clare*, pp 155–6.   **11** *BF*, i, pp 68–70.   **12** *BF*, i, pp 400–2; *BF*, v, pp 80–6.   **13** TCD MS 97, fos 178–186v; Colker, *Latin MSS*, I, pp 190–1.   **14** *YLC*, nos 10 & 96.   **15** C. Cenci & R.G. Mailleux, *Constitutiones generales ordinis fratrum minorum*, I (*saeculum xiii*) (2007), pp 67–104. Later constitutions are listed in Vauchez & Caby (eds), *L'histoire des moines*, pp 160–4.   **16** M. Bihl (ed.), 'Abbreviatio statutorum tam papalium quam generalium edita apud Barchinonam in conventu Beatae Mariae de Iesu Familiae

The Augustinians or Friars Hermits of St Augustine (OESA) emerged from a union of five groups of Italian solitaries in 1256.[17] In addition to adopting the rule of St Augustine, the first friars adopted statutes and legislation to regulate their lifestyle. The earliest surviving version of the Augustinian constitutions is that promulgated by the general chapter meeting in Ratisbon in 1290.[18] In addition to incorporating some of the order's earlier legislation, the Ratisbon text also borrowed material from the Dominican constitutions.[19] The Ratisbon constitutions consisted of a prologue followed by fifty-one chapters governing all aspects of the friars' lifestyle and the order's administration. Subsequent chapters amended the constitutions and, in 1345, the order's general chapter meeting in Paris commissioned the prior general, Friar Thomas of Strasbourg, to revise the additions. His revision took the form of an appendix to each chapter of the Ratisbon text and was approved by the chapter of Pavia in 1348. The revised constitutions remained normative for the order until 1551.[20]

The Carmelite friars (OCarm.) or the Order of Friars of Our Lady of Mount Carmel, emerged in the late twelfth century from groups of hermits living in the Holy Land. Granted a rule of life *c*.1207 by St Albert, the Latin patriarch of Jerusalem, they claimed the prophet Elijah as their inspiration in the contemplative life and their main centre was on Mount Carmel above Haifa in Northern Palestine, where they had a church dedicated to the Virgin Mary.[21] By the mid-thirteenth century, the political instability of the region led many of the hermits to migrate to Europe and the order's centres of gravity shifted to Cyprus, Sicily, England and the South of France.[22] In tandem with this geographical shift, the friars adopted many of the practices of the Dominicans and Franciscans, establishing priories in towns and cities, adopting a ministry of public preaching and developing an educational system closely modelled on that of the Friars Preachers. These developments were endorsed by a series of papal bulls issued in the mid-thirteenth century that copperfastened the transformation from hermits to mendicants.[23] The earliest surviving constitutions are those enacted by the general chapter meeting in London in 1281. From 1318, the decisions of the general chapters were recorded in the *Liber ordinis*, from which delegates to the chapter

Cismontanae de Observantia [1451]' (1942), pp 106–97. The text of the Adare copy of the statutes was published by R. Howlett, *Monumenta Franciscana* (1882), ii, pp 81–119. For an overview of Observant legislation, see Etzi, *Iuridica Franciscana*, pp 140–66.   **17** B. Van Luijk (ed.), *Bullarium Ordinis Eremitarum S. Augustini periodis formationis, 1187–1256* (1964), provides texts of the papal bulls authorizing the union. **18** I. Cendoya OSA, *Las primitivas constituciones de los Augustinos* (1966).   **19** D. Guttierrez, *The Augustinians in the Middle Ages, 1256–1356* (1984), pp 55–61.   **20** Ibid., p. 56.   **21** C. Ciconneti, *La regola del Carmine: origine – natura – significato* (1973); see also the contributions to E.X. Gomes et al. (eds), *The Carmelite rule, 1207–2007* (2008).   **22** F. Andrews, *The other friars* (2006), pp 22–9.   **23** A. Staring, 'Four bulls of Innocent IV: a critical edition', *Carmelus*, 27 (1980), 273–85.

transcribed excerpts as required. The *Liber ordinis* was then transferred to the priory at which the next general chapter would take place.[24]

The Franciscan and Dominican 'tertiary' or 'Third Order' movement emerged from a pre-existing religious group, the 'Order of Penitents', in thirteenth-century Italy.[25] As a result of the friars' pastoral activities, some groups of penitents became more markedly 'Franciscan' or 'Dominican' in character, appropriating SS Francis or Dominic as their patron. In 1284 Friar Munio of Zamora, the master general of the Dominicans, organized the Dominican tertiary groups into the Dominican order of penitents.[26] In 1289, Pope Nicholas IV issued a formal rule for the Franciscan penitents, embodied in the bull *Supra montem*.[27] The earliest reliable reference to the Franciscan Third Order in Ireland occurs in 1425, when Pope Martin V granted a copy of this bull to the Irish tertiaries.[28] In the winter of 1426–7, a copy of the Dominican Third Order rule was issued to the Observant friars in Portumna, indicating that they also promoted the tertiary vocation among their lay followers.[29]

In addition to the legislation enacted by each order's general chapter, the local Irish units or provinces gathered in regular provincial or vicarial chapters. No statutes enacted by any Irish mendicant chapter survives, however, depriving us of the local insights that such legislation affords elsewhere. One notebook of the antiquarian Sir James Ware (d. 1666) contains references to the *Codex statutorum* of the Irish Observant Franciscans, though none of the excerpts is of legislative significance.[30]

In the period between the general chapters, authority in each order was vested in its major superior and his council of advisors. These superiors were known by different titles: the 'priors general' in Augustinian and Carmelite usage; the 'master general' for the Dominicans; and the 'minister general' in Franciscan terminology. Where they survive, the registers of the major superiors provide some important information about the affairs of the friars in Ireland. The Irish material in the registers of the Dominican masters general was edited by Hugh Fenning OP.[31] The registers of the medieval ministers general of the Friars Minor are not extant, but some material relating to the Irish Conventual Franciscans dating to the late fifteenth century has recently been published.[32] A small amount of Irish material

**24** Andrews, *The other friars*, p. 22; G. Wessels, *Acta capitulorum generalium ordinis Fratrum B.V. Mariae de Monte Carmelo, vol. I, ab anno 1318 usque ad annum 1593* (1912).   **25** G.G. Meersseman, *Dossier de l'ordre de la penitence au XIIIe siècle* (1981); R.M. Stewart, *De Illis qui faciunt penitentiam: the Rule of the Secular Franciscan Order* (1991); M. D'Alatri, *Aetas Poenitentialis: l'antico Ordine Francescano della Penitenza* (1995). **26** W.A. Hinnebusch, *History of the Dominican order*, i (1965), pp 400–4.   **27** *BF*, iv, pp 94–7.   **28** A transcript of this bull is preserved in the Representative Church Body Library, Dublin, C.6.1.6.2., *Registrum novum*, vol. ii, pp 652–8.   **29** H. Fenning OP, 'The Dominicans of Kilcorban' (1987), p. 10.   **30** BL Add. MS 4821.   **31** Hugh Fenning OP (ed.), 'Irish material in the registers of the Dominican masters general (1360–1649)' (1969), 249–336.   **32** G. Parisciani, *Regesta Ordinis Fratrum Minorum Conventualium, 1:*

is preserved among the registers of individual Carmelite priors general and the Irish material from the extant registers of the Augustinian priors general was published by F.X. Martin OSA.[33] No material remains to illustrate how the superiors of each order in Ireland governed their respective jurisdictions.

IRISH MENDICANT SOURCES

The surviving references and transcripts indicate that Irish friars had a keen interest in the history and traditions of their respective institutes. Unfortunately, nothing of what survives is comparable to the detailed narratives of the English Franciscan pioneer, Friar Thomas of Eccleston, or the sixteenth-century German Observant chronicler, Friar Nicholas Glassberger.[34] The surviving Irish mendicant annals are terse documents, providing a minimum of information for each year with little attempt at interpretation or narrative. They also contain relatively little material of specifically mendicant interest. Of the nine such annals that are extant, the Annals of Multyfarnham, the Kilkenny Chronicle, the Annals of Friar John Clyn, of Ross and of Nenagh are Franciscan in origin.[35] A small amount of annalistic material relating to the Friars Minor is also preserved in TCD MS 667.[36] Dominican material is represented by the work of the fourteenth-century Dublin chronicler Friar John Pembridge[37] and by seventeenth-century extracts from the annals of the priories of Trim and Ross.[38] Some annalistic material is preserved in the calendar of the missal from the Carmelite priory at Kilcormac, Co. Offaly.[39] No annalistic or historical material is extant from any Irish Augustinian priory.

*1484–1494* (1989); ibid., *Regesta Ordinis Fratrum Minorum Conventualium, 2: 1504–1506* (1998).   **33** F.X. Martin & A. de Meijer, 'Irish material in the Augustinian general archives, Rome, 1354–1624' (1956).   **34** A.G. Little (ed.), *Fratris Thomae (vulgo dicti de Eccleston), tractatus de adventu Fratrum Minorum in Angliam* (1951); 'Chronica Fratris Nicolai Glassberger', *Analecta Franciscana*, ii (1887). Both of these sources contain important information about the history of the Irish Franciscan province.   **35** A. Smith (ed.), 'Annales de Monte Fernandi' (1842); R. Flower (ed.), 'The Kilkenny chronicle in Cotton MS Vespasian B XI' (1931); B. Williams (ed.), *The Annals of Ireland by Friar John Clyn* (2007); R. Butler (ed.), *Annals of Ireland by Friar John Clyn and Thady Dowling, together with the Annals of Ross* (1849); D.F. Gleeson, 'The annals of Nenagh' (1943). For the relationship between these texts, see Clyn, *Annals*, pp 19–35; B. Williams, 'The "Kilkenny Chronicle"' (1995); eadem, 'The Dominican annals of Dublin' (2001). Dr Williams is currently preparing an edition and translation of the Annals of Multyfarnham.   **36** TCD MS 667, p. 66; Colker, *Latin MSS*, pp 1132–3.   **37** J.T. Gilbert (ed.), 'Annals of Ireland, AD1162–1370' in *Chartularies of St Mary's Abbey, Dublin* (1884), pp 303–98. A revised edition and translation of this work is in preparation by Bernadette Williams.   **38** *Chronicle of Ross*, Bodl. MS Rawl. B 4789, fos 68r–69r; *Chronicle of Trim*, BL Add. MS 4789, fos 206v–207v. I owe these references to B. Williams.   **39** J.J. Todd (ed.), 'Obits of Kilcormick' (1846).

Internal evidence indicates that portions of the Annals of Inisfallen were copied from a Franciscan exemplar in the early fourteenth century and other non-mendicant annalistic sources also contain references to the friars.[40]

As a matter of course, each friary maintained a necrology or register that recorded the deaths of friars, dignitaries and benefactors of the community. These documents often detailed the specific benefactions made. This ensured that the community continued to pray for their deceased *confrères* and benefactors and particular care was taken to preserve these documents. A number of seventeenth-century extracts from necrologies and registers from various friaries survive, along with extensive transcripts of the register of the Dominican priory at Athenry and the necrology of the Franciscan house in Galway.[41]

## OTHER SOURCES

In his magisterial survey of medieval Latin authors from Great Britain and Ireland, Richard Sharpe lists several Gaelic or Anglo-Irish mendicant writers.[42] While not all of their writings has survived and what has may not have circulated to an equal extent, the works listed indicate a broad and healthy intellectual climate among the Irish friars. In addition, the survival of manuscripts belonging to individual friars and that of the library catalogue of the Franciscan friary in Youghal, Co. Cork, gives further indication of their intellectual culture. The Youghal catalogue was compiled in stages between 1491 and 1523 and lists 150 volumes.[43] Primarily pastoral in focus, these books prepared the friars for their principal work as preachers and confessors, and the Youghal collection is comparable to the library holdings of mendicant communities in England and elsewhere in Europe.[44]

In their ministry as preachers, the Irish mendicants, particularly the Franciscans, demonstrated the same willingness to use poetry as did their *confrères* elsewhere. The earliest surviving examples are the fourteenth-century poems attributed to Friar Michael of Kildare in BL MS Harley 913 and the hymns compiled by the Franciscan bishop of Ossory, Richard Ledrede (d. *c.*1360).[45] The expansion of the friars in Gaelic territories in the fourteenth and fifteenth centuries brought

---

40 S. Mac Airt, *The annals of Inisfallen* (1951), pp xxxvi–vii.   41 A. Coleman (ed.), 'Regestum Monasterii Fratrum Praedicatorum de Athenry' (1912); M.J. Blake, 'The Obituary Book of the Franciscan monastery at Galway, with notes thereon' (1909–10).   42 R. Sharpe, *A handlist of the Latin writers of Great Britain and Ireland before 1540* (1997).   43 Ó Clabaigh, *Franciscans*, pp 158–80.   44 E. Schlotheuber, 'Late medieval Franciscan statutes on convent libraries and education' (2008).   45 W. Heuser (ed.), *Die Kildare Gedichte* (1904); A.M. Lucas (ed.), *Anglo-Irish poems of the Middle Ages* (1995); R.L. Greene, *The lyrics of the Red Book of Ossory* (1974); E. Colledge (ed.), *The Latin poems of Richard Ledrede OFM, bishop of Ossory, 1317–1360* (1974).

members of the hereditary learned families into their ranks, a development reflected in the poetry of individual friar-poets such as Tadhg Camchosach O'Daly, Philip Bocht O'Higgins and Eoin O'Duffy.[46]

The concerted attacks on the mendicant movement initiated in the mid-fourteenth century by Archbishop Richard Fitzralph of Armagh and subsequently pursued by other Oxford educated Anglo-Irish clerics such as Henry Crumpe OCist., John Whitehead and Philip Norris fostered the friars' aptitude for polemics.[47] The spirited response of mendicant champions such as the Augustinian Adam Payn represents a rare and still neglected Irish contribution to late medieval intellectual life.[48]

The survival of a small number of liturgical manuscripts, in addition to the material listed in the Youghal catalogue, gives an insight into the liturgical resources, musical repertoire and devotional practices of Dominican and Franciscan friars in late medieval Ireland. The fifteenth-century breviary and missal from the Carmelite priory at Kilcormac, Co. Offaly, represent a unique survival in the British Isles and provide a comprehensive picture of the liturgical life of Irish Carmelites. No liturgical texts remain from any Irish Augustinian priory or from houses of the Dominican or Franciscan tertiaries.[49]

## PAPAL RECORDS

A number of references to Irish mendicant affairs occur in various series of medieval papal registers.[50] These are accessible in a variety of formats. Of particular interest, however, are contemporary collections of papal bulls or *bullaria* assembled by the Irish friars themselves, such as those contained in the fifteenth-century Franciscan codex Trinity College Dublin MS 250, or in Lambeth Palace MS 61 ii, which contains papal privileges granted to the Carmelite friars.[51]

From the seventeenth century onwards, the friars printed their own *bullaria*, which provided each order with accessible versions of its papal grants and privileges.[52] The Franciscans are the best served in terms of modern critical editions, as the *regestum pontificum* in each volume of Luke Wadding's *Annales*

46 C. Mhág Craith, *Dán na mBráthar Mionúr*, 2 vols (1967, 1980); L. McKenna (ed.), *Philip Bocht O Huiginn* (1931).   47 See below, pp 153–60.   48 See below, pp 158, 165–8.   49 See below, pp 171–6.
50 M. Haren, 'Vatican archives as a historical source to 1530' (1984); P. Connolly, *Medieval record sources* (2002), pp 38–50.   51 See below, pp 165–6.   52 T. Ripoll & A. Bremond (eds), *Bullarium ordinis fratrum Praedicatorum* (1729–40); E. Monsignano, *Bullarium Carmelitanum*, 2 vols (1715); J.A. Ximenez, *Bullarium Carmelitanum* (1768).

*Ordinis Minorum*,[53] and two series of the *Bullarium Franciscanum* provide reliable modern editions of the texts.[54] In addition, much material relating to the Irish friars is available in the *Calendar of papal registers relating to Great Britain and Ireland*. A small number of mendicant entries are also found in the two volumes of *Hibernia Pontificia*.[55]

EPISCOPAL RECORDS

The Irish mendicant material preserved in the papal registers in some measure compensates for the almost complete loss of material from Irish episcopal sources. The comprehensive series of English bishops' registers make it possible to trace a variety of mendicant activities in medieval England that are barely evident in the equivalent Irish records. The most extensive set of episcopal *acta* that survives are those of the archbishops of Armagh, which have to varying degrees been calendared or published.[56] The Franciscan material in the Armagh registers has been published separately by Anthony Lynch.[57]

A number of mendicant references are found in the small amount of material that survives from the archdiocese of Dublin and the seventeenth-century Franciscan chronicler Francis O'Mahony (Matthews) has preserved decrees from the bishops of Cork and Cloyne relating to disputes between the mendicants and the secular clergy in Munster at the end of the fifteenth and beginning of the sixteenth century.[58] Occasional references to the friars survive in certain medieval Irish synodal *acta*, which have recently been published in a modern edition.[59]

**53** L. Wadding et al., *Annales Ordinis Minorum* (1931–64). **54** Sbaralea et al. (eds), *Bullarium Franciscanum Romanorum Pontificum constitutiones, epistolae, ac diplomata continens tribus ordinibus minorum clarissarum et poenitentium a seraphica sancto Francisco institutis concessa ab illorum exordio ad nostra usque tempora* (1759–1904); U. Hüntemann & C. Schmitt (eds), *Bullarium Franciscanum continens constitutiones epistolas diplomata Romanorum pontificum, nova series* (1929–). **55** *Calendar of entries in the papal registers relating to Great Britain and Ireland: papal letters* (1893–); M.P. Sheehy (ed.), *Pontificia Hibernia: medieval papal chancery records relating to Ireland, 640–1261* (1962–5). **56** Connolly, *Medieval record sources*, pp 41–4; D.A. Chart (ed.), *The register of John Swayne, archbishop of Armagh and primate of Ireland, 1418–1439* (1935); W.G.H. Quigley & E.F.D. Roberts (eds), *Registrum Johannis Mey: the register of John Mey, archbishop of Armagh, 1443–1456* (1972); B. Smith (ed.), *The register of Milo Sweetman, archbishop of Armagh, 1361–1380* (1996); M.A. Sughi (ed.), *Registrum Octaviani*, 2 vols (1999); B. Smith (ed.), *The register of Nicholas Fleming, archbishop of Armagh, 1404–1416* (2003); L.P. Murray & A. Gwynn, 'Archbishop Cromer's register' (1929–44). **57** A. Lynch (ed.), 'Documents of Franciscan interest from the episcopal archives of Armagh, 1265–1508' (1989–90). **58** N. White (ed.), *Registrum diocesis Dublinensis: a sixteenth-century precedent book* (1959), p. 30; B. Jennings (ed.), *Wadding papers, 1641–38* (1953), pp 113–14. **59** G. Bray (ed.), *Records of Convocation XVI: Ireland, 1101–1690* (2006).

RECORDS OF CENTRAL AND LOCAL GOVERNMENT

As with the ecclesiastical records of late medieval Ireland, the records of central and local government are extant in fragmentary and uneven form. The destruction of the Public Record Office in Dublin in 1922 was but the most comprehensive of several disasters that befell the records of the English administration in Ireland throughout the centuries.[60] Fortunately, a great deal of this information was available in other formats and repositories and, although not available for consultation in the course of the present work, the publication in 2011 of the CIRCLE database has made the surviving records of the Irish chancery available in a calendared and searchable electronic format. The chancery was the secretariat of royal administration in Ireland and issued letters in the king's name sealed with the Irish great seal.[61] These documents took the form either of a 'letter patent', which had a general application, or a 'letter close', addressed to an individual or to a body such as a religious community. Both categories of letter contain references to the friars and their activities. As recipients of royal alms, individual friars and mendicant communities regularly feature in the surviving exchequer records.[62] Their involvements in court cases as defendants, plaintiffs or witnesses meant that they sometimes appear in the justiciary rolls, while their appeals to the king's council in England resulted in their appearance in these sources as well.[63]

The clearest indication of the incomes, landholdings and economic resources that sustained the friars derives from the extents compiled by the officials charged with dissolving the religious orders in Ireland in the sixteenth century. The most comprehensive material relates to houses that were suppressed during the 1539–40 campaign.[64]

Municipal records such as those of Dublin, Kilkenny and Galway also give indications of the activities and influence of the friars in local milieux and demonstrate both their interactions with their neighbours and their involvement in civic life.[65] Likewise, occasional references to the friars in the muniments of Anglo-Irish families such as the Butlers of Ormond and the Blake and Lynch familes of Galway and Athenry illustrate their dealings with their aristocratic and mercantile patrons.[66]

---

60 Connolly, *Medieval record sources*, pp 9–13; P. Crooks, 'Historical Introduction', www.irishchancery. net/irish_chancery_rolls.php, accessed 7 July 2011.   61 Connolly, *Medieval record sources*, pp 15–18. 62 P. Connolly (ed.), *Irish exchequer payments, 1270–1446* (1998).   63 Connolly, *Medieval record sources*, pp 23–6; G.O. Sayles, *Documents on the affairs of Ireland before the king's council* (1979).   64 N.B. White, *Extents of Irish monastic possessions, 1540–1541* (1943).   65 See below, pp 97–117.   66 M.J. Blake, *Blake family records, 1300–1600* (1902); G. Mac Niocaill (ed.), *Crown surveys of lands, 1540–41, with the Kildare rental begun in 1518* (1992); E. Curtis (ed.), *Calendar of Ormond deeds* (1932–43).

## EARLY MODERN SOURCES

Much of the Irish mendicant source material survives because of its preservation or transcription by antiquarians from the late sixteenth and seventeenth centuries onwards. In the wake of the Reformation, ecclesiastical history was regarded as a form of apologetics, and this encouraged interest in the records and history of the early Irish church on both sides of the confessional divide. Among the reformers, the earliest figure to gather material on Irish friars was the Edwardian bishop of Ossory and former Carmelite John Bale, who included a number of Irish references in his 1536 work *Anglorum Eliades* ['The English sons of Elijah'].[67] James Ussher (d. 1656), bishop of Meath and later archbishop of Armagh, also played a major part in the preservation of many important sources, but the most assiduous labourer in the field was the antiquarian Sir James Ware (d. 1666), whose notebooks and published work remain key sources for the study of medieval Irish monastic and ecclesiastical history.[68] Ware exploited his contacts with antiquarians in England and his position as auditor general of Ireland to assemble a remarkable collection of primary texts and transcripts that he drew on in his *De Hibernia et antiquitatibus ejus disquisitiones*.[69] This seminal work contained a hand-list of medieval Irish religious houses arranged alphabetically by county and was used by scholars of all persuasions. Ware's work was quarried, translated and expanded by scholars such Louis Alemand (d. 1728),[70] John Stevens (d. 1726),[71] Walter Harris (d. 1761)[72] and Mervyn Archdall (d. 1791).[73] Others such as Archbishop William King (d. 1729), Bishop John Stearne (d. 1795) and Dr John Madden (d. 1703) also assembled important collections of manuscripts and transcripts, of which the most significant was the nineteen-volume *Collectanea de rebus Hibernicis* assembled by Walter Harris.[74]

The religious and political situation in Ireland from the mid-sixteenth century made it extremely difficult to form candidates for the religious and priestly life to the standards set by the Council of Trent. To remedy this, between 1578 and the end of the seventeenth century, approximately forty-five secular and religious foundations were established on the Continent to train candidates for the Irish mission or to prepare them for the life of the cloister. Of these, almost 60 per cent

**67** J. Bale, 'Anglorum Eliades', BL MS Harleian 3838.    **68** On Ware's work as an ecclesiastical historian, see particularly M.T. Flanagan, *Irish royal charters: texts and contexts* (2005), pp 391–7; W. O'Sullivan, 'A finding list of Sir James Ware's manuscripts' (1997); idem, 'Ware, Sir James', *DIB*, 9, pp 798–9.    **69** J. Ware, *De Hibernia et antiquitatibus ejus disquisitiones* (1654). His first published work, *Archiespiscoporum Casseliensium et Tuamensium vitae duobus expressae ...* (1628), also contained a handlist of Irish Cistercian monasteries.    **70** L. Alemand, *Histoire monastique de d'Irlande* (1690).    **71** J. Stevens, *Monasticon Hibernicum; or, The monastical history of Ireland* (1722). This is a translation of Alemand's work.    **72** W. Harris (ed. & trans.), *The antiquities and history of Ireland by the Right Honourable Sir James Ware, Knt* (1705).    **73** M. Archdall, *Monasticon Hibernicum* (1786).    **74** Calendared in C. McNeill, 'Harris:

were houses established for male and female religious, with seven Franciscan houses, six Capuchin, four Dominican and one Augustinian foundation being established.[75] They also acted as centres for the preservation of much Irish literary, historical and hagiographical source material and as focal points for Irish *émigré* communities. The Irish Franciscan colleges of St Anthony, Louvain (1607), and St Isidore, Rome (1625), were particularly important in this regard. The college in in Louvain provided the framework for the hagiographical and historical endeavours of friars John Colgan, Patrick Fleming, Hugh Ward and Michael O'Clery.[76] The community at St Isidore's, under the direction of Friar Luke Wadding, produced an edition of the works of Duns Scotus and developed into a leading Scotist academy.[77] Wadding also edited the writings of St Francis of Assisi and produced a monumental history of the Franciscan order, the *Annales minorum*.[78] Much of the Irish material in this latter work derived from two important seventeenth-century sources: Brussels MS 3947 *De provincia Hiberniae S. Francisci* by Friar Donatus Mooney,[79] and the *Brevis synopsis provinciae Hiberniae FF Minorum* of Friar Francis O'Mahony.[80] The former was compiled in Louvain in 1617–18 and is the single most important source for the history of the Franciscans in late medieval and early modern Ireland. The compiler, Donatus Mooney, was minister provincial from 1615 to 1618, and gathered what historical information he could about the Irish friaries while conducting his visitations of communities. The *Brevis synopsis* was also the work of another minister provincial and was completed by 1629. Though working considerably later than the period covered in the present work, both writers had access to late medieval material that has since been lost. An Irish translation of the *Brevis synopsis* was made between 1632 and 1635 by Friar Maurice Ultach MacShane, and this was used by Friar Michael O'Clery as the source for many of the Franciscan entries in the Annals of the Four Masters.[81] O'Clery also produced a chronological list of the houses of the Irish province, which is of great importance for charting the progress of the Observant reform movement.[82]

collectanea de rebus Hibernicis' (1934).   **75** M.A. Lyons, 'St Anthony's College, Louvain and the Irish Franciscan college network' (2009), p. 28; J.J. Silke, 'The Irish abroad, 1534–1691' (1976), p. 616.   **76** B. Cunningham, 'The Louvain achievement I: the Annals of the Four Masters' (2009); P. Ó Riain, 'The Louvain achievement II: hagiography' (2009); M. Mac Craith, 'Collegium S. Antonii Louvanii' (2009). **77** M.W.F. Stone, 'The theological and philosophical accomplishments of the Irish Franciscans' (2009). **78** L. Wadding, *Annales ordinis minorum* (1931–64).   **79** 'Brussels MS 3947'.   **80** 'Brevis synopsis'. **81** J. O'Donovan (ed.), *Annála ríoghachta Éireann: Annals of the Four Masters from the earliest period to the year 1616* (1851).   **82** J. Moloney (ed.), *Micheál Ó Cléirigh, A chronological list of the foundations of the Irish Franciscan province* (1934), pp 192–202.

Sources for the medieval Irish Dominicans are scarcer, and what remains owes its survival largely to its inclusion in John O'Heyne's *Epilogus chronologicus* (1706) and Thomas de Burgo's *Hibernia Dominicana* (1762).[83] The former was edited and translated in 1902 by Ambrose Coleman OP, who supplemented entries on various houses with material drawn from a range of published and archival sources. Apart from the small number of Irish references that occur in general histories of each order, the Irish Augustinians and Carmelites produced no significant historical material or narratives in the early modern period. Francis Bordoni featured references to the Irish houses of Franciscan regular tertiaries in his 1658 history of the Franciscan Third Order, but these are derived from information quarried from Wadding's *Annales minorum*.[84]

The main modern works on the friars and their activities in Ireland are listed in the footnotes and bibliography of the current volume. Two works are of particular importance as they collate and summarize many of the medieval and early modern sources described above: E.B. Fitzmaurice OFM and A.G. Little, *Materials for the history of the Franciscan province of Ireland* and A. Gwynn and R.N. Hadcock, *Medieval religious houses: Ireland*.[85] Despite some deficiencies in content and methodology, these texts remain the indispensable starting points for research on any aspect of medieval Irish monastic or mendicant history.

Where possible throughout this work, personal names and surnames have been given as found in the contemporary sources cited or standardized to their modern English forms. Likewise, the locations of friaries are given with reference to the modern county system. Unless otherwise stated, all photographs are by the author.

---

**83** J. O'Heyne, *Epilogus chronologicus* (1706); A. Coleman, *The Irish Dominicans of the seventeenth century by Fr John O'Heyne OP* (1902); T. de Burgo, *Hibernia Dominicana* (1762, 1772). For a useful survey of Irish Dominican historiography, see T.S. Flynn OP, *The Irish Dominicans, 1536–1641* (1993), pp xix–xxiii. **84** F. Bordoni, *Cronologium fratrum et sororum Tertii Ordinis S. Francisci* (1658). **85** E.B. Fitzmaurice & A.G. Little, *Materials for the history of the Franciscan province of Ireland* (1920); A. Gwynn & R.N. Hadcock, *Medieval religious houses: Ireland* (1970 [repr. 1988]).

# CHAPTER ONE

# The coming of the friars

AD 1224 *The preachers entered Ireland* [1]

The emergence of the friars in the thirteenth century heralded a revolution in the development of the religious life. The new orders represented both a response to the needs of the church and a reaction against the values of an increasingly urbanized society and profit-based economy.[2] Whereas the monastic orders emphasized withdrawal from the world, the friars sought to evangelize it and they naturally gravitated to urban settlements and to the newly established universities. Paradoxically, each order also maintained a strong contemplative dimension, with the Carmelites and Augustinians in particular remaining loyal to the eremitical roots from which they had sprung. The friars depended on alms for their support, hence the use of the word 'mendicant' (from the Latin *mendicare* – to beg) to describe them. Their emergence corresponded with a period of upheaval within the church as it responded to challenges from political leaders determined to curb its power and from dissident, heterodox groups bent on a return to radical, evangelical values. In the person of Innocent III (d. 1216), the papacy recognized in the friars the means to push forward the programme of reform and pastoral renewal proposed by the Fourth Lateran Council in 1215.[3] The friars' commitment to evangelical poverty provided the means of harnessing a tremendous energy for the good of the church, although this commitment proved to be a source of ongoing division for the Franciscans.

## THE FRIARS IN IRELAND

The earliest indication of the presence of the mendicants in Ireland is a laconic entry in the Annals of Ulster and various Anglo-Irish annals, which records that in 1224 'The preachers entered Ireland'. Their arrival, closely followed by that of the Franciscans, brought Irish society into contact with one of the most vibrant

---

**1** 'Annals of Multyfarnham' in A. Smith (ed.) *Tracts relating to Ireland*, ii (1842), p. 12.   **2** L.K. Little, *Religious poverty and the profit economy in medieval Europe* (1978), pp 146–69.   **3** C.H. Lawrence, *The friars: the impact of the early mendicant movement on Western society* (1994); M. Robson, *The Franciscans in the Middle Ages* (2006); F. Andrews, *The other friars* (2006).

movements within Christendom. Though few details survive of the early years of any of the mendicant orders in Ireland, their initial settlement pattern is indicative of missions staffed by English pioneers. These first friars gravitated to the towns and boroughs of the Anglo-Irish colony concentrated in southern and eastern Ireland. Here, cultural and linguistic affinity assured a welcome and provided a forum for their ministry and the necessary support for their mendicant lifestyle. In this they followed the pattern of their *confrères* in England and on the Continent. In England, for example, the Franciscans established foundations at Canterbury, London and Oxford within six months of their arrival at Dover in 1224. By 1230 they had established another twelve houses in the principal towns of what Knowles described as the country's 'central parallelogram'. Within twenty years of their arrival, the Friars Minor could be found in the ecclesiastical and civil capitals of England, at its two university centres, fifteen out of its nineteen cathedral cities and twenty-five of the towns that were (or would become) the English county towns.[4]

The arrival and spread of the Dominicans and Franciscans in Ireland in the 1220s and 1230s coincided with a period of economic prosperity and territorial expansion for the Anglo-Norman colony and the friars quickly secured the support of patrons keen to erect religious houses in their newly established boroughs. As elsewhere in Europe, such foundations enhanced the status of a settlement, consolidating its urban character and, in conjunction with markets, castles, town walls and burgage plots, the presence of a friary is regarded by historical geographers as one of the defining features of the Anglo-Norman borough in Ireland.[5] Their mendicant lifestyle meant that, unlike monastic orders, the friars did not require large endowments of land to sustain themselves. This made their houses relatively inexpensive and cost-effective to endow, rendering them particularly attractive to lower income patrons.[6]

Gaelic Ireland was a rural society and consequently during this first phase of expansion was less attractive to the mendicants who relied on the alms of town-dwellers for their support. The Carmelites and Augustinians, arriving towards the end of the thirteenth century, established no houses in Gaelic territories and the Augustinians do not appear to have recruited Gaelic novices initially.[7] In general, however, it was not until the late fourteenth and fifteenth centuries and the

**4** D. Knowles, *The religious orders in England*, I (1948), pp 132–3. A similar, if slightly more cautious, settlement pattern is evident among the English Dominicans, see W.A. Hinnebusch, *The early English Friars Preachers* (1951), pp 56–71. See also J. Burton, *Monastic and religious orders in Britain, 1000–1300* (1994), pp 109–19.   **5** B. Graham, 'Anglo-Norman colonization and the size and spread of the colonial town in medieval Ireland' (1985).   **6** For the English situation, see J. Röhrkasten, *The mendicant houses of medieval London* (2004), pp 379–409.   **7** Martin, 'Augustinian friaries', 356–7.

emergence of the Observant movement that the mendicants made any widespread expansion into Gaelic territories.

This initial phase of expansion is more complex than at first appears. Though the friars showed a preference for the colonial settlements, it is equally clear that from the outset these early foundations also enjoyed widespread support from the Gaelic aristocracy. The Dominican house in Athenry, Co. Galway, though founded by Miler de Bermingham in 1241, had most of its claustral complex built by Gaelic benefactors and was the burial place of the Gaelic bishops of the neighbouring diocese of Kilmacduagh. Their *confrères* in Cork, founded by Lord Philip de Barry, were patronized by the Mac Carthy family. Gaelic clerics and aristocrats also established a small number of houses in their own territories including the Franciscan friaries at Ennis, Cavan and Armagh and the Dominican houses at Roscommon and Derry. The friars in Ireland had to operate in areas that were characterized by shifting allegiances and localized power bases. This gave a particular cast to their identities and alliances that defies classification as either 'Gaelic' or 'Anglo-Irish' and indicates their ability to adapt to the fluid world of the border.[8] As will be demonstrated below, racial tension within the mendicant orders emerged in the context of the wider crises facing the Anglo-Irish colony towards the end of the thirteenth century.

A notable feature of these early foundations in Gaelic territories was the extent to which the friars gravitated towards pre-existing religious sites.[9] In Armagh, the Franciscans coexisted with communities of Augustinian canons and Celí Dé. The Dominican foundations at Roscommon and Lorrha, Co. Tipperary, also shared early Christian sites with houses of Augustinian canons. The Dominicans followed the rule of St Augustine and the canons may therefore have felt an affinity with the newcomers. It is more likely however that the new foundations represented an attempt by the friars' patrons to reinvigorate a pre-existing religious site by introducing a vibrant new expression of the religious life. This latter consideration provided the impetus for many of the later foundations discussed in chapter three.

FIRST CONTACTS

The identities and backgrounds of the first friars in Ireland are unknown, as are the channels by which their patrons became aware of the mendicant movement.

---

**8** For the fluid relationship between the ethnic groups in Ireland at this period, see R. Frame, 'Power and society in the lordship of Ireland' (1977). See also B. Smith, *Colonisation and conquest in medieval Ireland: the English in Louth, 1170–1330* (1999, [2007]), pp 74–92. I am grateful to John McCafferty for discussion of this point.  **9** This was also a feature of the houses established by the Cistercians and Augustinian canons in the twelfth and thirteenth centuries. See G. Carville, *The occupation of Celtic sites in Ireland by the Canons*

The chronicle of Friar Thomas of Eccleston indicates that the Franciscan mission to England included English friars who had joined the order elsewhere and the pioneers in Ireland may have included Anglo-Irish or Gaelic friars who had done likewise.[10] Bernadette Williams argues that the Irish delegates to the Fourth Lateran Council in 1215 would have become aware of the Dominican and Franciscan movements whose emergence was discussed by the Council fathers.[11] This may explain the rapid expansion of the friars in Ireland and the remarkable readiness of thirteenth-century Gaelic cathedral chapters to elect Dominicans and Franciscans to bishoprics.[12] Many of the early friaries were established by Anglo-Norman magnates with estates and connections in England where their families already patronized the mendicants. These links doubtless played a part in the decision to support their *confrères* in Ireland and may well have been the channels by which the friars were first introduced.[13]

### ORIGIN LEGENDS

The dearth of primary sources dealing with the early years of the friars may account for the subsequent circulation of apocryphal narratives concerning the origins of the Dominican and Franciscan orders in Ireland. The earliest surviving expression of this is the account of the coming of the Friars Minor published in 1587 by Francisco Gonzaga in the *De origine seraphicae religionis Franciscanae ejusque progressibus* ['on the origin and development of the seraphic Franciscan order']. He states that

> This province of Ireland, though it does not lack antiquity, produced no other province in the order, but had as its founder one of the companions of the seraphic father Francis, who, crossing thither from Compostella, built some monasteries in the island and at length died there with the greatest reputation for holiness.[14]

Regular of St Augustine and the Cistercians (1982).   **10** A.G. Little (ed.), *Friatris Thomae ... tractatus De Adventu Fratrum Minorum in Angliam* (1951), pp 29–30. Writing *c.*1672, Dr John Lynch claimed that the Dominican pioneers included two Irish friars, Peter Madden and Anthony Geoghegan, but this is without foundation. O'Sullivan, *MIDS*, p. 16.   **11** B.A. Williams, 'The Latin Franciscan Anglo-Irish annals of medieval Ireland' (1991), pp 25–77.   **12** Cotter, *Friars Minor*, pp 132–42; W.R. Thomson, *Friars in the cathedral: the first Franciscan bishops, 1226–1271* (1975), pp 137–48.   **13** For further discussion of this point, see below, pp 93–5.   **14** F. Gonzaga, *De origine seraphicae religionis Franciscanae* (1587), iii, p. 845. Translated in *FL*, p. xi. 'Brevis synopsis', pp 181–2, gives 1214 as the date of his arrival and adds that he was buried in Youghal. See also 'Brussels MS 3947', p. 15, and *AM*, i, p. 203.

Gonzaga was minister general of the Franciscans from 1579 to 1587 and used his position to solicit material concerning the history of the various provinces of the order from their respective ministers provincial so it is likely that his information came from an Irish source. This claim was accepted and developed by the Irish Franciscan historians of the seventeenth century for whom the province's early establishment by a companion of St Francis and during the saint's lifetime would have been a source of considerable pride.

Similar traditions circulated among the seventeenth- and eighteenth-century Irish Friars Preachers and are first recorded in a report on the state of the Irish province compiled in 1622 by the prior provincial, Friar Ross MacGeoghegan. He asserted that

> This is a most ancient province, in which there are thirty-eight priories, in addition to many residences and chapels, very many of which were founded and erected in the time of the most holy father Dominic, as a letter from the same St Dominic to the most illustrious Prince of Tyrconnel in favour and recommendation of two friars sent by him to Ireland confirms. That letter was preserved with the fullness of the friars' faithful veneration and singular devotion in our convent in Derry until it was lost as a result of fire and the devastation wrought by heretics recklessly oppressing the said convent and the friars living in it. The same is confirmed by an ancient manuscript of our Limerick convent, in which, among other records of antiquity, the death and burial of the most illustrious Prince Donal O'Brien, first founder of that convent in 1233 is recorded, and from many other fragments of our ancient records, which, by God's providence, have escaped the hands of the heretics.[15]

A variation of the legend alleges that after the destruction of the friary in Derry that the letter was then taken to Spain and placed in a Spanish Dominican archive, where it was subsequently lost.[16]

The similarities between the two accounts are quite striking. In each instance the friars were keen to establish the antiquity of their institutes and their juridical independence *ab initio*. They achieved this by attributing the establishment of both provinces to an initiative of their respective founders and alleging that a number of houses were established during their lifetimes. By inventing such direct connections with SS Dominic and Francis the Irish friars were able to ignore the English roots from which they had in fact sprung. This is particularly evident in

---

**15** The Latin text is given in T.S. Flynn, *The Irish Dominicans, 1536–1641* (1993), pp 323–5 at p. 323. See also J. O'Heyne, *Epilogus chronologicus*, ed. A. Coleman (1902), p. 2.   **16** For the various versions of this legend, see T. de Burgo, *Hibernia Dominicana* (1762, 1772), pp 36–43 and O'Sullivan, *MIDS*, pp 13–16.

the Dominican account in which the two patrons nominated were both of Gaelic stock. In the context of the destruction of the English Franciscan and Dominican provinces in the 1530s and the changed circumstances of early modern Ireland such fictitious accounts of Continental origins may have had an additional political attraction for the friars.

Comparable narratives exist for the Scottish Dominicans and Franciscans. The Scottish historian Hector Boece, writing in 1527, claimed that St Dominic had personally sent friars on a mission to establish the Dominicans in Scotland in 1219.[17] In January 1586, Friar John Hay, the minister provincial of the Scottish Observant Franciscans, completed the account of the history of the Friars Minor in Scotland that he had compiled at Gonzaga's request while exiled in Cologne. Whereas Hay's chief interest was the history of the Scottish Observant friars, he also emphasized that the Scottish province had been founded in 1224, 'during the lifetime of the Blessed Francis'.[18] While, as with the Irish material, these claims are not historically tenable, they demonstrate a comparable desire on the part of the Scottish friars to emphasize the antiquity and independence of their respective provinces. In the case of Hay, a desire to distance the Scottish Franciscans from the English roots whence they had sprung may also have been an additional motivating factor.

No narratives survive concerning the origins of the Augustinian or Carmelite friars in Ireland. A brief reference to the presence of the Carmelites to Ireland is preserved in *The ten books on the way of life and great deeds of the Carmelites* written by the Catalan friar Felip Ribot around 1385.[19] The Irish reference is contained in the ninth book, which drew on the chronicle of Friar William of Sandwich (fl. *c.*1287) and dealt with the spread of the Carmelites to England, Scotland and Ireland in the wake of the approval given to the White Friars in 1245 by Pope Innocent IV.[20] Although the reference adds little to what is known of the origins of the Irish Carmelites, it is of great interest in the overall context of Ribot's work. The *Ten books* formed part of a process of historical revisionism by which the Carmelites invented an apocryphal history that traced their origins back to the prophet Elijah and his disciples on Mount Carmel in Palestine.[21]

In his 1536 work *Anglorum Eliades* ['The English sons of Elijah'], John Bale, the English historian and former Carmelite friar, recorded that the English prior provincial Henry de Anna sent friars eminent for their learning and sanctity to

17 H. Boece, *Heir beginnis the history and croniklis of Scotland* (1540), Book 13, chapter xiiii. See also A. Ross OP, *The dogs of the Lord: the story of the Dominican order in Scotland* (1981), p. 2. I am grateful to Richard Fawcett for this latter reference.    18 W. Moir Bryce (ed.), 'Chronicle of the Observantine province of Scotland by Father John Hay OM' in idem, *The Scottish Grey Friars* (1909), ii, p. 173.    19 R. Copsey OCarm. (ed.), *The ten books on the way of life and the great deeds of the Carmelites* (2005).    20 Ibid., p. 137. 21 A. Jotischky, *The Carmelites and antiquity: mendicants and their pasts in the Middle Ages* (2002), pp 136–50.

Ireland *c.*1256. According to Bale, these pioneers were received with 'open arms' by the earl of Ormond and other noblemen.[22] This account is not entirely reliable and the earliest contemporary evidence for the White Friars' presence in Ireland dates to 1271. Despite this, Bale's narrative is significant for the evidence it provides of close links between the Carmelites and the Butler family from the earliest years of the order in Ireland.[23]

## THE FOUNDATIONS TO 1348

Although the precise details and circumstances of the foundation of many of the first Irish friaries are obscure, it is clear that the pattern of rapid expansion that characterized the mendicant movement on the Continent and in England was replicated in Ireland. In terms of the number of friaries, both the Dominicans and Franciscans had peaked by *c.*1270, with each order making relatively few foundations after that date. In contrast, the recently arrived Carmelite and Augustinian friars experienced rapid growth from the 1270s onwards, with both groups securing patronage and establishing houses until well into the 1320s, despite the economic and political upheavals of the period.

### THE DOMINICANS

Uniquely among the Irish mendicants, a list detailing the foundation dates of the Dominican houses established before 1300 survives (fig. 1.1). It was first published by Sir James Ware in 1639, and although it preserves a genuine medieval source, it must be treated with some caution as the speed of expansion that it recounts is at variance with what the Dominican constitutions permitted and with what is known to have been Dominican practice elsewhere. Otherwise, sources for the early chronology of the Friars Preachers in Ireland are fragmentary and imprecise. The Annals of Multyfarnham, a late thirteenth-century Franciscan text, records the arrival of the Preachers in 1224 and most subsequent writers have accepted this.[24] A later tradition records that, like the Franciscans, the Preachers owed their introduction to the patronage of Maurice Fitzgerald, whose descendants proved notable benefactors of both orders throughout the Middle Ages.[25] Another tradition attributes the foundation to William Marshal, and Bernadette Williams

---

**22** BL MS Harleian 3838, fo. 21. See O'Dwyer, *Irish Carmelites*, p. 1, for alternative arrival dates. I am grateful to Richard Copsey OCarm., for this reference.   **23** See below, pp 81–2, 94.   **24** T. de Burgo, *Hibernia Dominicana* (1762), i, p. 38.   **25** Marquis of Kildare, *The earls of Kildare and their ancestors from 1057 to 1773* (1864), p. 11.

8

1.1 Map of Dominican
foundations to 1291.

Coleraine
Derry
Newtownards
Rathfran
Sligo
Strade
Roscommon
Trim
Drogheda
Mullingar
Athenry
Dublin
Lorrha
Athy
Arklow
Kilkenny
Limerick
Cashel
Kilmallock
Rosbercon
Tralee
Waterford
Cork
Youghal

Carrickfergus
Armagh
Downpatrick
Cavan
Dundalk
Drogheda
Multyfarnham
Trim
Athlone
Monasteroris
Galway
Claregalway
Dublin
Killeigh
Kildare
Wicklow
Ennis
Nenagh
Castledermot
Limerick
Kilkenny
Cashel
Ardfert
New Ross
Clonmel
Wexford
Buttevant
Carrickbeg
Waterford
Cork
Youghal
Timoleague

1.2 Map of Franciscan
friaries in Ireland to 1336.

plausibly argues that he was the more likely candidate as he was a major benefactor of the Preachers in London and his appointment as justiciar in 1224 would have enabled him to invite the friars to Ireland and assure them of support.[26] Their first foundation was established in Dublin in 1224, where they received a site on the north bank of the River Liffey from the Cistercian monks of St Mary's Abbey in return for an annual offering of a lighted candle to the abbot in acknowledgment of the donation. This subsequently developed into the priory of St Saviour, the order's principal house in Ireland and the site of a major *studium* or house of studies.[27] In the same year, at the invitation of Luke Netterville, archbishop of Armagh, the friars established the priory of St Mary Magdalene in Drogheda, where the bell tower of the medieval church still stands on the north side of the River Boyne.[28] In 1225, William Marshal, earl of Pembroke, established the priory of the Holy Trinity in Kilkenny. Most of the friary's conventual buildings have now disappeared but the nave and transept remain in use for worship and give a good indication of the liturgical environment of a medieval friary church.[29] In 1226, the Preachers arrived in Waterford but only received royal permission for the construction of St Saviour's Priory there in 1235.[30] The Limerick house, also dedicated to St Saviour, was founded in 1227 by Donal Cairbreach O'Brien, king of Thomond, and the Cork foundation of St Mary of the Isle was established by Philip de Barry in 1229.[31] St Mary's Priory in Mullingar, Co. Westmeath, was established by either the Nugent or the Pettit family in 1237. A medieval seal matrix belonging to the priory still survives. It depicts the Holy Trinity, to whom the priory was subsequently re-dedicated.[32] In 1243, Archbishop David MacKelly, the first Irish Dominican bishop, founded St Dominic's Priory in Cashel, where the well-preserved remains of the priory church still remain.[33] Holy Cross Priory, Tralee, Co. Kerry, was also established in 1243 by John FitzThomas Fitzgerald (John of Callan).[34] The following year, 1244, saw the foundation of two priories

**26** Bernadette Williams, pers. comm.   **27** *MRH*, pp 224–5; B. O'Sullivan, 'The Dominicans in medieval Dublin' (1947); O'Sullivan, *MIDS*, pp 18, 19–20, 32. Williams disputes O'Sullivan's attribution of the foundation to Archbishop Henry on account of the antipathy towards the archbishop shown by the Dublin Dominican chronicler, Friar John Pembridge.   **28** *MRH*, p. 224; H. Fenning [Anonymous], *St Magdalen's Church Drogheda: centenary, 1878–1978* (1978); O'Sullivan, *MIDS*, p. 32.   **29** *MRH*, p. 226; H. Fenning, *The Black Abbey: the Kilkenny Dominicans, 1225–1996* (1996), pp 5–6; O'Sullivan, *MIDS*, pp 32–3.   **30** *MRH*, p. 231; H. Fenning, *The Waterford Dominicans* (1990); O'Sullivan, *MIDS*, p. 33.   **31** BL Add. MS 4783, fo. 58. I am grateful to Bernadette Williams for this reference. *MRH*, pp 226–7, 224; M. Nolan OP, *St Saviour's priory Limerick, 1227–1977* (1977), pp 1–20; M.F. Hurley and C.M. Sheehan, *Excavations at the Dominican priory, St Mary's of the Isle, Crosse's Green, Cork* (1995), pp 7–10.   **32** *MRH*, pp 227–8; H. Fenning, 'The Dominicans of Mullingar' (1964). Coleman gives May 1238 as an alternative date and asserts that the house was first dedicated to the Holy Trinity. R. Ó Floinn, 'Medieval seal matrix from Gaulstown, Co. Meath' (1978–9), 84–8. I am grateful to Hugh Fenning for this reference.   **33** *MRH*, p. 223; O'Sullivan, *MIDS*, pp 34, 37.   **34** BL Add. MS 4783, fo. 58; *MRH*, p. 231; L. Dunne, 'Murder, pillage and destruction: archaeological finds from medieval Tralee (2010).

in Ulster: St Columba's at Newtownards, Co. Down, and St Mary's of the Bann, later the site of Coleraine, Co. Derry.[35]

The Anglo-Irish invasion of Connacht in 1235 led to the establishment of mendicant houses in the west and northwest of Ireland. The Dominicans, in particular, benefited from the expansion and more foundations were made for them than for any other mendicant order. This may be partly because the invasion was led by Richard de Burgh, whose cousin, Hubert de Burgh, was one of the order's most influential benefactors in England. In 1241, Miler de Bermingham established the important foundation of SS Peter and Paul at Athenry, where the remains of the large friary church are extant.[36] Maurice Fitzgerald founded Holy Cross Priory in Sligo in 1252 and extensive remains of the priory still stand on the south bank of the Garavoge River.[37] 1252 was also the year in which the Dominicans replaced the Friars Minor at the Dexter foundation at Strade (or Athleathan), Co. Mayo, at the behest of Basilia de Bermingham, daughter of the founder of Athenry.[38] The remains of the priory church, with some particularly fine late-medieval sculpture, still survive there. Despite their initial association with the invaders, the Dominicans quickly garnered the support of the Gaelic aristocracy in Connacht. As noted above, the register of the de Bermingham foundation at Athenry indicates that Gaelic benefactors were responsible for building much of the claustral complex there. In 1253, Felim O'Connor, king of Connacht, founded St Mary's Priory in Roscommon, which became one of the order's most important houses in Ireland and where extensive remains of the large priory church survive.[39] He also sponsored the building of the friars' refectory in Athenry.

The friars continued to expand elsewhere in Ireland. In 1253, a priory was established in Athy, Co. Kildare, at a strategic crossing point on the River Barrow by either Maurice Fitzgerald or the de St Michael baron of Reban.[40] The house was dedicated to the proto-martyr of the Dominican order, St Peter of Verona (d. 1252), and was the first expression of his cult in Ireland. This initial period of rapid expansion slackened somewhat and no new foundation was made for a decade until the foundation of St Mary's priory, Trim, by Geoffrey de Geneville, lord of Meath in 1263.[41] The priory of the Holy Cross in Arklow, Co. Wicklow, was established in 1264 by Thomas Theobald Fitz Walter, Butler of Ireland.[42] The Anglo-Norman families of Grace and Walsh are credited with founding the priory

35 *MRH*, pp 228, 223; O'Sullivan, *MIDS*, pp 39–43.   36 *MRH*, pp 221–2; M.J. Blake, 'The abbey of Athenry' (1902); R.A.S. Macalister, 'The Dominican church at Athenry' (1913).   37 *MRH*, pp 229–30; H. Fenning OP, *The Dominicans of Sligo* (2002).   38 Coleman, 'Regestum', pp 204–5; Y. McDermott, 'Strade priory: patronage and development at a medieval mendicant friary' (2009).   39 *MRH*, p. 229; L. Taheny, *The Dominicans of Roscommon* (1990), pp 1–9.   40 *MRH*, pp 229, 222. H. Fenning OP, *Dominicans of Athy, 1257–2007* (2007), p. 2.   41 *MRH*, p. 230; H. Fenning OP, 'The Dominicans of Trim: 1263–1682' (1963); M. Potterton, *Medieval Trim: history and archaeology* (2005), pp 318–31.   42 *MRH*, p. 221; D. Walsh, 'The Dominicans in Arklow (1264–1793)' (1963–4). O'Sullivan, *MIDS*, p. 50.

at Rosbercon, Co. Kilkenny, on the west bank of the River Barrow opposite New Ross, where the friars arrived in 1267. Although subsequently recorded as dedicated to St Dominic or to the Virgin Mary, the foundation may originally have been dedicated to the Holy Cross as an annual fair was held in Rosbercon on the feast of the Triumph of the Cross (14 September).[43] In 1268, Thomas FitzMaurice Fitzgerald established Holy Cross priory in Youghal, Co. Cork. This dedication was later changed to Our Lady of Graces on account of the priory's wonderworking image of the Virgin Mary (pl. 1). Fragmentary remains of the priory church survive in the town's North Abbey graveyard.[44] In 1269, the priory of St Peter Martyr at Lorrha, Co. Tipperary, was established by Walter de Burgh, earl of Ulster. In 1274, the Dexter family established Holy Cross priory at Rathfran, Co. Mayo, where extensive remains of the church and the foundations of the convent are extant. St Dominic's Priory, Derry, was also founded in 1274, possibly by Donal O'Donnell, who was buried there in 1281.[45] St Saviour's Priory, Kilmallock, Co. Limerick, one of the best preserved of the medieval Dominican foundations, owes its origins to the friars themselves, who purchased the site from John Bluet, a burgess of the town in 1291. Despite having royal license for the foundation, they were ejected by agents of the bishop of Limerick. The friars in turn appealed to King Edward I, who ordered the justiciar, William de Vescy, to investigate the case.[46] The foundation of Killmallock marked the end of the first phase of Dominican expansion in Ireland as no further foundations were made by the Preachers for over half a century until the establishment of the priory of St Eustace at Naas, Co. Kildare, c.1355.

THE FRANCISCANS

The Irish Franciscan province was erected by the general chapter of the order meeting in Assisi in 1230 (fig. 1.2).[47] The first minister provincial was Friar Richard of Ingworth, a man of considerable standing in the order,[48] though it is possible that some Franciscans were already active in Ireland before this, and later writers record various arrival dates between 1214 and 1232.[49] The tradition among the Observant reformers of the late fifteenth century was that the friars arrived in 1224 in Youghal, where they established a friary dedicated to St Nicholas, and that

**43** *MRH*, p. 229; T.S. Flynn, *The Dominicans of Rosbercon (1267–c.1800)* (1981), pp 11–17; O'Sullivan, *MIDS*, pp 50–1. **44** *MRH*, pp 231–2; U.G. Flanagan, 'Our Lady of Graces, Youghal' (1990); O'Sullivan, *MIDS*, pp 51–2. **45** *MRH*, pp 228, 224. **46** *MRH*, p. 226; A. Hogan, *Kilmallock Dominican priory* (1991), pp 1–4. **47** The most thorough account of the origins and early expansion of the Irish Franciscan province is N. Gallagher, 'The Irish Franciscan province: from foundation to the aftermath of the Bruce Invasion' (2010). **48** Thomas of Eccleston, *De Adventu*, p. 4. **49** For analyses of the sources, see Cotter, *Friars Minor*, pp 11–16; Gallagher, 'Irish Franciscan province', pp 19–27.

the province expanded from there.[50] Francis Cotter has presented an alternative case for Dublin as the Irish proto-friary.[51] Developing a proposition first made by J.A. Watt, Cotter argues that a foundation in a royal, capital city would be more in keeping with the pattern of contemporary Franciscan settlement in England and consonant with that of the other mendicant orders in Ireland. Expansion from Dublin rather than Youghal would also explain some of the peculiarities of the first Franciscan foundations in Ireland, particularly the *c.*1239 foundation of Athlone, Co. Westmeath, in the midlands, and the late date of the house in Cashel, seat of the metropolitan archbishop in Munster, which was established *c.*1265. Though plausible in a number of respects, Cotter's proposition lacks contemporary support and dismisses all subsequent traditions. The fact that Dublin was the first house for which a contemporary record survives (a grant of alms by Henry III in 1233) and its pre-eminence on the earliest surviving list of the friaries in Ireland, compiled in 1331, are by no means conclusive.[52] More significantly, it does not take account of the central role of Maurice II Fitzgerald, justiciar of Ireland, in introducing the Friars Minor to Ireland. His principal seat was at Imokilly, the barony in which Youghal is situated, and he subsequently retired to the friary and was buried there in 1257, thereby establishing the foundation as one of the main burial places of the Fitzgeralds of Desmond. This Fitzgerald role as the founders of the both the Franciscan and Dominican orders in Ireland was later assiduously promoted both by the friars and by the Fitzgeralds themselves. The friary library in Youghal possessed material relating to the early history of the Irish province as well as a chronicle relating to the Fitzgeralds and these may have been the sources for the tradition of Youghal as the Irish proto-friary.[53]

Notwithstanding the uncertainty over the date and place of their arrival, it is clear that the early Irish Friars Minor shared in the experience of rapid expansion common to their *confrères* throughout thirteenth-century Europe and to the other mendicant orders in Ireland. Whereas no medieval list of foundation dates and dedications survives for the earliest Franciscan houses, there is contemporary evidence for their presence in ten different locations by 1250: Athlone, Co. Westmeath; Carrickfergus, Co. Louth; Castledermot, Co. Kildare; Cork; Downpatrick, Co. Down; Drogheda, Co. Louth; Dublin; Dundalk, Co. Louth; Kilkenny and Waterford.[54] It is likely that a number of other important houses, such

---

**50** BL Add. MS 4821, fo. 101, 'Youghill fundatorem habuit Maur. Geraldin', An. 1224. Vid Stat. ord. minorum in Hibernia et lib. de Kilconnill. Is obiit 1257. Vid. lib. conv. de Athdare.'; *AFM*, iii, p. 217, gives the same information, but without the sources. See also D. O'Sullivan, 'Youghal, the first house of the Friars Minor in Ireland' (1953) and P. Ó Riain, *Feastdays of the saints: a history of Irish martyrologies* (2006), pp 257–8.  **51** Cotter, *Friars Minor*, pp 12–17.  **52** *FL*, pp 23, 133–4.  **53** *YLC*, no. 102. See also the mendicant references included in the brief obituary list of 'dyvers lordys and gentyllman of the Geraldys' included in the sixteenth-century Kildare rental. G. Mac Niocaill (ed.), *Crown surveys of lands, 1540–41, with the Kildare rental begun in 1518* (1992), p. 354.  **54** *MRH*, pp 243, 244, 246–7, 248–9, 250, 257, 260.

as Nenagh, Co. Tipperary; New Ross, Co. Wexford and possibly Ennis, Co. Clare, were also founded by mid-century. The Franciscans also benefited from the colonial expansion into Connacht in 1235 with the establishment of houses at Claregalway (*c.*1250), Co. Galway, by John de Cogan II and at Galway (1296) by William de Burgh.[55]

The friary at Ardfert, Co. Kerry, was founded before 1253 by Thomas FitzMaurice FitzRaymond and was dedicated to St Francis.[56] The friary at Kildare was established between 1254 and 1260 by William de Vescy and Gerald FitzMaurice, Baron Offaly and ancestor of the Fitzgerald earls of Kildare, many of whom were later interred there.[57] Gerald was also credited with the foundation of the friary in Clane, Co. Kildare, in 1258, and a damaged effigy of a knight in the friary church is reputed to represent him.[58] Patrick O'Scannail, the Dominican archbishop, introduced the Franciscans to Armagh in 1264. This late date for a foundation in the primatial city is somewhat puzzling. In England, a foundation was made in Canterbury, the ecclesiastical capital, within six weeks of their arrival in 1224. The delay in Armagh is perhaps attributable to the fact that most of the medieval primates resided at their manors of Termonfeckin and Dromiskin in Co. Louth, using St Peter's Church, Drogheda, as their pro-cathedral. In November 1241, two friars, John de Alnoto and Thomas de Bartoun, probably members of the Drogheda community, witnessed a grant of land by Hugh de Lacy to Archbishop Albert Suerbeer of Armagh.[59] The late foundation date of the friary in Cashel, the metropolitan see of Munster, is also puzzling, particularly in light of its later position as the head house of a custody. Here, the founder was Lord William Hacket and the friars were introduced *c.*1265. A Dominican house had been established in the town in 1243, and it is possible that the townspeople were unable to support a second mendicant community (in addition to contributing to the building of the new cathedral) at any earlier stage.[60] The 1267 foundation of the Limerick friary is attributed to a member of the de Burgh family, possibly Lord Thomas.[61] Various dates between 1236 and 1276 are given for the foundation of the house at Multyfarnham, Co. Westmeath. Of these, the most reliable seems to

F. Grannell, *The Franciscans in Athlone* (1978); I. Fennessey, 'Castledermot and the Franciscans' (1998–9). C. Mooney, 'The mirror of all Ireland' (1953); P. Conlan, *The Franciscans in Drogheda* (1987); G. Cleary, *The Friars Minor in Dublin, 1233–1939* (1939); H. O'Sullivan, 'The Franciscans in Dundalk' (1960–1); C. Mooney, 'The Franciscans in Waterford' (1964); D.F. Gleeson, 'The Franciscan convent at Nenagh' (1938); N. Gallagher, 'Irish Franciscan province', pp 27–34. **55** *MRH*, pp 250–1; B. Jennings, 'The abbey of St Francis, Galway' (1947). **56** *MRH*, p. 242; K. Walsh, 'Franciscan friaries in pre-Reformation Kerry' (1976). **57** *MRH*, p. 252; I. Fennessy, 'The Franciscan friary at Kildare' (1996/7). **58** *MRH*, p. 245. Gerald FitzMaurice was also reputed to be buried in Kildare. **59** *MRH*, p. 242; *FL*, p. 7; B. Smith (ed.), *The register of Nicholas Fleming* (2003), p. 202; E.B. Fitzmaurice, 'The Franciscans in Armagh' (1900). **60** *MRH*, p. 244. A monastery of Cistercian monks was established at Hore Abbey, beneath the Rock of Cashel, in 1272. **61** *MRH*, pp 253–4; B. Egan, *Franciscan Limerick* (1971).

be 1268. The founder was Lord William Delamar, although the Nugent barons Delvin later assumed patronage of the house.[62] Very little is known about the early years of the friars in Wexford, but it can be provisionally dated to *c.*1268 and may owe its origins to Fitzgerald patronage.[63] The same provisional date is given for the establishment of the Wicklow community, with the O'Byrne and O'Toole families being credited as patrons.[64] The Kilkenny friar-chronicler John Clyn records the erection of the friary in Clonmel, Co. Tipperary, in 1269. The founder was reputedly Sir Otho de Grandison with the Desmond Fitzgeralds also playing an important role as benefactors.[65] The friary at Buttevant, Co. Cork, was founded by David de Barry, lord of Buttevant, sometime before his death in 1279.[66] The friary at Trim in Meath was dedicated to St Francis and was in existence before 1282, though the first contemporary reference concerns a burial dispute in 1318.[67] Killeigh friary, Co. Offaly, was in existence by 1303 and may have been founded in 1293 by the O'Conor Faly.[68] The origins of the house at Timoleague, Co. Cork, are particularly confused, with various dates between 1240 and 1376 being given in the sources. The earliest contemporary record refers to 1331, when Friar John Clyn listed it among the houses of the custody of Cork.[69] The patrons were the de Barry and MacCarthy families.

The friary at Monasteroris, Co. Offaly, was founded in 1325 by John de Bermingham, earl of Louth, on the strength of a papal bull of John XXII. It is therefore one of the earliest friaries for which papal approbation survives. The friary derived its name from de Bermingham's Gaelic patronymic Mac Feorais.[70] The friary at Cavan was built by Giolla Iosa O'Reilly sometime before his death in 1330, possibly after 1325 though a date as early as 1300 has been proposed.[71] The friary at Carrickbeg or Carrickmagriffin, Co. Waterford, on the south bank of the River Suir, was founded in 1336 by James Butler, first earl of Ormond and the annalist Friar John Clyn was appointed its first guardian.[72] Papal approval for the friary was secured in 1347.[73] Carrickbeg was the last Irish foundation before the Black Death and can be fairly said to represent the end of the first phase of Franciscan expansion in Ireland.

**62** *MRH*, p. 256; T O'Donnell, *The Franciscan friary at Multyfarnham* (1951). **63** *MRH*, p. 261; F. Grannell, *The Franciscans in Wexford* (nd). **64** *MRH*, p. 261; B. Millett, 'The Franciscans in County Wicklow' (1984). **65** Clyn, *Annals*, p. 149; *MRH*, p. 246. **66** *MRH*, p. 243; G. de Barra, 'Buttevant' (1953). **67** *MRH* p. 260; Potterton, *Medieval Trim: history and archaeology*, pp 331–42. **68** *MRH*, p. 273. **69** *MRH*, pp 259–69; J.T. Collins, 'The friary at Timoleague' (1953). **70** *MRH*, p. 255; *FL*, p. 126–7; **71** *MRH*, p. 245; F.J. McKiernan, *St Mary's Abbey, Cavan* (2000). **72** *MRH*, p. 243; Clyn, *Annals*, p. 221; P. Conlan, 'The Franciscans in Carrick-on-Suir' (2003). **73** *CPL*, iii, pp 263–4.

1.3 Map of
Augustinian,
Carmelite and
Friars of the Sack
foundations to
1341.

15

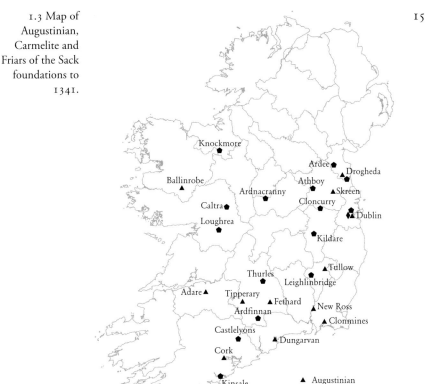

Knockmore

Ardee
Drogheda
Ballinrobe
Athboy
Ardnacranny
Skreen
Caltra
Cloncurry
Loughrea
Dublin

Kildare

Tullow
Thurles
Leighlinbridge
Adare
Tipperary
Fethard
Ardfinnan
New Ross
Clonmines
Castlelyons
Dungarvan
Cork

Kinsale

▲ Augustinian
⬟ Carmelite
◆ Friars of the Sack

THE CARMELITES, AUGUSTINIANS AND FRIARS OF THE SACK

The emergence in Ireland during the last third of the thirteenth century of the
Carmelites, Augustinians and Friars of the Sack corresponded with a time of flux
within each order and of turmoil and uncertainty in the affairs of the Anglo-Irish
colony (fig. 1.3).[74] Unlike the Dominicans and Franciscans, with their strong sense
of pastoral purpose and mendicant identity, the Austin and Carmelite friars had
originated as hermits and both groups had to negotiate the transition from an
eremitical, contemplative lifestyle to that of a mendicant order engaged in an
urban, pastoral ministry. Their emergence in Europe in the mid-thirteenth
century also occurred at a time of general hostility towards the mendicants on the
part of the secular clergy and the monastic orders. A number of mendicant groups
were doomed to extinction by a decree of the council of Lyon in 1274 that forbade
them to receive any further novices. The Dominicans and Franciscans were
permitted to continue because of their 'manifest utility' to the church, but the

**74** Discussed in greater detail below, p. 89.

Augustinian and Carmelites were only granted a stay of execution until a future council passed a definitive judgment regarding them. Thus, the very right to exist remained an open question for both orders for several decades and in England and the Continent this uncertainty resulted in a reluctance on the part of donors to support their foundations.[75] The Friars of the Sack were less fortunate and, despite the large number of their foundations, they gradually withered into oblivion by the early fourteenth century.[76] There is insufficient evidence to demonstrate how these conflicts affected the friars in Ireland, but both numerically and in terms of influence the newcomers remained subordinate to their Dominican and Franciscan colleagues throughout the later Middle Ages.

In England, concern over the transfer of land and other real estate to undying corporations such as religious orders and monasteries led to the enactment in 1279 of the Statute of Mortmain, which forbade such alienations without royal permission. As enacted, the statute only held force in England but was adopted in Ireland by no later than 1289.[77] Though the amounts of land and other properties alienated to the Irish friars were usually quite small, they were still subject to inquisitions *ad quod damnum* that determined what losses the crown would suffer from such grants. As the enforcement of mortmain legislation corresponded with the emergence of the Augustinians and the Carmelites in Ireland, it meant that both orders were well represented in the surviving inquisitions and extents, the details of which give invaluable insights into the process of founding friaries.[78]

### THE CARMELITES

The earliest contemporary reference to the Carmelite friars in Ireland occurs in 1271 when a letter of protection was granted for five years to 'the brothers of the order of the Blessed Mary of Mount Carmel in Ireland.'[79] This document, renewed in 1274, is similar to those granted to English representatives of other religious orders conducting business in Ireland and may indicate that the recipients were English friars engaged in establishing the order's first Irish houses.[80] The White Friars had made their first English foundations at Hulne in Northumberland and Aylesford in Kent by 1242 and when the first Irish references

---

**75** N.P. Tanner, *Decrees of the Ecumenical Councils* (1990), i, p. 326; Andrews, *The other friars*, pp 17–21. **76** Ibid., pp 207–23. **77** P.A. Brand, 'King, church and property: the enforcement of restrictions on alienations into mortmain in the lordship of Ireland in the later Middle Ages' (1983); idem, 'The licensing of mortmain alienations in the medieval Lordship of Ireland' (1986). **78** The surviving Irish *Ad quod damnum* material is calendared in P. Dryburgh & B. Smith, *Inquisitions and extents of medieval Ireland* (2007). I am grateful to Hugh Fenning for this reference. **79** *CDI*, ii, p. 154. **80** For other Irish examples, see C. Ó Clabaigh, 'The Benedictines in medieval and early modern Ireland' (2005), pp 98–9; A. Hogan, *The priory of Llanthony Prima and Secunda in Ireland, 1172–1541* (2008), p. 145 n. 25.

occur, eighteen Carmelite friaries had been established in England.[81] The friary at Leighlinbridge, Co. Carlow, was founded by a member of the Carew family at a strategic crossing point on the east bank of the River Barrow towards the close of the reign of Henry III (d. 1272) and is traditionally regarded as the first Carmelite priory in Ireland.[82] As was customary with Carmelite foundations, the house was dedicated to the Virgin Mary. The first attempt to establish a community in Dublin occurred in 1274 and the friars were beneficiaries of a will in 1275. The friars' patron was Sir Robert Bagot, the chief justice. The friars encountered difficulties in their attempts to establish the Dublin house and only secured a permanent site in 1278.[83] Two other foundations were made at unspecified dates early in the reign of Edward I (1272–1307). Ralph Pipard, lord of Ardee, Co. Louth, established a priory there and granted the friars a share from the produce of his manor. The other house, at Drogheda, was erected by the townspeople on the southern or Co. Meath bank of the River Boyne.[84]

The Carmelites in Kildare owed their origins to William de Vescy, who had previously established a Franciscan house in the town.[85] The de Vescy family were longstanding supporters of the Carmelites in England, being patrons of one of their earliest priories at Hulne in Northumberland, and this connection probably provides the context for the Kildare foundation. The priory at Ardnacranny, Co. Westmeath, was founded *c*.1291 by Robert Dillon, while at the same time members of the Butler family established a house in Thurles, Co. Tipperary, although practically nothing else is recorded of either of these convents until their dissolution.[86] In about 1300, Richard de Burgh, the earl of Ulster, founded a Carmelite friary dedicated to St Mary at Loughrea, Co. Galway, the church of which remains. Earl Richard endowed the community again in 1305, but no further reference to it occurs before 1437, when Pope Eugene IV granted an indulgence to all who visited their church and contributed to its repair.[87] The remains of the Carmelite priory at Castlelyons, Co. Cork, are the most extensive of all the order's medieval Irish houses. In 1309, the founder, John de Barry, received royal permission to grant a small parcel of land at Castlelyons to the prior and community of the Carmelites in Drogheda. The friars may already have been

**81** R. Copsey, *Carmel in Britain 3: the hermits from Mount Carmel* (2004), p. vii; K.J. Egan, 'Dating English Carmelite foundations' (1992). The English province eventually numbered thirty-nine foundations. **82** *MRH*, pp 290–1; P. O'Dwyer, *The Irish Carmelites* (1988), pp 3–4; M. Kavanagh, 'The White Friars and the white castle of Leighlin' (1996, for 1995). **83** *MRH*, p. 289; O'Dwyer, *Irish Carmelites*, pp 4–6. The significance of the Statute of Mortmain for Irish mendicant foundations is discussed in greater detail below, pp 89–90. **84** *MRH*, pp 286, 288. O'Dwyer, *Irish Carmelites*, 10–13; D. Mac Íomhair, 'The Carmelites in Ardee' (1983). **85** *MRH*, p. 290. **86** *MRH*, pp 286–7, 291–2. **87** *MRH*, p. 291; O'Dwyer, *Irish Carmelites*, p. 14; C. Ó Clabaigh, 'The mendicant friars in the pre-Reformation diocese of Clonfert' (2007). I am grateful to Commandant Kevin MacDonald for advice on this point.

present since 1307, as Ware refers to a foundation there but gives the order as Franciscan. The house was established without papal permission and on 5 January 1314 Pope Clement V forbade the prior and community to live there for a period of seven years, after which they might petition for permission to return. As no further reference to this occurs in any of the papal registers, it is possible that the friars came to some alternative arrangement or ignored the prohibition altogether.[88] On the same date, however, the pope issued another bull in favour of the Irish friars, permitting them to establish convents in the dioceses of Cashel, Cork, Elphin, Limerick and Lismore.[89] The only house that can be attributed directly to this licence is that at Ardfinnan, Co. Tipperary, in the diocese of Lismore.

In October 1317, William de Loundres was permitted to grant the Carmelites at Athboy, Co. Meath, the land on which their priory stood. This indicates that the friars were already in possession of the site and the community was sufficiently well established to host a provincial chapter in 1325. The de Bermingham family of Athenry were responsible for establishing a friary at Caltra, Co. Galway, *c.*1320, but nothing else is known of its pre-dissolution history.[90] The community at Knockmore, Co. Sligo, was also established *c.*1320, but here even the identity of the order is uncertain, with a number of early sources ascribing it to the Dominicans.[91] The founders were members of the O'Gara family. In 1347, Edward III licensed the establishment of the house at Cloncurry, Co. Kildare, by John Roche, but again nothing else is known of the community before its dissolution in 1539.[92] The last foundation to be made before the Black Death was at Kinsale, Co. Cork, which was erected sometime during the reign of Edward III, possibly in 1334. Here, the founder was Robert FitzRichard Balrain, who granted an additional quarter of land to the community in 1350.[93]

### THE AUGUSTINIANS

The first contemporary reference to the Augustinian or Austin friars in Ireland occurs in 1282, when the community of Holy Trinity Priory, Dublin, was the beneficiary of a will.[94] Sir James Ware dated the foundation of the Dublin house to 1259, but as the Augustinians were not listed with the other mendicant legatees of Elizabeth le Grant in 1275, F.X. Martin concluded that this date was too early. The priory occupied an extensive site on the south bank of the River Liffey now

---

88 *MRH*, p. 288; *CPL*, ii, p.120; *Bull. Carm.*, I, p. 544; O'Dwyer, *Irish Carmelites*, pp 22–3. 89 *Bull. Carm.*, I, p. 545. 90 *MRH*, p. 287. 91 *MRH*, p. 290. 92 Ibid. 93 *MRH*, p. 291; O'Dwyer, *Irish Carmelites*, pp 23–4. 94 H.J. Lawlor, 'The calendar of the Liber Niger and the Liber Albus of Christ Church, Dublin' (1908/9), p. 31. The testator, William de Stafford, was about to embark on pilgrimage to the Holy Land and left legacies to a number of Dublin churches and religious houses.

occupied by Cecilia Street and the northern part of Crowe Street, where a portion of the friary precinct wall survives. The founder was reputedly a member of the Talbot family and in 1284 Edward I permitted the mayor and corporation of Dublin to allow the friars acquire an acre of land to extend their site, notwithstanding the Statute of Mortmain. The house was the order's principal convent in Ireland and the site of a general *studium* from the latter part of the fourteenth century.[95]

St Augustine's Priory, Abbeyside, Dungarvan, Co. Waterford, was erected *c*.1290 by Thomas Fitzgerald, Lord Offaly, who became justiciar of Ireland in 1295 and died in 1296. The MacGraths of Sleady and O'Briens of Commeragh also endowed the community and the tomb of Donal MacGrath (d. 1400) is situated in the north-west corner of the church, near the high altar, a position normally reserved for founders or other prominent benefactors.[96] The date of the friars' arrival in Drogheda is unknown, but they were well established by 1300, when the prior successfully asserted their right to a burgage in the town. Nothing further is known of the early history of the house apart from the fact that it was restored by members of the Brandon family, 'English men of quality', at some unspecified date.[97]

The first reference to the Augustinian priory or 'Red Abbey' in Cork occurs in the 1306 will of John de Wynchedon, a wealthy merchant who sought burial in their cemetery. He left a bequest for Masses for the repose of his soul and also bequeathed eight marks for the repair of the friars' choir stalls.[98] The friary precinct stretched to the gate of the city and it was customary for Cork merchants to make an offering to the friars before embarking on foreign trading trips.[99] Stephen Butler is thought to have founded the friary at Tipperary *c*.1300, but otherwise nothing is known of its pre-Reformation history.[1] In contrast, the origins of the priory in Fethard, Co. Tipperary, are remarkably well documented, giving a comprehensive impression of the legal process by which a friary was erected. Walter Mulcote established the foundation sometime before 1305, when

95 F.X. Martin, 'The Augustinian friaries in pre-Reformation Ireland' (1956), 372–3; T.C. Butler, *John's Lane: history of the Augustinian friars in Dublin, 1280–1980* (1983), pp 17–24; *MRH*, pp 298–9; D. Kelly, 'The Augustinians in Dublin' (2005); S. Duffy & L. Simpson, 'The hermits of St Augustine in Dublin' (2009). 96 Martin, 'Augustinian friaries', 373–4; *MRH*, p. 299; T.C. Butler, 'Augustinian foundations in the south-east' (1978), 9–11. 97 J. Stevens, *Monasticon Hibernicum* (1722), p. 314; Martin, 'Augustinian friaries', 371; *MRH*, p. 298; P. Duffner, *The Low Lane church: the story of the Augustinians in Drogheda, 1300–1979* (1979), pp 9–15. 98 D. O'Sullivan (ed.), 'The testament of John de Wynchedon of Cork anno 1306' (1956), p. 77. This is the earliest will to survive from medieval Cork and provides an important snapshot of the religious life of the city at the beginning of the fourteenth century. 99 D. O'Sullivan, 'The Augustinian convent of medieval Cork' (1941), 144–5; Martin, 'Augustinian friaries', 369–71; *MRH*, pp 297–8; T.C. Butler, *The Augustinians in Cork, 1280–1985* (1986), pp 7–17. 1 Martin, 'Augustinian friaries', 383; *MRH*, p. 302.

he granted the friars an acre and a half of land that he held from the archbishop of Cashel. This grant received royal confirmation in July 1306 and the friars were pardoned for contravening the Statute of Mortmain.[2] Little else is known of the house's pre-Reformation history, apart from the fact that it was dedicated either to St Augustine or to the Holy Trinity. Three late medieval statues preserved in the National Museum of Ireland are thought to come from the friary church (pl. 17).[3] The priory at Tullow, Co. Carlow, was established in 1314 when Simon the Lombard and Hugo Talon donated a house and three acres of land to the friars in the village of St John adjoining Tullow. The Knights Hospitallers at Kilmainham, from whom Talon held the land, confirmed the grant in 1331. F.X. Martin suggested that Simon the Lombard was an Italian moneylender who financed the building of the monastery on land donated by Talon, who later died as a member of the community.[4]

The Augustinian friary at Adare, Co. Limerick, on the south bank of the River Maigue, was founded by John FitzThomas Fitzgerald, first earl of Kildare, some time before his death in 1316. His initial grant of lands and tenements in the town was confirmed in a charter granted to his son Thomas in December 1317 by the lord deputy, Roger Mortimer. The remains of the complex which now serve as the Church of Ireland church and parochial school, are among the best preserved medieval structures in Ireland.[5] Permission to alienate land to establish the priory of St Nicholas at Clonmines, Co. Wexford, was granted to members of the Kavanagh family in 1317, and Nicholas FitzNicholas granted the community a messuage and garden in 1385. The impressive ruins of the priory church indicate that it was well endowed at the time of its construction.[6] The earliest indication of an Augustinian presence at New Ross, Co. Wexford, occurs in a letter of Pope John XXII dated December 1320. This concerned the transfer of a number of friars from the Augustinians to the Friars Minor. One of these, John de Ros, later returned to the Augustinians and was readmitted to the convent at New Ross, which the Franciscans alleged was an excommunicable offence. The papal letter absolved the Austin friars from any censure.[7] The founder of the house was William Roche.

---

**2** Martin, 'Augustinian friaries', 375; *MRH*, pp 299–300. T.C. Butler, *The friars of Fethard* (1976).  **3** They depict God the Father from a Throne of Grace ensemble, John the Baptist and Christ on the Cold Stone. **4** Martin, 'Augustinian friaries', 383–4; *MRH*, p. 302.  **5** Caroline, Lady Dunraven, *Memorials of Adare Manor* (1845), pp 68–74. The Latin text of the confirmation charter with an English translation is given on pp 68–9; R.F. Hewson, 'The Augustinian priory, Adare' (1938); Martin, 'Augustinian friaries', 359–60; *MRH*, p. 295; T.C. Butler, *The Augustinians in Limerick* (1988), pp 1–7.  **6** Martin, 'Augustinian friaries', 368–9; Butler, 'Augustinian foundations', 9–11.  **7** Martin, 'Augustinian friaries', 380–1. The February 1320 response of Edward II to Adam, guardian of the Franciscans of New Ross, concerning the apostasy of Friar John de Wynton may be connected to this dispute. *FL*, p. 109.

The date for the foundation St Mary's Priory at Ballinrobe, Co. Mayo, is uncertain. Martin suggested that it may have been established *c.*1312 by Elizabeth de Clare and John de Burgh in thanksgiving for the birth of a son and heir. Elizabeth was the grandchild of Edward I, and in 1248 another ancestor, Richard de Clare, had established the first English Augustinian friary at Clare in Suffolk. Her husband was the son and heir of Richard de Burgh, earl of Ulster, who had ceded them the manor of Lough Mask (with Ballinrobe as its manorial caput) on the occasion of their wedding in 1308. The earliest contemporary reference to the foundation occurs in 1338 when Edmund de Burgh, son of Richard, the 'Red Earl' of Ulster, was taken from the friary by his cousin Edmund Albanach de Burgh, placed in a sack and drowned in Lough Mask.[8]

In 1341, Lord Francis de Feipo introduced the Augustinians to Skreen in Meath, leasing them a property at a peppercorn rent for ninety-nine years. He also leased them another twelve acres at Ponestown for an annual rent of twelve pence with grazing rights for three horses at Skreen. This grant was confirmed by Edward II in May 1342. The priory was dedicated to the Holy Trinity, and a reference to Friar John Keppocke of the Drogheda Austin friars indicates that the first friars may have come from there. Little else is known of the early history of the house.[9] The foundation at Skreen was the last Augustinian house to be established in Ireland before the Black Death.

### THE FRIARS OF THE SACK

The Friars of Penitence of Jesus Christ (known as the Friars of the Sack from the sackcloth cloak they wore over their habits), emerged in Provence in the 1240s, when two laymen, inspired by the preaching of the Franciscan dissident, Friar Hugh of Digne, adopted an eremitical lifestyle.[10] By 1251, they had received papal approbation and, as their numbers grew, they followed the example of the Augustinians and Carmelites and embraced a mendicant lifestyle and an urban preaching ministry. They also adopted many Franciscan practices and placed a strong emphasis on evangelical poverty, thereby incurring the hostility of some Friars Minor. Their constitutional and educational structures owed much to the Dominicans. The friars expanded rapidly in Provence, France, Northern Italy, France, Spain and the Low Countries. They arrived in England in or before 1256, when they and their property were granted royal protection by Henry III.[11] In 1257, Friar Peter of Tewkesbury, minister provincial of the English Franciscans, recommended them to the Franciscan provincial chapter meeting in London,

---

8 Martin, 'Augustinian friaries', 361–2; *MRH*, p. 296.   9 Martin, 'Augustinian friaries', 382–3; *MRH*, pp 301–2.   10 Andrews, *The other friars*, pp 175–223.   11 Ibid., pp 183–4. W. Emery, 'The Friars of the

where the Sack friars had that year established their first foundation.[12] By 1274, when the order fell victim to the recruitment ban imposed by the second council of Lyon, the Friars of the Sack had eighteen houses in England and a single Scottish priory in the border town of Berwick.

The earliest reference to the Friars of the Sack in Ireland occurs in 1268, when two members of the order received royal protection for three years to conduct business in Ireland. This presumably was connected to the establishment of the order's only Irish house in Dublin. The Franciscan Annals of Multyfarnham also record their arrival in 1268.[13] The precise location of the friary is not known, but Archdall suggested that it may be identified with the monastery of Witeschan, mentioned in an inquisition conducted during the reign of Richard II (1377–99). This was situated in the Coombe area of Dublin, on the boundary of the lands of St Thomas' Abbey.[14] The new foundation received royal grants of alms of ten pounds in 1272 and of five marks in 1274.[15] In addition, like the other Dublin mendicants, they also attracted bequests in wills. In March 1275, they were among the beneficiaries of Elizabeth le Grant, while William Stafford left them a bequest in 1282.[16] Nothing further is known of their activities in Ireland. They obviously maintained a public church as Thomas Thonnyr was indicted in 1309–10 of harbouring Adam Cauntelon and others who had broken into the 'church of the friars *de penitentia Jesu Christi*', robbing them of forty shillings.[17]

## CONSTITUTIONAL ARRANGEMENTS

The administrative structures of all the mendicant orders were very similar. The fundamental unit of each order was the convent (priory or friary), governed by a prior (or, in Franciscan terminology, a guardian or warden). The prior or guardian was responsible for the spiritual and temporal affairs of the friars, for maintaining discipline and for representing the community in its relations with patrons, ecclesiastical authorities and the rest of the province.[18] Ideally, a convent's full complement consisted of a superior and twelve friars, but many houses contained larger communities while some were smaller. Each convent had a fixed geographical area or 'limit' within which the friars of the house exercised their ministry as preachers and confessors and in which they were permitted to beg or quest for alms. Within a wider geographical or linguistic territory, a number of

Sack' (1943); idem, 'A note on the Friars of the Sack' (1960).  **12** A.G. Little (ed.), *De adventu*, pp 102, 103.  **13** *FL*, p. 35.  **14** Archdall, *Monasticon Hibernicum*, p. 174.  **15** *CDI*, ii (1877), pp 147, 149.  **16** M.J. McEnery & R. Refaussé (eds), *Christ Church deeds* (2001), no. 106, p. 54; Lawlor, 'Calendar of the Liber Niger and the Liber Albus of Christ Church, Dublin' (1908–9), p. 31.  **17** *MRH*, p. 306.  **18** L. Viallet, 'Le rôle du gardien dans le couvents franciscains au XV^e siècle' (2010).

convents were often grouped together for administrative purposes. The terminology for this arrangement differed between orders. Among the Franciscans it was known as the custody, and among the Augustinians these subdivisions were known as *plagae*. The superiors of these subdivisions usually exercised ordinary jurisdiction over communities in their territories. Collectively, all the convents made up an order's province, and this was governed by a provincial prior (or minister provincial in Franciscan usage). This officer in turn was answerable to the respective superior general of each order: the master general in the case of the Dominicans; the minister general of the Franciscans; and the priors general in Augustinian and Carmelite usage.

In each order, the provincial chapter met regularly at anything from annual to triennial intervals. Legislation enacted at this gathering was binding on all the friars of the province and formed the basis of each order's provincial constitutions, none of which survive for any Irish order. The supreme legislative body for each mendicant order was its general chapter that met regularly at different locations throughout Europe. These gatherings, at which the provincial superiors and other delegates represented their respective regions, enacted and promulgated the general constitutions that governed each order.[19]

Each order also maintained standards of discipline and uniformity of observance through the system of visitation, whereby each convent and province was subject to regular tours of inspection by the superior general or, more commonly, by delegated friars known as visitators. At the conclusion of each visitation, a report (*tabula* or *carta*) was drawn up by the visitators indicating what abuses were to be corrected and, where necessary, deposing superiors and correcting delinquents. No contemporary visitator's *tabula* survives from medieval Ireland, but the Franciscan visitation of 1325 discussed below gives some indication of its impact.

The success with which these administrative structures operated varied between orders and between the different provinces of the same institute. An additional complicating factor in Ireland was the fact that, among the mendicants, only the Franciscans enjoyed full autonomy as a province, with the Dominicans, Augustinians and Carmelites forming, for varying periods, subordinate parts of the English provinces of their respective orders.

### THE DOMINICANS

The rapid and widespread expansion of the Dominicans in Ireland and the difficulties of regularly travelling to England meant that from the outset the Irish

---

**19** For discussion of the rules and general constitutions of each order, see above, pp xiii–xviii.

Friars Preachers enjoyed a considerable degree of self-government, but the denial of full autonomy was a cause of resentment.[20] Various attempts were made in the fourteenth and fifteenth centuries to secure independence but, despite these, the Irish friars remained subject to the English prior provincial and his delegates until an Irish Dominican province was definitively established in 1536.

The earliest reference to Dominican organization in Ireland occurs in 1242, when a 'provincial' chapter was held in Athenry.[21] While the term is inaccurate, it indicates that regular assemblies presided over by a representative of the English provincial were being held by the Irish friars. The first reference to the vicar provincial of Ireland occurs in March 1256, when he was instructed by Pope Alexander IV to send two friars to combat heresy in the diocese of Raphoe.[22] In May 1256, Laurence de Somercote, a fundraiser for the crusades, referred to Friar Karolus (Charles) as the Irish vicar provincial and indicated that a chapter was to be held in Cashel in June that year.[23]

The system of vicariates, whereby Dominican provinces were subdivided into smaller units governed by a vicar or delegate of the prior provincial, was formally established by the order's general chapter meeting in Bologna in 1275.[24] It is clear, however, that the system was already the norm in Ireland before this date. In 1314, following the order's general chapter in London, the master general, Berengar of Landorra, issued a charter outlining the canonical status of the Irish vicariate and confirming the norms for its governance.[25] Friar Berengar's charter was incorporated in the bull *Sacrae religionis*, issued to the Irish friars by Pope Boniface IX on 21 February 1400. The charter decreed that the Irish vicar provincial was to be selected by the English Dominican provincial from a list of three names proposed by the priors of the Irish houses, a representative of each community and by the Irish preachers general. Once appointed, the vicar was to enjoy all the privileges of a prior provincial, except when the prior provincial of England conducted a visitation of the Irish vicariate. The vicar was instructed to hold an annual chapter to which he was accountable, as were the priors of the individual convents. The Irish vicariate chapter could suspend the vicar or any local superior, but dismissal from office was reserved to the prior provincial and chapter of England. The Irish friars were represented at the annual English chapter by two

**20** This section is based on O'Sullivan, *MIDS*, pp 177–93; Flynn, *The Irish Dominicans*, pp 1–11; U. Flanagan, 'The formative development of the Dominican and Franciscan orders in Ireland, with special reference to the Observant reform' (1947), pp 130–56; D. Pochin-Mould, *The Irish Dominicans* (1957), pp 14–27.   **21** A. Coleman, *Ancient Dominican foundations in Ireland* (1902), p. 79; *MRH*, p. 221; Archdall, *Monasticon Hibernicum* (1786), p. 273.   **22** M. Sheehy, *Pontificia Hibernica*, II (1965), nos 421, 422. The bishop of the diocese, Patrick O'Scanaill, was a Dominican.   **23** *FL*, pp 23–4.   **24** Reichert, *Acta capitula generalium*, i, p. 177. For Dominican organization in general, see W.A. Hinnesbusch, *The history of the Dominican order*, i (1965), pp 169–93.   **25** For studies, see below, pp 271–80.

priors or preachers general from Ireland and the vicar provincial was obliged to attend in person every four years. The charter also granted the Irish friars the right to send two delegates to the order's annual general chapter. In keeping with the long established custom, the prior provincial of England continued to nominate visitators for an annual visitation of the Irish convents.[26] The charter had the effect of erecting the Irish vicariate as a province in all but name, and established the basic canonical position of the Irish Dominicans until the end of the fifteenth century and the emergence of reform congregations among the friars in Ireland. It was not entirely satisfactory, and the difficulty of getting Gaelic, Anglo-Irish and English friars to agree on appointments soon became apparent. The political context of the Bruce invasion of Ireland, which formed the backdrop to these developments, was undoubtedly significant and is discussed in greater detail below. The order's general chapter meeting at Lyon in 1318 condemned those members of the Irish vicariate who had refused to accept the vicar provincial appointed by the English provincial. Their leader, Friar Henry Glam, was banished from Ireland, deprived of active voice in the order and condemned to a penitential regime, while the prior provincial of England was ordered to go to Ireland and discipline the friars.[27]

## THE FRANCISCANS

The Irish Franciscan province was formally established by the general chapter of Assisi in 1230 with the appointment of Friar Richard of Ingworth, a veteran of the 1224 Franciscan mission to England, as its first minister provincial. He had been the first custos of the custody of Cambridge and governed the Irish province for fifteen years before going to work as a missionary in Syria.[28] His successor was another English friar, John of Kethene, who was appointed by the general chapter in 1239 and ruled the province until 1254. Friar John had previously been the guardian of the friary in London before being appointed provincial of the short-lived Franciscan province in Scotland.[29] Thomas of Eccleston recorded that his reputation for compassion and gentleness was such that friars who found life difficult elsewhere transferred to Ireland to live under his regime.[30]

Like the other Franciscan provinces, the Irish province was divided into smaller administrative units known as custodies, each one of which was governed by a superior, called a *custos*, who exercised ordinary jurisdiction over the friars of the

---

**26** T. Ripoll, *Bullarium OP*, vii, pp 74–5. See also de Burgo, *Hibernia Dominicana*, pp 49–50; Flanagan, 'Formative development', pp 139–50; Pochin-Mould, *Irish Dominicans*, pp 245–7. **27** Reichert, *Acta*, ii, pp 112–13. **28** A.G. Little (ed.), *De adventu*, pp 4, 6, 9–10, 35. **29** Watt, *A tender watering: Franciscans in Scotland from the 13th to the 21st century* (2011), pp 41–58. **30** A.G. Little (ed.), *De adventu*, pp 41–3, 69, 101.

custody. The *custos* was entitled to appoint or depose guardians and was expected to make an annual visitation of the houses in his custody. Initially, the minister general or minister provincial appointed the *custodes*, but after 1336 they were elected by the delegates from the houses of each custody attending the provincial chapter.[31] The earliest reference to custodies in Ireland occurs in a list enumerating the friaries in each of the order's provinces that was compiled between 1263 and 1270. The Irish province then consisted of twenty-two friaries divided into four custodies.[32] By 1325, the province consisted of thirty-two houses, which were divided into five custodies.[33] A list compiled for the general chapter meeting at Perpignan in France in 1331 indicated that the number of houses had increased to thirty-seven, while the number of custodies remained at five.[34] The increase in the number of custodies from four to five occurred at a period of great tension between the Anglo-Irish and Gaelic members of the province and was designed to ensure that the Anglo-Irish friars maintained their position of dominance. The Gaelic houses were grouped together in the custody of Nenagh that became, geographically, the most extensive custody in the province. In 1345, the provincial chapter meeting at Clane recognized four custodies and in 1385 a list of the houses of the Irish province compiled for the order's general chapter meeting in Ragusa (Dubrovnik) also listed four.[35]

Whereas the Irish province was an independent entity from its inception in 1230, it was one of three provinces in the order that was subject to restrictions concerning its minister provincial, whose appointment was reserved to the minister general.[36] Though this restriction was first expressed in the 1312 papal bull *Exivi de paradiso*, it confirmed a pre-existing practice rather than marking an innovation.[37] The ministers provincial appointed were always either English or Anglo-Irish friars, which indicates that by the fourteenth century both the papacy and the ministers general of the order were alert to the issue of race relations within the Irish province. The province did not gain the right to elect its minister provincial until the mid-fifteenth century and the election of the Gaelic friar, William O'Reilly.

**31** R.M. Huber, *A documented history of the Franciscan order* (1944), pp 652–6.   **32** *MRH*, pp 235–9; Cotter, *Friars Minor*, pp 18–19; *FL*, p. 49.   **33** 'Brevis synopsis', pp 142–3.   **34** *FL*, pp 133–4. The custody of Dublin had seven houses (Dublin, Castledermot, Clane, Kildare, Monasterorois, Wexford and Wicklow); that of Drogheda had six (Drogheda, Carrickfergus, Downpatrick, Dundalk, Multyfarnham and Trim); Cashel also had six houses (Cashel, Kilkenny, New Ross, Waterford, Clonmel and Youghal); Cork had five (Cork, Buttevant, Limerick, Timoleague and Ardfert) and the Nenagh custody consisted of eight foundations (Nenagh, Armagh, Athlone, Cavan, Claregalway, Ennis, Galway and Killeigh).   **35** Clyn, *Annals*, p. 233. The friaries of Kilkenny and New Ross were transferred from the Cashel custody to that of Dublin. A.G. Little suggests that the Cork custody may have been abolished at this stage with its houses being divided between Cashel and Nenagh. *FL*, pp 138–9.   **36** The other provinces were Romania and the Holy Land. For the formulary document appointing the Irish minister provincial in the fourteenth century, see M. Bihl OFM, *Formulae et Documenta e cancellaria Fr Michaelis de Caesena OFM, Ministri Generalis, 1316–1328* (1930), p. 153.   **37** *BF*, v, p. 85; *FL*, p. 94.

Though the surviving references are few, it seems that the ministers provincial of Ireland were regular attendees at the order's general chapters. In 1251, Friar John of Kethene led the opposition to the relaxation of the vow of poverty proposed at the general chapter at Genoa. In 1254, he was released from office at the chapter of Metz.[38] Friar John Tancard died while returning from the general chapter at Pisa in 1272,[39] and in 1294 Friar William of Tadyngton was granted royal permission to sail with seven other friars from Yarmouth to the general chapter meeting that year in Assisi. In 1301, similar permission was given to Friar Thomas de Thorpe to attend the chapter meeting in Genoa.[40] In 1354, the group of six friars accompanying the provincial Friar John Tonebrigg to the general chapter in Assisi included two Gaelic friars: Patrick Makeregh and Galfridus O'Hogan.[41] The perils inherent in the journey and the high status of the Irish minister provincial are evident in the experience of Friar John Wabergen who was kidnapped by Flemish pirates while returning from the general chapter in Munich in 1405. He was ransomed for twenty marks, the other friars in the party for five.[42]

## THE AUGUSTINIANS

The Augustinians in Ireland formed the largest and poorest of the five administrative units known as 'limits' into which the English province was divided.[43] Each limit was ruled by a vicar provincial and by the mid-fourteenth century, when the first references to Ireland occur in the registers of the order's priors general, it is clear that, like the Dominicans, a considerable degree of autonomy had been granted to, or assumed by, the friars in Ireland. To an even greater degree than the other mendicants, the Augustinians identified themselves with the Anglo-Irish colony and initially established no foundation in Gaelic territories. There is no evidence of recruitment of Gaelic members to the order before the late fourteenth century. When tension emerged over the governance of the limit, it was between the Anglo-Irish members of the order in Ireland and their superiors and *confrères* in England and this is discussed in greater detail below.[44]

**38** *FL*, p. 22.   **39** *FL*, p. 39.   **40** *FL*, pp 66, 76. Thorpe was requested to ask the chapter to pray for the king and the royal family.   **41** *FL*, p. 145. Hogan was one of the compilers of the Annals of Nenagh. **42** *FL*, p. 172.   **43** F. Roth, 'A history of the English Austin Friars' (1961), 542–6; F.X. Martin & Alberic de Meijer, 'Irish material in the Augustinian general archives, Rome, 1354–1624' (1956); Martin, 'The Augustinian friaries', 355–8.   **44** See below, pp 45–7.

## THE CARMELITES

Like the other mendicant orders, the Carmelite order in Ireland was established
by members of the English province, and the Irish friars were initially subject to
the prior provincial of England: Roger Crostwick, who was prior provincial of
England from 1272 until 1277, conducted a visitation of the Irish houses during
his term of office.[45] By 1291, six foundations had been established in Ireland and
an attempt was made to combine these with the five Scottish foundations to erect
a Hiberno-Scottish province. In 1294, the order's general chapter, meeting in
Bordeaux, gave the newly erected province the right to send one student annually
to the order's *studium* at Paris.[46] This attempt at separation was bitterly resented
by the English provincial, Friar William Ludlington, and by other high-ranking
English friars. The conquest of large areas of Scotland by Edward I in 1296
effectively put paid to any hopes of independence for the Scottish priories, but the
order's prior general, Friar Gerard of Bologna, continued with efforts to enforce
the decision of the general chapter. In January 1303, he secured a letter from
Edward I instructing Sir Roger Brabazon and other members of the royal council
to assist his delegates, Friars William Pagham de Hanabergh and William
Newenham, who had been thwarted by English members of the order in their
attempts to conduct a visitation. At Pentecost in 1303, the general chapter,
meeting in Narbonne, again ordered the separation of the Irish and Scottish
houses, but encountered further resistance from a number of English and Irish
friars. Eventually, the prior general was forced to appeal to the pope and obtained
permission for two commissaries, Friars Gobelinus, the prior provincial of
Germany, and Conrad of St George, a former provincial of Germany, to represent
him at the English provincial chapter that was held in London in 1305. Here, they
presided over the election of the more amenable Friar Richard Welwen as prior
provincial, and enforced the decision of the general chapter. Those who had
opposed the granting of independence, including the Irish friar David O'Buge,
were sent into exile. The first prior provincial of the newly independent Irish
province was Friar William Newenham, who was confirmed in office by the
general chapter of the order meeting in Genoa in 1309 and who ruled the
province until 1311.[47]

   Though relatively little evidence survives to illustrate the origins and expansion
of the mendicant orders in Ireland, it is clear that the Irish friars shared in the
experience of rapid growth that was the lot of their *confrères* elsewhere. The
foundation of the Augustinian priory at Skreen in 1341 marked the end of the first
wave of mendicant expansion and the combined total of mendicant houses in

---

45 BL MS 3838, fo. 22b; O'Dwyer, *Irish Carmelites*, p. 4.   46 R. Copsey, 'The Scottish Carmelite province
and its provincials' (2004), pp 116–19.   47 O'Dwyer, *Irish Carmelites*, pp 20, 48.

Ireland then stood at ninety-six, all but eight of which were located in the towns and boroughs of the Anglo-Norman colony.[48] Their arrival during a period of expansion and prosperity for the colonists was a major factor in the success of this first wave of foundations but, despite this association, many communities also secured the support of aristocratic Gaelic patrons. The mounting ethnic tensions and economic stagnation that characterized Irish affairs in the late thirteenth century also affected the friars who, like their secular counterparts, experienced the fourteenth century as a period of discord, decline and division.

---

**48** Cotter, *Friars Minor*, p. 186.

# CHAPTER TWO

# Discord, division and death, 1290–1390

AD1325 *There was discord, as commonly reported, among virtually all the mendicants of Ireland, some of them upholding, favouring and promoting the side of their nation, blood and language, others canvassing for achievement and high office.*[1]

The widespread and rapid expansion that characterized all the mendicant orders in Ireland faltered at the beginning of the fourteenth century as the friars shared in the colony's experience of recession, depopulation and loss of confidence in the face of Gaelic resurgence. Climatic and environmental changes also contributed to a decline in agricultural productivity and prosperity, as did the three years of havoc that followed on the Bruce invasion in 1315. This experience of decline and debility was compounded by the Great Famine of 1316–18 and by the catastrophic impact of the Black Death that erupted in Ireland in the summer of 1348. The late thirteenth and early fourteenth centuries witnessed bitter divisions between the Gaelic and Anglo-Irish sections of the Dominican and Franciscan orders. Tension was evident too in the relationship between the Anglo-Irish Augustinians and Dominicans and their English *confrères*. The Great Schism (1378–1417) also had a negative impact on the religious observance and *esprit de corps* of the friars in Ireland.

## RACIAL TENSION AND THE FRIARS IN IRELAND

The surviving evidence suggests that Irish mendicant internal relations were characterized by peace and stability from their arrival until the final decades of the thirteenth century.[2] This was in marked contrast to the experience of the Cistercians who were beset by bitter divisions between their Gaelic and Anglo-Irish members, which culminated in a radical restructuring of the order's Irish

---

1 Clyn, *Annals*, pp 182–3.  2 Gallagher, 'Irish Franciscan province', pp 35–41; Cotter, *Friars Minor*, pp 31–50; Ó Clabaigh, *Franciscans*, pp 36–41. See also J.A. Watt, *The church and the two nations in medieval Ireland* (1970); idem, *The church in medieval Ireland* (1998); idem, 'The church and the two nations in late medieval Armagh' (1989). An important, if neglected, assessment is C. Ó Maonaigh, 'Ciníochas agus náisiúnachas san eaglais in Éirinn, 1169–1534' (1964–5).

houses in 1227–8.[3] The impression of mendicant harmony was confirmed by the compiler of the *Liber Exemplorum*. Writing about Thomas O'Quinn, the Franciscan bishop of Clonmacnois (1252–78), he described him as 'a good and faithful and well educated man',[4] and gave a glowing account of the efficacy of his preaching. O'Quinn had served as *custos* or regional superior of the Drogheda custody in 1252 and the presence of a Gaelic friar in this capacity in a stronghold of the colony indicates that racial tension and questions of loyalty were not yet issues.[5]

This harmonious state of affairs can be ascribed to a number of factors and bears comparison with the initial experience of the friars in other border areas.[6] Chief among these was the novelty of the mendicant ideal and the presence of a number of first-generation Franciscans and Dominicans among the pioneers in Ireland. Among the Franciscans, the wise government of the first two provincials, Friars Richard of Ingworth (1230–9) and John of Kethene (1239–54), as the province was established was particularly important. This idealism in following a common purpose initially seems to have been sufficient to unite members of different ethnic backgrounds.

The first possible indication of disquiet about the friars occurs in a letter from Nicholas Cusack, Franciscan bishop of Kildare (1279–99), to Edward I composed sometime between 1283 and 1299. He reported that trustworthy sources had informed him that

> The peace of the land is frequently disturbed by the secret counsels and poisonous colloquies which certain religious of the Irish tongue, belonging to diverse orders, hold with the Irish and their rulers.[7]

Cusack further alleged that these meetings led to unrest as the errant religious incited the Gaelic rulers and their subjects to attack the English settlers and to take their possessions without fear of any ecclesiastical sanctions claiming that this was in keeping with both the divine will and human law. As a solution he suggested that religious with Gaelic sympathies be removed from houses in volatile areas and that reliable Englishmen, with likeminded companions, should be sent among the Irish in future. As bishop of Kildare and a member of a prominent Anglo-Irish family established at Killeen in Co. Meath, Cusack's sympathies naturally lay with the king and the colony. It is not clear if the friars were among the offenders in this instance but, given their reputation as vernacular preachers and their role in subsequent events, it is very likely that they were.

---

**3** B. O'Dwyer, 'The problem of reform in the Irish Cistercian monasteries and the attempted solution of Stephen of Lexington in 1228' (1964); Watt, *The church and the two nations*, pp 85–107. **4** *Lib. ex.*, pp 85–6; Jones, *Friars' tales*, p. 113. **5** *FL*, xx, p. 18. **6** J.B. Freed, 'The friars and the delineation of state boundaries in the thirteenth century' (1976). **7** *FL*, p. 52.

Definite evidence for concern over the friars' activities and their Gaelic contacts came in a report on the organization of the exchequer in Dublin in 1285.[8] One of the complaints was that the Dominicans and Franciscans were granted money at the audit of accounts without any writ or warrant. Some friars were also criticized for 'making much' of the Irish language. The conspicuous loyalty of other friars to the crown is evident in the exchequer payments to individuals for services rendered. The earliest surviving example also occurred in 1285 when the Franciscan friar Stephen Dexter was granted forty shillings for expenses incurred in travelling to England to expound matters to the king.[9] In 1316, Friar Philip of Slane, a Dominican and subsequently bishop of Cork, was granted £3 for his expenses in going to Munster as the king's special envoy during the Bruce invasion to verbally apprize magnates there of the king's wishes. Shortly afterwards, he was granted £8 for his expenses in going to England to advise the king on behalf of the Irish council.[10] He received a further payment of £5 in 1318 for expenses incurred in the royal service and, later that year, an additional payment of £20 for his expenses in going to Rome.[11]

A series of payments between 1326 and 1338 indicates the extent to which the friars were regarded as reliable royal representatives for sensitive missions. The exchequer accounts for 1326–7 record a payment of £2 to Friar Henry Cogery, a high-ranking member of the Dublin Franciscan community, for going to Scotland on royal service.[12] In 1331, Friar Richard MacCormogan, the prior of the Dublin Dominicans, received three payments for negotiating with the O'Tooles of Wicklow and other Irish leaders on behalf of the justiciar. The final payment was for going to O'Toole and pronouncing a sentence of excommunication against him as a rebel against the king.[13] These contacts may provide the context for the interest in the O'Byrne and O'Toole families evident in the chronicle of Friar John Pembridge, who was also a member of the Dublin community at this time.[14] The exchequer records for 1335–6 record payments for four other friars engaged on diplomatic missions. Friar Andrew Leynagh, guardian of the Franciscan house at Kildare, received £3 for going to the Isles of Scotland to negotiate with John de Insula. Friar Alexander Lawless of the Dublin Dominican convent received £1 for his expenses in going to Ulster to negotiate with Henry de Mandeville, while

---

8 *FL*, p. 53.   9 *FL*, pp 53–4. Friar Stephen may be identical to the compiler of the *Annals of Multyfarnham*. 10 Connolly, *Irish exchequer payments*, pp 242, 245.   11 Ibid., pp 257, 267. For the significance of the Roman mission, see below, pp 38–9.   12 Connolly, *Irish exchequer payments*, p. 321. Friar Henry was the lector of the Dublin Franciscan community and played a prominent role in the trial of the Irish Templars as well as in attempts to establish the University of Dublin. See below, pp 279–80.   13 Ibid., pp 337, 339, 347. Friar Richard may be identical to the Dublin Dominican Richard Ocornegan who received a payment for negotiating with the O'Byrnes of Wicklow in 1337–8.   14 Pembridge, *Chronicle*, pp 336, 338, 341, 348, 349, 356, 371, 374, 378, 395. I am grateful to Bernadette Williams for this observation.

Friars Henry Holywode and William Jordan of the same community received payments for going to Connacht to negotiate with O'Connor 'concerning the security and keeping of the king's peace and the safety of the king's people in Ireland.'[15] In 1337–8, two payments were made to Friar Richard de Bokhampton, vicar provincial of the Dominicans in Ireland, for his expenses in going to England to 'further and expedite very important business touching the state of the land of Ireland'. Friar Gerald Lawless received a payment for going to Wicklow to negotiate peace with the O'Byrnes while Friar Richard Ocornegan was recompensed for his expenses in negotiating peace with 'certain Irish'. Both friars were members of the Dublin Dominican community.[16] It is noteworthy that these payments increased markedly during periods of crisis in the affairs of the colony and that, with their linguistic skills and Gaelic contacts, the friars were regarded by the crown authorities as reliable negotiators and intermediaries.

CORK 1291

The alleged deaths of sixteen Friars Minor at the hands of their *confrères* during a provincial chapter in Cork in 1291 is the most frequently cited and notorious example of racial tension within the medieval Irish church.[17] Knowledge of the incident comes from two English Benedictine sources. One of these, the Annals of Worcester Abbey, recorded that on 10 June 1291

> there was held a general chapter of the Friars Minor at Cork in Ireland, to which the Irish brothers came armed with a certain bull. Contention arose over this bull and they fought with the English and many were killed and wounded to the scandal of the order until finally the English with the help of the town prevailed.[18]

Further details are given in the *Historia Anglicana* of Bartholomew of Cotton, who gives the number of deaths:

> The minister general of the Order of St Francis, making visitation throughout the whole world came to Ireland to visit there and in his general chapter, sixteen brothers with their brethren were slain, several were wounded and some more were imprisoned by action of the king of England.[19]

**15** Connolly, *Irish exchequer payments*, p. 379. Friar William's surname suggests a Connacht origin. He may have been a member of the Dominican priory at Strade, Co. Mayo, with which the Jordan family (alias Dexter) was closely associated. **16** Ibid., p. 392. **17** Cotter, *Friars Minor*, p. 191, n. 19. **18** *FL*, p. 64. Translated in Cotter, *Friars Minor*, p. 34. **19** Ibid.

As reported, the incident presents a number of difficulties and both accounts have been the subject of detailed scrutiny by Francis Cotter.[20] He notes that the bull to which the Worcester chronicle refers has never come to light[21] and queries the objectivity of the sources as both emanate from English Benedictine monasteries and reflect the contemporary anti-mendicant bias of the black monks.[22] They are demonstrably unreliable in some of their accounts of foreign events and the *Historia Anglicana* account of the incident occurs, as an insertion in a much later hand, in only one of the four surviving manuscripts of the text. Most puzzling of all is the complete silence of all the contemporary Irish sources about the event. Among the Franciscans, both the author of the Kilkenny chronicle, writing within a few years of the alleged incident, and Friar John Clyn refer simply to the *capitulum Cork* – 'the chapter of Cork'.[23] Whereas it is possible that both writers preferred to draw a veil over a painful event in the province's history, this seems unlikely in the case of Clyn, who openly recorded later instances of racial tension in the province. Likewise, the chronicle of the Dublin Dominican John Pembridge is also silent about the alleged Cork incident. This is significant as a Dominican chronicler would not be bound by the same constraints of self-censorship as his Franciscan counterparts. The *acta* of the Franciscan general chapter meeting in Paris in 1292 makes no reference to the incident in its legislation; a significant omission as the minister general, Raymond Gaufredi, conducted a visitation of the Irish province in September 1291 and, according to the *Historia Anglicana* report, was actually present at the Cork chapter when the incident took place.[24]

What is clearly mistaken is the frequently expressed view that the provision in the bull *Exivi de paradiso* reserving the appointment of the minister provincial of the Irish Franciscans to the minister general was a direct result of this incident. From its foundation, the Irish province was one of three provinces which, for reasons of their distance from the central administration of the order and the difficulty of conducting visitations, had their provincial minister appointed by the minister general. The provincials were always English or Anglo-Irish friars, however, indicating the sensitivity of the ministers general to the issue of race relations in the Irish province.[25] The Irish Franciscans did not gain the right to choose their own provincial until the mid-fifteenth century and the election of the Gaelic friar, William O'Reilly.[26]

20 Cotter, *Friars Minor*, pp 33–40.   21 TCD MS 250 contains, *inter alia*, fifteenth-century transcripts of forty-seven thirteenth-century papal bulls relating to the Franciscans. It is the unique source for a number of bulls relating to the Irish friars, but contains no contentious material. See Colker, *Latin MSS*, i, pp 442–8. 22 W.R. Thomson, 'The image of the mendicants in the chronicles of Matthew Paris' (1977).   23 R. Flower (ed.), 'The Kilkenny Chronicle' (1931), p. 333; Clyn, *Annals*, p. 10.   24 Cotter concludes that the Cork incident is apocryphal.   25 Cotter, *Friars Minor*, pp 38–4.   26 See below, pp 70–2.

## THE BRUCE INVASION

The most significant event in polarizing the Irish mendicants along ethnic lines was the invasion of Ireland in May 1315 by Edward Bruce, earl of Carrick and brother of Robert I, king of Scotland. This event must be viewed in the broader context of political relations within the British Isles from the end of the thirteenth century that saw the English crown involved in a succession of military interventions in Scotland, Ireland and Wales.[27] The mendicant friars, particularly the Dominicans and the Franciscans, played significant roles both as mediators between the warring groups and as partisans allied with them. In consequence, each order experienced deep internal divisions between those friars loyal to the English crown and those others sympathetic to the Bruces and their supporters.[28] As will be shown below, the invasion and its aftermath had a number of important constitutional consequences for the Franciscan friars in Ireland. The impetus towards independence on the part of the Carmelite friars in Ireland and Scotland and the Dominican friars in Ireland described in the previous chapter should also be interpreted in this contemporary political context.[29]

Before Edward Bruce's expedition, his brother Robert had sought the support of Irish secular and ecclesiastical leaders by appealing to a sense of common Gaelic identity uniting the Scots and the Irish against the English foe.[30] Shortly after landing with a force of six thousand soldiers at Larne or Glendun in modern Co. Antrim, Edward Bruce was recognized as king of Ireland and, with his Gaelic allies, embarked on a campaign against the towns and boroughs of the colony. The friars did not escape the hardship that followed, but Bruce was selective in his treatment of the mendicant communities, possibly reflecting the extent to which they or their founders and patrons supported him. The Franciscan community at Carrickfergus was apparently unmolested during the lengthy siege of the town's castle in June 1315, but later that month Friar Clyn's source recorded the burning of the Franciscan friary at Dundalk and the destruction of its books, vestments and sacred vessels by the Scots.[31] A seventeenth-century source recorded the deaths of the guardian and twenty-three members of the community in the course of the raid.[32] The founders and principal patrons of this friary were the de Verdon family, whose antipathy towards Bruce may account for the rough treatment meted out

**27** S. Duffy (ed.), *Robert the Bruce's Irish wars* (2002). **28** This section draws on two important recent studies: N. Gallagher, 'The Franciscans and the Scottish wars of independence: an Irish perspective' (2006); A. Müller, 'Conflicting loyalties: the Irish Franciscans and the English crown in the High Middle Ages' (2007). **29** For the response of the Scottish Franciscans to these developments, see A. Müller, 'Nationale Abgrenzung in universalen Verbänden? Zur Entwicklung und Autonomiebestrebung der schottishen Franziskaner im 13. und 14. Jarhundert' (2004). I am grateful to Dr Müller for this reference. **30** J. Lydon, 'The impact of the Bruce invasion' (1987), p. 283. **31** Clyn, *Annals*, p. 163. **32** 'Brevis Synopsis', p. 173.

to the community. The support of some Gaelic friars for the invaders was evident in the arrest on 21 June at Caernarfon in Wales of a messenger of the bishop of 'Ennadens' bearing suspicious letters. Seán Duffy argues that this prelate was the Franciscan friar Gilbert O'Tierney, bishop of the western Irish diocese of Annaghdown, and that the suspect letters were Bruce's invitation to the Welsh to join forces with the Irish and Scots and drive out the English from their respective homelands. At the time, O'Tierney was acting as a suffragan bishop in the English border diocese of Hereford and was therefore ideally situated to act as an intermediary between Bruce and the Welsh.[33]

In late July, while withdrawing from a force led by Richard de Burgh, earl of Ulster, Bruce's forces burned Coleraine and destroyed the bridge over the River Bann, but spared the town's Dominican priory, possibly because it enjoyed the patronage of the O'Catháin family, one of his Irish allies.[34] The Carmelite friars in Ardee were not so fortunate: a Dublin source records the destruction by fire of their church, full of men, women and children, by Bruce's followers in 1315.[35] Edward Bruce continued his campaign in Ireland throughout 1316 and was joined by his brother Robert in December of that year. Early in 1317, the Scottish forces moved southwards out of Ulster and by 23 February 1317 they were encamped at Castleknock on the outskirts of Dublin. Anticipating a siege, the citizens had demolished St Saviour's Dominican priory and used the rubble to reinforce the city's defences.[36] In February or March 1317, the Franciscan friary at Casteldermot, a royal foundation that also enjoyed Geraldine patronage, was destroyed by the Scots along with its books, vestments and altar vessels.[37]

From the outset, the support the invaders received from Irish secular and mendicant clergy was a cause of grave concern to the English crown. In September 1315, Edward II wrote to Edmund Butler, the justiciar of Ireland, instructing him to inquire into the activities of Gaelic clergy and friars whose presence among the English in Ireland was perceived as a threat to security.[38] The friars' activities were still a cause for concern in 1316 when the king wrote to the Franciscan minister general, Friar Michael of Cesena, urging him to correct those Gaelic Friars Minor who had actively supported the Scots. One of the king's informants was Friar Thomas Godman, the Irish minister provincial, indicating the degree to which the Irish Franciscan province had been divided by the Bruce incursion.[39] Similar representations were made to the Holy See and, in April 1317, the newly elected Pope John XXII wrote to the archbishops of Dublin and Cashel condemning those friars who had incited the Gaelic population to rebellion.[40]

**33** S. Duffy, 'Ireland and the Irish sea region', p. 218.   **34** S. Duffy, 'The Bruce invasion of Ireland: a revised itinerary and chronology' (2002), p. 16.   **35** *MRH*, p. 286, Pembridge, *Chronicle*, p. 345.   **36** Pembridge, *Chronicle*, p. 353.   **37** J.T. Gilbert (ed.), *Chartularies of Saint Mary's Abbey, Dublin* (1884), ii, pp 299–300.   **38** *FL*, pp 94–5.   **39** Ibid., pp 98–9.   **40** Ibid., p. 100.

The alternative perspective of the Gaelic population found expression in the strongly worded Remonstrance presented to John XXII by Donal O'Neill, king of Tyrone, in late 1317. This was a forceful and articulate apologia for supporting Bruce that detailed the outrages suffered by the Gaelic population at the hands of the Anglo-Irish community. The identity of its author is unknown but a plausible case has been made for Friar Michael Mac Lochlainn, lector of the Franciscan *studium* in Armagh.[41] In detailing the offences of Anglo-Irish churchmen, the author identified the views of Friar Simon le Mercer, a member of the Drogheda Franciscan community, as being particularly notorious:

> For not only their laymen and their secular clergy but even some of their regular clergy make the heretical assertion that it is no more of a sin to kill an Irishman than a dog or any brute creature … and in the same way Friar Simon of the Order of Friars Minors is a particular exponent of this heresy. For in the year just past, unable to remain silent from the malignancy overflowing in his heart, he burst out shamelessly into speech like this in the court of the noble lord Sir Edward Bruce, earl of Carrick, in the presence of the same lord (as he himself testifies), claiming that it was no more a sin to kill an Irishman, and if he himself were to commit such a deed he would nonetheless celebrate Mass.[42]

The activities of the Bruces corresponded almost exactly with the outbreak of a major famine in Ireland, part of a wider European crisis that exacerbated the hardship caused by the military campaign. The Dominican chronicler John Pembridge saw this famine as divine retribution for the rebellion and specifically for the fact that the Scottish rebels had flouted church precepts by eating meat during Lent.[43] The defeat and death of Edward Bruce at the battle of Faughart in October 1318 brought the immediate crisis to an end, but the ethnic faultlines it established continued as sources of bitter division between the Gaelic and Anglo-Irish Dominicans and Franciscans for many years afterwards.

In 1324, in response to charges made against the Irish Friars Minor by Edward II, Pope John XXII established a commission to investigate the Irish province. The pope appointed the dean of St Patrick's Cathedral, William de Rodierd, as the judge delegate, and his findings were announced to the provincial chapter held in Dublin in April that year.[44] Two visitators appointed by the Franciscan minister general, Friars Durandus and Romanus, also attended this gathering. The

**41** J.R.S. Philips, 'The Remonstrance revisited: England and Ireland in the early fourteenth century' (1993), p. 18.   **42** Walter Bower, *Scotichronicon* (1991), vi, p. 397.   **43** Pembridge, *Chronicle*, pp 357–8.   **44** NLI D.679; *Ormond deeds*, i, 240–2; trans. 238–9.

commission found that the loyalty of communities at Ardfert, Athlone, Buttevant, Claregalway, Cork, Galway, Limerick and Nenagh was suspect and instructed that the Gaelic members of these friaries be reassigned to other houses of the province. It also decreed that no Gaelic friar was to be appointed guardian or lector in any of these houses except Claregalway and Galway. Gaelic friars were also barred from ever holding the offices of minister provincial or vicar provincial. A month later, presumably in response to lobbying, de Rodierd had to modify his decrees. Four other houses were allowed to have Gaelic guardians and, along with Claregalway and Galway, these came to form the nucleus of the Gaelic custody of Nenagh. A final prescription instructed that the communities should be racially mixed and the bishops of Ossory, Waterford and Connor ratified the decree.[45] The manuscript containing the legislation, National Library of Ireland (NLI) D.679, is a fragment of a fourteenth-century roll that gives the texts as consecutive entries in a contemporary hand. As these are the only entries on the roll, it indicates that it was compiled for someone with an interest in monitoring the affairs of the Gaelic friars. An obvious candidate is Richard Ledrede, the controversial English Franciscan bishop of Ossory from 1317 to 1361. His cathedral city, Kilkenny, became, in 1391, the seat of the Butler family, among whose muniments the roll is now preserved. Given the bishop's role in ratifying the decrees, it is highly likely that he received a copy of them. The preservation of legislation hostile to the Gaelic section of the province by the Anglo-Irish friars was to have a long history. When Friar William O'Reilly became the first Gaelic minister provincial of the Irish province *c.*1445, he faced bitter opposition from a number of Anglo-Irish friars who, in 1450, were able to produce royal and papal legislation from the 1320s forbidding the appointment of Gaelic friars as provincial ministers.[46] As his opponents were based in friaries within Butler territory and their objections bear striking similarity to the decrees of the 1324 commission preserved in NLI D.679, it is possible that this was one of the sources to which they had access.

Evidence for ongoing polarization of the Irish Dominicans was demonstrated by the activities of Friar Philip of Slane, who became bishop of Cork in 1321. He had been a member of the Irish council since 1318 and received an annual fee of five marks for his services. In 1324, he undertook the first of two embassies to the pope at the behest of Edward II, seeking approbation for a reform programme for the Irish church. This consisted of three main proposals. Firstly, that Irish clergy should preach loyalty to the crown and that those preaching rebellion should be punished. Secondly, that dioceses with an annual income of less than £60 would

**45** The bishop of Ossory was Richard Ledrede. See A. Neary, 'Richard Ledrede: English Franciscan bishop of Ossory' (1984).   **46** *FL*, pp 203–7.

be united to larger ones, thereby reducing the number of Irish sees from thirty-four to ten, each having its episcopal seat in a royal city. This would ensure that each diocese had adequate financial resources and would also discourage Irish bishops from undermining royal authority. Finally, the petition requested that the pope condemn the practice whereby English candidates were not accepted as novices in Gaelic religious houses. Whereas all religious orders were accused of this fault, the friars were singled out as being particularly egregious offenders.[47] To assist the pope in his deliberations, Friar Philip presented him with a *Libellus de descriptione Hibernie*, his abridgment of the *Topographica Hibernica* of the twelfth-century writer, Gerald of Wales.[48]

Although received sympathetically by Pope John XXII, further clarification of the scheme was requested and Friar Philip returned to Avignon with a revised draft in 1325, the result of consultations with the archbishops of Dublin and Cashel, the council of Ireland and the royal council in England. Though he secured a papal decree uniting the diocese of Cloyne to his own see of Cork, nothing further came of the petition and he died in March 1327.

In Ireland, the annals of Friar John Clyn corroborate the extent of this ethnic tension among the friars. For the year 1325, he recorded that

> There was discord, as commonly reported, among virtually all the mendicants of Ireland, some of them upholding, favouring and promoting the side of their nation, blood and language, others canvassing for advancement and high office.

He also added that the Franciscan general chapter held at Lyon that year had transferred the friaries of Ardfert, Buttevant, Cork and Limerick from the control of the Irish friars to that of the English with the erection of the custody of Cork.[49] It is likely that this decision was in response to the de Rodierd commission and may even have been taken on the advice of Friars Durandus and Romanus, the visitors who had attended the Dublin chapter in 1324.

Further evidence for unease over the activities of the Gaelic section of the Franciscan province came in 1327, when the annual royal alms to the Athlone friary were transferred to the community at Cashel because the former house no longer had any English friars.[50] This indicates that the racial integration ordered by de Rodierd had not been strictly followed.

---

**47** J.A. Watt, 'Negotiations between Edward II and John XXII concerning Ireland' (1956). The text of the petition and the papal response is given at 16–18.   **48** BL MS Add. 19513, fos 164r–188v; R. Sharpe, *A handlist of the Latin writers of Great Britain and Ireland before 1540* (1997), p. 438.   **49** Clyn, *Annals*, p. 182. For Williams' assessment of Clyn's nuanced response to the issue of ethnic tension within the Irish Franciscan province, see pp 85–101.   **50** The loyalty of the Athlone friars remained suspect for many years;

## THE BLACK DEATH

The Black Death marked a watershed for the religious orders in Ireland as it did for Irish society in general.[51] The sources for the progress of the plague in Ireland are relatively few, with the principal witnesses being the Franciscan annalists John Clyn and Galfridus O'Hogan and the Dominican continuator of the chronicle of Friar John Pembridge.[52] Of these, Clyn devoted the most attention to the pandemic, making it possible to trace the plague's progress from its first manifestation at Drogheda and Howth (or Dalkey) in August 1348 to its arrival in Kilkenny during the season of Lent in 1349.[53] He recorded that twenty-five Franciscans died in Drogheda and twenty-three died in Dublin before Christmas 1348 and that eight Dominicans died in Kilkenny between Christmas Day and 6 March 1349. The number of deaths in the Dublin and Drogheda friaries probably represented the majority of friars in each community, as even the largest mendicant houses in Ireland seldom numbered more than thirty members.[54]

Clyn's account is of particular interest for the incidental information that it gives on the nature and spread of the pestilence. His description of the speed of the contagion and the symptoms of the disease indicates that it first appeared in Ireland in its most infectious pneumonic form. Likewise, his remark that 'those touching the dead and even the sick were immediately infected and died, and the one confessing and the confessor were together led to the grave'[55] may reflect the experience of his *confrères* who contracted the disease while ministering to the dying. His account of the large numbers of pilgrims to the shrine of St Mullins in Carlow chillingly conveys the extent of panic and desperation that gripped his contemporaries. Somewhat surprisingly, despite the social upheaval caused by the outbreak, Clyn continued to receive news of Continental affairs and recorded the establishment of a cemetery for plague victims in Avignon by Pope Clement VI in May 1348. His work also provides unique evidence for the circulation of the apocalyptic 'Cedar of Lebanon' prophecy in Ireland.[56]

As the plague progressed, Friar Clyn became increasingly alarmed at the scale of the mortality and his account of its arrival in Kilkenny, where he was stationed, in 1349 is almost unbearably poignant

---

deprived of alms in 1327, they were restored to favour in 1334, but were again deprived in 1354 in favour of the Wicklow community. *FL*, pp 129, 136, 145.   **51** M. Kelly, *A history of the Black Death in Ireland* (2001); eadem, *The great dying: the Black Death in Dublin* (2003).   **52** Williams believes that Friar Pembridge may have been a victim of the plague: pers. comm.   **53** Clyn, *Annals*, pp 111–12, 246–52. **54** In 1380, the Dominican community in Dublin numbered twenty-nine friars. *MRH*, p. 225. O'Sullivan postulates that large houses would have held thirty friars. O'Sullivan, *MIDS*, pp 91–2.   **55** Clyn, *Annals*, p. 250.   **56** This apocalyptic text emerged in the context of the Mongol threat to Western Europe in the mid-thirteenth century. It continued to circulate for centuries afterwards, re-emerging at times of crisis as a harbinger of dire events. See Clyn, *Annals*, pp 110–12, 248–50; R.E. Lerner, *The powers of prophecy: the*

This pestilence gathered strength in Kilkenny during Lent, for between Christmas Day and 6 March, eight Friars Preachers died. There was scarcely a house in which only one died but commonly man and wife with their children going one way, namely, crossing to death. Now I, Friar John Clyn of the Order of Minors and convent of Kilkenny, have written in this book the noteworthy deeds that happened in my time, that [I know] by faithful eye witness or by worthy reliable report. And lest these notable records should be lost with time and recede from the memory of future people, [I] seeing these many evils and the whole world as it were in a bad situation, among the dead expecting death when it should come, I have brought together in writing just as I have truthfully heard and examined. And lest the writing should perish with the writer and the work fail together with the worker, I am leaving parchment for the work to continue if, by chance, in the future a man should remain surviving, and anyone of the race of Adam should be able to escape this plague and [live] to continue this work [I] commenced.[57]

Clyn survived the crisis until at least June 1349, when he recorded the increased price of corn and spices and the death of his friend and possible patron, the Kilkenny nobleman, Fulk de la Freigne. In the original manuscript, a later hand recorded that 'here it seems the author died' and Clyn has often been cited as a victim of the Black Death, though Bernadette Williams has recently challenged this interpretation.[58]

The impact of the plague in Gaelic mendicant communities is even more difficult to gauge. The principal source for the period, the Franciscan Annals of Nenagh, recorded the deaths of Friars Robert O'Fynain and William O'Mullchacha in the Nenagh community in August 1349 and that of Friar Thadeus MacMahowne in Limerick in late October of the same year. While it is not stated that they died of plague, the entries occur in the context of an account of unprecedented mortality and it seems plausible that they were victims of the pestilence. All three were senior members of the order: O'Mullacha and McMahowne were the lectors respectively in Nenagh and Limerick and O'Fynain had been guardian of a number of friaries. It is possible that the mortality rate in both communities was much higher but that the annalist only recorded the deaths of senior figures and officeholders. A mortality rate of 45 per cent has been posited for monastic houses in England, and the priory of Augustinian nuns at Lismullin,

*cedar of Lebanon vision from the Mongol onslaught to the dawn of the Enlightenment* (1983), passim, but see particularly pp 114–34 for the context of Clyn's version of the prophecy.   **57** Clyn, *Annals*, pp 250, 252. **58** Williams argues that Clyn's annals may have been intended for or sponsored by Fulk de la Freigne and that Clyn ceased writing on the death of his patron. Clyn, *Annals*, p. 83.

Co. Meath, showed a decline of 42.6 per cent between 1348 and 1367, which a contemporary observer attributed to the Black Death and later outbreaks of the plague.[59] It is likely that comparable mortality rates applied in other Irish religious houses.

FOUNDATIONS, 1350–67 (fig. 2.1)

The Black Death wrought tremendous upheaval in all aspects of Irish social and ecclesiastical life.[60] It exacerbated a pattern of decline that had characterized church life since the late thirteenth century as clerical incomes dropped, benefices became impoverished and pluralism and absenteeism increased. The impact on the religious orders was particularly severe, pushing their crisis management abilities to the limit.[61] After the initial loss of life to the pestilence, all orders struggled to replenish their ranks, often accepting unsuitable, unqualified or underage candidates to do so. In 1354, the Irish Augustinian friars received permission to appoint men who were unable to speak Latin to the office of local prior.[62] While these stratagems addressed some of the orders' immediate needs, they also sowed the seeds of future difficulties. Friar Luke Wadding attributed the decline in standards among the Franciscans in the aftermath of the Black Death to the policy of accepting unsuitable candidates for the novitiate and to the failure to provide them with a suitable grounding in the discipline of the religious life.[63]

The monastic orders and Regular Canons made no new foundations in Ireland in the fourteenth century and existing monasteries were often severely compromised as economic and religious entities. Paradoxically, the mendicants demonstrated a remarkable resilience and, despite their reduced manpower, the Carmelite, Dominican and Franciscan orders each established a small number of new foundations in Ireland in the immediate aftermath of the pestilence. Increased numbers of legacies and bequests from plague victims may have bankrolled this expansion and the phenomenon occurred elsewhere in Europe. The Carmelites in Catalonia made a number of new foundations immediately after the Black Death and the Augustinian friars in Winchester caused outrage by their attempts to acquire some of the most lucrative properties in the city in the immediate aftermath of the outbreak.[64] Such was the concern over the English friars' expanding property portfolios that in 1349 and 1350 Edward III ordered first the sheriffs of London and then all the escheators of England to inquire into

**59** Kelly, *Black Death in Ireland*, p. 118.   **60** Ibid., pp 109–30.   **61** A. Müller, 'Managing crises: institutional re-stabilisation of the religious orders in England after the Black Death (1347–1350)' (2005).   **62** Martin & de Meijer, 'Irish materal', no. 1, p. 64; Müller, 'Managing crises', pp 215–16.   **63** Wadding, *AM*, viii (1932), p. 25.   **64** Andrews, *The other friars*, p. 41; Müller, 'Managing crises', p. 217.

2.1  Map of foundations, 1350–67.

the property acquired by the mendicants and to seize all buildings that they had leased to laypeople.[65]

St Mary's Carmelite priory at Horetown, Co. Wexford, may have been established by a member of the Furlong family as early as 1350, but an alternative date of *c.*1387 is also given and is perhaps more likely. Nothing further is known about this foundation until its dissolution in January 1541.[66] In 1352, an inquisition *Ad quod damnum* found that it would not be to the king's disadvantage to permit the town of Carlingford and thirteen other named benefactors to grant land to the Dominican friars to establish the church and priory of St Malachy.[67] In 1353, the first reference to the Franciscan friary at Kilconnell, Co. Galway, occurs and a chalice and ciborium belonging to the house and possibly dating to the late fourteenth/early fifteenth century were recorded in various

65 A.G. Little (ed.), 'A royal inquiry into property held by the mendicant friars in England in 1349 and 1350' (1933). Cited by Müller, 'Managing crises', p. 217.   66 *MRH*, p. 289; O'Dwyer, *Irish Carmelites*, p. 36. The earlier date is given by W.H. Grattan-Flood in *History of the diocese of Ferns* (1916), p. 100, but without any supporting authority.   67 Dryburgh & Smith, *Inquisitions and extents* (2007), no. 302, pp 185–6. *MRH*, p. 222, gives an incorrect date for the foundation. See also A. Curran, 'The Dominican order in Carlingford and Dundalk' (1968); O'Sullivan, *MIDS*, pp 62–5. I am grateful to Hugh Fennning and

seventeenth-century inventories of the friary's church plate.[68] The first references to the Carmelite foundations at Knocktopher, Co. Kilkenny, and Ballynahinch, Co. Galway, both occur in 1356. The Knocktopher foundation was the subject of a 1356 petition by James Butler, second earl of Ormond, seeking permission to grant a messuage and thirteen acres to the friars who were already established in the town. The proposal contravened the Statute of Mortmain and was initially refused, although permission was eventually granted in 1358. Unusually for a Carmelite house, the foundation was not dedicated to the Virgin Mary but to Christ under the title of St Saviour, a designation normally found in Dominican foundations. Alemand noted that the house was a popular place of pilgrimage, and the priory well, dedicated to the Holy Trinity, still exists. Elements of the priory buildings survive incorporated into Knocktopher House, the (former) residence of the Langrishe family.[69] The priory at Ballynahinch, Co. Galway, was founded by an O'Flaherty in the same year, but nothing further is known of its history.[70] The foundation of the Dominican priory of St Eustace in Naas was licensed by Edward III c.1355–6. Here, the founders were members of the Eustace or FitzEustace family, but nothing else is known about the priory before its dissolution in March 1540.[71] In December 1367, Pope Urban V permitted the Irish Franciscans to establish a convent for twelve members on the lands of William Montacute, earl of Salisbury, at Ballabeg on the Isle of Man. The friary church was consecrated in 1373 and two members of the community subsequently became bishops of Man.[72]

### ANGLO-IRISH SEPARATISM

If tension between Gaelic and Anglo-Irish friars was a defining feature of the Irish mendicants in the early fourteenth century, the latter half of the century was characterized by heightened antipathy between the Anglo-Irish members and their English *confrères*. The friars presumably shared in the aspirations of the 'middle nation', as the English of Ireland were sometimes known.[73] Despite their numerical strength, the Dominicans and Augustinians in Ireland remained under the jurisdiction of their English superior and at times this burden chafed.

Raymond Gillespie for advice on this point.   **68** Ó Floinn, 'Irish Franciscan church furnishings' (2011), p. 9. Other sources give c.1400 and 1414 as the foundation date. See below, p. 66.   **69** Dryburgh & Smith, *Inquistions and extents*, no. 319, p. 191; *MRH*, p. 290; O'Dwyer, *Irish Carmelites*, p. 38; Stevens, *Monasticon Hibernicum*, pp 336–7; W. Carrigan, *Ossory* (1905), iv, pp 24, 26.   **70** *MRH*, p. 287.   **71** *MRH*, p. 228.   **72** Conlan, *Franciscan Ireland*, p. 147; J.K. Barratt, 'The Franciscan Friary of Bymacan' (1964).   **73** R. Frame, 'Exporting state and nation: being English in medieval Ireland' (2005). I am grateful to

## THE AUGUSTINIANS

Very little is known about the constitutional arrangements of the Austin friars in Ireland for the first seventy years of their existence. As noted in the previous chapter, the Irish friars formed one of the five *plagae* or limits into which the English province was divided. Like the Dominicans, it appears that the Augustinians in Ireland had been granted (or had assumed) a large degree of autonomy in conducting their affairs and that they were accustomed to appointing their own regional superiors by the mid-fourteenth century. This did not go unchallenged and the earliest surviving references to Irish affairs in the registers of the priors general relate to disputes between Anglo-Irish and English friars over the degree of freedom the friars in Ireland enjoyed. In September 1359, Friar Matthew of Ascoli, the newly elected prior general of the order, permitted Friar Thomas Thornton, prior provincial of England, to nominate the vicar provincial of the Austin friars in Ireland. The Irish vicar provincial was instructed to summon a chapter of the friars in Ireland from which he would select four advisors to assist him in making appointments, transferring friars and otherwise governing the region. They would also appoint two delegates to attend the English provincial chapter and report the decisions of the Irish chapter (fig. 2.2). The prior general also appointed a vicar general, Friar John Dale, as his representative in Ireland, presumably to ensure that the remaining rights and privileges of the Irish limit were preserved. Dale was permitted to move friars, absolve excommunicates, issue dispensations and accept up to four apostates back into the order; prerogatives normally reserved to the prior general himself.[74]

Although similar in its constitution to the provincial chapters of the order's other provinces, the Irish chapter lacked executive force and its subordinate status exacerbated tensions between the Anglo-Irish friars and their English brethren. In 1365, the order's general chapter, meeting in Siena, confirmed the recently enacted statutes of Friar Matthew of Ascoli relating to the friars in Ireland and Hungary. Though the text of these decrees has not survived, it seems likely that they represented further attempts to defuse the situation in Ireland.[75]

F.X. Martin suggested that mounting tension between the different ethnic groups provided the context for one of the more bizarre incidents in Irish mendicant history: the implication of eight named Anglo-Irish Augustinians in the death of another friar, Richard Dermot, described as an Englishman (*anglicus*), in May 1379.[76] The crime was committed in Holy Trinity priory, Dublin, and the victim's

Brendan Smith for advice on this point.  **74** Martin & de Meijer, 'Irish material', pp 68–9, nos 9, 10. **75** Ibid., p. 69, no. 12.  **76** F.X. Martin, 'Murder in a Dublin monastery, 1379' (1988).

2.2 Provincial seal of the English Augustinian friars. Found near Christ Church Cathedral, Dublin (from Thomas Butler, *John's Lane*, p. 22).

body was initially concealed in the well of Adam Bron, a neighbour of the friars. A few nights later, the body was removed secretly by six named friars and buried in the friary cemetery. The jury found that the accused were not guilty of murder but that two of them, Friars John Foster and Reginald Newton, were guilty of concealing the body and of failing to notify the coroner, for which they were sentenced to imprisonment. The sentence was later commuted to a fine of forty pence. Those implicated included Friar Nicholas Bodenham, the vicar provincial of the Augustinians in Ireland, and Friar John Holywood, a distinguished theologian.

In their recent study of the Dublin Augustinian community, Duffy and Simpson challenged Martin's interpretation and argued that Dermot was in fact an Anglo-Irish friar, a member of a prominent Pale family.[77] Their case is strengthened by a reference to another Augustinian with the same surname in a 1425 entry in the register of the order's prior general. Regardless of the precise background to the incident, the involvement of the most senior figures of the order in Ireland in the illicit and sacrilegious disposing of a *confrère*'s corpse indicates a high degree of tension and dysfunction within the Dublin community.

In 1385, the Augustinian general chapter, meeting at Gran in Hungary, granted Friar Henry Tesdale, the English prior provincial, the right to do as he pleased with the privileges of the Irish limit. The result was that the Irish limit was

---

77 Duffy & Simpson, 'The hermits of St Augustine in Dublin' (2009).

deprived of many of its accumulated rights, which was resented by the friars who entrusted their resistance campaign to three of their most able members.[78] Friar John Holywood, whose involvement in the Richard Dermot affair has already been noted, was professor of theology in the order's *studium* in Dublin. Friar Gerald Caneton was a lector in theology and would become bishop of Cloyne in 1394. The last spokesman, Friar Adam Payn, was the youngest of the three and was at the beginning of a career trajectory as a theologian and controversialist that would see him defending his *confrères* in England, all the mendicant orders at the Council of Pisa in 1409–10 and eventually succeeding his *confrère* Caneton as bishop of Cloyne in 1413.[79] In 1391, Caneton and Payn were commissioned to lobby the order's general chapter at Würzburg on behalf of the Irish limit. As a result of their representations, the chapter delegates instructed the prior general, Friar Bartholomew of Venice, to either restore the rights of the Irish limit or to establish acceptable alternative arrangements for governing it. He opted for the former course and confirmed the privileges of the Irish friars in a series of lengthy decrees issued from Ferrara in May 1392. These were confirmed by the general chapter meeting in Rimini in 1394. All penalties that the three spokesmen had incurred in their defence of the rights of the Irish limit were annulled. In addition, Caneton was appointed to the important position of procurator general of the order, responsible for channeling all official business between the Augustinian friars and the Holy See. He was also given the right to visit and inspect at will any English house of the order. In Ireland, John Holywood was appointed the prior general's representative or vicar general and was to remain in office until he decided to call an election for a successor. Adam Payn, whose academic career in England had been jeopardized by his stance, was permitted to pursue his studies in Oxford as a lector, even though he had not completed the required course for this promotion.[80] Their actions represented a remarkable victory for the Irish friars and initiated a period of closer contacts between the Irish Augustinians, the central authorities of the order in Italy and the papacy. They also occurred when the Observant reform was emerging in the order as a whole. The registers of the priors general between 1394 and 1419 are no longer extant, but when records resume it is clear that the centre of gravity had shifted to Connacht and to those new foundations, mostly in Gaelic territories, which formed the nucleus of the Observant movement among the Irish Austin friars.

---

**78** Martin & de Meijer, 'Irish material', p. 85, no. 46.   **79** F.X. Martin, 'An Irish Augustinian disputes at Oxford: Adam Payn' (1975).   **80** Martin & de Meijer, 'Irish material', pp 72–3, nos 22, 23, 24.

## THE DOMINICANS

As with the Augustinians, the second half of the fourteenth century witnessed a concerted effort by the Friars Preachers to establish an independent Irish province.[81] The movement encountered considerable opposition from the English Dominican authorities, supported by King Edward III, and was part of wider campaign to resist the reform of the English province proposed by the master general of the order, Friar Elias Raymond, following his provincial visitation in 1372. The visitation corresponded with a period of xenophobia in England on account of the war with France and, as the master general was a native of Toulouse, opposition to him quickly assumed an ethnic dimension. In 1369, Edward III ordered the expulsion of foreign students, including Dominicans, from Oxford. A group of friars, both English and foreign, barricaded themselves into the convent in protest and, as a result, the situation within the Oxford house remained tense for several years afterwards. The master general presented his report on the affairs of the English province to the general chapter meeting at Florence in 1374 and a number of developments ensued. The first was a proposal that the Irish vicariate be erected as an independent province of the order. Although this received approval from the chapter, the Dominican constitutions required the consent of three consecutive general chapters for motions of this nature to be carried definitively. In addition, the chapter issued a number of ordinances for the English province that were entrusted for dispatch to Friar Stephen Coulying. What the precise nature of these were is not known, but they were greeted with uproar in England, and in August 1374 Edward III ordered the English prior provincial not to accept any foreign friars at Oxford and specifically forbade the reception of Coulying or any friar acting as visitator of the master general. The English friars received the decree enthusiastically, refused to acknowledge Friar Stephen's authority and eventually secured his arrest and imprisonment.

The action of the English friars constituted an unprecedented rebellion against the central authority of the order, which responded forcefully. The English provincial, Friar Thomas Rushook, and his vicar for Ireland, Friar John of Leicester, were deposed by the master general, who appointed Friar John of Paris as his vicar for England and Friar Robert Cusack for Ireland. In addition, the priors of twelve English convents were deposed and other rebels reassigned to different priories. In 1378, the English provincial chapter petitioned the king and parliament to hear

---

81 The most thorough account of this period is Flanagan, 'Formative development', pp 276–91. Summary accounts are given by O'Sullivan, *MIDS*, pp 185–200; Pochin Mould, *Irish Dominicans*, pp 56–65; F.X. Martin, 'Murder in a Dublin monastery', pp 477–9.

their complaints against John of Paris, whom they accused of acting against the honour of the kingdom and the safety of the order.

Against this backdrop, the proposal for Irish independence was working its way through the Dominican constitutional system: in 1376, the general chapter meeting at Bourges approved the petition and, two years later, in June 1378, the chapter of Carcassonne brought forth the Irish province as an independent entity. Conceived in conflict, the fraught circumstances of the order in England and the looming crisis in the church at large meant that its birth was inauspicious and its existence proved to be of short duration. Two months before the chapter, on 29 March 1378, Pope Gregory XI had died at Rome. The conclave to elect a successor chose Bartholomew Prignano, archbishop of Bari, who became Pope Urban VI. A group of disaffected cardinals withdrew from Rome and, after several months spent in different locations in central Italy, on 20 September elected the French cardinal Robert of Geneva as Pope Clement VII, thus initiating the Western Schism.

Within a year, the church had divided into rival obediences and religious orders were split in two by their allegiances to the rival claimants. Friar Elias Raymond, a native of Toulouse, sided with the Clement VII at Avignon, the English friars with Urban VI at Rome. The deposed prior provincial of England, Thomas Rushook, and John of Leicester, his vicar in Ireland, appealed against the penalties and decrees of the master general and the chapter of Carcassonne to Pope Urban who, in 1379, issued a decree annulling all the acts of the chapter, reducing the status of the Irish province to that of a vicariate as established by Berengar of Landorra and the chapter of London of 1314 and reinstating Rushook and John of Leicester to their former positions.[82] The Dominican province of Ireland had ceased to exist within a year of its establishment.

This development occasioned a violent reaction in Ireland that, fortuitously, can be reconstructed from the records of a court case and royal pardon granted to those involved in the affray. In August 1380, Friar John of Leicester arrived in Dublin to assert himself as vicar provincial of Ireland. He already enjoyed some stalwart local support as Friar Thomas Bron, who came to his aid on this occasion, had already appeared in court in 1377 charged with assaulting two of his *confrères* in Drogheda, Friars John Rosse and Philip Holywood.[83] In the event, the newly restored vicar provincial was able to muster fifteen friars, armed and wearing coats of mail under their habits, and the party went to take possession of St Saviour's Priory on his behalf. The resident community was already apprized of their intentions and when the party broke into the priory they were confronted by another group of armed friars led by the prior of St Saviours, Friar William Roche.

**82** T. de Burgo, *Hibernia Dominicana*, pp 52–7.   **83** Archdall, *Monasticon Hibernicum*, pp 455–6; O'Sullivan, *MIDS*, pp 197–200.

In the ensuing fracas, one of the Dublin friars, Richard Ferrars, was robbed of an iron breastplate worth twenty shillings. The citizens of Dublin were alerted to the developing crisis by the sounding of the priory bell and, as pre-arranged, an armed band led by the mayor, John Hull, hurried over Dublin bridge to defend their beleaguered community. In the face of these odds, John of Leicester prudently decided to surrender and he and his companions were imprisoned in Dublin Castle. The case was brought before Edmund Mortimer, the justiciar, and his council on 6 December 1380. From the proceedings, it is clear that the dispute centred on the status of the Irish vicariate and on who had the right to govern it. In September 1382, Richard II issued a pardon to those involved in the affray. However, the tenor of this document indicates that the king regarded as the offending party those who had resisted John of Leicester. While the incident indicates that there was a separatist movement among the Anglo-Irish friars, the fact that their opponents also bore Anglo-Irish names indicates that a desire to establish an independent Irish province was by no means universal. The fact that it occurred shortly after the death of the Friar Richard Dermot at the hands of his Anglo-Irish Augustinian *confrères* indicates that tension within religious orders was not an isolated phenomenon. The Irish Knights Hospitaller at Kilmainham were also at odds with their English colleagues at precisely this period, and the religious orders seem to reflect in microcosm the wider contemporary tension between the Anglo-Irish community and the English administration.[84]

## THE FRIARS AND THE GREAT SCHISM

The Great Schism (1378–1417) divided the Latin Church into two and eventually three camps, each supporting the claims of rival claimants to the papacy. Faced with a choice between a Roman pontiff and a French one, the English parliament, meeting at Gloucester in 1378, joined Italy, Flanders and most of Germany in opting for Urban VI and the Roman obedience. Scotland, France, Spain and the rest of Europe held with Clement VII and the Avignon succession. In general, Ireland sided with the Urbanist cause but there were pockets of support for Clement VII.[85] In the province of Dublin and those areas under English influence, allegiance was immediately given to Urban VI and the Roman obedience, while Clement VII initially garnered support in the ecclesiastical provinces of Tuam and Armagh and among certain houses of Augustinian canons.[86] Despite the fact that

84 C.L. Tipton, 'The Irish Hospitallers during the Great Schism' (1970); F.X. Martin, 'Murder in a Dublin monastery', pp 480–2. 85 K. Walsh, 'Ireland, the papal curia and the schism: a border case' (1980); A. Gwynn, 'Anglo-Irish church life in the 14th & 15th centuries' (1968), pp 51–64. 86 C. Burns (ed.), 'Papal letters of Clement VII of Avignon (1378–94) relating to Ireland and Scotland' (1982).

Urban VI had suppressed the newly established Irish province, there is no evidence for support for his rival's cause amongst the Irish Dominicans. The Clementine obedience did attract support from some high-ranking Franciscans, however, and, although slight, the surviving evidence suggests that the Irish Franciscan province was somewhat divided in its allegiance.[87]

The most outspoken defender of the Roman obedience among the mendicants in Ireland was Friar Philip Torrington, an Oxford-trained theologian and member of the English Franciscan province who had been appointed archbishop of Cashel in 1373. On his return to London from a trip to Rome in 1379, he preached a sermon against Clement VII, declaring that he and his supporters were excommunicates and that the time was opportune to stage an invasion of France. Luke Wadding recorded that in 1381 Urban VII issued letters to the archbishop and guardian of Cashel and the guardian of the friary in Galway instructing them to act against the followers of Clement VII. The implication is that these included other members of the order, possibly including the minister provincial.[88]

In January 1381, Pope Clement dispensed the lector of the Armagh *studium*, Friar Thomas O'Colman, from the impediment of illegitimacy to enable him to accept appointment as archbishop of Armagh in succession to Milo Sweetman who had died the previous year.[89] Friar Thomas had already received a dispensation from this impediment from Gregory XI in March 1375.[90] The earlier mandate also stated that he was descended from noble and powerful ancestors on both sides of his family and that he had studied theology in Oxford, Cambridge and Paris. He was rendered eligible for appointment to all dignities within the Franciscan order, with the exception of that of minister general. In recognition of his defence of the rights and liberties of the church in Ireland, often at danger to his life, he was also declared eligible for appointment as a bishop. Despite his prominence and standing in the locality, Friar Thomas was unable to secure recognition as archbishop and, at an unknown date in 1381, Urban VI provided John Colton to the primatial see.

The death of Archbishop Philip Torrington of Cashel in 1381 removed one of Clement's most vocal critics in Ireland and created a vacancy in the southern metropolitan see. Clement VII provided Friar Michael, the Franciscan minister provincial of Ireland, as his successor and on 22 October 1382 issued letters of appointment to the candidate, the clergy and people of the diocese and Richard II of England. In the letter of provision, Friar Michael was described as a master of theology but otherwise nothing further is known of him.[91] He proved unable

---

**87** For what follows, see Cotter, *Friars Minor*, pp 130–2.  **88** *AM*, ix, pp 47, 48, 51. But see Cotter, *Friars Minor*, p. 131 for the difficulties with this reference.  **89** Burns, 'Papal letters', p. 24.  **90** *CPL*, iv, p. 206.  **91** Burns, 'Papal letters', p. 30.

to assert himself in face of the Urbanist candidate, Peter Hackett, and in July 1387 was appointed bishop of Sodor in the Isles of Scotland, where he remained until death *c.*1398.

Although the fourteenth century marked a low point in many aspects of the Irish mendicant experience, it also witnessed developments that would subsequently be of immense significance. Of these, the foundation of new friaries in Gaelic territories, the Irish friars' increased contacts with their Continental *confrères* and the emergence of the Observant reform movement became major contributing factors in the renaissance of mendicant life that occurred in Ireland in the century and a half before the Reformation.

CHAPTER THREE

# Recovery and reform, 1390–1530

*We have been informed that the house of the Order of Preachers
at Portumna in the diocese of Clonfert – a place isolated from
cities and from earthly commerce – was begun by some friars of
the order that there under regular observance they might be able
to serve God more peaceably.*[1]

The period between the late fourteenth and the early sixteenth century witnessed
a remarkable second flowering of the mendicant movement in Ireland. In terms
of the number of friaries established, it was reminiscent of the first wave of
expansion in the thirteenth century, although with some significant differences.
Whereas the earlier foundations were overwhelmingly concentrated in the towns
and boroughs of the Anglo-Norman colony, the latter wave was more rural in
character and the new houses were largely located in the territories of the Gaelic
chieftains and Anglo-Irish magnates of Munster, Connacht and Ulster. These
imposing gothic friaries with their distinctive tapering towers and extensive
claustral complexes became as much a symbol of that newly prosperous and
confident society as the castles and tower houses of their patrons.

This period is also notable for the emergence of vigorous reform parties within
the Dominican, Franciscan and Augustinian orders. These reformers, known as
Observants, were an Irish manifestation of the reform movements that reanimated
late medieval religious life on the Continent.[2] The fifteenth and sixteenth centuries
also witnessed a revival in many of the earlier mendicant foundations, expressed
both in the renewal of the fabric of the buildings as well as by the adoption of the
Observant reform by a significant number of the older communities.

The emergence of the Observance coincided with the shift of each order's
political centre of gravity to Gaelic territories and reignited the smouldering issues
of racial tension, jurisdiction and autonomy. The pastoral zeal of the reformers led
to a quickening of devotion among their lay followers. This found expression in a
variety of ways, which are discussed in chapter ten. Of these, the most significant

---

**1** 1426 bull of Pope Martin V. Cited in Flanagan, 'Formative development', p. 308. See also, *CPL*, vii,
p. 506. **2** For this broader context, see the various articles in K. Elm (ed.), *Reformbemühungen und
Observanzbestrebungen im spätmittelalterlichen Ordenswesen* (1989).

was the emergence of the Tertiary or Third Order movements among the lay followers of the Dominican and Franciscan friars. From these lay fraternities, a new form of communal religious life arose – the regular tertiaries – for whom forty-nine foundations were made in Ireland between 1425 and 1511.[3]

## THE OBSERVANT REFORM

The emergence in Ireland of the Observant movement at the end of the fourteenth century connected the Irish friars with the most vibrant reform current in the late medieval church.[4] Within each order, the Observants promoted a return to rigorous discipline and strict adherence to their respective rules and constitutions as antidotes to the laxity of lifestyle known as 'conventualism'. To facilitate this trend, Continental Observants received papal and conciliar permission to appoint their own superiors, thereby gaining a great degree of autonomy while remaining nominally subordinate to the orders' general superiors. This stratagem facilitated a workable compromise among the Dominicans, Augustinians and Carmelites who, on occasion, even elected Observant friars to the offices of prior general or master general of each order. Among the Franciscans, however, divisions over the observance of poverty and fidelity to the ideals of St Francis proved so divisive that, in 1518 and 1528, they resulted in a division of the Friars Minor into three distinct orders: the Conventuals, the Observants and the Capuchins.[5]

In the Irish context, the Observants' mechanism of parallel jurisdiction proved politically attractive to Gaelic friars who, by adopting the reform, could effectively withdraw almost completely from the jurisdiction of the Anglo-Irish and English friars who had dominated each order's political affairs since the thirteenth century. Although this may have contributed to the initial success of the reform in Gaelic areas, the genuine religious zeal of the reformers was recognized by their contemporaries and led to many of the older foundations in the Pale and the towns of the colony adopting the reform in the late fifteenth and sixteenth centuries. The Observants were highly regarded by all sections of lay society as confessors, preachers and moral authorities and attracted widespread and influential patronage.

3 See below, pp 305–17.   4 F.X. Martin, 'The Irish friars and the Observant movement in the fifteenth century' (1960).   5 This topic has generated a vast literature. For recent surveys, see T. MacVicar, *The Franciscan spirituals and the Capuchin reform* (1986); D. Nimmo, *Reform and division in the medieval Franciscan order* (1987); Ó Clabaigh, *Franciscans*, pp 19–32; M. Robson, *The Franciscans in the Middle Ages* (2006), pp 119–40, 181–91, 202–22.

## THE DOMINICAN OBSERVANT MOVEMENT

The first reference to the Observant movement among the Friars Preachers in Ireland occurs in 1390, when the master general of the order, Friar Raymond of Capua, designated Friar Nicholas Hil as vicar of Ireland, commissioning him to establish the priory at Drogheda as a house of regular observance.[6] This was in keeping with Raymond's policy of designating a house in each province as a centre for the solemn celebration of the Dominican liturgy and where the order's constitutions would be observed with particular fidelity.[7] Hil's appointment was annulled in 1393 and no further references to the Observance in Ireland occur in the registers of the masters general until 1484. Despite this, other sources indicate that the movement continued to flourish and that, as with the Augustinians and Franciscans, it was intimately connected with the establishment of new priories in the west of Ireland. The friary at Athenry played a seminal part in these developments, even if precise details of its role are irrecoverable. First established in 1241, this community underwent a process of physical and religious renewal in the first half of the fifteenth century. In 1400, a papal indulgence was granted to those who contributed to the restoration of the friary.[8] In September 1423, Pope Martin V granted another indulgence to those who contributed to its repair after a serious fire.[9] This facilitated a major rebuilding campaign, details of which were recorded in the community's register.[10] A series of papal letters issued in the winter of 1426–7 shows the extent to which the Athenry friars collaborated with their *confrères* in Portumna and Roscommon to promote the work of reform and expansion in the region. On 8 October 1426, Pope Martin confirmed the transfer of the property at Portumna from the Cistercians of Dunbrody to the Dominicans.[11] Two days later, on 10 October, the pope granted an *inspeximus* or notarized copy of the Dominican Third Order rule at the request of the Irish male and female tertiaries.[12] The friars appear to have already started work on their new foundation, as on 23 November 1426 the pope also granted an indulgence to those who assisted the work of completing the church and priory at Portumna. The bull's description of the site as 'a place isolated from cities and from earthly commerce'[13] gives an indication of the values that inspired the new foundation.

The priory at Longford, though established *c.*1400, was first described as Observant in 1429. The western expansion continued with the establishment of

---

6 Fenning, 'Irish material', p. 254, no. 1.   7 Flynn, *The Irish Dominicans*, pp 1–11; Flanagan, 'Formative development', pp 303–19, 320–55, 410–50; D. Pochin Mould, *The Irish Dominicans* (1957), pp 56–73.   8 *MRH*, p. 221; de Burgo, *Hibernia Dominicana*, p. 230.   9 *Bull OP*, ii, p. 625; cited in Flanagan, 'Formative development', p. 321; de Burgo, *Hibernia Dominicana*, p. 231.   10 Coleman, 'Regestum', p. 209.   11 *Bull OP*, ii, p. 670; Flanagan, 'Formative development', p. 328.   12 *Bull OP*, ii, p. 328. In May 1425 he had granted a similar *inspeximus* of the Franciscan Third Order rule to the Irish tertiaries. *FL*, p. 226.   13 *Bull OP*, ii, p. 672;

new houses at Tombeola, Co. Galway (1427), Urlar, Co. Mayo (1434), Tulsk, Co. Roscommon (1448), Burrishoole, Co. Mayo (1486), Galway (1488), Cloonameehan, Co. Sligo (1488), and Ballindoon, Co. Sligo (1507).[14] While the sources do not indicate the extent to which these foundations were expressions of reform, their establishment in relatively remote locations in the west of Ireland suggests a desire for prayer, solitude and withdrawal that characterized contemporary Augustinian and Franciscan Observant foundations.

## MASTER MAURICE MORALIS O'MOCHÁIN OP

The impetus towards reform and autonomy was greatly advanced by the rise to prominence of Friar Maurice Moralis O'Mocháin in the last quarter of the fifteenth century. Friar Maurice was a member of a hereditary learned family with branches in the Uí Fiachrach territories of Aidhne (south Galway) and Killaraght, Co. Sligo, where they were the hereditary custodians of the cross of St Attracta and erenaghs of Killaraght. His attachment to the convent of Athenry suggests that he belonged to Uí Fiachrach Aidhne group, based in the diocese of Kilmacduagh in south Galway. The first reference to Friar Maurice occurs in 1460, when he was ordained subdeacon and deacon by Bishop Richard Beauchamp of Salisbury. He was then based in the city's Dominican convent, presumably studying theology. By 1462, he had moved to Worcester, where Bishop John Carpenter ordained him priest. In 1474, the Dominican master general, Friar Leonard Mansuetis, permitted him to study for a doctorate in theology at Oxford.[15]

His prominence in Irish Dominican affairs became evident in 1484 when the Irish delegates to the order's general chapter in Rome successfully petitioned for the erection of the Irish vicariate as an independent province and Friar Maurice was appointed prior provincial.[16] In this capacity, he continued to promote the Observant reform and, in 1488, he was authorized by the master general, Friar Joachim Torriani, to establish the reform in Drogheda, Coleraine, Cork, Youghal and elsewhere in Ireland as he saw fit.[17]

His career as prior provincial and the independence of the province proved equally short-lived. In 1491, the English Dominican authorities secured the reduction of the Irish province to its former status as a vicariate of the English province. Friar Maurice resigned his office and received permission to pursue

translation in Flanagan, 'Formative development', p. 308.    **14** This section summarizes Flynn, *Irish Dominicans*, pp 4–8.    **15** A.B. Emden, *A survey of Dominicans in England based on the ordination lists in the episcopal registers (1268–1538)* (1967), pp 177–8, 209, 406; Fenning, 'Irish material', p. 257, no. 10. **16** Fenning, 'Irish material', pp 259–60, no. 21; *MOPH*, viii, pp 383–4.    **17** Fenning, 'Irish material', p. 261, no. 26. He was also licensed to promote fifteen friars aged twenty-three to the priesthood. As a

further studies wherever he wished.[18] In 1493, he was reappointed vicar of Ireland and his reform of the convent at Youghal was approved. He was also permitted to reform other houses and given wide-ranging authority to correct friars of 'corrupt and evil manners'.[19] In 1496, he was succeeded as vicar provincial by Master Richard Hart but was appointed vicar of the reformed friars and friaries in Ireland. He died sometime in the early years of the sixteenth century.[20] He was affectionately remembered in his native convent: after his death, Lord Thomas de Bermingham and his wife Anablina gave ten ounces of silver to the community to pray for the repose of his soul and to embellish the chapel dedicated to SS Catherine of Alexandria and Catherine of Siena, which he had established in the priory church.[21] The choice of patrons was significant: St Catherine of Alexandria was the patron saint of philosophers and students and particularly venerated by Dominicans. St Catherine of Siena (d. 1380) was a Dominican tertiary, a keen supporter of church reform and a confidant and supporter of Friar Raymond of Capua in his attempts to promote the Dominican Observant movement.

## THE DEVELOPMENT OF THE DOMINICAN OBSERVANT REFORM

The impetus towards renewal evident in the new foundations in Connacht was contemporary with the emergence of the Observant reform among the Irish Friars Preachers. Though initially a Gaelic phenomenon, its adoption by the communities in Cork, Drogheda, Kilkenny and Youghal demonstrated its appeal in Anglo-Irish areas as well and the emergence of an Irish Observant congregation was a further indication of its strength. While attempts to gain independence from the English province were ultimately thwarted, they demonstrated the confidence of the Irish Dominicans in their ability to conduct their own affairs.

As with the Franciscan and Augustinian Observants, the reform brought the Irish Friars Preachers into closer contact with their Continental *confrères*, particularly those of the *Congregatio Hollandiae* – the Congregation of Holland. This group had already collaborated with the Scottish Observant friars and was the most vigorous expression of Dominican reform in northern Europe.[22] The earliest evidence for Irish contacts dates from 1501, when Friar Thomas Machascule of the Cork community was permitted to transfer to the Continental reformers.[23] In 1503, the superior of the Congregation of Holland was given responsibility for the reform movement in Ireland and was instructed to send a vicar to Ireland, initially for three years, to oversee its progress.[24] The vicar assigned

personal concession, he was allowed to dispose of his goods within the order and to ride on horseback. **18** Ibid., p. 263, no. 37.　**19** Ibid., p. 263, no. 39.　**20** Ibid., p. 264, no. 44.　**21** Coleman, 'Regestum', pp 218–19, 220.　**22** S.P. Wolf, 'Dominikanische Observanzbestrebungen: Die Congregation Hollandiae (1464–1517)' (1989), p. 274.　**23** Fenning, 'Irish material', p. 265, no. 49.　**24** Ibid., p. 265, nos 50, 52.

was Friar John de Bauffremez, a distinguished lector and former superior of various houses in Flanders and Germany. He was confirmed in office by papal authority in 1504.[25] On 4 September 1505, Friar John Coyn succeeded him as vicar of the Irish reformed friars, while Friar Richard Hart was simultaneously appointed vicar of the non-reformed convents.[26] The emergence of an Observant vicariate further complicated the Irish Dominicans' governmental structures and led to a 'very tangled triple jurisdiction'.[27] In addition to the Observant superior, there was the vicar of the provincial of England, whose authority was recognized by the houses in the Pale and in Anglo-Irish strongholds, while another vicar held jurisdiction over houses in Gaelic areas. The exasperation that this induced is evident in the instruction issued by the master general, Thomas of Vio Cajetano, to the Irish friars in 1506:

> To the three [friars] bearing themselves as vicars in Ireland, one over three reformed convents, the other over the whole nation as instituted by Master Vincent Bandelli, the third calling himself vicar of the provincial of England. It is ordered that each describe his institution and authority, from whom, over which convents, with what exemptions and which superior they recognize [and] which contributions they pay. They are to provide their letters of institution or authentic copies of the same.[28]

Friar Thomas' irritation is contextualized by the next entry in the register, which indicated that the Irish friars had fallen into substantial arrears with their contributions to the master general's finances. Regardless of which vicar they recognized, each house was ordered to pay its dues to Master Simon Lacy, the vicar of the English prior provincial in Ireland.[29]

The general chapter of 1518 recognized only two bodies in Ireland: the reformed friars and the vicariate of the English province, and in 1524 the master general, Friar Anthony of Ferraria, intervened to clarify issues of jurisdiction between the two superiors.[30] The desire of the Irish friars for an independent province remained unabated, but was again thwarted in 1525 by the master general Francis Silvestri, who reasserted that the Irish 'province' was subject to the province of England and was to be governed by a vicar.[31] In 1529, mandates of the master general Friar Paul Butigella indicated that the Irish friars were divided into two vicariates, Observant and Conventual, with each being governed by its own

In the same year, Friar Gerard of Lira was assigned to Ireland or to the Congregation of Holland.   **25** A. de Meyer, *La Congrégation de Hollande ou la réforme dominicaine en territoire Bourguignon, 1465–1515* (1946), p. 395. For de Bauffremez's career and appointments, see pp 329–30; *CPL* xix, p. 547.   **26** Fenning, 'Irish material', p. 266, nos 56, 57.   **27** Flynn, *Irish Dominicans*, p. 6.   **28** Fenning, 'Irish material', p. 267, no. 61.   **29** Ibid., p. 267, no. 62.   **30** Ibid., p. 268, no. 66.   **31** Ibid., p. 269, no. 69.   **32** Ibid., pp 269–70,

vicar.[32] Eventually, after two centuries of struggle, an independent Irish province was finally erected in 1536 by a now lost decree of Pope Paul III, at the instance of Friar David Brown. The order itself belatedly confirmed this arrangement in 1558 at the general chapter in Rome, by which stage the Irish Dominicans were struggling for their very survival.

## DOMINICAN FOUNDATIONS, 1383–1507 (fig. 3.1)

The foundation of the priory of St Canice at Aghaboe, Co. Laois, in 1382 by Finghin Mac Gilla Pátraic, lord of Ossory, was the first foundation established for the Dominicans since 1355. It marks a watershed in the history of the Irish Friars Preachers as, with two exceptions, all subsequent foundations were established in Gaelic territories and enjoyed predominantly Gaelic patronage.[33] The new foundation was established on the site of the ancient monastery of St Canice and extensive remains of the church and transept survive, though nothing remains of the conventual buildings. A list of the 'abbots' of the priory is given by Mervyn Archdall, but this is unreliable.[34]

The priory of the Holy Cross at Cloonshanville, Co. Roscommon, was founded *c.*1385 by the MacDermot Roe as a burial place for him and his descendants.[35] Nothing else is known of its early history and little remains of the structure today, apart from the belfry and fragments of the transept and chancel. St Brigid's Priory in Longford was established by a member of the O'Farrell family *c.*1400, possibly at the instigation of the English Dominican bishop of the diocese of Ardagh, Friar Adam Leyns. The priory church was destroyed by fire in 1427 and in 1429 Pope Martin V granted an indulgence to those who bestowed alms for its restoration, by which stage the community had become Observant. Further indulgences were granted in 1433 and 1438, and three friars died during a bout of disease in 1448 but otherwise nothing further is known of the community.[36]

The priory of the Blessed Virgin Mary and SS Peter and Paul at Portumna, Co. Galway, was established by Murchadh O'Madden, lord of Uí Maine, sometime before 1414, when a chapel there, which previously belonged to the Cistercian monks of Dunbrody, Co. Wexford, was granted to the Dominicans. Substantial remains of the church and priory remain. As already demonstrated, the foundation played an important role in the promotion of the Observant reform among

nos 72, 73.   **33** *MRH*, p. 221; O'Sullivan, *MIDS*, pp 67–9.   **34** Archdall, *Monasticon Hibernicum*, p. 590. Fenning notes that this lists includes the name of many secular priests. O'Sullivan, *MIDS*, p. 69, no. 4. **35** *MRH*, p. 223; O'Sullivan, *MIDS*, pp 69–72; Y. McDermott, 'The priory of the Holy Cross, Cloonshanville' (2009).   **36** *MRH*, p. 227; O'Sullivan, *MIDS*, pp 72–3; D. Mac Firbis, 'The annals of Ireland, from the year 1443 to 1468' (1846), p. 221; J.J. McNamee, *History of the Diocese of Ardagh* (1954), pp 211–19, 246.

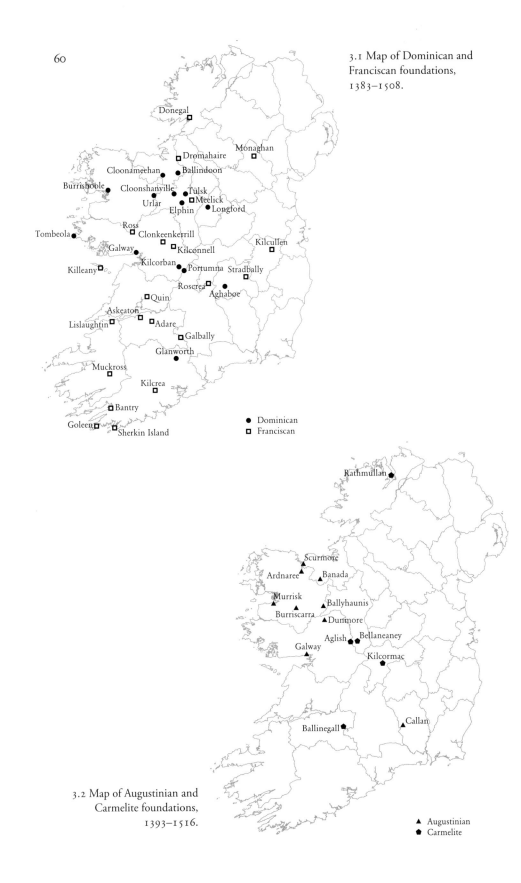

3.1 Map of Dominican and
Franciscan foundations,
1383–1508.

Donegal

Monaghan

Dromahaire

Cloonameehan
Ballindoon

Burrishoole
Cloonshanville
Tulsk

Urlar
Meelick
Elphin
Longford

Ross
Clonkeenkerrill
Kilcullen

Galway
Kilconnell

Kilcorban
Killeany
Portumna
Stradbally

Tombeola
Roscrea

Quin
Aghaboe

Askeaton
Lislaughtin
Adare

Galbally
Glanworth

Muckross
Kilcrea

Bantry
Goleen
Sherkin Island

● Dominican
□ Franciscan

Rathmullan

Scurmore
Ardnaree
Banada

Murrisk
Ballyhaunis
Burriscarra
Dunmore

Aglish
Bellaneaney

Galway
Kilcormac

Ballinegall
Callan

3.2 Map of Augustinian and
Carmelite foundations,
1393–1516.

▲ Augustinian
⬟ Carmelite

the friars in Connacht. The inclusion of SS Peter and Paul in the dedication suggests that the founding community came from Athenry, where the thirteenth-century de Bermingham foundation was similarly dedicated.[37] St Patrick's Priory, Tombeola, Co. Galway, was founded on foot of a papal licence of 1427 permitting the Athenry friars to establish two new foundations. Though little is known of its subsequent history, the founder was an O'Flaherty and the community, situated in a remote but populous district, normally numbered eight members.[38] The priory of St Thomas at Urlar, Co. Mayo, was founded by a member of the Nangle or Mac Costelloe family *c.*1430, with papal licence being granted in 1434.[39] The well-preserved remains of the convent survive on the banks of Lough Urlar and the house's remote location meant that it survived the suppressions of the sixteenth century. It functioned as a general novitiate house for the Irish friars in the early seventeenth century, which may represent a continuation of the medieval practice.

In 1446, Bishop Thomas de Burgh of Clonfert granted the chapel of Kilcorban in east Co. Galway, with some adjoining land, to the brothers and sisters of the Third Order of St Dominic.[40] This grant was confirmed by license of Pope Eugene IV.[41] Kilcorban was the only house established for Dominican regular tertiaries in late medieval Ireland and is discussed further below.[42] St Patrick's Priory, Tulsk, Co. Roscommon, was founded in 1448 by Felim O'Connor.[43] He granted a quarter of land to the friary and was later buried there, having died of wounds received in battle.

St Mary's Priory, Burrishoole, Co. Mayo, picturesquely situated on the north-eastern shore of Clew Bay, was established *c.*1469 by Richard de Burgh, Lord Mac William Uachtar, who died in the habit of the order and was buried there in 1473. Papal confirmation of the foundation was granted in a license of 1486 that also delegated the archbishop of Tuam to absolve the friars from the excommunication they had inadvertently incurred as a result of establishing a new convent without papal permission. Extensive remains of the church survive, and a community of Dominican tertiary sisters lived in the vicinity of the priory during the late sixteenth and early seventeenth centuries.[44] Very little is known of the history of Holy Cross Priory, Glanworth, Co. Cork. Its principal patrons were members of the Roche family, whose impressive castle lies adjacent to the priory. Fr Urban Flanagan gives 1475 as the date of foundation and the remains of the church (all that survives of the claustral complex) are fifteenth century in date.[45] The erection

37 *MRH*, p. 228; O'Sullivan, *MIDS*, pp 73–4; M. McMahon, *Portumna priory* (1978).   38 *MRH*, p. 230; O'Sullivan, *MIDS*, p. 74.   39 *MRH*, p. 231; O'Sullivan, *MIDS*, pp 75–7.   40 *MRH*, pp 225–6; O'Sullivan, *MIDS*, p. 87; H. Fenning, 'The Dominicans of Kilcorban' (1987).   41 *CPL*, ix, p. 495.   42 See below, pp 308–9.   43 *MRH*, pp 230–1; O'Sullivan, *MIDS*, pp 77–8; K. O'Conor et al., 'Tulsk Abbey' (1996), 67–9. 44 *MRH*, p. 222; O'Sullivan, *MIDS*, pp 79–80; Y. McDermott, 'The Dominican priory of Burrishoole' (2010). 45 *MRH*, p. 225; O'Sullivan, *MIDS*, pp 78–9; C. Manning, *The history and archaeology of Glanworth Castle,*

of the priory at Cloonameehan, Co. Sligo, was a joint initiative involving both friars and laymen. In 1488, Pope Innocent IV, on the petition of three noblemen, licensed the establishment of new Dominican foundations in the dioceses of Kildare, Achonry and Meath. The Achonry foundation, at Cloonameehan, was sponsored by Eoghan Mac Donnchadha. The register of the Dominicans in Sligo credited Friar Bernard Mac Donnchadha, prior and lector of the Sligo community, as the founder. Initially, the house was a dependency of the Sligo convent and housed a small community. A full complement of friars was resident there in 1584.[46] The involvement of clerical and lay members of the same family in the foundation is significant, and similar joint initiatives were features of some contemporary Augustinian, Franciscan and tertiary foundations.

The priory of St Mary on the Hill at the Claddagh in Galway was one of the most important of the late medieval Dominican foundations and owed its origins to the patronage of the Lynch family, wealthy merchants and notable benefactors of the friars in Athenry. In 1488, Pope Innocent VIII permitted the friars to take possession of a disused chapel, formerly the property of the Premonstratensian canons of Tuam. The mayor of the city, John FitzStephen Lynch, built the choir of the church in 1493.[47]

The last Dominican foundation erected in late medieval Ireland, the priory of St Mary, Ballindoon, Co. Sligo, was begun by Thomas O'Farrell in 1507. Situated near the shore of Lough Arrow, it is architecturally the most puzzling of the surviving Dominican remains, with an unusual tower incorporating an elaborate rood loft with little remaining of the convent. The prior of Burrishoole, another Thomas O'Farrell, was slain in 1527, otherwise nothing else is known of the early years of this house.[48]

THE FRANCISCANS

The Franciscans experienced the most widespread growth of all the mendicant orders in late medieval Ireland, with both the Conventual and Observant branches establishing twenty-one new foundations between 1400 and c.1510.[49] The success of the Observant reform among the Friars Minor led to the erection of a quasi-autonomous Irish Observant vicariate in 1460 and, in addition to specifically Observant foundations, many older houses adopted the reform. The Observants

*Co. Cork* (2010), pp 2, 9–11.  **46** *MRH*, p. 223; O'Sullivan, *MIDS*, pp 82–3.  **47** *MRH*, p. 225; O'Sullivan, *MIDS*, pp 80–1; E. Ó Héideáin (ed.), *The Dominicans in Galway, 1241–1991* (1991). **48** *MRH*, p. 222; O'Sullivan, *MIDS*, p. 86; *Ballindoon abbey, 1507–2007* (2007).  **49** This section summarizes Ó Clabaigh, *Franciscans*, pp 42–79.

were also keen promoters of the tertiary movement among their lay followers and maintained close links with the Franciscan regular tertiaries.[50]

## REFORM AND REGULAR OBSERVANCE

The earliest evidence for a reform movement among the Irish Franciscans comes from Friar Francis O'Mahony, the seventeenth-century provincial and chronicler, who recorded:

> I gather that this province of the order of Minors in Ireland was governed, according to the system of the seraphic institute, by ministers provincial from the year 1239 from this historical account in an ancient codex: In the year of the Lord 1239, Br Simon was made minister of Ireland, and from that time on others took his place in continuous succession, according to custom. There were never wanting those eager for their manner of life and rule and [who] even encouraged others in regular discipline, although in other parts of the world, the order underwent some distress. Timidly nevertheless, on account of the power of others, until the year 1417, in which time, greater in heart and numbers, they withdrew from the more relaxed discipline and exhorted and attracted many others to the pure observance of the rule, though still under the government of the ministers provincial.[51]

The source cited by O'Mahony has not survived, but it was clearly the work of an Observant author with access to sources relating to the early years of the province and the progress of the reform. The Friar Simon mentioned as minister provincial in 1239 is otherwise unknown, and Friar John of Kethene ruled the province from 1239 to 1254. Despite this anomaly, the passage is significant as it shows the existence of a *sui generis* reform party before 1417. Its emergence was contemporary with other indigenous reform groups in France, Italy and Spain and it may have drawn on a tradition of unease about the observance of poverty in the Irish province for which some fourteenth-century evidence exists.[52] The reformers succeeded in establishing two houses: the Macnamara foundation at Quin, Co. Clare (pl. 12), in 1433 and the MacCarthy foundation at Muckross, Co. Kerry, *c.*1448. Whereas both of these were described as being 'under regular observance', it is clear that until 1460 the reform in Ireland was a *sub ministris* one, that is one which followed a reformed lifestyle but remained under the jurisdiction of the Conventual authorities. It is likely that many of the Conventual foundations described below formed part of this reform movement, though no contemporary evidence for this exists.

By the mid-fifteenth century, the number of reform-minded friars in Ireland had reached a critical mass and they were increasingly aware of the privileges that their Continental colleagues enjoyed. In 1458, one of the leading reformers, Friar Nehemias O'Donoghue, attended the Observant general chapter in Rome and spent two years learning the customs of the reformed friars in France.[53] The year of his return, 1460, was hailed as 'year of the Observance' as it was the year in which the Observant vicariate of Ireland was established with Friar Nehemias as its first vicar provincial.[54] This development initiated a phase of rapid expansion as new houses were founded for Observants and as older convents adopted the reform. It was also marked by intense disputes between the Conventual and Observant authorities concerning jurisdiction and the transfer of houses to the reform.[55] Opposing factions existed even within individual communities: in 1516, the Annals of Ulster recorded the drowning in Lough Erne of some friars from the Conventual friary at Cavan. The only two identified by name were John Mac Grath and Nicholas O'Catháin, who were described as 'friars of stricter observance'.[56]

In many cases, members or descendants of the founding families insisted that the communities adopt the Observance.[57] The community at Kilconnell was reformed in 1460 on the instructions of Malachy O'Kelly, son of the founder.[58] In August 1497, the friary at Carrickfergus was reformed at the behest of the local chieftain Niall O'Neill, with sixteen Observant friars from Donegal forming the nucleus of the new community. The Annals of Ulster record the transfer of the Cavan friary to the Observants at the request of John O'Reilly, lord of Breifne, in 1502.[59] In 1534, the friary in Limerick became Observant at the request of the mayor and corporation of the city, who had petitioned the provincial chapter for its reform.[60] This is the only Irish instance of a common Continental phenomenon whereby civic corporations intervened to secure the reform of a mendicant community. In 1540, the community at Ennis adopted the reform at the instigation of Murrough O'Brien and the chief men of Thomond.[61]

From 1460 until 1517, the Irish Observant vicariate was governed by a vicar provincial elected for a triennial term by the delegates to the Observant vicariate chapter. The Conventual minister provincial had to ratify this election, though in

---

53 'Brevis synopsis', p. 165.   54 The Observants in Ireland had already elected a vicar provincial, Malachy O'Clumhain, sometime before August 1460 but no further references to him occur and the list of Observant vicars provincial begins with Nehemias O'Donoghue. See Ó Clabaigh, *Franciscans*, pp 53–4. 55 Ó Clabaigh, *Franciscans*, pp 64–9.   56 *AU*, iii, p. 527.   57 Such interventions by patrons were also common on the Continent. See L. Ceyssens, 'Les ducs de Bourgogne et l'introduction de l'observance à Malines (1447–1469)' (1937).   58 BL Add. MS 4821, fo. 105v.   59 *AU*, iii, pp 423, 461.   60 'Brevis synopsis', p. 148. This chapter was held in Kilconnell friary.   61 *Ann. Conn.*, p. 713; *AFM*, v, p. 1455.

the event of his refusal to do so, confirmation automatically occurred after three days.[62] This practice ceased after the division ordered by Pope Leo X in 1517 at the *capitulum generalissimum* in Rome. In consequence, the Observant superiors were recognized as the juridical superiors of the Friars Minor and assumed the roles and titles of ministers provincial and ministers general. The impact of this decision is evident in the dossier of Observant material preserved in Bodleian Rawlison MS C.320, where every reference to the vicars of the Observants has been corrected to read 'minister'. The extent of the Observants' strength and reputation in Ireland is evident in the account of the 1517 Rome chapter given in the Annals of Ulster:

> A general chapter was held in Rome this year by the Friars Minor in their entirety, through the grace of the Holy Spirit and through favour of Pope Leo X and amongst the things that were determined therein, it was decided that the minister of the friars of strict observance should be over the friars in their entirety and that only a vicar or master should be over the friars of common life. And every monastery of common life which should have two-thirds of the community unanimous to have it of strict observance, it should be obliged on the minister of strict observance to take it to him and that it should be under their obedience from that out.[63]

By 1540, in addition to the ten houses founded specifically for Observants, approximately twenty-three older foundations had adopted the reform, while twenty-four convents, including a number of new foundations, remained under the jurisdiction of the Conventual authorities.

## CONVENTUAL FOUNDATIONS, 1400–85

The friary at Askeaton, Co. Limerick, on the banks of the River Deel, was founded for the Friars Minor by Gerald Fitzgerald, fourth earl of Desmond, shortly before 1400 and marked the beginning of the order's remarkable revival in Ireland (pl. 11).[64] In 1414, Pope John XXIII instructed the bishop of Clonfert, Thomas O'Kelly, to licence the foundation of three Franciscan friaries.[65] Two were in his own diocese; the third, at St Mullins (Co. Carlow), was not established. These were the first houses established by the Irish Franciscans since the foundation of Kinalehin friary, also in the diocese of Clonfert, in the mid-

---

62 *AS*, vii, nos 12, 13, 17. A formulary letter seeking such confirmation is found in TCD MS 250. See Ó Clabaigh, *Franciscans*, pp 183–4. **63** *AU*, iii, p. 527. **64** *MRH*, pp 242–3; T.J. Westropp, 'Notes on Askeaton, part iii' (1903). **65** *FL*, p. 177; *BF*, vii, p. 482; *CPL*, vi, p. 467.

fourteenth century, and Bymacan on the Isle of Man in 1373.[66] The presence of
three Franciscan friaries in Clonfert provides clear evidence the shift of the order's
centre of gravity to Connacht.[67] The friary at Kilconnell, Co. Galway, was
certainly in existence by 1414, and the death of its founder, William O'Kelly, lord
of Uí Maine, in 1420 was recorded in the obituary book of the community.[68]
Varying dates in the 1460s are given for the introduction of the Observant reform,
which was also done at the behest of the local lord.[69]

The earliest contemporary reference to Quin Friary, Co. Clare, occurs in 1433
when Pope Eugene IV granted permission to MacCon Macnamara to found a
house for the Friars Minor *sub regulari Observantia*. As noted above, the term
'Regular Observance' was more a recognition of the lifestyle of the friars than an
indication of its constitutional position. Quin remained under the jurisdiction of
the Conventuals until it was officially dissolved in 1541 and did not become
Observant until a community was reconstituted there in 1612.[70]

The first reference to the friary at Muckross, Co. Kerry, occurs in a 1468 bull
of Pope Paul II, which indicated that the community had been in existence for
about twenty years, implying that it had been founded sometime in the period
1440–8. The community was described as living a life of penance and strict
observance under their guardian, Richard Chilvart: the first reformer to be known
by name from a contemporary source. Again, it appears that the friars followed a
reformed lifestyle under the jurisdiction of the Conventual authorities. They did
not join the Observant vicariate and remained, like Quin, subject to Conventual
governance until they were dispersed in 1587.[71]

The friary at Meelick on the banks of the River Shannon in Co. Galway was
established by Breasal O'Madden and the O'Maddens continued as the principal
patrons of the house. In 1445, Pope Eugene IV granted an indulgence to those
who contributed to the restoration of the convent. At this stage, the community
was described as *sub regulari observantia*, but the Observant reform proper was
only introduced in 1479 at the instance of the O'Madden chieftain.[72] In 1442,
Pope Eugene IV granted an indulgence to those who contributed to the repair of

**66** J.K. Barratt, 'The Franciscan friary of Bymacan' (1964).   **67** C. Ó Clabaigh, 'The mendicant friars in
the medieval diocese of Clonfert' (2007).   **68** 'Fundatus circa anno 1400 per D. O'Kelly cuius obitus his
verbis describitur in libro eiusdem conventus: 3 cal. nov. 1420 obitus Wm Magnus Ykelly, omnium
Hibernicorum suo tempore nominatissimi ac principalis istius conventus fundatoris'. BL Add. MS 4821,
fo. 105v. The date 1400 seems to be a conjecture of the compiler, as Ware in BL Add. MS 4814, fo. 6v gives
the same founder but the date 1414.   **69** *MRH*, p. 251; F.J. Bigger, 'The Franciscan friary of Kilconnell'
(1900–1); P. Conlan, *The Franciscan friary, Kilconnell, Co. Galway* (2007).   **70** *MRH*, p. 257; *BFNS*, i, p. 58;
*AM*, x, p. 526; *CPL*, viii, p. 427 (which omits any mention to regular observance); 'Brussels MS 3410', p.
202; A. Gwynn & D. Gleeson, *A history of the diocese of Killaloe* (1962), pp 487–92.   **71** *MRH*, p. 256;
*BFNS*, ii, pp 733–4; *AM*, xiii, p. 645 (see also p. 498); K. Walsh, 'Franciscan friaries in pre-Reformation
Kerry' (1976).   **72** *MRH*, pp 254–5; BL Add. MS 4814, fo. 7v; P.E. MacFhinn, *Milic* (1943), pp 4, 8–14.

the friary at Gahannyh in Cork diocese. This has been identified as Goleen near Mizen Head in west Cork, but nothing further is known of this foundation, and nothing remains on the site. A noteworthy feature was that the founder was a friar, Donal O'Scully, and not some secular patron, a situation paralleled in some contemporary Dominican and Augustinian foundations.[73] The origins of the friary at Stradbally, Co. Laois, are also obscure, and it has frequently been confused with other friaries and religious houses. In the early seventeenth century, Friar Francis O'Mahony gave *c.*1447 as the date of foundation and an O'Moore as the founder. There is no record of it becoming Observant and it probably remained Conventual until its dissolution *c.*1568.[74]

In 1453, Pope Nicholas V instructed the Franciscan bishop of Clonfert, Cornelius O'Cuinnlis, to licence the foundation of a number of friaries in the ecclesiastical province of Tuam.[75] His mandate indicates that the friars had already been offered the parish church of St Patrick in Elphin, Co. Roscommon, by the Franciscan bishop of the diocese, Cornelius O'Mullally, with the consent of the canons of the chapter, the clergy and the people of the parish, including Tomaltach MacDermott, the local chieftain. The new foundation was exempted from pastoral responsibilities and ecclesiastical taxes and was granted land for the support of the community. Nothing further is known of the friars in Elphin, but obituary references in the Annals of Connacht indicate that they enjoyed the patronage of the local aristocracy including the O'Mulconrys, a hereditary learned family of historians and poets.[76]

In the same year as the foundation of Elphin, David O'Mulkerrill received papal permission for the transfer of the house of the Franciscan tertiaries at Clonkeenkerrill, Co. Galway, to the Friars Minor.[77] This may have been connected to the permission to found friaries addressed to the bishop of Clonfert cited above, as Clonkeenkerill is also in Clonfert diocese.

The Conventual friary at Monaghan was established in 1462 by Felim MacMahon, king of Oriel.[78] By 1466, a friary existed at Bantry, Co. Cork. It owed its origins to a papal licence granted in 1449 to Donatus Omabba (O'Mahony?) and was initially established for the Conventual friars. Sir James Ware gave 1460 as the date of foundation and Dermot O'Sullivan of Beare as founder.[79] The community became Observant during one of the terms of office of Friar David O'Herlihy as minister provincial.[80] In 1471, Aunfrun O'Brien founded a house for Conventual friars at Galbally, Co. Tipperary. Despite being sacked the

73 *MRH*, p. 251; *FL*, p. 196; *CPL*, ix, p. 249.   74 *MRH*, p. 259; 'Brevis synopsis', pp 157–8.   75 *MRH*, p. 249; *CPL*, x, pp 641–2; *BFNS*, i, p. 848; C. Giblin, 'The Franciscans in Elphin' (1988).   76 See below, pp 262–3.   77 *MRH*, p. 246; *CPL*, x, pp 649; *BFNS*, i, pp 844–5.   78 *MRH*, p. 255; *AU*, iii, p. 207; 'Brussels MS 3947', p. 19; C. Giblin, 'The Franciscan ministry in the diocese of Clogher' (1970).   79 *MRH*, p. 243; BL Add. MS 4814, fo. 4v.   80 O'Herlihy was minister provincial from 1521 to 1524 and

following year, the friars remained until their dispersal in 1540 and did not adopt the Observant reform.[81]

The presence by 1477 of a Conventual community in Roscrea, Co. Tipperary, is attested by a colophon in Lambeth Palace Library, MS 46.[82] Donatus Mooney, quoting a now vanished inscription in the cloister, attributed the foundation to Mulrony O'Carroll.[83] The community remained Conventual until its dissolution, and Mooney recorded an encounter he had with a former inmate that confirms this.[84]

The final foundation established for the Conventuals was near Killeany on Inishmore, Aran Islands, Co. Galway. O'Mahony dated its foundation to 1485, but gives no information about the founder.[85] It was still Conventual in 1506 when Pope Julius II gave the friars permission to keep forty cows to supply them with milk products during Lent.[86]

### OBSERVANT FOUNDATIONS, 1460–1508

After the erection of the Observant vicariate in 1460, the majority of new Franciscan foundations were for the reformed branch of the order. Foundation dates between 1455 and 1462 are given for the houses at Moyne, Co. Mayo, Enniscorthy, Co. Wexford, and Sherkin Island, Co. Cork. The foundation of the first specifically Observant community in 1464 at Adare, Co. Limerick, by the earl and countess of Kildare is exceptionally well documented and is discussed in detail in the next chapter (pl. 10).[87]

Various dates are given for the foundation of the friary at Kilcrea, Co. Cork, of which the most reliable is 1465. An alternative foundation date of 1478 is too late, as a manuscript written in the friary in 1472 survives. The founder was Cormac Láidir MacCarthy, who was killed by his brother in 1495 in a dispute over the chieftaincy.[88] He was buried in the Franciscan habit and was the first of a line of MacCarthy chiefs to be buried there. The Four Masters describe him as 'an exalter and reverer of the church who ordered the strict observance of the Sabbath in his territory', which may owe something to the influence of the friars. The MacCarthys had been among the principal patrons of the Franciscan house at Cork since the thirteenth century, so Cormac Láidir's choice of the Observant branch for the new foundation was not surprising. His other religious foundation

between 1530 and 1533.   **81** *MRH*, p. 250; BL Add. MS 4814, fo. 5v; *AFM*, iv, p. 1070; D. Ó Riain, *The Moor Abbey, Galbally* (1992).   **82** *MRH*, p. 258; see below, p. 142; A. Gwynn & D. Gleeson, *A history of the diocese of Killaloe* (1962), pp 493–8.   **83** The text is given in BL Add. MS 4821, fo. 106r, 'Claustrum ea extructus [*sic*] 1523 Orate pro anima Molrony: f: Joh: Carroll qui fuit D. Eliae et princeps Hiberniae tunc anno 1523 qui me fieri fecit'.   **84** 'Brussels MS 3947', pp 75–6.   **85** *MRH*, p. 242; 'Brevis synopsis', p. 161.   **86** *MRH*, p. 242.   **87** See below, pp 95–7.   **88** *AU*, iii, p. 385; O'Mahony, quoting the inscription on his tomb in the choir of the friary church, gives the date as 1494. 'Brevis synopsis', p. 159.

was for the Franciscan Third Order Regular at Ballymacadane. He also built three tower houses in his territory, including his principal residence at Kilcrea, adjacent to the friary.[89]

The origins of the friary at Rosserrilly, Co. Galway, are particularly confused, with various sources giving dates ranging from 1351 to 1498 for its foundation.[90] Fr Canice Mooney OFM has discussed these at length and favours a foundation date of *c*.1460. He believes that it was an Observant foundation from the start and that references to it transferring from the Conventuals to the reform in 1470 are mistaken.[91]

The earliest reference to Lislaughtin, Co. Kerry, occurs in May 1477 when Pope Sixtus IV instructed three neighbouring prelates to licence the Observant foundation that John O'Connor had begun to build in his territory. O'Connor also endowed the church with altar vessels and other furnishings, and the fine gilt processional cross donated by his son Cornelius in 1479 survives.[92]

The Observant house at Donegal, in the diocese of Raphoe and the territory of Tyrconnell, became one of the most famous and influential of the friars' houses in the sixteenth and early seventeenth century. It was founded in 1474 by Red Hugh O'Donnell at the urging of his mother, Nuala O'Connor.[93] The community grew rapidly, and in 1497 sixteen friars from Donegal introduced the reform to Carrickfergus, while in 1508 Donegal friars formed the nucleus of the new Observant community at Dromahair (alias Creevelea), Co. Leitrim.[94] The O'Donnell chieftains proved generous benefactors, providing the friars with chalices and vestments and, in 1530, defraying the expenses of a provincial chapter held in Donegal.[95] Red Hugh died and was buried in the friary in 1505, his widow, Nuala O'Brien, died in 1528 having spent over twenty years as a secular tertiary living in retirement near the friary.[96] The friary was the burial place of the O'Donnells and many of the most prominent Ulster families, and the friars were highly influential in the locality. Donatus Mooney did his novitiate in Donegal and his account of the year of probation there provides a rare insight in the daily routine of an Irish mendicant community.[97]

The friary at Kilcullen, Co. Kildare, at the bridge over the River Liffey on the boundaries of the archdiocese of Dublin was founded in 1486 by Roland FitzEustace, Baron Portlester. It was the only Observant house established in the

**89** *MRH*, p. 251; A. Ó Gibealláin, 'The Franciscan friary of Kilcrea' (1965); E. Bolster, *A history of the diocese of Cork* (1972), pp 442–5; D. Maher, *Kilcrea friary* (1999).   **90** *MRH*, p. 258; C. Mooney, 'The friary of Ross: foundation and early years' (1960–1).   **91** Ibid., p. 13.   **92** *MRH*, p. 254; *CPL*, xiii, pp 572–3; *BFNS*, iii, p. 474; K. Walsh, 'Franciscan friaries in pre-Reformation Kerry (1976).   **93** 'Brussels MS 3947', pp 38–48, esp. pp 38–9; C. Mooney, 'The founding of the friary of Donegal' (1954–5). **94** *AU*, iii, p. 417.   **95** 'Brussels MS 3410', p. 198; *Ann. Conn.*, p. 675.   **96** *Ann. Conn.*, p. 667. **97** 'Brussels MS 3947', pp 41–7.

Pale, but little else is known of its early years.[98] FitzEustace was buried there in 1496 and his daughter Alison, wife of Gerald Fitzgerald, eighth earl of Kildare, in 1517.[99] The friars were involved in a dispute with the secular clergy in March 1494 and were declared contumacious for three times refusing to answer summonses to provincial councils.[1] A 1554 petition from the guardian and friars of Kilcullen to Queen Mary appealing for the return of their property and that of other named friaries has survived.[2]

The last new Observant foundation made in this period was Dromahair, Co. Leitrim, which was founded by Margaret O'Brien, wife of Eoghan O'Rourke, in 1508.[3] She was a sister of Nuala O'Brien, who had been a keen patron of the Donegal friars and, according to Mooney, it was from Donegal that the first friars came to the new foundation.[4] Thomas MacBrady, bishop of Kilmore, died there in 1511, possibly while visiting to consecrate the friary church, and in 1512 the Annals of Ulster record the burial of Margaret O'Brien in the wooden church she had built for the friars.[5] Her husband, Eoghan O'Rourke, was buried there in 1526.[6] Two friars, Eremon O'Donnell and Mael Sechlainn Mac Govern, died in the fire that destroyed the friary in 1536;[7] on the evidence of his surname, it would appear that the former was one of the original group of pioneers from Donegal. The house was restored by Brian Ballach O'Rourke, and much of the stone complex that survives was probably constructed at this stage.

### FRIAR WILLIAM O'REILLY OFM

The period of expansion that both the Conventual and Observant friars underwent corresponded with the provincialate of the first Gaelic minister provincial, William O'Reilly.[8] His surname suggests a Breifne (Cavan/Leitrim) origin, though there is no reference to him in any of the surviving O'Reilly genealogies and nothing is known of his early years. He may have entered the order in the friary at Cavan, which had been founded by the family in the early fourteenth century and which was the only Franciscan house in O'Reilly territory. He was described as both an inceptor and professor in theology, indicating that he had studied at the University of Oxford.

98 *MRH*, pp 251–2; BL Add. MS 4814, fo. 3r; 'Brussels MS 3947', p. 85.   99 BL Add. MS 4821, fo. 106v.   1 N. White (ed.), *Registrum diocesis Dublinensis* (1959), p. 30.   2 BL Harl. MS 416, fo. 73. 3 *MRH*, p. 248; 'Brussels MS 3410', p. 198; J.J. MacNamee, *History of the diocese of Ardagh* (1954), pp 226–30.   4 'Brussels MS 3947', pp 48–9. He notes that it was in this convent that he was ordained and celebrated his first Mass.   5 *AFM*, v, p. 1309; *AU*, iii, p. 501.   6 *AFM*, v, p. 1393.   7 *AU*, iii, p. 607. 8 G. Mac Niocaill, 'Uilliam Ó Raghallaigh OFM' (1961).

His rise to prominence in the province reignited the tension between its Gaelic and Anglo-Irish members. In June 1445, he was granted a letter of denization by Henry VI.[9] Since the enactment of the Statute of Kilkenny in 1366, this was necessary for any Gaelic cleric wishing to minister within the Anglo-Irish colony. The letter also permitted him to be advanced to any office in the Franciscan order, including that of minister provincial, and may have been issued in retrospective confirmation of his appointment. Friar William soon encountered stiff opposition from his Anglo-Irish subjects: on 10 September 1446, Pope Eugene IV instructed the archbishop of Tuam and the bishops of Clonmacnois and Clonfert to investigate O'Reilly's petition for confirmation in office.[10] The letter indicated that O'Reilly had been appointed by the minister general, Friar Anthony Rusconi (1443–9), rather than elected by the provincial chapter. It is also clear that those who opposed him had access to earlier legislation forbidding the appointment of Gaelic friars to the position of minister provincial, and the survival of such legislation from the fourteenth century has already been noted above.[11] The letter also noted that the Gaelic friars were more numerous and vigorous than the Anglo-Irish, a point confirmed by the extent of their expansion into Gaelic territory as already demonstrated. As O'Reilly was still in office in 1448, it appears that the judges delegate (all mendicant friars) had found in his favour.

The opposition to O'Reilly continued, and many guardians rebelled against his authority and brought their case to the king who appealed the appointment to Pope Nicholas V. The pope appointed Robert Power, bishop of Lismore, and John Cantwell, dean of Cashel, to examine the case and in the interim the province was governed by Friars David Carrewe and Nicholas Walsh.[12] The 1454 papal letter that restored O'Reilly as minister provincial indicated that he had not attended the process that had deposed him from office.[13] O'Reilly appears to have appealed to Rome in person and may have remained there until his restoration.

Friar William also faced opposition on the secular front: in 1450 and again in 1451, Henry VI wrote to Richard, duke of York and lord lieutenant of Ireland, on the matter. The 1450 letter, which only survives in a draft version,[14] is the more detailed and alleged that O'Reilly, 'oure enemy borne and of Irrysche blode, name and nacion', secured his confirmation as minister by deceiving the pope and the king's procurator in Rome. He ordered that O'Reilly and his supporters were to be arrested if they ever came into the duke's jurisdiction and instructed him to write to the earl of Desmond and Patrick FitzMaurice Fitzgerald of Kerry, ordering them to act likewise. Friars David Carrewe and Gilbert Walshe were also urged to

---

**9** *FL*, pp 198–9.  **10** *BFNS*, i, p. 507; *FL*, pp 199–200.  **11** See above, pp 37–8.  **12** *AM*, x, pp 10–11. Wadding had access to a bull of Nicholas V endorsing the actions of Carrewe and Walsh and confirming Gilbert Walsh as provincial, but this has not survived.  **13** *BFNS*, i, pp 857–8.  **14** Bodl. MS Rawl. B 484,

see that the friars observed the injunctions against appointing Gaelic friars to positions of authority. In July 1451, the king again wrote to the duke of York ordering that O'Reilly be summoned to answer charges that he had caused the legislation forbidding the appointment of Gaelic friars as provincial to be overturned, and to be punished if it were found to be true. The king ordered that no Gaelic friar was to be admitted to any house of the order within the colony without first swearing an oath of allegiance before the chancellor of Ireland.[15]

O'Reilly weathered the opposition and continued to function as minister provincial throughout. He was active in founding new houses in 1453 and was re-elected at the provincial chapter in Waterford in 1469.[16] He was still minister provincial in 1470, when he witnessed an oath of fidelity taken before Archbishop John Bole of Armagh by the bishop of Down and Connor.[17] He may have continued in office until 1471, when the first reference to Friar Tadhg O'Donoghue as minister provincial occurs.[18]

The emergence of William O'Reilly as the first Gaelic minister provincial, his survival in the face of concerted opposition, and the succession of another Gaelic provincial, demonstrate the extent to which the balance of power had tipped towards the Gaelic section of the province. The expansion of the Conventual friars into Gaelic territories and the emergence of the Observant vicariate provide further corroboration of this.

## THE AUGUSTINIAN OBSERVANT MOVEMENT

Attempts to trace the emergence of the reform movement among the Irish Augustinians are hampered by the fact that the principal source for the period, the registers of the Augustinian priors general, are missing for the crucial period from 1394 to 1419. As indicated above, the late fourteenth century was a time of tremendous tension within the Irish Augustinian limit, as Anglo-Irish friars sought greater autonomy from their English *confrères*. When records resume in 1419, they indicate that, like the Dominicans and Franciscans, the order's political centre of gravity had shifted to Connacht and that a strong impetus towards reform had emerged among its Gaelic members.[19]

This development brought them into closer contact with their Continental brethren, where reform currents had been animating the Augustinians since 1385

fo. 18; *FL*, pp 203–4.   **15** *FL*, pp 205–6.   **16** *BFNS*, i, pp 848–9; *CPL*, x, pp 641–2; *FL*, p. 207. This is the first unambiguous reference to an Irish minister provincial being elected.   **17** Lynch, 'Franciscan documents', p. 40.   **18** *BFNS*, iv, pp 19–20.   **19** Unless otherwise stated, this section is based on Martin & de Meijer, 'Irish material'; F.X. Martin, 'The Irish Augustinian reform movement in the fifteenth century' (1961).

when the prior general, Friar Bartholomew Veneto, had selected the priory of Leccetto near Siena as a model of strict religious observance for the whole order. From Leccetto, the movement spread to other Italian houses and beyond the Alps, with the first Observant houses in Germany being established in 1419 and in Spain in 1420. The priors general promoted the reform by assembling the reformed priories into congregations and taking them under their direct jurisdiction, thereby affording the reformers a greater degree of protection and autonomy. By the end of the fifteenth century, six such Observant congregations existed in Italy, with two in Spain and one each in Germany and Ireland.[20]

The earliest reference to the Irish Observant movement occurs on 19 September 1423 in the register of the prior general, Friar Augustine Favaroni. In a lengthy entry, he licensed the establishment of the newly founded friary of Corpus Christi at Banada, Co. Mayo, as a house of Regular Observance at the behest of Friar Charles O'Hara, its founder. Friars from other Augustinian communities were permitted to transfer to Banada as long as the reformers were willing to receive them. Before transferring, they were instructed to make a full inventory of any goods that had been conceded to them by the order and leave it with their former communities. Anything they brought with them on transferring to the Observance was to be returned to their erstwhile *confrères* after their deaths. The prior general took the house under his immediate jurisdiction, but permitted the Irish Augustinian vicar provincial or his commissary in Connacht to visit and correct members of the community short of removing them from it. An annual election for the office of prior was also enjoined on the community.[21]

Whereas Augustinian priories had already been established at Ardnaree, Co. Mayo, *c.*1400, and at Burriscarra before 1413, the establishment of Banada was the catalyst for a further expansion in the west of Ireland. The priory at Dunmore, Co. Galway, was established by 1425, Ballyhaunis, Co. Mayo, by *c.*1430, Scurmore, Co. Sligo, in 1454 and Murrisk, Co. Mayo, in 1457. The presence of a Friar Mahon O'Hara at Dunmore in 1427 may indicate that the founding community came from Banada, an O'Hara foundation, while Friar Hugh O'Malley, the founder of Murrisk, was explicitly stated to be a 'friar of the house of Corpus Christi, Benfada in the diocese of Achonry' in the papal bull authorizing its foundation issued on 12 February 1457.[22] The local chieftain, Tadhg O'Malley, had granted the site for the foundation and was presumably a relative of Friar Hugh.

**20** Martin, 'Irish Augustinian reform', pp 237–8. See also F.X. Martin, 'The Augustinian Observant movement' (1989) and K. Walsh, 'The Observance: sources for a history of the Observant reform movement in the order of Augustinian friars in the fourteenth and fifteenth century' (1977). **21** Martin & de Meijer, 'Irish material', pp 81–2, where the date is incorrectly given as 29 December. Martin, 'Irish Augustinian reform', pp 238–42. **22** *CPL*, vii, pp 568–9; *CPL*, xi, p. 294.

FRIAR HUGH O'MALLEY OESA

The expansion of the order in Connacht, the emergence of the Observance and the increased autonomy of the Gaelic friars coalesced in the actions of Friar Hugh O'Malley during his visit to Italy in early 1457.[23] Having secured papal approval for the foundation of Murrisk, he proceeded to Naples where, on 5 March 1457, he secured various privileges for himself and his *confrères* in Connacht from the prior general, Friar Julian Falciglia. Among these was the appointment of Friar Cornelius O'Hely as rector of the friars in Connacht. He was to enjoy the same authority over his subjects as the vicar provincial of Ireland did. However, to preserve the unity of the order, the Connacht friars were ordered to honourably receive the vicar provincial when he visited them and to continue making their contributions to the expenses of the Irish limit. The vicar provincial retained his right to discipline the friars of the Connacht houses and the nomination of the rector for Connacht rested with him and his definitors.[24]

The prior general confirmed the privileges granted to the Observant friars at Banada by two of his predecessors and granted the prior of the house greater authority in the correction, transfer and expulsion of disobedient friars.[25] In recognition of his efforts to promote reform, Friar Hugh was appointed to the position of lector and granted its attendant privileges. More importantly, at the wish of the Irish brethren, the prior general nominated him as his vicar general to preside at the forthcoming chapter of the Irish limit at Tullow, Co. Carlow, in June 1458.[26] This convent was located within the territory of the Butler earls of Ormond and Martin plausibly argues that O'Malley's presidency of the chapter and the subsequent dominance of Connacht friars in the administration of the vicariate provides the context for the establishment of a priory at Callan, Co. Kilkenny, in 1461.[27]

In February 1472, two friars of Callan, Dermot O'Kane and Hugh Gavigan, acting on behalf of the majority of the community, sought permission from the prior general, Friar James of Aquila, to adopt the Observant reform.[28] In acceding to their request, the prior general also granted them a wide range of privileges and exemptions, establishing Callan as the flagship of the Observants in Ireland and placing it under his direct jurisdiction and that of his successors. In addition, he affiliated the Callan friars to the priory of Santa Maria del Popolo in Rome and to the Lombard Observant congregation, the most vibrant of the reform congregations in Italy, of which the Roman house was a member. Four months later, on

23 Martin, 'Irish Augustinian reform', pp 242–4.   24 Martin & de Meijer, 'Irish material', pp 88–9, no. 56.   25 Ibid., p. 89, no. 57.   26 Ibid., 'Irish material', p. 90, nos 58, 59.   27 Martin, 'Irish Augustinian reform', pp 246–8.   28 Martin & de Meijer, 'Irish material', pp 92–4, no. 67.

15 May 1472, he instructed three friars from Callan to introduce the reform in Adare and Cork, if the communities themselves desired it.[29] The attempt to reform the Cork community was unsuccessful and they were released from their association with the reformers in February 1475, returning to the jurisdiction of the Irish vicar provincial.[30]

Friar James of Aquila's successor as prior general, Ambrose Massari, was also a keen promoter of the Observance and continued to favour the Irish reformers during his term of office. In February 1477, he appointed Friar Donal O'Carra as his vicar and instructed that he preside at the next chapter of the Irish limit, which took place at Callan.[31] In January 1479, he took the convent under his direct protection, and in June that year granted almost complete autonomy to the community and to the Observants in Ireland. The Callan community was permitted to receive friars in good standing from other convents; if the majority of friars in another community wished to adopt the Observance, they could become affiliated to the Callan friars, who were entitled to hold an annual chapter, electing a vicar general to preside at it. 'On account of the great distance', the prior of Callan was allowed the same jurisdiction over his convent as that of a provincial and no friar could withdraw from the community without his express permission. If other convents united with Callan and adopted the reform, they were permitted to elect their own vicar general, who would possess the same authority as the vicars general of other Observant congregations. The English provincial was forbidden under pain of excommunication to interfere with the affairs of the Observants at Callan.[32] Further privileges were conceded on 10 April 1480, when Massari ordered the provincial of England not to exact more than the customary taxes from the Callan friars. He also confirmed that the Observants had the right to elect and confirm their own priors and to participate in the election of the vicar provincial of the Irish limit, even though this official had no effective jurisdiction over them.[33] The balance of power had now tipped definitively towards the Observant party in the Irish limit and to the Gaelic friars who dominated it.

Unlike the Franciscans, where divisions between Conventuals and Observants proved insurmountable, it was possible for Irish Observant Augustinians to coexist with their Conventual *confrères*, endeavouring to communicate the spirit of the reform to other houses without altering their constitutional position.[34] This was the course adopted in Ireland, as Observant friars were appointed as superiors in Conventual houses and as presidents of the general chapters of the limit. Massari's

29 Ibid., p. 94, no. 68.   30 Ibid., p. 87, no. 92.   31 Martin, 'Irish Augustinian reform', pp 250–1; Martin & de Meijer, 'Irish material', pp 99–100, no. 93.   32 Martin & de Meijer, 'Irish material', pp 100–1, nos 96, 98.   33 Ibid., p. 101, no. 101.   34 Martin, 'Irish Augustinian reform', pp 251–2.

orders of 10 April 1480 also instructed the vicar provincial of the Irish limit to reform as many friaries as possible. On 24 March 1484, a specific instruction was issued to reform the communities at Cork and New Ross.[35]

The predominance of Gaelic names in the registers of the priors general of this period is indicative of their continued support for the Observance in Ireland and of close links between the Gaelic section of the order and its central authorities. This did not mean that the Anglo-Irish section was neglected, although references to older foundations in the Pale are less frequent. On 19 March 1493, the prior general, Friar Anselm of Montefalco, wrote to the Irish vicar provincial assuring him that all the privileges of the limit were intact and could not be derogated by the prior provincial of England.[36]

On 6 June 1495, the new prior general, Marianus of Genazzano, permitted the friars at Banada and Callan to elect a vicar general for themselves and for a third foundation to be made for the Observant friars with the consent of the vicar provincial and chapter of the Irish limit.[37] Martin proposed that this refers to the priory in Galway established by members of the Athy and Lynch families at the behest of Friar Richard Nangle in 1506.[38] Nangle presided over the chapter of the Irish limit in 1514, was lector in theology in Galway in 1517 and was elected vicar provincial of the Irish limit in 1518.[39] During his tenure of office, the policy of reforming individual houses continued, with Dublin and Drogheda being reformed in 1517 and 1519. In June 1519, he was permitted to remain in office as vicar provincial until the next chapter, and he held the office and that of prior of Dublin in 1539.[40] He accepted the royal supremacy and was appointed bishop of Clonfert by Henry VIII in 1536, although he was unable to gain possession of his see in the face of local opposition. He remained in Dublin, where he was much valued for his erudition and ability to preach in Irish by the first reformed archbishop, George Browne, himself a former prior provincial of the English Augustinians.[41]

### AUGUSTINIAN FOUNDATIONS, 1400–1506 (fig. 3.2)

The foundation of St Mary's priory at Ardnaree, Co. Mayo, sometime shortly before 1400, marks the beginning of the Augustinian revival in late medieval Ireland.[42] This was the first house of Austin friars to be established since the foundation of Skreen, Co. Meath, in 1342. The new foundation was situated at a

---

35 Martin & de Meijer, 'Irish material', p. 102, no. 104.  36 Ibid., p. 107, no. 120.  37 Ibid., p. 108, no. 124.  38 Martin, 'Irish Augustinian reform', p. 257.  39 Ibid., p. 261.  40 Ibid., p. 262.  41 B. Bradshaw, 'George Browne, first Reformation archbishop of Dublin, 1536–1554' (1970).  42 *MRH*, p. 295; Martin, 'Augustinian friaries', pp 360–1.

strategic crossing point on the River Moy around which the town of Ballina subsequently developed. It was only the second house to be established for the order in Connacht since the foundation of the priory at Ballinrobe *c.*1312, and it is likely that the pioneering friars came from there. The earliest reference to Ardnaree in the papal registers occurs in 1401, when a member of the community was granted a dispensation.[43] Donal O'Dowd had gained possession of the castle of Ardnaree and the surrounding territory in 1371 and the friary became the family's principal religious foundation and place of burial.[44] It is possible that Muirchertach O'Dowd, who was buried there in 1402, was the founder, though Tadhg Riabhach O'Dowd is also given the title. In 1410, an indulgence was granted to those contributing to the work of restoring the priory.[45] Though the conventual buildings have disappeared, the extensive remains of the priory church suggest that the community was a large one.

The next foundation, St Mary's Priory at Burriscarra, Co. Mayo, was originally a Carmelite house established towards the end of the thirteenth century, but which was abandoned by 1383.[46] In January 1413, the anti-pope John XXIII instructed Thomas O'Kelly, bishop of Clonfert, to confirm the Augustinians in possession of the site provided that their claim that the Carmelites had abandoned it for over thirty years was correct. Friar Matthew Omaan and other friars from Ballinrobe had been invited to take over the foundation by Edmund and Richard Staunton, descendants of the founder, and with the permission of the archbishop of Tuam and the rector of the parish church.[47] In 1430, another papal letter granted an indulgence to all who contributed to the repair of the house following a fire.[48] The Carmelites later contested the Austin friars' occupation of their former foundation and in 1438 Friar Gerard of Rimini, the Augustinian prior general ordered Friar William Wells, provincial of the Austin friars in England, to conduct an impartial investigation into the circumstances of the transfer.[49] As the Augustinians remained in possession of the site until the early seventeenth century, it appears that whatever process ensued found in their favour.

As noted above, the foundation in 1423 of Corpus Christi priory at Banada, Co. Sligo, was a singularly important development in the affairs of the Irish Austin friars. By decree of the prior general, Friar Augustine Favoroni, the house was established as the first house of Augustinian Regular Observance in Ireland and was placed under the prior general's direct jurisdiction. It would eventually become the cradle from which the Augustinian Observant movement in Ireland sprang.[50] The priory was founded by, Donagh Dubh O'Hara at the instigation of

---

**43** *CPL*, v, p. 493.   **44** *AFM*, iii, pp 654–5.   **45** *CPL*, vi, p. 220.   **46** *MRH*, pp 296–7; Martin, 'Augustinian friaries', 366.   **47** *CPL*, vi, pp 387–8.   **48** *CPL*, viii, p. 162.   **49** Martin & de Meijer, 'Irish material', p. 87.   **50** *MRH*, p. 296; Martin, 'Augustinian friaries', 364–6.

his relative Friar Charles, who was appointed its first superior. The founder retired to the friary in 1439, having resigned the lordship to his brother Cormac.[51] The O'Haras maintained an intense, if not always constructive, interest in the affairs of the house: in 1460, Friar Cormac O'Casey complained to the pope that the prior and most of the community were all related in the third or fourth degree of kindred, and disposed of the property of the house without reference to other members of the convent. The pope ordered that if this were true then no future property was to be alienated without the consent of Friar Cormac and other members of the community.[52] In 1444–5 and again in 1460, indulgences were granted to those who visited the church and contributed to the support of the friars and the maintenance of the fabric of the priory.[53]

The earliest evidence for the existence of St Mary's Priory, Dunmore, Co. Galway, occurs in passing reference of December 1425 in the register of the Augustinian prior general.[54] The founder was Walter Mór de Bermingham, ninth Baron Athenry, and the Berminghams and O'Kellys were generous benefactors of the community.[55] In 1430, indulgences were granted to those who contributed to building the priory and equipping the church. The well-preserved remains of the nave, chancel and tower survive, and evidence for the claustral buildings is visible on the north side of the church.

A number of dates in the mid-fourteenth century are given for the establishment of St Mary's Priory, Ballyhaunis, Co. Mayo.[56] The surviving fabric suggests a fifteenth-century date, and Martin argues that this foundation is to be identified as the *Hanahannassa* described as newly founded in September 1432 in the register of the prior general, Augustine Favaroni. The patrons were the MacCostello/Nangle family and a Friar Philip Nangle is referred to in the 1432 entry.[57] Little else is known of the early history of the house. Though nothing survives of the conventual buildings, the priory church was restored for worship in the nineteenth and twentieth centuries and the interior provides a good indication of the layout of a medieval priory church.

The priory of the Holy Trinity at Scurmore, Co. Sligo, was established by Thady O'Dowd at the behest of Friars Eugene O'Cnáimhín and Tadhg MacFirbis sometime before 1454.[58] Despite their benefactor's donation of certain lands for their sustenance, the community was so impoverished that the friars supported themselves by cultivating the land and by fishing. The foundation had also been

51 *AFM*, iv, pp 916–17.   52 *CPL*, xii, p. 88.   53 *CPL*, ix, p. 455; *CPL*, xii, p. 103.   54 Martin & de Meijer, 'Irish material', pp 84–5. The entry concerns the transfer of Friar Matthew O'Clery from Ardnaree to Dunmore.   55 *MRH*, p. 299; Martin, 'Augustinian friaries', 374–5.   56 *MRH*, p. 296; Martin, 'Augustinian friaries', 363–4.   57 Martin & de Meijer, 'Irish material', p. 87.   58 *MRH*, p. 301; Martin, 'Augustinian friaries', 381–2. MacFirbis was a member of one the hereditary learned families, noted as historians.

made without the requisite papal licence and, in December 1454, Pope Nicholas V absolved the friars from the censures incurred by this omission and allowed them to establish a priory. He also granted permission to maintain a fishing boat on the River Moy.[59] Poverty remained a besetting issue for the community and, for this reason, in 1493 the prior general gave permission to Friar Odo Caewayn to take his meals in private houses.[60] Nothing further is known of the subsequent history of the foundation.

As noted above, the priory at Murrisk, Co. Mayo, was established on foot of a papal mandate issued in 1456 at the behest of Friar Hugh O'Malley, a member of the Observant community at Banada.[61] The site of the friary had been donated by Tadhg O'Malley, 'captain of his nation', and the O'Malleys remained the principal patrons of the house. Another source attributed the foundation to Maeve O'Connor, wife of Diarmuid Baccach O'Connor. Situated on an inlet of Clew Bay, the house was dedicated to St Patrick and preserved a number of his relics. It acted as the starting point for pilgrims ascending Croagh Patrick. The stated purpose of the foundation was evangelical, as 'the inhabitants of those parts have not hitherto been instructed in the faith'.[62] Only the church and the east range of the priory survive, and it appears that the full complement of claustral buildings was not completed. This probably indicates the presence of a very small community. A residential tower stands at the west end of the church, comparable in location, if not in scale, to those at the west ends of the Franciscan house at Ardfert, Co. Kerry, and at the Dominican priory in Kilkenny.

The foundation of the priory at Callan, Co. Kilkenny, was licensed by Pope Pius II on foot of a petition of Richard Butler and his wife in 1461.[63] Richard was defeated in battle in 1462 and the task of building the friary fell to his son, James Butler, who was buried there as its founder in April 1487. Canon Carrigan suggests that James' involvement with the foundation may have been an act of reparation for living in concubinage with his cousin Sadbh Kavanagh.[64] He also states that the house was noted for its care of the poor and for its fine library, which allegedly contained copies of all the works to be found in the nearby Cistercian monastery of Jerpoint. As shown above, the community played a central role in the affairs of the Irish Augustinian Observant movement. This was introduced in Callan in 1472, and by 1479 the priory had become the principal house of the reformers in Ireland.

**59** *CPL*, x, p. 677.   **60** Martin & de Meijer, 'Irish material', p. 106, 'Concessimus Fratri Odoni Ycaewayn quod propter conventus paupertatem posit amore Dei in domo alicuius persone honeste et bone fame refici, cum benedictione tamen prioris'.   **61** *MRH*, p. 300; Martin, 'Augustinian friaries', 378–9.   **62** *CPL*, xi, p. 294.   **63** *MRH*, p. 297; Martin, 'Augustinian friaries', 366–8. W. Carrigan, *History of the diocese of Ossory*, iii (1905), pp 310–13.   **64** Carrigan, *History of the diocese of Ossory*, iii, pp 311–12.

The priory of St Augustine at Galway was the last foundation established by the Austin friars in Ireland before the Reformation.[65] Different authorities give either 1500 or 1506 as the date of foundation, with recent scholarship favouring the latter date.[66] The house was established by Margaret Athy, at the request of Friar Richard Nangle, professor of theology and later vicar provincial of the Irish Augustinian limit. Her husband, Stephen FitzDominick Dubh Lynch, was a wealthy merchant and had for many years been mayor of the city, and the building of the friary was begun during his absence on an overseas journey. The priory's strategic position on a hill overlooking the harbour meant that it was the first thing to greet him on his return. While his initial reaction to his wife's initiative is not recorded, he proved to be a major benefactor of the new foundation. He died in 1536 and in his will particularly commended the Austin friars to his heirs, making specific reference to 'Master Doctor Na(n)gle'. He also bequeathed to the community all his arable land east of the city, amounting to nine named properties.[67]

CARMELITE REFORM IN LATE MEDIEVAL IRELAND

The pattern of decline and reform that characterized the other mendicant orders was replicated among the Carmelite friars. From the mid-fourteenth century, various attempts were made by the general chapter to redress discipline, observance and the abuse of privileges, but these were often undermined by the facility with which the priors general granted dispensations. Despite this, the impetus towards reform gathered momentum and found a variety of expressions throughout the fifteenth century. The earliest of these emerged in central Italy where, from 1413, reformers emerged, first in the convent of Le Selve in Tuscany and then in the convent of Mantua in the Bologna province of the order from which the Observant Mantuan congregation derived its name. The reform was adopted by many convents in central and northern Italy, and by 1428 had spread to the convent of Gironde in Switzerland. These reformed communties were under the direct jurisdiction of the order's prior general, who delegated much of his authority to the vicars general of the Mantuan congregation. These reform attempts occurred during the term of office of the prior general John Grossi, who was sympathetic to the project.[68]

65 *MRH*, p. 300; Martin, 'Augustinian friaries', 377–8.   66 P. Walsh, 'The foundation of the Augustinian friary at Galway' (1985–6); J. O'Connor, *The Galway Augustinians* (1979).   67 W. Battersby, *History of the hermits of the order of St Augustine in Ireland* (1856), pp 277–8.   68 J. Smet, 'Pre-Tridentine reform in the Carmelite order' (1989); idem, *The Carmelites*, i, pp 61–77.

The earliest indication of a reform current among the White Friars in Ireland occurs in a letter of Friar Thomas Netter, prior provincial of England, to James Butler, fourth earl of Ormond, dating to *c.*1419–20:

> I know both your sincere faith and the Catholic mentality with which your lordship acts upon for the restoration of the order, whose founder and patron you are in Ireland. Since you, like another Joas, wish that the broken roofs of the temple be restored and the observance of religious life return with effect to its ideal state, hoping that an opportunity offers itself, I am sending to your dominion a certain bachelor sent by our Revered Father, the prior general. This is with a view to this business of reforming the whole order and you can communicate confidently with him concerning all that relates to this purpose. Now it only remains that he should be supported by the protection of your lordship as is fitting and as the business with which he is to deal requires. So I hope that your sacred wish may be effectively realized and that you attain the heavenly reward for your holy concern.[69]

From this, it is evident that the reform in Ireland was contemporary with other Continental reform movements and that it was supported both by the friars' principal Irish patron and by the order's prior general. It was also contemporary with reform attempts among the other mendicant orders in Ireland. Whereas the Irish province had acquired independence in the early fourteenth century, Netter's letter demonstrates that the prior provincial of England could intervene in the affairs of the Irish brethren. Unfortunately, no evidence survives of the success or otherwise of this attempt at reform.

The fifteenth-century reform movement reached its peak during the generalate of Friar John Soreth, a Norman friar elected prior general by the general chapter of Avignon in 1451.[70] In addition to fostering reform, he also promoted the Carmelite Third Order movement and regularized the position of Carmelite nuns.[71] As prior general, he engaged in widespread visitations of the Carmelite provinces in France, Germany, Sicily and the Low Countries. In Italy, he supported the attempts of the Mantuan reformers to effect the reform of the friars, and in 1469 he appointed a vicar to promote the reform of the convents in the Iberian Peninsula. The revised constitutions he composed for the order were accepted by the 1462 general chapter and confirmed by the 1469 chapter.[72]

**69** K. Alban (ed.), 'The letters of Thomas Netter of Walden' (1992), pp 353–4. See also O'Dwyer, *Irish Carmelites*, pp 55–75.   **70** G. Grosso, *Il B. Jean Soreth (1394–1471): priore generale, riformatore e maestro spirituale dell'ordine Carmelitano* (2007) provides the most comprehensive account of his career. See also Smet, *The Carmelites*, i, pp 78–101.   **71** Grosso, *Il B. Jean Soreth*, pp 191–250; Smet, *The Carmelites*, i, pp 87–101.   **72** Ibid., pp 93–152.

Although Soreth visited neither Ireland nor England, the fortuitous survival of an inscription from medieval stained glass panels, reputedly from the priory at Ardnacranny, Co. Westmeath, indicates that the Irish friars were sympathetic to his efforts at reform:

> Blessed John Soreth, a Norman, twenty-fifth general, a man of subtle genius and devout life, the glory, splendour and reformer of the Carmelite order, completely committed to God and prayer ended this life in a most holy manner AD1471.[73]

The Irish priors provincial attended the order's general chapters intermittently and it is difficult to ascertain the impact that contemporary reform currents had on the Irish houses. In 1472, Friar Donald Connell was nominated as prior provincial of Ireland. Described as a 'venerable and learned man but with many extravagant habits', he ruled the province until 1488 when he was succeeded by Friar Cornelius Connell, who held office until 1504.[74]

The register of Friar Peter Terrasse (prior general, 1503–11) contains a series of entries relating to the visitation he conducted of the English province in 1504–5.[75] A number of these related to the affairs of the Irish brethren and, when combined with entries in the *acta* of the general chapter, clearly indicate that the Irish friars were divided over issues of observance and discipline at the beginning of the sixteenth century.[76] Central to the controversy was Friar William Carew, an Oxford bachelor of theology, who, in November 1504, was absolved from the excommunication imposed on him by the Irish prior provincial. In December 1504, Carew was made vicar-general and visitator of the Irish province and permitted to receive the insignia of a master of theology. He was removed as vicar-general in October 1505 and Friar Cornelius Connell, the former prior provincial, was appointed in his place. Connell and three provincial definitors were instructed to investigate a dispute between Carew and another Irish friar, William de Castro. The outcome of this case is not recorded, and in June 1507 Friar William Connell was appointed prior provincial of Ireland and given power to deal with rebellious friars.[77] He may have employed these powers a little too enthusiastically, as he was removed from office at the request of his subjects in April 1509. His successor as prior provincial was Friar William Carew, who was also appointed the prior general's vicar in Ireland, with responsibility for reforming the province and

**73** J. Moran, 'The shattered image' (2006), p. 133. See below, pp 247–8.   **74** Wessels, *Acta capitulorum*, pp 257, 262, 265, 285. His name is also given as Donald Gnormel, Connail and Connell.   **75** R. Copsey, 'The visit of the prior general, Peter Terrasse, to England in 1504–5' (2004), pp 260, 266.   **76** This section summarizes O'Dwyer, *Irish Carmelites*, pp 78–9.   **77** O'Dwyer suggests that he may have been a kinsman of Friar Corenlius Connell. Ibid., p. 78.

recovering the arrears in taxes owed by the Irish province to the prior general. Connell contested his deposition and the prior general deputed Carew to excommunicate him if he did not hand over the prior provincial's seal of office to his successor. By June 1509, the situation had reversed and Connell had been restored as provincial. In September, the delegates to the Irish provincial chapter were ordered to examine depositions from several Irish prelates in favour of Carew and, if they proved true, Connell was to be deposed from office. If they proved false, Carew was to be taken into custody and not released without the permission of the prior general.

CARMELITE FOUNDATIONS, 1393–1516

The attempts at reform provide the context for the order's modest expansion, which witnessed five new foundations being established between 1393 and 1516. The first of these at Eglish or Monteanchoe, near Ahascaragh, Co. Galway, is very poorly documented and uncertainty surrounds which order actually occupied the site.[78] The earliest reliable reference to a Carmelite presence occurs in a papal letter of 1437, in which Pope Eugene IV, in response to a petition of the Carmelite prior general, instructed the bishop of Clonfert to regularize the position of the friars of Monteanchoe in the diocese of Elphin. The friars had been given possession of a chapel there during the episcopate of Bishop William O'Cormican (1393–8) but, like a number of other foundations of the period, it appears not to have received papal licence.[79] The chapel had originally been erected where a 'venerable cross' had been discovered sixty years previously, and another papal letter from 1437 granted an indulgence to those who visited and gave alms for the upkeep of the Carmelite houses at Monteanchoe and Loughrea on the feast of the Exaltation of the Cross and the other principal feasts of the liturgical calendar.[80] The later history of the house is obscure and it is described as being Franciscan in some seventeenth-century sources.

St Mary's Priory, Kilcormac, Co. Offaly, was founded by Odo son of Nellan O'Mulloy in 1406. The foundation became the principal burial place of the O'Mulloy family and the founder was buried before the high altar of the church in 1454.[81] A fifteenth-century breviary and missal belonging to the community are preserved in Trinity College Dublin. Marginal entries in the calendar of the missal list a number of fifteenth- and sixteenth-century obituaries. These principally record the (generally violent) deaths of members of the O'Mulloy family and other benefactors of the community, along with those of the friars themselves.[82]

**78** *MRH*, p. 289.   **79** *CPL*, viii, pp 639–40.   **80** *CPL*, viii, p. 636.   **81** *MRH*, pp 289–90.   **82** J.H.

Although nothing survives of the friary buildings, a fine sixteenth-century pieta from the priory church is preserved in the modern Roman Catholic parish church in Kilcormac.

As with the foundation at Eglish described above, very little is known of the Carmelite foundation at Bellaneeny, Co. Roscommon, apart from a single reference in a papal letter of 1437. Seventeenth-century sources list it as a Conventual Franciscan foundation, and it is possible that it was taken over by the Friars Minor or the Franciscan Regular Tertiaries at some stage in its history. Patrick Egan suggested that it functioned as a small cell or place of religious retreat for friars from other Carmelite communities in the vicinity.[83] A revived interest in the eremetical or anchoritic life was a notable feature of contemporary Carmelite foundations in England.[84]

The earliest reference to the priory at Milltown or Ballinegall, Co. Limerick, occurs in a letter of Pope Pius II dating to 1459–60. At the petition of Friar Thomas Wallse, prior provincial of the Carmelites in Ireland, the pope instructed the archbishop of Cashel to investigate the claims of Friars Donald Ygormellay and William de Burgh that they were hindered in establishing a priory at Milltown by the bishop of Emly. Three benefactors, the brothers Torieleus and Kennedy Macbriayn and James Deles, had granted the site to build a priory in honour of the Virgin Mary. The friars had accepted the site without the requisite papal license and had been excommunicated by the bishop of Emly for celebrating the liturgy illicitly. They had subsequently withdrawn from the foundation. The pope instructed that if the facts were as stated, the archbishop was to absolve the friars from the penalties they had incurred and to license the foundation of the house with its necessary buildings and offices without requiring the permission of the local bishop.[85] Nothing further is known of the foundation until its surrender by Prior Donagh O'Dangane in 1556–7.

The final foundation made by the Carmelites before the Reformation was at Rathmullan, Co. Donegal, in 1516. Dedicated to the Virgin Mary, it was situated on the shores of Lough Swilly and became the principal burial place of its founders, the Mac Sweeney Fanad. It is unique among the later Carmelite foundations because of the detailed account of its foundation preserved in the early sixteenth-century *Leabhar Chlainne Suibhne*:

> And it was this MacSuibhne (Eoghan Rua?) who first built the castle of Rath Maoláin, and it was his wife, Máire, daughter of Eoghan, son of

Todd, 'Obits of Kilcormick', *Miscellany of the Irish Archaeological Society*, 1 (1846), 99–106 at 100. **83** *MRH*, p. 287; P.K. Egan, 'The Carmelite cell of Bealanney' (1954–6). **84** Johan Bergstrom-Allen, 'The Whitefriars return to Carmel' (2005). **85** *MRH*, p. 291; *CPL*, xii, p. 62.

Diarmaid Bacach Ó Máille, who erected the monastery of Rath Maoláin. It was Suibhne and his wife who brought to that monastery a community from the south, from Munster. The prior who introduced the community was Suibhne, son of Donnsléibhe, of Clann Suibhne Connachtach. The year of the Lord when the monastery was founded was 1516. At the end of two years after founding of this monastery MacSuibhne died – he who was the constable of the greatest name and fame, and who, of all that came in this latter age, bestowed most on schools and poets. He had been forty-six years in the chieftainship of his family and was seventy-eight years of age when he died, having gained victory over the devil and the world, in the habit of the friars of Mary, in the monastery which he himself had founded in her honour, on the seventh of April, on the Wednesday between the two Easters, in his own seat of Rath Maoláin. At the end of four years after that, his noble, lovable wife, the daughter of Ó Máille, the most generous and best mother, and the woman of most fame in regard to faith and piety of all who lived at her time, died. This is the manner in which she passed her days: she used to hear Mass once each day, and sometimes more than once; and three days each week she used spend on bread and water fare, with Lenten fast and winter fast and the Golden Fridays. She also caused a great hall to be erected for the Friars Minor in Donegal, not only that, but many other churches we shall not here enumerate that woman caused to be built in the provinces of Ulster and Connaught. It was also she who had this book of piety copied in her own house, and all affirm that in her time there was no woman who passed her life better than she. And the manner of her death, after victory over the devil and the world, she was clothed in the habit of the friars of Mary in the monastery which she herself had founded. The following were the children of that couple we have spoken of: Ruaidhrí Óg, son of Ruaidhrí son of Maolmhuire (he was the elder son, and a noble princely man he was; he travelled many of the countries of the world and could speak all the common languages; he died in the town of Rath Maoláin ten years before his father's death, and was buried in the church of Rath Maoláin; his was the first body ever buried there, and it was mainly on account of it that the monastery was erected and completed; let everyone who reads this line bestow a blessing on the soul of Ruaidhrí Mac Suibhne, and Ruaidhrí left no descendants), and Toirrdhealbhach was the second son of that famous couple that we have spoken of, and he was Mac Suibhne of Fanad.[86]

---

**86** P. Walsh (ed.), *Leabhar Chlainne Suibhne* (1920), pp 66–9.

The passage is significant from a number of perspectives. The reference to MacSweeney establishing both a castle and priory at Rathmullan indicates that both structures were considered appropriate expressions of lordship along with the patronage of poets, scholars and churches. The reference to the founding community coming from Munster is indicative of the founders' widespread contacts throughout Ireland. It is also significant the first prior was himself a Mac Sweeney. The reference to the Carmelites as the 'friars of Mary' suggests a strong Marian devotion on the part of the founders and may explain their preference for the Whitefriars over the other mendicant orders with which they had links. Perhaps the most poignant statement concerns the motivation for the erection of the priory: the desire to provide a fitting burial place for Rory MacSweeney, the couple's much-loved eldest son. Reference to Máire's devotional practices and recent analysis of her 'Book of Piety' give a rare insight into the spiritual and religious mentality of a late medieval Gaelic noblewoman, which owed much to the influence of the friars.[87] In all, the passage gives a unique insight into the motivations for founding a late medieval friary and illustrates the complex ties of mutual dependence that underlay the friars' relationship with their patrons.

**87** S. Ryan, 'Windows on late medieval devotional practice' (2006).

# CHAPTER FOUR

# The friars and their patrons

AD1351 *Kenwric Sherman, formerly mayor of the city of Dublin, died and was buried beneath the belfry of the Friars Preachers of the same city. This belfry he himself had erected, as well as glazing the east window of the choir and roofing the church and many other good deeds. He died in that convent on 24 February. At the end of his life he made his will, to the value of three thousand marks, and left many goods to churches, priests – religious and secular – for twenty miles around the city.*[1]

The expansion of the mendicant movement in Ireland, detailed in the previous chapters, depended on the support given to the friars by their patrons and benefactors. Unlike the Regular Canons and the older monastic orders whose endowments of lands, rents and tithes provided their incomes, the friars, as mendicants, were almost entirely dependent for their support and sustenance on what they received from others. This reliance on continual almsgiving brought them into contact with a wide cross-section of society, creating relationships of mutual dependence and influence that became one of their most characteristic features.

This chapter examines the support given to the friars in Ireland by various elite groups: the English crown and its representatives; Anglo-Irish and Gaelic aristocrats; noble women and merchants. It also examines the manner in which the friars benefited from testamentary bequests and concludes by exploring the ways in which they responded to their benefactors' expectations.

## ROYAL PATRONAGE

The arrival and initial expansion of the mendicant friars in England and Ireland corresponded with the lengthy reigns of the Plantagenet kings, Henry III (1216–72) and his son Edward I (1272–1307). Both rulers proved to be influential

---

1 Pembridge, *Chronicle*, p. 391.

supporters of the new orders and established a tradition of royal patronage that lasted until the Reformation. The support of Henry III, who assumed personal rule in 1227, was particularly beneficial for the Dominicans and Franciscans, who arrived in England in 1221 and 1224 respectively, as it was simultaneously an expression of genuine piety and an example that other aristocratic benefactors emulated.[2] In the overall context of his religious patronage, Henry III's support of the mendicants was relatively modest, but he nonetheless became the most significant benefactor of the friars in London.

Royal support took a number of forms and is relatively well documented. The mendicant pioneers in both Ireland and England were beneficiaries of letters of royal protection. These documents instructed royal officials to show the friars support and ensured they were not molested in establishing new foundations. Between 1244 and 1272, Henry III issued letters of protection for the Augustinians, the Carmelites, the Crutched friars, the Friars of the Sack and the Pied Friars in England.[3] The earliest evidence for the practice in Ireland occurred in 1271, when the Carmelite friars were granted letters of protection, which were renewed in 1274.[4]

A small number of mendicant houses in England and Ireland owed their foundation directly to royal patronage. In England, Henry III was credited with establishing seven mendicant friaries, while in 1317–18, Edward II, a notable supporter of the Carmelites, donated Beaumont Palace, near the north gate of the city of Oxford, to establish a foundation for their student friars.[5] In the late fifteenth century, after lengthy contact with their Continental superiors, Edward IV introduced the Observant Franciscans into England, establishing their first house at a site adjacent to the royal palace at Greenwich in 1482.[6] The English Observants also benefited from the support of Henry VII, who first encountered the movement while exiled in the court of Duke Francis II of Brittany between 1471 and 1484.[7] He was the founder of the friary at Richmond and secured the transfer of the Conventual houses at Canterbury, Newcastle and Southampton to the reformed friars.[8]

In Ireland, such royal foundations are harder to trace. In June 1285, Edward I instructed the justiciar and treasurer of Ireland to increase the annuity paid to the Dominicans in Limerick by ten marks on account of the special affection he bore for the community. He also claimed that his ancestors had established the priory,

**2** J. Sever, *The English Franciscans under Henry III* (1915); J. Röhrkasten, *The mendicant houses of medieval London, 1221–1539* (2004), p. 390.   **3** Röhrkasten, *Mendicant houses*, pp 340–2, esp. no. 1510.   **4** See above, p. 16.   **5** D. Knowles & R.N. Hadcock, *Medieval religious houses: England and Wales* (1971), pp 216, 218, 236.   **6** A.G. Little, 'Introduction of the Observant friars into England' (1921–3).   **7** V.K. Henderson, 'Rethinking Henry VII: the man and his piety in the context of the Observant Franciscans' (2004).   **8** See below, p. 89.

though this was elsewhere ascribed to Donal Cairbreach O'Brien.[9] Edward I was also credited with founding the Franciscan friary at Castledermot with Walter Riddlesford sometime before 1247. While this is impossible chronologically, it may indicate that his father Henry III played some part in its establishment.[10]

The friars frequently enlisted the moral authority of kings, princes and rulers in the British Isles in times of crisis. This was particularly evident in their response to the Second Council of Lyon's suppression of a number of mendicant orders in 1274. The Carmelites and Augustinians received a stay of execution 'until decided otherwise'.[11] This created a great deal of anxiety for both orders as they were establishing their first foundations in Ireland and during the pontificate of Martin IV (1281–5) the Carmelite prior general, Friar Peter of Millau, lobbied to redress the situation as it hindered recruitment and discouraged potential patrons. His appeal won the support of bishops based in the Holy Land as well as that of the Grand Masters of the Knights Hospitaller and the Knights Templar. He also secured the support of Edward I of England who, in 1282, wrote to a number of cardinals in support of the Carmelites and requested that their status be confirmed.[12] In 1451, an anonymous petitioner enlisted the support of Henry VI on behalf of the four mendicant orders during the campaign against them waged by Dean Philip Norris of St Patrick's Cathedral, Dublin.[13] In 1507, Henry VII of England and James IV of Scotland were among the many European rulers enlisted by the Observant Franciscans to lobby Pope Julius II against the diminution of their privileges in favour of the Conventual wing of the order.[14] The contemporary Franciscan chronicler, Nicholas Glassberger, alleged that Henry VII would have expelled all the Conventual friars from the fifty houses in his realm rather than lose any of the five reformed communities.[15]

Another expression of royal support took the form of waiving penalties incurred for violation of the Statute of Mortmain. This statute, enacted by Edward I in 1279, sought to limit the amount of real estate that passed into the inalienable possession of the church, thereby depriving the crown of its feudal dues.[16] Before a religious corporation could acquire real estate, an inquisition *ad quod damnum* was held to ascertain its value and what, if any, loss its alienation would ensue to the king, overlord or borough. Once this was established and arrangements made for the discharge of feudal obligations, the property could be transferred. In comparison with the older monastic orders, the amount of land

---

9 *CDI*, iii, pp 38–9; BL Add. MS 4783, fo. 58; *MRH*, pp 226–7. **10** *MRH*, p. 244. **11** N.P. Tanner, *Decrees of the Ecumenical Councils* (1990), i, p. 326. **12** A. Staring (ed.), 'The letter of Pierre de Millau to King Edward I of England, 1282' (1989). **13** A. Fletcher, *Late medieval popular preaching in Britain and Ireland* (2009), pp 262–3. See below, pp 158–60. **14** For the text of James IV's letter, see Moir Bryce, *Scottish Grey Friars* (1909), ii, pp 276–9. **15** Glassberger, *Cronica*, p. 542. **16** S. Raban, *Mortmain legislation and the English Church, 1279–1500* (1982).

granted to Irish mendicant foundations was relatively small, but the principle remained and found expression in the records.[17] As shown above, inquisitions concerning the granting of properties to the Carmelites of Dublin (1278), the Dominicans in Kilmallock (1291) and the Carmelites in Knocktopher (1356) survive and give important insights into the process of founding and endowing a friary.[18] The inquisitions and their outcome did not always go in the friars' favour. In 1297, the three tenements granted to the Franciscans in Kildare by William de Vescy were taken into the king's hand as permission to alienate them had not been obtained. A similar fate befell the 240 acres given to the Franciscans at Carrickbeg in 1385 by James Butler, third earl of Ormond, which was granted without license of Richard II.[19]

The most frequent expression of royal support was the granting of royal alms to various Irish friaries. This took the form either of a donation for a specific purpose or of an annuity from the Irish exchequer.[20] The earliest example occurred in 1233, when Henry III granted the Franciscans in Dublin twenty marks for the repair of their friary. As the Franciscans were forbidden to handle money themselves and initially took this prohibition very seriously, the grant was received by their proctors, Geoffrey de Turvill, archdeacon of Dublin, and Robert Pollard, mayor of the city.[21] The practice of granting regular royal alms to the Franciscans was first recorded in 1245. This consisted of twenty pounds granted to purchase one hundred habits for the friars in Dublin, Waterford, Drogheda, Cork, Athlone and Kilkenny. In 1246, this payment was commuted to assist the friars in Waterford in a building project.[22] The earliest example of royal almsgiving to the Irish Dominicans occurred in 1253 when, along with the Franciscans and the hospital of St John in Dublin, they shared a grant of one hundred marks.[23]

Comprehensive records for the Irish exchequer survive from between 1270 and 1446 and these give a clearer indication of the extent of royal almsgiving.[24] While the payments fluctuated with the royal fortunes, in theory the Dominican and Franciscan orders in Ireland each received an annuity of thirty-five marks (£23 6s. 8d.). The only other religious to receive such grants were the Victorine canons of St Thomas' Abbey in Dublin, who received twenty marks (£13 6s. 8d.) annually.[25] In 1270, the Dominicans received £46 13s. 4d. in alms from the Lord Edward,

---

**17** A.G. Little, 'The Franciscans and the statute of mortmain' (1934), 673–6.   **18** *MRH*, pp 226, 289. See also P.A. Brand, 'The licensing of mortmain alienations in the medieval Lordship of Ireland' (1986).   **19** Cotter, *Friars Minor*, p. 65; *FL*, pp 70, 164.   **20** For royal alms to the Irish Franciscans before 1400, see Cotter, *Friars Minor*, pp 54–9.   **21** *CDI*, i, p. 298, no. 2004. For Irish attitudes to evangelical poverty, see Cotter, *Friars Minor*, pp 51, 71–4; Ó Clabaigh, *Franciscans*, pp 19–32, 116–21.   **22** Cotter, *Friars Minor*, p. 55. This sum proved insufficient and was later increased by five marks.   **23** Archdall, *Monasticon Hibernicum*, p. 200. O'Sullivan, *MIDS*, pp 170–6.   **24** Connolly, *Irish exchequer payments*, p. xxiii and passim.   **25** St Thomas' Abbey was established by Henry II in 1177 as an act of reparation for the murder of Archbishop Thomas Becket.

son of Henry III.[26] In 1285, the making of unaccounted payments to the Dominicans and Franciscans was one of complaints made about the Irish exchequer but, despite this, the annuities continued.[27] Irregularities of another order were discovered in October 1325 when, in the course of an audit of the Irish treasury records, evidence emerged for massive peculation by Alexander de Bicknor, archbishop of Dublin and former treasurer and justiciar of Ireland. Among the stratagems employed to disguise the fraud was the forging of letters of receipt for alms that were either never granted or only paid in part. Although most of the irregularities concerned payments to former Knights Templar, the friars' annuities were also embezzled. Thus, the chancery roll recorded a false payment to the Franciscan Richard Copyn, while a forged letter dated 30 March 1313 acknowledged receipt of a grant of thirty-five marks by the Dominicans of Dublin, who had in fact only received five marks.[28]

Grants to the friars were normally paid to the superiors of the Dublin houses for distribution to other foundations, usually situated in towns with a royal castle. In 1292, the standard amount of thirty-five marks was issued for distribution among the Dominicans and Franciscans of Dublin, Cork, Waterford, Limerick and Drogheda.[29] Occasionally, the grants were anticipated, as in 1276–7, when the Franciscans received a prest or advance payment of £11 13s. 4d.[30] The annuities were more likely to fall into arrears, however, as political circumstances changed and the royal finances fluctuated: between 1314 and 1317, the financial pressure occasioned by the Bruce invasion led to a marked reduction in the amount paid to the mendicants.[31] The normal payments were only resumed in 1325–6, and in 1327 the alms paid to the Franciscans in Athlone were transferred to those in Cashel, as the former community no longer contained any English friars.[32] In 1327, the Dominican friars were forced to appeal directly to the king's council in England for payment of the customary royal alms that were several years in arrears.[33]

Although the other mendicant orders did not receive annuities from the exchequer, all groups benefited from occasional grants or from royal appointments. In 1270, the Friars of the Sack received the substantial sum of £3 6s. 8d.[34] The Carmelite friars at Ardee received an annuity from their founder Ralph Pipard out of the income of his manor there. When this reverted to the crown on his death, Edward I 'of his special grace in compensation for various alms' granted the friars an annual income of six pounds between 1303 and 1314.[35] This

---

**26** Connolly, *Irish exchequer payments*, p. 2.   **27** *FL*, p. 53.   **28** J.F. Lydon, 'The case against Alexander Bicknor, archbishop and peculator' (2009), pp 105–6.   **29** Connolly, *Irish exchequer payments*, p. 166. **30** Ibid., p. 18.   **31** Ibid., pp 227, 239, 247, 256, 260, 264, 272, 276.   **32** Ibid., p. 314; *FL*, p. 129. **33** G.O. Sayles, *Documents on the affairs of Ireland before the king's council* (1979), p. 130.   **34** Connolly, *Irish exchequer payments*, p. 2. This was their only recorded royal alms.   **35** Ibid., pp 178, 185, 192, 221.

arrangement fell into arrears, and in 1331 the community had to petition the royal council in England for its restitution.[36]

In the fourteenth century, the lucrative positions of chaplains to the royal chapels in Dublin were granted to the Carmelite and Augustinian friars. In 1316 the Dublin Carmelites were appointed to serve the exchequer chapel and were granted an annual income of fifty shillings in return for providing a priest to celebrate the liturgy. This was increased to one hundred shillings in 1335 and the friars retained the chantry until the dissolution of the religious houses in Dublin in 1539.[37] In 1354, the city's Augustinian community was granted an annuity of £2 13s. 4d. in perpetuity to provide a friar to celebrate daily divine service in the chapel of Dublin Castle for the welfare of the king, the queen and the royal family and for the souls of the king's ancestors.[38] The Carmelites in Leighlinbridge received payments 'of the king's gift' in 1348 and 1360 for maintaining the bridge over the River Barrow and for offering protection to travellers. The community was granted an annuity of £6 13s. 4d. for this purpose in 1374.[39] Once conceded, royal annuities continued as a matter as course. The extents compiled at the dissolution of the monasteries in 1540–1 indicate that the Dominican communities in Dublin and Drogheda were each in receipt of an annuity of £6 13s. 4d., while the Carmelite friars in Dublin continued to receive their annual grant of one hundred shillings.[40]

Relative to their *confrères* in England, the Irish friars received little by way of gifts in kind from the crown.[41] In 1248, Henry III ordered that the Franciscans of Downpatrick and Carrickfergus be supplied with 'food and raiment' to the value of ten marks.[42] In 1285, Edward I ordered the justiciar in Ireland to grant thirty oaks to the Dominicans in Dublin for the repair of their church.[43] The Franciscans in Drogheda received sixteen crannocks and thirteen pecks of oats by order of Edward II in 1324, while in 1356 their *confrères* in Wicklow received ten cows and half a vat of beer by order of Edward III.[44] Royal interventions also took other practical forms: in 1377 Edward III ordered the corporation of Limerick to reimburse the city's Dominican community for the 1,050 ash trees they had supplied to help rebuild the city after it had been burned in 1369.[45]

As noted above, individual friars occasionally received casual alms or payments for services rendered to the crown, incidentally demonstrating their role as trusted emissaries in the royal service.[46] Such reliance on the mendicants, particularly the

---

**36** Sayles, *Documents on the affairs of Ireland*, pp 147–8.   **37** O'Dwyer, *Irish Carmelites*, pp 26, 31. They also received an annual grant of two shillings and four pence for wax. See also M.V. Ronan, 'The ancient Chapel Royal, Dublin Castle' (1923), p. 367.   **38** Two friars were to celebrate on Sundays. Connolly, *Irish exchequer payments*, pp 475, 489, 510, 513, 525, 532.   **39** Connolly, *Irish exchequer payments*, pp 427, 507, 532, 535, 538.   **40** N.B. White, *Extents of Irish monastic possessions, 1540–1541* (1943), pp 54, 121, 244.   **41** Cotter, *Friars Minor*, p. 56.   **42** *FL*, p. 15.   **43** *CDI*, iii, p. 38.   **44** *FL*, pp 222, 224.   **45** A. Coleman, *Appendix*, p. 55.   **46** See above, pp 32–3.

Dominicans and Franciscans, for sensitive affairs of state was a common feature of contemporary English, European and papal diplomacy.[47]

Although the crown and its representatives played an important role in supporting the friars in Ireland, the majority of Irish friaries owed their origins to the patronage of aristocratic families. While these included some of the upper echelons of the aristocracy, many smaller landowners and members of knightly families also patronized the friars, attracted by the fact that their foundations were architecturally unpretentious and did not require large endowments of land. This pattern of modest piecemeal patronage and small-scale endowment was similar to the early experience of the mendicants in England.[48]

The friars' early benefactors in Ireland included individuals who belonged to families with extensive lands and estates in England, where they had also patronized the mendicants. The patronage of Hubert de Burgh, earl of Kent and justiciar of England, was particularly important for the Dominicans and Franciscans following their arrival in England. The earl was one of the primary benefactors of the London Friars Preachers when they made their first foundation at Holborn in the early 1220s.[49] Relatives of both de Burgh and William Marshal were prominent in the affairs of the colony in Ireland in the first half of the thirteenth century. Bernadette Williams argues that Marshal's son, William Marshal II, may have been responsible for introducing the Friars Preachers to Ireland in 1224 during his term of office as justiciar. He also founded the Dominican priory in Kilkenny in 1225.

Richard de Burgh, a cousin of Hubert de Burgh, led the invasion of Connacht in 1235 and the subsequent erection of towns and boroughs provided the opportunity for a modest mendicant expansion in the province. Dominican foundations were established by Maurice Fitzgerald at Sligo (1253), by Miler de Bermingham at Athenry (1241) and by members of the Dexter family at Strade (1252) and Rathfran (1274).[50] John de Cogan founded a Franciscan friary at Claregalway before 1252 and William de Burgh established another in Galway in 1296.[51] The Carmelite and Augustinian friars each made one foundation in Connacht. The Carmelite house at Loughrea was founded by Richard de Burgh *c.*1300 and Lady Elizabeth de Clare established the Austin friars at Ballinrobe

47 C.H. Lawrence, *The friars*, pp 166–201; W.A. Hinnesbusch, 'Diplomatic activities of the English Dominicans in the thirteenth century' (1942). 48 Röhrkasten, *Mendicant houses*, pp 379–408. 49 Ibid., pp 30–1. 50 *MRH*, pp 221, 228, 229. See also H. Fenning, *The Dominicans of Sligo* (2002), pp 7–10. 51 *MRH*, pp 245, 250–1; B. Jennings, 'The abbey of St Francis, Galway' (1947).

*c.*1312. The de Clare family introduced the Augustinian friars to England in 1248, establishing their first house at Clare in Suffolk, and this family association probably influenced the decision of Lady Elizabeth's de Clare to establish the friars in Connacht.[52]

Once established, the link between the friars and their aristocratic patrons often endured for several centuries. The Butler earls of Ormond were recognized as the principal patrons of the Carmelite order in Ireland, and in 1419/20 the English prior provincial, Thomas Netter, corresponded with James Butler, fourth earl of Ormond, about his desire to reform the Irish houses.[53] The Fitzgerald earls of Kildare and Desmond regarded themselves as the founders and principal patrons of the Franciscan order in Ireland and Maurice Fitzgerald, tenth earl of Desmond, expressly invoked this status when intervening on the friars' behalf in a dispute with the secular clergy in Dungarvan in 1515.[54] As noted above, some Gaelic chieftains used their positions as patrons to induce the Franciscan convents at Carrickfergus, Cavan and Kilconnell to adopt the Observant reform in the late fifteenth century.[55]

Although the establishment of a friary was often attributed to an individual patron, the foundation accounts of the Dominican priory at Athenry and the Franciscan house at Adare reveal that the process was normally a collaborative exercise involving a number of benefactors. The foundation at Athenry was an initiative of Miler de Bermingham, first baron Athenry, who, in addition to providing the site, also provided sustenance for the builders and horses to draw stone to the site, and granted the friars a portion of the harvest from his own lands, prevailing on his followers to do likewise.[56] In return, he and his descendants received the most honourable burial place in the priory church: a tomb on the north side of the high altar. His son, William, archbishop of Tuam, granted the friars a dole of wine for their general chapter and included St Dominic in his recitation of the *Confiteor*.[57] Miler's daughter, Basilia, played a dramatic part in establishing the Dominican foundation at Strade, Co. Mayo.[58] The Athenry register recorded the successions, marriages, obituaries and notable achievements the de Bermingham family until the early sixteenth century.[59] Successive barons confirmed the grants made to the friars by their ancestors, often adding further

---

**52** Martin, 'Augustinian priories', 361–2; *MRH*, p. 296. For de Clare patronage of monastic foundations in England, see K. Stöber, *Late medieval monasteries and the patrons: England and Wales, c.1300–1540* (2007), pp 162–71. **53** Alban (ed.), 'The letters of Thomas Netter of Walden', pp 353–4. **54** B. Jennings (ed.), *Wadding papers, 1614–38* (1953), pp 113–15. See below, pp 166–7. **55** See above, p. 64. **56** Coleman, 'Regestum', pp 204–5. **57** Members and devotees of religious orders frequently included an invocation of the founder in the *Confiteor*. See S. Ryan, 'A wooden key to open Heaven's door: lessons in practical Catholicism from St Anthony's College, Louvain' (2009), p. 226. **58** Coleman, 'Regestum', pp 204–5. **59** Ibid., pp 212–17.

donations of lands, properties or livestock and many were described as 'great friends of the community' or of 'loving the friars greatly'. The ninth baron, Thomas III de Bermingham (d. 1500) and his wife Anablina de Burgh, proved particularly generous benefactors of the community. The register contains two lengthy lists of their donations to the friars including, poignantly, the benefactions made by the couple following the death of their son John de Bermingham in 1488.[60]

The Athenry friars also enjoyed the support of the de Burgh earls of Clanrickard, who chose it as their burial place over the Augustinian abbey at Athassel, at the end of the fourteenth century. As with the de Berminghams, the friars carefully recorded the succession, benefactions and burial places of the de Burghs.[61] The community also received support from the local Gaelic aristocracy from an early stage in their history. Cornelius O'Kelly built the chapter house and Eugene O'Heyne built the dormitory at Athenry as well as that of the de Cogan Franciscan foundation at Claregalway.[62] Lord Felim O'Connor, king of Connacht, built the refectory at Athenry in addition to founding the Dominican priory at Roscommon.

The connection between the friars and the various branches of the Fitzgerald family further illustrates the enduring link between the mendicants and their benefactors. Although among the first Anglo-Normans to arrive in Ireland in 1169, the family's rise to prominence was consolidated during the lifetime of Maurice II Fitzgerald, second baron Offaly and justiciar of Ireland from 1232 to 1245.[63] The arrival of both the Dominican and Franciscan pioneers in Ireland corresponded with his career and he proved an important benefactor and protector of both orders. His involvement in the 1235 conquest of Connacht brought him extensive territories in the west and north-west of Ireland and he erected both a castle and a Dominican priory in Sligo. He retired to the Franciscan friary he had founded in Youghal, where he assumed the Franciscan habit and died on 29 May 1257.[64] As noted above, the Franciscan friaries at Ardfert (*c.*1253), Askeaton (*c.*1420), Clane (1258), Clonmel (1269) and Kildare (*c.*1254) and the Dominican houses at Sligo (1252), Tralee (1243) and Youghal (1268 or 1271) acknowledged members of different Geraldine families as their founders and principal benefactors. Other early foundations, such as the Dominican priories at Limerick and Kilmallock, received substantial Fitzgerald support at later stages in their history.

Friar Donatus Mooney recorded the names of the principal benefactors of the Franciscan foundation at Adare.[65] The document, which was read each Friday in

60 Ibid., pp 218–21. 61 Coleman, 'Regestum', pp 211, 212, 216, 217, 221. 62 Ibid., pp 213, 215. 63 B. Smith, 'Fitzgerald, Maurice (*c.*1194–1257)', *ODNB*, 19 (2004), pp 832–3. 64 Ó Clabaigh, *Franciscans*, p. 115; P. Ó Riain, 'Deascán lámhscríbhinní: a manuscript miscellany' (2003), pp 62–8; B. Jennings (ed.), 'Brevis Synopsis', p. 182. 65 'Brussels MS 3947', pp 63–4; James Ware in BL Add. MS 4821, fo. 107v.

chapter to remind the friars to pray for their benefactors, provides a unique insight into the process of founding a friary and demonstrates how the expectations of patrons and the needs of the friars coalesced to their mutual advantage.

The church of the Friars Minor at Adare was dedicated in honour of St Michael the archangel, on the 19th November 1464, the feast of St Pontianus, Martyr, and St Elizabeth, widow. Thomas, earl of Kildare and his wife Johanna, daughter of James, earl of Desmond, built the church and the fourth part of the cloister at their own expense. They also furnished the windows of the church with glass and presented the bell and two silver chalices. The convent was accepted, on behalf of the order, at the provincial chapter held at Moyne, on the feast of the apostles SS Peter and Paul in the same year, and the brethren of the family of the Observance entered into possession on the feast of All Saints following. The church was consecrated in honour of St Michael the Archangel, on his feast, in the year 1466. The following places outside the church were also consecrated that they might be used for burial of the dead: the whole circuit of the cloisters, inside and outside, both sacristies and the entire cemetery, except a portion at the south, which was set aside for those who might die without the right to Christian burial.

The other parts of the edifice were built by the following: the bell tower by Cornelius O'Sullivan, a pious and devout stranger who had settled amongst us (so the ancient book described him). He also presented us with an excellent chalice gilt with gold. Margaret Fitzgibbon, wife of Cunlaid O'Daly, the good poet, erected the great chapel. One of the small chapels was built by John, son of the earl of Desmond; the other by Leogh de Tulcostyn, and Margaret, wife of Thomas Fitzmaurice. We owe another fourth part of the cloister to a tertiary, Rory O'Dea, who also gave us a useful silver chalice. Another tertiary, Marianus O'Hickey, erected the refectory, and the wooden choir on the north side. He entered the order later on and died in this convent, having spent a most holy life. Donald, the son of O'Dea and Sabina, his wife, finished another fourth of the cloister. Edmond Thomas, Knight of the Glen, and his wife, Honora Fitzgibbon, erected the infirmary. The latter died on the 13th May 1503. Johanna O'Loughlin, widow of Fitzgibbon, added ten feet to the sanctuary, under which she directed a burial place to be formed for herself. Conor O'Sullivan, who built the belfry, died on the 16th of January 1492; Margaret Fitzgibbon, who built the Lady Chapel, on the 23rd January 1483; Donough O'Brien, son of Brian Duv who constructed the dormitory, on the vigil of St Francis, 1502; Thomas, earl of Kildare, founder of the convent, on the 25th March 1478; his wife Johanna, on the feast of St Anthony of Padua, 1486. The first to receive the habit in the convent was Theoderic Fitzmaurice, who died on the 18th June 1484. There lived here also another laybrother named Quirke, who was held in great esteem for his sanctity. He died on the 13th December 1532. John, Prior of Holy Cross, Limerick, who was the ordinary protector of the Fathers of Adare, died on the 2nd August 1531.[66]

Like the Dominicans in Athenry, the Franciscans in Adare received support from both Anglo-Irish and Gaelic patrons. The most striking feature of the account, however, is the extent to which all the branches of the Fitzgeralds were involved in the foundation. In addition to the earl and countess of Kildare, as the senior representatives of the family, the families of the earl of Desmond, the Fitzmaurice lords of Kerry, the Knight of the Glen and the White Knight were also represented. Given the contemporary popularity of the Observant Franciscans with magnates elsewhere in Britain and Europe this support may represent a desire for religion *à la mode*. It is more likely that all branches of the Geraldines were aware of their descent from the original patron of the Friars Minor in Ireland and that they wished to establish a dynastic association with the first house of a vibrant new reform of the Franciscan movement.

### URBAN AND MERCANTILE PATRONS

From shortly after their arrival in Ireland, the friars cultivated close links with members of the merchant class and civic leaders. The earliest reference to the Franciscans in Dublin in 1233 indicates that one of their proctors was Robert Pollard, mayor of the city.[67] Later mayors also proved stalwart supporters: John le Decer (d. 1332) built the Lady Chapel in the Franciscan church and provided the altar stone for the high altar of the Dominican priory, while a successor, Kenwric Sherman, built the tower and glazed the east window of the Dominican church before entering the community shortly before his death in 1351.[68]

The survival of several documents relating to the Lynch family of Galway and Athenry illustrates the close relationship between the friars and their merchant benefactors.[69] By the mid-fifteenth century, the Lynches had emerged as major

66 Jennings, 'Brussels MS 3947', pp 63–4; trans. from *Franciscan Tertiary* (Apr. 1895), 354–7.  **67** *CDI*, i, p. 298, no. 2004.  **68** *FL*, p. 89, Pembridge, *Chronicle*, pp 337, 391; O'Sullivan, *MIDS*, pp 115, 119, 156.  **69** M.J. Blake, *Blake family records, 1300–1600* (1902).

patrons of the Dominican community at Athenry, where the family burial vault was located in St Dominic's Chapel in the transept of the priory church. By the end of the century, the family's business interests had shifted to the port town of Galway but they maintained close links with the Athenry friars. Edmund Lynch kept an open house for the Dominicans whenever they visited Galway, as did Margaret Ballach Lynch.[70] These contacts provide the context for the erection of a Dominican priory in Galway in 1488, of which the Lynches were the principal patrons.[71] The mayor of Galway, John FitzStephen Lynch, built the choir of the church in 1493. This new foundation was part of the family's campaign to aggrandize the city and their position within it and they quickly came to dominate its political, economic and ecclesiastical life. In 1484, at the request of Dominic Dubh Lynch, King Richard III granted the city a charter of incorporation confirming all previous grants and permitting the election of a mayor. He also conceded the privileges of the city of Bristol in place of the laws of Breteuil. This effectively established Galway as an independent enclave and put it on a par with the royal cities of Dublin, Cork, Waterford and Limerick. The first mayor was Dominic's brother, Peter Lynch, who took office in 1485.[72]

The move towards independence also found expression in the ecclesiastical sphere.[73] In 1485, in response to an appeal by the townspeople, Pope Innocent VIII established the parochial church of St Nicholas in Galway as a collegiate foundation under the control of a warden and college of priests.[74] The community's prosperity was also reflected in the number of new mendicant friaries established in Galway. In addition to the new Dominican foundation, the thirteenth-century Franciscan foundation also underwent renewal. In 1438, an advanced school of theology was established there and Edward MacPhilbin de Burgh constructed a new dormitory for the friars sometime before his death in 1496.[75] In 1460, the first of three attempts was made to induce the community to accept the Observant reform.[76] In 1506, Margaret Athy and her husband Stephen Lynch established a house of Augustinian friars on the outskirts of the city at the behest of Friar Richard Nangle while in 1511 Walter Lynch established a house for the 'Poore nonnes of St Francis' near the church of St Nicholas, where his daughter was a member of the community.[77] The references to Lynches and other Galway merchants in the Athenry register and their bequests to the friars discussed below demonstrate both the wealth of the Galway merchant class and the high regard in which they held the friars.

---

70 Coleman, *Regestum*, pp 210, 211.   71 O'Sullivan, *MIDS*, pp 80–2.   72 The Lynch brothers' names also indicate a close Dominican connection, being christened after the founder of the order, St Dominic, and possibly its protomartyr, St Peter of Verona.   73 F. Grannell OFM, 'Galway' (1981), cols 925–53, esp. cols 936–41.   74 M. Coen, *The wardenship of Galway* (1984).   75 *FL*, p. 68.   76 *MRH*, pp 250–1; O'Mahony, 'Brevis synopsis', p. 151, where the date is misprinted as 1260; M. Ó Cleirigh, 'Brussels MS 3410', p. 199.   77 *MRH*, p. 317.

## WOMEN AND THE FRIARS

The friars also benefited from the support of women from aristocratic or mercantile backgrounds for whom patronage and charitable works were the conventional means by which they expressed piety, demonstrated status and hoped to merit salvation.[78] The Annals of Dudley Firbhisigh encapsulated societal expectations in its 1451 eulogy of Margaret O'Carroll, whom it commended for her patronage of

> philosophers, poets, guests, strangers, religious persons, soldiers, mendicant or poor orders … And she was the only woman that made the most of preparing highways and erecting bridges, churches and Mass books and of all manner of things profitable to serve God and her soul, and not that only but while the world stands, her very many gifts to the Irish and Scottish nations shall never be numbered. God's blessing, the blessing of all saints, and every other blessing from Jerusalem to Inis Gluair be on her going to heaven, and blessed be he that will read and hear this, for blessing her soul. Cursed be that sore in her breast that killed Margaret.[79]

In connection with establishing religious houses, women were usually recorded as acting in consort with their husbands. Thus, the foundation of the Dominican friary at Urlar in 1434 was presented as a joint initiative of Edmund MacCostelloe and his wife Fionnuala, while the erection of the Observant Franciscan house at Adare in 1464 was jointly credited to Thomas, earl of Kildare and Johanna, his countess and daughter of the earl of Desmond. The presence of the Kildare and Desmond arms above the late fifteenth-century gatehouse of the nearby Augustinian priory in Adare may also indicate joint patronage of this foundation by the earl and countess (fig. 8.29). Though conventionally represented as subordinate to their husbands in these contexts, some aristocratic women were both forceful and persuasive as occasion demanded. Sometime *c.*1252, Basilia, daughter of Miler de Bermingham and wife of Stephen Dexter, lord of Athleathan, went on hunger strike and secured the expulsion of the Franciscans from her husband's foundation at Strade in favour of the Dominicans whose house at Athenry had been established by her father.[80] The Observant Franciscan house at Donegal was founded in 1474 by Red Hugh O'Donnell at the behest of his mother, Nuala

---

**78** For this neglected aspect of Irish women's history, see M.A. Lyons, 'Lay female piety and church patronage in late medieval Ireland' (2002); D. Hall, *Women and the Church*; G. Power, *Anglo-Irish and Gaelic women in Ireland, c.1170–1540* (2007), pp 48–51, 159–68.   **79** As cited in *AFM*, iv, pp 972–3. **80** Coleman, 'Regestum', p. 204. The Athenry friars regarded this as a victory and as an extension of the patronage Miler de Bermingham bestowed on their own house.

O'Conor, and his wife, Fionnuala O'Brien. Donatus Mooney records that the chieftain's mother was so determined to secure the new foundation that she travelled to the vicariate chapter of the Irish Observants at Rosserrilly and appealed in person to the delegates. When they declined her invitation because of commitments elsewhere, she so harangued the gathering that the newly elected vicar provincial and some other officeholders resigned their positions and accompanied her back to Donegal.[81]

Less frequently, women were acknowledged as founders or major benefactors of friaries in their own right. In 1321, Isabella Palmer built the choir of the Franciscan church in Kilkenny. In Adare, Johanna O'Phelan extended the sanctuary of the Franciscan church by ten feet and incorporated her own tomb in the extension, while Margaret Fitzgibbon (d. 1483) built the church's Lady Chapel. As noted above, Margaret Athy was responsible for establishing the Augustinian priory in Galway in 1506, while Margaret O'Brien (d. 1512/13), wife of Eoghan O'Rourke, lord of Breifne, built the wooden church of the Observant Franciscan friary at Dromahair.[82]

The Athenry register provides numerous examples of how women from mercantile backgrounds, particularly widows, supported the town's Dominican community.[83] Isabel Bodkin built a portion of the friary infirmary, to which she retired after the death of her husband. Joanna Wyffler secured the translation of the body of her husband David Wydyr (d. 1408) from Bristol to Athenry, where she entertained all the friars of Connacht for a fortnight at his obsequies. She subsequently re-glazed the great east window of the church and the windows of the choir, built a stone bridge connecting the friary and the town and provided a wooden chest for the ornate vestments that the couple had previously donated to the community. Sylina Lynch donated casks of fish and wine at the beginning of Lent and Advent for a period of twenty years, while Joanna Godsun presented the community with vestments for the chapel that she and her late husband had endowed. Katalyn Brayneoc also donated vestments and statues for the roodbeam in the church. Joanna O'Kelly was a major benefactor of all the Dominican houses in Connacht and presented the Athenry friars with a graduale containing the music of the Mass and a gilded pyx for reserving the Eucharist. The friars rewarded her generosity with a *memento* in all Masses celebrated in honour of the Virgin Mary at the high altar of the church.[84] The hospitality of Margaret Ballach Lynch to members of the community visiting Galway earned her the sobriquet *hospita fratrum* – the hostess of the friars. The register described her as

**81** 'Brussels MS 3947', pp 38–48, esp. pp 38–9. See also C. Mooney, 'The founding of the friary of Donegal' (1954–5).   **82** Lyons, 'Female piety', pp 60–1.   **83** For widows' patronage, see Kenny, *Anglo-Irish and Gaelic women*, pp 159–68.   **84** Coleman, 'Regestum', pp 207, 208, 209, 210.

a great almsgiver to all the friars and not only to the friars but to all those in manifest necessity and she was the wife of Thomas Martin, sometime burgess of the town of Galway, who for many years after the death of her husband, lived in honest widowhood, distributing her largesse to the poor for the love of God.[85]

LITURGICAL ITEMS

The donation of items for use in the liturgy was particularly popular with the friars' benefactors and included such costly items as altar vessels, processional crosses, statues, vestments, hangings and liturgical books. These high-status gifts often bore inscriptions or heraldic devices that reminded the friars to pray for the donor during the Divine Office and particularly at Mass. Often richly decorated, they formed an integral part of the decor of friary churches and helped to shape the mendicants' devotional milieu and are discussed in greater detail below.[86]

The friars also benefited from endowments that ensured supplies of the bread, wine and wax used in the celebration of the Eucharist and the Liturgy of the Hours. In 1351/2, William Folyn, the sovereign of Kilkenny, and the city's corporation granted the annual rent income from two tenements to the city's Dominican and Franciscan communities to provide bread and wine for the Masses celebrated in the friary churches.[87] In 1394, Thomas Holbeyn granted the Dominicans the income of another tenement in Kilkenny for the same purpose.[88] The Friars Preachers at Athenry were recipients of similar grants: for thirty years at the turn of the fourteenth and fifteenth centuries, Christina Lynch, wife of Thomas Bonnanter, a wealthy merchant of the town, supplied them with candles for use during the night office of Matins. In the late fifteenth century, Lord Thomas de Bermingham, and his wife, granted an annuity of one shilling from the rent of a tenement in the town for the same purpose.[89] Subsequent occupiers of the properties did not always comply with the pious intentions of their predecessors. In 1376, the archdeacon of Ossory, Robert de Tunbrigge, excommunicated Philip Leget of Kilkenny for refusing to supply the friars with bread and wine as required by his rent contract while in 1509 Oliver Cantwell, the Dominican bishop of Ossory, excommunicated Edmund Sleger for the same offence.[90]

85 Ibid., p. 210.   86 See below, pp 253–5.   87 C. McNeill, *Liber primus Kilkenniensis* (1931), pp 25–6. The rents accruing came to forty shillings per annum.   88 Coleman (ed.), *The Irish Dominicans of the seventeenth century* (1902), appendix, p. 27.   89 Coleman, 'Regestum', pp 208, 210, 219.   90 Coleman, *Irish Dominicans*, appendix, p. 27; N.B. White, *Irish monastic and episcopal deeds, AD1200–1600* (1936), p. 112. This latter dispute was particularly bitter.

BEQUESTS AND FUNERAL OFFERINGS

Testamentary bequests constituted one of the most important sources of income for the friars. Throughout Europe, the making of wills and testaments became more common in the twelfth century and Irish examples survive from the thirteenth century onwards. The estate of the deceased was generally divided into three portions after the discharge of outstanding debts. Of these, one-third was reserved to the spouse, one-third to offspring and the remaining portion was assigned for *pro anima* purposes, the various charitable and religious bequests believed to benefit the soul of the deceased. The disposition of these *pro anima* legacies frequently brought the friars into conflict with the secular clergy, a point discussed more fully in chapter six. These bequests often illustrated the devotional practices and piety of the testator and demonstrated the extent of the friars' influence and popularity. In England, sufficient material survives to permit detailed analyses of this aspect of the friars' income in centres such as York, Lincoln and London.[91]

In Ireland, the surviving wills and testaments are fewer in number and much less representative, emanating almost entirely from the towns of the Anglo-Irish colony and representing the interests of relatively wealthy individuals.[92] Only one register of wills remains from medieval Dublin, containing seventy-four wills proved during the pontificates of Archbishops Michael Tregury and John Walton (1457–83).[93] Another twenty-four testaments are preserved in various Dublin records, giving a total of ninety-eight wills, ranging in date from 1270 to 1500. As noted in chapter one, the earliest references to the Augustinians in Dublin and Cork and the Carmelites in Dublin occur in wills, while two of the three surviving references to the only Irish house of the Friars of the Sack occur in Dublin wills of 1275 and 1282.[94] Although the surviving material is weighted in favour of the capital, sufficient material survives from Cork, Dundalk, Galway, Kilkenny, Kinsale and Limerick to indicate that the friars enjoyed similar support in other areas. Most bequests were made to friaries in the testator's locality, but a number of late medieval merchants' wills from Galway contained bequests to mendicant houses throughout Connacht and further afield.

The earliest surviving bequest dates from 1267, when Richard FitzRobert, rector of Inisnag near Thomastown in the diocese of Ossory, bequeathed five

**91** M. Robson, 'Benefactors of the Greyfriars in York: alms from testators, 1530–1538' (2001); idem, 'The Greyfriars of Lincoln' (2010), pp 125–8; Röhrkasten, *Mendicant houses*, pp 261–76.   **92** Cotter, *Friars Minor*, pp 59–62. See also the important article by M. Murphy, 'The high cost of dying: an analysis of *pro anima* bequests in medieval Dublin' (1987).   **93** TCD MS 552; H.F. Berry, *Register of wills and inventories of the diocese of Dublin in the time of Archbishops Tregury and Walton, 1457–1483* (1898).   **94** *MRH*, p. 306.

marks to the Franciscans of Waterford in whose church he sought burial. He also left bequests to the city's Dominican community and to the Friars Minor and Preachers of Kilkenny as well as to other religious bodies.[95] This practice of including the friars among other religious groups was a generic one, as was that of leaving a sum for distribution between all the mendicant houses in a city or town. In Dublin, such bequests often consisted of multiples of ten pence, to be divided equally between the 'four orders of friars'.[96] Very occasionally, testators expressed a preference for one group over the others, by granting them a more substantial legacy. In 1471, William Nele of Clondalkin left six shillings and eight pence (eighty pence) to the Dominicans and three shillings and four pence (forty pence) to each of the other three orders, while in 1476 Agnes Laweles left twelve pence each to the Carmelites and Franciscans of Dublin and nothing to the Dominicans or Augustinians. Walter Sale left twenty pence to each of the capital's mendicant houses in 1476 and an additional twenty pence to the building fund of the Franciscan community, among whom he wished to be buried.[97]

Robert de Moenes, a former mayor of Dublin, whose will was proved in 1326, may have used his will to express dislike for the Dominicans, who alone received nothing in a will remarkable for its generosity to the city's other religious houses. His daughter or niece, Gilliana de Moenes, also ignored the Preachers in her 1348 will, which may indicate a long-running antipathy between the de Moenes family and the order.[98]

The 1306 will of the wealthy Cork merchant, John de Wynchedon, indicates the close personal ties that bound a testator and the friars.[99] In addition to substantial bequests to the fabric funds of various parish churches and to the secular clergy, anchorites, lepers, infirm and crippled of the region, the testator generously endowed the Augustinian friars among whom he sought burial. He left ten marks and two hundred pounds of wax for his funeral and a further ten marks for distribution to the poor. He also bequeathed eight marks for the erection of choir stalls in the priory church, left twenty shillings for the sustenance of the Augustinian provincial chapter and gave three marks for a friar to celebrate Mass for the repose of his soul each day for a year after his death. The city's Dominican and Franciscan communities received similar if slightly smaller bequests. De Wynchedon's preference for the Austin friars is all the more interesting as two of his sons were, respectively, Franciscan and Dominican friars.

95 *FL*, pp 32–4. He wished to be buried beside his brother in the Waterford friary.   96 Berry, *Register*, pp 15, 16, 28, 30, 71, 78, 82, 90, 98, 113, 122, 131, 150, 153, 163.   97 Ibid., pp 77, 98, 135.   98 J.G Smyly (ed.), 'Old (Latin) deeds in the library of Trinity College' (1946), 8–11; idem, 'Old (Latin) deeds in the library of Trinity College' (1947), 31–2. I owe both these references to Bernadette Williams.   99 O'Sullivan (ed.), 'Testament of John de Wynchedon' (1956), 77, 80.

In Limerick, the Dominican and Franciscan communities received bequests from members of the Arthur merchant family in the fourteenth and fifteenth centuries. Martin Arthur (d. 1376) was a notable benefactor of the city's Dominican community. In addition to building the priory's cloister, his *pro anima* legacies included payments of forty-two shillings to have the friars pray for his soul and attend his funeral, a half mark for his burial in the Dominican habit and twenty shillings to construct his tomb in the priory church. He also left ten shillings to the city's Franciscan community and individual bequests of two shillings each to Friars Simon Medin and Maurice O'Cormacaine.[1] His widow, Juliana Beoufor, was also interred in the Dominican priory and paid a half mark for burial in the habit. In addition, she left two marks for repairs to the chapter house and a half mark for repairs to the Franciscan church. Her individual bequests included payments of twenty pence to Friar William Allo and forty pence to Friar Simon Mody. John Arthur continued the family's support for the friars and bequeathed 6s. 8d. to the Franciscans and three shillings and four pence to the Dominicans in his 1425 will.[2] The small number of wills proved before the consistory court of Armagh in the early sixteenth century consistently record bequests to the Franciscan community at Dundalk.[3]

In the majority of cases, the bequests were made in cash, but occasionally the friars received goods in kind: in 1311, the Franciscans and Dominicans of Dublin received a bequest of cattle from the estate of John, son of Ririth, while in 1471, John Kempe left a pig to the appropriately named Friar Bull of Drogheda, but the order to which he belonged is not specified.[4] In 1473, Jonet Cristor of Glasnevin willed that each of the city's mendicant houses would receive eight measures of wheat and ten of malt on the day of her burial. She also left six shillings and eight pence (eighty pence) for division among them.[5]

Occasionally, individual friars were the beneficiaries of wills. The above-mentioned John de Wynchedon left five pounds to each of his two friar-sons and ten shillings to Philip Michis, prior of the Cork Dominican community. He also left individual sums to Friars Geoffrey Lumley, William Ludesop, Thomas de Calle, and William FitzAdam.[6] John Oge Blake of Galway (d. 1420) left sums of money to seven named Franciscans in addition to substantial bequests to all of the region's mendicant houses. John FitzHenry Blake (d. 1468) also left bequests to all the mendicant friaries of Connacht in addition to a gift of four pence to each Franciscan priest in Galway. His bond of personal affection with one friar was

---

1 BL Add. MS 31885, fo. 242 (330).    2 BL Add. MS 31885, fo. 244 (332v–331r. [*sic*]).    3 H.A. Jefferies, 'The role of the laity in the parishes of Armagh *inter anglicos,* 1518–1553' (1998), p. 80. Significantly, Jefferies concludes that teastators' primary loyalty lay with their parish rather than with the mendicants. 4 M. Murphy, 'The high cost of dying'; Berry, *Register*, p. 15.    5 *FL*, p. 219; Berry, *Register*, p. 56. 6 O'Sullivan, 'Testament of John de Wynchedon', 80, 81.

evident in the bequest of his mantle to Friar Malachy O'Dubayn of the Galway community.[7]

Canon law dictated that a testator's parish priest should be present at the making of a will unless the testator died outside the parish. This was to ensure that the rights of the parochial church were not infringed. In 1455, testators in the diocese of Armagh were warned that their wills would be void if the rector, vicar or chaplain of the parish were not present when they were drawn up.[8] The secular clergy feared that friars at deathbeds would entice testators to seek burial in friary cemeteries or to leave them bequests that might otherwise have gone to the parish church. This may explain why friars do not appear as witnesses to any of the surviving Dublin wills, as the parochial clergy were better able to enforce their rights in the city's parishes. In contrast, friars frequently occur as witnesses, and occasionally as executors, in wills from other parts of the country. John de Wynchedon's witnesses in 1306 included both his parish priest and two Friars Preachers in addition to a number of laymen. One of the Dominican witnesses, Friar Thomas de Calle, was charged with arranging the celebration of Masses for his soul. John Oge Blake's will was drawn up in the Franciscan friary in Galway in 1420 and included Friar Thomas O'Clumayn among its witnesses. For his troubles, Friar Thomas received a bequest of two marks, double what the other friar legatees were given. Friar Donatus O'Malley, prior of the Observant Augustinian foundation at Callan, was the principal witness to the will of Sir James MacRichard Butler, who was buried in the priory church *c.*1437.[9] In 1510, Friars John Wydram and John O'Nycholl of the Franciscan community at Ennis acted as witnesses and executors for the will of the rather colourful Renalda O'Brien.[10] Her will provides the unique example of the testament of a Gaelic noblewoman. Although she was the abbess of the Augustinian community at Killone, Co. Clare, she wished to be buried in the nearby friary church at Ennis. She left a bequest to the guardian and community of the Observant Franciscans at Adare, subsequently remitted to them by Piers Butler, earl of Ossory.[11]

Although the presence of friars as witnesses was indicative of the respect with which they were regarded, it occasionally led to conflict with disgruntled parties when the will was proved. In 1305, an unidentified Franciscan from Ardfert and

7 R. O'Flaherty, *A chorographical description of West or H-Iar Connaught* (1846), pp 201, 209.   8 D.A. Chart, *The register of John Swayne* (1935), p. 200.   9 E. Curtis (ed.), *Calendar of Ormond deeds*, iii, pp 322–5, no. 329.   10 Daughter of Tadhg an Chomhaid O'Brien who became ruler of Thomond in 1459. She was successively mistress to John Butler, sixth earl of Ormond, to whom she bore Sir John Butler, and wife to Richard Butler of Knockgraffon. She ended her life as the abbess of the Augustinian nunnery at Killone near the O'Brien stronghold at Ennis. See B. Ó Dálaigh, 'Mistress, mother and abbess: Renalda Ní Bhriain (*c.*1447–1510)' (1990), where a translation of her will is provided on pp 62–3.   11 NLI D.2014. Calendared in E. Curtis (ed.), *Calendar of Ormond deeds*, iv, p. 27.

the Cistercian abbot of Abbeydorney were accused of a deathbed connivance with Thomas Fitzmaurice to deprive Nicholas, his son and heir, of a parcel of land in favour of his younger son Gerald.[12] In 1318, Friar John de Nasse, procurator and clerk of works at the Franciscan friary in Clonmel, brought a case against Raymond de Valle, who had taken forty pounds from a chest in the friary. Raymond's father, William de Valle, had bequeathed the money to the friary to build a chapel in honour of the Virgin Mary. As the matter concerned probate, the judge was the archbishop of Cashel, who found in favour of the friars and ordered Raymond to return the money.[13] Although the secular clergy's fear of mendicant sharp practice was occasionally well founded, the friars were also capable of great probity when it came to probate. The *Liber exemplorum* contains two cautionary stories concerning the fates of executors who failed to discharge their duties.[14] Sometime in the 1530s, Sir Walter Delahide of Moyclare near Dublin connived in the destruction of his mother-in-law's will by his wife and her sisters. Racked by conscience after the event, he approached a friar for counsel. The friar advised disclosure of the conspiracy and persuaded Sir Walter to have the matter brought to court.[15]

Perhaps the clearest example of the complex network of ties that bound the friars to their contemporaries comes from the 1456 will of Moldina Whitechurch, a wealthy widow of Drogheda. In a previous will, which she revoked, she had left her goods to Robert Walsh. In her new will, she wished Friar William Kynton, a Dominican in the Drogheda community, to be her executor and principal beneficiary. Friar William was her grandson and it was her hope that their ties of kinship and affection would expedite matters. As the statutes of the Friars Preachers impeded Friar William in the task of executor, she made a deed of gift of all her goods to a third party, John More of Payneston, who was to hold them in trust for her grandson until he was free to dispose of them. She then, in the manner of medieval testators, bequeathed her soul to God, the Virgin Mary and all the saints, and her body to be buried in the parish church of St Peter in Drogheda. She left thirty shillings for her obsequies and gave twenty pence to the Dominicans and a shilling to each of the other three mendicant communities in the town to pray for her soul. The residue of her considerable estate she left to her grandson, Friar William, to purchase a missal and chalice with which for the rest of his life he was to offer Mass for the repose of her soul. He in turn was instructed to bequeath both items to another priest who would perform the same service for him, for Moldina, her husband and for all the faithful departed.[16]

---

**12** *FL*, p. 217.   **13** *FL*, p. 221.   **14** *Lib. ex.*, pp 81–3; Jones, *Friars' tales*, pp 109–11.   **15** *Calendar of patent rolls, Ireland Henry VIII–Elizabeth*, i, 98; cited in B. Bradshaw, *The dissolution of the religious orders in Ireland under Henry VIII* (1974), p. 12.   **16** Chart (ed.), *Register of Primate Swayne*, pp 200–2.

4.1 Portrait of a female donor, north-western tower corbel, Dominican priory, Sligo. The angels hold a stone shield on which a heraldic device was formerly painted (Edwin Rae © TRIARC, Irish Art Research Centre).

EXPECTATIONS OF PATRONS (fig. 4.1)

The relationship between the friars and their benefactors was a symbiotic and reciprocal one. In addition to the spiritual benefits believed to accrue from supporting a religious community, the friars offered a wide variety of more tangible benefits to their patrons.

### MEMORIALIZATION

The most valued service that the friars performed for their benefactors occurred post-mortem. Burial in the friary church or cemetery ensured the continual intercession of the community for the deceased and established an abiding link between the friars and their patrons. The elaborate tombs of founders and patrons, occupying prominent positions in the friary churches, reminded the friars of their

4.2 Founder's tomb, Dominican priory, Strade, Co. Mayo (photograph by Karena Morton).

obligation to pray for their benefactors (fig. 4.2).[17] Ornamented with effigies of the deceased, saintly intercessors and heraldic devices, these memorials also functioned as statements of power, prestige and social hierarchy. The place of honour, reserved for the founder and his descendents, was in the north-eastern corner of the sanctuary, immediately adjacent to the side of the altar from which the gospel was proclaimed. Surviving examples demonstrate that these founders' tombs were often elaborate structures ornamented with tracery, stucco and mural paintings (fig. 8.27).[18] Their location meant that they also doubled as an Easter sepulchre, the structure into which the cross and Blessed Sacrament was placed during the Easter Triduum. The elaborate MacMahon tomb at the Franciscan friary in Quin and the carved stone panels depicting scenes from Christ's passion from the founder's tomb at Ennis illustrate this dual purpose (fig. 8.23).

**17** R. Gillespie, 'Irish funeral monuments and social change, 1500–1700: perceptions of death' (1994), pp 156–8; C. Tait, *Death, burial and commemoration in Ireland, 1550–1650* (2002), pp 59–84.  **18** R. Moss, 'Permanent expressions of piety' (2006), pp 72–3.

In death as in life, a strict social hierarchy reigned and governed the positioning of graves within friary churches and precincts.[19] The register of the Athenry Dominicans indicates that burial within the chancel and sanctuary of the church was reserved to the principal aristocratic benefactors of the priory: the de Bermingham barons Athenry and the de Burgh earls of Clanrickard. The latter family had previously been buried with the Augustinan canons at Athassel, Co. Tipperary, and their decision to transfer to Athenry necessitated the rebuilding of the east end of the priory church. A similar spatial hierarchy is evident in the list of burials that survives from the Franciscan church in Waterford.[20]

The area around the high altar and the three steps of the predella leading up to it were also reserved for the burial of notable benefactors: William de Bermingham, the pugnacious archbishop of Tuam (d. 1312), was buried in the deacon's step at the Dominican church in Athenry.[21] In the Carmelite priory in Castlelyons, the predella consisted of three broad, shallow steps of sufficient width to each accommodate a row of burials.[22] A tomb directly in front of the high altar was also much coveted and Johanna, countess of Kildare, was buried in this position in the Franciscan church in Adare in 1486. The sedilia or ornamental seats for the ministers at Mass also doubled as tombs on occasion. The tomb of Johanna O'Phelan was incorporated into the sedilia of the Franciscan church at Adare, while the tomb of the O'Brien barons Inchiquin served as the sedilia at the friary in Ennis.[23]

Non-aristocratic patrons were usually buried in the nave and transept of the church, where Masses were daily celebrated by the community's friar-priests at side altars and chapels. These locations consequently came to function as chantries for the wealthy benefactors who had endowed them. In the Dominican priory at Athenry, the Lynch family vault was situated before the altar in the chapel of St Dominic, while in their Sligo priory, the tomb of the O'Crean family occupied a prominent position at the north-east end of the nave. Patrons often supplied the liturgical accoutrements for the family mortuary chapel, an expression of piety and prestige to which subsequent generations contributed. In Athenry, John Blake and his wife, Joanna Godsun, donated a chalice and missal to the chapel they had endowed in the priory church. Joanna further embellished the chantry after the death of her husband and donated a wooden altar, two silk chasubles and other vestments. Their son, William Blake, continued his parents' patronage, presenting

**19** R. Gilchrist & B. Sloane, *Requiem: the medieval monastic cemetery in Britain* (2005), pp 56–8.   **20** J. Walton, 'A list of early burials in the French church, Waterford' (1973). I am grateful to Rachel Moss for this reference.   **21** Coleman, 'Regestum', p. 205.   **22** A similar feature occurs in the Franciscan church in Carmarthen in Wales. Gilchrist & Sloane, *Requiem*, p. 57.   **23** A recent excavation of the sedilia at the Premonstratensian abbey, Lough Key, revealed that it was repeatedly used for interments. M. Clyne, 'Archaeological excavations at Holy Trinity Abbey, Lough Key, Co. Roscommon' (2005), p. 86.

a valuable altar cloth, two bronze candlesticks worth sixteen shillings and a holy water stoup.[24] The deep attachment to these family mausolea and the value placed on the friars' intercession is particularly evident in the 1468 will of John FitzHenry Blake, who instructed that his body be buried in the 'monastery of the Friars Minor in Galway, in the tomb of my brethren, the nation of the Blakes, under the protection of St Francis and with the suffrages of his order'.[25]

In addition to praying for their deceased benefactors, the friars also functioned as the custodians of their memory, genealogy and reputation. This sometimes took the form of marginal entries in liturgical books such as those recording the deaths of members of the O'Mulloy family in the calendar of the Kilcormac missal or entries relating to the O'Briens found in the martyrology of the Dominican priory in Limerick.[26] Most mendicant communities maintained a necrology listing the obits of their patrons and principal benefactors along with those of members of the community. Extensive transcripts of those belonging to the Franciscan friary in Galway and the Dominican priory in Athenry still survive.[27] The Galway necrology contained a succession list of the Fitzgerald family and annalistic material relating to the family was preserved in the 'Book of Antiphonalles' belonging to the Dominicans of Sligo.[28] The friars also produced or preserved more extensive genealogical records of their patrons: the fourteenth-century Dominican chronicler, Friar John Pembridge, included a lengthy genealogy of the Marshal family in his annals, and the Franciscans in Youghal had a chronicle of the Fitzgeralds in their library in 1523.[29] In the seventeenth century, the Dominican friar Dominic O'Daly compiled a history of the Fitzgeralds in which he recorded many of the early legends of the family and its association with the Dominican priory in Tralee.[30] This mnemonic service was not just confined to noble families: the charters of the liberty of Meath were preserved by Franciscan community at Trim.[31]

RETIREMENT AND RECRUITMENT

The friaries provided secure and worthy places in which founders could pass their declining years and there are numerous annalistic references to patrons and their descendants dying 'in the habit of a friar, after the victory of unction and

---

24 Coleman, 'Regestum', p. 208.    25 R. O'Flaherty, *A chorographical description of West or H-Iar Connaught* (1846), p. 206.    26 J.H. Todd, 'Obits of Kilcomick' (1846); BL Add. MS 4783, fo. 58. I owe this latter reference to Bernadette Williams.    27 M.J. Blake, 'The obituary book of the Franciscan monastery at Galway' (1909–10); Coleman, 'Regestum', pp 215–18.    28 Blake, 'Obituary book', p. 229; Coleman, *Appendix*, p. 98.    29 Pembridge, *Annals*, pp 312–14; *YLC*, no. 102.    30 D. de Rosario O'Daly OP, *Initium, incrementa, et exitus Familiae Geraldinorum Desmoniae Comitum, Palatinorum Kyrriae in Hybernia* (1655) trans. C.P. Meehan, *The rise, increase and exit of the Geraldines, earls of Desmond* (1878).    31 J. Mills & M.J. McEnery (eds), *Calendar of the Gormanston register* (1916), p. 7.

penance'.[32] In 1308, Geoffrey de Geneville resigned the lordship of Meath and spent the remaining six years of his life as a Dominican in the priory he had founded at Trim.[33] The Athenry register recorded that Lord Thomas de Burgh, son of the second earl of Ulster, repeatedly expressed the hope that 'God would not snatch him from the world' without allowing him to assume the Dominican habit in the convent, which he did shortly before his death in 1316.[34] In 1365, 'Cucconaught O'Reilly, lord of Breifne, retired among the friars and resigned the lordship to his brother Philip.'[35] In 1421, Murrough O'Conor Faly resigned the lordship of Offaly and joined the Franciscan community at Killeigh, and in 1439 Donogh O'Hara, lord of Leyney, did likewise and entered the Augustinian community he had founded at Banada.[36] Nor was this practice confined to male patrons and benefactors: in 1447, Finola, daughter of Calvagh O'Conor Faly and wife of the O'Donnell and Hugh Boy O'Neill, 'retired from this transitory world, to prepare for life eternal' in the Franciscan friary at Killeigh.[37] The annals also record the death in 1528 of Nuala O'Brien, who had spent over twenty years of her widowhood living as a tertiary attached to the friary in Donegal.[38] In Athenry, Isabel Bodkin also passed her widowhood in the infirmary of the Friars Preachers, the building of which she had in part financed.[39]

The presence of lay pensioners or corrodians within the friary precinct was an almost inevitable consequence of aristocratic patronage and was a besetting problem for those monastic orders which relied on it for revenue. The practice meant that in return for an endowment of land or another source of income, benefactors received a corrody that permitted them to live *en pension* with the community in their declining years. The practice was well-attested among the Irish Knights Hospitaller in the fourteenth century, and O'Sullivan suggests that a number of Irish Dominican foundations may have acquired their land holdings in like manner.[40] These arrangements rarely worked to the advantage of the religious community and frequently undermined monastic discipline. Consequently, the practice was often criticized by reformers, which may explain why, in 1492, Friar Anselm of Montefalco, the prior general of the Augustinians, ordered Friar David, prior of the Augustinian priory at Banada, to immediately expel from the friary precincts all laymen and women living there. He also decreed that no laypeople were to reside within the precincts unless they were oblates of the order or servants of the house.[41]

---

**32** See, for example, the 1528 obituary of Eoghan O'Rourke, lord of Breifne, *AFM*, v, pp 1392, 1393. **33** Potterton, *Medieval Trim: history and archaeology*, p. 89. **34** Coleman, 'Regestum', pp 210–11. **35** *AFM*, iii, pp 630, 631. **36** *AFM*, iv, pp 850, 851, 916, 917. **37** *AFM*, iv, pp 954, 955. **38** *AFM*, v, pp 1392, 1393; *Ann. Conn.*, p. 667; *ALC*, ii, p. 265. **39** Coleman, 'Regestum', p. 206. **40** C. Mc Neill (ed.), *Registrum de Kilmainham, 1326–39* (1932); E. Massey, *Prior Roger Outlaw of Kilmainham, 1314–1341* (2000), pp 12–20. N. Byrne, *The Irish crusade* (2007), pp 253–4; O'Sullivan, *MIDS*, p. 157. **41** Martin & de Meijer, 'Irish material', p. 105, no. 115.

The 'family friary' also provided a suitable place for those members intent on the religious life as a career. The first to receive the religious habit in the Fitzgerald Franciscan foundation at Adare was Theodoric Fitzmaurice, presumably of the lineage of the Fitzmaurice lords of Kerry, and in 1616 the surviving altar plate from Adare was in the custody of Friar Thomas Fitzgerald.[42] In 1394, the Athenry register recorded the death of Friar Henry de Burgh, presumably a member of one of the branches of the de Burgh family that patronized the house.

Men and women of merchant backgrounds also entered the mendicant communities supported by their families. Friars John and Adam de Wynchedon, members of the Dominican and Franciscan communities in Cork, were the sons of a wealthy city merchant.[43] The necrology of the Athenry Dominicans records the deaths of twenty-two members of the community between 1394 and 1457, including Friars John Bonnanter (d. 1405), John Wallys (d. 1408) and Nicholas Brayneog (1431).[44] These were presumably related to the Thomas Bovanter, Agnes Bonanter, Wyllyn Wallys and Robert,[45] Walter, Thomas and Kathaline Braynach[46] listed in the register as benefactors of the community who were buried in the priory church. In 1511, in a rare reference to mendicant nuns, Walter Lynch, a Galway merchant, established a house for the 'Poore nonnes of St Francis' near the city's Collegiate Church of St Nicholas, where his daughter was a member of the community.[47]

### HOSPITALITY

The dearth of large-scale public buildings in medieval Europe meant that the churches and chapter rooms of religious houses frequently hosted civic and political gatherings.[48] In February 1395, the earl of Nottingham received the submissions of various Irish chieftains to Richard II in the Franciscan church in Castledermot, while the king himself received the submission of Turloch O'Connor Don in the Franciscan church in Waterford.[49] From at least 1428, the annual election of the sovereign or mayor of Kilkenny took place in the chapter room of the city's Dominican priory.[50] The Dominican priory in Trim hosted meetings of the Irish parliament in 1446, 1484, 1487 and 1491. Friaries also

42 'Brussels MS 3947', pp 63–4.   43 O'Sullivan, 'Testament of John de Wynchedon', 80.   44 Coleman, 'Regestum', pp 215–17. A number of these friars had entered the order in Athenry but died elsewhere. 45 Ibid., p. 204. Miler de Bermingham purchased the site for the monastery from Robert Braynach, a knight.   46 Ibid., p. 209.   47 *MRH*, p. 317.   48 J. Röhrkasten, 'Secular uses of mendicant priories of medieval London' (2006), provides numerous examples of the phenomenon throughout England and Europe.   49 Cotter, *Friars Minor*, p. 151; D. Johnson, 'Richard II and the submissions of Gaelic Ireland' (1985).   50 C. McNeill, *Liber Primus Kilkenniensis* (1931), p. 57 and passim.

proved popular venues for clan gatherings of Gaelic or Anglo-Norman families. These often occurred on anniversaries and feastdays, but were normally recorded only when someone got killed. In 1338, Edmund de Burgh, son of the earl of Ulster, was abducted by his cousin Edmund Albanach de Burgh from the Augustinian priory in Ballinrobe, put in a sack and drowned in Lough Mask.[51] The obituary list of the Carmelite priory at Kilcormac recorded that on the octave of the Epiphany in 1525, Hugh and Constantine O'Mulloy were violently dragged from the priory church by Charles O'Mulloy and his followers and killed in front of the friary gates.[52] Donatus Mooney recorded that the nobility in the vicinity of Multyfarnham gathered at the friary there to celebrate the feast of St Francis with the community each year. According to Dr Henry Jones, Anglican dean of Kilmore, this annual gathering later provided the occasion for plotting the 1641 rebellion.[53]

In addition to the long-term lay residents discussed above, the friars also maintained short-term accommodation for their benefactors and other guests.[54] The west ranges of many of the fifteenth-century foundations such as the Franciscan houses at Moyne, Sherkin Island, Rosserrilly, Adare and Quin, and the Carmelite priory at Castlelyons provided accommodation of a higher standard than that found in the friars' dormitory in the east range and these were probably reserved for the reception of guests and visitors.[55]

A number of friaries also possessed freestanding guest quarters within their precincts. In describing the Franciscan friary at Clonmel, Mooney referred to the 'Earl's Hall' (*aula Comitis*) and noted that many Irish nobles maintained such places of retreat within the bounds of the friaries they patronized.[56] Luke Wadding likewise recorded that Dermot MacCarthy, founder of the Franciscan house at Cork, reserved apartments for his own use within the friary.[57] The O'Brien chieftains of Thomond maintained a residence beside the gate of the friary at Ennis.[58] In Waterford, the guest accommodation of the Dominican community was very extensive, perhaps on account of having to cater for large numbers of overseas travellers. In addition to the normal claustral building, the extent of the priory taken in January 1541 listed the 'Baron's Hall' with its three upper rooms, the 'Little Hall' with its kitchen and upper room and the Great Hall with upper rooms and other appurtenances among the buildings in the compound.[59] At Askeaton, the remains of the medieval hospice still stand within the precinct of the Franciscan friary (pl. 11).

**51** *MRH*, p. 296; Coleman, 'Regestum', p. 217.   **52** Todd, 'Obits of Kilcormick', p. 100.   **53** Ó Clabaigh, 'The other Christ', p. 162.   **54** For Franciscan examples before 1400, see Cotter, *Friars Minor*, pp 151–2. **55** Discussed below, p. 232.   **56** 'Brussels MS 3947', p. 79.   **57** Wadding, *AM*, ii, p. 310.   **58** J. Bradley et al., 'Urban archaeology survey xv: County Clare' (1988), p. 49. I owe this reference to Edel Bhreathnach. **59** White, *Monastic possessions*, p. 351; O'Sullivan, *MIDS*, pp 135–6.

Friaries also provided suitable accommodation for royal officials on business and, on rare occasions, for the king himself. In 1324, the justiciar, treasurer and chancellor of Ireland all stayed with the Franciscans in Kilkenny during the witchcraft trial of Dame Alice Kettler.[60] In 1360–1, the Dominicans in Kilmallock received a payment of five pounds for repairs to the accommodation the justiciar used when on circuit.[61] In January 1395, Richard II of England, in Ireland at the head of an army, stayed with the Franciscans in Drogheda for eighteen days. Through no fault of the friars, a less cordial welcome awaited Sir Richard Edgecombe when he lodged with the Dominicans in Dublin in 1488. Sent to reconcile to royal favour those noblemen who had supported Lambert Simnel in his rebellion against Henry VII, he was snubbed by the earl of Kildare and forced to remain in the friary guest quarters for several days until the earl deigned to receive him.[62]

Merchants were also familiar guests in medieval friary guest houses as the convent and its precinct provided a secure base for them and their merchandise. This was particularly true in rural Gaelic territories where such secure bases were scarcer that in the towns of the Anglo-Irish colony. The earliest example of friaries being used as repositories occurred in 1252 when Canon John de Frosinone, papal nuncio in Ireland, controversially deposited sums of money given for the crusades in Franciscan and Dominican friaries and at the Cistercian monasteries of Mellifont and Dublin.[63] In 1290, John le Juvene, a ship's skipper, brought a case against Nicholas de Clere, treasurer, and the justices of Ireland alleging that having had all his goods stolen from his ship by the people of Waterford, he was denied justice by the Irish courts. He furthermore alleged that on his departure for England, Nicholas had sent the sheriff of Cork to the Franciscan church in Youghal where they broke into the vestry and removed the box he had stored there along with his jewels, muniments and treasure to the value of one hundred pounds.[64] In 1307, three people were accused of trespass in the church of the Friars Minor in Ardfert, where they stole grain from a chest belonging to Sibilla la Gras.[65] In 1506, Donal O'Crean, 'a pious and conscientious merchant', died suddenly one morning while attending Mass in the Franciscan friary in Donegal.[66] He was probably a member of the Sligo merchant family who were generous patrons of that town's Dominican priory and may well have passed his last night in the guest quarters of the Donegal friary.

Merchants also used the friaries as venues in which to conduct their business affairs. An interesting example of this occurred in 1407 when Walter Lawless of

---

**60** T. Wright, *A contemporary narrative of the proceeding against Dame Alice Kyteler* (1843), p. 26. I owe this reference to Bernadette Williams.   **61** Connolly, *Irish exchequer payments*, p. 506.   **62** O'Sullivan, *MIDS*, p. 136.   **63** *FL*, pp 2–3.   **64** *FL*, p. 60. The plaintiff may be identical to the Cistercian laybrother of the same name who was hanged for piracy in Dublin in 1294.   **65** *FL*, p. 86.   **66** *AFM*, v, pp 1286, 1287.

Galway granted his share in eel weirs on the River Corrib and of a tenement in the city to John Blake of Athenry. The transaction took place in the Dominican house in Sligo and the deeds relating to it were endorsed by the conventual seal.[67] In 1443, the Franciscan house in Galway was the scene for a grant by Henry Blake to his son John of all his lands and tenements in the city and its environs. Among the witnesses to the transaction was Friar Cornelius, the guardian of the community.[68] In disputed cases, merchants sometimes invoked the moral authority of the friars as arbitrators. In 1445, a dispute over property arose between William Blake and the aforementioned Henry and John Blake. All parties agreed to accept the arbitration of William de Burgh, earl of Clanrickard, and Master John, a Dominican of Athenry. Perhaps the most interesting example, however, is the involvement of Friar Henry Joyce, a Dominican, probably of Athenry, in the 1468 marriage settlement between John Blake and Peter Lynch of Galway. In return for a dowry of sixty marks, Peter Lynch, later first mayor of the city, agreed to marry John Blake's daughter, Evelyn. As both parties were related within the prohibited degrees of consanguinity, a dispensation had to be procured from Rome, the cost of which was to be divided equally between the bride's father and her betrothed. In the interim, Peter bound himself to regard as legitimate any offspring born before the dispensation was obtained and the marriage solemnized.[69]

An unusual benefit to merchants staying in the various friaries in Galway was the ability to claim sanctuary to avoid the payment of debts. This became a cause of contention between the civil authorities and the friars in the mid-1530s. In 1536, one of the ordinances for the reformation of the city issued by Henry VIII prohibited the friars, and specifically the Franciscans on St Stephen's Island, from offering sanctuary to robbers and malefactors.[70] In 1537, the city's corporation enacted a byelaw forbidding citizens from sending food to those keeping sanctuary 'in the abbeys, easte or weste, fearing to come into the town to pay their debts', thereby implicating the city's Augustinian and Dominican communities with their Franciscan colleagues. In 1541, another byelaw prohibited debtors from claiming sanctuary for more than twenty-four hours.[71] Despite the corporation's best efforts, the friaries' role as privileged havens was destined for a lengthy future: Mooney noted that sometime around 1616 the lay occupier of the Franciscan precinct in Galway continued to assert the property's civil immunity, refusing to let the city magistrates either exercise authority or carry the mace or civic emblems beyond the centre of the bridge over the river that separated St Stephen's Island from the town.[72]

**67** M.J. Blake, *Blake family records, 1300–1600* (1902), p. 17, nos 16 & 17.   **68** Ibid., pp 25–6, nos 33 & 34.   **69** Ibid., p. 39, no. 60.   **70** J.S Brewer & W. Bullen (eds), *Calendar of the Carew manuscripts, 1515–1574* (1867), pp 91–2.   **71** J. Hardiman, *The history of the town and county of Galway* (1820 [1926]), pp 84, 210.   **72** 'Brussels MS 3947', p. 55.

The international character of the mendicant orders gave their merchant-benefactors access to an extensive network of contacts and bases right across Europe. Foreign merchants lodged in Irish friaries and Irish merchants routinely exploited their mendicant links when travelling abroad, as is evident from a late fifteenth-century formulaic letter of introduction from the vicar provincial of the Observant Franciscans in Youghal to his *confrères* on the Continent. In it, he asked his colleagues to afford whatever assistance and protection they could to the bearer, a 'particular friend' of the Youghal community, and to his merchandise:

> To the venerable in Christ, the fathers, guardians and all other friars of our family, and especially those of province N and specifically the convent of N in that province to whom these present letters pertain. Friar N vicar provincial in the province of Ireland over all the friars of the said vocation commonly called *de Obsevantia*. Everlasting greetings in the Lord. Since we are bound by a rule of perfect charity that knows no wavering, we ought to pay back to our devoted friends and to those loving us tenderly [all] permissible and possible repayments of mutual charity and to share with them any help, advice and favour in upright and permissible things. For which reason I make recommendation, as deeply as I can, for the welfare of this particular friend of ours [insert name] beginning a voyage with his merchandise for the purpose of private and public gain, and I beseech you, for the sake of God, to show him in deed and word, as though to special and spiritual friends, whatever is suitable and permissible to you, should the need arise. From our convent N in the year of the Lord. Signed in testimony of sincere recommendation of him.[73]

So routine were these arrangements that they often only come to light when something went wrong. In 1295, Richard de Saham sequestered and sold the property that two Flemish merchants had stored in the Franciscan friary at New Ross, while in Dublin in 1315 the guardian of the Franciscan friary was ordered to surrender the chest and letters that the late Francis Bectory, a merchant of Lucca, had entrusted for safekeeping to Friar John of Ross.[74] In 1408, David Wydyr, a merchant of Athenry, became seriously ill in Bristol while returning from a trading trip to Flanders. As a friend and benefactor of the Dominicans in Athenry, he turned to their *confrères* in Bristol for assistance and remained with them until he died and was buried in their church. His remains were subsequently repatriated to Athenry and his widow handsomely remunerated both communities.[75]

---

73 Latin original in J.A. Gribbin & C. Ó Clabaigh (eds), 'Confraternity letters of the Irish Observant Franciscans and their benefactors' (2002), pp 470–1.  74 *FL*, pp 66, 220.  75 Coleman, 'Regestum', pp 207, 215.

The friars' mendicant lifestyle was predicated on a network of support that aroused reciprocal affection, support and dependence among their benefactors. As Mooney noted in the early seventeenth century:

> Very many of the nobility throughout the kingdom held the monasteries of
> our order as dear to them as their own personal property. They had been
> founded by their predecessors. There was the burial place of their families.
> There they hoped to rest themselves. The nobles were themselves, moreover,
> united to the friars in most intimate friendships, and could not imagine how
> they were to exist without them.[76]

Though ostensibly pledged to a life of asceticism and renunciation, such intimate contact with members of the social and economic elites of late medieval Ireland inevitably influenced the friars and their lifestyle.

---

**76** 'Brussels MS 3947', p. 17. Trans. in *Franciscan Tertiary*, 4:10 (1894), 295.

CHAPTER FIVE

# The lifestyle of the friars

*There was a plentiful supply of fish, an immense, I might say, a superabundant quantity of vegetables, while such was the profusion of shellfish that they could be collected at any time on the seashore without the slightest trouble. The convent stood close by the sea ... while at low tide you could walk to the island of Bartragh, which is at least a mile distant. This island abounded in rabbits. Indeed it would seem as if God wished to supply all our necessities with his own hand, so that we had no need to seek fish, vegetables or meat from an earthly benefactor.*[1]

The friars' reliance on ongoing patronage and continual almsgiving brought them into contact with a wide cross section of society. This chapter examines the manner in which the friars' benefactors met their needs for clothing and food and explores the wider spiritual context in which this support occurred. It pays particular attention to the friars' diet and examines the practice of questing, whereby they regularly begged for food from the people in their localities.

## THE RELIGIOUS HABIT

The friar's habit was the external sign of his religious calling and was regarded as a sacramental, a consecrated item of which particular care had to be taken.[2] The Observant Franciscans were forbidden to wear secular clothes or to lend their habits to lay people for use in plays, and deprivation of the habit or the imposition on a professed friar of the novice's habit were features of the disciplinary procedures of each order. The friars normally slept in their habits or portions thereof and worn out garments were used to shroud the corpses of benefactors.[3] In each order, the habit and undergarments were normally made from woollen cloth as an expression of poverty and asceticism, and superiors had

---

1 Description of Moyne Friary, 'Brussels MS 3947', p. 51.   2 E. Boaga, 'L'abito degli Ordini mendicanti' (2000), discusses the form and symbolism of the habit in each mendicant order.   3 *AS*, iv, nos 10, 13; vi, no. 16.

to ensure that all the friars wore habits of uniform quality and design.[4] As a concession, elderly or sick friars or those travelling were occasionally permitted to wear less abrasive linen underwear instead of woollen garments. In 1431, the Augustinian prior general granted Friar William Macgoreolitaidh of Ireland permission to 'ride a horse, take baths and use linen cloth'. The Dominican master general made similar concessions to Friars Patrick Ohydrichda and Donatus Odublane of the Aghaboe convent in 1475.[5]

The Dominican habit consisted of a white woollen tunic reaching from the shoulders to the ankles and girded at the waist with a leather belt (fig. 5.1). Over this, the friar wore a white scapular consisting of two strips of cloth that fell, front and back, from the shoulders to a little below the knees and reaching from elbow to elbow when the arms were folded. Where the two strips joined, there was an opening to allow the scapular slip over the friar's head. At the opening, a hood or capuce was joined to the scapular. This spread over the shoulders and dropped to the small of the back, where it came to a point. By the mid-fourteenth century, the hood was a separate garment distinct from the scapular. The Dominican habit was completed by a black cloak or *cappa*, with a hood, which the friars wore in choir during the winter, while preaching and hearing confessions or whenever they left the friary. As these were the occasions on which they were most visible to the laity, the Dominicans were commonly called the Blackfriars after the colour of their outer garments. Dominican laybrothers wore a black or grey scapular over the white tunic within the friary and a black bell-shaped scapular in place of the cleric's *cappa* when outside it. The Dominicans also wore hose, stockings and shoes.[6] The surviving Irish images of St Dominic and the marginal illustrations of Friars Preachers in Oxford Bodleian manuscript Douce 104, a copy of *Piers Plowman* produced in Dublin in 1427, indicate that the Irish Dominican habit was in line with that worn by their English and Continental *confrères* (pl. 3).[7]

The Franciscan habit was the simplest of all those worn by the mendicant orders and consisted of a long, grey woollen tunic, 'the colour of ashes', and tailored in the form of a cross (pl. 6). It was girded at the waist by a cord that extended down the front of the tunic between the friar's legs. From these two distinctive features, the Friars Minor became popularly known as the Greyfriars or the Cordeliers. The cord was often embellished with decorative knots symbolizing the friars' vows of poverty, chastity and obedience and was

**4** Ó Clabaigh, *Franciscans*, p. 117; *AS*, iii, 1–7, 9–10; Hinnebusch, *History of the Dominican order*, 1, pp 339–43.   **5** Martin & de Meijer, 'Irish material', p. 86, no. 50; Fenning, 'Irish material', p. 257, no. 12. **6** Hinnebusch, *History of the Dominican order*, 1, pp 340–1.   **7** Bodleian MS Douce 104, fo. 44r; K.L. Scott, 'The illustrations of Piers Plowman in Bodleian Library MS Douce 104' (1990).

5.1  A Dominican friar, from Mervyn Archdall, *Monasticon Hibernicum* (1786).

occasionally worn by the friars' lay associates as a mark of their devotion to St Francis.[8] Items such as penknives, pens, *vademecum* books and other trinkets were stored in pouches suspended from the cord. These pouches also allowed the friar receive alms without having to physically handle money. The surviving Irish images of St Francis show that the tunic was puckered up at the waist and allowed to hang over the cord . While Irish depictions of the saint normally show him barefooted, the sepulchral effigy of the Franciscan bishop of Ossory, Richard Ledrede (d. *c.*1360) in St Canice's Cathedral, Kilkenny, depicts him wearing sandals over unstockinged feet and this was probably the norm among the Irish Friars Minor.[9]

The divisions over the observance of the vow of poverty between the different branches of the Franciscans found expression in the amount of material used to make the habit and the manner in which its hood or capuce was designed. The Conventual Franciscan habit was the most ample and had a capuce that came midway down the chest at the front, covering the upper arms and coming to a point at the back (fig. 5.2). The images of SS Francis and Anthony are depicted in this form of the habit on a tomb from the friary in Galway (fig. 7.2). The hood of the Observant habit formed a semicircle over the chest, leaving the arms free, and tapered to a point at the back. It is well illustrated by the image of St Francis from the Franciscan friary in Ennis (fig. 5.3). The Capuchin habit was the most constricted and had a long, pointed capuce (from which the movement derived its name) attached directly to the tunic.The Franciscan tertiary habit consisted of tunic bound with a cord with a capuce that extended downwards at the chest and back, coming to a point at the waist at front and back .

The Carmelite habit initially consisted of a tunic of undyed wool fastened at the waist by a leather belt. Over this, clerics wore a scapular of the same material, to which the hood was originally attached. Until the late thirteenth century, the most distinctive feature of Carmelite dress was the striped mantle or *cappa*, composed of alternating dark and light strips of cloth that the friars wore over the tunic and scapular. This piebald arrangement led to derision from other religious and, as a result, a white mantle was adopted by the general chapter meeting in Montpellier in 1287. The colour's links with the Virgin Mary strengthened the order's Marian identity and, in England and Ireland, this led to the Carmelites' popular designation as the 'Whitefriars' or the 'Friars of Mary'. By the fifteenth century, the hood had become detached from the scapular and covered much of the chest and upper arms at the front, coming to a point at the back (fig. 5.4).[10]

---

**8** See below, p. 305.    **9** Donatus Mooney records that, as an ascetic act, Friar Eoin O'Duffy (minister provincial, 1580–3) habitually went barefoot, rejecting even the use of sandals. 'Brussels MS 3947', pp 49–50.
**10** Boaga, 'L'abito degli Ordini mendicanti' (2000), pp 369–75; Andrews, *The other friars*, pp 20–1.

5.2 A Conventual Franciscan friar, from Archdall, *Monasticon Hibernicum.*

Following a period of fluidity, the general chapter of the Augustinian friars at Ratisbon in 1290 decreed that the Augustinian habit should consist of a white woollen tunic, scapular and hood worn beneath a black tunic and hood that was bound at the waist with a long leather belt, the end of which hung down between the friar's legs. This combination of colours sometimes led to confusion and conflict with the Dominicans.[11] No images of the Augustinian habit survive from medieval Ireland (fig. 5.5).

The habits themselves or bolts of cloth for making them were routine gifts to friars in England and on the Continent, and this practice also occurred in Ireland.[12] In 1245 and 1246, Henry III granted twenty pounds to purchase habits for the Franciscans in Dublin, Waterford, Drogheda, Cork, Athlone and Kilkenny.[13] For a period of twenty-two years in the fourteenth century, Nicholas Godsun of Athenry (d. 1338) annually presented twenty-four members of the town's Dominican community with an 'English cloak' while his wife gave them habits of 'English cloth'.[14] The residents of the hospital of St John at the Newgate in Dublin wove the cloth for the habits of the city's Franciscan community, which they presented to the friars during their annual visit to the hospital on the feast of St John. In recompense, the friars allowed the inmates to keep one tenth of the cloth they had woven.[15]

An account by the sixteenth-century Scottish Observant Franciscan provincial, Friar John Hay, illustrates how many benefactors perceived the religious habit:

> The dress of the friars was humble and lowly, of the colour of ashes. Indeed, the woollen stuffs for the under and upper tunics were not purchased for gold or silver, but were made by the hand labour of high-born ladies. For these ladies, deeming it to be an act of religion, thought that, as imitators of the saintly women Dorcas and Elizabeth, they were highly honoured if they could complete with their own hands during the year webs of cloth sufficient for the garments of the friars. Thus, there sprang up a holy rivalry among these noble matrons, who vied with each other as to who should be the first in the year to get ready the webs of cloth for the habits of the friars; which, when worn out by the friars, were eagerly sought after by these same ladies and laid aside as cherished relics, to be used as the burial wrappings for the bodies of their deceased children and kinsmen.[16]

---

**11** B. Rano, 'Agostiniani' (2000), pp 378–83; Andrews, *The other friars*, p. 89.  **12** Röhrkasten, *Mendicant houses*, p. 341.  **13** Cotter, *Friars Minor*, p. 55. This amount was later deemed insufficient and increased by five marks.  **14** Coleman, 'Regestum', p. 208.  **15** Archdall, *Monasticon*, p. 205. The inmates also provided the cloth for the habits of the Augustinian canons of St Thomas' Abbey, as well as for the city's University of St Patrick.  **16** J. Hay, 'Chronicle of the Observantine province of Scotland' (1909), vol. ii, p. 179. Trans. at p. 190.

5.3  St Francis, Ennis
friary, Co. Clare.

Though no evidence survives of Irish noblewomen weaving cloth for the friars, there are numerous references in both the Anglo-Irish and Gaelic sources to the friars' benefactors being buried in the habit.[17] The attribution of apotropaic power to the friars' habits was a constant irritant to their critics, as the 1538 outburst of the royal official Thomas Agarde against the Observant Franciscans demonstrated:

> Here as yett the blude of Criste is cleane blottyed owte of al mens herttes, what with that monsttyr, the Byschope of Roome, and his adherenttes, in espechially the false and crafty bludsukkers, the Observauntes, as they wilbe called most hollyeste, soo that ther remaynz more vertu in on of ther cootes and knottyd gyrdylles, than ever was in Criste, and his Paschion.[18]

**17** See above, pp 110–11.   **18** State papers: King Henry the Eighth; part iii: 2, p. 570.

## THE FRIARS AND FOOD

Recent analyses of monastic kitchen accounts in England have shed considerable light on this important aspect of religious life.[19] In Ireland, the only domestic accounts for monasteries that survive are for the Augustinian canons at Holy Trinity Priory, Dublin, and Kells Priory, Co. Kilkenny. Though fragmentary, both sets indicate that, like their colleagues in England, the canons enjoyed a rich diet with a high protein content and consumed significant quantities of imported luxury items such as saffron, pepper, figs and oil.[20] Excavations of English monastic cemeteries have revealed that, relative to the general population, a disproportionate number of monks suffered from diffuse idiopathic skeletal hyperostosis (DISH), a disorder caused by dietary excess and a sedentary lifestyle.[21] Such evidence as is available from Irish friary excavations shows some slight parallels with the English findings.[22] In 1998, twenty-four medieval skeletons were uncovered during excavations of the east walk of the cloister in Ennis. Burial in this location was generally reserved for members of the order, and the lowest stratum of burials in Ennis consisted of uncoffined male burials, presumably those of friars.[23] One skeleton, of an elderly male, showed signs of DISH to an extent that would have affected his mobility and possibly his breathing. The dental remains of these skeletons also showed a lower prevalence of caries and a less severe incidence of dental calculus, which suggests that they enjoyed a better standard of oral hygiene and a more varied diet than their contemporaries.[24]

## FASTING

Although the Irish friars probably enjoyed a better diet than many of the laity, their ascetic regime meant that they also observed a greater number of fasts. Fasting entailed eating one meal per day, often taken at around two o'clock in the afternoon. This consisted of Lenten fare, which excluded meat, eggs, oil, animal fats and dairy products. The extent to which this regime was actually observed is impossible to ascertain but, in principle, both the Dominicans and the

**19** B. Harvey, *Living and dying in medieval England, 1100–1540: the monastic experience* (1993), pp 34–71; M. Threfall-Holmes, *Monks and markets: Durham cathedral priory, 1460–1520* (2005), pp 34–74.   **20** A. Empey, 'The Augustinian priory of Kells' (2007), pp 10–11.   **21** J. Rogers & T. Waldron, 'DISH and the monastic way of life' (2001).   **22** M. Murphy & M. Potterton, 'Investigating living standards in medieval Dublin and its region' (2005), pp 249–50.   **23** Evidence for friars' burials in the east cloister walk also exists for the Franciscan communities at Quin and Sherkin Island. See below, pp 219–20. I am grateful to Anne Lynch for advice on this point.   **24** J. O'Sullivan et al., 'Archaeological excavation of medieval, post-medieval and modern burials at Ennis Friary, Co. Clare' (2003).

5.4  An Augustinian friar, from Archdall, *Monasticon Hibernicum.*

Carmelites fasted from the feast of the Exaltation of the Cross (14 September) until Easter.[25] The Franciscans and Augustinians were bound to fast from the feast of All Saints (1 November) until Christmas and to observe the customary Lenten fast of the church. The Franciscan rule also commended those friars who voluntarily undertook a forty-day fast from the feast of the Epiphany (6 January).[26] In addition to the Friday fast enjoined on all Christians, the friars, like many religious, also fasted on Wednesdays and Saturdays and undertook additional fasts in preparation for certain feastdays of the liturgical calendar. Superiors had the authority both to dispense their subjects from fasting and to impose it as a punishment for delinquent behaviour.

## ABSTINENCE AND MEAT CONSUMPTION

Like all other religious, the mendicants were restricted in their consumption of the flesh of quadrupeds. Unless they were ill, the Dominicans and Carmelites observed perpetual abstinence from eating meat. These restrictions were relaxed in the case of the Irish Dominicans in 1347, when they were permitted to eat meat outside their priories, and for the Carmelite order as a whole in 1432.[27] The dissolution records indicate that some Dominican communities' commitment to perpetual abstinence was more aspirational than real. The Friars Preachers at Athy received quarters of beef each Christmas from two of their tenants, while their *confrères* at Trim also received a quarter of beef as part of their rent income. Ironically, this latter payment fell due on the feast of St Dominic (4 August), suggesting that the friars had swallowed their principles and dined well in honour of their patron.[28] In mitigation, it is clear from other sources that the patronal feastday was one on which religious communities were accustomed to entertain their patrons, friends and benefactors.[29] Renders of meat or livestock formed part of the rents and services due to the other orders as well. The Augustinians in Cork received pigs from their tenant Thomas Conyll, while the Franciscans in Castledermot received a sheep and a kid from their tenants each summer, and a pig in winter. Care MacArte, a tenant of the Augustinians in New Ross, owed the friars a quarter of beef at Christmas as part of his rent.[30] The Franciscan friars at Moyne maintained a warren on a nearby tidal island that supplied them with

**25** Hinnebusch, *History of the Dominican order*, 1, pp 358–60; B. Edwards (ed.), *The rule of St Albert* (1973), p. 87. **26** Esser (ed.), *Opuscula*, pp 229–30; Gutierriez, *The Augustinians in the Middle Ages, 1256–1356*, pp 114–15. **27** Clyn, *Annals*, p. 242. The friars were permitted to eat meat outside the priory. Smet, *The Carmelites*, 1, p. 72. **28** White, *Extents*, pp 308–9. **29** Ó Clabaigh, 'The other Christ', p. 162; 'Brussels MS 3947', p. 94. **30** White, *Extents*, pp 141, 170, 365.

5.5  A Carmelite friar, from Archdall, *Monasticon Hibernicum.*

rabbits. This was an unusual feature, as the right to maintain warrens was a seigneurial prerogative and was normally associated with monastic estates or secular manors.[31]

## DAIRY PRODUCTS

Many mendicant communities owned herds of cows that provided them with milk products. The Dominicans in Athenry maintained a dairy herd to which Lord Thomas de Bermingham donated eighteen milch cows following his son's burial in the priory in 1488. His wife, Anablina, later bequeathed four cows with their calves to the community. Another benefactor of the community, Lord Richard de Burgh (d. 1536), granted sixty cattle along with the services of a cowboy, a cowgirl and a herdsman. He forbade the friars to sell or otherwise dispose of the cattle and ordered that each animal be replaced when it died. He also gave eight horses to the community as well as a full complement of agricultural equipment, including a plough.[32] The Dominicans in Dublin possessed an interest in Helen Hore's meadow that presumably provided fodder for their cattle. In 1503, the Carmelites of Kilcormac undertook to give seventeen cows to John, Theobald and the son of Mortagh O'Mulloy. The description of these as 'beautiful, fat and in calf cows' indicates that they were bred from the friars' dairy herd.[33] In 1506, Pope Julius II permitted the Conventual Franciscans at Killeany on Inis Mór, the largest of the Aran Islands, to keep a herd of cattle and allowed them to eat milk products during Lent.[34]

Dairy products constituted an important part of the friars' diet and were often received from tenants and benefactors or were sought by the friars while questing. Although it is likely that, like other religious, the friars consumed cheese and curds, the surviving Irish sources only mention butter. In Athenry, Lord Thomas de Bermingham gave two ounces, probably of silver, to the friars to purchase butter each autumn, while his wife Anablina included a large vat of butter in the bequests she left to the community.[35] The Carmelites at Drogheda customarily received a portion of butter from each load entering through St John's Gate for sale in the town.[36] The dissoulution records indicate that Conor Mackee paid the Dominicans in Arklow three gallons of butter as part of the rent for his messuage. Their *confrères* at Aghaboe received a gallon of butter from their tenants as part of

**31** 'Brussels MS 3947', p. 51; K. O'Conor, 'Medieval rural settlement in Munster' (2004), pp 237–8; M. Murphy & M. Potterton, *The Dublin region in the Middle Ages* (2010), pp 342–5. **32** Coleman, 'Regestum', pp 217–21; O'Sullivan, *MIDS*, pp 148–9, 155. **33** J.H. Todd (ed.), 'Obits of Kilcormick' (1849), pp 103–4. **34** *MRH*, p. 242. **35** Coleman, 'Regestum', pp 219–20. **36** O'Dwyer, *Irish Carmelites*, p. 13; J. D'Alton, *History of Drogheda* (1863), i, p. 42.

the rent they owed. The Franciscans at Castledermot received a portion of butter from their tenants on every Wednesday between 3 May and 14 September and a dish of butter at Easter.[37]

FISH

Abstinence from flesh meat meant that fish figured prominently in the domestic economy of Irish mendicant communities and provided the friars with one of their principal sources of protein. Consequently, many Irish friaries were located near rivers or sea inlets and possessed weirs and fishing rights that they jealously guarded.[38] The Dominicans in Cork had rights to half the catch from a fishing pool and a salmon weir on the Lee.[39] In 1309 or 1310, a number of people in Athy, including the prior of the monastery of Crutched Friars, were indicted for stealing a net and fish from the Dominican weir there.[40] In 1380, Edmund Mortimer, earl of March, granted the Friars Preachers in Coleraine the right to keep a fishing boat on the Bann and to receive half the fish caught in the Lyn pool on St John's Eve.[41] The Franciscans in Galway were granted fishing rights on the River Corrib in April 1520 by William fitzWilliam de Burgh, and the community was also entitled to a salmon from the city's great weir each Wednesday, Friday and Saturday, in addition to a day's haul every week from each of the twenty eel weirs on the river.[42] The 1540–1 dissolution records contain references to the weirs and fishing rights of the Carmelite house at Leighlinbridge, the Dominican and Augustinian priories at Cork and the Franciscan friaries at Trim and New Ross.[43] Mooney refers to a number of Franciscan fisheries and described how the friars in Donegal were able to catch an immense quantity of fish with one cast of a net from beside the wall of their infirmary. He also noted that the O'Donnell had granted them a fishery to provide them with sustenance during times of fast.[44] In the summer of 2010, a series of fishweirs was recorded on the bed of the River Shannon when water levels dropped (fig. 5.6). The remains consist of a series of drystone V-shaped funnels that directed the fish into the nets or wicker baskets employed by the fisherman. Situated in the townland of Friarsland, 100m to the east of the

---

37 White, *Extents*, pp 170, 334, 373.  38 These are listed and discussed in A.E.J. Went, 'Irish monastic fisheries' (1955).  39 White, *Extents*, p. 139; O'Sullivan, *MIDS*, p. 150.  40 O'Sullivan, *MIDS*, p. 150. 41 O'Sullivan, *MIDS*, p. 151. Went notes that as St John's Eve falls at the peak of the fishing season the friars would have been entitled to several hundred, if not thousands, of fish. 'Irish monastic fisheries', p. 50. 42 M.J. Blake, 'The obituary book of the Franciscan monastery at Galway' (1909–10), p. 229. B. Jennings, 'The abbey of St Francis, Galway' (1947), pp 104, 106. These days were observed as days of fast and abstinence on which the friars would have required a supply of fish.  43 White, *Extents*, pp 135, 139, 140, 307, 364.  44 'Brussels MS 3947', pp 39, 43.

5.6 Fish weir, Meelick, Co. Galway (photograph by Christy Cunniffe).

Franciscan friary at Meelick, Co. Galway, it is quite likely that they once belonged to the medieval Franciscan community there.[45]

Once caught, fish had to be either kept alive or preserved until they were required for consumption. At the Franciscan friary at Rosserrilly and the Dominican house at Tulsk, a series of earthworks may represent fishponds in which fish were stored or bred.[46] The friary kitchen at Rosserrilly contains a fine stone fish tank used to store live fish until they were required for use (fig. 5.7). While fresh fish doubtless constituted a major part of the friars' diet, they also consumed pickled and dried varieties. For a period of twenty years, Sylina Lynch presented the Dominican community at Athenry with 'pipes' or large casks of fish and wine at the beginning of the penitential seasons of Advent and Lent.[47] Salted salmon was among the items of food stolen from the Franciscan friary in Dundalk in 1438.[48] Mooney's account of the use of blessed salt by Friar Bernard MacGrath to perform a miracle at the friary fish weir in Donegal may indicate that the friars there pickled the fish themselves.[49] In coastal and estuarine areas, shellfish formed another important element of the friars' diet. Excavations at the Dominican friary in Limerick in 1975 uncovered substantial quantities of oyster shells in various parts of the complex.[50] Mooney noted the abundance of oysters and other

45 I owe this information to Christy Cunniffe and Donal Boland, maritime archaeologist. 46 K. O'Conor et al., 'Tulsk Abbey' (1996), 67–9. 47 Coleman, 'Regestum', p. 210; O'Sullivan, *MIDS*, p. 173. Fenning notes that such 'pipes' had a capacity of 105 gallons. 48 *FL*, p. 190; D.A. Chart (ed.), *Register of Primate John Swayne* (1935), p. 59. 49 'Brussels MS 3947', p. 43. 50 Shee Twohig, 'Excavations at St

5.7  Fish tank, Rosserrilly friary, Co. Galway.

shellfish on the seashore near the Franciscan friary at Moyne. He also recorded
that after consumption, the shells were burned and formed the strong cement
used to construct the friary buildings.[51]

POULTRY

Although eggs and poultry must have formed a major element of the Irish
mendicant diet, little evidence for this remains in the archaeological or written
record. In Adare, the remains of a three-storey dovecote belonging to the
Augustinian community survive, while the dissolution commissioners' survey of
Dominican possessions at Drogheda in October 1540 recorded 'a close called le
Culverhousse parke' (fig. 5.8).[52] Such dovecotes were normally found on the
demesne lands of manorial or monastic estates where the doves fed on the owners'
grain, rather than that of their neighbours. The relatively small size of the friars'
landholdings may explain why dovecotes were not a widespread feature of their
domestic economy in comparison with the monastic orders.[53] Flocks of hens,

Saviour's Dominican priory' (1995), pp 120, 121, 124, 125.  **51** 'Brussels MS 3947', p. 51.  **52** White,
*Extents*, p. 244. A culverhouse was an alternative name for a dovecote.  **53** For the role of dovecotes in the
domestic economies of Cistercian and Augustinian monasteries, see G. Carville, *The impact of the Cistercians on*

5.8 Dovecote,
Augustinian priory,
Adare, Co. Limerick.

geese and ducks must also have been a familiar sight within the precincts of mendicant houses, but little evidence survives to illustrate this. The tenants of the Franciscans in Kildare each rendered four hens as part of their annual rent, while those of the Dominicans in Athy each owed the community six hens. The Carmelites in Kildare and the Dominicans in Arklow also received a hen from each of their tenants annually.[54]

## AGRICULTURE AND HORTICULTURE

The friars addressed their need for cereals, vegetables, fruit and firewood in a variety of ways. Of these, the quest or begging tour discussed below was the most characteristic. They also exploited their own landholdings and, while these were relatively small, they were sufficient to supply the friars with many of their necessities. Mooney noted that the Franciscans at Moyne did not have to depend

---

*the landscape of Ireland, 1142–1541* (2002), p. 170; A. Hogan, *The priory of Llanthony Prima and Secunda in Ireland: lands, patronage and politics* (2008), pp 185, 187, 199, 213.   **54** White, *Extents*, pp 167, 168, 172, 373.

on their benefactors for meat, fish or vegetables, as they were able to supply these items from their own resources.[55] The agricultural equipment and horses bequeathed to the Athenry Dominicans by Richard de Burgh in 1536 indicates that either the friars or their servants worked the lands themselves. In like manner, the services owed to some friaries by their tenants indicate that they exploited the land by direct labour. The tenants of the Carmelites at Leighlinbridge each owed three 'boondays' or days of compulsory labour and one weeding day to the friars. Tenants of messuages belonging to the Franciscans at Kildare owed their masters eight ploughdays, eight cartdays, eight weeding days and eight reaping days, while the two cottiers each owed two weeding days and two reaping days. The holder of a messuage belonging to the town's Carmelite community owed one weeding day and one reaping day, while the tenants and cottiers of the Dominicans at Aghaboe each owed three boondays and two weeding days.[56]

Wood for cooking, heating and structural repairs came from a variety of sources. In Galway, the Franciscan community customarily received some firewood from each consignment brought for sale to the city.[57] A number of houses possessed small acreages of forest at their dissolution. These included the Franciscan friary at Multyfarnham and the Dominican priories in Kilkenny, Limerick and Mullingar.[58] Occasionally, the friars employed more robust stratagems to procure fuel, as in 1363, when Friar Maurice Hamond, guardian of the Franciscan friary at Cashel, and three of his *confrères* cut down timber belonging to Sir Robert Preston, the lord chief justice, and drove off some of his cattle.[59]

Many friaries possessed orchards, which supplied their communities with fruit. In 1438, 'apples, pears and other fruits' were among the foodstuffs stolen from the Franciscan friary in Dundalk.[60] In Limerick, the orchards of the Dominican and Franciscan communities were contiguous to each other on the King's Island.[61] The 1540–1 dissolution extents record the presence of orchards in the precincts of the Dominican convents in Athy, Cashel, Drogheda, Kilkenny, Mullingar and Trim, the Franciscan friaries at Castledermot, Dundalk, Enniscorthy, Kilcullen, Kilkenny, Limerick, Multyfarnham and Youghal, the Augustinian priory in Cork and the Carmelite houses at Athboy, Drogheda and Dublin.[62] Excavations of the monastic latrine drain at Tintern Abbey, Co. Wexford, indicated that the Cistercian monks there consumed blackberries, raspberries, wild strawberries, figs, prunes, sloes and haws, in addition to apples and pears. It

55 'Brussels MS 3947', p. 51. Mooney makes no reference to growing cereals but refers to the friars' mills. This indicates that they depended on their benefactors for grain.   56 White, *Extents*, pp 135, 166–8, 334. 57 'Brussels MS 3947', p. 55.   58 White, *Extents*, pp 275, 291; O'Sullivan, *MIDS*, p. 147.   59 *FL*, pp 149–50; Archdall, *Monasticon Hibernicum*, p. 651.   60 *FL*, p. 190; D.A. Chart (ed.), *Register of Primate John Swayne* (1935), p. 59.   61 'Brussels MS 3947', p. 62.   62 O'Sullivan, *MIDS*, p. 147; White, *Extents*, pp 121, 138, 140, 170, 173, 198, 210, 244, 246, 247, 266, 275, 308, 334, 374.

is highly likely that the friars supplemented their diets with many of the same fruits and berries.[63]

Although the landholdings and properties of the mendicants in Ireland were in no way comparable to those of the monastic and canonical orders, they did provide a source of income for the friars. The ownership of property sat uneasily with some mendicants, particularly the Franciscans, and Mooney records that whenever the Observants took possession of a Conventual foundation they disposed of any lands or properties that guaranteed them a fixed income.[64]

## THE QUEST AND DONATIONS OF FOOD

The friars' most characteristic economic activity was the quest: the regular begging for alms by designated friars on behalf of their convents.[65] This took place within clearly defined territories or limits, often coextensive with the areas within which the friars were licensed to preach and hear confession. In England, the questing limits of a friary could extend up to twenty or thirty miles from the home base.[66] It is how most people outside of friary towns would have encountered a friar and, though often attacked by their critics, the practice frequently led to an intimate and enduring relationship between the friars and their benefactors over a widespread area.[67] Where the territory to be covered was very large, smaller residences were occasionally constructed for use as bases and the territories themselves divided up into smaller units and entrusted to particular teams of friars. This practice may provide the context for the foundation of some of the smaller Dominican and Carmelite houses in the west of Ireland in the fifteenth century. The Dominicans in Tralee possessed a small property at Dingle that O'Sullivan suggests served as a base for questing and preaching tours in south-west Kerry.[68] Otherwise, the questing friars depended on the support of friends and benefactors for hospitality while on their begging tours.[69]

The object of the quest was to gather non-perishable foodstuffs, particularly grain, and it was most frequently undertaken at harvest time. The Athenry register indicates that the friars' patrons there, beginning with their founder in the thirteenth century, customarily set aside a fixed portion of their harvest for the town's Dominican community. The phrase used to describe this was *redecimare* or to re-tithe, which suggests that this arrangement was additional to

---

**63** S. Geraghty, 'The plant remains' (2010), p. 233.   **64** 'Brussels MS 3947', p. 54. For a summary of Dominican landholdings, see O'Flynn, *Irish Dominicans*, pp 26–39, 315–20; O'Sullivan, *MIDS*, pp 143–9. **65** For earlier treatments of this subject, see Cotter, *Friars Minor*, pp 52–4; Ó Clabaigh, *Franciscans*, pp 119–20; O'Sullivan, *MIDS*, pp 163–9.   **66** M. Robson, 'The Greyfriars' itinerant ministry inside their limitatio' (2008), p. 9.   **67** A. Williams, 'The "limitour" of Chaucer's time and his "limitacioun"' (1960). **68** O'Sullivan, *MIDS*, p. 167.   **69** Robson, 'Greyfriars' itinerant ministry', p. 18.

the tithe that benefactors were obliged to pay to the parochial clergy.[70] Such multiple tithing arrangements were common on the Continent and often led to disputes over the complex division of the sheaves.[71] The Dominican communities at Cloonameehan, Rathfran, Roscommon, Tralee, Tulsk and Urlar also benefited from similar allocations of grain at harvest time.[72]

In addition to ensuring a regular corn supply, these tithing arrangements consolidated the relationships between the friars and their benefactors, with successive generations often confirming the grants made to the friars by their ancestors. On his accession as Baron Athenry, Richard de Bermingham (d. 1322) confirmed the tithes granted to the Athenry convent by his father and grandfather, as did his own son and grandson in their turn.[73] Benefactors of lower social standing also confirmed grants of grain made by their ancestors. In addition to entertaining two friars each day at his table, William Styvyn granted the Athenry community a tithe of his harvest. His son, William junior, not only confirmed his father's grant but carted the corn to the community's barn when the friars were otherwise engaged.[74] Incidental evidence for questing by the Donegal Franciscans occurs *c.*1600, when they declined Hugh O'Donnell's offer to provide all their needs, preferring to continue the quest instead. The Donegal community also relied on lay representatives with whom benefactors deposited their alms[75] The questing limits of the Dominican priory in Athy extended to the surrounding towns of Baltinglass, Stradbally, Kilcullen and Dunlavin.[76]

The right to quest was a frequent cause of contention with the secular clergy and other religious, and much of the evidence for the practice in Ireland comes from the ensuing disputes.[77] In 1297, in the course of a bitter dispute between the archbishop and archdeacon of Tuam on one side and the Dominicans of Athenry and the Franciscans of Claregalway on the other, the friars' representatives claimed that the archdeacon had forbidden the faithful to give them food. The archbishop denied responsibility, expressed his affection for the friars and undertook to have the archdeacon withdraw any proclamations injurious to them.[78] In 1320, the provincial constitutions of Archbishop Alexander de Bicknor of Dublin condemned questors who deceived simple people in their preaching and forbade them to quest without episcopal licence.[79] These injunctions were repeated

---

70 Coleman, 'Regestum', pp 204, 205, 208, 209, 210, 212.   71 See, for example, C. Harline & E. Put, *A bishop's tale: Mathias Hovius among his flock in seventeenth-century Flanders* (2000), pp 139–42. 72 O'Sullivan, *MIDS*, pp 166–7.   73 Coleman, 'Regestum', pp 205–6.   74 Ibid., p. 209.   75 'Brussels MS 3947', pp 39–40, 43.   76 H. Fenning OP, *Dominicans of Athy, 1257–2007* (2007), pp 3, 8.   77 See below, pp 143–68.   78 James Mills, *Calendar of the justiciary rolls or proceedings in the court of the justiciar of Ireland, 1295–1303* (Dublin, 1905), pp 108–9, 114–15. The archbishop in question was William de Bermingham, otherwise recorded as a benefactor and friend of the Athenry friars. See above, pp 94–5. 79 G. Bray (ed.), *Records of convocation XVI: Ireland, 1101–1690* (2006), p. 155.

by his successor, Archbishop Thomas Minot, in the provincial constitutions he issued in Lent 1367.[80] In August 1453, the provincial synod of Cashel decreed that friars were to confine themselves to their traditional limits when begging, and forbade them to quest at those times when the secular clergy collected their dues. The synod also forbade questors to operate without episcopal licence, indicating that this was a recurrent abuse.[81] The only surviving Irish examples of such licences occur in the register of Primate Octavian de Palatio of Armagh. In March 1489, he permitted the Franciscan friar Innocent de Castrucio de Monte Regali to seek alms for his convent in Paris, while in 1496 he licensed Friar Cornelius Gerald, the Dominican prior of Drogheda, to quest throughout the diocese for funds to renovate the priory.[82] Occasionally the friars approached the secular authorities over the right to quest: in 1375, William of Windsor, governor of Ireland, granted permission to the guardian and friars of Ennis to quest for food within the terrritory of the English Pale.[83]

The right to quest occasionally caused disputes between various convents within the same order. In September 1431, the prior of the Augustinian community at Ballinrobe was empowered by the prior general of the order to arrest and imprison friars from other Augustinian houses who quested within the Ballinrobe limit.[84] In 1491, the Franciscan friars at Askeaton secured a judgment from the Conventual Franciscan minister general, Francis 'Samson' Nanni, against their *confrères* in Ennis. The boundaries of their respective questing areas had traditionally been set mid-way between the two houses, but the Ennis friars had hindered the Askeaton questors in their activities. The minister general confirmed the rights of the Askeaton community and threatened the Ennis friars with excommunication if they did not accept the judgment. He also threatened the Franciscan minister provincial and the other officials of the Irish province with deprivation of office and excommunication if they did not uphold his ruling.[85] The fact that both these disputes had to be resolved at the highest level of their respective orders suggests that they were long-running and divisive. Similar disputes between convents were probably addressed by the local superiors.

In addition to what they gathered on the quest, the friars also received grain, malt, bread and beer as gifts and rents from their benefactors and tenants. John le Decer, mayor of Dublin, imported three shiploads of corn from France at a time of great shortage in Ireland. He presented one to the garrison of Dublin Castle, another he reserved for himself, while the third was divided between the city's

**80** Ibid., pp 176–7. **81** Ibid., pp 255–6. **82** M. Sughi (ed.), *Registrum Octaviani*, ii, nos 416, 475, 517, 518, 519. Friar Innocent was also permitted to admit members into the confraternity of SS Francis and Anthony. **83** *FL*, pp 157–8. **84** Martin, 'Irish material', p. 86, no. 51. **85** G. Parisciani, *Regesta Ordinis Fratrum Minorum Conventualium, 1484–1494* (1989), p. 197, no. 1529.

Dominican and Augustinian convents.[86] In 1404, the prior of the Carmelites in Kinsale was one of three inhabitants permitted to import grain into the town.[87] Conor Mackee, who rented a property from the Dominicans in Arklow, paid them six cakes as part of his rent. The Augustinians in New Ross received six cakes and six gallons of beer from their tenant Care MacArte. In Kildare, the Franciscans' tenants paid them twenty-four cakes and twenty-four gallons of beer as part of their rent. Some communities also brewed their own beer. The Franciscans at Multyfarnham had their own brewhouse, while in 1473 Jonet Cristor of Glasnevin bequeathed eight measures of wheat and ten measures of malt to the four houses of friars in Dublin.[88]

Wine also played an important role in the friars' domestic economy as it was necessary for the celebration of the Eucharist, and benefactors took great care to ensure an adequate supply for the liturgy.[89] From the early thirteenth century, wine was imported to Ireland from the Bordeaux area, along with distinctive green glazed jugs from the Saintonge region. The presence of Saintonge pottery provides a clear indication of the wine trade with France, and fragments of these jugs are found on almost all Anglo-Irish sites in Ireland, including the Dominican friaries in Cork and Limerick.[90] Miler de Bermingham and his son William, archbishop of Tuam, donated casks of wine to the Dominicans in Athenry, as did Wylln Wallys, a burgess of the town. In the fifteenth century, Sylina Lynch presented them with a cask of wine at the beginning of Advent and Lent for a period of twenty years and wine and other drinks were among the comestibles presented by Lord Thomas de Bermingham and his wife Anablina de Burgh on the occasion of the burial of their son John in 1488.[91]

The consumption of wine was not solely a liturgical or religious phenomenon: in 1451, the friary in Cavan burned down as a result of a mishap with a candle on the part of Friar Ua Mothlain, 'he being inebriate after drinking wine'.[92]

## HOSTING THE FRIARS

Benefactors also provided support for the friars by entertaining them in their own households, hosting them when travelling or by providing food for each orders' chapter meetings. The right to entertain religious at table was regarded as an act of charity from which the benefactor derived spiritual benefit, and aristocrats

**86** Archdall, *Monasticon Hibernicum*, p. 206; O'Sullivan, *MIDS*, p. 173.   **87** E. Tresham (ed.), *Rotulorum patentium et clausorum cancellariae Hiberniae calendarium* (1828), p. 179. I owe this reference to Bernadette Williams.   **88** *FL*, p. 219; Berry, *Register*, p. 56.   **89** See above, p. 101.   **90** C. McCutcheon, 'Pottery' (1995), pp 85–7; C. McCutcheon, 'Pottery' (1996), p. 68.   **91** Coleman, 'Regestum', pp 204, 205, 210, 219.   **92** *AU*, iii, pp 170–3.

frequently sought the privilege from the papacy in the fourteenth and fifteenth centuries. In 1343, Maurice Fitzgerald, son of Maurice, first earl of Desmond, petitioned Pope Clement IV for permission for mendicant and non-mendicant religious to eat meat when they dined at his court.[93] The practice was not just confined to the nobility: in the early fourteenth century, John Le Decer, mayor of Dublin, entertained the city's Dominican community at his table each Friday.[94] The burgesses of Athenry were particularly hospitable to their local Friars Preachers: Nicholas Godsun (d. 1338) daily entertained two friars and a priest at his table, while his wife fed four Dominicans each day during Lent. Likewise, Wylln Wallys (d. 1344) and William Stywyn both entertained two friars at table each day. A century later, Walter Blake (d. 1452) was accustomed to entertain one friar each day.[95]

The friars also benefited from the hospitality shown them by benefactors whenever they were on a journey. The accounts of the Augustinian canons of Holy Trinity priory, Dublin, record a payment for oysters and salmon to entertain Dominicans from Arklow in the prior's chamber on Monday of the first week of Lent, 1338.[96] Edmund Lynch (d. 1462) accommodated the Dominicans of Athenry in his household whenever they came to Galway on business, while the kindness shown to them by the Galway widow Margaret Lynch earned her the title 'the hostess of the friars'.[97] In 1567, a group of Franciscans from Moyne who sought hospitality from Sir Roger O'Shaughnessy at Ardamullivan Castle near Gort inadvertently occasioned the arrest of their distinguished travelling companion, Richard Creagh, the Limerick-born archbishop of Armagh.[98]

In return for the hospitality they received, the friars were expected to edify their table companions with some spiritual table talk or moral exhortation. Writing in 1586, John Hay, the exiled provincial of the Scottish Franciscans, vividly portrayed what must also have been a common occurrence in Ireland:

> If, on occasion, the friars halted at the houses or castles of the nobles to preach, they were held in such veneration that the earl or baron would himself bring a basin of water for the friar to wash his hands, and the lady, his wife, would in like manner bathe his feet. Before any dishes were laid for the meal, the signal was given by the chapel bell, and the whole

**93** W.H. Bliss, *Calendar of the entries in the papal registers relating to Great Britain and Ireland: petitions to the pope, vol. I: AD1342–1419* (1896), p. 15.   **94** Archdall, *Monasticon Hibernicum*, p. 206.   **95** Coleman, 'Regestum', pp 206, 208, 209, 210.   **96** J. Mills, *Account roll of the priory of the Holy Trinity, Dublin, 1337–1346* (1891), p. 10. The friars may have been conducting a Lenten preaching mission in Dublin. **97** Ibid., pp 210, 211.   **98** C. Lennon, *Archbishop Richard Creagh of Armagh, 1523–1586* (2000), p. 88.

household assembled to receive the bread of life from one of the friars. If any great noble or even bishop happened to be at the castle on a friendly visit, that honour was none the less proffered and paid to the despisers of the world against their will. However unwilling to do so, they were compelled to accept the first place at the tables of the nobles, where, instead of shafts of mirth producing wit, the tales of the Old and the New Testament, or the history of well-known holy fathers, suitable for the time, place and company, were narrated by the senior friar, and often drew tears from those seated around.

Why enlarge further? So dear to all was the companionship of the friars, that they thought they had entertained or accompanied an angel of the Lord if they had a friar as their guest or accompanied one on his way.[99]

The experience of Friar Bernard MacGrath (d. 1546), a saintly member of the Donegal Franciscan community, corroborates Hay's account. He was invited to preach before Gerald Fitzgerald, ninth earl of Kildare and lord deputy of Ireland,

The lord deputy then invited him to a banquet laid for the noblemen who accompanied him, and placed him in the seat of honour next to himself. While a variety of subjects was being discussed by the guests, Fr Bernard remained silent. At length, the earl requested him to tell them something of the perfections, of the privileges, and the eminent virtues of our Holy Father St Francis. He replied, 'It seems to me sufficient to call to your attention to what you witness in this hall even now. Here I am, a man of little account, one of the common people and unworthy at that, clad in a mean habit, and yet I am preferred at your table to so many lords of rank and nobility. What other proof do you need of the prerogatives which our Holy Father St Francis enjoys in the heavenly court than to see his unworthy son honoured as he is here in the court of the lord deputy?'[1]

Whereas the friars viewed such honours as a providential reward for a life of renunciation and as a form of pastoral ministry, their critics were less indulgent. The Luttrell Psalter, produced *c.*1320–40 for Sir Geoffrey Luttrell, has a marginal image of two rather glum-faced Dominicans and a suitably edified host, but other sources suggest that the Irish friars' table-fellowship was not always so restrained (pl. 2). The copy of *Piers Plowman* illustrated in Dublin in 1427 and contained in Bodleian MS Douce 104 contains a marginal drawing depicting an obese Dominican at table. One of the woodcuts contained in John Derricke's 1581

---

**99** Moir Bryce, *Scottish Grey Friars*, ii, p. 190.   **1** 'Brussels MS 3947', p. 46. Translation in *The Franciscan*

5.9 John Derricke, *Image of Ireland* (1581), 'The MacSweeney Fanad feasting'. Friar Smellfeast (B) is depicted preaching to the assembly and then occupying the place of honour at the table.

work an *Image of Ireland*, depicts the MacSweeney Fanad feasting. Prominent in the gathering is the satirically named Friar Smellfeast, who is depicted blessing the meal and occupying the place of honour at table. The whole company is entertained by a harper, rhymer and a pair of professional farters, and the friar used the occasion to incite the MacSweeney to rebel against the crown (fig. 5.9). The MacSweeneys had founded the Carmelite friary at Rathmullan in 1516 and were notable benefactors of the Franciscans in Donegal, and it is possible that Friar Smellfeast represented a member of one of these communities.

The regular chapter meetings of each order constituted another occasion on which benefactors provided for the material needs of the friars. These were often very large assemblies and outstripped the friars' capacity to cater for themselves. Consequently, throughout Europe, royalty, aristocrats, bishops and other benefactors vied to supply the friars' needs.[2] In return, they received a remembrance in the prayers and Masses offered by the assembled delegates.[3] The earliest surviving record of such support in Ireland occurs in 1306, when the Cork merchant John de Wynchedon bequeathed twenty shillings to the Augustinian friars and two marks each to the Franciscan and Dominican orders to provide sustenance for their chapter meetings in Ireland.[4] The Athenry register records that 280 friars attended the chapter there in 1482, while 360 were present at the chapter held there in 1524. At the 1482 chapter, Thomas de Bermingham and his

*Tertiary* 5 (1894), 165–6.   **2** Röhrkasten, *Mendicant houses*, pp 260–1, 343, 349.   **3** Hinnebusch, *History of the Dominican order*, 1, pp 183–4.   **4** O'Sullivan (ed.), 'Testament of John de Wynchedon, 1306' (1956), 77.

wife Anablina, entertained the entire body twice in one day. At another chapter held in 1491, they again fed the capitular delegates on two occasions and presented twenty pence to the priors of all the Irish houses. Their son and heir, Miler de Bermingham, and his wife, Honora de Burgh, contributed a large sum to defray the expenses of the 1524 chapter and entertained the friar-delegates twice in one day, 'with great solemnity'.[5] The O'Donnell showed similar generosity to the Franciscan provincial chapter meeting at Donegal in 1530, and 'provided for it entirely, from first to last, with great expense and magnificent honorific bounty'.[6] In addition to enjoying the spiritual suffrages of the chapter delegates, rulers were also not above trying to enlist the authority of the chapter for their own ends: in 1532, the marital difficulties of Henry VIII were one of the items on the agenda of the Carmelite general chapter meeting in Padua.[7]

A combination of lavish hospitality, local politics and a provincial chapter may provide the context for the orgy of drunken rioting that convulsed the Franciscans in Roscrea in 1477. Knowledge of the event comes from Lambeth Palace library MS 46, a copy of the *Clementinae*, a canon law text transcribed in 1477 by Rodericus O'Lachtnain, an Augustinian canon of Lorrha, Co. Tipperary. The colophon to the work records that is was completed in the year that the Friars Minor had gathered at Roscrea and joined forces with Eugene O'Carroll, William O'Carroll and MacGillapoil to destroy the castle of John O'Carroll along with the church of St Cronan and their own friary. While it is not stated that this was a chapter meeting, it is clear that a large number of friars were present at the gathering, including the minister provincial. An oblique indication of the contents of the friars' buttery is found in the account's reference to whiskey, wine, mead and 'beer without measure' being among the items stolen by the rioters.[8]

The widespread extent of the friars' patronage was a measure of the regard in which they were held by their contemporaries. It provided them with the necessities of life and the material security to enable them to pursue their vocations and ministry. It also brought them into close contact with the aristocratic and mercantile elites of late medieval Ireland. While this was a welcome development for the friars, it became a major contributing factor to the vehement hostility that developed between the mendicants and their clerical critics.

5 Coleman, 'Regestum', pp 218–20; O'Sullivan, *MIDS*, pp 175–6.  6 *Ann. Conn.*, p. 675.  7 G. Wessels, *Acta Capitulorum Generalium* (1912), pp 384, 398–9.  8 M. Rhode James & C. Jenkins, *A descriptive catalogue of the manuscripts in the library of Lambeth Palace* (1937), p. 63.

# CHAPTER 6

# The friars and their critics

*At this time, a great controversy began between Master Richard Fitzralph, archbishop of Armagh, and the four mendicant orders, but the friars at length prevailed and silence was imposed on Armagh by the pope.*[1]

The Fourth Lateran Council (1215) outlined a programme of pastoral practice and renewal that definitively shaped medieval and early modern Catholicism.[2] The Dominicans and Franciscans were swiftly coopted to implement its pastoral programme, and successive popes granted wide-ranging privileges and exemptions to enable them to do so more effectively.[3] Although highly effective as pastoral agents, the very success of the friars was an implied criticism of the secular clergy who, in Ireland as elsewhere, were usually less educated than the mendicants. In consequence, the friars encountered resentment from certain sections of the clerical and monastic establishments who opposed the newcomers' usurpation of their traditional positions.[4]

The friars' opponents maintained that the mendicants' pastoral activity damaged the spiritual relationship between a priest and his parishioners.[5] Here, the critics invoked Lateran IV as central to their argument was the interpretation of the phrase *proprio sacerdoti* ('to one's own priest') in the conciliar canon *Omnis utriusque sexus fidelis*.[6] This enjoined annual confession and reception of communion on all the faithful and the friars' critics insisted that the right to administer these sacraments pertained to secular clergy as holders of the *cura animarum* – the care of souls. The many papal privileges granted to the mendicants raised the question of papal competence to grant dispensations from conciliar

---

**1** Pembridge, *Chronicle*, p. 393.   **2** N. Tanner, 'The Middle Ages: pastoral care – the Fourth Lateran Council of 1215' (1999).   **3** *Il papato duecentesco e gli ordini mendicanti*, SISF, 25 (1998).   **4** This controversy has generated a vast literature. What follows draws on H. Lippens, 'Le droit nouveau des mendiants en conflit avec le droit coutumier du clergé séculier du concile de Vienne à celui de Trente' (1954); C.M. Erickson, 'The fourteenth-century Franciscans and their critics', *Franciscan Studies*, 13 (1975); 14 (1976); C.H. Lawrence, *The friars* (1994), pp 152–65; R.N. Swanson, 'The mendicant problem in the later Middle Ages' (1999).   **5** For the ecclesiological and legal backgrounds to the dispute, see Y. Congar, 'Aspects ecclésiologiques de la querelle Mendiants-Séculiers' (1961); M.J. Haren, 'Friars as confessors: the canonist background to the fourteenth-century controversy' (1984).   **6** N.P. Tanner (ed.), *Decrees of the Ecumenical Councils* (1990), i, p. 245.

decrees, a particularly sensitive issue in the later Middle Ages, when the Western Schism pitted popes and church councils against each other.

Critics, lay and clerical, were untiring in exposing the friars' shortcomings: the facility with which they granted absolution, their predilection for ministering to the rich, the manner in which their preaching undermined clerical authority and how their exemption from episcopal oversight made them arrogant and incorrigible. The presence of the friars in the universities brought them into contact and conflict with the elite cadre of the secular clergy: the university masters. Though initially welcomed to the nascent institutions, resentment soon emerged as the friars attracted the most able students to their lectures and to their ranks, thereby depriving the secular masters of both income and recruits. The mendicants' reluctance to side with the secular masters in defence of university rights and privileges eventually provided the flashpoint from which the dispute erupted at the University of Paris in 1253. The dispute was invested with a greater degree of intensity as it occurred against the background of intense apocalypticism caused by the circulation of the prophecies of the late twelfth-century Cistercian abbot, Joachim of Fiore (d. 1202).[7] Both the mendicants and their enemies assimilated his doctrine to demonstrate that the end was nigh and that Antichrist was at hand in the form of their opponents.

Although the theological and legal aspects of the dispute were fought out in the universities, the law courts and the papal curia, they found more mundane expression at parochial level. The visit of a friar questing for alms, the penchant for burial in the friars' habit or in a friary cemetery and the privileges claimed by mendicant preachers and confessors were all to the detriment of the parish priest, who frequently found both his authority and his income diminished by the activities of the mendicants.

In this chapter, the key elements of the debate as it developed in Paris in the mid-thirteenth century are first presented, before its early manifestations in Ireland are examined. The anti-mendicant campaigns of four prominent Anglo-Irish clerics active between 1350 and 1448 are then explored. In conclusion, the evidence for popular anti-mendicant sentiment in Ireland and an analysis of the manner in which the Irish friars defended their rights are also presented.

## PARIS: THE DISPUTE BEGINS

In March 1253, tension between the secular clergy and the friars erupted at the University of Paris.[8] The flashpoint was an assault on four of the university's

---

**7** M. Reeves, *The influence of prophecy in the later Middle Ages: a study of Joachism* (1969).  **8** D. Douie,

students by members of the city's constabulary, during which a student died. Outraged, the university masters called a strike, which the friars refused to support, and the mendicant schools remained open. The friars' action exacerbated a fraught situation as the secular masters of theology already resented the friars' occupancy of three of the twelve magisterial chairs in the theology faculty. In 1252, the faculty had decreed that no candidate for the *magisterium* in theology could qualify unless he had attended one of the university's approved colleges or schools. It also banned any religious order from possessing more than one chair in theology. This decision targeted the Dominicans who, since 1231, had held two of the chairs.[9] They refused to surrender their second chair and consequently were expelled from the faculty.

Against this background, the friars' refusal to respect the strike in 1253 was particularly provocative and led to the excommunication and expulsion of the three mendicant masters of the theology faculty. The friars responded by appealing to the king and the pope, and in July 1253 Pope Innocent IV overturned the decree of excommunication and instructed that the expelled masters be reinstated. He also ordered that the friars and the secular masters send delegates to the papal curia for arbitration of the substantive issues. The Burgundian theologian, William of St Amour, led the university delegation and, in addition to material relating to the dispute, also presented the curia with excerpts from the *Introduction to the Eternal Gospel* by the Franciscan friar, Gerard of Borgo San Donnino, which he and his Parisian colleagues considered heretical. This work drew heavily on the writings of Joachim of Fiore and predicted the imminent emergence of a third age of the church, the age of the Holy Spirit, in which the Eternal Gospel would be preached by new religious orders, the mendicants. The introduction of this apocalyptic element raised the stakes and enabled the secular masters to focus on the friars' orthodoxy and thereby challenge their very right to exist.

William and the secular masters won a significant victory on 21 November 1254, when Innocent IV issued the bull *Etsi animarum*, which curtailed the mendicants' privileges. The friars were ordered to seek the permission of the parish priest before hearing confessions, they had to pay him one quarter of any offerings resulting from burials in their cemeteries and they could not celebrate Mass in their churches at the same time as it was celebrated in the parish church.[10] This arrangement proved short-lived as Pope Innocent died in December 1254 and his successor, Alexander IV, a former cardinal protector of the Franciscans, swiftly annulled his predecessor's ruling and supported the friars in their dispute with the

*The conflict between the seculars and the mendicants at the University of Paris in the thirteenth century* (1954); P.R. Szittya, *The antifraternal tradition in medieval literature* (1986), pp 11–18; Lawrence, *Friars*, pp 127–65. **9** A third chair was held by the Franciscans. **10** *BF*, v, pp 259–61, 281.

University of Paris, where they were finally readmitted to membership in October 1257.[11]

The publication of William of St Amour's *De periculis novissimorum temporum* ('On the perils of the end times') in early 1256 marked an important development in the debate.[12] In it, he presented thirty-nine scriptural signs to identify the false prophets and pseudo-preachers whose emergence would herald the coming of the Antichrist. While the friars were not explicitly identified as such, the implication was clear and, even though condemned in October 1257, the text was 'destined to become the most influential antifraternal work of the next two centuries',[13] providing the exegetical apparatus for the friars' subsequent critics.

Through the influence of the poets Rutebeuf and Jean de Meun, the anti-mendicant doctrine of William of St Amour quickly passed into French vernacular poetry, eliciting similar responses from the friars' supporters and opening the debate to a much wider audience.[14] Between 1254 and 1275, Rutebeuf composed more than a dozen poems attacking the friars, championing the cause of the secular clergy and invoking William of St Amour as his authority. In the 1270s, Jean de Meun incorporated a two-thousand-line condemnation of the friars in the allegorical love epic *Le roman de la rose*. In it, the allegorical figure *Faus Semblant* was presented as a hypocritical, lecherous mendicant, embodying many of the attributes of the false prophets found in *De periculis*.

The friars responded to the assault on their lifestyle by appointing some of their most able members as their defenders. In 1256, the Franciscan Thomas of York attempted a systematic refutation of *De periculiis* in his *Manus qui contra Omnipotentem tenditur* (1256). St Thomas Aquinas, for the Dominicans, responded with the *Opus contra impugnantes Dei cultum* (1256) and the *Contra retrahentes a religionis ingressu* (1270). The most persuasive defence came from the pen of St Bonaventure who, as master of the Franciscan *studium* in Paris since 1253, had been intensely involved in the dispute since its beginning.[15] Bonaventure became minister general of the Franciscans in 1257 and faced opposition on two fronts. In addition to defending the friars from external assault, he also had to contend with divisions among the Friars Minor themselves. These centred on observance of the vow of poverty, the precise status of St Francis' Testament and on whether or not the pope could dispense from the precepts of the Franciscan rule. Since the 1240s, the growing influence of groups of zealots known as the Spirituals or *Fraticelli* also threatened the order's unity and their extreme

11 Thomas of Eccleston records that, after promulgating *Etsi animarum*, Innocent IV lost the use of his voice and died more 'miserably than any other man'. Eccleston, *De Adventu*, pp 94–6. 12 William of Saint-Amour, *De periculis novissimorum temporum*, ed. G. Geltner (2007). 13 Szittya, *Antifraternal tradition*, p. 17. 14 Ibid., pp 183–90. 15 J.G. Bougerol, 'Saint Bonaventure et la défence de la vie évangélique de 1252 au Concile de Lyons' (1974).

Joachitism left it open to further accusations of heresy.[16] Not surprisingly, a highly apologetic tone informs all of Bonaventure's writings on mendicant life and evangelical poverty, particularly his classic exposition, the *Apologia pauperum*.[17] In this treatise, Bonaventure further developed the theme of evangelical poverty as a perfect form of Christian discipleship that he had outlined in some of his earlier works. The position he adopted provided the basis for the defence of mendicancy embodied in the second authoritative pronouncement on the Franciscan rule, the bull *Exiit qui seminat* of Pope Nicholas III (1279).[18] With this, the Franciscans were given definitive papal approbation, the doctrine of evangelical poverty was canonically established and their critics, in theory, were silenced.

As noted in chapter one, the dispute over the status of the friars flared up at the Second Council of Lyon in 1274. The council attempted to resolve the conflict with the decree *Religionum diversitatem* that reiterated the prohibition on new religious orders enacted by the Fourth Lateran Council in 1215.[19] While this addressed some of the grievances of the secular clergy, the substantive issues of the friars' right to exist and their extensive pastoral privileges went unchallenged. In 1281, with the bull *Ad fructus uberes*, Pope Martin IV permitted the mendicants to perform pastoral work anywhere without the permission of the local clergy.[20] This was greeted with outrage in France, where various synods instructed the secular clergy to uphold the provisions of *Omnis utriusque sexus* and insist that the obligatory annual confession should be made to the parish priest. Appeals to have the provisions of *Ad fructus uberes* annulled led Pope Nicholas IV to establish a papal commission headed by Cardinals Gerard of Santa Sabina and Benedict Gaetani. The legates convened an assembly in Paris in November 1290 that dismissed the objections of the bishops and the university masters. After a further decade of disputes, Cardinal Gaetani, elected pope as Boniface VIII in 1294, came to an uneasy compromise solution with the bull *Super cathedram*, promulgated in 1300. This instructed that the friars could only preach in parishes with the permission of the local priest, that friar-confessors had to be licensed by the diocesan bishop, and that a quarter of all burial offerings made to the friars had to be given to the deceased's parish priest.[21] Although *Super cathedram* attempted to redress the balance between the traditional rights of the secular clergy and the friars' privileges, it failed to resolve the most important issue: the definition of *proprius sacerdos* in *Omnis utruisque sexus*. It was to this point that all the friars' subsequent critics would return.

---

**16** D. Burr, *The spiritual Franciscans: from protest to persecution in the century after St Francis* (2001). **17** St Bonaventure, *Doctoris seraphici Sancti Bonaventurae: opera omnia*, viii (1898), pp 233–330. **18** *BF*, iii, pp 404–16. **19** Tanner, *Decrees*, i, pp 242, 326–7. **20** *BF*, iii, p. 480. **21** *BF*, iv, pp 498–500.

During the council of Vienne in 1311, the Dominican friar Hervé Nedelec advanced the proposition that the pope, as *proprius sacerdos* of every Christian, could delegate the power of absolution to whomever he wished. The Parisian theologian John of Pouilly strenuously rejected this proposition in lectures delivered in Paris in 1312 and again at a church council in Senlis in 1313. His attacks provoked a reaction from the mendicants who, in 1318, cited thirteen of his propositions as heretical. Later reduced to three, these were condemned in 1321 by Pope John XXII in the bull *Vas electionis*.[22] The propositions condemned were that confessions made to a friar had to be repeated to the penitent's parish priest and that the pope could dispense neither from the obligation of annual confession to the parish priest nor from the obligation of repeating that confession if already made to a friar. Although John of Pouilly retracted his opinions, they remained influential throughout the fourteenth and fifteenth centuries and were subsequently revived by later participants in the debate, including the friars' Anglo-Irish critics, discussed below. Although neither decree definitively resolved the conflict, *Super cathedram* and *Vas electionis* became the touchstone texts of the controversy and were frequently invoked and reissued whenever the dispute flared up.

### THE DISPUTE IN IRELAND

Although there is no evidence of any Irish involvement in the theoretical aspects of the anti-fraternal conflict before the middle of the fourteenth century, it is clear that some members of the Irish Franciscan province were aware of the order's internal difficulties in the late thirteenth and early fourteenth centuries. TCD MS 347 contains two apocalyptic texts attributed to Joachim of Fiore. The first of these foretold the coming of the Antichrist and various political and ecclesial events that would take place in 1250.[23] The second text is unique to TCD MS 347 and cited a pseudo-Joachimist work, the *Super Hieremiam prophetam*. It discussed the three ages of the world and predicted the coming of two orders of spiritual men in the church who would oppose Antichrist. One would be an order of preachers in the spirit of Elijah, the other would be hermits in the spirit of Moses.[24]

---

22 *BF*, v, pp 208–9.   23 TCD MS 347, fos 388v–389; Colker, *Latin MSS*, i, p. 738. The text is edited by Reeves, *Influence of prophecy*, p. 50. See also Cotter, *Friars Minor*, p. 73.   24 TCD MS 347, fos 388v–389; Colker, *Latin MSS*, i, p. 738. Reeves, *Influence of prophecy*, p. 527.

The stigmata of St Francis gave him a unique apocalyptic significance in medieval hagiography and rendered the order's internal disputes over poverty particularly divisive.[25] Attempts to mitigate it were forcefully resisted and rejected as the work of Antichrist by the rigorists. The English friars were noted for their commitment to an austere lifestyle and this was also a feature of the early Irish province. At the general chapter of the order in Genoa in 1251 or 1252, the Irish minister provincial, John of Kethene, along with his English counterpart, fought vigorously to rescind the relaxations in the observance of poverty permitted in 1245 by Innocent IV in the bull *Ordinem vestrum*.[26]

An excerpt from chapter eight of Bonaventure's life of St Francis – the *Legenda maior* – in BL MS Harley 913 indicates unease with standards of observance on the part of at least one Irish Franciscan. The text relates how Francis, disturbed by the scandalous behaviour of some of the friars, prayed to God for them. He received assurance that it was God himself who was the order's chief protector and shepherd. While this reference is indicative of a friar with what Neil Cartlidge terms a 'Franciscan conscience', the Spirituals and their programme otherwise received little or no support in the Irish province.[27] In 1311, the Annals of Innisfallen condemned them and their leader Peter of John Olivi:

> There arose at this time in the order of the Friars Minor a dangerous sect, the members of which were called the Sarabaites. They wished to deviate from the common rule of the order, and desired (they claimed) to sweat under the rigours of sterner life. Under the guise of religious scruple and false piety, they spread the poison of their devilish ingenuity and dishonestly placed themselves, their sect and their erroneous doctrine under the immediate protection of the Holy See and of certain members of the [papal] curia who supported them. On this account, the Community of the Order appealed, not unadvisedly, from the aforesaid supporters and the unjust auditors (who had been appointed from among them) to the pope and the said council, requesting nonetheless that in the meantime the pernicious doctrine of the others, that enunciated by Friar Peter John, be wholly checked lest from the deadly draught the Lord's flock contract the disease of the erroneous leprosy.[28]

The dispute between the mendicants and the University of Paris exacerbated the tensions between the papacy and the French church, which claimed a privileged

**25** C. Ó Clabaigh, 'The other Christ: the cult of St Francis of Assisi in late medieval Ireland' (2006), pp 149, 153–9. **26** Eccleston, *De Adventu*, p. 42. **27** N. Cartlidge, 'Festivity, order and community in fourteenth-century Ireland: the composition and context of BL MS Harley 913' (2003), p. 38. **28** S. Mac Airt (ed.), *Annals of Inisfallen* (1951), p. 411.

quasi-independent relationship to papal authority. In 1303, in reaction to the papal support for the mendicants expressed in *Vas electionis*, King Philip IV of France appealed for an ecumenical council to resist Pope Boniface VIII. He received widespread support, including letters of adhesion from some members of the mendicant communities in Paris. The king's appeal was supported by thirty-eight of the city's Augustinian friars and eighty-four Franciscans, including Friars Odo and Dionysius of Ireland.[29]

Although little evidence survives to illustrate the origins of the dispute in Ireland, it engendered tremendous antipathy towards the friars among Anglo-Irish clerics. Most of the surviving Irish evidence corresponds with periods when these critics were at their most vocal. The decision of Pope Innocent VI in 1359 to reissue *Vas electionis* at the request of the Irish Franciscan provincial was probably prompted by the Fitzralph controversy. In 1400, the same bull was reissued, probably in connection with the contemporary dispute between the Dominicans of Drogheda and Archbishop Colton of Armagh, Henry Crumpe and John Whitehead.[30]

The friars were not always the victims of clerical aggression and their own behaviour occasionally warranted correction. In 1367, the bishop of Limerick complained of their infringement of the conditions of *Super cathedram*, and the bishop and chapter of Meath made a similar complaint in 1371.[31] The Limerick dispute proved long running and acrimonious. In August 1376, Pope Gregory XI ordered Simon Sudbury, archbishop of Canterbury, to investigate charges made by the Franciscan archbishop of Cashel, Philip Torrington, against Bishop Peter Curragh of Limerick. Torrington alleged that he had been physically assaulted when, as conservator of the friars' privileges in Ireland, he attempted to investigate the complaints of the Limerick friars against Bishop Curragh, who responded by excommunicating anyone who attended the friary church or sought burial there.[32]

### BURIALS AND FUNERAL OFFERINGS

At a local level, disputes frequently arose over the right of sepulture. Since the mid-thirteenth century, the Dominicans and Franciscans had been allowed to bury members of the laity in their churches and cemeteries. This privilege infringed the rights of the secular clergy and deprived them of a significant source of income, the *funeralia* or canonical portion, customarily paid to the rector for his services at funerals and which sometimes included wax, candles and offerings for anniversary Masses. The earliest recorded dispute in Ireland occurred in 1291,

29 W.J. Courtenay, 'The Augustinian community at Paris in the early 14th century' (2001); idem, 'The Parisian Franciscan community in 1303' (1993); *FL*, p. 79.   30 *CPL*, v, p. 324; *BF*, vii, p. 104; *FL*, p. 170. 31 *BF*, vi, pp 410–11, 451.   32 *BF*, vi, p. 576; *FL*, pp 158–9.

when the Cistercians of St Mary's Abbey and the Franciscans in Dublin contended over the body of Milo Talbot, who had wished to be interred with the friars. The abbot and monks disrupted the funeral procession and attempted to take possession of the corpse by force.[33] In 1309–10, Friar William of Bristol, guardian of the Franciscans in Ardfert, brought a case against Bishop Nicholas and the canons of the nearby cathedral for forcibly removing the body of John de Cantilupe from the friary. Some friars were manhandled during the removal and the court ordered that the accused be arrested and their goods distrained.[34] Occasionally, disputes arose between the mendicants themselves: in 1317, the Franciscans in Armagh brought a case against the Dominican friars of Drogheda for removing the body of Sir Thomas de Mandeville from the Armagh friary. In 1318, the prior of the Augustinian canons in Tristernagh was delegated to adjudicate in a dispute between the Dominicans of Mullingar and the Franciscans of Trim over the body of Rohesia de Verdon, which the Franciscans claimed but which the Dominicans would not surrender.[35] In each case the surnames indicate that the disputed remains were those of members of leading local families and that prestige and substantial burial fees were at stake. That such funeral offerings could be significant is evident from the account of the obsequies of a wealthy Irish merchant, David Wydyr, who died in Bristol in 1408 and who was subsequently reinterred in the Dominican priory at Athenry, of which he and his wife were notable benefactors:

> David Wydyr, a worthy former burgher of Athenry, travelled to Flanders and returning from Flanders to England was by divine will overtaken by death in the city of Bristol. Because of his affection for the order of St Dominic, he chose burial in the friar's habit with the Friars Preachers at Bristol and for whose soul that convent received twenty pounds. He bequeathed to the convent of his native town of Athenry one hundred marks, a silk choir cope for the use of the cantor in choir and two bronze candlesticks. The cost of the silk cope was sixteen marks and the cost of the bronze candlesticks was twenty shillings.
>
> The noble matron Joanna Wyffler, wife of the said David Wydyr, on the advice of the friars, caused the bones of her husband to be transferred, honourably and with great expense, from the convent of Bristol to the convent of Athenry by Friar Thomas Nasse, lector of the Athenry convent. And the said matron kept with her for fifteen days all the Friars Preachers in Connacht … from Roscommon, Sligo, Athleathan, Rathfran, Lohrra and *de portu Dei* (Portumna?) and all other mendicant orders, the Minors,

33 *FL*, pp 62–3.    34 *FL*, p. 91.    35 *FL*, pp 104, 105; *CPL*, ii, p. 171.

the Augustinians and the Carmelites as well as the poor and indigent, both spiritual and otherwise for the funeral rites of her husband. She gave food and drink to them in abundance and silver to the poor religious and clerics and she caused the great window over the high altar and all the windows in the choir to be glazed and it is said that it cost more than one hundred marks for the glass and for all pertaining to the glazing. For the same [funeral], she gave one hundred pounds of wax and innumerable other gifts.[36]

In addition, Joanna Wyffler also imported a sculptured tombstone for her husband, paid for some additional building work in the priory, built a bridge over the stream dividing the convent from the town and bought a chest to preserve the choir copes and other vestments that the couple had previously donated to the community. Significantly, perhaps, the record of her largesse contained no reference to representatives of the local secular clergy. While this may be an oversight, it contextualizes Archbishop Fitzralph's bitter assertion in the *Defensio curatorum* that just as a vulture could smell carrion over five hundred miles of ocean, so a friar could sniff out the corpse of a wealthy man.[37]

The recurrent nature of these disputes is evident from the inclusion of a formulary document for claiming corpses in TCD MS 250.[38] In addition to asserting their right to bury the body, the document invoked the friars' apostolic privileges and threatened their opponents with papal sanctions. In their determination to uphold these rights, the friars were sometimes capable of not only ignoring the prerogatives of the secular clergy but also their own internal legislation. The copy of the Observant Franciscan statutes produced in 1482 for the community in Adare included a chapter dealing with the vow of poverty. This concluded with the clause:

> The general chapter orders and wishes that the friars freely grant to the curates the canonical portion of those funeral offerings given them by those buried among them and warns that they studiously avoid litigation over the canonical portion with curates at the Roman curia.[39]

This section was later so thoroughly erased that it is now only legible with the aid of ultraviolet light.

36 Coleman, 'Regestum', p. 207.  37 T.P. Dolan, 'Richard FitzRalph's *Defensio curatorum* in transmission' (2006), p. 181.  38 TCS MS 250, fo. 167v; Colker, *Latin MSS,* i, p. 449.  39 Oxford Bodleian MS Rawl. C. 320, fo. 33.

IRISH CONTRIBUTORS TO THE DEBATE

## *Richard Fitzralph (1350–60)*

The emergence of the Anglo-Irish cleric Richard Fitzralph as the principal opponent of the friars in the mid-fourteenth century marked the beginning of the Irish contribution to the theoretical aspects of the debate. Though best known as a controversialist, he enjoyed a considerable contemporary reputation as an academic, theologian and prelate and, posthumously, as a saint.[40] His violent reaction against the friars occurred in the last decade of his life and was surprising for a number of reasons. Born into a prosperous family in Dundalk at the end of the thirteenth century, Fitzralph had close childhood associations with the town's Franciscan community and may have received his early education from the friars.[41] In a sermon preached to the Franciscans in Avignon on the feast of St Francis, 1349, he attested that at least one member of his family had always been a member of the Dundalk community since its foundation. Likewise, he may also have been related to Friar John Fitzralph, the Irish minister provincial in 1332. Katherine Walsh suggests that one of his relatives may have been among the twenty-two members of the Dundalk community killed by the forces of Edward Bruce in 1315.[42] There was no evidence of a conflict with any of the mendicant orders during his time in Oxford, and in his early years at the papal court in Avignon he was a much sought after guest preacher in the city's friary churches. His *volte face* was inexplicable to the contemporary friars, and the Franciscans in particular viewed it as a betrayal of his earlier friendship. Writing in the seventeenth century, Luke Wadding alleged that a dispute over the removal of an ornament from the Franciscan church in Drogheda was the cause of the controversy, but this seems unlikely.[43]

Fitzralph began his Oxford studies c.1314–15 and graduated as a master of arts in 1325, by which stage he was already studying theology.[44] In 1328, he graduated as a bachelor of theology and had by then attracted the attention of an influential patron, John Grandisson, bishop of Exeter, who became his mentor and lifelong friend. Fitzralph became tutor to the bishop's nephew, who was studying in Paris, and thus came into contact with several prominent Parisian theologians and exegetes. He graduated as a doctor of theology in Oxford in 1331 and within a year was elected chancellor of the university. During his term of

---

**40** K. Walsh, *A fourteenth-century scholar and primate: Richard Fitzralph in Oxford, Avignon and Armagh* (1981). For summary accounts of his career, see K. Walsh, 'Richard Fitzralph of Armagh (d. 1360): professor–prelate–saint' (1990) and K. Walsh, 'Fitzralph, Richard', *ODNB*, 19 (2004).   **41** H. O'Sullivan, 'The Franciscans in Dundalk' (1960–1), p. 35.   **42** Walsh, 'Richard Fitzralph of Armagh', pp 112–13; M. Haren, 'Richard Fitzralph of Dundalk, Oxford and Armagh: scholar, prelate and controversialist' (2009).   **43** Wadding, *AM*, viii, p. 127.   **44** Walsh, *A fourteenth-century scholar*, pp 15–84.

office (1332–4), he dealt with the Stamford schism, during which the university's northern masters and students seceded to the town of Stamford in Lincolnshire. Although this was a cause of embarrassment to Fitzralph, he continued to enjoy the confidence of the university authorities and was chosen to present the Oxford cause to Pope Benedict XII in Avignon in 1334. This was the first of Fitzralph's four visits to the papal curia and marked an important development in his ecclesiastical career.[45] While in Avignon, he became involved in a theological dispute on the nature of the beatific vision, which established his reputation as a controversialist and preacher. In July 1334, the pope appointed him chancellor of the diocese of Lincoln, and in December 1335 he became dean of Lichfield. Despite these English appointments, Fitzralph spent the period from 1337 to 1344 at Avignon becoming deeply involved in discussions with representatives of the Greek and Armenian churches who sought papal support in the face of Islamic expansion. His engagement with them inspired one of his most theologically sophisticated works, the *Summa de quaestionibus Armenorum*, which dealt at length with issues relating to papal primacy and ecclesiastical authority and which subsequently influenced the deliberations of the councils of Basel and Ferrara-Florence (1431–49) in their efforts to promote unity with the eastern churches.[46]

In May 1346, the cathedral chapter of Armagh elected Fitzralph to succeed Archbishop David O'Hiraghty. Pope Clement VI quashed the election as it violated the papal prerogative of appointment, but nonetheless appointed Fitzralph to the vacant see in July 1346.[47] Having done homage to Edward III in April 1347 and received the temporalities of the see, Fitzralph was ordained bishop by John Grandisson in Exeter Cathedral on 8 July 1347. He spent some time acting as suffragan to Grandissson before returning to Ireland early in 1348 and embarked on a preaching tour of his diocese *inter anglicos* during the Easter octave of that year. His sermon diary shows that he frequently condemned the ethnic violence that divided his Gaelic and Anglo-Irish subjects. He also condemned those Anglo-Irish merchants whose sharp practice deprived the church of tithes and material support. While in his diocese, Fitzralph became increasingly critical of the friars' lenient pastoral practices, the manner in which they exercised their ministry for gain and how they undermined his authority and that of his clergy. Though he criticized all four orders, it was the Franciscans who particularly drew his fire and he devoted considerable energy to undermining the doctrine of voluntary poverty, so important to their identity.[48]

The first evidence of his change of heart occurred in a sermon, the *Proposicio*, preached before Pope Clement VI and the papal curia in Avignon on 5 July 1350,

**45** Ibid., pp 85–106.  **46** Walsh, *A fourteenth-century scholar*, pp 129–81.  **47** Ibid., pp 239–48. **48** Ibid., pp 349–451.

in which he attacked the friars' abuse of their pastoral privileges. He developed the theoretical aspects of his argument in the treatise *De pauperie salvatoris*, which he published in London and Oxford in 1356. In this latter work, he developed a theory of dominion whereby all ownership and the valid exercise of authority were founded on God's gift to the individual soul. On exegetical grounds, he also challenged the friars' assertion that Christ had been a mendicant. He elaborated on these themes in a series of sermons he preached in late 1356 and 1357 at the request of his friend Richard Kilvington, dean of St Paul's Cathedral, at St Paul's Cross in London, the foremost pulpit in the city. Although primarily aimed at the Franciscans, the sermons also aroused the ire of the other mendicant orders who, in March 1357, drafted a united response to his criticism. The result was an *Appellacio*, listing twenty-one errors in Fitzralph's arguments, which was delivered to his lodgings by Friar John Arderne, the prior of the London Augustinians, on 10 March. Fitzralph responded with a strongly worded sermon in English that he delivered at St Paul's Cross on 12 March and which subsequently circulated widely.

The friars appealed to King Edward III, who forbade Fitzralph to leave England without royal permission in a vain attempt to prevent him taking his case to the papal curia. The legal case between the archbishop and the friars opened in Avignon when he delivered his *proposicio*, later known as the *Defensio curatorum*, in a sermon preached to the pope and curia on 8 November 1357. A commission of four cardinals was appointed to investigate his allegations. While the case was in process, Fitzralph completed the eighth book of his *De pauperie salvatoris*, in which he clarified his position and responded to some of his critics. The commission had not reached a decision by the time of Fitzralph's death in November 1360 and, with the deaths of Dean Richard Kilvington and Friar Richard Conway in 1361, the matter was allowed to lapse.

Despite his failure at Avignon, Fitzralph's posthumous influence remained powerful.[49] His theories on dominion and authority profoundly influenced the thought of John Wycliffe, and the Lollards venerated him as a saint. His autograph copy of the *De pauperie salvatoris* came into the possession of the Bohemian scholar and anti-mendicant campaigner, Adalbert Ranconis de Ericinio, demonstrating the channels through which Fitzralph's positions and those of Wycliffe came to influence the followers of John Huss in Prague.[50] The opening folio of the late fourteenth-century copy of *De pauperie salvatoris* commissioned by the English Benedictine monk Nicholas Easton, depicts Fitzralph writing under the inspiration of the Holy Spirit while representatives of

**49** Ibid., pp 452–68.   **50** K. Walsh, 'Wyclif's legacy in Central Europe in the late fourteenth and early fifteenth centuries' (1987).

the four mendicant orders are assailed by devils (pl. 4).[51] The *Defensio curatorum* also circulated widely throughout Europe and over eighty copies of the text survive, including one that belonged to the Augustinian canons at Duleek, Co. Meath.[52] The translation of the text into English by John Trevisa *c.*1380 broadened its circulation and his principal themes were adopted by other Oxford-educated Anglo-Irish clerics.

Despite his notoriety, Fitzralph came to enjoy a reputation for holiness. His bones were translated from Avignon by Bishop Stephen Wall of Meath and enshrined in the church of St Nicholas in Dundalk, though the Dominican continuator of Pembridge's chronicle expressed reservations about their authenticity.[53] A cult of 'St Richard of Dundalk' developed, and a liturgical office was composed in his honour. His feastday was celebrated on 27 June and was included in a number of late medieval Irish liturgical texts.[54] Attempts to include him in the general calendar of the church proved less successful. A commission to inquire into his life and sanctity was established *c.*1380 by Pope Urban VI, but nothing came of this attempt at canonization.

### Henry Crumpe (1376–1401)

The emergence of Henry Crumpe as a campaigner against the friars was the first indication of the persistence of Fitzralph's legacy in Ireland. Crumpe, a monk of Baltinglass, Co. Wicklow, was a controversial figure who came to prominence through his involvement in various disputes in Ireland and England.[55] He first emerged in Oxford in 1376 as an opponent of John Wycliffe's views on church–state relations, and Friar Thomas Netter, the English Carmelite prior provincial, recorded both his anti-Wycliffite and his anti-mendicant views in his work *Fasiculi Zizaniorum*.[56] By this stage, Crumpe was a doctor of theology and probably regent of the Cistercian *studium* in the city. His opposition to Lollardy incurred the wrath of Wycliffe's Oxford supporters and forced him to flee England sometime after July 1362. Returning to Ireland, he renewed his campaign against the friars and in March 1385 William Andrew, the Dominican bishop of Meath, condemned eight propositions that Crumpe had enunciated in sermons preached in the diocese and elsewhere. Of these, seven concerned his denial of the friars' rights to hear the confessions of the laity, while the eighth concerned his views on the Eucharist, which, ironically, were heavily influenced

---

**51** Cambridge, Corpus Christi College MS 180, fo. 1r; Walsh, *A fourteenth-century scholar*, pp 472–3. **52** Lambeth Palace Library MS 357, fos 30b, 45b–72; Hogan, *Priory of Llanthony*, p. 41. **53** Pembridge, *Chronicle*, p. 393. I am grateful to Bernadette Williams for this reference. **54** For example, TCD MS 77, fo. 50, 'Ricardi Row archiescopi Armachani'. **55** K. Walsh, 'Crumpe, Henry', *ODNB*, 14 (2004); J. Catto, 'The Cistercians in Oxford' (1997), p. 111. **56** T. Netter, *Fasiculi Zizaniorum* (1858), pp 113, 289, 311–14, 343–59.

by Wycliffe. Crumpe himself regarded his position on the friars as identical to Fitzralph's and ignored the condemnation. He continued to promulgate his views after his return to Oxford and consequently was suspended from all scholastic acts in March 1392. In May 1393, he was summoned to answer related charges before a council that included the archbishops of Canterbury, York and Dublin, nine other bishops and a number of theologians. They forbade him to engage in any academic activity until permitted by the archbishop of Canterbury. This probably was a more lenient sentence than he might have expected, as documents relating to his earlier condemnation in Ireland were found in the Dominican friary in Oxford in June 1392, too late to be of use in the trial. Crumpe was unchastened by the experience and in 1401, along with Archbishop John Colton of Armagh and John Whitehead, rector of Stabannan, Co. Louth, he became involved in a dispute with the Dominican friars of Drogheda over their promotion of the Portiuncula indulgence. An appeal to Rome found in favour of the friars and Crumpe, Colton and Whitehead were threatened with excommunication if they did not desist. The dispute concerned the friars' right to hear the confession of those wishing to avail of the indulgence and their seeking alms for the maintenance of the friary church.[57] It formed part of a wider dispute as, in 1400, Pope Boniface IX had intervened to protect the friars and ordered the archbishops of Dublin and Cashel and the bishop of Kildare to see that *Vas electionis* was observed in Ireland.[58] Nothing further is heard of Crumpe after the Drogheda incident, though as John Bale was aware of two of his anti-mendicant texts in the sixteenth century, it is likely that his views continued to be influential.[59]

## John Whitehead (1401–10)

Henry Crumpe's successor in the dispute was John Whitehead, who became rector of Stabannan in September 1389, but was granted leave to pursue studies and subsequently divided his time between Ireland and Oxford. It is almost certain that they knew each other before the dispute with the Drogheda Dominicans, as their university careers overlapped. Whitehead was a doctor of theology by 1408 and Archbishop Nicholas Fleming of Armagh appointed him as his representative at the Council of Pisa in 1409, along with Robert Montayne, bishop of Meath.[60]

His attack on the friars in the treatise *Determinatio in materia de mendicitate* brought him into conflict with Friar Peter Russell, a future Franciscan provincial of England. Whitehead's work survives in one fifteenth-century manuscript and

---

57 *CPL*, v, pp 432–3.  58 *CPL*, v, p. 324; *BF*, vii, p. 104, *FL*, p. 170.  59 R. Sharpe, *A handlist of Latin writers of Great Britain and Ireland before 1540* (1997), p. 167. These were the *Determinationes mendicantes* and the *Contra religiosos mendicantes*, neither of which are known to survive.  60 B. Smith (ed.), *The register of Nicholas Fleming, archbishop of Armagh, 1404–1416* (2003), pp 97–8, no. 104.

his intellectual debt to Fitzralph is immediately evident in the incipit: *Suppositio secundum dominum Ardmachanum*.[61] Another treatise preserved in the same manuscript, the *Determinatio de confessione et absolutione*, was his response to the Dominican William Eddesburgh.[62]

Whitehead's presence at the council of Pisa provided the opportunity to present his case to the most authoritative body possible: an ecumenical council.[63] As such, it caused great alarm to the friars in Ireland and elsewhere, who, in 1409, launched a coordinated campaign to oppose him and appointed Friar Adam Payn, an Augustinian, and Friar John Cuock, a Franciscan, as their representatives.[64] Whitehead first defended himself before Archbishop Thomas Arundel of Canterbury in London in February 1410, but was unsuccessful.[65] The same charges were also brought to Rome and Pope Alexander V condemned nine of his propositions with the bull *Regnans in excelsis*.[66] In effect, Whitehead's positions were merely restatements of the perennial points of conflict alleging the necessity of repeating confessions made to friars and the inability of popes to dispense from conciliar decrees and asserting the traditional rights of the secular clergy. He also proposed that penitents could not confess to the friars without the permission of their parish priests, that *Vas electionis* was the work of a heretic and was therefore invalid, and that friars who appealed to the papacy for permission to hear confessions and bury the dead were in a state of mortal sin, as were the popes who had granted such faculties. The polemic assertion that the friars were not shepherds but rogues, thieves and wolves was also condemned. The bull's condemnation of John of Pouilly by name was significant, as it demonstrated the extent to which Whitehead's dependence on the views of the Paris master was obvious to his contemporaries.

## Philip Norris (1431–67)

The most bitter and long running of the disputes between the friars and their Anglo-Irish critics was with the Dublin priest, Philip Norris. Like Crumpe and Whitehead, Norris was an Oxford graduate and conducted his campaign both at the university and in Ireland.[67] The earliest reference to him occurs in July 1427, when he became vicar of St Nicholas' Church, Drogheda. The first sign of tension with the friars emerged in June 1431, when he was granted a testimonial letter by the university to protect him from the attacks of the Dominican friar,

61 Oxford Bodleian Digby MS 98, pt 6, fos 200r–208; Sharpe, *Latin writers*, p. 345.   62 Oxford Bodleian Digby MS 98, pt 6, fos 208r–216; Sharpe, *Latin writers*, p. 345.   63 F.X. Martin, 'An Irish Augustinian disputes at Oxford: Adam Payn, 1402' (1975), pp 297–304.   64 Glassberger, *Cronica*, pp 233, 238–40.   65 Sharpe, *Latin writers*, p. 345. His response to the charges was copied into the archbishop's register and subsequently printed in D. Wilkins, *Concilia Magnae Britaniae et Hiberniae* (1737), iii, pp 324–5.   66 *FL*, pp 172–6; *BF*, vii, p. 420.   67 K.Walsh, 'Norris, Philip', *ODNB*, 41 (2004).

Thomas Hore, who had denounced him to the pope. In 1435, Cardinal Dominic Firmano cautioned Norris over his references to the friars in his university sermons. In 1438, an Oxford Augustinian, Friar William Musselwycke, initiated proceedings against him and Bishop John Stafford, the chancellor of England, cited him for heresy. This citation constituted an infringement of the university's privileges, and Norris received its full support: Musselwycke was expelled from Oxford and another testimonial letter was issued, contesting the charges against Norris and denying that he had ever been expelled from the university or excommunicated. The convocation of Canterbury appointed a committee to examine the matter in October 1438, and this found in Norris' favour. The friars appealed to Rome and both this process and that of Cardinal Firmano were decided in August 1440. In both cases, Pope Eugene IV found in favour of the friars and ordered Norris to recant his position or to face condemnation for heresy. Norris appealed this sentence to the Council of Basel in 1443 and it does not appear to have been executed. Norris also enjoyed support in Dublin: in 1441, the friars complained that Thomas Walsh, a lawyer, had obstructed Archbishop Talbot of Dublin from promulgating the bulls issued in their favour against Norris. The friars complained to King Henry VI because of this, and Norris was imprisoned from 1441 to 1443. During this time, the friars brought the case to Rome and, in 1448, they secured confirmation from Pope Nicholas V of the original sentence of Eugene IV.[68] For a second time, the sentence was not executed and Norris was appointed rector of St Patrick's, Trim, in 1450.[69] His relations with the friars remained strained, and in 1456 he secured a bull from Pope Callixtus III that refuted claims that he had deviated from orthodoxy at the time of the Council of Basel and ordered the Franciscans to stop molesting him.[70] In 1457, he was appointed dean of St Patrick's Cathedral, Dublin, which post he held, despite increasing infirmity, until his death in 1465.

Quite apart from the perennial issues of jurisdiction and rights, the terms in which the debate was conducted give some idea of the passions it aroused. In the 1440 sentence passed against Norris by Cardinal Firmano, he was accused of asserting that

> as the walls of Jerusalem were destroyed by four different princes, so the Church of Christ will be destroyed by the friars of the four mendicant orders. Also, as the prince of the tribes came into Jerusalem with a great throng, so the friars have entered the church and are like a throng, which disturbs the church. Also, as the prince of the tribes sent from Antioch to

**68** *BFNS*, i, p. 621, no. 1217.   **69** Potterton, *Medieval Trim*, p. 278. I am grateful to Michael Potterton for this reference.   **70** *CPL*, xi, pp 100–2.

Jerusalem deceitfully spoke to them words of peace, so the friars of the four mendicant orders entered the church with deceit, and are destroying it according to their designs and ability. Also, as the prince of the tribes came to the city of Jerusalem with a great crowd (*turba magna*) and as crowd (*turba*) comes from 'I disturb, you disturb' (*turbo, turbas*) so the friars have entered the church and are in her like a crowd (*turba*) that disturbs (*perturbant*) the church. Also, as the Gabonites came to Joshua with lies, so the four mendicant orders have entered the church with lies. He asserted that just as there were four general councils in which different heretics were condemned, so the friars of the four mendicant orders are worse heretics than they were. Also, that the friars of the four mendicant orders are the worst licentious bawds. Also, that the friars of the four mendicant orders are robbers and thieves who despoil Holy Church. Also, that the friars of the four mendicant orders are worse than Judas the traitor. Also, that the friars of the four mendicant orders are ravaging wolves. Also, that the friars of the four mendicant orders are anti-Christ and leaders against Christ. Also, that the friars of the four mendicant orders are disciples of Mohammed.[71]

The calibre of the friars' opponents from the mid-fourteenth until the mid-fifteenth century provides a clear indication of the depth of anti-fraternalism among the Irish secular and monastic clergy. Indeed, the only significant contributions that Irish scholars made to late medieval theology concerned the questions of jurisdiction, dominion, pastoral care and ecclesiology that the secular-mendicant dispute raised.

### POPULAR ANTI-MENDICANT LITERATURE IN IRELAND

As noted above, a remarkable feature of the anti-mendicant campaign was the manner in which it found expression in contemporary literature. In France, the work of the poets John de Meun and Rutebeuf translated abstract theological concepts into popular verse and introduced the conflict to a wider audience. This process continued in the late-fourteenth century in England, where Geoffrey Chaucer, John Gower and William Langland produced works with a strong anti-mendicant flavour. Although Chaucer is sometimes credited with a partial English translation of the *Roman de la rose*, his most influential contribution was the unsympathetic depiction of friars in the *Canterbury Tales*. These range from the morally ambivalent figure of the general prologue 'a frere ther was, a wantown and

71 *BFNS*, i, pp 231–3, no. 484. See also ibid., pp 229–30, no. 480.

a merye' to Friar John of the Summoner's Tale, who, being bequeathed a fart to divide equally among his *confrères*, did so in a blasphemous parody of Pentecost.[72]

William Langland's work *Piers Plowman* provided the most extensive critique of the friars in late-medieval English literature. Little is known of the author, but his work, regarded as one of the greatest pieces of medieval alliterative poetry, circulated widely and profoundly influenced subsequent writers.[73] *Piers Plowman* survives in three different versions, A, B and C, composed and revised over a twenty-year period between *c.*1367 and *c.*1386, and these are found in over fifty different manuscripts. Part satire, part Christian allegory, part vision or dream poem, the role of the mendicants is so central to the work that a recent commentator speculated that it may be the work of a former Friar Minor.[74] Langland was fully aware of the eschatological role of the friar as harbinger of the end times and servant of Antichrist.[75] In *Piers Plowman*, the friars are mentioned more often and at greater length than any other type of cleric. They appear at all the major structural and psychologically significant points in the poem and are noteworthy only for their depravity. With the exception of fleeting references to SS Dominic and Francis, every aspect of mendicant life and ministry was presented in a negative light. Thus, in *passus* (ch.) iii, it was to a 'confessour ycoped as a frere' that Lady Mede, the allegorized figure of bribery and corruption, made her blasphemous confession. He granted her easy absolution and as penance proposed that she erect a stained glass window in the friary church on which her name would be engraved. He also offered to admit her to confraternity with his order.[76] In *passus* vi, where the seven deadly sins come forward to make their confessions, the figure of wrath described the manner in which he pitted friars and parish priests against each other in defence of their respective rights.[77] In *passus* xxii, the final chapter of the poem, when the church, 'the fortress of unity', was besieged by the agents of Antichrist, and its defenders complained of the harsh treatment of their own confessor, Doctor Shrift, the figure of Conscience made the mistake of sending for a friar to hear the confessions of its defenders. The friar, Doctor Friar Flatter, returned bearing the necessary episcopal licences and was introduced to the castle under the alias Sir Pentrans Domos, one of the titles given to false teachers and pseudo-prophets by William of St Amour in *De periculis*. By offering easy penances in return for Mass stipends and gifts of money, he undermined Conscience and removed all fear of sin, leaving the church vulnerable to the attack of the enemy.[78]

---

**72** A. Williams, 'The "limitour" of Chaucer's time and his "limitacioun"' (1960); Szittya, *Antifraternal tradition*, pp 231–46.   **73** A. Hudson, 'The legacy of *Piers Plowman*' (1988).   **74** L.M. Clopper, *"Songes of rechlesnesse": Langland and the Franciscans* (1997).   **75** Szittya, *Antifraternal tradition*, pp 247–87; W. Langland, *Piers Plowman: a new annotated edition of the C text* (2008), pp 22–4.   **76** Langland, *Piers Plowman*, pp 81–2.   **77** Ibid., p. 125.   **78** Ibid., pp 371–8.

The evidence for the circulation of such anti-mendicant popular literature in Ireland is slight but significant. The library catalogue of the earl of Kildare listed the ninety-two volumes contained in the library of Maynooth castle in 1526. These included a French copy of the *Roman de la Rose*.[79] Its presence in the library of one of the principal patrons of the friars in Ireland is not necessarily indicative of any anti-mendicant sentiment on the earl's part, as the work was very popular in aristocratic circles.

Evidence for the circulation of *Piers Plowman* in Ireland comes from Bodleian MS Douce 104, which was probably written in Dublin in 1427.[80] The codex contains a version of the C text of the poem and, in addition to being the only known copy to be produced outside England, it is also unique on account of seventy-two detailed marginal illustrations that accompany the text. These show a remarkable similarity to the satirical depiction of the Irish exchequer preserved in the contemporary *Red Book of the Irish exchequer*, and have led one scholar to suggest that they were the product of the same school, if not of the same individual.[81] As Derek Pearsall notes, the illustrations also 'provide a record of a response to the text of an early fifteenth-century reader of considerable intelligence and interpretative acumen'.[82] The manner in which the friars are depicted is therefore of particular significance, as it demonstrates how they were perceived by the illustrator and presented to the volume's readers. In all, five images of friars are found in the manuscript. These include depictions of Dominicans giving absolution to a young woman (Lady Mede) (pl. 3) and preaching from a pulpit (pl. 5).[83] The text's description of a false friar and its references to Sir Penetrans Domos are also illustrated by images of Friars Preachers. In the latter instance, the friar is shown holding the jordan or urine flask commonly used for medieval medical diagnoses.[84] A single image of a Franciscan friar occurs in the text, but without any apparent pejorative overtones (pl. 6).[85]

The evidence for anti-mendicant motifs in Gaelic literary sources is also very slight. Although there are numerous references to friars and mendicant themes in Gaelic bardic poetry, very few of these are hostile and there is nothing comparable to the opprobrium found in English or Continental literature.[86] A number of

**79** G. Mac Niocaill (ed.), *Crown surveys of lands, 1540–41 with the Kildare rental begun in 1516* (1992), p. 314.   **80** This section is based on D. Pearsall & K. Scott, *Piers Plowman: a facsimile of Bodleian Library, Oxford, MS Douce 104* (1992). I am grateful to Alan Fletcher for advice on various points.   **81** K. Kerby-Fulton & S. Justice, 'Langlandian reading circles and the civil service in London and Dublin, 1380–1427' (1997); K. Kerby-Fulton, 'Professional readers of Langland at home and abroad: new directions in the political and bureaucratic codicology of *Piers Plowman*' (2000), pp 117–29. See also K. Kerby-Fulton & D. Despres, *Iconography and the professional reader: the politics of book production in the Douce Piers Plowman* (1999).   **82** Pearsall & Scott, *Piers Plowman*, p. ix.   **83** Bodleian MS Douce 104, fos 11v, 47r. This latter figure may represent an Augustinian Canon Regular.   **84** Bodleian MS Douce 104, fos 44r, 111v.   **85** Ibid., fo. 46r.   **86** E. Bhreathnach, 'The friars and vernacular Irish learning' (2011).

factors may have contributed to this. In the late fourteenth and fifteenth centuries, when the friars made numerous foundations in Gaelic territories, it was most frequently in the context of the Observant reform, a movement notable for the high regard in which its members were held. Many Gaelic friars were members of the traditional learned families, who consequently may have been reluctant to satirize the mendicants. It is also likely that the debates over the *cura animarum* that exercised the minds of Anglo-Irish university graduates were less relevant in Gaelic areas where parochial structures were somewhat looser.[87] Even when negative incidents concerning friars are reported in Gaelic sources, care is taken not to exploit them in general terms. Thus, in 1451, when a text of the Annals of Ulster recorded the destruction by fire of the Franciscan friary in Cavan, the disedifying origins of the conflagration were later carefully erased and the entry simply read 'The monastery of Cavan was burned this year, namely about the feast of St Brenann [nine lines erased]'.

The full context is provided by the unedited entry in the B text of the annals:

> The monastery of Cavan was burned by the friar Ua Mothlain, he being inebriate after drinking wine. And it happened thus: the candle that he took with him to his chamber was left lighting and he himself fell asleep and the chamber took fire and the whole monastery afterwards.[88]

A similar discretion is evident in Lambeth Palace Library MS 46, a copy of a canon law text, the *Clementinae*, transcribed by the Augustinian canon, Rodericus O'Lachtnain, in 1477. The colophon recorded that it was written in the same year as the Friars Minor in Roscrea looted and destroyed their own friary, the church of St Cronan and the castle of John O'Carroll, carrying off clothes, food and vast quantities of alcohol. While recording a spectacular breakdown of regular discipline, the scribe was at pains to exonerate the minister provincial and the guardian and lector of Roscrea from any culpability. A later hand also erased a number of words in the text, which perhaps described even greater excesses.[89]

One exception to the generally positive image of the friars in Gaelic literature is the poem *Bráthar bréige* (A false friar), composed by the bardic poet Tadhg Dall O'Higgins (d. 1591).[90] In its thirteen stanzas, the poet satirized a 'melodious, beloved' friar from Connacht for wandering around the province, decked out in a

87 H. Jefferies, *Priests and prelates of Armagh in the age of reformations, 1518–1558* (1997), pp 57–82 at pp 81–2. Idem, *The Irish church and the Tudor reformation* (2010), pp 15–55. In both works Jefferies counters the conventional bleak assessment of late medieval Irish church life and pastoral care. 88 *AU*, iii (1895), pp 170–3. 89 M. Rhode James & C. Jenkins, *A descriptive catalogue of the manuscripts in the library of Lambeth palace* (1937), p. 63. 90 E. Knott (ed.), *Tadhg Dall Ó hUiginn*, 2 vols (1922), i, pp 262–3 (text);

fine habit, hose, shoes and cloak, but offering to sell a stolen, battered and
worthless hat. The word used for 'hat' in the poem is *atán* which also translates as
'little swollen thing', a pun which suggests that the offending article was not an
item of dress.[91] From the description of the habit and the places in Connacht
visited, the friar in question was probably a Dominican. Although the poem
echoes many of the anti-mendicant themes found in medieval English literature,
it appears to be a satire on an individual rather than a condemnation of the friars
as a body. Likewise, the Donegal chieftain Manus O'Donnell's description of
Friar Aodh recovering from a drinking session seems more like an affectionate
ribbing than a biting satire:

> Bráthair bocht brúite ó fhión –
> Ná dúisgthear é gion gur choir;
> Gabh go ciuin ceannsa re a thaobh;
> Leigtear d'Aodh an tsrann-sa go fóill.

> [Poor friar overcome with wine!
> Wake him not, though waked he should be;
> Step by him gently, quietly;
> Let Aodh have a snore for himself for a while.][92]

As the pre-eminent composers of popular hymnody and religious verse in Ireland,
the friars were well positioned to respond to their critics' literary onslaughts. The
clearest expression of this is found in the Hiberno-English, French and Latin
material contained in BL MS Harley 913.[93] While much of this was religious in
nature and presumably intended for preaching purposes, a number of the pieces
are satires on various estates in society, with members of monastic orders
attracting particular opprobrium. The Latin material includes such goliardic
compositions as the 'Abbot of Gloucester's feast', a rollicking account of a
debauched drinking session in the Benedictine priory at Gloucester, a short
treatise against monks, a hagiographical parody entitled 'The passion of a monk
according to Bacchus' and a satire on the niggardliness of monastic hospitality.[94]
The most trenchant criticisms occur in two of the volume's Hiberno-English
poems, 'Satire' and 'The land of Cockayne'.[95] In 'Satire', the monks were but one

ii, pp 173–4 (trans.). I am grateful to an tOllamh Pádraig Ó Macháin for this reference and for advice on
its significance.   **91** Pádraig Ó Macháin, pers. comm.   **92** C. Mhág Craith, *Dán na mbráthar mionúr*
(1967), p. 375. Cited in P. Corish, *The Catholic community in the seventeenth and eighteenth centuries*
(1981), pp 14, 141.   **93** W. Heuser, *Die Kildare gedichte* (1904); A.M. Lucas, *Anglo-Irish poems of the
Middle Ages* (1995).   **94** BL Harley MS 913, fos 10r–11; 57r; 60r–v; 60v.   **95** BL Harley MS 913, fos
7–8; 3–6v; Lucas, *Anglo-Irish poems*, pp 58–65; 46–55.

of the estates in society ridiculed, in their case for excessive drinking. The Dominican, Franciscan and Augustinian friars were also mocked, which suggests that the poet was not himself a friar. The inclusion of anti-mendicant verse in mendicant codices was not unusual, and examples occur in other contemporary manuscripts.[96] The most extended attack on the monastic order is found in the 'Land of Cockayne', a composition only found in this manuscript, though influenced by a French work, the *Fabliau de Cocagne*. Here, the poet described in Rabelaisian detail the gluttonous and licentious antics of a community of Cistercians, which P.L. Henry identified as that of St Mary's Abbey at Inishlounacht on the banks of the River Suir near Clonmel.[97]

## THE FRIARS DEFEND THEIR RIGHTS

The persistent tension that existed between the friars and their clerical critics made the mendicants more conscious of their rights and the need to defend them. In consequence, they carefully preserved copies of the privileges and exemptions granted them by the papacy and secular authorities. Irish evidence for this occurs in TCD MS 250, a fifteenth-century Observant Franciscan codex. In addition to two confessor's manuals and a number of formulary administrative documents, the codex contains a dossier of texts detailing rights, privileges and exemptions recorded in its final folios.[98] These include transcripts of forty-eight thirteenth-century papal bulls granted to the Friars Minor by Popes Gregory IX, Alexander IV and Clement IV. Only two of these bulls were specifically addressed to the Irish friars;[99] the remainder were addressed to the order in general or to other provinces and friaries, but were obviously regarded as having universal application. These included confirmations of the friars' right to be buried in their own cemeteries, to have their own oratories and celebrate the liturgy during time of interdict, to accept the necessities of life from excommunicates and to govern their internal affairs without interference from prelates or bishops. Franciscan superiors were permitted to present candidates for ordination to prelates of their choice and they could not be coerced into executing ecclesiastical commissions against their will. The right to hear confession and preach, even during episcopal vacancies, was also confirmed, as was their exemption from episcopal and legatine authority. Prelates were also encouraged to receive the friars charitably and to facilitate their ministry. Other practical provisions included an injunction

---

**96** Cartlidge, 'Festivity, order and community', p. 35; D.L. Jeffrey, 'Authors, anthologists and Franciscan spirituality' (2000). **97** P.L. Henry, 'The Land of Cokayne: cultures in contact in medieval Ireland' (1972). Cartlidge challenges this identification, see Cartlidge, 'Festivity, order and community', p. 43. **98** TCD MS 250, fos 149–68. **99** M. Sheehy, *Pontificia Hibernica*, II, pp 46–7, 52–3.

prohibiting the foundation of another mendicant house within three hundred perches (*cannae*) of a Franciscan friary, and one rebuking those who denied the stigmata of St Francis.

As occasion demanded, the Irish friars routinely sought copies of relevant papal privileges from church authorities. In May 1457, the Augustinian reformer, Friar Hugh O'Malley, was granted confirmation by Pope Callixtus III of the privileges granted to the Irish Austin friars by his predecessors Boniface VIII (1294–1303), Urban VI (1378–89), Alexander V (1409–10), Martin V (1417–31) and Eugene IV (1431–47).[1] In June 1465, Friar William O'Reilly, the Franciscan minister provincial, petitioned Archbishop John Bole of Armagh for a copy of the bull *In quibusdam locis*, issued by Pope Clement IV in Perugia in 1265, which excommunicated anyone who occupied or damaged the friars' churches.[2] A copy of this bull also occurs in TCD MS 250, and it was obviously regarded as having universal application.[3]

The high point of papal support for the mendicants came during the pontificate of Pope Sixtus IV (1471–84), who endorsed the privileges granted by his predecessors to each of the mendicant orders and confirmed the communicability of these privileges between each order. These bulls, widely referred to as *Mare magnum* – the great ocean – because of the latitude of their concessions, were known to the friars in Ireland. A copy of the Carmelite *Mare magnum*, heavily underlined and with annotations in Irish, survives in Lambeth Palace MS 61 ii.[4] The Franciscans in Youghal were able to invoke the provisions of their *Mare magnum* in the course of a dispute with the rector of Dungarvan in 1515.[5]

## EXEMPTIONS AND CONSERVATORS

The friars' exemption from episcopal oversight was often a cause of conflict with the secular clergy and other religious orders. A document preserved in TCD MS 250 indicates that, in 1315, the Franciscans in Dublin refused to accept a summons from Abbot Ralph of St Thomas' Abbey to attend his abbatial court, arguing that only the pope had jurisdiction over them.[6] In March 1494, the guardian of the Franciscan friary at Kilcullen was declared contumacious for three times refusing to answer summonses to attend provincial councils convoked by Archbishop Walter Fitzsimons.[7]

**1** Theiner, *Vetera monumenta*, p. 402; *CPL*, xi, p. 143. F.X. Martin suggests that these were sought in connection with the dispute between the friars and Dean Philip Norris: 'Irish Augustinian reform', p. 244, n. 59. **2** Lynch, 'Franciscan documents', p. 17. The text of the bull is given in *BF*, iii, pp 15–16. **3** TCD MS 250, fo. 156; Colker, *Latin MSS*, i, p. 445. **4** The underscorings relate principally to privileges connected with hearing confessions. **5** See below, p. 167. **6** TCD MS 250, fos 166v–167v; Colker, *Latin MSS*, i, p. 449. **7** N. White (ed.), *Registrum diocesis Dublinensis: a sixteenth-century precedent book* (1959), p. 30.

To ensure that the friars' rights and privileges were protected, various popes appointed high-ranking prelates as conservators or protectors of each order and of their provinces. The earliest evidence for the practice in Ireland dates to 18 August 1245, when Pope Innocent IV extended the provisions of the mandate *Nimis iniqua* to Ireland and appointed the archbishop of Dublin and the bishops of Ossory and Kildare as conservators of the Franciscans' rights and privileges.[8] On 17 September 1245, he issued a similar mandate to the archbishop of Cashel and the bishops of Cloyne and Cork, ordering them to defend the Irish Dominicans.[9] The bull sought to protect the friars from those prelates and clergy who forced them to receive the sacraments from their hands and to attend councils and courts, and who refused to allow them to possess their own cemeteries or church bells, forcing them to bury deceased friars in secular graveyards. Other points of contention included prelates seeking to limit the numbers within each mendicant house, demanding a share of all gifts or offerings made to the friars, excommunicating the friars' benefactors and attempting to appoint the superiors of mendicant friaries.

As noted above, in 1376 the Franciscan archbishop of Cashel, Philip Torrington, came into conflict with his suffragan, the bishop of Limerick, in his role as conservator of the friars. In 1514, Bishop John Fitzgerald of Cork and Cloyne found in favour of the Franciscans in a dispute over burial dues between the friars and John Fitzgibbon Fitzgerald, warden of the college in Youghal. The judgment also included the Dominican friars in the town and was subsequently confirmed by Maurice Fitzgerald, archbishop of Cashel, who described himself as the 'conservator of privileges of the four orders of friars in the kingdom or province of Ireland'. In confirming his suffragan's ruling, the archbishop extended it to the Dominican and Augustinian friars of Cork and ordered the local Gaelic and Anglo-Irish magnates to enforce it.[10] In 1515, Maurice Fitzgerald, tenth earl of Desmond, backed the friars of Youghal in their dispute with Maurice Hobert, rector of Dungarvan, over the question of burial dues. He declared that he was enforcing Bishop John Fitzgerald's ruling and emphasized his descent from the founder of the Friars Minor in Ireland and his particular role as protector of the Observants. He also referred to the *Mare magnum* of Sixtus IV as the authoritative papal statement of mendicant privileges.[11]

---

**8** *BF*, i, pp 372–4; *CPL*, i, p. 226; Sheehy, *Hibernica pontificia*, pp 113–14. **9** M.H. MacInerney, *A history of the Irish Dominicans*, pp 31–5; Sheehy, *Hibernica pontificia*, p. 118. The archbishop of Cashel was the Dominican David McKelly, while another Friar Preacher, Alan O'Sullivan, was bishop of Cloyne. **10** B. Jennings (ed.), *Wadding papers, 1614–38* (1953), pp 108–13. These documents were transcibed in 1625 by Friar Francis O'Mahony to strenghten the friars' case in contemporary disputes over privileges with the secular clergy. **11** Ibid., pp 113–15.

Although the friars' conservators were usually bishops with a countrywide brief, individual houses also enjoyed the protection of senior prelates in their localities. The Adare necrology cited by Donatus Mooney recorded the death of Prior John of Holy Cross priory, Limerick, on 2 August 1531, and noted that he was the protector of the Observant Franciscan community in Adare.[12]

While the friars' concerns with secular matters and defending their rights often led them into conflict with the secular clergy and other critics, it did not completely extinguish, in the words of St Francis, 'the spirit of prayer and devotion to which all things must be subjected'.[13]

12 Jennings, 'Brussels MS 3947', p. 64.   13 Esser, *Opuscula*, p. 95.

CHAPTER SEVEN

# Liturgy and devotion

*May St Francis, St Dominic and Patrick of Macha, saving me,*
*bring my soul to the kingdom where Thou art, O Father.*[1]

## THE LITURGY

The daily celebration of the Liturgy of the Hours and the Eucharist was central to
the spiritual lives of mendicant communities. However, in order to devote more
time to intellectual and pastoral work, the friars adopted a pragmatic approach to
the Divine Office celebrating it 'briefly and succinctly',[2] and spending less time in
choir than the older monastic orders for whom it was the *raison d'être* of the
religious life. Individual friars could even be dispensed from the communal
recitation of the office in order to devote more time to study, though those
excused were expected to celebrate it privately.[3] In the course of the thirteenth and
early fourteenth centuries, each order consolidated its liturgical practices, which
were articulated in their respective ordinals: liturgical books that contained the
officially sanctioned editions of the liturgical texts and detailed each order's rubrics
and ceremonial. This ensured a high degree of liturgical uniformity, and Irish
practice may be inferred both from the general norms as well as from the extant
texts. This uniformity did not preclude adaptation to local circumstances, and the
surviving Irish material contains examples of how the friars celebrated distinctively
Irish feasts and celebrations.

## THE HORARIUM

The Liturgy of the Hours provided the framework around which the conventual
life of the friary was structured. A considerable degree of flexibility was given to
local superiors in arranging the daily timetable and the sacristan was the official
delegated to ring the bells that summoned the friars to their various engagements.
At the Franciscan friaries at Askeaton and Muckross a small sun dial or Mass dial

1 Baothghalach Mac Aodhagáin, 'A Athair nua neamhdhasa' in L. McKenna, *Aithdioghluim Dána*, ii (1939),
p. 127.   2 Hinnesusch, *The history of the Dominican order*, i, pp 351, 371.   3 A. Gonzalez Fuente OP, *La
vida liturgica en la orden de Predicadores* (1981), pp 67–87.

with an arrow marking north is located in the north arcades of the cloisters. These dials were used to mark the times of the various hours of the Divine Office, though their effectiveness in the Irish climate must have been sporadic.[4] The detailed Dominican constitutions make is possible to reconstruct in broad outline the daily timetable in a typical, if imaginary, medieval friary and it is likely that a similar schedule was observed in the houses of the other mendicant orders.[5] There were two basic schedules governing the friars' daily routine. The winter schedule began on 14 September, the Feast of the Exaltation of the Cross, and ended at Easter, when the summer schedule came into force. Each day began with the recitation of the nocturnal offices of Matins and Lauds sometime between midnight and three in the morning, after which the friars returned to bed. These lengthy offices and the broken sleep that they entailed were regarded as one of the greatest hardships of the religious life, and elderly or sick friars were occasionally dispensed from attending them. In 1490, Friar Maurice Ochonoret, an aged member of the Dublin Augustinian community, was dispensed from the night vigil on account of his ill health.[6] Enthusiasm for the Midnight Office was regarded as a sign of virtue, and the poet Tadhg Óg O'Higgins (d. 1448) asked that his own negligence in this regard would be counterbalanced by the zeal of St Dominic: 'I am slow to rise in time for Matins; pardon me for this, setting it against the cold nights he arose.'[7]

When the friars arose again, they celebrated the short office of Prime at around six-thirty during the dark winter mornings and considerably earlier in the summer schedule. A meeting of the conventual chapter in the chapter room usually followed, during which the martyrology of the day was read and other domestic business transacted.[8] The chapter-meeting was also the lynchpin of each order's disciplinary structure. It was here that the superior encouraged or rebuked his subjects and imposed penances on those friars who confessed their failings at the chapter of faults. Humble confession of shortcomings was regarded as a virtue in a friar and was especially commended in those whose senior positions usually exempted them from the practice. Bishop Carbry O'Scoba, the Dominican bishop of Raphoe, was accustomed to accuse himself at the chapter of faults whenever a visitator came to his convent. His attempts to do so when staying with the Dominicans at Lyon while attending the general council there in 1274 were

---

**4** Aisling O'Donoghue, 'Mendicant cloisters in Munster' (2011), p. 126.   **5** Hinnebusch, *The history of the Dominican order*, i, pp 349–53; idem, *Early English Friars Preachers*, pp 219–26. For the Augustinian horarium, see Andrews, *The other friars*, pp 124–7.   **6** Martin & de Meijer, 'Irish material', p. 104, no. 111. He was also confirmed in the possession of his own room.   **7** L. McKenna, *Dán Dé: the poems of Donnchadh Mór Ó Dalaigh, and the religious poems in the duanaire of the Yellow Book of Lecan* (1922), pp 74–5, verses 14–15. I am grateful to Edel Bhreathnach for this reference.   **8** The martyrology was a day-by-day listing of the feasts and celebrations of the liturgical year.

thwarted by the master general, Friar John of Vercelli.[9] Friar Richard Brady (d. 1607), the Franciscan bishop of Kilmore, had to be dissuaded from confessing his faults in chapter whenever he stayed with his *confrères* at Multyfarnham.[10]

The office of Terce was chanted around eight and that of Sext at around midday, after which the conventual Mass was celebrated. After Mass, the friars had their dinner, which was the only meal of the day during the winter season. In the summer schedule, dinner was followed by a short siesta, at the end of which the office of None was celebrated. In winter, the friars sang Vespers in the late afternoon at around four-fifteen, while it was still light. This was followed by Compline at around five o'clock. During the summer season, Vespers was celebrated around six-thirty and Compline at around seven forty-five, while there was still sufficient light for reading. The summer schedule also made provision for a collation (a light meal or drink) in the refectory between Vespers and Compline. After Compline, the friars had an opportunity for private prayer, during which time some visited the various shrines and altars in the church, while others remained in choir, before retiring for the night.

### LITURGICAL RESOURCES

An impression of the liturgical resources typically available in a late medieval Irish friary comes from the liturgical books listed in the library catalogue of the Franciscan community in Youghal.[11] The 1491 section of the catalogue shows that the friars then had eight missals for the celebration of Mass, five large choir psalters for use during the Divine Office, five graduals containing the texts of chants sung at Mass, two *collectoria* containing the prayers recited at the end of each office, a *pulpitarium* containing the texts chanted from the lectern in the centre of the choir or from the choir loft, and four antiphonaries containing the antiphons and hymns sung during the Liturgy of the Hours.[12] All these volumes were used for services in the friary church and were probably kept in the church itself or in the sacristy. The Youghal community also possessed two martyrologies listing the feastdays of the saints and other celebrations proper to the order, and two volumes containing the instructions or rubrics that governed the conduct of the liturgy. These latter volumes were normally preserved in the chapter house of

**9** MacInerney, *Irish Dominicans*, pp 292–3; O'Sullivan, *MIDS*, pp 56–7. Bishop O'Scopa was one of thirty Dominican bishops attending the council and died during it. **10** 'Brussels MS 3947', p. 98. **11** The Youghal liturgical books are very similar to those bequeathed in 1468 by Dean John Collyn to Waterford Cathedral and to the chantry chapel of St Saviour that he had established there. See G. Mac Niocaill (ed.), 'Registrum cantariae S. Salvatoris Waterfordensis' (1966). **12** *YLC*, nos 1–9. One of these antiphonaries was a large format, two-volume work that was may have resembled TCD MS 109.

the friary, where the friars could more readily consult them. Later additions to the catalogue included breviaries and small missals in the possession of individual members of the community. These were used by friars when travelling or celebrating Mass privately and may well have been printed books.[13]

## MUSIC AND THE LITURGY

Instruction in music formed an integral part of the training of novices in each order.[14] The Youghal library contained a volume for instruction in music, and a 1493 concession by the Augustinian prior general to Friar Thaddeus Okeallay of Dunmore noted that he was responsible for instructing the friars how to chant.[15] The presence of an allegorical interpretation of the tonic scale in TCD MS 667 also indicates familiarity with basic musical concepts.[16] Donatus Mooney recorded that the day and night hours of the Divine Office were celebrated with great solemnity by the friars in Donegal, that he himself had reintroduced the singing of the office at Kilconnell and that a large notated gradual survived from the friary at Youghal. He also noted that the individuals who gained possession of the friars' property at Drogheda after its suppression had their sleep disturbed by the sound of ghostly friars singing the night offices.[17]

While much of the psalmody was chanted on a monotone (*recto tono*), the presence of musical notation in the Franciscan codex TCD MS 109 and in the Carmelite missal from Kilcormac indicates that the friars also employed plainchant in the liturgy. References to organs in the Dominican church at Athenry and the Franciscan friary at Killeigh indicate that the chant in these communities was accompanied by music and such instruments were probably to be found in many other friary churches.[18]

## LITURGICAL LEGISLATION

### Dominicans and Franciscans
After an initial period of fluidity, the definitive version of the Dominican liturgy was established by the master general Humbert of Romans and promulgated by

**13** The books reserved for the use of Friar Maurice Hanlan included a breviary, missal and diurnale (*YLC,* no. 86) and, apart from the choir books discussed here, the 1491 section of the catalogue refers to another breviary in the possession of Friar William Bretonicus (*YLC,* no. 30). The 1523 section notes the addition of seven breviaries (*YLC,* nos 106, 109, 120, 126, 133, 142) and seven missals (nos 107, 112, 124, 128, 135, 137, 150), three of which were printed.  **14** See below, pp 265–7.  **15** *YLC,* no. 76; Martin & de Meijer, 'Irish material', pp 106–7, no. 119.  **16** TCD MS 667, p. 149; Colker, *Latin MSS,* ii, p. 1150.  **17** 'Brussels MS 3947', pp 40, 73.  **18** Coleman, 'Regestum', pp 218, 219; W.H. Grattan Flood, 'Irish organ-builders from the eighth

the order's general chapter meeting in Paris in 1256.[19] In an encyclical letter to the order, Friar Humbert instructed the friars to correct their liturgical manuscripts in light of the revisions and listed the fourteen volumes that comprised the authoritative edition of the order's liturgy. The diligence with which this was observed is evident from BL Add. MS 23935, a portable copy of the Dominican liturgical texts with which the master general corrected the errors in the liturgical books of the priories that he visited.[20] Given this strong concern for uniformity, it seems certain that the liturgical books of the Irish Friars Preachers conformed to the general norms and that, for instance, the missals, antiphonaries and other liturgical books donated to the friars in Athenry by their benefactors were themselves copied from Dominican exemplars.[21]

The only surviving Irish manuscript with Dominican liturgical material is Lambeth Palace MS 534, a thirteenth-century copy of the Bible that the Dominican community at Arklow acquired in the fifteenth century.[22] Although not originally intended for liturgical use, the inclusion of rubrics in the body of the text and the addition of a list of scriptural pericopes indicates that it was used as a lectionary at Mass. The presence of rubrics in the psalter may also indicate that it was used during the Divine Office.[23]

Franciscan liturgical practice was codified by the English minister general, Friar Haymo of Faversham, in the ordinal *Indutus planeta*, which he presented to the general chapter meeting at Bologna in 1243. His revision of the Franciscan missal and breviary drew heavily on the practice of the contemporary papal court. This was because the abbreviated liturgy of an itinerant papal curia was more suited to the friars' peripatetic lifestyle than the lengthy and elaborate liturgies of monks or regular canons.[24] Friar Haymo's reforms in turn influenced the development of the Roman liturgy, as the rapid spread of the Franciscans introduced Roman liturgical norms to parts of Europe that hitherto had their own distinctive customs.[25] That Irish Franciscan liturgy conformed to the norms of *Indutus planeta* is evident from Berlin Staatsbibliothek Preussicher Kulturbesitz MS theol. lat fol. 703, a late fifteenth-century Franciscan manuscript from Youghal that contains copies of the

to the close of the eighteenth century' (1910), p. 232. The friary is mistakenly described as an Augustinian house. **19** W.R. Bonniwell OP, *A history of the Dominican liturgy* (1945); Hinnesbusch OP, *English Friars Preachers*, pp 217–26; Fuente, *La vida liturgica*, pp 45–65. See L.E. Boyle OP et al. (eds), *Aux origines de la liturgie Dominicaine: le manuscrit Santa Sabina XIV L1* (2004) for important reassessments of the development of the early Dominican liturgy. **20** G.R. Galbraith, *The constitution of the Dominican order, 1216–1360* (1925), p. 195. See also M. Huglo, 'Comparison du "prototype" du couvent Saint-Jacques de Paris avec l'exemplaire personnel du maître de l'Ordre des Prêcheurs' (2004). **21** See below, pp 283–4. **22** W. Hawkes, 'The liturgy in Dublin, 1200–1500: manuscript sources' (1957–8), 64–7. **23** G. Dahan, 'Les texts bibliques dans le lectionnaire du "prototype" de la liturgie dominicaine' (2004). **24** P. Rocha SJ, 'Liturgia della Cappella Papale, liturgia dei Frati Minori e liturgia dei Frati Predicatori' (2004). **25** S.J.P. Van Dijk & J. Hazelden Walker, *The origins of the modern Roman liturgy* (1960), pp 292–320. I am grateful to Placid Murray OSB for advice on this point.

Franciscan missal, breviary and the texts for the prayers at mealtimes.[26] The bulk
of the codex consists of the martyrology of Usuard adapted for Franciscan use in
the south of Ireland.[27]

The other Franciscan liturgical text to survive from late medieval Ireland is
TCD MS 109,[28] a late fifteenth-century antiphonary containing the antiphons,
texts, hymns and music for various feasts. The late thirteenth-century codex TCD
MS 347 provides additional, if incidental, evidence for the Irish friars' familiarity
with Franciscan liturgical norms. The bulk of the volume's contents consists of
model sermons and other homiletic material arranged according to the cycle of the
liturgical year and, by and large, following the cursus of the Franciscan
lectionary.[29] Its sanctoral section contains extensive material for the feastdays of
various saints, including SS Anthony of Padua and Francis of Assisi.[30]

## Carmelites and Augustinians

The eremitical Middle Eastern origins of the Carmelites gave rise to distinctive
liturgical practices and commemorations that endured even after the order's centre
of gravity had shifted to Europe. Many of these derived from the liturgy of the
Holy Sepulchre in Jerusalem that the crusaders had introduced to the Holy Land
and which eventually became the established liturgy of the Latin Kingdom of
Jerusalem.[31] Though French in origin, the rite gradually gathered accretions proper
to the Holy Land, incorporating the feasts of Old Testament figures and
introducing a distinctive commemoration of the resurrection on the Sunday
before the beginning of Advent.[32] The friars gradually adopted many features of
the papal liturgy as well as commemorations proper to themselves. Towards the
end of the thirteenth century, the English Carmelites attempted to standardize the
liturgy by producing an ordinal, the earliest surviving copy of which is preserved
in TCD MS 194.[33] This ordinal was subsequently revised by the order's prior
general, Sibert of Beka, and adopted by the order *c.*1312.

**26** P.J. Becker & T. Brandis, *Die theologischen lateinischen Handschriften in folio der Staatsbibliothek
Preussicher Kulturbesitz, Berlin* (1985), ii, pp 237–40. The texts are found at fos 106r–123r; 126v–149v; 150r.
**27** Berlin Staatsbibliothek Preussicher Kulturbesitz MS theol. lat fol. 703, fos 2r–105v. **28** TCD MS 109.
Described in Colker, *Latin MSS*, i, pp 234–5. Its Observant provenance is indicated by the extensive service
for St Bernardine of Siena (fos 103v–109), while the inclusion of antiphons and responsories for St
Bonaventure (fos 109–114v) indicates that it was produced sometime after his canonization in 1482.
**29** TCD MS 347, fos 61–156v; Colker, *Latin MSS*, i, pp 714–26. M. O'Carroll SND, 'The lectionary for
the proper of the year in the Dominican and Franciscan rites of the thirteenth century' (1979). **30** TCD
MS 347, fos 122rv; 150. Curiously, this latter text consists of only two lines. **31** For the development of
the Carmelite liturgy, see J. Boyce, *Praising God in Carmel: studies in Carmelite liturgy* (1999), pp 1–45,
329–69. **32** Ibid., p. 5. **33** TCD MS 194, fos 168–237v; Colker, *Latin MSS*, i, pp 383–4.

The missal and breviary that survive from the Carmelite foundation at Kilcormac, Co. Offaly, give an indication of the liturgical practices of the Irish Carmelites. A colophon in the missal indicates that Friar Dermot Offlanagan of the Carmelite community at Loughrea transcribed it in 1458 for the prior of Kilcormac, Edward Obracayn.[34] While this demonstrates a concern to conform to the order's general liturgical norms, Paschalis Kallenberg notes that the Kilcormac missal was copied from an exemplar produced before 1339, as it lacks many of the celebrations prescribed by the order for liturgical observance after that date.[35] Curiously, while the missal's calendar contains references to Carmelite celebrations such as the feasts of the prophet Elisha, SS Simon Stock, Nicholas, Albert of Sicily and Angelus, the protomartyr of the order, its *sanctorale* section does not contain any services for Carmelite saints.[36] The manuscript has some musical notation with blank spaces left for the addition of neumes.

A memorandum at the beginning of the Kilcormac breviary indicates that it was transcribed in 1489 by Malachias O'Lachtnain, a cleric of the diocese of Killaloe.[37] Kallenberg notes that it was copied from an exemplar written between 1411, when the feast of St Albert of Jerusalem was introduced, and 1425, when the feast of St Maurus was upgraded in the Carmelite liturgy.[38] While both texts demonstrate that the Irish Carmelites conformed to the order's liturgical norms, the use of outdated exemplars suggests that they were not familiar with subsequent developments in the order's liturgy.

Like the Franciscans, the Augustinians also adopted the liturgy of the papal court and their liturgical norms were consolidated in the legislation and *ordinarium* promulgated by the prior general Friar Clement of Osimo *c.*1290. These gave detailed instructions on the celebration of the liturgy as well as providing the authoritative liturgical texts and music. Augustinian liturgical practice was heavily though selectively influenced by that of the Franciscans. Eight manuscript versions of the *ordinarium* survive and it was first published in 1508.[39] No examples of Augustinian liturgical material survive from medieval Ireland.

**34** TCD MS 82, fo. 154; Colker, *Latin MSS*, i, pp 145–6.   **35** P. Kallenberg, *Fontes liturgiae Carmelitanae* (1962), pp 138–9.   **36** Colker, *Latin MSS*, i, p. 146. For an edition of the calendar, see H.J. Lawlor, 'The Kilcormic missal: a manuscript in the library of Trinity College, Dublin' (1900).   **37** Dublin, TCD MS 86, fo. 1v; Colker, *Latin MSS*, i, pp 154–6.   **38** Kallenberg, *Fontes*, pp 206–7; S. Furlong OSB, 'Officium S. Patricii: the medieval office of St Patrick' (2008), i, pp 39–41.   **39** Guttierez, *The Augustinians in the Middle Ages, 1256–1536* (1984), pp 107–14.

CULTS AND DEVOTIONS

The devotional interests of the friars were also expressed in the saints to whom their churches were dedicated and whose images were found on their shrines and altars. The churches of the Dominican priory in Kilkenny and the Augustinian houses in Dublin and Scurmore were dedicated to the Holy Trinity and the medieval patronal image still survives in Kilkenny (pl. 7).[40] Particular emphasis was placed on devotion to Christ and his passion and, as was standard in most medieval churches, the rood or principal crucifix in each friary church was an object of great veneration, often having a dedicated altar or perpetual lights burning before it. Burial before the rood was also much sought after: William Thorpe, a medieval benefactor of the Friars Minor in Waterford, was buried before the rood in the friary church there.[41] The Dominican churches at Arklow, Cloonshanville, Glanworth, Rathfran, Sligo, Strade, Tralee and Youghal were dedicated to the Holy Cross, while those at Dublin, Kilmallock, Limerick and Waterford were dedicated to Christ under the title of St Saviour. The Carmelite Kilcormac missal contains the texts of two of the most popular votive Masses to Christ in the later Middle Ages: the Mass of the Holy Name of Jesus and the Mass of the Five Wounds of Christ.[42] The Observant Augustinian foundation at Banada was also dedicated to Christ under the title of Corpus Christi and is the only known occurrence of this dedication in medieval Ireland.

MARIAN DEVOTION

Devotion to the Virgin Mary was a major feature of mendicant spirituality, with each order appropriating and promoting distinctive aspects of the Marian cult. In addition to the Divine Office, the Dominican, Carmelite and Augustinian friars also recited the Office of the Virgin, an abbreviated form of the Liturgy of the Hours celebrated in honour of St Mary. The Dominican priories at Ballindoon, Burrishoole, Coleraine, Cork, Galway, Mullingar, Portumna, Rosbercon, Roscommon and Trim were dedicated to the Virgin Mary, as were the Franciscan friary at Cork and the Augustinian foundations at Ardnaree, Ballinrobe, Ballyhaunis, Burriscarra and Dunmore.[43] Each friary, as a matter of course, had an

---

40 Martin, 'Augustinian friaries', pp 372, 381.   41 J.C. Walton, 'A list of the early burials in the French Church, Waterford' (1973), p. 71. I am grateful to Rachel Moss for this reference.   42 TCD MS 82, fos 97–99rv; Colker, *Latin MSS*, i, p. 82. It also includes material attributed to Pope Boniface VIII concerning the efficacy of these devotions. See also S. Ryan, '"Reign of blood": aspects of devotion to the wounds of Christ in late medieval Gaelic Ireland' (2002).   43 *MRH*, pp 222–5, 227–30; Martin, 'Augustinian friaries', pp 360, 361, 363, 366, 374.

7.1 Image of the
Virgin Mary,
Franciscan friary,
Ennis, Co. Clare.

altar dedicated to the Virgin, or a 'Lady Chapel', often located in the transept of the church. Wooden statues of the Virgin survive from the Franciscan friaries at Adare, Askeaton (pl. 8) and Waterford and from the Dominican tertiary foundation at Kilcorban. The sixteenth-century image of the pieta belonging to the Carmelite friars at Kilcormac is preserved in the modern Roman Catholic parish church there. Two images of the Virgin Mary were donated to the Dominicans in Athenry in the early fifteenth century, while their *confrères* in Youghal venerated a thirteenth-century ivory image of the Madonna and child that became a major focus of devotion in the sixteenth and seventeenth centuries (pl. 1).[44] Stone sculptures of the Virgin occur on tombs in a number of friaries, and fine examples survive in the Franciscan friary in Ennis (fig. 7.1) and the Dominican priory at Athenry.

44 Coleman, 'Regestum', pp 209, 210–11; C. Tait, 'Art and the cult of the Virgin Mary in Ireland, *c.*1500–1660' (2006), p. 180.

Devotion to the Virgin Mary was particularly important for the self-identity of the Carmelites, who, in the absence of the cult of a founder, emphasized the apocryphal Marian origins of the order in their liturgy.[45] They also promoted the wearing of the scapular and the Sabbathine privilege as distinctive Carmelite practices. Originally, these were two separate Marian devotions that became conflated in the fifteenth century, leading to the widespread belief among the friars and their lay clients that those who died wearing the scapular of the Carmelite habit would be released from purgatory through the intercession of the Virgin on the Saturday following their death. The Virgin herself had allegedly granted these privileges to the elusive thirteenth-century prior general, St Simon Stock.[46] The inclusion of his feastday in the calendar of the Kilcormac breviary indicates that the Irish friars were aware of his cult and, presumably, of its Marian aspects.[47] Contemporary references to the Carmelites in Kinsale and Rathmullan as the 'Friars of Mary', and the dedication of almost all their Irish priories to her provides further evidence of the strength of their Marian devotion.[48]

A distinctive feature of the Domincian liturgy was the procession in honour of the Virgin Mary with which the office of Compline concluded. During it, the friars passed from the choir of the church into the nave, singing the Marian antiphon *Salve Regina* and kneeling with the congregation as they sang the final strophes. At the conclusion of the hymn, the prior of the community sprinkled all present with holy water. This devotion held great appeal for the friars and their lay devotees and many miracles and apparitions of the Virgin were recorded as occurring during it.[49] A depiction of one such apparition in an early sixteenth-century Flemish painting now preserved in the St Catherine's Museum, Utrecht, also serves to illustrate the interior appearance of a medieval mendicant church (pl. 9).

## THE CULT OF THE SAINTS

The evidence for the Irish friars' devotion to the other saints of the church is scanty. The Franciscan church in Youghal and the Augustinian house at Clonmines were both dedicated to St Nicholas.[50] The Franciscan church in Waterford had altars dedicated to the Magi and St Appolonia. It also housed an image of St Christopher as well as a chapel of St Francis and an altar dedicated to St Clare.[51] A number of statues from medieval Waterford were preserved in the city's Hospital of the Holy Ghost, which occupied part of the claustral complex of

**45** C. O'Donnell, 'Mary and the liturgy' (2007).   **46** R. Copsey, 'Simon Stock and the Carmelite vision' (2004).   **47** Ibid., p. 107.   **48** P. Walsh (ed.), *Leabhar Chlainne Suibhne* (1920), pp 66–9.   **49** Bonniwell, *A history of the Dominican liturgy* (1945), pp 148–66.   **50** P. Ó Riain, *Feastdays of the saints: a history of Irish martyrologies* (2006), pp 257–8; Martin, 'Augustinian friaries', p. 368.   **51** Walton, 'List of early burials',

the dissolved Franciscan friary. These may originally have come from the friary church and are now displayed in the Waterford Museum of Treasures. The collection includes an early-fourteenth-century wooden statue of the Madonna and child; two images of St John the Baptist (one a fifteenth-century sandstone image of the saint's head on a dish, the other a wooden statue depicting him clad in camel-skin, holding a book and the *Agnus Dei*); a gothic statue of St Stephen; a thirteenth- or fourteenth-century wooden statue of a saint or angel and a fifteenth-century English alabaster image of St Catherine of Alexandria.[52] Statues of St Catherine also survive from the Dominican priory at Kilkenny and the Dominican tertiary foundation at Kilcorban, while in Athenry a chapel in the Dominican church was jointly dedicated to her and to St Catherine of Siena. The Franciscan church at Adare was dedicated to St Michael the archangel and four wooden statues from the friary church still survive. These represent the Madonna and child, St Joseph and St Louis of France, patron of the Franciscan tertiaries, as well as an image of a friar-saint, possibly St Francis.

With the exception of the specifically Franciscan material, all of these images represent cults that were well established throughout western Christendom. The images of SS Appolonia, Christopher and Catherine indicate devotion to the auxiliary saints or 'holy helpers', who were widely invoked for particular needs: St Appolonia was the patron of those suffering from toothache and St Christopher was invoked by travellers. The cult of St Catherine of Alexandria was particularly strong and she was the patroness of a wide clientele, including students, philosophers, theologians and young women.[53]

## MENDICANT TYPOLOGIES OF SANCTITY

The emergence of the Dominican and Franciscan orders corresponded with the consolidation of the church's canonization process. Though previously regarded as a matter for local bishops or popular acclamation, by the late twelfth century the process of 'making saints' had increasingly become a papal prerogative.[54] The close links between the friars and the papacy and their role as champions of orthodoxy meant that the causes of mendicant candidates for canonization were processed rapidly and included for commemoration in the church's general calendar. The network of mendicant friaries acted as nodal points from which distinctive cults, devotions and liturgical practices radiated, both within the orders and throughout the church.

pp 72, 74.   **52** E. McEneaney, 'Politics and devotion in late fifteenth-century Waterford' (2006), pp 46–9. He argues that they represent the patronal images of a number of the city's churches and religious houses. **53** E. Duffy, *The stripping of the altars* (1992), pp 155–205; S. Ryan, 'Popular religion in Gaelic Ireland, 1445–1645' (2002), pp 211–94.   **54** A. Vauchez, *Sainthood in the later Middle Ages* (2005), pp 59–144.

In his definitive examination of medieval sanctity, André Vauchez argues that 'the sainthood of the mendicants constituted from the beginning a coherent and profoundly original reality'.[55] By analyzing the cults of a number of thirteenth-century friar-saints, including St Dominic, he demonstrates that this new model of sanctity was expressed through certain recurrent *topoi*. These included setting aside promising secular careers or renouncing an exalted birthright to follow Christ more perfectly. Although friar-saints were often capable of great asceticism and gifted with a capacity for prayer, devotion and study, mendicant sanctity was essentially centrifugal and bore its greatest fruit in the apostolate as the 'zeal for souls' drove the friars to the service of their fellows. Other hallmarks of male mendicant sanctity included a disregard for personal appearance and clothing, a passion for chastity and probity in their dealings with women, obedience to the precepts of the order and the will of their superiors and a concern for orthodoxy. These values were communicated to the friars and their lay followers through liturgy, hagiography and preaching, and friar-saints were presented as exemplars of orthodox Christian living, effective intercessors and wonder-workers.[56]

### MENDICANT CULTS IN IRELAND (fig. 7.2)

Evidence for the early impact of these new cults in Ireland occurs in a number of thirteenth-century liturgical sources. The mid-thirteenth-century codex TCD MS 576 was the chapter book of the Augustinian canons of Holy Trinity Cathedral priory, Dublin, and contains the texts that were read at the beginning of the daily chapter meeting.[57] These included the martyrology, which listed the liturgical commemorations that occurred each day. The latest additions to the Christ Church martyrology in the hand of the original scribe are nine thirteenth-century feastdays. Of these, four were mendicant celebrations: St Peter Martyr (29 April); the translation of the relics of St Francis (25 May); St Anthony of Padua (9 June); St Francis of Assisi (4 October).[58] The feast of the Dominican Peter Martyr (d. 1252, canonized 1253) is the latest in the original scribal hand and thus provides the *terminus* for the compilation of the manuscript. The late thirteenth-century martyrology from the abbey of St Thomas in Dublin contains numerous mendicant entries.[59] It shows a close affinity with the Dominican martyrology promulgated by Humbert of Romans in 1256 and Pádraig Ó Riain argues that the exemplar used by the canons of St Thomas' may have been borrowed from St Saviour's Dominican priory on the opposite bank of the River Liffey.[60]

---

55 Ibid., p. 344.  56 Boyce, *Praising God in Carmel*, p. 330.  57 TCD MS 576; Colker, *Latin MSS*, ii, pp 1038–40.  58 Ó Riain, *Feastday of the saints*, pp 122–3.  59 TCD MS 97; Colker, *Latin MSS*, i, p. 187. 60 Ó Riain, *Feastday of the saints*, pp 253–4.

7.2 Frontal from the tomb of Sir Peter French, Franciscan friary, Galway. Mendicant saints depicted in the lower register (l–r) include SS Clare (1), Anthony (2), Francis (5) and Dominic (7) (Lawrence Collection © National Library of Ireland).

Even when included in the general calendar of the church, the manner in which mendicant saints were commemorated liturgically outside the churches of their orders was usually a matter for local legislation.[61] Irish evidence for this occurs in the calendar of TCD MS 78, a late fifteenth-century antiphonary known as the 'Clondalkin Breviary' but originally produced for use in the diocese of Ossory. A number of feasts in the calendar are marked *per constituciones*, indicating that their observance had been imposed by episcopal or synodal decree. These included the feasts of SS Dominic (4 August) and Francis (4 October), but none of the surviving Irish synodal legislation indicates when, where or by whom these decrees were enacted.[62]

The presence of a friary could also influence the manner in which other local religious communities commemorated mendicant saints. TCD MS 84, a breviary from St Mary's Augustinian abbey at Trim, contains extensive material for the

---

**61** I am indebted to Dom Senan Furlong for advice on this section.   **62** Colker, *Latin MSS*, i, p. 128; S. Furlong, 'Officium S. Patricii', i, p. 28. The feast of St Francis is given the higher rank of a duplex or double feast, i.e. one that began with the celebration of the first Vespers on the evening preceding the feast and concluded with the second Vespers celebrated on the evening of the feast itself.

feasts of SS Dominic and Francis, and Aubrey Gwynn proposed that the canons acquired these texts from the town's mendicant communities.[63] The late fifteenth-century martyrology from the Observant Franciscan friary at Youghal, Co. Cork, provides an interesting example of liturgical adaptation to local circumstances. A marginal entry for 29 May commemorates the death in 1257 of the founder of the friary, Maurice Fitzgerald, and ennumerates the indulgences granted by local bishops to those who prayed for him. Another entry in the main body of the text for 9 September commemorates the dedication of the friary church in honour of St Nicholas. The presence of marginal entries in a later hand commemorating St Vincent Ferrer (5 April), the death of St Dominic (5 August) and the translation of his relics (24 May) presumably represent the influence of the town's Dominican community on their Franciscan colleagues.[64]

## THE CULTS OF SS FRANCIS, DOMINIC AND AUGUSTINE

The Irish Friars Minor enthusiastically promoted the cult of their founder and more sources relating to St Francis survive than for any other mendicant saint.[65] This material consists principally of copies of his writings, hagiographical and liturgical material and a significant number of effigies and images.[66]

The earliest evidence for knowledge of St Francis' writings in Ireland occurs in the late thirteenth-century codex TCD MS 347, which contains three of the saint's shorter devotional works: the letter sent to the entire order, the praises to be said before the Divine Office and his Testament.[67] The first of these concerned the friars' worthy celebration of the Eucharist, the second was a series of biblical quotations and a collect to be recited before each hour of the Divine Office. The third document, a copy of the Testament that Francis composed shortly before his death in 1226, is particularly interesting as it subsequently became highly controversial within the order and the church. In it, Francis gave a brief and moving account of his conversion before reiterating certain points of observance for the friars. Although Pope Gregory IX decreed that the Testament did not bind the friars, it became a rallying point for disaffected literalists within the order and attempts were made to suppress the document shortly after Francis' death. The copy in TCD MS 347 is of great interest as it is one of the very earliest copies of the text to survive.[68]

---

**63** A. Gwynn, 'A breviary from St Mary's Abbey, Trim' (1966), 290–8.   **64** Ó Riain, *Feastdays of the saints*, pp 256–7.   **65** Ó Clabaigh, 'The other Christ'.   **66** J.R.H. Moorman, *The sources for the life of S. Francis of Assisi* (1940).   **67** Esser, *Opuscula*, pp 135–50, 183–7, 305–17. Translations in Armstrong et al., *Francis of Assisi*, i, pp 116–21, 161–2, 124–7.   **68** Moorman, *Sources*, pp 35–7.

The order's official life of its founder was that composed by St Bonaventure, which he presented to the general chapter of Pisa in 1263. This work, known as the *Legenda maior*, was recognized as a theological masterpiece and became the standard text for the rest of the Middle Ages. All earlier works were suppressed by order of the chapter of Paris in 1266.[69] That the Irish friars were familiar with the *Legenda maior* is evident from two fourteenth-century sources. One of these, BL MS Harley 913, is one of the best known of all late medieval manuscripts from Ireland, on account of its corpus of Hiberno-English poetry.[70] Interest in its literary content has until recently obscured the significance of its Latin and specifically Franciscan elements.[71] One of the texts included in the codex is an extract from chapter eight of the *Legenda maior*, concerning the friars' fidelity to the Franciscan rule. In addition, one of the poems in the volume, entitled *Satire*, contains a reference to St Francis preaching to the birds, an incident recorded in chapter twelve of the *Legenda maior*:

> Hail, Seint Franceis with thi mani foulis-
> Kites and crowis, reuenes and oules,
> Fure and tuenti wildges and a poucok!
> Mani bold begger siwith thi route.
> [Hail, Saint Francis, with your many birds, kites and crows, ravens and owls, twenty-four wild geese and a peacock! Many a stout beggar follows your company].[72]

The account by Friar Simon Fitzsimon of his pilgrimage to Jerusalem in 1323 mentions the miraculous appearance of St Francis while St Anthony was preaching to a chapter of the friars at Arles, an incident recorded in chapter four of the *Legenda maior*.[73] It is also likely that the *Legenda maior* was one of the several unidentified works of St Bonaventure listed in the Youghal catalogue.

In addition to the officially sanctioned life of the saint, an alternative hagiographical tradition existed. These memoirs, emanating from the saint's circle of intimates, provided a rallying point for the literalist or Spiritual wing of the order.[74] With the emergence of the Observant movement in Ireland in the fifteenth century, this literature gained a wider audience and the Youghal library contained two examples of this literature genre in 1491, the library possessed two copies of the *Flores Francisci*, while the *Actus beati Francisci* had been acquired by 1523.[75]

**69** Moorman, *Sources*, pp 136–51; Armstrong et al., *Francis of Assisi*, ii, 525–683.   **70** A.M. Lucas (ed.), *Anglo-Irish poems of the Middle Ages* (1995).   **71** N. Cartlidge, 'Festivity, order and community in fourteenth-century Ireland: the composition and contents of BL MS Harley 913' (2003).   **72** Lucas, *Poems*, pp 58–9.   **73** M. Esposito (ed.), *Itinerarium Symonis Semeonis ab Hybernia ad Terram Sanctam* (1960), p. 32.   **74** See above, pp 148–50; D. Nimmo, *Reform and division in the medieval Franciscan order* (1987), pp 240–349.   **75** Ó Clabaigh, *Franciscans*, pp 165, 178.

The defining moment for the perception of St Francis in medieval hagiography occurred in September 1224, when, while on retreat at La Verna in central Italy, the saint had an intense religious experience. After a vision, he discovered that his breast, hands and feet bore the stigmata or marks of Christ's passion. The historicity of the event and its subsequent promotion by the friars was controversial. The friars saw it as the 'divine seal' of approval for his way of life and by extension, for their own. Their insistence on Francis as a unique figure, an *alter Christus* – another Christ – frequently aroused the ire of their critics, and the thirteenth-century papal bulls preserved in TCD MS 250, a fifteenth-century Irish Observant manuscript, include one condemning those detractors who denied the stigmata.[76]

The Dominican and Franciscan movements emerged at a period when apocalypticism and the influence of the Calabrian exegete and mystic, Joachim of Fiore (*c.*1135–1202), was particularly acute. In his chief works, Abbot Joachim outlined a prophetic theory of salvation history based on an allegorical understanding of the Trinity. Salvation was presented in three ages: the Age of the Father, lived under the law of the Old Testament; the Age of the Son, lived under the grace of the New Testament; and the Age of the Holy Spirit, during which new religious orders would emerge to convert the world, ushering in the *Ecclesia spiritualis* – the Spiritual Church.[77] This final age of the world would be heralded by the Angel of the Sixth seal, referred to in the Apocalypse:

> Then I saw another angel ascend from the rising of the sun, with the seal of the living God, and he called with a loud voice to the four angels who had been given power to harm earth and sea, saying, 'Do not harm the earth or the sea or the trees, till we have sealed the servants of our God upon their foreheads'. (Revelation, 7:2–3)

The reference to bearing 'the seal of the living God' led many to identify the stigmatized Francis as the fulfilment of this prophecy. That Joachim and his prophecies were known to the friars in Ireland is evident from TCD MS 347, which contains two texts attributed to him. The first of these, the *prophecie Ioachim in maiori volumine de concordanciis*, foretold the coming of the Antichrist and various political and ecclesial events that would take place in 1250.[78] The second prophecy is unique to the Dublin manuscript and cites a pseudo-Joachimist work, the *Super Hieremiam prophetam*. It discussed the three ages of the world and predicted the coming of two orders of spiritual men in the church who

---

76 TCD MS 250, fo. 163v; Colker, *Latin MSS*, ii, p. 447.   77 M. Reeve, *The influence of prophecy in the later Middle Ages: a study in Joachism* (1969).   78 TCD MS 347, fos 388v–389; Colker, *Latin MSS*, i, p. 738. The text is edited by Reeves, *Influence of prophecy*, p. 50. See also Cotter, *Friars Minor*, p. 73.

would oppose the Antichrist. One would be an order of preachers in the spirit of Elijah, the other would be hermits in the spirit of Moses. Their identification with the Dominicans and Franciscans is made clear in the final line of the document, which is written in capitals, 'Explicit prophecia Ioachim de ordine fratrum minorum et predicatorum' – here ends the prophecy of Joachim concerning the order of Friars Minor and Preachers.[79]

All these elements found expression in the work of the bardic poet and Observant friar Philip Bocht O'Higinns (d. 1487), described as 'the best versifier of devotion' in his obituary in the Annals of Ulster. Of the twenty-nine surviving poems attributed to him, three are devoted entirely to St Francis, while he invoked his intercession in another twenty-three. The poems are remarkable for their fusion of the conventions of bardic literature with material drawn from Latin hagiography, preaching material and works such as the *Legenda aurea* of James of Voragine. In the poems relating to Francis, however, he depends almost entirely on Bonaventure's *Legenda maior* as well as on another unidentified Franciscan source.[80]

There is much less evidence to indicate how the Irish Dominicans and Augustinians promoted devotion to their respective founders. As a matter of course, each Dominican church had a chapel or altar dedicated to the order's patron. In Athenry, St Dominic's Chapel was the burial place of the Lynch family, and the burning of the saint's statue from the priory in Cork in 1578 was the cause of much sorrow to the friars and their lay supporters. Attempts to destroy the saint's image in Coleraine in 1611 allegedly resulted in the death of two men.[81] Stone images of St Dominic survive at the Dominican friaries in Sligo and Athenry, at the Franciscan houses at Askeaton, Galway and Kilconnell, and at Clonmacnois Cathedral (fig. 7.3; pl. 15), while a wooden effigy of the saint is preserved in the Dominican priory in Kilkenny. St Dominic is also represented on the seal of the Dominican house at Mullingar. His life and virtues form the subject of three fifteenth-century bardic poems, two of which are attributed to Tadhg Óg O'Higgins (d. 1448), who was buried in the Dominican priory at Strade, while the third is attributed to the Observant Franciscan poet Philip Bocht O'Higgins. In each instance, the poets were familiar with the stock motifs of Dominic's *vita*.[82]

St Augustine is commemorated in one bardic poem, which its most recent editor attributes to an anonymous Augustinian Observant friar, writing in the later

**79** TCD MS 347, fo. 389; Colker, *Latin MSS*, i, p. 738. Reeves, *Influence of prophecy*, p. 527. **80** L. McKenna (ed.), *Philip Bocht O hUiginn* (1931), pp 1–5 (trans. pp 129–31) and pp 32–5 (trans. pp 149–51). See also L. McKenna, *The Irish Monthly* (1930), 150–3. **81** *MRH*, pp 223–4. Bishop Babington of Derry, who ordered the destruction of the Coleraine image, also died shortly afterwards. **82** Bhreathnach, 'The mendicant orders and vernacular Irish learning', p. 366; S. Ryan, 'Popular religion

7.3 St Dominic from Dean Odo's doorway, Clonmacnois Cathedral. The saint wears the Dominican habit and *cappa* and holds a book. He wears a lector's academic cap (photograph by Christy Cunniffe).

fifteenth or sixteenth century.[83] The poem praises the saint's wisdom, gives a lengthy account of the manner in which St Monica's prayers led to his conversion, and invokes him as an advocate on the poet's behalf. It also alludes to the fact that the rule of St Augustine was followed by two groups, the canons regular and the friars and urged that

> His brethren should follow
> St Augustine on the straight path;
> fruitful, fragrant clustered branch
> humblest source of lore for clergy.[84]

> [Sint Aibhisdin san iúl díreach
> dual dá bhráitribh breith a luirg,
> géag mheasa na mogal gcumhra
> tobar feasa is umhla an uird.]

in Gaelic Ireland, 1445–1645', i, pp 258–66.   **83** D. Ó Catháin (ed.), 'Some Augustinian material in Irish' (1998), p. 32.   **84** Ibid., p. 35.

OTHER MENDICANT CULTS

If the Irish Friars Preachers were diffident in prompting the cult of St Dominic, they compensated for it by enthusiastically promoting devotion to the order's proto-martyr Peter of Verona, or St Peter Martyr.[85] Raised in a Cathar household, Peter became a Catholic while a student and entered the Dominicans in Bologna in 1221. After his initial training, he devoted much of his energy as a preacher to combating heresy, and in 1251 Pope Innocent IV appointed him inquisitor for Lombardy. His activities antagonized his former Cathar colleagues and, on 6 April 1252, the saint and his friar-companion were assassinated as they travelled between Como and Milan. The inquisitor was hacked to death as he inscribed the opening words of the Apostles' Creed on the ground using his own blood. In consequence, his iconographic attribute is a gaping head wound often with a sword or hatchet protruding from it. Eleven months later, on 9 March 1253, Peter became the fastest candidate to be formally canonized in the history of the church when Innocent IV declared him a saint in Perugia. His cult spread quickly through the Dominican order and the wider church.[86] The order's general chapter meeting in Budapest in 1254 ordered that his feast and that of St Dominic be celebrated with the fullest liturgical honours, that their names be inscribed in the order's calendars and litanies and that their images be displayed for veneration in the friars' churches.[87] Shrines and altars dedicated to the new martyr became routine features of Dominican establishments. In Ireland, the dedication of the priory at Athy was changed from St Dominic to St Peter Martyr and the priory at Lorrha was dedicated to him sometime before 1269.

The foundation at Lorrha became a major centre for the promotion of St Peter's cult in north Munster and the earliest account of the saint's life, composed by the Italian Dominican friar Thomas Agni *c.*1270, contains vivid accounts of thirteen miracles wrought through his intercession in the dioceses of Limerick, Killaloe and Emly.[88] In each instance, the miracle was worked through the medium of water that had been blessed with a relic of the martyr. Agni's account of the cure of a boy at Lorrha serves to illustrate the strength of the cult:

> In the village of Lorrha in the Irish province in the diocese of Limerick [sic] there was a boy named Elias who was tormented by a terrible tumour in the foot and he found it intolerable. He was unable to rest or to travel or even to take any food. After he had fasted in such agony for two days, for three days he tasted only the water that had been sanctified by contact with the martyr's relics. On the first day he felt better, on the second day more

---

85 D. Prudlo, *The martyred inquisitor: the life and cult of Peter of Verona (+1252)* (2008).   86 Ibid., pp 90–5.
87 Prudlo, *Martyred inquisitor*, p. 91.   88 Ibid., pp 161–2, 258–60.

improvement and on the third he felt and declared himself fully healed. He washed his tumour with the same water and immediately the pain was relieved, and he was able to walk with strength, and he ate with joy. On account of this, the inhabitants of the village, moved with remarkable wonder, went with the clerics to the church and rang the bells, and they began to devoutly sing the *Te Deum*, to the glory of God and the holy martyr Peter who alone had accomplished this great miracle.[89]

The other Irish miracles included cases of healing from diseases, safe delivery in childbirth, relief from paralysis and the preservation from destruction of a wooden vessel holding water blessed by the saint's relics during a house fire in Limerick. The most remarkable feature of the Irish material in Agni's account is the manner in which it demonstrates the efficiency of the friars' communication network. Within a relatively short period of time, a detailed knowledge of the martyr's cult was available to the friars in Ireland who, in return, swiftly transmitted accounts of his Irish miracles to the order's central authorities in Italy.

A number of Franciscan saints enjoyed widespread cults in late medieval Ireland. Of these, St Louis of Toulouse (d. 1297) was the most popular. Friar John Clyn recorded his canonization in 1318.[90] In 1323, the Anglo-Irish friars, Simon Fitzsimon and Hugh the illuminator, visited his shrine en route to the Holy Land,[91] and the friar-poet Tadhg Camchosach O'Daly composed a poem in his honour at the end of the fourteenth century.[92] A fifteenth-century copy of his *vita* and account of his miracles by John of Orta is found in TCD MS 175 and in its sister manuscript, Marsh's Library MS Z3.1.5, which belonged to the friary in Clane in the sixteenth century.[93] His effigy, along with that of St Francis and other saints, is found on a late fifteenth-century tomb in Kilconnell friary (fig. 7.4). Evidence for devotion to St Anthony of Padua comes from the presence of his *vita* in TCD MS 175[94] as well as from his depiction on a tomb from the Franciscan friary in Galway, while references to St Clare in the poetry of Philip Bocht O'Higgins[95] and her representation on the Galway tomb indicates awareness of her cult (fig. 7.2). As noted above, a statue of St Louis IX, king of France, survives from the Franciscan friary in Adare and the dedication of the friary church there occurred on the feast of another tertiary Franciscan, St Elizabeth of Hungary, in 1464.[96]

**89** Ibid., p. 258.   **90** Clyn, *Annals*, p. 169.   **91** Esposito, *Itinerarium Symonis Semeonis*, pp 32–3.   **92** R. Flower, *The Irish tradition* (1947), pp 117–18 gives an account of O'Daly and a translation of the poem. **93** TCD MS 175, fos 48–56; Colker, *Latin MSS*, ii, p. 334.   **94** TCD MS 175, fos 58–66v. Colker, *Latin MSS*, i, p. 334. It is also found in Marsh's Library MS Z3.1.5. Both of these were copied from the same exemplar. For the history and relationship of the two codices, see R. Sharpe, *Medieval Irish saints' lives* (1991), pp 94–119.   **95** McKenna, *Ó Huiginn*, p. 2 (trans. p. 129).   **96** 'Brussels MS 3947', p. 63.

IRISH MENDICANT 'SAINTS'

Although no Irish friar was ever formally canonized, Dominican and Franciscan sources indicate that some medieval Irish friars enjoyed reputations for sanctity within the orders or in their immediate localities. The *Vitas fratrum*, a mid-thirteenth-century compilation of the noteworthy deeds of holy Dominicans compiled by Gerard of Frachet, contains an account of the post-mortem appearances of Friar Walter, a holy member of the Cork community.[97] The mid-fourteenth-century *Catalogue of the saints of the Friars Minor* commemorates two holy friars of Waterford: Friar Nicholas, who predicted the day of his own death to his *confrères*, and Friar John, at whose tomb the sick were cured and the dead restored to life. Friar John was commemorated on 5 September and one source gave 1245 as the year of his death.[98] The sixteenth-century friar-historian Marianus of Florence recorded the death of Friar Thomas of Ireland in Aquila in Italy in 1270. An excess of humility drove him to cut off his thumb, thereby rendering him ineligible for ordination as a priest. He was noted as a miracle worker during his life and after his death and was also credited with the authorship of the *Promptuarium morale*, edited by Luke Wadding in 1654.[99]

Donatus Mooney recorded a number of sixteenth-century friars who enjoyed reputations as saints or wonder-workers in various Irish friaries. These included the laybrothers Andrew Nugent of Multyfarnham and Friar Cuvéa of Adare and the priest-friar Fergal O'Treain of Ennis, whose presence at the deathbed of the chieftain Conor na Srón O'Brien saved him from despair. The community at Kilconnell was noted for the sanctity and learning of several of its lay and clerical members, one of whom, Friar Farrell MacEgan, was so steadfast in prayer that he developed calluses on his knees.

The most extensive account, however, concerned the life and virtues of the Donegal Franciscan, Friar Bernard MacGrath, who died in 1546. The author, Friar Donatus Mooney, had himself been a novice in Donegal in 1600 and his account probably derives from the oral tradition of the convent, as he cites no written sources. Mooney's account is remarkable for the degree to which it conforms to Vauchez's typology of mendicant sanctity discussed above. He records that Friar Bernard was born of a noble family who provided him with a good Christian education.[1] His family, the MacGraths of Termonmacgrath, in the diocese of Clogher, were the traditional custodians of the sanctuary of St Patrick's Purgatory. A later generation of the family produced one of the Franciscan order's most notorious apostates in the person of Friar Miler MacGrath, and Mooney's promotion of Friar Bernard's sanctity may have involved a compensatory element.[2]

Although a handsome and well-dressed young man, such was his piety and regard for chastity that he abandoned his studies after being propositioned by a woman and became a novice in the Donegal friary. Here his devotion to poverty was such that he was known as the 'poor man', a designation that echoed that of

97 Gerard of Frachet, *Vitas Fratrum*, p. 268. The incident is also recounted in the compendium of *exempla* compiled by a Dominican friar in Cambridge. Jones, *Friars tales,* p. 175.   98 *FL*, pp 12–13.   99 *FL*, pp 36–7.   1 'Brussels MS 3947', pp 41–7.   2 I owe this observation to an tOllamh Mícheál Mac Craith OFM.

the *poverello* – the 'little poor man' of Assisi. He was remarkable for his obedience and two of his miracles occurred in response to commands from his guardian. Humility led him to attribute cures wrought by him to the power of God rather than his own merits, as on the occasion when he cured his former novitiate companion of a tumour.[3] His concern for orthodoxy was also evident in his use of sacramentals such as water and salt 'blessed by ecclesiastical ritual' to produce fish from an empty weir and cause barren furrows to bring forth corn. He had particular faith in the efficacy of holy water, urging one suppliant not to have recourse to the charms and spells of witches to cure his cattle but instead to recite the Our Father, Hail Mary and the Creed together with his family and then to sprinkle the herd with water which Friar Bernard had blessed.[4] His powers of clairvoyance enabled him to predict the imminent death of an abbot who contradicted him during a sermon and to foretell the arrival of the funeral cortege of a benefactress for burial in the friary. In keeping with a well-established hagiographical convention, he predicted that his own death would occur simultaneously with that of his friend, the saintly dean of Armagh.

## PRAYER AND MEDITATION

The liturgy provided the context within which the medieval Irish friar pursued his quest for holiness while the example of the saints embodied the ideals towards which he strove. These complemented his personal prayer life and ascetic efforts and helped shape his individual spirituality. Given the highly personal nature of this process, it is very difficult to discuss it with certainty but some patterns can be traced in broad outline.[5]

In keeping with monastic custom, all the mendicant orders recognized the necessity for silence at certain times and in certain places to foster an atmosphere conducive to mental prayer or meditation.[6] The friar's cell in the dormitory was the place where private prayer most frequently occurred, but it was also common for communities to engage in meditation together in the friary church. In describing the destruction of the Franciscan friary in Multyfarnham by Sir Francis Shane in 1601, Mooney recorded that the attack occurred as the friars were returning to their cells from the church after the evening meditation.[7]

---

**3** 'Brussels MS 3947', pp 44–5. His companion had left the novititate and became a secular priest. After his cure, at Friar Bernard's urging, he resigned his benefice and rejoined the friars.   **4** Ibid., p. 46.   **5** Ó Clabaigh, *Franciscans*, pp 110–12.   **6** For Franciscan practice, see *AS*, ii, no. 3; I. Brady, 'The history of mental prayer in the Order of Friars Minor' (1951), pp 317–19; B. Roest, 'The discipline of the heart: pedagogies of prayer in medieval Franciscan works of religious instruction' (2007).   **7** 'Brussels MS 3947', p. 92.

The type of meditation in which the Irish friars engaged probably consisted of intense reflection on incidents in the life of Christ and the saints that, from the twelfth century onwards, had dominated late medieval spirituality.[8] As Colum Hourihane notes, 'the art and texts of this period move the worshipper over time from *compassio* to *imitatio* – from an understanding to an actual involvement in Christ's pain and suffering'.[9] Such emphasis on the use of the imagination and the conscious imitation of Christ led to a proliferation of spiritual writings marked by an affective and devotional quality. The presence of a number of works of this ilk in the library of the Youghal Franciscans indicates that the Irish friars were in touch with the mainstream currents of late medieval devotion. The Youghal library possessed copies of the pseudo-Bonaventuran *Meditationes vitae Christi*, the *Vita Christi* of the fourteenth-century Carthusian, Ludolph of Saxony, and two copies of Lothar de Segni's *De miseria humanae conditionis*.[10] Each of these works was influential in shaping late medieval devotion, encouraging the use of the imagination and emotions in meditating on Christ's suffering and on the human condition. The *Meditationes vitae Christi* was translated into Irish before 1462 by Thomas O'Bruachain, a canon of Killala, and is found in a number of late fifteenth-century manuscripts.[11] The *Vita Christi* was an encyclopaedic life of Christ that urged its readers to imagine themselves present at the events described. Each chapter of the work concludes with a prayer that summarized the material of the meditation.[12] The *De miseria* of Lothar of Segni owed much of its popularity to the fact that its author later became Pope Innocent III. It presents a very negative and bleak view of the human condition, stressing man's sinfulness and need of redemption. An Irish translation was completed in 1443 and a copy of this is found in the Rennes MS, written in Kilcrea friary in 1475.[13]

At the end of the fourteenth century, an influential movement known as the *Devotio moderna* emerged from the circle of the Dutch reforming preacher Geert Groote (1340–84). His lay followers were known as the Brethren of the Common Life, and other disciples formed a congregation of Augustinian canons. The movement spread into France, Germany and northern Italy, but their spirituality found its classic and most influential expression in the *Imitatio Christi* of the Augustinian canon, Thomas à Kempis (*c.*1380–1471), which circulated from 1418. This work is divided into four books; the first two giving instruction for the conduct of the spiritual life, the third dealing with the qualities of the soul, and the fourth, dealing with the reception of communion, profoundly influenced the

---

8 G. Constable, 'The ideal of the imitation of Christ' (1995).    9 C. Hourihane, 'Foreword' (2006), p. xvii.
10 *YLC*, nos 108[a], 22, 78[d] and 141[a].    11 C. Ó Maonaigh (ed.), *Smaointe beatha Chríost* (1944).
12 Texts and translations given in M.I. Bodenstedt, *Praying the life of Christ* (1973).    13 J.A. Geary (ed.), *An Irish version of Innocent III's De Contemptu Mundi* (1931).

Eucharistic practice of the church. By 1523, the Youghal library held two copies of the *Imitatio*.[14]

From the beginning of the fifteenth century, devotional woodcuts produced on the Continent became an important and inexpensive way of disseminating religious images. These prints circulated widely, as single leaves or in book form, and it is likely that the various works described as *liber devotus, pectorale passionis* and *libellus de passione* in the Youghal library catalogue were of this nature.[15] Images of Christ and his passion were particularly popular and influenced other artistic media as well. The stone carving of Christ as the *Ecce homo* or Man of Sorrows in Ennis friary ultimately derives from a woodcut. Bernadette Cunningham notes that the image of Christ's passion in the late sixteenth-century *Seanchas Búrcach* manuscript shows striking parallels with contemporary German woodcuts. She suggests that the artist's inspiration may have come from devotional images circulated by the friars in north Mayo, where the manuscript was produced.[16]

The Youghal Franciscans were also familiar with some classic treatises on the spiritual life. By 1523, they had acquired a copy of St Bonaventure's *Soliloquium*,[17] an influential introduction to prayer that dealt with the various stages through which the soul arrives at the contemplation of God. The reference to *Ricardus eremita* is to one of the works of the fourteenth-century English mystic Richard Rolle, whose writings circulated elsewhere in fifteenth-century Ireland, and whose style was similar to many of the other devotional works in the library.[18] All these works were designed for private reading and meditation, but other works such as the sermons of St Bonaventure, the *Legenda aurea* and the collections of sermons in the Youghal library would also have furnished material for devotional reading and meditation, even if their primary purpose was to provide material for preaching or teaching. The sermons of St Bernard, the Dialogues of St Gregory the Great, and the *Diadema monachorum* of Smaragdus of St Mihiel were also suitable for spiritual reading, even if they were more markedly monastic in character.[19]

The discovery of a set of *paternoster* beads during excavations at the Domnican priory in Cork illustrates another aspect of medieval mendicant devotion (fig. 7.5).[20] Although the discovery context suggests that they may have belonged to a layperson buried in the priory church in the sixteenth century, friars would

**14** *YLC*, nos 94, 121.   **15** *YLC*, nos 41, 100[b] & [c].   **16** B. Cunningham, 'Illustrations of the passion of Christ in the *Seanchás Búrcach* manuscript' (2006).   **17** *YLC*, nos 102[a], 147[b].   **18** *YLC*, no. 41. A number of Rolle's works are also found in Lambeth Palace MS 357, written for the Augustinian canons at Duleek in the late fifteenth century.   **19** *YLC*, nos 60, 69, 14.   **20** M.F. Hurley & C.M. Sheehan, *Excavations at the Dominican priory of St Mary's of the Isle, Cork* (1995), pp 112–14.

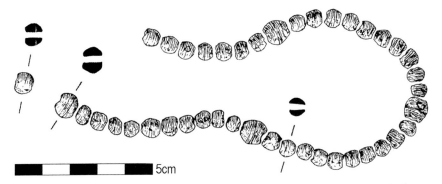

7.5 *Paternoster* beads found during excavations at St Mary's Dominican priory, Cork.
Reproduced by permission of Maurice Hurley.

also have used such beads as devotional aids. Laybrothers in particular would have used *paternoster* beads to count the multiple recitations of the Our Father by which they fulfilled their obligation to participate in the Liturgy of the Hours. From the late fifteenth century, the Dominican friars began to promote the rosary, a Marian devotion, among their lay followers.[21]

## PILGRIMAGE

Pilgrimage was an important feature of the spirituality of late medieval friars, as it was for their lay contemporaries. The presence of images of the Magi, St Thomas Becket and SS Peter and Paul on a tomb in the Dominican priory in Strade (fig. 7.6) indicates that its occupant had been a pilgrim to Cologne, Canterbury and Rome, and the friars were also aware of the significance of these shrines as places of pilgrimage. This is confirmed by presence of an altar dedicated to the Magi in the Franciscan church in Waterford, as well as the two images of Thomas Becket that survive in the Franciscan church in Ennis (fig. 7.7).

The most comprehensive indication of the importance of pilgrimage for the friars is the account of a pilgrimage to Jerusalem undertaken in 1323 by two Anglo-Irish Franciscans, Friars Simon Semeonis and Hugh the Illuminator. On his return, Friar Simon compiled his narrative, possibly while staying in the Franciscan friary in Norwich, and it survives in a single manuscript, Corpus

---

**21** C. Tait, 'Art and the cult of the Virgin Mary in Ireland, *c.*1500–1660' (2006), esp. pp 172–7, where she discusses the emergence of the devotion in Ireland in the mid-sixteenth century.

7.6 The Magi, Christ displaying his wounds, SS Thomas Becket, Peter and Paul and a suppliant pilgrim. Dominican priory, Strade, Co. Mayo (photograph by Karena Morton).

Christi College Cambridge MS 447. The account is incomplete and the narrative breaks off during the description of the shrines of the Holy Land.

Very little is known about the author Friar Simon Semeonis. Aubrey Gwynn suggested that his surname is a scribal error for Simonis and should be rendered *Filius Simonis* or FitzSimons, a family name that was established in Tipperary, south Kilkenny, Kerry and Dublin by the early fourteenth century. A Friar Simon Demeonis appears as a witness to a document in TCD MS 250 and may be identical to the author of the *Itinerarium*.[22] Internal evidence indicates that Friar Simon was a high-ranking member of the Irish Franciscan province who had received a solid education within the order's network of studia in Ireland, but who had not pursued advanced studies abroad. In the first line of the document, he alludes to having turned down the 'highest honour' in order to go on pilgrimage, and in the same context he refers to a provincial chapter of the Irish Franciscan province held in Clonmel in October 1322. His presence as a chapter delegate indicates that he was probably the guardian of a friary or *custos* of one of the

---

22 TCD MS 250, fo. 166v; Colker, *Latin MSS*, i, p. 449.

7.7  St Thomas Becket with the arrest of Christ, MacMahon tomb, Ennis friary, Co. Clare.

custodies into which the Irish Franciscan Province was divided. He may even have been elected minister provincial, declining the position in order to go on pilgrimage, a common practice in an age when such journeys were often undertaken in fulfilment of a vow. His travelling companion, Friar Hugh the Illuminator, was a witness in the trial of the Knights Templar in Ireland in 1310. Unlike his companion, Friar Hugh did not reach his destination and died of dysentery in Cairo on 26 November 1323.

Although the friars' destination was Jerusalem, the account indicates that they made the most of their journey and visited many other sights and shrines en route. They sailed from Ireland on 16 March 1323 and landed at Holyhead in Wales. Reaching Chester on 24 March, they spent Easter there before travelling on to London. Here, Friar Simon was impressed by the liturgy in the Lady Chapel of St Paul's Cathedral 'in which daily at the celebration of Mass the English chant sweet and joyous melodies to Mary quite unlike the shouting of Lombards and the howling of Germans'.[23] He also noted the famous chapel of St Thomas Becket on London Bridge. From London, the pilgrims travelled to Canterbury. Despite its popularity with Irish pilgrims and the cathedral priory's links with Ireland through its estates in Wexford, Friar Simon's description of the Becket's shrine is the only one to survive from an Irish source:

23 Esposito, *Itinerarium*, p. 27.

> After several days, we proceeded by way of Rochester to Canterbury, where is the shrine containing the body of St Thomas the martyr … in the monastery of the Black Monks, all of gold and adorned with innumerable precious stones and pearls, glittering like a gate of Jerusalem and even crowned with an imperial diadem. According to the inhabitants, there exists no similar shrine under the moon.[24]

In the cathedral, the friars also noted the tomb of John Pecham, the Franciscan theologian and archbishop of Canterbury who had died in 1292. From Dover they sailed to Wissant and travelled through Boulogne – where they venerated the famous image of the Virgin Mary – and Amiens – where the head of St John the Baptist was enshrined – Beauvais and St Denis, before arriving at Paris. They spent some time here, and Friar Simon was greatly impressed by the splendour of the city and its reputation for learning. Given the object of their trip, it is not surprising that the Sainte Chapelle with its relics of the passion received the greatest attention. From Paris, they travelled to Dijon but had to make a detour, as conflict between Milan, Naples and the papacy had closed the pilgrim route through Lombardy. They passed instead through Lyon and sailed down the Rhone, passing through Valence and Vienne until they came to Avignon, where Pope John XXII was in residence. At Tarascon, they venerated the relics of St Martha before sailing to Arles and then to Marseilles where they visited the shrine of St Louis of Toulouse, a Franciscan friar who had died in 1297. At Nice, they took ship for Genoa and made their way across Italy to Venice, where they remained for seven weeks. En route, they visited the shrine of the Irish abbot St Columbanus as well as that of St Anthony in Padua. From Venice, they sailed along the Adriatic coast and into the Mediterranean ocean, making landfall en route at Pola, Ragusa (Dubrovnik), Durazzo, Corfu and Cephalonia before arriving at Candia in Crete. Here, they encountered an encampment of gypsies and Simon's uncomplimentary description of their campsite is one of the earliest accounts to survive. On the 10 October 1323, the pilgrims sailed from Crete and arrived in Alexandria on 14 October. Here, the customs officials who interrogated them spat upon the various religious artefacts they had, before alerting the authorities at Cairo of the arrival of their ship by carrier pigeon. While waiting for permits to travel into Egypt, the friars were kept under guard inside the gates of the city and exposed to taunts from Muslims and Christian renegades. Having secured permission, they then travelled to Cairo, arriving there on 23 October. Friar Hugh's illness and death meant that Simon remained in Cairo until 1 December, and the delay enabled him to acquire a detailed knowledge of the

---

**24** Ibid., pp 28, 29, 30, 31. See also M. Staunton & C. Ó Clabaigh, 'Thomas Becket and Ireland' (2011).

social, religious and economic conditions of the city. He was intrigued by the game of polo, the three elephants and giraffe owned by the Sultan and by the special egg-hatching unit that incubated large numbers of chicks. Despite his disdain for Islam, Friar Simon recorded many aspects of Muslim society that impressed him. He noted the humane way in which Christian slaves were treated and how all were equal before the law. He also recorded that poor pilgrims received permits to travel to Jerusalem *gratis*, a policy of which he was a beneficiary. He procured his travel permit from the Sultan through the intervention of three apostate Christians, one a former Franciscan, who worked as interpreters and departed for Jerusalem by camel on 1 December 1323. He spent seven weeks visiting the shrines in Jerusalem and Palestine and was back in Cairo by 2 February 1324. While he omitted any account of the return journey, internal references indicate that his route home took him through Rome, Milan and Germany.

Although Friar Simon's account is the most comprehensive narrative of a medieval Irish pilgrimage, neither he nor his companion were the only friars to undertake one. Friars travelling abroad for studies or visiting Rome and other Continental centres on business of the order routinely visited the various shrines they encountered en route.[25] An incidental reference in the 1425 correspondence between the Carmelite prior provincial of England, Friar Thomas Netter, and his counterpart in Ireland, Friar Philip Raythey, indicates that the letters had been borne by Friar Nicholas, an Irish friar-pilgrim to the shrine of St Thomas at Canterbury.[26]

The registers of the Augustinian priors general and the Dominican masters general contain a number of entries permitting Irish friars to undertake pilgrimages to various Continental shrines. In 1431, Friar William Macgoreolitaidh and his companion were granted permission by the Augustinian prior general to visit various 'devout places [*loca devota*]' in Ireland and abroad. In like manner, in 1479, Friar Donatus, an Irish Augustinian laybrother, was given permission to visit the shrines of the apostles in Rome, but was ordered, under pain of excommunication, to return immediately to Ireland and present himself to his superior.[27] In 1491, Friar Thomas Lawless, a Dominican from Waterford, was permitted to visit Rome by the master general Friar Joachim Turriani, while in 1520, Friar David of the Athenry convent was granted leave to visit the shrine of St James in Compostella by the master general Friar Garcia of Loaisa.[28]

**25** Fenning, 'Irish material', pp 256, no. 9; 259, no. 17; 270, no. 77. Martin & de Meijer, 'Irish material', pp 87, no. 54; 102, no. 103.   **26** K. Alban (ed.), 'The letters of Thomas Netter of Walden' (1992), no. 36, p. 372.   **27** Martin & de Meijer, 'Irish material', pp 86, no. 50; 100, no. 95. Friars who went on pilgrimage without permission or who dallied unduly en route ran the risk of being labelled apostates.   **28** Fenning, 'Irish material', pp 262, no. 35; 268, no. 64.

## HERMITS AND ANCHORITES

If religious zeal prompted some friars to wander abroad as pilgrims, it encouraged others to embrace a more solitary existence as hermits and anchorites.[29] Each mendicant order combined a strong pastoral and apostolic identity with a yearning for the contemplative life. In the case of the Carmelites and Augustinians, this was a legacy of their origins as hermits. It may be significant that the Carmelite friars were charged with the maintenance of the bridge at their first foundation of Leighlinbridge, as this was a task frequently entrusted to hermits.[30] The eremitical impulse was a notable feature of the various medieval reform movements within the Franciscan order.[31] St Francis had written a rule for friar-hermits and, while there is no evidence that this text circulated in Ireland, the Irish friars were aware that Francis himself had spent time as a hermit, from their reading of the *Legenda maior* of St Bonaventure.

As an act of charity, monasteries and friaries occasionally undertook the support of a recluse, providing him or her with an anchorhold to live in and with some or all of his or her daily sustenance.[32] It is in this context that the earliest possible reference to friars and anchorites occurs in Ireland. In 1326, Robert de Moenes, a wealthy Dublin merchant and former mayor of the city, included bequests to two women described as Minorite sisters (*sororibus minoribus*) in his will. This term was normally used to describe Franciscan or Poor Clare nuns, but as no such community existed in Dublin at this date it may refer to anchoresses attached to the city's Franciscan friary.[33] In addition to supporting recluses, mendicant communities occasionally permitted their own members to embrace the solitary life. In these cases, the friar-anchorites remained under the jurisdiction of their religious superiors rather than that of the local bishop.[34] In July 1490, the Augustinian prior general permitted Friar Cornelius, an Irish friar, to live the solitary life and exercise a ministry of preaching, a faculty that recalled the Augustinians' origins as preaching hermits in central Italy in the mid-thirteenth century.[35] In July 1508, Octavian de Palatio, archbishop of Armagh, granted an indulgence of forty days to those who supported Friar Meylerus Bratnagh, an Observant Franciscan friar who, despite being old and blind, henceforth proposed to adopt a stricter religious life by becoming an anchorite in a cell adjacent to the cathedral at Cashel, Co. Tipperary.[36] To benefit from the indulgence, contributors had to be in a state of grace and the archbishop noted that Friar Meylerus had

**29** C. Ó Clabaigh, 'Anchorites in late medieval Ireland' (2010).   **30** J. Bergström-Allen, 'The Whitefriars return to Carmel' (2005).   **31** G.G. Merlo, 'Eremitismo nel francescanesimo medievale' (1991).   **32** For the English evidence, see Warren, *Anchorites*, pp 265–79.   **33** TCD MS 1207/85–26. Cited by Hall, *Women and the Church*, pp 186–7.   **34** Ó Clabaigh, 'Anchorites', p. 167.   **35** Martin & de Meijer, 'Irish material', p. 104, no. 110.   **36** M.A. Sughi (ed.), *Registrum Octaviani* (1999), i, p. 30; ii, pp 123–4.

7.8  Anchorite's cell, Franciscan friary, Moyne, Co. Mayo
(photograph by Yvonne McDermott).

undertaken this project with the support of his superiors. The fact that the archbishop of Armagh issued an indulgence for the support of an anchorite in the archdiocese of Cashel indicates that Friar Meylerus employed the services of a proctor to quest for alms on his behalf throughout the country. The use of proctors and indulgences to garner support for medieval English hermits and anchorites is well attested, and there is evidence for the practice in Ireland in the early fifteenth and late seventeenth centuries.[37]

The tertiary movement also provided a framework for the solitary life, as both the Dominican and Franciscan tertiary rules could be adapted for a variety of vocations. In Ireland, evidence for this comes entirely from the Franciscan tertiaries. In 1512, the baron of Slane, Christopher Fleming, and his wife, Elizabeth Stuckley, restored the cells at St Erc's hermitage on their demesne at Slane, Co. Meath, for the use of Father Malachy O'Byren and Brother Donagh O'Byrne, both hermits and Franciscan tertiaries.[38] Though much of the fabric that currently survives at the site dates to this restoration, the hermitage was first mentioned in a deed of 1344.[39] Mooney recorded the tradition that one of the

37 Ó Clabaigh, 'Anchorites', pp 164–5, 176–7.  **38** *MRH*, pp 274–5.  **39** J. Mills & M.J. McEnery, *Calendar of the Gormanston register* (1916), pp 55–6. I am grateful to Charles Smith for this reference.

early barons of Slane, also a Franciscan tertiary, had been enclosed as an anchorite there.[40]

Architectural features in a number of the late medieval mendicant foundations in the west of Ireland also suggest the presence of recluses in these communities. The Franciscan tertiary foundations at Rosserk, Co. Mayo, and Court, Co. Sligo, and the Observant Franciscan house at Moyne, Co. Mayo, have curious cells embedded in the walls of the transepts of the friary church. Each is equipped with a doorframe, a squint looking onto the altar in the adjoining chapel, and a narrow external window (fig. 7.8). Whereas their dimensions are extremely confined, it is hard to envisage what function they could have fulfilled other than as an anchorhold. Other mendicant foundations, such as the Augustinian priory at Adare and the Dominican priory at Kilmallock, both in Co. Limerick, have first-floor cells above stone-vaulted sacristies to the north of the chancel, equipped with hagioscopes overlooking the high altar. At the Franciscan friary in Askeaton and the Dominican friary in Athenry, similar features have a line of vision on altars in the nave of the church.[41] The Franciscan friary at Ennis, Co. Clare, also has a cell in this position, equipped with a fireplace, though it is equally possible that it may have functioned as another well-documented medieval monastic phenomenon – the house prison.

---

**40** 'Brussels MS 3947', p. 104.   **41** O'Sullivan, *MIDS*, pp 131–2.

## CHAPTER EIGHT

# Architecture and art

*The walls are built of excellent stone, a great part of which is elegantly chiselled. The roof is of wood, fashioned in the form of tiles, while the ceiling of the church is exceedingly beautiful. There are seven altars. The campanile is lofty, and in it hangs a large and sweet toned bell ... Almost all of the nobles of the country have erected burial places for themselves in the church, many of which are of marble, beautifully polished and ornamented with sculpture.*[1]

Collectively, the surviving mendicant friaries constitute some of the most remarkable and best-preserved examples of Ireland's medieval built heritage. In comparison with mendicant houses in England, Scotland and on the Continent, the Irish friaries have only recently begun to attract the attention of architectural historians and many aspects of their design and construction remain problematic.[2] This relative neglect is all the more surprising considering the large number of well-preserved remains that survive, making Ireland, in Maurice Craig's phrase, the *locus classicus* for the study of mendicant architecture in the British Isles.[3] No friary or friary precinct has been the subject of a full-scale archaeological investigation and the essential painstaking work of analyzing architectural features, moulding profiles and masons' marks has only recently been systematically pursued.[4] The surviving buildings of all four mendicant orders display a remarkable homogeneity with little variation in design between the different orders.

---

**1** Description of Kilconnell friary, 'Brussels MS 3947', p. 56. **2** A.R. Martin, *Franciscan architecture in England* (1937); J.P. Greene, *Medieval monasteries* (1992), p. 171; W. Schenkluhn, *Architettura degli ordini mendicanti* (2003); R. Fawcett, *Scottish architecture from the accession of the Stewarts to the Reformation, 1371–1560* (1994), pp 128–41. **3** The standard works, on which much of what follows is based, are C. Mooney, 'Franciscan architecture in Pre-Reformation Ireland' (1955–7); H. Leask, *Irish churches and monastic buildings* (1955–60); E.C. Rae, 'Architecture and sculpture, 1169–1603' (1987); R. Stalley, 'Gaelic friars and Gothic design' (1990); idem, 'The end of the Middle Ages: Gothic survival in sixteenth-century Connacht' (2003); P. Conlan, 'Irish Dominican medieval architecture' (2002); A. O'Donoghue, 'Mendicant cloisters in Munster' (2011); M. O'Neill, 'Irish Franciscan friary architecture: late medieval and early modern' (2009); O'Sullivan, *MIDS*, pp 107–42; R. Moss, 'Dominican order' (forthcoming). **4** C. Hourihane, *The mason and his mark* (2000); D. O'Donovan, 'Building the Butler lordship, 1405–c.1552' (2007); eadem, 'Holycross and the language of Irish late Gothic' (2011).

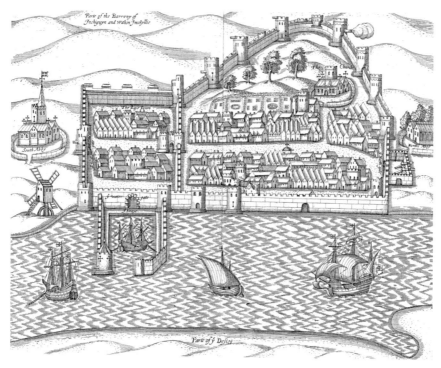

8.1 The town of Youghal from Thomas Stafford, *Pacata Hibernia* (1633). The Dominican and Franciscan houses are situated at the northern and southern entrances to the town.

Where differences occur, they are usually indicative of the relative sizes of the communities and, for this reason, Franciscan and Dominican friaries tend to be larger and more complex than Augustinian or Carmelite houses.

As a comprehensive analysis of every aspect of mendicant architecture and art is beyond the scope of the present study, this chapter examines how sites were chosen and buildings planned, what functions the component parts of the claustral complex fulfilled and how the friary churches were furnished and decorated. It concludes by showing how the friary building itself became a symbol of the religious life as its various architectural elements were allegorized and acquired ascetic and moral overtones.

LOCATIONS AND SITES

As noted in chapter one, the first mendicant foundations in Ireland clustered, with few exceptions, around the cities, towns and boroughs of the Anglo-Norman colony. The presence of a mendicant foundation enhanced the status of an urban settlement and provided a convenient indication of its prosperity. In keeping with English and Continental practice, friaries were frequently situated on sites adjacent to a main thoroughfare but outside the town walls (fig. 8.1).[5] Here, the friars were near their supporters and benefactors but were also able to acquire sufficient land for their house, precinct, cemetery and gardens in a location that afforded them the solitude conducive to the religious life. Conflict between the friars and existing religious bodies over revenues and seeking alms led to the decree that no mendicant house was to be established within three hundred perches (*cannae*) of an existing foundation.[6] The Irish friars were aware of this constraint, as a copy of the relevant bull is included in the Franciscan codex TCD MS 250.[7] The original distance proved impractical, and in 1268 Pope Clement IV reduced the distance to 140 cannae.[8]

In Cork and Limerick, the Friars Preachers had their own gates in the city walls, while in Kilkenny the 'Freren Gate' in the town walls was so named because it was close to the Dominican priory. In Drogheda, the Dominican house was situated near one of the city's gates, which was named St Sunday's Gate in consequence.[9] While these locations gave greater freedom and occasional exemption from urban rates and charges, they also left the communities exposed in times of war and social upheaval. In 1316, under threat of attack by Edward Bruce, the mayor and citizens of Dublin demolished the Dominican church on the north bank of the Liffey and used the stones to shore up the city walls.[10] In Galway, the Augustinian priory was converted into a fort *c.*1603, while the Dominican convent was demolished to secure the city's defences in 1651.[11] Occasionally, friaries were built within the town walls and in some cases the precinct wall formed part of the fortifications. At Carlingford, Co. Louth, the Dominican church had a machiolation, battlements and turrets at its west end and was described in 1540 as being a 'strong mansion needing no expenditure on repairs, but on every side strongly fortified, and will be a very sure defence for the town in case of attack through rebellions of those living close by'. Similarly, the Franciscan church in Waterford was described as being necessary for 'the comfort, defence and ease of the city.'[12] At Drogheda, the town walls incorporated the east window of the Franciscan church, while in Limerick the city walls partially enclosed the precinct of the Dominican priory.[13]

5 J. Röhrkasten, *The mendicant houses of medieval London, 1221–1539*, pp 501–13; P. Volti, *Couvents des ordres mendiants et leur environment à la fin du moyen âge* (2003), pp 187–220.   6 A perch was equivalent to five-and-a-half yards; three hundred *cannae* was slightly less than a mile.   7 TCD MS 250, fo. 157rv. 8 Andrews, *The other friars*, p. 27, n. 7.   9 St Sunday was a popular alternative name for St Dominic resulting from the similarity between the Latin form of his name (*Dominicus*) and that of Sunday (*Dies Dominica*).   10 Pembridge, *Chronicle*, p. 353; *MRH*, p. 225.   11 J. O'Connor, *The Galway Augustinians* (1979), pp 74–5; H. Fenning, 'The Dominicans of Galway, 1488–1988' (1991), p. 27.   12 White, *Extents*, pp 245, 350.   13 'Brussels MS 3947', p. 28.

As the friars expanded in Ireland, their settlement pattern became more diverse, and, while continuing to gravitate towards urban settlements, a number of foundations were made at existing religious sites. This was particularly true of foundations made in Gaelic territories. The Franciscans established a house in 1263–4 at Armagh, where a community of Augustinian canons already existed. The Dominican foundations at Lorrha (1269) and Aghaboe (1382) also shared early Christian sites with pre-existing communities of canons. A similar pattern can be discerned at a number of fifteenth-century foundations: the Franciscan friary in Elphin owed its origins to the decision of the bishop and chapter of the diocese to grant the parish church of St Patrick to the friars *c.* 1450, while that at Kilconnell (1414) occupied the site of an early monastic enclosure. The Franciscan tertiary foundation at Killybegs, Co. Donegal, was also established on an early Christian site.[14] On occasion, friaries occupied the sites of defunct monasteries or abandoned religious properties. The Franciscans acquired an abandoned priory of the Crutched Friars for their foundation in New Ross sometime before 1256.[15] The Dominican foundation at Portumna occupied a property previously owned by the Cistercian monks of Dunbrody, while their site in Galway was formerly the property of the Premonstratensian canons of Tuam.[16] In 1583, the Franciscans took over the abandoned house of Augustinian canons at Lisgoole, Co. Fermanagh.[17] The most intriguing transfer occurred at Clonkeenkerrill, Co. Galway, where a community of Franciscan tertiaries not alone took over an existing church site but also assimilated the hereditary clerical family associated with it. This foundation subsequently became a house of Friars Minor.[18]

A number of friaries occupied the sites of secular dwellings or fortifications. The Franciscan proto-friary at Youghal began as a castle for Maurice Fitzgerald, while that at Carrickbeg, Co. Waterford, was built on the site of a Fitzgriffin castle granted to the friars in 1336 by the earl of Ormond.[19] The Dominican house at Waterford occupied the site of an old tower, and existing towers were incorporated into the friary complexes at the Franciscan foundation in Buttevant and the Dominican church in Kilkenny.[20] The Franciscan friary at Quin (1433) occupied the site of a de Clare castle, destroyed *c.* 1286 (fig. 8.2), while the Augustinian Observant house at Banada was reputedly built from the stones of seven towers of a de Burgh castle that were dismantled for the purpose.[21] Swords Castle, one of the principal residences of the medieval archbishops of Dublin, also incorporated a residence for an unspecified group of mendicants and is the only known Irish

---

**14** http://monasticon.celt.dias.ie, accessed 14 September 2010.   **15** *MRH*, p. 257.   **16** *MRH*, pp 225, 228.   **17** *MRH*, p. 254. K.W. Nicholls, 'The Lisgoole agreement of 1580' (1960).   **18** *MRH*, pp 269–70; Ó Clabaigh, *Franciscans*, pp 96–7.   **19** 'Brussels MS 3947', p. 27, 80; Clyn, *Annals*, pp 218, 220. I am grateful to Conleth Manning for clarification of this point.   **20** De Barra, 'Buttevant', p. 56; Fenning, *The Black Abbey*, p. 7.   **21** *MRH*, p. 296; Martin, 'Irish Augustinian reform', p. 241, n. 42.

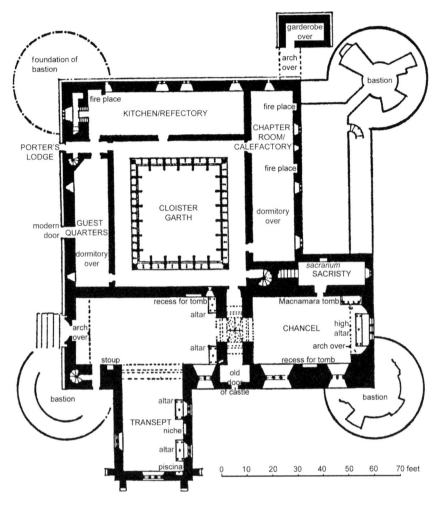

8.2 Plan of the Franciscan friary, Quin, Co. Clare, showing the foundations of the dismantled De Clare castle (after Leask, *Irish churches and monastic buildings*, III, p. 103).

instance of a practice common elsewhere whereby high-ranking prelates and secular rulers maintained some friars at their courts.[22]

Another notable feature of Irish mendicant sites was their close proximity to the castles and tower houses of their patrons. The thirteenth-century Franciscan foundation at Ennis was adjacent to the O'Brien stronghold at Clonroad, while at Athenry the Dominican priory was within sight of the castle of the de Bermingham barons. This pattern is particularly noticeable with the second wave

22 R. Stalley, 'The archbishop's residence at Swords: castle or country retreat?' (2006), pp 166–7; Lawrence,

of foundations in the late fourteenth and fifteenth centuries, when Observant friaries of all orders were built in close proximity to Gaelic or Anglo-Irish strongholds. The Dominican foundations at Ballindoon, Glanworth and Portumna, the Franciscan houses at Adare (pl. 10), Askeaton (pl. 11), Donegal, Kilcrea, Lislaughtin and Quin (pl. 12), the Augustinian friaries at Ardnaree, Callan and Dunmore and the Carmelite priory at Rathmullan all stand adjacent to a residence of their principal patrons. This arrangement was mutually beneficial. It afforded the friars protection and material support while enhancing the reputation of the magnates as benefactors with a serious commitment to the spiritual wellbeing of their people. Many of the friaries are coeval with the tower houses of their patrons and often formed part of the same building campaign, with both structures functioning as manifestations of lordship and authority. At Askeaton, there is a close parallel between the east dais window of the great hall of the Desmond Castle and the north choir window of the nearby Franciscan friary, both dating to *c.*1420. At Glanworth, Co. Cork, the Dominican priory founded *c.*1475 by David Mór Roche was probably constructed at the same time as a major rebuilding project in the nearby Roche castle.[23] As already noted in chapter four, the friaries functioned as worthy mausolea for the founders and their descendants, with the friars acting as intermediaries, intercessors, counsellors and confessors to their aristocratic patrons. This juxtaposing of an aristocratic or royal residence and an austere religious foundation was a feature of mendicant friaries elsewhere in late medieval Europe.[24] James IV of Scotland established an Observant Franciscan house in 1494 at Stirling, where he was accustomed to join the community for the Holy Week liturgy.[25] In England, Observant Franciscan houses were established adjacent to the royal palaces at Richmond and Greenwich and the friars functioned as quasi court chaplains. It was in the Greenwich friary that Henry VIII married Catherine of Aragon in June 1509. Their son Henry was baptized in the Richmond friary in January 1511, while their daughter, the future Queen Mary, was christened in the friary church at Greenwich in February, 1516.[26]

WATER

Whether rural or urban, friaries were invariably located adjacent to a permanent water source. This enabled them to harness water to power mills and provide

*The friars*, pp 169–73.   **23** T.E. McNeill, 'The larger castles of later medieval Limerick' (2011), p. 176; C. Manning, *History and archaeology of Glanworth Castle* (2009), p. 143.   **24** For this phenomenon in northern France and the Netherlands, see Volti, *Les couvents des ordres mendiants*, pp 189–90.   **25** D.E. Easson, *Medieval religious houses: Scotland* (1957), p. 113; C.A. Strauch, 'Royal connections: the Scottish Observants and the house of Stewart' (2007), p. 165.   **26** MacCraith, 'Collegium S. Antonii Louvanii', p. 236.

8.3 Moyne friary, Co. Mayo, showing the friary complex, boundary walls and watercourse
(© National Monuments Photographic Unit).

domestic sanitation using a system of dams and sluices. Although well
documented among monastic orders, the use of hydraulic power has received little
attention in an Irish mendicant context.[27] In describing the Franciscan foundation
at Moyne, Co. Mayo, Donatus Mooney conveys something of the friars' hydraulic
expertise. Within the friary precinct, they channelled a spring, making use of it for
drinking and sanitation purposes at six or seven different locations within the
enclosure in addition to using it to power two mills.[28] This watercourse still
functions at Moyne and flows under the north range of the cloister complex,
where it serviced the kitchen and latrines, before flowing through the remains of
a mill on its way to the sea (fig. 8.3). At the Observant Franciscan house at Adare,
the watercourse diverted from the River Maigue is still extant. Though now dry,
it too flowed through the domestic offices of the north range, flushing the latrines,
and servicing the kitchen, bakery and brewing areas before turning a mill and
rejoining the river downstream of the friary. Also in Adare, on the opposite bank
of the Maigue, the water channel that serviced the nearby Augustinian priory still
survives in part. The Franciscans at Cashel were credited with building the
aqueduct that conveyed water to the town from a source two miles distant, and in
the early seventeenth century the remains of the water courses were still evident in

27 Greene, *Medieval monasteries*, pp 109–32.   28 'Brussels MS 3947', p. 51.

the ruins of the friary.[29] The remains of a millrace and fishponds can still be traced in the precincts of the Dominican priory at Tulsk, Co. Roscommon, as well as at the Franciscan house at Rosserrilly, Co. Galway.[30] These complex drainage and sanitation systems were laid out before the erection of any of the friary buildings and recent excavations at the Franciscan house on Sherkin Island, Co. Cork, have revealed the drainage system servicing the east range of the claustral buildings.[31]

Potable water came from a variety of sources, including streams, wells and public water supplies. A number of friary wells still survive, and in some instances became the focus of pilgrimages in the early modern period. St Augustine's Well at Lough Atalia on the outskirts of Galway served the Augustinian community there and still functions as a place of devotion.[32] The 'abbey well' in Callan was the principal water supply for the Augustinian friars there and remains in use to the present day.[33] Wells dedicated to St Dominic survive in the vicinities of the Dominican priories at Urlar and Glanworth.[34] Excavations in 2008 revealed a well adjacent to the north domestic range of the friary complex at Ennis (fig. 8.4).[35] Mooney's description of the Franciscan well at Kilkenny demonstrates both the friars' hydraulic skill and the well's cultic significance:

> Close to the infirmary, and not far from the river, rises a spring of most excellent and palatable water. It is called the well of St Francis, and was formerly surrounded by a wall erected by the friars. The waters flow in such abundance that it rises high enough to enter all the buildings of the monastery through various channels and inlets when its course to the river is dammed up. It is there turned to several uses and, finally, passing through the sinks and sewers, flushes them, on its way to the river. The wholesome waters of this well are certainly most useful and refreshing, whether its existence be due to natural causes or, as many think, to the merits of St Francis. This belief is widely diffused, and numbers come from distant places to drink of its water, or to carry it to others, who, through illness, are unable to make the journey – many of whom have been restored to health.[36]

In some urban centres, the friars were occasionally beneficiaries of private water supplies granted by benefactors. In Dublin, the Dominicans were the first religious community to acquire such a supply from the public watercourse and cistern constructed in 1244. This privilege was granted some time between 1250 and

**29** Ibid., p. 77.   **30** K. O'Conor et al., 'Tulsk Abbey' (1996), 67–9.   **31** A. O'Donoghue, 'Mendicant cloisters', pp 128–9; Ann Lynch, pers. comm.   **32** P. O'Dowd, 'Holy wells of Galway city' (2008). **33** Conleth Manning, pers. comm.   **34** Pochin-Mould, *Irish Dominicans*, p. 40; Manning, *History and archaeology of Glanworth Castle*, p. 11.   **35** Frank Coyne and Tracy Collins, pers. comm.   **36** 'Brussels MS 3947', p. 83. Trans. in *Franciscan Tertiary*, 6 (1895), 194.

8.4  Well adjacent to the north cloister range, Franciscan friary, Ennis, Co. Clare
(photograph courtesy of Br Cathal Duddy OFM).

1255. The pipe conducting the water the lengthy distance from the city's New Gate to the priory passed over Dublin Bridge and had a calibre of five thumb-breadths along its length. Within the priory, the pipe was reduced to the dimensions of a man's little finger and the friars were forbidden to enlarge it on pain of forfeiting the grant.³⁷ In 1247, Bishop Geoffrey de Turville of Ossory granted the Black Friars in Kilkenny a supply of water from St Canice's (alias St Kenny's) Well. The diameter of the pipe carrying the water to the friary was the same as the bishop's pontifical ring, narrowing to the dimensions of a man's little finger within the house. The charter granting the supply is preserved in the Kilkenny municipal archives and has attached a copper ring of the requisite calibre (pl. 13).³⁸ The Franciscans in Dundalk enjoyed a similar arrangement, as in 1311, Richard Touker was charged with breaking their water conduit and stealing lead from the spring to the value of more than 20s.³⁹

The communities situated at riverbank, estuarine and island sites also depended on water for transport, and contemporary references indicate that many friaries possessed boats. In December 1454, two Augustinian friars of Holy Trinity priory,

37 B. O'Sullivan OP, 'The Dominicans in medieval Dublin' (1990), p. 89. The citizens agreed to submit to the archbishop's sanctions if they interfered with the supply.  38 'Charter of Geoffrey de Turville, bishop of Ossory, to the Friars Preachers of Kilkenny' (1850), pp 264–7. I am grateful to Aideen Ireland for this reference. H. Fenning, *The Black Abbey*, pp 7–8.  39 *FL*, p. 218.

Scurmore, Co. Sligo, were permitted to maintain a fishing boat on the River Moy on account of the poverty of the community.[40] At the Franciscan friary at Askeaton, the principal entrance to the friary precinct was through a large water-gate that opened onto a quay on the banks of the River Deel. Their *confrères* at Multyfarnham owned an island on which they dried the nets from their fishing boats.[41] In 1516, the Annals of Ulster recorded the death by drowning in a boating accident on Lough Erne of a large party of friars from the Franciscan house at Cavan.[42] Their colleagues at Moyne were more fortunate in 1578, when they escaped a raid on the friary by putting to sea in their boats.[43] In Youghal, the Franciscan community received an income from a ferry crossing on the River Blackwater, which had been granted to them, probably by one of the early earls of Desmond. In 1489, after the community adopted the Observant reform, they renounced the income as incompatible with their vow of poverty and returned it to Maurice Fitzgerald, tenth earl of Desmond.[44]

SITES, PLANS AND BUILDERS

Although no account survives of the coming of the friars to Ireland, it is likely that their initial attempts to find accommodation resembled those of their *confrères* elsewhere in Europe. A rented room or space in a pilgrims' hospice or in a monastery guest house would have sufficed for the first pioneers. Even when the first friaries were built, they were often simple wooden structures. Archaeological excavations have not yet revealed evidence for pre-existing wooden structures at any Irish mendicant sites, but the Annals of Ulster record the burial in 1512 of Margaret O'Brien in the wooden church she had constructed for the Franciscans at Dromahair.[45] This was destroyed by fire in 1536 and replaced by a stone building, the remains of which still exist. Even when the friary churches were built in stone, it is likely that some of the domestic building remained wooden structures for a considerable period of time. Excavations at the site of the Augustinian priory at Cecilia Street in Dublin in 1996 revealed the remains of the lime-kiln and slaking pit used to produce the mortar for the walls and buildings.[46]

Both St Dominic and St Francis had a horror of large churches and costly stone convents. In the Testament that Francis composed shortly before his death, he ordered the Friars Minor not to receive 'churches and poor dwellings or anything which is built for them, unless it is harmony with the holy poverty we have

40 *CPL*, x, p. 677; *MRH*, p. 301; Martin, 'Augustinian friaries', pp 381–2.   41 White, *Extents*, p. 275.
42 *AU*, iii, p. 527.   43 'Brussels MS 3947', p. 52.   44 National Library of Ireland, Lismore papers, MS 41,981/ 2. I owe this reference to Rhiannon Carey Bates and David Kelly.   45 *AU*, iii, p. 501.
46 S. Duffy & L. Simpson, 'The hermits of St Augustine in Dublin' (2009), pp 229–33.

promised in the Rule'.[47] This unease found expression in their respective orders' subsequent legislation, although the frequency with which both orders' general chapters had to address the issue in the thirteenth century indicates that the founders' injunctions were not always heeded. The Dominican constitutions addressed the issue of buildings on five separate occasions between 1220 and 1300 and, despite Humbert of Romans instruction that the friars' houses be 'mediocre and humble', many friaries developed into magnificent expressions of civic pride and mercantile munificence.[48] A similar pattern is evident among the Franciscans. In treating of the observance of poverty, the 1260 general constitutions of Narbonne fobade 'curiosity and superfluity' in the buildings themselves and in their internal furnishings and ordered that transgressors in this regard be severely punished.[49] Less information is available for Carmelite and Augustinian attitudes to buildings, but in general these followed the pattern and tenor of the Friars Minor and Preachers.[50] The Observant reformers in each order likewise stressed poverty and simplicity in buildings and the 1451 Barcelona statutes prohibited the Franciscans from incurring excessive debts for building projects and forbade excess in their churches, convents and liturgical ornaments.[51]

At the Cistercian monasteries of Corcomroe, Co. Clare, Abbey Owney, Co. Limerick, and Kilcooley, Co. Tipperary, fragments of architectural designs remain incised on the walls of the churches or used as decorative motifs on stonework.[52] No such evidence survives from any mendicant site and the architectural models and inspiration for the Irish houses remain obscure. For Franciscan foundations, Michael O'Neill has recently demonstrated that ground plans based on the square root of two and golden section triangles underlie many of the surviving thirteenth-century foundations. The later Franciscan foundations also employed the same principles as their thirteenth-century counterparts.[53] In a pioneering study of the fifteenth-century Franciscan house at Muckross, Co. Kerry, Roger Stalley showed that the proportions of the building were established using the dimensions of the cloister garth as a base line and calculating the layout of the rest of the building using a ratio based on the square root of two.[54] These proportions were not particular to the mendicants, and they determine the layout of many Augustinian and Cistercian monasteries as well.[55]

The ground plan deriving from this system could easily be laid out with a set of pegs and ropes and, once established, meant that the friary could be completed

47 Esser, *Opuscula*, p. 312.   48 R.A. Sundt, 'Mediocres domos et humiles habeant fratres nostri: Dominican legislation on architecture and architectural decoration in the 13th century' (1987).   49 C. Cenci & R.G. Mailleux, *Constitutiones generales* (2007), p. 75. The issue of architecture was a recurrent problem for the Franciscans also: cf. pp 116, 167, 295–6.   50 Andrews, *The other friars*, pp 39–40, 112–19.   51 *AS*, p. 132, nos 18, 19.   52 R. Stalley, *The Cistercian monasteries of Ireland* (1987), pp 49, fig. 9, 68–75, 204.   53 M. O'Neill, 'Irish Franciscan friary architecture: late medieval and early modern' (2009), pp 309–16.   54 R. Stalley, 'Gaelic friars', pp 198–202.   55 T. Fanning & M. Clyne, *Kells priory, Co.*

8.5  Reconstruction of Cork Dominican priory, phase 1
(reproduced by permission of Maurice Hurley).

in a piecemeal but harmonious fashion over a longer period of time. The 'additive' nature of Irish friaries is another noteworthy feature of their construction, and many foundations only achieved their final form after centuries of addition, renovation and rebuilding.[56] This process can often be traced in the physical structure of the buildings themselves: at many sites, the bell towers are fifteenth-century insertions into fourteenth-century churches that obscure earlier windows and other architectural features. Good examples of this survive at the Carmelite house in Loughrea, the Dominican church in Kilkenny and the Franciscan friary in Claregalway (fig. 8.19). At the Franciscan house at Quin, the domestic ranges of the convent are not bonded together, indicating that they were constructed as discrete units at various times even though they follow a basic ground plan. Likewise, architectural differences in the cloister arcade of the west range of the Franciscan friary in Adare indicate that it was constructed at a later stage than the rest of the convent. At the Franciscan house at Muckross, differences in the

*Kilkenny: archaeological investigations* (2007), pp 487–90.   **56** Stalley, 'The end of the Middle Ages'. Stalley's thesis has major implications for dating the later friaries, many of which, he argues, attained their final forms only in the late sixteenth or early seventeenth centuries.

8.6 Reconstruction of Cork Dominican priory, phase 2
(reproduced by permission of Maurice Hurley).

vaulting patterns of the integrated cloister walks indicate that they also were
constructed at different stages. In each of these instances, the buildings follow the
proportions of the basic ground plan laid out at the beginning of the construction
process.

Excavations at the site of the Dominican priory in Cork and recent analyses of
the fabric of the Dominican priories in Athenry and Roscommon have revealed
distinct construction phases in the thirteenth and fifteenth centuries, by which
latter stage the buildings had been renovated almost beyond recognition.[57] The
Cork excavations demonstrated that the original friary church was likely to have
been a simple elongated one-storey rectangular structure, possibly with a transept
on the south side of the church built as part of the same building campaign in the
second quarter of the thirteenth century (fig. 8.5). This relatively simple complex
was radically overhauled in the late fourteenth and fifteenth centuries, when

---

**57** Hurley and Sheehan, *Excavations*, pp 46–51; J. McKeon, 'The Dominican priory of Saints Peter and
Paul, Athenry' (2009).

several additions were made to the original church and priory complex. The discovery of two subtantial stone plinths in the church indicates that a tower was added at the junction of the choir and the nave. The cloister was also substantially altered, possibly to accommodate a new north aisle. A layer of lime mortar discovered in the church was interpreted as a sub-floor surface underlying a tiled floor (fig. 8.6).[58] At Roscommon, recent work has revealed that it too was extensively renovated in the fifteenth century when a tower and new windows were added to the church and the domestic ranges rebuilt and provided with stone vaulted cloister walks.[59] Not every friary received such attention. The remains of the small Augustinian priory at Murrisk, Co. Mayo, suggest that only the east range of the domestic building was constructed in stone and that the rest of the claustral complex was either built in wood or never built at all.

Practically nothing is known of the identities of the master builders, masons and other craftsmen who designed and built the Irish friaries, with the single exception of the *Ioannes* who carved his name on the transom of a window in the Dominican house at Portumna in the late fifteenth century.[60] Elsewhere in Europe, individual friars were noted as architects, glass makers and painters, and some Irish friars may have operated in these capacities: Friar John de Nasse was 'master of the works' (*magister operum*) for the building of the Lady Chapel at the Franciscan friary in Clonmel in 1318.[61] The Irish exchequer records for 1280–1 note a payment of £3 to Brother Roger de Chester, a glazier, of which £2 was payment for glazing the windows of the exchequer itself.[62] It does not specify to which order he belonged. It seems likely, however, that the friars depended on external labour both for the construction of the friaries and subsequent maintenance of their fabric. Mooney records that the friars at Timoleague employed a carpenter to maintain their house in the early seventeenth century, and this was probably a standard practice among all the orders.[63] The image of an axe on a grave-slab in the nave of the friary church at Quin allegedly marks the grave of a carpenter killed in a fall, while a grave-slab at Buttevant Friary commemorated John O'Dowling, *carpentarius* to the Franciscan community there.[64]

If the identities of the craftsmen remain largely unrecoverable, recent analyses of architectural features and masons' marks give some indication of their movements and of the buildings on which they laboured.[65] In most cases, the mason(s) involved worked on other non-mendicant projects and the friaries can

**58** M. Hurley & C.M. Sheehan, *Excavations at the Dominican priory*, pp 44–51.   **59** Kieran O'Conor, pers. comm.   **60** The name also appears on the screen dividing the nave and chancel at the nearby Augustinian monastery at Clontuskert, Co. Galway.   **61** *FL*, p. 221.   **62** P. Connolly, *Irish exchequer payments, 1270–1446* (1998), i, p. 73; J. Moran, 'Painted and stained glass in Ireland' (2006), p. 131.   **63** 'Brussels MS 3947', p. 68.   **64** Mooney, 'Franciscan architecture', ii, pp 125–6.   **65** O'Donovan, 'Building the Butler lordship', pp 135–92, 245–7.

be situated within the context of regional 'schools' of masons. The earliest example identified is the Cashel School, where a single mason can be traced by his mark to five of the most important religious buildings constructed in the mid-thirteenth century: Cashel Cathedral; St Canice's Cathedral, Kilkenny; Athassel Priory (Augustinian canons); and the Dominican priories at Cashel and Youghal. Similarities in design between the windows in the choir of Cashel Cathedral and those of the Dominican priory in the town suggest that the two sites may also have shared some of the same workforce.[66]

In the fifteenth century, masons from the 'Holycross School' who worked at the Cistercian monasteries of Hore, Kilcooly and Holycross also laboured on a number of the region's mendicant friaries. The work of this school is notable for its exceptionally high standard and detail, particularly evident in some of the decorative stonework at Holycross. The Franciscan house at Ennis shares a number of sculptural features with Holycross and indicates that the friary was rebuilt at considerable expense in the mid-fifteenth century.[67] Individual masons' marks from this school are found on stonework at the Franciscan friaries at Ennis and Quin and at the Augustinian priory in Fethard.

A mason from the 'Limerick School', another fifteenth-century group of craftsmen, contributed to the building of the Franciscan friaries at Adare, Askeaton, Ennis and Muckross, buildings that share architectural similarities with the Franciscan foundations at Moyne and Rosserrilly. The work in these houses is not of the same quality as the other fifteenth-century schools, and this is particularly evident in the poorly finished dressing of stone and the lack of architectural detail.[68] The friaries at Adare, Muckross, Moyne and Rosserrilly were at the forefront of the Observant reform, and this simplicity of design and execution may have been ideologically motivated.

## THE FRIARY BUILDINGS

### The cloister

At the heart of all but the smallest Irish mendicant houses lay the cloister alleys and garth. This enclosed area served a number of practical and symbolic functions, of which the most basic was to provides axes of communication between the different domestic ranges and the church.[69] In churches where the crossing tower formed the division between the nave and the chancel, the friars' principal entrance to the church was normally through a doorway in the north walk of the

---

66 Hourihane, *The mason and his mark*, pp 28–9.  67 Ibid., pp 34–9, 63–4.  68 Ibid., pp 39–40.
69 For what follows see, A. O'Donoghue, 'Mendicant cloisters in Munster' (2011).

8.7 Plan of the
Franciscan friary,
Muckross, Co. Kerry
(from Leask, *Irish
churches and monastic
buildings*, III, p. 105)

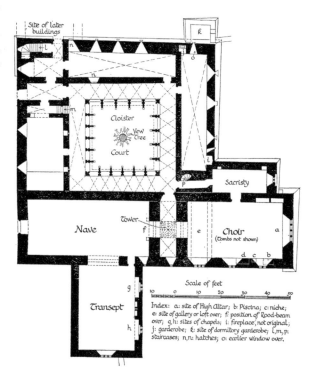

cloister underneath the tower.[70] Stairways situated at the junctions of each range gave access to first-floor domestic apartments, such as the dormitories, guest quarters and, in some cases, refectories, while slypes or passages at ground-floor level communicated with the rest of the precinct. The principal entrance to a friary was normally situated in the west range of the claustral complex (fig. 8.7).

The earliest mendicant cloister ambulatories in Ireland were single-storey structures covered by lean-to roofs (fig. 8.8). This model was the norm in monasteries and remained in vogue with monks and canons even when the cloisters were subsequently rebuilt.[71] The dearth of stone cloister fragments from thirteenth-century friaries and the large number of fifteenth-century remains possibly indicates the replacement of wooden cloisters by stone structures in the later Middle Ages.[72] Even among the fifteenth-century foundations, stone-built cloisters were not universal. At the Augustinian house at Murrisk, the presence of stone corbels in the ranges surrounding the cloister garth indicate that the cloister was a wooden lean-to structure, while the Franciscan tertiary foundation at

---

**70** Or through the south wall if the cloister was on the south.  **71** J. Montague, 'The cloister arcade' (2007), pp 187–206.  **72** Stalley, *Cistercian monasteries*, p. 160; M. Quinlan, *Athassel Augustinian priory* (2009), p. 36.

8.8  Lean-to cloister arcade, Adare Franciscan friary, Co. Limerick.

Rosserk, though arranged around a central garth, does not appear to have had any cloister ambulatories or arcades.

At other fifteenth-century friaries, the cloisters were elaborate stone-vaulted structures that integrated the cloister ambulatories and their arcades into the adjoining domestic ranges (fig. 8.9). This produced a compact structure in which the pillars of the arcade had a substantial load-bearing function and led to the emergence of distinctive arcade pillars, often described as dumb-bell piers, to cope with the increased stress. Quite why this transition took place is difficult to ascertain. The compact cloisters that resulted were more suited to urban environments, where space was at a premium, than to the rural convents of late medieval Ireland.[73] The integration of the ambulatories and the ranges resulted in small dark rooms on the ground floor, a situation exacerbated by their position on the north side of the church. Although the first floor rooms were correspondingly brighter and more spacious, the abiding impression of sites like Quin and Muckross is of an unpleasant claustrophobia (fig. 8.10). A number of these integrated cloisters occur in houses that were rebuilt following fires in the fifteenth century, and their stone vaulting may have been intended as a preventative measure. The Dominican community at Athenry received papal indulgences in

73 Stalley, 'Gaelic friars and Gothic design', p. 195.

8.9 Integrated cloister, Dominican priory, Sligo (photograph by Fr Fergal MacEoinín OP).

1423 and 1445 to assist rebuilding campaigns after fires. Similar indulgences were granted to the Dominicans in Sligo in 1415 and Roscommon in 1445 and at each of these sites evidence survives for integrated, stone-vaulted fifteenth-century cloisters.

The cloister ambulatories and garth were also used as burial places, principally for the friars themselves, but also on occasion for their benefactors and prominent ecclesiastics. Mooney records that the ambulatories and garth of the Observant Franciscan cloister in Adare were consecrated as cemeteries in 1466, while recent excavations at the Franciscan friaries at Ennis, Galbally and Sherkin Island as well as at the Dominican priory in Limerick have revealed large numbers of burials in the cloisters of those foundations.[74] The earliest stratum of burials in Ennis consisted entirely of male skeletons, and male remains also predominated in the burials excavated in the east range of the cloister at Sherkin Island friary. These presumably represent the graves of members of the community. A pectoral cross was discovered during excavations of the south range of the cloister at Moor

74 For discussion of burials within friaries and in friary cemeteries, see above, pp 107–10.

8.10  Integrated cloister, Franciscan friary, Quin, Co. Clare
(note the dormitory cubicle windows overhead).

Abbey, Galbally, Co. Tipperary, and presumably came from the grave of a bishop. Mooney remarked that Friar Thaddeus O'Sullivan, a noted preacher, was buried in the east range of the cloister at Kilcrea, 'just where the brethren enter the chapter room'.[75] Fragments of a tin or lead chalice and paten were discovered during restoration work in the cloister at the Franciscan friary in Adare in the mid-nineteenth century. Though now lost, their form suggests a fifteenth-century date and they may have come from the grave of a priest or bishop.[76] The longevity of the practice is demonstrated by a grave-slab in the east ambulatory of the Franciscan friary at Quin commemorating Friar John Hogan, the last member of the community, who was buried there in 1820.

## DOMESTIC BUILDINGS

With the exception of some of the smaller fifteenth-century foundations in the west and north of Ireland, the convents almost invariably conform to the standard monastic layout of conventual buildings arranged around a cloister to the south

---

**75** 'Brussels MS 3947', p. 71.   **76** R. Ó Floinn, 'Irish Franciscan church furnishings in the pre-Reformation period' (2011), pp 10–12. He notes that a lead grave chalice found in Kilcrea friary, Co. Cork, was sold in 1868.

or, more frequently, north of the church.[77] This preference for placing the domestic apartments on the darker side of the claustral complex has consistently puzzled Irish architectural historians.[78] A possible explanation lies in the different emphases that monastic and mendicant communities placed on the purpose of their churches. For monks, the church was primarily the place for the choral recitation of the Divine Office and so oriented that it received the maximum amount of light during the morning. By placing the cloister on the south side, monks also ensured that there was sufficient light in the north or 'reading cloister' each evening for the daily reading from the *Conferences* of John Cassian enjoined on them by the rule of St Benedict. For mendicants, the friary church was primarily pastoral in function. It was where congregations assembled to hear the friars preach and to participate in the popular devotions they promoted. Many of these, such as Lenten sermons or *collationes*, were afternoon or evening activities. The most popular liturgical office for the Dominicans and their lay devotees was that of Compline, the last of the canonical hours, during which the friars opened the screen that divided the choir from the nave and processed through the church singing the Marian antiphon *Salve Regina* (pl. 9).[79] Mooney noted that in the early seventeenth century it was customary for people in Galway, Clonmel and Waterford to visit the Franciscan churches in the evening to perform their devotions, and this probably represented the survival of a medieval practice.[80] By placing the domestic buildings on the north side of the complex, the friars maximized the amount of natural light that the nave and transept of the friary church received during the late afternoon and evening. The presence of large windows in the gables of many of the transepts in friary churches also facilitated this.

## THE EAST RANGE

The east range of the friary complex was usually the first to be constructed, as it contained the rooms most essential to monastic living. On the ground floor, these consisted of the sacristy, the chapter house and the parlour or calefactory. Overhead, the first floor of the range was occupied by the friars' dormitory with the garderobe or latrine block being accessible from a door in the north-east corner.

---

**77** An exception to this is the Carmelite priory at Ballinasmale, Co. Mayo, where the church and domestic buildings do not conform to any recognizable pattern. Patrick Conlan OFM suggests that this is in keeping with the original eremitical arrangements of the Carmelites, with hermits' cells arranged around a central oratory. P. Conlan, pers. comm.   **78** See O'Neill, 'Irish Franciscan friary architecture', p. 314 and A. Hogan, *Kilmallock Dominican priory*, p. 53 for the locations of the cloisters in surviving Franciscan and Dominican houses.   **79** W.R. Bonniwell, *A history of the Dominican liturgy* (1945), pp 150–1, 161–6. **80** 'Brussels MS 3947', pp 55, 78, 81.

THE SACRISTY

The sacristy in mendicant houses was invariably situated on the ground floor adjacent to the chancel or presbytery of the church to which access was gained through a door in the north or south wall of the choir (depending on the position of the claustral buildings). Here, the vessels, vestments and service books required for the celebration of the Eucharist and the Liturgy of the Hours were stored in a secure environment. At the Franciscan friary in Ennis, a series of recesses in the north and south walls of the sacristy indicate the position of storage presses. The sacristy was also one of the first parts of the convent to be provided with a stone vaulted ceiling to protect its contents from fire. Remnants of such vaults survive at the Dominican priories at Kilmallock and Sligo, at the Franciscan friaries at Ennis, Quin, Askeaton (fig. 8.11) and Muckross and at the Augustinian house at Adare. The sacristy was also where preparations for the liturgy took place. At the Franciscan friaries at Kilcrea and Quin, an alcove with a drainage channel indicates the location of a *sacrarium*, the place in which altar vessels and altar linen were ritually washed after Mass. The *sacrarium* in Quin is decorated with a miniature vault and equipped with sockets for a rail from which an aquamanile or double-headed water-jug was suspended. At Rosserrilly, the sacristy is located in the ground floor of a seventeenth-century extension at the north-eastern corner of the complex. It contains the remains of a small oven that may have served for baking the hosts for use at Mass.

THE CHAPTER ROOM

Following standard practice, the chapter room of the friary was normally situated in the east range of the cloister. Unlike their more elaborate monastic counterparts, the chapter room of an Irish friary was usually a compact, unprepossessing affair with the doorway leading from the cloister into a ground-floor room generally being the only indication of its purpose. In the Franciscan friary at Adare and the Augustinian foundation at Murrisk, a small window to the north of the chapter room doorway provides another indication of its function (fig. 9.1). These windows permitted such individuals as novices, laybrothers and members of the laity who, canonically, were not members of the chapter, to follow its deliberations while standing outside in the cloister walkway.[81] The chapterhouses of the Dominican foundation at Sligo and possibly of those at Cork and Roscommon

---

**81** These windows were a common feature in monasteries of monks and canons. Examples may be seen in the chapter rooms of the Augustinian priories at Kells, Co. Kilkenny, Athassel, Co. Tipperary, and of Holy Trinity (Christ Church), Dublin.

are unusual among Irish mendicant examples in that they projected *en echelon* from the wall of the east range. This was a common arrangement in Irish Cistercian monasteries and in houses of Augustinian canons.[82]

The chapter room played a vital role in the maintenance of discipline and the cultivation of a community's sense of identity. It was here that the friars gathered each morning after Prime to listen to a reading of a chapter of their rule and the day's martyrology.[83] It was the venue in which the superior addressed the friars, where elections were conducted and matters affecting the community were discussed. It was also where the community's regular chapter of faults took place. At this gathering, which normally took place on Fridays but sometimes more frequently, each friar accused himself of any infractions of the rule or constitutions that he had committed or which he had noticed others doing. More serious disciplinary matters were also addressed in the chapter room and it was

**82** Stalley, *Cistercian monasteries*, pp 162–6.   **83** P. Ó Riain, *Feastdays of the saints* (2006), pp xvii–xviii.

here that punishments, deprivations, imprisonments and excommunications were proclaimed.[84] Novices were admitted to each order and received the religious habit in the chapter room and it was also where they were instructed in each order's liturgical observances, which were contained in the 'chapter books', volumes that were permanently stored there to facilitate consultation. The chapter book from the Youghal Franciscan friary contains two formulary documents indicating that the friars issued confraternity letters and letters of introduction for overseas travel to their benefactors in the chapter room.[85] Notwithstanding their central place in the religious life of the community, the rooms were often used for more secular purposes. As noted in chapter four, they occasionally provided the venue for meetings of parliament or royal councils, for the election of civic officials or for conducting business transactions. As was the custom in monastic houses, burial in the chapter room was a privilege reserved to high-ranking prelates in each order. Mooney notes the burial of Friar Raymond de Burgh, bishop of Emly, in the Franciscan chapter room in Adare in 1562.[86]

## THE DORMITORY

The upper storey of the east range normally housed the principal dormitory or sleeping area of the convent. In the early phases of each order's development, this consisted of a long, open room in which the friars slept in single beds, with cubicles and private cells being reserved for each order's administrative and intellectual elite. In the later Middle Ages, private accommodation had become the norm, and the surviving evidence indicates that most friars in Ireland occupied individual dormitory cells by the late fifteenth or early sixteenth century. These cubicles were divided by wooden partitions and accessed from a central passageway running the length of the room from north to south. Mooney makes incidental references to these cells in his accounts of the Franciscan friaries at Ennis and Multyfarnham, and the dissolution records of 1540–1 refer to removal of the dormitory cells at the Augustinian friary in Naas.[87] A grant of Kilconnell in 1595 refers to twenty-eight small chambers called 'dortors', which presumably were the friars' dormitory cubicles. The remains of ten cells were evident in the Dominican priory at Aghaboe in 1786.[88] At the Franciscan friary in Quin, a pair of socket holes remain in the west wall of the dormitory. These held the beams

---

**84** *AS*, pp 126, no. 8; 128, no. 9; 135, no. 14; 149, no. 1.   **85** J.A. Gribbin & C. Ó Clabaigh, 'Confraternity letters of the Irish Observant Franciscans and their benefactors' (2002).   **86** 'Brussels MS 3947', p. 64.   **87** 'Brussels MS 3947', pp 61, 93; White, *Extents*, p. 165.   **88** C. Mooney, 'Franciscan architecture', iii, p. 28; Archdall, *Monasticon Hibernicum*, p. 590.

8.12 East range, Lislaughtin friary, Co. Kerry. The windows of the dormitory cubicles are visible on the first floor.

that supported the panelling that enclosed a friar's cell and indicate that it had a width of approximately two metres. A small rectangular window lit each cubicle and the number of these gives some indication of the residential capacity of the convent (fig. 8.12).

In addition to its dormitory function, the cell was the only personal or private space a friar possessed. It was in the cell that activities such as dressing, attending to personal hygiene and study took place. Silence was maintained at all times in the dormitory and a friar was appointed to supervise the conduct of the friars in their cells. Although forbidden to possess any property of their own, each religious was assigned materials for their personal use, such as writing tablets, pens, books, footwear and undergarments. The small rectangular recess beneath each dormitory window in the Franciscan friaries at Askeaton, Lislaughtin and Kilcrea probably formed part of a cupboard or storage area for this material. Similar, if more elaborate, features incorporating study carrels survive in the dormitory of the Dominican house at Gloucester in England.[89]

The cell also provided a space for private prayer. Mooney's account of the deathbed conversion of Conor na Srón O'Brien by the Ennis Franciscan Fergal O'Trean in 1496 shows the friar retiring to his dormitory cell, shutting the door and spending twenty-four hours praying for repose of the chieftain's soul. In

89 W.A. Hinnebusch, *Early English Friars Preachers* (1951), pp 171–5, illustrations pp 173–4.

Continental foundations, the friars' cubicles contained religious images and paintings designed to foster prayer and devotion, with the cycle of frescoes painted by Fra Angelico in the cells of the Observant Dominican priory of San Marco in Florence in 1440–1 being the most famous. While nothing comparable survives from Ireland, such devotional images were not unknown. Fragments of wall paintings remain in the embrasures of eight of the dormitory windows in Muckross, one of which depicts a cross on a stepped platform. At the Franciscan friary at Askeaton, a large image of the *Imago pietatis* or Christ as the Man of Sorrows and the instruments of the passion occupies the north wall of an upper room in the west range. Although the dormitory function of this latter room is uncertain, it demonstrates the deployment of sophisticated religious imagery in parts of the convent other than the church.

The privilege of having an enclosed or larger cell was reserved to lectors and other officials in each order whose duties demanded more privacy, and the 'doctor's chamber' mentioned in the 1540 extents of the Dominican priory in Waterford may have been one such structure.[90] In a number of friaries, the room over the stone-vaulted sacristy may have provided such private accommodation. Accessed through the first floor dormitory, this was usually a large, well-lit chamber. In the Augustinian priories at Adare and Fethard and the Dominican priory at Kilmallock, an internal window overlooking the high altar allowed the occupant to watch as Mass was celebrated in the church. Similar windows occur in the Franciscan friaries at Askeaton, Donegal and Kilcrea and in the Dominican house in Athenry, but in these places they overlook altars in the nave. These cells may also have provided accommodation for infirm friars or for members of the community living as anchorites.

Private cells and appartments were occasionally granted to individual friars as a privilege by the major superiors of the orders. In 1397, Raymond of Capua, master general of the Dominicans, granted Friar Cornelius of Ireland the right to his own chamber.[91] In 1451, the master general, Friar Guido Flamochetti granted another Irish Dominican, Friar Philip Verdon, the right to the cell and garden that he had acquired and repaired.[92] In March 1423, Friar Richard Madden of the Augustinian community in Ballinrobe was permitted to have his own cell though he was deprived of this privilege shortly afterwards because of his scandalous behaviour.[93] Similar concessions of cells and gardens were made to Friar John Dermot in 1425, to Friar Richard de Burgh of Ballinrobe in 1473 and to Friar Thaddeus O'Kelly of Dunmore in 1492, all of whom were Augustinians.[94]

---

90 White, *Extents*, p. 351.  91 Fenning, 'Irish material', p. 256, no. 6. Friar Cornelius could not be deprived of this privilege by anyone other than the master general.  92 Ibid., no. 8.  93 Martin & de Meijer, 'Irish material', pp 80–1, no. 35; 83, no. 38.  94 Ibid., pp 85, no. 46; 96, no. 74; 106–7, no. 119.

8.13 Lavatory block and library, Adare Franciscan friary, Co. Limerick.

## THE GARDEROBE

At the north end of the dormitory, a door normally gave access to the convent's principal garderobe or latrine block. At the Franciscan friaries at Adare, Kilconnell, Lislaughtin, Muckross, Moyne and Quin, the Dominican houses at Urlar and Sligo and the Carmelite foundation at Castlelyons, the garderobe was an elaborate two-storey structure. The first floor contained a long wooden bench on which the friars sat, the waste dropping into the pit below. At Quin, the stone supports for this bench survive, as does a lamp niche in the west wall of the garderobe. The waste either accumulated in a cesspit at ground level or was flushed away through the drain. As noted above, the watercourses that serviced the lavatories, kitchens and workrooms of the friaries can still be traced at a number of sites. At the Franciscan friaries in Kilconnell and Adare (fig. 8.13), a small door in the ground floor of the garderobe gave access to the cesspit, while at the Franciscan house at Kilcrea and the Dominican foundation at Urlar, an archway at ground level facilitated removal of the accumulated material.

Fear of homosexual impropriety meant that conduct in both the dormitory and the garderobe received particular attention in mendicant formation literature. Bernard of Bessa's *Speculum Disciplinae*, which circulated widely among the Irish

Observant Franciscans, warned friars against frequenting each other's cubicles and instructed them to urinate while sitting to avoid exposing themselves.[95] Similar concerns are alluded to in the *Abbreviatio statutorum*, and are also evident in David of Augburg's *De informatione iuvenum*, which deals at length with the issue of emotional attachment between friars and inappropriate physical contact.[96]

THE LIBRARY

While every mendicant house had a collection of books, not every convent had a library room. Such dedicated spaces were normally features of large communities and *studia*. The library of the Dominican priory in Waterford occupied a separate room, and Bishop John Edmund de Coursey (d. 1518) built a library for the Franciscans at Timoleague.[97] The Augustinian friars at Callan reputedly possessed a large library that may have required a separate chamber,[98] but otherwise the friars' modest book collections were stored in book chests in the chapter room or cloister or in aumbries in the sacristy, such as those that survive in the Franciscan friary at Ennis. Cistercian monasteries in England had book presses in the east range of the cloister, generally in the wall space between the processional door to the church and the entrance to the chapter house. In the north range of the Franciscan friary in Claregalway, a large arched recess may have served a similar function, though it may equally indicate the position of the lavabo. At the Franciscan houses at Adare and Lislaughtin, the library and scriptorium were situated in large, well-fenestrated rooms above the garderobe. In the Franciscan friary in Kilcrea, the library doubled as the scriptorium and was situated in a room above the sacristy lit by ten sets of double-light windows, with a fireplace in the east wall of the room.[99] At the Franciscan friary in Adare, the library was lit by three sets of double lancet windows that provided light for two or three bookcases or reading desks set at right angles to the lateral walls of the room (fig. 8.3). The shelf marks in the catalogue of the Observant Franciscan house at Youghal indicate that the books there were arranged in two bookcases according to subject categories, and similar cataloguing systems from English and Continental libraries give an indication of the internal arrangement and organization of the friars' libraries.[1]

**95** Bernard of Bessa, *Speculum disciplinae*, cap. xxvi, p. 610.   **96** *AS*, vi, no. 4; David of Augsburg, *De exterioris et interioris hominis compositione* (1899), cap. xxxv, pp 236–45.   **97** White, *Extents*, p. 352; *MRH*, p. 259.   **98** W. Carrigan, *History of the diocese of Ossory* (1905), iii, p. 312.   **99** D. Maher, *Kilcrea Friary* (1999), p. 14.   **1** N. Senocak, 'Book acquisition in the medieval Franciscan order' (2003); eadem, 'Circulation of books in the medieval Franciscan order: attitude, methods and critics' (2004).

*The refectory*

The refectory or main dining room of a mendicant convent normally occupied the range of the cloister opposite the church. In most Irish friaries, this meant that it was situated in the north cloister range. In the case of the Franciscan friary at Askeaton, the refectory occupies a position at right angles to the south range of the cloister, with a dormitory overhead. While this arrangement is a standard one in Cistercian monasteries, its occurrence in Askeaton is due to the peculiarities of the site. In convents where the cloisters were freestanding, non-integrated structures, as at Franciscan houses at Moyne, Adare and Dromahair and the Dominican priory in Cork, the refectory occupied a position on the ground floor. In houses where the cloister was a stone-vaulted structure integrated into the ground floor range, as at the Dominican house in Sligo, the Franciscan friary at Muckross, the Augustinian convent in Adare and the Franciscan tertiary foundation at Rosserk, the refectory was located on the first floor and accessed by a stairs from the cloister alley below. This first-floor location had the practical advantage of providing a more spacious and better-lit location for the refectory, but also had a symbolic resonance, as it recalled the *cenaculum* or upper room in Jerusalem in which Christ had celebrated the Last Supper with his disciples.[2]

Following monastic tradition, the consumption of food in a friary was a highly ritualized event. Before entering the refectory, each friar washed his hands in a lavabo positioned near the refectory door. In Augustinian and Cistercian monasteries, this was often a highly elaborate architectural feature, but simpler arrangements were the norm in mendicant houses. At the Augustinian friary in Adare, the lavabo consists of a simple niche in the north wall of the cloister beside the stairs leading to the refectory. In the Franciscan house in Claregalway, a large arch in the south wall of the cloister may indicate the presence of the lavabo there. On entering the refectory, each friar venerated the image of the crucifix positioned on the end wall of the room before taking his seat. The refectory seats and tables were arranged around the side-walls of the refectory, and each friar took his place in order of seniority in the community, with the prior or guardian occupying the place of honour at the top table beneath the crucifix. Friars sat on benches ranged along the walls of the refectory and occupying only one side of the table. This arrangement left the centre of the room free for those serving the meal and for the performance of public penances by members of the community. At the Dominican priory in Cork, the raised dais on which the refectory tables stood and the stone benches lining its walls were exposed during excavations in 1993.[3]

**2** R. Gilchrist, *Contemplation and action: the other monasticism*, pp 144–5. **3** Hurley & Sheehan, *Excavations*, pp 19–43, 54–5.

8.14  Reader's desk (projecting) at Rosserilly friary, Co. Mayo.

8.15  Reader's desk in the Dominican priory, Sligo (photograph by Fr Fergal MacEoinín OP).

1 Thirteenth-century ivory image known as 'Our Lady of Graces', Dominican priory, Youghal, Co. Cork (photograph by Fr Joseph McGilloway; image reproduced by permission of Fr Joe Kavanagh OP).

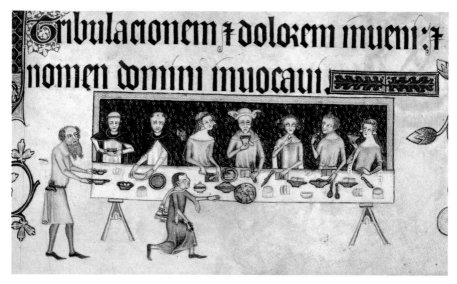

2 The Luttrell family at table, with two Dominican friars in attendance (© The British Library Board, BL Add. MS 42130 (the Luttrell Psalter), fo. 208r).

**3** A Dominican friar hearing confession. The Bodleian Library, Oxford, Douce MS 104, fo. 11v, a copy of *Piers Plowman* produced in Dublin in 1427.

**4** Cambridge, Corpus Christi College MS 180, fo. 1r. The beginning of Archbishop Richard Fitzralph's anti-mendicant treatise *De pauperie salvatoris*, written for Adam Easton OSB. The prelate is depicted writing under the inspiration of the Holy Spirit. In the margin, demons assail representatives of each of the mendicant orders (image reproduced by permission of the Master and Fellows of Corpus Christi College, Cambridge).

5 A Dominican friar preaching. The Bodleian Library, Oxford, Douce MS 104, fo. 47r.

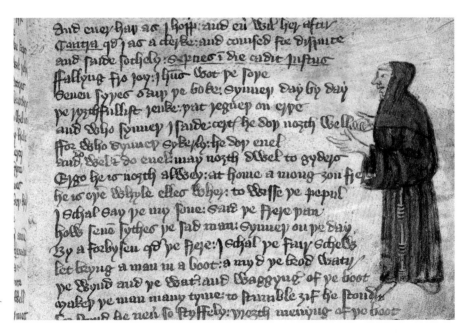

6 A Franciscan friar. The Bodleian Library, Oxford, Douce MS 104, fo. 46r.

7 (*right*) Fifteenth-century English alabaster image of the Holy Trinity, Dominican priory, Kilkenny (photograph by Fr Louis Hughes OP).

8 (*left*) Statue of the Madonna and Child, Franciscan friary, Askeaton, Co. Limerick (© National Museum of Ireland).

9 (*this page*) Interior of a sixteenth-century Flemish Dominican church depicting an apparition of the Virgin Mary during the *Salve Regina* procession at the end of Compline. Note the screen and rood loft dividing the chancel from the nave of the church and the black-clad lay brothers in the background (Museum Catariijneconvent, Utrecht. Inventory no. ABM S00071).

10 (*opposite*) Adare, Co. Limerick. The Franciscan friary (1464) is in the foreground, with the Fitzgerald castle and parish church in the background. The Augustinian priory is just out of sight in the upper left-hand corner of the picture on the opposite bank of the River Maigue (© National Monuments Photographic Unit).

**11** Askeaton, Co. Limerick. Aerial view showing the church, claustral complex and boundary walls of the Franciscan friary with the River Deel in the background (© National Monuments Photographic Unit).

**12** Quin, Co. Clare. Aerial view showing the fifteenth-century church and friary complex built on the ruins of the earlier de Clare castle. The River Rine is visible in the foreground and the remains of house platforms and field boundaries are evident in the background (© National Monuments Photographic Unit).

**13** (*above*) The 1247 grant by Bishop Geoffrey de Turville of a water supply from St Kenny's Well to the Dominican community, Kilkenny. The diameter of the water pipe is indicated by a copper ring attached to the charter, which was the same size as the bishop's pontifical ring (Kilkenny City Archive. Image © Tom Brett, photographer, Kilkenny).

**14** (*left*) Fifteenth-century stained glass quarries from St Saviour's Dominican priory, Limerick (photograph by Josephine Moran).

**15** Dean Odo's doorway, Clonmacnois Cathedral, Co. Offaly. The three figures above the doorway depict SS Dominic, Patrick and Francis (photograph by Michael Potterton).

16 Augustinian priory, Adare, Co. Limerick. Interior of the chancel showing the sanctuary area and (modern) altar and choir stalls (photograph by Michael Potterton).

**17** God the Father, from a Throne of Grace ensemble. Possibly from the Augustinian priory, Fethard, Co. Tipperary (© National Museum of Ireland).

**18** The de Burgo–
O'Malley Chalice
(© National Museum
of Ireland).

**19** (*this page*) Late fifteenth-century processional cross associated with the Franciscan friary, Multyfarnham, Co. Westmeath (© National Museum of Ireland).

**20** (*opposite*) Processional cross presented to the Observant Franciscan community, Lislaughtin, Co. Kerry, by Cornelius O'Connor and Avelina Fitzgerald in 1479 (© National Museum of Ireland).

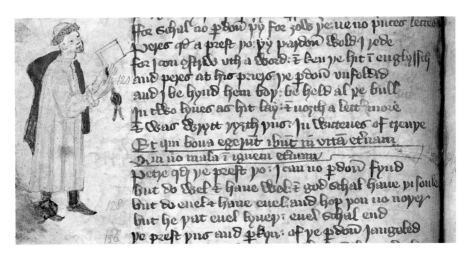

**21** A cleric bearing an indulgence or a letter of confraternity.
The Bodleian Library, Oxford, Douce MS 104, fo. 44v.

**22** An Observant Franciscan letter of confraternity issued by the friars in Youghal to Sir John Arundell, his wife and two sons in 1515 (Cornwall Record Office, Truro, AR 27/6).

In keeping with monastic custom, meals in the refectory were eaten in silence and accompanied by the reading of suitably edifying material.[4] This practice meant that each community was exposed to a regular cycle of hagiography, travel accounts, legislation and other hortatory literature. The presence of readers' desks in a number of Irish convents provides physical evidence for the practice. In the Franciscan houses at Moyne and Rosserrily, the reader's desk is recessed into the wall of the east wall of the refectory and is well lit by external windows. At the Dominican house at Sligo, where the refectory occupies a first-floor position, the reader's desk was lit by an elaborate oriel window that projects into the cloister (figs 8.14, 8.15). In the ground-floor refectory of the Dominican convent at Cork, the desk was an elaborate affair mounted on the north wall of the room and accessed by a narrow intramural stairway. It is also possible that the fine example that forms the entrance to the Blessed Sacrament chapel of the Collegiate Church of St Nicholas in Galway was salvaged from the refectory of one of the city's three mendicant communities after their dissolution.

## THE KITCHEN

The friary kitchen was normally adjacent to the refectory in the north range of the cloister. At the Franciscan friary in Quin, its position is indicated by the presence of a large fireplace and oven in the north-western corner of the building. Here, it was also adjacent to the porter's lodge in the west range, thereby facilitating the delivery of foodstuffs and pittances, the supplying of food to visitors and guests and the distribution of alms. At the Franciscan friaries in Kilcrea and Multyfarnham, the kitchen, buttery and refectory were contiguous to each other on the ground floor.[5] At Kilcrea, a doorway in the external wall of the north range gave access to both the kitchen and the refectory. The kitchen of the Augustinian friary in Adare occupied the ground floor of the north range, with the refectory overhead. Here, the hatch for passing food to those serving at table still survives in the wall of the refectory stairwell. At the Franciscan tertiary foundation at Rosserk, both the refectory and the kitchen were situated on the first floor of the north range. In houses with integrated cloister walks, the small, dark rooms on the ground floor of the north range were probably used for the storage of food, beer, wine and other comestibles. The 1540–1 dissolution records refer to such cellars in the Carmelite

---

**4** For a discussion of this material, see below, pp 281–2.   **5** White, *Extents*, p. 275.

house at Dublin, the Franciscan friary in Youghal and the Augustinian convent in Cork.[6]

Occasionally, the kitchens were located in buildings close to but separated from the main north range. This arrangement reduced the threat of fire to the main complex. At the Franciscan friary in Adare, the presence of ovens and fireplaces in buildings to the north of the friary indicates that they were used for preparing food, baking and possibly brewing. The Franciscan house at Multyfarnham possessed a free-standing brewhouse and bakery as well as a stone building roofed with tiles for the storage of malt.[7] In larger houses such as the Franciscan friaries at Moyne and Roserrilly and possibly the Dominican priories at Portumna, Rathfran and Carlingford, this arrangement developed into a second cloister housing the domestic offices. At Rosserrilly, the presence of two large fireplaces, an oven and a fish tank (fig. 5.7) in adjacent rooms of this second north cloister indicate the position of the kitchen, bakery and brewhouse.

## THE WEST RANGE

In Benedictine and Cistercian monasteries, the west range of the claustral complex was normally used for accommodating laybrothers. In friaries, it functioned as the principal interface between the community and the outside world, acting as a buffer zone between secular and sacred spaces and containing the principal entrance to the house. It was here that visitors were received, alms dispensed and hospitality offered. At the Franciscan friaries at Quin and Muckross, small chambers adjacent to the main door functioned as the porter's lodge. Here, the laybrother charged with receiving guests had his station, vetting visitors and deciding on how to deal with them. In both houses, a doorway opened into the kitchen area, allowing for the delivery of food. The functions of the other rooms in the west range are often difficult to determine. The presence of large windows on the first floor of the west range at Quin may indicate that it was used as a classroom. The west ranges of the Franciscan houses at Adare and Sherkin Island have garderobes, large fireplaces and dormitory style windows, indicating that they may have been used for accommodating guests and laybrothers. At Rosserrilly, a large building projects from the west range, indicating that it may also have functioned as a guest house.

6 Ibid., pp 121, 137.   7 Ibid., p. 275.

## THE FRIARY CHURCH

The surviving remains of Irish friary churches indicate that they were architecturally unpretentious affairs, consisting of long, narrow rectangular halls on an east–west axis, divided into a nave for the laity in the west, and a choir (or chancel) for the friars in the east. Unlike Benedictine and Cluniac monasteries, the friars did not need elaborate aisled churches and chancels for liturgical processions. Neither do examples of apses nor feretory chapels survive in any Irish friary church. Similarly, there is no example in Ireland of aisled chancels such those found in Continental and English friaries.[8] Nor is there any example of an Irish friary church being redesigned to serve the needs of pilgrims, as occurred at the basilicas of St Francis in Assisi, St Anthony in Padua and St Dominic in Bologna.[9] With the exception of the transept chapels in Ennis friary, no evidence survives for stone-vaulted ceilings in any Irish mendicant church. In many of the churches, the nave was flanked by an aisle with a large transept abutting its northern or southern side, depending on the position of the claustral buildings.

The laity entered the nave of the church through its principal door, normally situated in the west gable of the church. In the Franciscan church in Adare, the main entrance was in the south-west wall, while at Askeaton another door gave direct access to the transept. The surviving doorways are usually relatively plain features, well proportioned but with little in the way of heraldic or iconographic ornament. This is in marked contrast to such elaborate portals as Dean Odo's door at Clonmacnois Cathedral (pl. 15), or those at the Augustinian monasteries at Clontuskert, Co. Galway, and Lorrha, Co. Tipperary. Even parochial churches like St Mary's Church, Callan, Co. Kilkenny, Stackallan Church, Co. Meath, and Tullaroan Church, Co. Kilkenny, had ornamental portals incorporating sculpture and heraldry.[10] A possible explanation for this lies in the use of the church door as a backdrop for solemnizing marriages, a parochial event that did not normally occur in a friary. At the Dominican priories at Cashel, Lorrha and Portumna, the Augustinian priory at Adare and the Franciscan house at Castledermot, the presence of corbels over the doorways indicates that a wooden lean-to porch sheltered the main doors of these churches.[11] A holy water stoup was sometimes incorporated into the door-frame, as at the Augustinian foundation at Dunmore, or positioned adjacent to it, as at the Franciscan friaries in Adare and Kilconnell.

The nave of the friary was a large rectangular hall designed to facilitate the friars' preaching activities. It was also a popular location for burials, and niches

---

**8** Martin, *Franciscan architecture in England* (1937), the plate between p. 22 and p. 23 shows the comparative plans of English Franciscan churches. **9** Schenkluhn, *Architettura degli ordini mendicanti* (2003), pp 34–43. **10** Moss, 'Permanent expressions', p. 75. **11** I am grateful to Con Manning for advice on these features.

8.16 Tomb niches and lancet windows in the south nave wall of the Dominican priory, Roscommon.

recessed into the walls with the burial vaults set in the foundation are a feature of number of churches (fig. 8.16). Normally, these are relatively plain structures, but fine examples of ornamented canopied tombs survive in the north walls of the naves of the Dominican church in Sligo and the Franciscan foundation at Kilconnell (fig. 7.4). Burials also occurred in the floor of the nave and could be quite densely concentrated. The naves were lit by large windows set in the west gable and by smaller ones set in the north and south walls. At the Franciscan friary in Quin, a gallery in the western end of the nave increased the capacity of the church and gave a privileged vantage point to guests staying in the west range of the friary.

### THE TRANSEPT OR LADY CHAPEL

A distinctive feature of Irish mendicant churches is the frequent occurrence of a large transept abutting the nave of the church. These were often dedicated to the Virgin Mary and a number references to the 'Lady Chapel' occur in contemporary sources. These chapels housed the church's principal image of the Virgin and were normally later additions to earlier foundations (as at the Franciscan church in Ennis and the Augustinian friary in Adare). In the case of some of the later foundations, like the Observant Franciscan foundation at Adare, they were incorporated in the design from the outset. These features are generally found on the south side of the church and are of varying dimensions, some exceeding the dimensions of the nave itself, as in the Franciscan houses at Moyne, Kilcrea and Rosserrilly and the Augustinian priory at Adare. In addition to increasing the congregational capacity of the church, the transepts also provided additional space for extra altars and chapels, an indication of an increase in the size of the communities and of the emergence of new cults and devotions. They also demonstrate the continued support of aristocratic and mercantile patrons, as many of these chapels functioned as mausolea for their donors.

The additional altars were normally situated in the window alcoves of the east wall of the transept, as at Quin, Rosserk, Rosserrily and Kilmallock. Occasionally, these altars were situated in distinct chapels abutting the east wall of the transepts, as at Adare, Rosserrilly and Kilconnell. Even when the altars themselves have disappeared, their locations are indicated by aumbries and piscinae in the walls. A curious feature of a number of the Franciscan and tertiary foundations at Moyne, Rosserk and Court is the presence of a small cell or alcove between the east-facing windows of the transept. The purpose of these features is uncertain, but they may have functioned as anchorites' cells (fig. 7.8).[12]

## THE SCREEN AND ROOD LOFT

The nave and choir of the churches were separated by a screen that often incorporated the pulpit and rood beam of the church. In early churches, like the Franciscan house at Nenagh, the Dominican friary at Rathfran and the Augustinian church at Murrisk, no physical evidence of this division survives and it probably consisted of a simple wooden structure separating the two areas. In most mendicant churches, the cross-walls of the belltower divided the church into its respective parts with wooden screens, and doors in the western crossing arch providing communication between the nave and the choir. When opened, these doors also afforded a view of the high altar to worshippers in the nave. On the western side of the belltower, facing into the nave, a wooden platform or rood loft spanned the width of the tower and provided a pulpit from which the preacher could address the congregation gathered in the nave and transept. The stone corbels for supporting this loft survive in many locations, and in the case of the Franciscan house at Rosserrilly and the Dominican church in Ballindoon, the platforms were stone structures spanning the width of the tower (fig. 8.17). In the Dominican church in Sligo, the now reconstructed rood loft is a stone feature

12 C. Ó Clabaigh, 'The hermits and anchorites of medieval Dublin' (2010), pp 283–5, pl. 1.

8.17 Belfry tower with
rood loft, Rosserrilly
friary, Co. Galway. Note
the nave altars to either
side of the central
opening.

dating to the early fifteenth century that stands to the west of the crossing tower inserted in the later fifteenth century (fig. 8.18).

Above the rood loft, supported on a beam that spanned the width of the tower, stood the rood, or the principal crucifix in the church. The sockets for this beam are still visible in the west wall of the tower of the Franciscan friary at Ennis. This rood was generally flanked by images of the Virgin Mary and St John the Evangelist and was a major focus of devotion in medieval churches. The rood crucifix in the Franciscan friary in Kilcrea, Co. Cork, was an elaborate affair decorated with gold and silver images of the four evangelists on its four arms.[13] A small rood, thought to be from the house of Dominican tertiary friars in Kilcorban, is preserved in the Clonfert diocesan museum in Loughrea, Co. Galway.[14]

## THE BELFRY AND BELLS

The belfries of the mendicant friaries are their most distinctive feature, a fact commented on by Donatus Mooney in the early seventeenth century. In describing the tower of the Franciscan friary at Drogheda, he stated that 'the lofty bell-tower alone remains, a graceful and solid building of elegantly cut marble

---

**13** 'Brussels MS 3947', p. 70.  **14** P.K. Egan, 'Clonfert diocesan museum and its collections', (1956–7), p. 67.

8.18 Rood loft, Dominican priory, Sligo. Note the high altar in the background
(photograph by Fr Fergal MacEoinín OP).

blocks. This style of campanile is common to almost all our churches in Ireland, and is, I believe, peculiar to the country, for nowhere else have I seen the like.'[15] In most cases, the surviving structures represent insertions into earlier church buildings, and date, at the earliest, to the mid-fourteenth century. The first documented evidence occurs in 1347, when Friar Clyn noted the establishment of a confraternity in Kilkenny to erect a belltower in the Franciscan friary there.[16] Belfries continued to be added to friaries throughout the fifteenth and into the sixteenth centuries: that of the Dominican church in Kilkenny was erected by James Schortals, who died sometime after 1534. The tower in the Carmelite friary at Loughrea is a fifteenth-century insertion into an early fourteenth-century church, as are those in the Franciscan churches at Claregalway and Ennis. In each instance, the towers obscure earlier windows in the nave and choir of the church. A number of towers that subsequently collapsed are known from antiquarian drawings, and the foundations of the cross-walls that supported now vanished towers have been uncovered during excavations at the sites of the Dominican churches in Cork and Trim and the Franciscan friary in Armagh.[17]

The towers occur in two distinctive forms, of which the most common is a square, tapering structure that emerged through the roof of the friary church.

15 Ibid., pp 28–9.  16 Clyn, *Annals*, p. 243.  17 Hurley & Sheehan, *Excavations*, pp 48–9.

8.19  Belfry, Franciscan friary, Claregalway, Co. Galway.

Although normally associated with Franciscan sites, this design also occurs at the Augustinian friary at Adare, the Dominican church at Kilmallock and the Carmelite church in Loughrea (fig. 8.19). Another version is more rectangular in design, spanning the entire width of the church and dividing the roof of the nave and chancel into two distinct areas. This is normally found in Dominican

8.20 Belfry, Dominican priory, Burrishoole, Co. Mayo.

contexts, as in the priories at Cashel and Burrishoole (fig. 8.20). The towers of the Franciscan church at Muckross and the Carmelite church at Castlelyons also follow this design.

The bell chamber was housed in the top storey of the tower, with single- or double-light windows at the cardinal points allowing the sound to travel. Though very few medieval friary bells survive (from the Dominican friary in Waterford and the Franciscan friary in Askeaton),[18] surviving bell opes or rope holes in the crossing vaults of the towers indicate that most belfries housed between one and four bells (fig. 8.21). These consisted of smaller bells used by the sacristan to regulate the internal life of the convent, and larger ones used to summon the faithful to Mass and the Divine Office, to toll for the dead and to mark anniversaries.[19] In addition to their practical function, bells were believed to possess apotropaic powers and were rung at times of crisis to ward off evil. They were frequently dedicated to a patron saint, regarded as having an individual 'voice' or personality and, as noted

---

18 E. McEneaney & R. Ryan, *Waterford treasures* (2004), pp 108–9; T.J. Westropp, 'Bells of Askeaton Franciscan friary, Co. Limerick' (1914), 166. I owe this latter reference to Patrick Wallace.   19 Humbert, *Expositio,* pp 154–6; idem, *De officiis ordinis,* pp 247–8; R. Gilchrist, *Requiem,* p. 24.

8.21 Openings for bell ropes, Augustinian priory, Adare, Co. Limerick.

in chapter four, constituted a high-status donation on the part of benefactors. A bell inscription preserved in the Franciscan codex TCD MS 667, indicates how these different functions were perceived:

> The nature of a bell: I worship the true God, I call the people, I gather the clergy together, I intercede for the dead, repel the plague, I am the terror of all demons.

> [Natura campane. Deum colo verum, plebem uoco, colligo clerum, defunctos ploro, pestem repellem, cunctorum terror sum demoniorum][20]

### THE 'WALKING PLACE'

In addition to providing a division between the chancel and the nave, the space between the cross-walls of the tower provided the principal means of access to the church for the community through a door in the north wall of the cloister. This

---

**20** TCD MS 667, p. 37. Colker, *Latin MSS*, ii, p. 1124.

enabled the friars to pass from the convent to the choir of the church without being seen from the nave. At the Franciscan houses in Kilconnell and Rosserrilly, another door in the south wall of the tower allowed the friars direct access to the transept. In English friaries, this feature was known as the 'walking place' and, in addition to allowing access to the chancel, it permitted the friars to pass from the church to the friary precinct through an external door in the wall of the church.[21] Such a door is found in the Franciscan friary at Ennis.

### THE CHANCEL

The choir or chancel, in the eastern part of the building, was reserved for the friars. Here, the community celebrated the hours of the Divine Office, seated facing each other in choir stalls ranged along the northern and southern sides of the chancel (pl. 16). In the centre of the choir stood a large wooden lectern or *pulpitum*, from which the antiphons and lections at the liturgy were intoned and on which the large-format choir books used by the cantors were placed. The Youghal library catalogue lists one such *pulpidarium* among its books in 1491.[22] TCD MS 109, a large-format Franciscan antiphonary, is an example of the type of liturgical volume used at the *pulpitum*. In the Franciscan friaries at Adare, Kilconnell, Muckross, Rosserrilly and Waterford, corbels in the walls of the chancel and east face of the tower indicate the presence of wooden galleries. These provided additional accommodation for the community, a place of honour for distinguished visitors and a position for cantors at the liturgy.[23] Organs were recorded at the Dominican priory at Athenry and the Franciscan house at Killeigh, and were probably a feature of many other mendicant houses as well. These also may have been situated in the loft.[24]

### THE SANCTUARY

At the furthest east end of the church was the sanctuary, where the principal or high altar of the church was located, along with the sedilia or ceremonial seat for the ministers who presided at the daily conventual Mass, and the piscina in which

---

**21** Martin, *Franciscan architecture in England*, p. 19. **22** *YLC*, no. 4b. **23** At Adare, the only access to the curious chapel positioned over the north ambulatory of the cloister was through the gallery in the chancel. This may have functioned as a private chapel for patrons enabling them to participate in the liturgy from a private, prestigious vantage place. A similar feature occurs at the Franciscan friary at Kilconnell. **24** Coleman, 'Regestum', p. 218. This records the payment of three marks by Thomas de Bermingham and and Anablina de Burgh for the repair of the organ.

8.22  Sedilia and piscina, Augustinian priory, Callan, Co. Kilkenny (Edwin Rae © Triarc, Irish Art Research Centre).

the sacred vessels were washed after use at the Eucharist. At a number of sites, the sedilia was an elaborate stone structure and was almost invariably located in the south wall of the chancel.[25] A particularly fine example survives at the fifteenth-century Observant Augustinian foundation at Callan, Co. Kilkenny (fig. 8.22). Occasionally, as at the Franciscan houses at Adare and Ennis, the sedilia also incorporated the burial vault of prominent benefactors of the community. The sanctuary area was frequently distinguished from the rest of the choir by being located on a slightly higher level. In the Franciscan and Augustinian churches at Adare, these changes in floor levels are indicated by variations in the stone mouldings on the bases of tombs in the north wall of the chancels.

**25** Moss, 'Permanent expressions of piety', pp 82–3.

8.23 High altar, Quin friary, Co. Clare. Note the founder's tomb (Macnamara) in the north-east corner of the sanctuary.

## THE HIGH ALTAR

The friary's main or high altar was situated underneath the great east window of the church. Its position was both practical and symbolic. Its location underneath the largest window in the church meant that it received sufficient light for the early morning celebration of the Conventual Mass. The rising sun also recalled Christ's resurrection, an allusion recalled each morning in the words of the gospel canticle *Benedictus*, recited during the office of Lauds. The high altar generally stood on a higher level than that of the sanctuary and was approached by the three steps of the predella, which the priest, deacon and subdeacon occupied while celebrating the daily conventual Mass. These steps still remain at the Carmelite church in Castlelyons, where each one was sufficiently broad to incorporate a number of burials. At the Franciscan house at Quin, a gap between the base of the high altar and the current floor level indicates that a wooden predella once existed there (fig. 8.23). References to altar steps in the Dominican church at Athenry and the Franciscan friary in Kilkenny also indicate that the high altar in these churches occupied an elevated position at the east end of the sanctuary.

8.24 High altar, Dominican priory, Sligo (photograph by Fr Fergal MacEoinín OP).

The high altar was invariably a stone structure, of which relatively few survive.[26] The table of the high altar in the Dominican church in Sligo is decorated with five interlaced consecration crosses and preserves a partial inscription commemorating John, the donor (fig. 8.24). The front of the altar is divided into nine panels framed by cusped ogee-headed arches with foliate decoration. Though now blank, these may originally have borne painted images.[27] At the Franciscan friary in Quin, the high altar is a substantial structure cantilevered into the east gable of the church. In the Carmelite friary in Castlelyons and the Dominican church at Glanworth, only the bases of the high altars survive, indicating that they were free-standing structures.

## SUBSIDIARY ALTARS

The west wall of the belfry provided a backdrop for pairs of nave altars, which survive at the Franciscan friaries at Ennis, Muckross, Quin and Rosserrilly and at the Dominican priory at Lorrha. In contrast to the high altar, which was reserved for the solemn daily Conventual Mass, these smaller altars along with those in the transepts were used by individual friars for private celebrations of the Eucharist.

**26** Ibid., pp 81–2.   **27** JOHAN […] ME FIE[R]I FECIT.

Each altar was dedicated to a particular saint or devotion and acted as the focus for the promotion of their cult. Mooney records the presence of seven subsidiary altars at Kilconnell friary, and the Franciscan church in Waterford had altars dedicated to St Clare and the Magi.[28] Franciscan and Dominican churches invariably had altars or chapels dedicated to their founders and to the principal saints of each order. In Ennis, the retable of the surviving nave altar depicts St Francis (fig. 5.3), while a nearby image of the *Imago pietatis* – the man of sorrows – presumably also functioned as an altarpiece. There are contemporary references to the altars of St Francis in the friary churches at Kilkenny, Rosserrilly and Kilconnell, and to the chapels or shrines of St Dominic in the priory churches at Athenry and Limerick.[29] The Athenry church also had a chapel dedicated to St Catherine of Siena and St Catherine of Alexandria, who, because of their association with learning, were regarded as particular patrons of the Dominican order.[30] Altars and images of St Peter Martyr were routine features of all Dominican churches and presumably were also found in the Irish priories.

## ART AND ORNAMENTATION

As was demonstrated in chapter seven, the mendicant friars were at the forefront of popularizing devotion in late medieval Ireland.[31] In addition to celebrating the universal liturgy of the church, the friars also encouraged an interiorized form of spirituality that stressed the individual's connection with God and the saints and emphasized the role of the emotions in such a relationship.[32] This affective spirituality influenced all areas of the friars' ministry, but had a particularly important impact on the art of the mendicant movement.[33] Friary churches acted as devotional showcases in which the stained glass, wall paintings, woodwork, stone sculpture, statuary, vestments and altar plate complemented and confirmed the message delivered from the pulpit. The evidence for this art in Ireland is fragmentary, but enough survives to show that the iconography employed by the Irish friars was of a piece with that found elsewhere in Europe.

## STAINED GLASS

The scale and position of window tracery in Irish friaries bear witness to the significant role that stained glass played in the ornamentation of mendicant

**28** 'Brussels MS 3947', p. 56; Walton, 'List of early burials', pp 72, 74.  **29** See above, pp 182–6.  **30** Coleman, 'Regestum', pp 218–19.  **31** C. Hourihane, 'Foreword' (2006), pp xvii–xxii.  **32** G. Constable, 'The ideal of the Imitation of Christ' (1995).  **33** R.B. Brooke, *The image of St Francis: responses*

churches.[34] The fragility of the medium and the practice of salvaging the lead cames or strips that held the panels or quarries of glass together mean that very little survives to illustrate the appearance or iconographic range of medieval Irish stained glass. In the earliest reference to glass in an Irish friary, the fourteenth-century text *Caithréim Thoirdhealbhaigh* refers to the '*gormfuinneoig*' or 'blue window' of the Franciscan friary in Ennis.[35] Mooney refers to glass windows in the Franciscan churches at Adare, Donegal, Kilconnell, Muckross, Roscrea and Timoleague, while Luke Wadding records that the Franciscan friary in Clonmel also had coloured glass windows.[36] The dissolution records of 1540–1 list window glass among the chattels of the Dominican priory in Dublin, the Carmelite house at Ardee and the Franciscan friaries at Kildare and Castledermot.[37]

The endowment of stained glass was a popular way of patronizing the friars and was criticized by the author of *Piers Plowman* and other anti-mendicant writers. Lady Isabella Palmer rebuilt the east gable of the Franciscan friary at Kilkenny sometime before her death in 1347, and it is likely that this included the decorative glass of the east window.[38] A former mayor of Dublin, Kenwric Sherman (d. 1351), paid for the glazing of the east window of city's Dominican priory, while Maurice Doncref (d. 1361) left £40 for the same purpose.[39] The register of the Dominicans in Athenry records that Johanna Wyffler, widow of David Wydyr (d. 1408) paid over one hundred marks for the glazing of the great east window and choir windows of the church, while another benefactor, Edmund Lynch (d. 1462) of Galway, provided the stone mullions and the glass for the windows of the chapel he established in the priory.[40]

Fragments of stained and painted glass have been discovered during archaeological excavations and gravedigging at the Franciscan friaries at Castledermot, Kilconnell and Muckross and at St Saviour's Dominican priory in Limerick. Of these, the Limerick find is the most significant, as it consists of glass quarries dating respectively to the thirteenth and fifteenth centuries, dates that correspond with the priory's foundation by the O'Brien kings of Thomond and its later restoration by the Fitzgerald earls of Desmond (pl. 14).[41] The thirteenth-century material was of poor quality, consisting of painted *grisaille* glass with floriate patterns. The fifteenth-century quarries are of a higher standard, ornamented with smear-shaded floral designs executed in dark grey and yellow stain. Both types of quarries formed the background or borders to coloured, figurative panels. Some

to sainthood in the thirteenth century (2006); L. Bordua & A. Dunlop (eds), *Art and the Augustinian order in early Renaissance Italy* (2007).   **34** J. Moran, 'The shattered image' (2006).   **35** S.H. O'Grady, *Caithréim Thoirdhealbhaigh* (1929), ii, p. 32.   **36** 'Brussels MS 3947', pp 40, 64, 65, 68, 75.   **37** White, *Extents*, pp 53, 166, 170, 227.   **38** Moss, 'Permanent expressions', p. 79.   **39** O'Sullivan, *MIDS*, pp 114–15. **40** Coleman, 'Regestum', pp 207, 211.   **41** Moran, 'Shattered image', pp 130, 140–1.

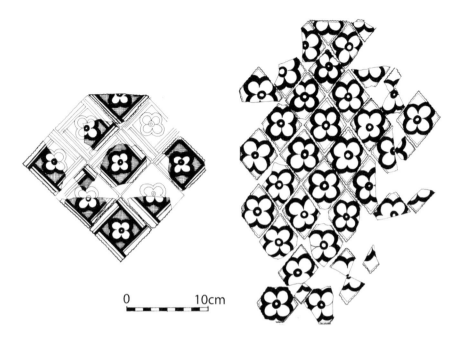

0      10cm

8.25 a & b  Line drawings of fifteenth-century stained glass quarries from St Saviour's
Dominican priory, Limerick (images courtesy of Josephine Moran).

fifteenth-century fragments of these coloured panels with inscriptions in black
letter script were also recovered (fig. 8.25).[42]

The Franciscan constitutions of Narbonne (1260) forbade historiated glass,
with the exception of images of the Crucifix, St Mary, St John, St Francis and St
Anthony in the principal window behind the high altar, but little remains to
indicate the subject matter of stained glass windows in Irish friary churches.[43] The
presence of a lily in a vase carved on the mullion of the east window in the
Franciscan friary at Dromahair indicates that it formed part of an Annunciation
scene in which the other narrative elements were composed of stained glass.[44] In
the mid-fourteenth century, the Franciscan bishop of Ossory, Richard Ledrede,
erected an elaborate historiated east window in St Canice's Cathedral, Kilkenny,
depicting scenes from the life of Christ, which won the admiration of the papal
nuncio Gianbattista Rinnucini three centuries later.[45] Though now lost, panels of
painted, stained glass reputedly from the Carmelite friary at Ardnacranny were
described in 1904. Dating to the late fifteenth century, one panel depicted the

**42** Ibid., pp 124, 130, 132. The inscribed fragments were too small to allow identification of the figures
represented.  **43** Cenci & Mailleux, *Constitutiones generales*, p. 75.  **44** Moss, 'Permanent expressions',
p. 79.  **45** Moran, 'The shattered image', pp 123, 132–3.

meeting between SS Dominic, Francis and Angelus at the Fourth Lateran Council in 1215, while inscriptions on the other panels commemorated the reforming prior general of the Carmelite order, Blesssed John Soreth (d. 1471).[46]

WALL PAINTINGS

The evidence for the wall paintings that once decorated the interiors of mendicant churches and convents is even more fragmentary, but it was obviously a widespread feature.[47] Recent conservation work has uncovered evidence for quite sophisticated cycles of wall paintings at secular and religious sites in Ireland. Paradoxically, most of the religious material comes from tower houses at Ardamullivan, Co. Galway, and Ballyportry, Co. Clare, while remains of hunting scenes are found in the Cistercian monasteries of Holy Cross and Clare Island. In mendicant contexts, fragments of wall paintings still survive or are recorded at the Franciscan friaries at Adare, Askeaton, Buttevant, Ennis, Moyne, Muckross and Rosserrilly, from the Franciscan tertiary foundation at Court and from the Augustinian friary at Adare.[48] Of these, the depiction of Christ as the Man of Sorrows at Askeaton, discussed above, is the most extensive. Fragments of graffiti and the outlines of ships survive at Ennis and Moyne. At Rosserrilly, a fragment of a black letter inscription on the south wall of the chancel once formed part of a now lost narrative sequence. Extensive remains of wall paintings survived in the Franciscan friary in Adare until the late nineteenth century and included figures of saints and floral and geometric motifs.[49] All that remains today are fragments of a red-orange marigold stencil pattern in the arch of the piscina and fragments of a black-letter inscription in a tomb niche, both in the south wall of the chancel. At Muckross, the underside of the aumbry arches in the transept are decorated with a stenciled design, while the image of a cross has been incised in the embrasure of one of the dormitory windows and was presumably painted. At the tertiary foundation at Court, a fragment of a crucifix survives, while decorative diapers and the fragments of three human figures were uncovered in the transept or Lady Chapel of the Augustinian priory at Adare during renovations in 1938.[50]

Mooney noted the presence of paintings at the Franciscan friaries of Kilcrea, Kilcullen and Timoleague, but it is not clear whether he refers to mural or panel paintings.[51] The latter were certainly known in Ireland: in the early fifteenth

---

**46** Ibid., p. 133. O'Dwyer, *The Irish Carmelites*, p. 64. **47** K. Morton, 'Aspects of image and meaning in Irish medieval wall paintings' (2006). **48** K. Morton, 'Later medieval Irish wall paintings, *c.*1100–*c.*1600 AD' (2007), ii, pp 35–9, 40–51, 85–9, 90–106, 117–21, 154–63, 164–73, 290–306, 320–32, 428–32, 441–50, 451–2, 513–20, 521–34, 544–54, 566–72, 573–6, 661–6. **49** Westropp, 'Paintings at Adare "Abbey", Co. Limerick', pp 151–2. **50** R.F. Hewson, 'The Augustinian priory, Adare' (1938), pp 110–11. **51** 'Brussels MS 3947', pp 68, 70, 85.

century, William Buttiler presented the Lady Chapel of the Dominican priory at Athenry with a Flemish altarpiece worth forty marks, depicting the death and burial of the Virgin Mary.[52] In the Augustinian priory at Adare, the base of the large east window in the Lady Chapel was recarved at some stage to accommodate a large retable or altarpiece, which may also have been a painted feature.[53]

STONE SCULPTURE

Stone sculpture was the most enduring form of ornamentation in friary churches, and its significance in promoting mendicant cults is discussed in chapter seven. The surviving sculpture is iconographically of a piece with what is found elsewhere in Ireland, with the crucifixion, images of the Virgin Mary, the apostles and auxiliary saints such as SS Catherine of Alexandria and Margaret of Antioch occurring in the friaries as well as in secular churches.[54] Occasionally, the iconography gives a snapshot of the patron's personal piety. The survival of an elaborate flamboyant canopied altar-tomb in the north-west corner of the nave of the friary at Kilconnell is a case in point. Its position near the principal door of the church meant that it would have been one of the first things seen on entering the building (fig. 7.4).[55] At the apex of the tomb, the figure of an unidentified bishop flanks that of the stigmatized St Francis of Assisi. The figures on the bast panel of the tomb depict St John the Evangelist, St Louis of Toulouse, St Catherine of Alexandria, John the Baptist, St James and St Denis. The inclusion of St James, garbed as a pilgrim with hat, scrip and cockleshell, may indicate that the patron had made the pilgrimage to Santiago de Compostella. The figure of St Denis is unusual and may indicate that he was a personal patron of the donor. However, as the figure is depicted in a Dominican habit, holding a lily and a book, the normal iconographic attributes of St Dominic, it may simply be a case of mistaken identity. At the Dominican church in Strade, another elaborate tomb occupies the place of honour in the north wall of the chancel, adjacent to the altar. Here, the donor kneels in supplication before a metropolitan archbishop, probably St Thomas Becket, and the apostles Peter and Paul. The other panel of the frontal depicts the Magi and Christ displaying his wounds, a common attribute of depictions of the Last Judgment (fig. 7.6).[56] The kneeling figure wears an unusual quasi-monastic habit that may indicate membership of the Dominican Third Order. The choice of saints indicates a strong personal preference and suggests that the patron had made pilgrimages to their cult sites at Canterbury, Rome and Cologne.

**52** Coleman, 'Regestum', pp 209, 210, 211.   **53** Hewson, 'Augustinian priory', p. 109.   **54** J. Hunt, *Irish medieval figure sculpture* (1974).   **55** Moss, 'Permanent expressions of piety', pp 86–9.   **56** R. Stalley, 'The abbey in its later Gothic context' (2005), p. 140, n. 20.

8.26  Retable depicting the pieta, Strade priory, Co. Mayo.

A stone carving of the Pieta at Strade constitutes the only surviving example of
an Irish mendicant retable or altarpiece. Flanked by the kneeling figures of the
male and female donors, the Virgin cradles the dead Christ in her lap, attended by
feathered angels underneath crocketted canopies (fig. 8.26).[57] As noted above,
such retables, in different media, were common ornaments in Irish friary and
secular churches. At the Franciscan church in Adare, the three sockets underneath
the great east window probably secured a retable over the high altar. Retables often
consisted of carved and painted alabaster panels held together in wooden frames.
Produced in Nottingham in England, they were exported all over Europe, even as
far as Iceland and Naples, and became a significant medium for the transmission
of iconography.[58] At the Franciscan friary in Ennis, a series of five carved limestone
panels depicting scenes from the passion of Christ were copied from English
alabaster models (fig. 7.7).[59] Likewise, the images of the head of St John the
Baptist from the Franciscan friaries in Ennis and Waterford, though rendered in
limestone and sandstone respectively, ultimately derive from English alabaster
models.[60]

57 Ibid., pp 82–3.   58 J. Hunt & P. Harbison, 'Medieval English alabasters in Ireland' (1976).   59 J. Hunt,
'The influence of alabaster carvings on medieval sculpture in Ennis friary' (1975).   60 E. McEneaney,
'Politics and the art of devotion', pp 46–7.

8.27 Thomas Dineley, sketch of a tomb at Quin friary, Co. Clare (reproduced by permission of the Royal Society of Antiquaries of Ireland).

### STUCCO, WOODWORK AND STATUARY

Although the most enduring expression of visual culture in late medieval Ireland, stone sculpture formed but one element of what were often quite complex visual programmes.[61] At the Franciscan friary at Quin, a fragment of a crucifixion scene in stucco survives above a limestone arch in the south wall of the chancel. When sketched by the English artist Thomas Dineley in 1681, the stucco work was much more extensive and included paintings of two figures on the rear wall of the tomb niche (fig. 8.27). Such multimedia approaches were probably characteristic of the decorative schemes of many mendicant churches where now only the stone elements survive.

The complete destruction of the wooden furnishings of the friary churches and convents is a case in point. The quality and detail of the carving in the canopied tombs, piscinae, sediliae and other stone features of the churches were presumably replicated in the choirstalls and other wooden furnishings of the friaries, but nothing survives to illustrate this. In describing the woodwork in the churches of the Franciscan friaries at Claregalway, Kilconnell and Kilcullen, Mooney noted that it was of a very high quality.[62] He also recorded that that the ceilings over the chapter house and refectory in Timoleague were supported by carved wooden beams.[63]

In a similar fashion, the loss of most of the wooden statuary from the friary churches leaves a major lacuna in any attempt at assessing mendicant iconography. The images that do survive indicate that the friars encouraged many of the same cults found elsewhere. Devotion to the Virgin Mary was assiduously promoted, and wooden statues of the Virgin Mary survive from the Franciscan friaries at Adare, Askeaton (pl. 8) and Waterford, while a particularly fine pieta survives from the Carmelite church at Kilcormac. Three late medieval statues preserved in the National Museum of Ireland are thought to come from the Augustinian church in Fethard. They depict God the Father from a Throne of Grace ensemble (pl. 17), St John the Baptist, and Christ on the Cold Stone.[64] A medieval alabaster image of the Trinity (pl. 7) and a freestanding statue of St Catherine of Alexandria survive *in situ* at the Dominican priory in Kilkenny. In addition to their image of the Virgin Mary, the Observant Franciscans at Adare possessed statues of St Louis of France, St Joseph and, possibly, St Francis.[65] The most complete ensemble of medieval statuary from Ireland comes from the Holy Ghost hospital in Waterford, established in 1544 in the church of the city's dissolved Franciscan friary. It is

---

61 Moss, 'Permanent expressions', pp 72–4.   62 'Brussels MS 3947', p. 54.   63 O'Neill, 'Irish Franciscan friary architecture', p. 320.   64 P.F. Wallace & R. Ó Floinn, *Treasures of the National Museum of Ireland* (2002), p. 269, illustration, p. 285.   65 Ó Clabaigh, 'The other Christ', pp 152–3.

likely that most of the images came from the friary church, though some may have come from other dissolved religious houses in the city.[66] These range in date from the thirteenth to the seventeenth century and include a fifteenth-century image of the head of St John the Baptist on a dish, as well as a wooden statue of the saint, a fifteenth-century alabaster statue of St Catherine of Alexandria and wooden statues of the Madonna and Child, St Stephen and an unidentified saint. All the wooden statues from Waterford reveal traces of polychrome.

Many of the statues and images in the priory church in Athenry were donated by benefactors, and the same pattern was doubtless repeated elsewhere. William Lynch, whose family's tomb was in St Dominic's Chapel, presented a crucifix and a statue of St Dominic worth 100s. Walter Fanyn presented an image of the Virgin Mary for the Lady Chapel in the priory church, while John Reed and his wife, Catylne Brayneoc, donated a crucifix and images of the Virgin Mary and St John the Evangelist costing thirty marks. This may refer to their sponsorship of the church's rood: the large crucifix mounted on a beam and flanked by images of the Blessed Virgin and St John that dominated the crossing arch of the tower. This was one of the principal images in a medieval church and the object of much devotion.[67] The most intriguing donation was that of William Buttiler and his wife, Agnes Bonanter, who presented the Lady Chapel with a Flemish altarpiece depicting the death and burial of the Virgin Mary.[68]

## LITURGICAL PLATE

Chalices were the most popular items of liturgical plate donated by benefactors because of their intimate association with the Eucharist. Mooney wrote that in 1600 the Franciscan community at Donegal possessed fourteen silver-gilt chalices, two silver ones and two ciboria for the reservation of the Blessed Sacrament.[69] The Athenry register records the donation of five chalices to the Dominican community there during the fifteenth century.[70] Gifts of chalices were also made as *ex voto* offerings or to mark important events. In 1466, the earl and countess of Kildare presented two silver chalices to the Franciscan community at Adare on the occasion of the consecration of the friary church. Mooney recorded that in 1616 a ciborium, six or seven chalices and a processional cross survived from the friary. The ciborium in particular attracted his attention for the quality of its craftsman-

**66** McEneaney, 'Politics and the art of devotion' (2006), pp 45–50. See also C. MacLeod, 'Medieval figure sculpture in Ireland: statues in the Holy Ghost hospital, Waterford' (1946). **67** The rood of the Franciscan friary in Kilcrea was ornamented with gold and silver medallions depicting the symbols of the four evangelists. 'Brussels MS 3947', p. 70. **68** Coleman, 'Regestum', pp 209, 210, 211. **69** 'Brussels MS 3947', p. 40. **70** Coleman, 'Regestum', pp 208, 210.

ship.[71] Once presented, these items were carefully preserved by the communities: as late as 1698, the Franciscan friars of Kilconnell had in their possession the chalices presented to them by the friary's founders two centuries previously.

The bullion value of altar vessels means that only four chalices from friaries survived to the modern period.[72] Of these, the 1494 de Burgh–O'Malley chalice, from either the Augustinian friary at Murrisk or the Dominican house at Burrishoole, both in Co. Mayo, is the most accomplished (pl. 18). A portable chalice commissioned for the use of the Dominicans of Roscommon by Friar Hubert O'Connor in the fifteenth century survived until at least 1980, when it was stolen from the museum of St Patrick's College, Maynooth. A silver-gilt chalice in the National Museum of Ireland has recently been identified as one presented to the Franciscan community at Kilconnell in 1532.[73] A small, beautifully proportioned chalice presented to the Franciscan community in Nenagh in 1589 also survives.[74] Apart from these, only three other items of mendicant liturgical plate remain: a bronze processional or altar cross of English manufacture associated with the Franciscan friary at Multyfarnham (pl. 19); a latten cross associated with the Dominican priory in Sligo; and the Ballylongford processional cross. This final item, a highly accomplished silver-gilt processional cross from the Observant Franciscan friary at Lislaughtin, Co. Kerry, gives an indication both of the standard of late medieval Irish church plate and the largesse of the friars' benefactors. It was presented to the friars in 1479 by Cornelius O'Connor, son of John O'Connor Kerry, the founder of the friary, and his wife, Avelina Fitzgerald, and is possibly the work of a Dublin goldsmith (pl. 20).[75]

## VESTMENTS

In comparison with most parochial churches and many Irish cathedrals, the vestries of Irish friaries were very well endowed with liturgical vestments. These were generally imported items and represented significant expenditure on the part of their donors. In 1600, Mooney recorded that the Donegal Franciscans possessed forty suits of vestments, mostly of silk but including some made of cloth-of-gold and cloth-of-silver. He also described those from Enniscorthy friary as being embroidered with figures and designs and noted that the friars in Adare once possessed a large number of vestments.[76]

71 'Brussels MS 3947', p. 64.    72 M. Krasnobebska-D'Aughton, 'Franciscan chalices, 1600–1650' (2009). 73 Ó Floinn, 'Irish Franciscan church furnishings', pp 10–11.    74 J.J. Buckley, *Some Irish altar plate* (1943), pp 14–18, 214; J.R. Bowen & C. O'Brien, *A celebration of Limerick's silver* (2007), pp 61 (illus.), 73. 75 C. Hourihane, 'Holye crossys: a catalogue of processional, altar, pendant and crucifix figures for medieval Ireland' (2000), pp 8–9; R. Ó Floinn, 'The Lislaughtin Cross' (2010), p. 92.

The Athenry register indicates that the Dominican community there was similarly well endowed.[77] David Wydyr (d. 1406), a merchant, presented them with a cope of silk and cloth of gold worth sixteen marks, for the use of the cantor in choir.[78] These were probably acquired in England or Flanders, where he had trading links. His widow Joanna provided a wooden chest in which to store the cope and other precious vestments that the couple had previously donated to the community. Edmund Lynch presented two particularly ornate sets of vestments for the ministers at High Mass. One, described as 'delightful to the eye of the beholders', consisted of the full ensemble of cope, chasuble, dalmatic, tunic, stoles, maniple, alb and amice in variegated colours, while the other set was of blue silk decorated with flowers and foliage embroidered in silver thread. Lord Thomas de Bermingham and his wife, Anablina de Burgh, also donated a full suit of red silk vestments to the community.

Although no vestments survive from any Irish friary, the late medieval sets that survive from Waterford Cathedral give some idea of how they may have appeared. While these vestments are a particularly opulent set of Italian and Flemish manufacture, combining silk, damask and detailed embroidery, the friars' contacts with the upper echelons of Anglo-Irish and Gaelic society suggests that at least some of their vestments may have been of similar quality.[79]

## PRECINCTS AND BOUNDARIES

The friary precincts were generally delineated by a substantial enclosing fence, earthwork or wall. This encircled the claustral complex as well as the cemetery, gardens and orchards, and provided the friars with a modicum of seclusion and security. In addition to keeping intruders out, the boundary wall also served to keep the friars in, especially after dark. It did not always succeed in this latter function: in August 1490, the Augustinian prior general forbade members of the Dublin community from entering the city after Vespers.[80]

The Franciscan friary precinct in Armagh was enclosed by Archbishop Patrick O'Scannail, while the precincts of the Dominicans at Athenry were completed by Joanna Wyffler. In the depiction of Youghal in *Pacata Hibernica*, the enclosures of both the Franciscan and the Dominican friaries are clearly illustrated (fig. 8.1). Though now vanished, seventeenth-century references to the gatehouse and precincts of the Franciscan friary at Ennis indicate that they were substantial

---

**76** 'Brussels MS 3947', pp 40, 63–4, 84.   **77** Coleman, 'Regestum', pp 208, 211, 218, 219.   **78** Ibid., p. 207.   **79** E. McEneaney, 'Politics and the art of devotion in late fifteenth-century Waterford' (2006), pp 40–6.   **80** Martin & de Meijer, 'Irish material', p. 104, no. 111.

8.28 Franciscan friary, Adare, Co. Limerick. Gateway with a recess for a heraldic plaque or a
devotional image.

structures.[81] The precinct walls of the Franciscan houses at Adare, Claregalway,
Lislaughtin, Moyne and Rosserrilly can still be traced, as can those of the
Augustinian friary at Adare. At each of these sites, an impressive gateway still
stands with openings designed to admit both pedestrian and vehicular traffic. In
each instance, a niche over the gateway housed either an image of the patronal
saint or the coat of arms of the founders. In Adare, the arms of the earl of Kildare
are positioned over the gateway of the Franciscan friary (fig. 8.28), while those of
the earls of Kildare and Desmond adorn the gatehouse of the nearby Augustinian
foundation (fig. 8.29). The care with which the friars chose their sites, their
hydraulic skill and the manner in which the claustral complex helped to sustain
their lifestyle is evident in Mooney's idyllic description of the site of the Franciscan
house at Moyne (fig. 8.3):

> The convent occupied a most agreeable situation. The buildings were
> spacious, of excellent workmanship, and almost entirely constructed of
> marble. Round the convent were gardens, meadows and orchards enclosed
> by a strong wall of stone. In the very cloister, a spring of water gushed forth
> from the rocky soil, and flowing through the premises, was made use of by
> the brethren in six or seven different places, it then rushed to the sea, about

**81** J. Bradley et al., 'Urban archaeology survey xv: County Clare' (1988), p. 58.

8.29 Heraldic devices of the earls of Kildare (*left*) and of Desmond (*right*) on the gatehouse of the Augustinian priory, Adare, Co. Limerick (photograph by Susan Saul Gibson).

three hundred paces distant, sweeping with it the refuse of the house. On its way, it turned two mills for grinding corn. The water was of an excellent and wholesome quality and flowed from this well in such abundance that it was never known to fail. There was a plentiful supply of fish, an immense, I might say, a superabundant quantity of vegetables, while such was the profusion of shellfish that they could be collected at any time on the seashore without the slightest trouble. The mortar used in the building of the church and convent was made from the shells of oysters and other such fish, which when burned forms a cement of wonderful binding power. The convent stood close by the sea. This was most convenient, for ships of heavy burthen could be moored at high water beside the infirmary and at the door of the cloister, while at low tide you could walk to the island of Bartragh, which is at least a mile distant. This island abounded in rabbits. Indeed, it would seem as if God wished to supply all our necessities with his own hand, so that we had no need to seek fish, vegetables or meat from an earthly benefactor. Would that we had been suffered to live there in peace.[82]

---

**82** 'Brussels MS 3947', p. 51. Trans. in *Franciscan Tertiary*, 5 (1894), 226–7.

THE CLOISTER OF THE SOUL

In addition to its practical functions, the conventual complex and particularly the cloister at its heart, became a powerful metaphor for the religious life itself – a secluded, silent place removed from secular concerns in which the life of the spirit was cultivated. In Continental friaries, as in most monasteries, the cloister provided a space for reading, meditation and prayer, but Irish examples, with their unglazed arcades on the north side of the friary church, seem unlikely to have held much contemplative appeal. Exceptionally, at the Augustinian friary at Adare, the remains of iron stantions in the cloister arches of the north arcade indicate that they were once glazed and this ambulatory may have housed reading or study carrels for the friars.

The positioning of devotional images in some Franciscan and Dominican cloisters enhanced their prayerful, recollected atmosphere. Unlike the Cistercian foundation at Jerpoint, with its veritable gallery of secular and saintly figures, the surviving images in mendicant cloisters are exclusively of the founders of each order.[83] Images of St Francis survive from cloister arcades in Adare, Askeaton, Dromahair, Killeigh and Meelick, while images of St Dominic survive from the cloisters of the priories at Athenry and Sligo. These images of the founders strengthened the friars' corporate sense of identity and acted as incentives to appropriate conduct within the cloister. At Askeaton, the image of St Francis appears within a crocketted ogee-headed niche on the north-east pier of the cloister arcade. It stands opposite the entrance to the chancel and acted as a visual summons to recollection for friars going to and from Mass and the Divine Office.

The notion of the cloister as metaphor for the religious life found expression in numerous late medieval devotional treatises, some of which are listed in the library catalogue of the Franciscan friary in Youghal. Of these works, the allegorical treatise *De claustro animae* ('on the cloister of the soul'), by the twelfth-century Augustinian Canon Regular, Hugh of Fouilloy (d. *c.*1172), was the most influential.[84] In its third section, the author attached a symbolic meaning to each part of the monastery, thereby establishing a meditative link between some spiritual or moral value and a familiar architectural feature. Thus, the four walls of the cloister represented contempt of oneself, contempt of the world, the love of God and the love of one's neighbour. Each wall faced a cardinal point and corresponded to a position of the sun in the sky. The twelve pillars of each arcade corresponded to a value or virtue appropriate to the range of the cloister in which it was situated: the range representing contempt of oneself included columns

**83** Moss, 'Permanent expressions', p. 79; Ó Clabaigh, 'The other Christ', pp 150, 160. **84** Hugonis de Foliceto, 'De claustro animae'. This section is based on C. Whitehead, 'Making a cloister of the soul in medieval religious treatises' (1998).

entitled love of subjection, contempt of fame and avoidance of praise. The allegory was further developed by reference to the processes of quarrying, carving and polishing each column while progress in the virtue it embodied was illustrated by reference to the base, shaft and capital of each pillar. The other parts of the monastery also embodied different monastic virtues. The guest house represented the compassion a religious extended to a delinquent *confrère*. The refectory became the time he devoted to nourishing his soul through the study of scripture, feeding upon its literal, allegorical and tropological senses at three different tables. The church represented the prayerfulness of his soul, while the dormitory became a figure of the tranquil soul reposing on the bed of conscience. This highly sophisticated allegory allowed the religious to sacralize every aspect of his life, dress and environment. Hugh's work proved hugely influential and its main tenets were incorporated into the widely read *Speculum maius* of Vincent of Beauvais and the *Rationale diviniorum officiorum* of Durandus of Mende, and copies of both these works along with the *de Claustro Animae* itself were to be found in the Youghal library.

Other writers produced less sophisticated but perhaps more memorable ways of allegorizing the cloister. The *Vitae Fratrum*, a collection of edifying tales about the early Dominican friars compiled by Friar Gerard of Frachet, contains a vivid account of a late-night tour of the friary in Bologna given to St Dominic by no less a guide than the devil himself:

> One time in the convent of Bologna, Dominic found the devil going around the entire house. Blessed Dominic said to him: 'Where are you going?' He answered: 'I go all around, I seek whether there is any among your brothers whom I may devour.' Said Blessed Dominic: 'What do you gain in the choir?' He answered: 'That I make them sleep, break silence, come late, leave quickly.' 'And in the refectory, what do you gain?' He answered: 'Sometimes I make them eat too much, sometimes I make them eat too fast.' 'And in the dormitory, what do you gain?' He answered: 'I prick them with desire, I make them rise late, and miss the office.' 'And in the parlour, what do you gain?' He answered, laughing, 'That place is all mine; for they cast rumours and words to the wind.' Finally, Blessed Dominic dragged him to the chapterhouse and said 'What do you gain here?' The devil answered: 'This place is my hell, because whatever I gain in a week I lose here in an hour, because here the brothers often accuse themselves, confess and are absolved; whence I hate this building above all others'.[85]

---

85 B. Jarrett (ed.), *Lives of the brethren of the Order of Preachers (1206–1259)* (1955), pp 52–3. I am grateful to Hugh Fenning for this reference.

CHAPTER NINE

# Forming the friars

*This city [Paris] is the home and nurse of theological and philosophical science, the mother of the other liberal arts, the mistress of justice, the standard of morals, and in fine the mirror and lamp of all moral and theological virtues.*[1]

The radical novelty of the mendicant vision drew thousands of idealistic young men into the friars' ranks, forcing them to address the issue of how best to form them as religious. The pastoral renewal called for by the Fourth Lateran Council emphasized the need for skilled preachers and confessors and the mendicants swiftly developed an educational system to produce them. The new approaches to scriptural exegesis, the emergence of theology as a distinct discipline, and the ongoing assimilation of the works of Aristotle that emerged in the twelfth century continued in the thirteenth as the young universities grew in confidence and prestige. Unlike the monastic orders, the mendicants harboured no suspicions of this new learning and gravitated to the universities where they attracted some of the most outstanding minds of the age to their ranks. The presence of these highly educated, idealistic members transformed the friars, who became increasingly clerical and learned. The most significant thinkers of the thirteenth and fourteenth centuries were mendicants whose work revolutionized the disciplines of theology, philosophy, the natural sciences and scripture and whose influence percolated to the grassroots of each order through a highly efficient system of *studia* or houses of study.

RECRUITMENT

Although the social background of the vast majority of medieval Irish friars remains irrecoverable, the surviving evidence suggests that the Irish mendicants conformed to the European pattern and recruited novices from the literate middle classes in the environs of their local convent.[2] In Europe, it was common for one

---

1 Esposito (ed.), *Itinerarium Symonis Semeonis*, pp 30–1.   2 P. Jacques, 'La signification sociale du Franciscanisme' (1984); Lawrence, *The friars* pp 34–5; Cotter, *Friars Minor*, pp 24–9; O'Sullivan, *MIDS*, pp 90–8; L.E. Boyle, 'Notes on the education of the *fratres communes* in the Dominican order in the

or two houses within a province to be designated as a novitiate, to which candidates were sent from other convents, and this was probably the case in Ireland.[3] Where references to a friar's family background survive, they usually relate to exceptional circumstances, as when Walter de Hereford, only son and heir of the lord of Otymy in Kildare, entered the Franciscans sometime between 1240 and 1250, leaving his inheritance to his two sisters.[4] Occasionally, the sources do shed incidental light on the origins of ordinary friars, as in 1310 when the trial proceedings of the Knights Templar in Dublin included judges and witnesses from the city's mendicant convents. The Franciscan participants included Friars Roger of Kilmainham, Gilbert of Sutton, Nicholas of Kilmainham, Ralph of Lusk, John of Ballymadan, Ralph of Kilmainham and Thomas of Ratoath, all villages in the hinterland of Dublin and presumably within the convent's limit, that area where the friars were entitled to preach and quest for alms.[5] The involvement in the trial of Friar Philip of Slane, a lector in the Dublin Dominican priory, and Friar John of Waterford, a member of the city's Augustinian community, indicates that other members of the communities came from further afield. The presence of Friar Roger of Eton as the guardian of the Dublin friary demonstrates the Irish Franciscans' ongoing conenction with the English province of the order. This was not unusual: the anonymous compiler of the *Liber exemplorum* was an English friar who had worked in both Cork and Dublin in the 1250s, and in 1309 Friar William of Bristol was the guardian of the Franciscans in Ardfert, Co. Kerry.[6]

The necrology of the Dominican friary in Athenry lists the names of twenty-three members of the community who died between 1394 and 1452.[7] Of these, ten bore Anglo-Irish surnames and were presumably local recruits from Athenry and its environs. These included Friars William Curtys, William Reydeymar (d. 1431), Thomas Naisse (d. 1431), Nicholas Brayneog (d. 1431) and Richard Gouer (d. 1447). Other evidence indicates that Friars John Bonnanter (d. 1405) and John Wallys (d. 1408) were members of Athenry merchant families that were prominent in the commercial and political life of the town and notable benefactors of the community.[8] Of the remaining friars listed in the necrology, twelve bore Gaelic surnames, and were presumably recruited from the region's Gaelic populace. These included Friars David Ymolayn (d. 1398), Nicholas Ymilikireayn (d. 1416), Maurice Ycorcran (d. 1438), Thomas Yscanlyn (d. 1439) and Friars Matthew Ydonalyn (d. 1439) and Eugene Ydonalyn (d. 1446), whose surnames were those of hereditary clerical and learned families in Connacht. Friars

thirteenth century' (1981).   **3** B. Roest, *Franciscan literature of religious instruction*, pp 208–9.   **4** *FL*, pp 16–17.   **5** H. Nicholson, 'The testimony of Brother Henry Danet and the trial of the Templars in Ireland' (2008); eadem, *The Knights Templar on trial: the trial of the Templars in the British Isles, 1308–1311* (2009), pp 14–69.   **6** *FL*, pp 41, 91–2.   **7** Coleman, 'Regestum', pp 215–16; O'Sullivan, *MIDS*, pp 94–5. **8** M.J. Blake, *Blake family records, 1300–1600* (1902), pp 6, 10, 12, 16, 18.

Cornelius Ydarmada and Bernard Ychonchur (d. 1452) bore the surnames of the princes of Moylurg and the kings of Connacht while Friar Henry de Burgh (d. 1394) was probably related to the earls of Clanrickard or to some other branch of the de Burgh family.[9]

The foundation of new friaries in Gaelic territories in the late fourteenth and fifteenth centuries brought the friars into increased contact with the hereditary learned families.[10] These constituted the intellectual elite of Gaelic society and enjoyed the patronage of its chieftains and rulers. They possessed considerable wealth in their own right and, as noted above, were often important benefactors of mendicant foundations. The Franciscans at Elphin enjoyed the support of the O'Mulconry family of historians and poets. In 1464, Lochlainn O'Mulconry was buried in the Elphin friary and, in 1468, Torna O'Mulconry, *ollamh* of poetry and history, was also interred there.[11]

Some members of these families also became friars themselves. Their background and professional training sat easily with the friars' educational structures and a number of them rose to positions of administrative or academic prominence within each order. The experience of the O'Daly family of bardic poets provides a representative example of the enduring links between the friars and the learned families. Members of this family were notable patrons of the Franciscan friaries at Kilconnell and Adare. At Kilconnell, their tomb occupies a prominent position in the north wall of the chancel, near the site of the high altar, a position normally reserved for founders and major benefactors. The earliest recorded member of the family to become a friar was the poet Tadhg Camchosach O'Daly, who joined the Franciscans in the fourteenth century.[12] Another Franciscan, Friar John O'Daly, a bachelor of theology, became bishop of Clonmacnois in 1444, while Friar Flann O'Daly governed the Observant Franciscans as vicar provincial from 1510 to 1513. Mooney records that Friar Philip O'Daly was noted for his prayerful ecstasies and for the Irish poems he composed in honour of the Virgin Mary. Friar Thadeus O'Daly of the Askeaton community was martyred at Limerick in 1579.[13] While the surviving evidence suggests that the connection was strongest with the Franciscans, the Dominican poet, diplomat and scholar Friar Dominic O'Daly (d. 1662) was a member of the branch of the family established at Kilsarkan, near Castleisland, Co. Kerry.

These links continued into the early modern period and the linguistic, historical and hagiographical projects of the Franciscan friars of St Anthony's College in Louvain were in large measure the achievement of members of the

---

9 See above, pp 110–12.    10 E. Bhreatnach, 'The mendicant orders and vernacular Irish learning' (2011). 11 *Ann. Conn.*, pp 519, 541.    12 R. Flower, *The Irish tradition* (1947), pp 117–18.    13 O'Mahony, 'Brevis synopsis', pp 168, 174, 183.

learned families. The college's founder, Friar Flaithrí O'Mulconry (d. 1629), demonstrates the facility with which friars from this background continued to flourish within the mendicant orders. Though initially formed in the practice of bardic poetry and *seanchas*, he subsequently became an influential commentator on St Augustine and translator of the devotional work *Desederius* or *Sgáthán an Chrábhaidh*. His diplomatic skills meant that he was a significant player in Irish, Spanish and papal politics. He became archbishop of Tuam in 1609 but never took possession of his see, functioning instead as an agent for Irish affairs in Louvain and Madrid.[14]

### POSTULANCY AND NOVITIATE

Very little evidence survives to show how the Irish friars fostered vocations to their respective orders. On the Continent, the practice of the Dominicans and Franciscans running grammar schools for potential candidates was widespread.[15] These schools, which were distinct from the *studia* conducted for the orders' clerical candidates, gave a grounding in literacy and the arts to postulants and other students. It is possible that the school of St Thomas Aquinas conducted by the Dominicans on Ushers Island in Dublin in the fifteenth century was one such academy.[16] As noted above, Luke Wadding's assertion that Richard Fitzralph received his early education from the Franciscans in Dundalk may indicate that the friars there ran a school that admitted external students.[17] The Franciscan Regular Tertiaries conducted such schools for boys, and portions of their monasteries were referred to as the schoolhouse.[18]

A candidate seeking admission to a medieval friary embarked on a process of scrutiny, initiation and formation designed to sustain him for the rest of his religious life.[19] Certain conditions were non-negotiable: the postulant had to be male, healthy, sane and preferably good-looking. He could not have contracted marriage, have any debts, be an unrepentant heretic, an excommunicate or a public sinner. Other impediments included illegitimacy or profession in another religious order, but such obstacles were surmountable by dispensation. The earliest extant papal document relating to the Irish Franciscans is a 1233 faculty allowing the minister provincial to absolve postulants from censures incurred for assaulting clerics and there are numerous examples of secular clerics and other religious

**14** B. Hazard, *Faith and patronage: the political career of Flaithrí Ó Maolchonaire, c.1560–1629* (2010). **15** Mulchahey, *First the bow is bent*, pp 85–97; Roest, *Franciscan education*, p. 68. **16** O'Sullivan, *MIDS*, p. 94. **17** Wadding, *AM*, viii, p. 127. Cited by K. Walsh, *A fourteenth-century scholar*, p. 361. **18** 'Brussels MS 3947', p. 102. **19** Mulchahey, *First the bow is bent*, pp 97–111, 126–9; Roest, *Franciscan education*, pp 238–50.

joining Irish mendicant communities.[20] In June 1475, the Dominican prior general, Friar Leonard Mansuetius, dispensed seven Gaelic friars from different communities from the impediment of illegitimacy and permitted their promotion to all offices in the order except that of prior. In June 1476 and July 1480, he likewise dispensed Friars Cormac Ogrugan of Urlar and Thomas Oluyn of the Derry community, but in these instances permitted their election as superiors.[21]

Unlike the older monastic orders, the friars initially refused to accept child oblates, recruiting only mature candidates to their ranks. This position fluctuated throughout the Middle Ages and the acceptance of very young candidates was one of the abuses most strongly condemned by Archbishop Richard Fitzralph in his campaign against the mendicants. Normally, candidates were aged between 14 and 18 at the time of their reception.[22] Friar Stephen Dexter, the compiler of the Annals of Multyfarnham, was 17 when he received the Franciscan habit in 1263.[23]

The recurring note in each order's novitiate legislation was caution: unsuitable candidates were to be dissuaded at an early stage. The early Dominican constitutions instructed that a candidate should be taken for a walk in the priory garden by three of the community's more senior and insightful brethren and interrogated, in Latin, about his intentions.[24] If the candidate persisted in his desire for admission he was led to the chapter room where the superior outlined the seriousness of the step he was taking and the difficulties inherent in the life. The candidate then stripped off his secular garments and was clothed in the novice's habit, which with the Augustinians and Franciscans differed from that of the professed brethren.[25] The community then processed into the chancel of the church where the novice received the kiss of peace and was assigned his place in choir.[26]

By the middle of the thirteenth century, a canonically valid novitiate customarily had to last a year and a day, during which the candidate was introduced to the ideals and practices of the order.[27] Responsibility for this induction lay with the novice master who, ideally, was a mature, exemplary friar, capable of forming the novice in the external behaviour appropriate to his new status and of inculcating the mental attitudes and spiritual outlook appropriate to their calling. The calibre of the novice master and the correct conduct of the novitiate were of fundamental importance to the wellbeing of each order and received a great deal

---

**20** TCD MS 250, fos 161v–162; M. Sheehy (ed.), *Hibernia pontificia*, ii (1965), pp 46–7. *Circa* 1230 David MacKelly, dean of Cashel, entered the Dominicans. He subsequently became bishop of Cloyne and then archbishop of Cashel. M.H. MacInerney, *A history of the Irish Dominicans* (1916), pp 1–52. In 1265, the bishop of Ross had vowed to become a Franciscan, *FL*, pp 30–1.  **21** Fenning, 'Irish material', pp 257–9, nos 13, 17, 20.  **22** Roest, *History of Franciscan education*, pp 240–1; Mulchahey, *First the bow is bent*, pp 83–5.  **23** *Ann. Mult.*, p. 14. I owe this reference to Bernadette Williams.  **24** Mulchahey, *First the bow is bent*, p. 75.  **25** An Augustinian novice's habit was white, that of a professed friar, black. The Franciscan novice's habit had a distinctive cape.  **26** Mulchahey, *First the bow is bent*, pp 76–85; Andrews, *The other friars*, pp 41–2, 121–4.  **27** J. Leclercq & A. Boni, 'Noviziato i & ii' (1980), cols 442–60.

of attention in mendicant legislation and hortatory literature. The Augustinian constitutions instructed priors to appoint as novice masters only learned, honest and upright brethren who were zealous for the precepts of the order.[28] The master general of the Dominicans, Friar Humbert of Romans (d. 1277), devoted the longest chapter of his influential treatise *De officiis ordinis* to the qualities expected of a Dominican novice master.[29]

The rapid expansion of monasticism in the eleventh and twelfth centuries and the emergence of the friars in the thirteenth led to an increase in literature and legislation dealing with the training of novices and junior friars. Mendicant writers frequently reworked existing ascetic literature, often from the Cistercian and Victorine traditions, with works such as Hugh of St Victor's *De institutione novitiorum* being particularly influential.[30] Mendicant novice masters and legislators were keenly aware of the value of older patristic and monastic sources for transmitting spiritual and ascetic values. Friar Humbert of Romans, for instance, listed the monastic classics that Dominican novices were expected to read during their year of probation. These included Hugh of St Victor's *Didascalion*; the treatise *On the cloister of the soul* by Hugh of Fouilloy;[31] St Bernard of Clairvaux's treatises *The steps of humilty and pride* and *On loving God*; the prayers and meditations of St Anselm and the *Golden epistle* of the Cistercian monk, William of St Thierry. Humbert also recommended that the novices read the *Confessions* of St Augustine, the *Conferences* of John Cassian, the *Lives and sayings of the Desert Fathers* and the *Lives of the Saints*, as well as the treatise on the virtues and the vices by the Dominican friar, William Peraldus.[32] Copies of many of these works were available in the Franciscan library in Youghal, where, presumably, they also formed a staple of the novitiate reading programme.

LEGISLATION AND NOVITIATE MANUALS

While no material survives to illustrate the formation experiences of the Dominican, Augustinian or Carmelite friars in medieval Ireland, the similarities in outlook and legislation between the mendicant orders means that a representative impression can be gained from the literature that circulated among the Irish

---

**28** Cendoya, *Las primitivas constituciones*, p. 59.   **29** Humbert of Romans, *Instructiones*, 'De officio magistri novitiorum', pp 213–33.   **30** B. Roest, 'Franciscan educational perspectives: reworking monastic traditions' (2000), pp 168–81. C. Walker Bynum, *Jesus as mother: studies in the spirituality of the high Middle Ages* (1982), pp 22–58 gives a concise summary of the spirituality and *mentalité* of regular canons. She concludes that 'it is in this new sense of responsibility for moral education that the writings and thought of the regular canons point towards the appearance of the friars in the early thirteenth century' (p. 58). **31** For its allegorical treatment of the architecture of the cloister, see above, pp 258–9.   **32** Humbert of Romans, *Instructiones*, p. 230; Mulchahey, *First the bow is bent*, p. 110.

Observant Franciscans from the late fifteenth century. This consisted of the relevant sections of the order's 1451 Barcelona statutes and the handbooks for novicemasters compiled by the thirteenth-century friars Bernard of Bessa and David of Augsburg.

The first chapter of the Barcelona statutes, *On the reception and instruction of novices*, detailed the requirements for admission to the novitiate and the norms by which it was conducted.[33] In keeping with the order's rule and in common with mendicant practice, candidates were not admitted without enquiring into to their suitability. Postulants had to be orthodox Catholics, at least sixteen years of age, of good health, not bound by marriage, of legitimate birth, free from debt, competently literate or fit for some useful work. They had to be of good character and 'untouched by the stain of any vulgar infamy.' Exceptions to these conditions could only be admitted to profession with the consent of the vicar provincial. The Franciscan Observants could not receive candidates from other mendicant orders and candidates transferring from monastic orders could only be accepted with their former superior's permission. During the year of probation, novices did not engage in formal academic work and devoted themselves to prayer, spiritual exercises and learning how to celebrate the Liturgy of the Hours correctly. No clerical novice could make profession until he could recite the Divine Office unaided. During the novitiate year, novices could not be ordained to Holy Orders or exercise pastoral responsibilities if they were already priests. They were also forbidden to leave the friary precinct or to converse with outsiders without the permission of their superiors.

Novices were free to leave at any stage during the novitiate year, and superiors, novicemasters and other friars were sternly warned not to impede their transfer to another order or their departure from the religious life altogether. At the end of the novitiate year, with the recommendation of those involved in his training and having disposed of his property, the novice made lifelong profession of the vows of obedience, poverty and chastity. The profession ceremony took place before the assembled brethren, generally in the chapter room. The newly professed friar then passed to the supervision of the junior master (*magister iuvenum*) under whose jurisdiction he remained until he was 25 years of age.

Something of the psychological, spiritual and intellectual influences to which the novice was exposed can be gained from the handbooks that were composed in the thirteenth century to assist novice masters in the instruction of their charges. In the Irish Franciscan context, two thirteenth-century works were of particular significance: the *Speculum disciplinae* of Bernard of Bessa, and the writings of David of Augsburg, the novicemaster of the Franciscan community in

---

**33** Mulchahey, *First the bow is bent*, pp 83–6.

Regensburg. Of these, the *Speculum disciplinae* was regarded as authoritative by the Irish friars and included in the *Scripta ordinis*, the normative texts of the Observant reformers. Bernard was secretary and companion to the minister general of the order, St Bonaventure, to whom the work was frequently attributed, as it is in the copy that survives from Adare. In compiling his work, Friar Bernard drew heavily on the *De institutione novitiorum* of Hugh of St Victor and other monastic sources. Following Hugh, Bernard argued that the exercise of discipline was the foundation on which the religious life was built. An attitude of humility and subjection was necessary before this could be achieved, and he outlined the principal elements of discipline in twenty-five chapters dealing with all aspects of the religious life. Though highly schematic and prescriptive, the work is not without occasional flashes of humour. In describing how a novice should conduct himself while serving Mass, Friar Bernard instructed that he should always wear a white surplice over his habit, 'the sleeves of which are not to be used for the wiping of the forehead or the cleaning of the nose'.[34]

Throughout the Franciscan order in general, the most influential Franciscan compendium of formation literature was that produced in the 1240s by David of Augsburg.[35] This consisted of three separate treatises that circulated under the title *De exterioris et interioris compositione hominis*. As with Bernard of Bessa, Friar David's work was frequently attributed to St Bonaventure, as it is in the catalogue of the Youghal Franciscan friary, where it had been acquired between 1491 and 1523.[36] Over 370 manuscripts of the Latin edition alone survive and, in the fifteenth century, it was translated into English and German for the use of regular tertiary communities and houses of nuns. It was first printed in Italy in Brescia 1485 and in Venice in 1487, and the copy owned by the Youghal friars may have been one of these early printed editions. Following Gregory the Great and William of St Thierry, the treatise first provided a guideline to exterior behaviour before outlining the processes by which the interior life was cultivated and the sevenfold steps by which the novice progressed on the path of spiritual perfection.

## LAYBROTHERS

In all the mendicant orders, laybrothers, or non-clerical members, formed a significant minority within each community. These friars were responsible for the manual and domestic work in the convent and, in treating of the gardeners,

---

**34** Bernard of Bessa, *Speculum disciplinae*, p. 599. **35** David ab Augusta, *De exterioris et interioris hominis compositione* (1899); Roest, *Franciscan literature of religious instruction*, pp 209–14; J.V. Fleming, *Introduction to the Franciscan literature of the Middle Ages* (1977), pp 216–24. **36** *YLC*, no. 147.

9.1 Franciscan friary, Adare, Co. Limerick. The door to the chapter room with a window for laybrothers and other non-chapter members to follow proceedings within. Note the windows for the dormitory cubicles on the first floor.

porters and cooks in Dominican priories, Humbert of Romans assumed that all these positions were held by laybrothers who were under the supervision of a cleric known as the master of the laybrothers.[37] Among the Dominicans, the laybrothers were identifiable by the black scapular and hood of their habit, those of the priest-friars being white. Augustinian laybrothers wore the order's black tunic, but without the cuculla and hood that covered the head and upper body of the clerical friars.[38] In the other orders, the laybrothers wore the same habit as the clerical members and, in general, lay friars were distinguishable from their clerical brethren by their lack of the clerical tonsure. Laybrothers did not have a voice or vote in conventual or provincial chapters, and in the Franciscan friary in Adare and the Augustinian friary at Murrisk, internal windows beside the chapter house door indicate that the brothers followed the proceedings within while standing outside in the cloister walk (fig. 9.1). Among the Franciscans, laybrother postulants had to be aged between 20 and 40, and older candidates were only received if their entry would be a cause of edification to the laity and clergy.[39]

**37** Humbert, *De officiis*, pp 233–6, 274–9, 317–20, 333–6.   **38** Cendoya, *Primitivas constituciones*, p. 62. **39** *AS*, i, no. 2.

Mooney refers to a number of these 'late vocations' to the Franciscan brotherhood in Ireland as well as to lay friars noted for their holiness. Andrew Nugent became a laybrother in Multyfarnham friary following the death of his wife, and he died with a reputation for sanctity. Friar Cuvéa, an early lay member of the Adare community, enjoyed a similar reputation, as did a number of unnamed lay friars of Kilconnell friary.[40] The most notable of these Franciscan laybrothers was the seventeenth-century friar Michael O'Clery. Although he was a member of a hereditary learned family and highly regarded as a historian and a hagiographer, his ignorance of Latin and the fact that he was 33 when he entered the friars seemingly rendered him ineligible for the priesthood.[41]

The subordinate status of the lay friars within each order means that little survives to illustrate their contribution to late medieval Irish mendicant life. A short seventeenth-century treatise for the instruction of Franciscan laybrothers sheds some light on what the experience of their late medieval counterparts may have been like. Printed in Louvain between 1610 and 1614, it survives in a single copy preserved in Marsh's Library, Dublin.[42] Written in Irish (as the laybrothers would not have read Latin), it consists of two pages of text printed on a single sheet and contains a summary of Christian doctrine and Franciscan precepts arranged in numerical and versified form. Its catechetical material consisted of a presentation of the articles of the creed, followed by an exposition of the ten commandments, the five precepts of the church, the seven deadly sins, the gifts of the Holy Spirit, the seven corporal and spiritual works of mercy and the eight beatitudes. The precepts of the Franciscan rule and the friars' observance were divided into twenty-five brief paragraphs. This was followed by a list of the fourteen cases in which absolution for transgressions was reserved to the minister provincial. The document concluded by enumerating the suffrages to be offered by the brothers for deceased friars, cardinal protectors of the order, benefactors buried in the friary cemeteries and cloisters, as well as the prayers to be offered for those who gave hospitality to friars on journeys and for the other benefactors of the order.

### APOSTATES AND FUGITIVES

While novices were free to leave at any stage during their novitiate year, religious profession was regarded as an irrevocable lifelong commitment, and abandoning it was deemed apostasy, a mortally sinful act inviting divine retribution on the

---

**40** 'Brussels MS 3947', pp 57, 64, 99.   **41** I am grateful to Bernadette Cunningham for discussion of this point.   **42** P. Ó Súilleabháin (ed.), *Rialachas San Fronsias* (1953), pp ix–x, 91–6. I owe this reference to

fugitive friar and those who abetted him. In 1258, the earl of Ulster, Walter de Burgh, sent an armed band to carry off his younger brother David, who had entered the Franciscans in Dublin. In the course of the raid, one of the party was killed and its leader died violently shortly afterwards, events that were portrayed as expressions of divine vengeance. Francis Cotter suggests that David de Burgh may have been a minor at this stage, as his brother, Earl Walter, came of age only in 1253.[43] In a similar vein, the Annals of Inisfallen record the death in battle in 1318 of an unnamed son of Mathgamain O'Brien, an apostate Franciscan subdeacon.[44]

The term also had a broader application, and friars who left their communities or transferred to another house without permission or who wore lay clothing while travelling ran the risk of being labelled apostates, even if they did not intend to abandon the religious life.[45] In 1425, Friar Thomas Netter, prior provincial of the Carmelites England, wrote a sharp letter to his counterpart in Ireland, Friar Philip Raythey, demanding the return of Friar John Arbour, who had gone to Ireland without the appropriate permission. Netter complained that other 'apostate and vagrant' English friars 'hardly worth our prisons', had been honourably received in the Irish priories in contravention of the order's legislation.[46] In 1479, Friar Donatus, an Irish Augustinian laybrother, was ordered under pain of excommunication to return immediately to Ireland from Rome and report to his superior. He appears to have undertaken a pilgrimage without the requisite permission.[47]

Fugitive religious were liable to arrest, and religious superiors could apply for a royal writ *de apostata capiendo*, invoking the secular authorities to pursue them.[48] If captured, the offenders were returned to their convents and subjected to such penalties as deprivation of the habit, corporal punishment, penitential fasting and, in extreme cases, lifelong imprisonment in the friary jail. In 1308, at the request of the prior provincial of the Dominicans, King Edward II ordered his bailiffs and ministers in Ireland to arrest and return a number of apostate Dominicans. A writ was issued in 1309 for the arrest of Friar William Portehors, an English Carmelite, who had absconded to Ireland.[49] In 1320, Edward II ordered royal officials in Ireland to apprehend John of Wynton, an apostate Franciscan, and return him to the custody of Friar Adam, guardian of the friary at New Ross.[50]

Fugitives sometimes contested the facts surrounding their departure. Around 1300, a cleric in Ireland, Master Walter de Ulvester, petitioned the king and council in England for protection against the 'false and malicious defamation' of

John McCafferty.  **43** *FL*, pp 27–8. The compiler laments the fact that the young man subsequently married. Cotter, *Friars Minor*, p. 26.  **44** *FL*, p. 106; *Ann Inisfallen*, p. 428.  **45** F.D. Logan, *Runaway religious in medieval England*, c.1240–1540 (1996), pp 9–34.  **46** K. Alban (ed.), 'The letters of Thomas Netter of Walden' (1992), p. 372, no. 36.  **47** Martin & de Meijer, 'Irish material', p. 100, no. 95. **48** Logan, *Runaway religious*, pp 97–120.  **49** Ibid., pp 181, 246.  **50** *FL*, p. 109.

the vicar provincial of the Irish Dominicans and the prior of the Dublin community that he was their subject and that he should be handed over to them. He offered to purge himself of the charge before the royal and ecclesiastical courts if given safe passage to Dublin. In this instance, the royal council decided that the matter did not pertain to the king.[51]

Although apostasy was regarded as a serious sin, it was possible for an errant friar to make amends. The Augustinian constitutions permitted a superior to accept an apostate back, up to three times, though with increasingly severe penalties after the first transgression.[52] Friar Gregory of Rimini, the Augustinian prior general, permitted the English prior provincial and his vicar in Ireland to reconcile apostates to the order in 1357.[53] In 1528, Friar Quentin Cogly of the Dominican community at Mullingar was reconciled to the Dominican order after apostatizing two years previously.[54] Mooney records that he reconciled an apostate Conventual Franciscan to the order after preaching a Lenten mission at Monaincha near Roscrea.[55]

## CLERICAL FORMATION: THE *STUDIA* SYSTEM

By the end of the thirteenth century, each mendicant order had established a system of *studia*, houses of studies wherein those friars destined for ordination received a basic grounding in grammar, the arts, philosophy and theology.[56] For the Dominicans, this posed no ideological difficulties: they were the Order of Preachers and study was integral to their vocation. The Dominican educational model greatly influenced Augustinian and Carmelite practice. Francis of Assisi had not envisaged this role for his friars and reluctantly permitted the study of theology, as long as it 'did not extinguish the spirit of prayer and devotion'.[57] Despite this, the Franciscans also developed their own *studia* and followed the Dominicans to the universities.

In addition to its pastoral and domestic functions, each mendicant friary also operated as a school and acted as a nodal point in a vast educational network through which ideas, texts and personnel circulated.[58] This gradated network of

---

**51** Sayles, *King's council*, pp 51–2, no. 63. **52** Cendoya, *Primitivas constitutiones*, pp 151–4. **53** Martin & de Meijer, 'Irish material', p. 65, no. 3. **54** Fenning, 'Irish material', no. 70, p. 269; Flynn, *Irish Dominicans*, p. 13. The nature of his offence was not specified and he subsequently became bishop of Dromore. **55** Mooney, 'Brussels MS 3947', p. 76. **56** The standard works, on which much of what follows is based, are E. Ypma, *La formations des professeurs chez les ermites de Saint-Augustin de 1256 a 1354* (1956); Mulchahey, *First the bow is bent*; Roest, *History of Franciscan education*; idem, *Franciscan literature of religious instruction*; R. Copsey, 'The formation of the medieval English friar' (2005). **57** Esser, *Opuscula*, 'Epistolum ad Sanctum Antonium', p. 95. **58** A. Kehnel, 'The narrative tradition of the medieval Franciscan friars' (2005).

*studia* and the international character of each order meant that the 'trickle down' effect was significant in each. The compiler of the *Liber exemplorum* provides a good illustration of this in an Irish context. An English member of the Irish Franciscan province, he had studied in Paris *c.*1264, where he met Roger Bacon before returning to work as a lector or teacher at different *studia* in Ireland, including Cork and Dublin.[59] His contacts in Paris included a Franciscan from Denmark and a number of Dominicans, all of whom provided him with *exempla*. He also recorded an *exemplum* that Friar Thomas d'Ufford, another member of the Irish province, heard while a student at Cambridge.[60] The breadth of references and sources on which he drew in the *Liber exemplorum* demonstrates the importance of Paris, both as a place of intellectual formation and as a centre for disseminating ideas and preaching resources.[61]

In addition to the local *studium*, a network of higher *studia solemne* and *studia particularia* within the provinces of each order allowed more talented students to follow advanced courses in philosophy and theology. At the apex of each order's network stood the *studia generalia*, to which outstanding students were sent to benefit from the experience of studying with leading theologians at international centres of excellence. A number of these *studia generalia* were located in university cities such as Paris, Oxford, Cambridge, Bologna and Naples, and some friars pursued university degrees in tandem with the internal lectorate programme of their order. The majority of friars at these *studia generalia* did not pursue degrees, however, and at all times university graduates constituted a small minority of each order's intellectual elite. Paradoxically, the intellectual formation of the vast majority of friars, the *fratres commune*, has, until recently, attracted least scholarly interest, with attention focusing instead on those friars whose careers in centres of higher study or in universities can be more readily traced.[62]

## THE LECTOR

The fundamental teaching qualification in each order was the lectorate, and the lector or doctor in each convent was the friar on whom each order's academic programme ultimately depended. The lector himself had been through the various levels of the order's *studia* system and might occasionally be a university graduate. In addition to training the younger friars, he was also responsible for providing ongoing formation for the rest of the community. If each friary was in some sense

---

**59** *Lib. ex.*, p. 22; Jones, *Friars' tales*, pp 48–9.   **60** *Lib. ex.*, p. 41; Jones, *Friars' tales*, pp 68–9. The *exemplum* is directed to lawyers and bailiffs.   **61** D. d'Avray, *The preaching of the friars* (1985).   **62** J. Cannon, 'Panorama geografico, cronologico e statistico sulla distribuzione degli Studia degli ordini mendicanti (Inghilterra)' (1978), pp 99–100; L.E. Boyle, 'Notes on the education of the *fratres commune* in the

a school, then each friar was a lifelong student, and the lector was responsible for organizing disputations, lecture courses and other academic exercises in which all the community were obliged to participate.[63] Lectors often moved between houses, and a friar's academic progress was interspersed with periods lecturing on philosophical and theological topics in the various *studia* of the province or of the order before he himself proceeded to further studies at another *studium*.

Within each order, the lectorate brought with it numerous privileges and exemptions. A lector was allowed his own chamber in the friary, a companion or secretary, a place of honour in the refectory and chapter, and was frequently exempted from communal recitation of the Divine Office. He was entitled to wear a distinctive lector's hat, and the image of St Dominic over Dean Odo's door at Clonmacnois Cathedral depicts him wearing such an academic cap (fig. 7.3; pl. 15). Among the Carmelites, lectors were permitted the use of a personal seal, effectively providing them with an independent income. The lector was also a significant figure in local secular society and frequently acted as a witness or intermediary in external affairs. A number of lectors from the Dominican priory in Athenry appear as witnesses to fourteenth- and fifteenth-century deeds and wills in the locality, while, as already noted, the lectors of the Dominican and Franciscan *studia* in Dublin were leading witnesses in the trial of the Irish Knights Templar in 1310.[64]

## THE IRISH *STUDIA*

### Dominicans and Franciscans

As one of the prerequisites for a Dominican foundation was the presence of a lector in the community, it is likely that most Irish Dominican foundations functioned as *studia* from their foundation. The earliest definite evidence occurs in the mid-thirteenth century, when Florence MacFlainn, archbishop of Tuam from 1250 to 1256, built the 'scholars' house' at Athenry and bequeathed a set of canon law books to the community.[65] His support may represent an Irish example of the widespread phenomenon whereby bishops regarded the presence of a mendicant *studium* in their dioceses as fulfilling the obligation imposed by both the Third and Fourth Lateran Councils to establish a theological school in each diocese.[66] If so, it indicates that the local secular clergy received their theological formation in the friars' *studium*, and similar arrangements may have been the norm elsewhere in Ireland. The Athenry register and other sources indicate that

Dominican order in the thirteenth century' (1981). **63** Mulchahey, *First the bow is bent*, pp 39–40. **64** See above, p. 261. **65** Coleman, 'Regestum', p. 213; *MRH*, pp 221–2. **66** Tanner (ed.), *Decrees of the Ecumenical councils,* i, Lateran council III, canon 18, p. 220; Lateran council IV, canon 11, p. 240.

the *studium* continued to flourish throughout the Middle Ages. The practice of transferring lectors between houses was demonstrated in 1397 when Friar John Halewyk, who had entered the order in London, was appointed as lector in Athenry for a three-year term. Before his appointment to Athenry, he had been a member of the Dominican community at Ipswich.[67] The appointment of English lectors to Athenry was a routine arrangement, as Lord Thomas de Bermingham (d. 1482) sponsored the restoration of the room of the 'English bachelors' in the friary.[68] That this was not a one-way traffic is evident from the obituary of Friar Gilbert Bron (d. 1451), a master of theology, who, though he died in London after a distinguished academic career in England, had entered the order in Athenry and had done 'much good' for his native convent. Another member of the community, Friar Thomas O'Corcoran (d.1428), also did much good for the community 'before he went to England', where he died at Chelmsford in 1428.[69] Evidence for the existence of a *studium* in Dublin by the early fourteenth century has already been noted, and a number of references to friars with academic qualifications (or aspirations) at Coleraine (1489), Limerick (1503), Sligo (1491) and Waterford (1491) respectively, suggest the existence of *studia* in these communities.[70]

As already noted, the right to have a private room or enclosed cubicle in the dormitory was one of the privileges most frequently conceded to lectors, and the 'doctor's chamber' listed in the 1540 extents of the Dominican priory in Waterford was presumably one such structure.[71] In 1489, Friar Eugene Obrym of Strade was granted the right to have his own chamber, which may indicate that he was the lector in that community.[72]

The first provincial of the Franciscans in Ireland, Richard of Ingworth, was one of the founding members of the friary in Oxford and had been the first custos of the Cambridge custody.[73] His successor as provincial, John of Kethene, procured a Bible with the Paris glosses for the Irish province, but otherwise there is no evidence for the educational activities of the friars for the first sixty years of the province's existence.[74] The earliest indication of a *studium* in Ireland comes from the anonymous compiler of the *Liber exemplorum*, who held the post of lector in Cork *c.*1267,[75] though it seems likely that some *studia* must have been established before this. The earliest reference to the Armagh *studium* occurs in 1303, when the lector, Michael MacLoughlin, was dispensed from the canonical impediment of illegitimacy.[76] In 1310, Friar William Prendergast, lector in the friary in Dublin,

67 Fenning, 'Irish material', pp 255–6, no. 5.  68 Coleman, 'Regestum', p. 220.  69 Ibid., p. 216.  70 Fenning, 'Irish material', p. 262, nos 31–4; p. 265, no. 53.  71 White, *Extents*, p. 351.  72 Fenning, 'Irish material', p. 261, no. 30.  73 For a summary of the situation before 1400, see Cotter, *Friars Minor*, pp 117–22.  74 *FL*, pp 1, 6.  75 *Lib. ex.*, p. 38; Jones, *Friars' tales*, p. 65.  76 *FL*, p. 80.

gave evidence at the trial of the Irish Templars, but again it is highly likely that the *studium* had been established long before this. The Dublin *studium* enjoyed considerable standing as Friar Henry Cogery, one of its lectors, was one of the three masters appointed to the short-lived University of Dublin in 1320.[77] The commission appointed to investigate the racial tension in the province in 1324 ordered the transfer of the Gaelic lectors at Ardfert, Athlone, Buttevant, Claregalway, Cork, Galway, Limerick and Nenagh, incidentally indicating the presence of *studia* at these houses.[78] The Annals of Nenagh record the deaths of the lectors at Armagh, Limerick and Nenagh during the plague in 1348–9, while in 1361 they record the death of Friar Thomas O'Holohan, *lector juvenis et valens*, at Ardfert. The description of a former vicar provincial, Tadhg O'Breasaill, who died at Clonmel in 1369, as a *lector solemnis* in different places indicates both his higher theological qualification and the existence of an advanced *studium* in Clonmel. It also shows that Franciscan lectors also moved between *studia* in the course of their careers. The numerous references to lectors in the Annals of Nenagh are particularly noteworthy and may indicate that Nenagh, the motherhouse of the Gaelic custody, was also a centre for more advanced theological studies.[79]

There are fewer references to *studia* in the Irish Franciscan province in the fifteenth and sixteenth centuries, but this is largely because the Annals of Nenagh, the principal source for the period, stops at 1371.[80] Such references as survive indicate that the various *studia* established in the thirteenth and fourteenth centuries continued to flourish and that the educational structures and achievements of the friars developed apace. In 1438, John White, the Irish Franciscan minister provincial, received permission to establish advanced *studia* at Galway and Drogheda. These were to prepare those friars who had shown an aptitude for theology to pursue advanced studies in the order's *studia generalia* or who were to take bachelor's, master's or doctor's degrees from a university.[81] These two houses were at the centre of a long-running dispute between the Conventuals and the Observants at the beginning of the sixteenth century, and it is possible that Conventual reluctance to allow Observants to either study at or take over these *studia* was the root of the problem.[82] In 1441, Thaddeus MacGillacundain was appointed lector at Ennis, while in the same year Matthew MacEgan, a member of a hereditary learned family, was appointed lector in Askeaton on his return from studies in Bologna.[83] In 1479, Sir James Butler and his wife Sadbh gave a substantial grant of land, tenements and other revenues to the proctors of the

---

**77** *FL*, pp 91–2; 107–8.    **78** NLI D.679; Curtis (ed.), *Ormond deeds*, i, pp 240–2.    **79** D.F. Gleeson (ed.), 'The annals of Nenagh' (1943), pp 160–2.    **80** Ibid., p. 163. There are five entries for between 1496 and 1528 but these are in a later hand and contain no reference to studies.    **81** *AM*, xi, pp 49–50; *FL*, p. 190.   **82** Such disputes were common on the Continent, see Roest, *Franciscan education*, pp 166–8.    **83** *AM*, xi, p. 144; *FL*, p. 192. This is the first reference to a *studium* at Askeaton.

Franciscans in Kilkenny for 'the use and utility of the said friars and the restoration of the place and the maintenance therein of the study of sacred theology'.[84] This provides a rare example of how such studies were financed.

As is frequently the case in other areas of Irish mendicant history, very little evidence survives to illustrate the educational structures of the Austin and Whitefriars in Ireland relative to the Dominicans and Franciscans. Most references to studies among the Augustinians relate to the Dublin community and initially were not very auspicious.[85] Twice in 1348 the community petitioned Edward III for financial assistance to send six friars from Irish houses to study in England, as they had nowhere to study the liberal arts and theology in Ireland.[86] In 1354, the friars in Ireland were granted permission to appoint as local priors members of the order who were not able to speak Latin, though similar concessions were granted to other provinces, reflecting the impact of the Black Death on the order's educational structures and the calibre of recruits.[87] Sometime in the mid-fourteenth century, a *studium* was established in the Dublin priory and the Austin friars gained a reputation for learning. In 1359, Friar John Dale, the recently appointed vicar of the Irish limit, was described as a professor of theology, as was Friar John Holywood in 1392. In 1364, at the behest of Prince Lionel of Clarence, the dean and chapter of St Patrick's Cathedral received the advowson of the church in Stackallen, Co. Meath, on condition that they maintained an Augustinian friar as a reader in theology at the cathedral's 'house of scholars'.[88] They also undertook to pay the prior and community at Dublin ten marks annually for the support of the appointed friar.[89] The Dublin priory functioned as the principal *studium* for the order in Ireland and, in 1479, the prior general decreed that no one was to be appointed prior or lector there unless they possessed suitable academic qualifications. The community's later reputation for learning is evident in an entry in the *Reportorium viride* of Archbishop Alen of Dublin (d. 1534), which stated that the Austin friars outshone all others in Dublin for their doctrine.[90]

Even less material survives concerning the Irish Carmelite friars. In 1325, Friar John Bloxham, the prior provincial of the English province, conducted a visitation

---

**84** White, *Irish monastic and episcopal deeds* (1936), pp 236–7.   **85** Martin, 'Augustinian friars', pp 372–3; Duffy & Simpson, 'Hermits of St Augustine', p. 215; T. Butler, *John's Lane: a history of the Augustinian friars in Dublin, 1280–1980*, pp 27–9.   **86** *MRH*, p. 298.   **87** Martin & de Meijer, 'Irish material', p. 64, no. 1. **88** Lionel of Clarence, third son of Edward III, was a notable benefactor of the English Augustinians. His remains were transferred to the order's proto-friary at Clare in Suffolk after his death in Italy in April 1368. Roth, *English Austin friars*, pp 55–6.   **89** Roth, *Sources*, p. 201.   **90** L. Alemand, *Monasticon Hibernicum*, p. 314; Martin & de Meijer, 'Irish material', p. 100, no. 97.

of the Irish houses and presided over a chapter of the order at Ardee that resulted in a series of reforms. John Bale, the source for this information, also claimed that he established a *studium* for the friars in Dublin, but otherwise nothing else is known of the Whitefriars' educational arrangements in medieval Ireland.

## STUDIES ABROAD

Each orders' lack of a *studium generalium* in Ireland meant that friars wishing to pursue studies to the highest level had to go abroad to do so. To facilitate this, each order made provision for a number of Irish friars to pursue studies, free of charge, in higher *studia* in England or on the Continent. Once this initial quota was exceeded, they had to pay the expenses of any additional students sent from Ireland. This facility was not unique to Ireland, and friars throughout Europe were entitled to send members or their respective provinces to study at their order's *studia generalia*. The right to appoint Irish friars to foreign *studia* lay with their superiors in Ireland and with the major superior of each order and was overseen by each orders' provincial and general chapters. While nothing survives to show how the Irish superiors exercised this prerogative, a number of references to Irish students and academic affairs occur in the surviving general registers of the Dominican, Augustinian and Conventual Franciscan friars and in the general constitutions of each order. Other sources occasionally shed incidental light on the presence of Irish friars in foreign studia. A.B. Emden's survey of the ordination lists in medieval English episcopal registers includes references to at least eighty-three Dominican friars whose surnames or toponyms indicate that they came from Ireland.[91] These often provide an indication of what *studium* they were attending and occasionally make it possible to trace their progress from house to house. The papal registers also refer on occasion to where a friar gained his educational qualifications, and further details can sometime be gleaned from records of grants of alms or details of court cases involving Irish friar students.

The Dominican constitutions initially allowed Irish and Scottish friars to send two friars annually to study at foreign *studia*, and the surviving sources indicate that Irish Dominicans availed of the opportunity. The educational arrangements of the Irish friars received more detailed treatment in the letter issued to the Irish Dominican vicariate by the master general, Berengar of Landorra, after the London general chapter of 1314.[92] As noted in chapter one, this letter conceded nearly all the privileges of an independent province to the Irish friars, while

---

**91** A.B. Emden, *A survey of Dominicans in England based on the ordination lists in Episcopal registers (1268 to 1538)* (1967), pp 25–6 and passim.   **92** Ripoll, *Bull. OP*, vii, pp 74–5. For what follows, see Flanagan, 'Formative development', pp 139–56.

preserving the right of the English prior provincial and chapter to appoint the Irish vicar provincial. The Irish vicar and his four definitors were permitted to appoint lectors for the Irish houses and to license them to engage in academic disputation and to assign (and recall) young friars to university studies.[93] They were also permitted to send two friars, *gratis*, to the order's *studia* at Oxford, Cambridge and London, and a third student was added to the quota of Irish friars studying in Paris. An unspecified number of promising students were to be assigned to *studia particularia* in England to study philosophy. In this last instance, they were to follow the practice of their English *confrères* when it came to paying student fees: if the English philosophy students were exempt from fees in any of these *studia*, then so were the Irish.[94] The letter further decreed that the books of deceased Irish friars were the property of the Irish vicar provincial, rather than of the prior provincial of England.[95]

The 1260 constitutions of Narbonne allowed each Franciscan province to send, free of charge, two young friars every year to the general *studium* at Paris. These were chosen by the minister provincial with the consent of the provincial chapter and were to have spent two or three years after their novitiate in a *studium* in their own province. These friars came to be known as *studentes de debito*, and the system was gradually extended to the other *studia generalia*, including those at Oxford, Cologne, Bologna and Strasbourg. Other students could be sent for studies to these places, but their expenses had to be paid by the province, and these were known as *studentes de gracia*. The minister general also had the right to appoint suitable students to these houses and exercised it in favour of a number of Irish friars in the fifteenth century.

Friar Nicholas Cusack, later bishop of Kildare and one of the earliest witnesses to the emergence of racial tension in the Irish province, seems to have been at Oxford in 1267,[96] and Friar Malachy, the author of a treatise on the seven deadly sins, completed his studies there in 1310.[97] In 1303, three Irish friars were among the eighty-four friars of the Grand Couvent at Paris who witnessed an appeal of King Philip the Fair against Pope Boniface VIII.[98] One of these may possibly be the Friar Odo O'Neill who became lector at the Franciscan *studium* in Armagh and then custos of the Nenagh custody, before dying during the plague in 1348.[99] The permission granted to two Ennis friars, Marianus Curydany and Laurence Omorth, to traverse England en route to Strasbourg in 1375 is the earliest reference to Irish friars at this important *studium*. They had been assigned there

---

**93** Ibid., pp 141, 144.   **94** Ibid., p. 143.   **95** Ibid., p. 145.   **96** *BRUO*, i, p. 530.   **97** *BRUO*, i, p. 1004.
**98** *FL*, p. 79. A.G. Little gives the names of Odo and Dionysius in the printed text but later added a marginal note to his personal copy of *FL* (now in Greyfriars, Oxford) in which he lists a *Ricardus Yberniensis* as well. His source for this addition is not specified.   **99** Cotter, *Friars Minor*, p. 225.

by the provincial chapter, which probably means that they were the *studentes de debito* of the Irish province for that year.[1] This arrangement was confirmed by the general chapter of Rome in 1411, at which Ireland was listed as one of the eight provinces allowed to send two students annually to Strasbourg.[2]

The right of the Franciscan minister general to send Irish students to English and Continental *studia* is confirmed by a number of sources. The earliest of these is a letter of Angelus Serpetri (minister general 1450–3) appointing an Irish friar, Richard Gilis, to a place in Oxford *c.*1450. It indicates that he was exercising a right granted to the Irish province by a general chapter held in Assisi (the year is not specified) to send a student *de debito* to the Oxford house.[3] The Conventual minister general, Francis 'Samson' Nanni, approved the appointment of Friar William of Ireland by the general chapter of Cremona to study theology in Milan in 1488. He also appointed two friars, Richard MacBryen and Roger Okreny, to study theology for three years in Oxford in 1491.[4]

## THE IRISH FRIARS AND THE UNIVERSITIES

One of the greatest obstacles to the development of the friars' educational system was the absence of a recognized university or *studium generale* in Ireland.[5] Members of all mendicant orders were involved in the various initiatives to establish one in the fourteenth and fifteenth centuries, none of which really succeeded. In 1312, Archbishop John Lech of Dublin secured permission from Pope Clement V for the establishment of a university at St Patrick's Cathedral. This was inaugurated in 1320 by his successor, Alexander de Bicknor, and the first three staff members, Friars William de Hardits, Henry Cogery and Edmund de Kermerdyn, were lectors at the Dominican and Franciscan *studia* in the city. The hopes that attended on this venture are evident in the enthusiastic account of initiative give by the Dublin Dominican chronicler John Pembridge.[6] The laconic account given by the Kilkenny Franciscan John Clyn is more telling: '1320: a university began in Dublin, a university as far as name, but if only it had been so in fact and reality'.[7] The venture was not a success, but appears to have struggled on in some attenuated form until 1464, when there is a record of a grant of land to the house and scholars of the dean and chapter at Dublin.

---

**1** *FL*, p. 157.   **2** Glassberger, *Chronicle*, p. 242.   **3** A.G. Little (ed.), 'A letter of Fr Angelus Christophori, minister general, appointing an Irish friar to a studentship at Oxford *c.*AD1450' (1930).   **4** Parisciani, *Regesta*, p. 107, no. 919; p. 197, no. 1530.   **5** For what follows, see A. Gwynn, 'The medieval university of St Patrick's, Dublin' (1938), pp 199–212, 437–54; F. MacGrath, *Education in ancient and medieval Ireland* (1979), pp 219–23; Ó Clabaigh, *Franciscans*, pp 127–9.   **6** Pembridge, *Chronicle*, p. 361.   **7** Clyn, *Annals*, pp 172–3.

In 1465, the mayor and corporation of Drogheda petitioned the parliament meeting in the town for the establishment of a university there. Though the parliament agreed to the proposal, nothing further came of it. In 1475, Pope Sixtus IV acceded to the request of the superiors of the four mendicant orders in Ireland to establish a university for the study of the liberal arts and theology in Dublin.[8] The proposed foundation was to be modelled on the University of Oxford and it was hoped that its establishment would obviate the need for Irish scholars to undertake the perilous journey to England or the Continent to pursue studies. The petition contained the significant statement that there were many friars in each order with the necessary qualifications to staff such a venture, but notwithstanding such resources, little seems to have come of the project. In 1496, the provincial synod of Dublin granted pensions for seven years to the lecturers of the university, and this is the last reference to the institution.

Thus, Irish friars wishing to take degrees had to travel abroad to do so. The surviving evidence indicates that the most popular destination for Irish students was Oxford, though the universities at Cambridge and Paris also numbered Irishmen among their graduates.[9] References to Irish friars in the papal registers indicate that there was a significant increase of friar graduates in the fifteenth century.[10] These chiefly concern the appointment of friars as bishops and frequently refer to the candidate's educational qualifications, but rarely indicate where they were gained.

## INFORMAL CIRCULATION OF TEXTS AND IDEAS

The formal educational structures established by the mendicant orders to train aspirants to the priesthood were not the only ways in which the friars were exposed to texts and ideas.[11] As they became increasingly settled in the course of the thirteenth century, the mendicants adopted many of the practices characteristic of the older monastic orders. The common celebration of the Divine Office exposed them to an annual cycle of scriptural, patristic and hagiographic material, as did the daily Conventual Mass, with its readings, collects and chants. The daily chapter meeting after the office of Prime, at which the martyrology was read and the legislative texts of each order were expounded, provided another forum for intellectual stimulus. It was also the occasion on which the friars were enjoined to pray for their deceased *confrères* and benefactors whose names and benefactions

---

8 *BFNS*, iii, pp 319–20.   9 M.H. Somers, 'Irish scholars at the universities of Paris and Oxford before 1500' (1979). The Oxford material is based on the *BRUO*.   10 Absentees have not been included. See M. Robson, 'Franciscan bishops of Irish dioceses active in medieval England' (1997).   11 A. Kehnel, 'The narrative tradition of the medieval Franciscan friars on the British Isles. Introduction to the sources' (2005); Ó Clabaigh, *Franciscans*, pp 122–3.

were recalled each Friday in Franciscan and Dominican houses.[12] Necrologies and other examples of this capitular material survive from the Franciscan houses at Adare, Youghal and Galway, the Dominican foundation at Athenry and the Carmelite foundation at Kilcormac in Co. Offaly. These gatherings were particularly important in fashioning each order's sense of identity through the commemoration of its saints and the articulation of its defining values.[13] Particular care was taken to preserve these chapter books, those volumes in which this information was preserved and which were kept in the convent's chapter room, and this type of commemorative, martyrological and legislative texts constitutes the largest body of material to survive from Irish mendicant sources. Annette Kehnel has demonstrated that informal recreational gatherings of the friars also provided a forum in which anecdotes, stories and information could be exchanged, and this is reflected in the surviving Irish literature.[14]

The practice of reading in the refectory was another occasion for exposure to a different sort of literature. Devotional works such as those found in the Youghal library or the lives of the saints found in the sister manuscripts TCD MS 175 and Marsh's Library MS Z3.1.5, both Franciscan compilations, would have provided suitable refectory reading material, and the careful, clear script of TCD MS 175 may indicate that it was intended for this public reading. The survival of refectory pulpits at the Dominican house in Sligo and in the Franciscan friaries at Rosserrilly and Dromahair friaries provides physical evidence for the practice (figs 8.14, 8.15). Refectory reading was not confined to devotional material, however, and the Irish friars had the same interest in travel literature and exotica as their continental *confrères*.[15] The late thirteenth-century Irish Franciscan codex TCD MS 347 contains a copy of the *Descriptiones Terrarum*, a work on the Tartars,[16] and a detailed account of the pilgrimage of two Irish friars, Simon FitzSimon and Hugh the Illuminator, to the Holy Land between 1322 and 1324 survives. The Irish Franciscans were also familiar with Friar Oderic (d. 1331) of Poderone's account of his travels to China and the Far East, as a copy of his work written in an Irish friary in 1422 survives.[17] The 1475 Rennes/Kilcrea manuscript contains a copy of the Irish translation of the voyage of Sir John Mandeville made by Finghin O'Mahony in 1472.[18] This very popular work purported to be an account of the travels of a fourteenth-century English knight to the Holy Land and beyond, and

---

**12** Marginal annotations in Bodl. MS Rawl C.320 show that the *Abbreviatio statutorum* was regularly read aloud to the community at Adare.   **13** For the role of hagiography in fashioning mendicant identity, see above, pp 179–91.   **14** A. Kehnel, 'The narrative tradition of the medieval Franciscan friars on the British Isles: introduction to the sources' (2005).   **15** For Franciscan interest travel writing, see B. Roest, *Reading the book of history* (1996), pp 101–23.   **16** TCD MS 347, fos 3–4v. Colker, *Latin MSS*, i, p. 711.   **17** *FL*, p. 133. His companion for some of his travels was a Friar James of Ireland.   **18** G. Dottin, 'Le manuscrit irlandais de la bibliothèque de Rennes' (1894), pp 87–8. See also W. Stokes, 'The Gaelic Maundeville'

described the fantastic creatures he encountered. Other texts of a similar nature are found in TCD MS 667, a mid-fifteenth-century Franciscan manuscript from Clare, and include the *De Inventione Sanctae Crucis*[19] and the Wars of Charlemagne.[20] It is impossible to gauge the impact that this exposure to liturgical, devotional and literary texts had on the friars, but it may be fairly assumed that it provided an ongoing intellectual stimulus for communities that complemented the formal studies programme.

### SCRIBES AND LIBRARIES

The friars were avid bibliophiles and the acquisition of books, their allocation to individual friars and their redistribution after death produced a significant body of legislation within each order.[21] Benefactors also bequeathed books to or commissioned books for their local friary. In October 1452, Richard Browne, alias Cardone, the archdeacon of Rochester, left four books of sermons to be divided between the Augustinian and Dominican communities at Naas.[22] The Athenry Friars Preachers received several missals, an antiphonary and a *pontificale* from their benefactors in the course of the fifteenth century. Of these, the missal sponsored by Adam Cryan *c.*1462 for use at the high altar is of particular interest, as such missals were usually large, ornately illuminated and costly items. The community also received a set of canon law texts from Archbishop Florence MacFlainn.[23] At Adare, the Franciscan community's copy of the *Scripta ordinis* contained in Bodleian Library MS Rawlison C320 was sponsored by Donough Macnamara and Margaret O'Brien in 1482.[24]

Each house possessed the requisite books for the celebration of Mass and the Divine Office, and these were stored in the church or in the sacristy. In 1491, the Franciscans in Youghal possessed five decorated parchment missals and three plain ones, five large choir psalters, five graduals, a large two-volume antiphonary, a volume containing the collects or prayers recited at the end of each service and a *pulpitarium*.[25]

The friars produced many of the surviving manuscripts themselves. These range from commonplace books such as TCD MS 667 and BL MS Harley 913

(1898–9), pp 1–63, 226–312 for an edition and translation of the text. **19** TCD MS 667, pp 68–71. Colker, *Latin MSS*, ii, p. 1134. **20** TCD MS 667, pp 107–30. Colker, *Latin MSS*, ii, p. 1141. **21** K.W. Humphreys, *The book provisions of the medieval friars* (1974); Roest, *Franciscan education*, pp 197–234; N. Senocak, 'Book acquisition in the medieval Franciscan order' (2003); Senocak, 'Circulation of books in the medieval Franciscan order: attitude, methods and critics' (2004). **22** Coleman, 'Regestum', p. 213; Anstey, *Monumenta Academica Oxon.*, 2 (1868). I owe this latter reference to Hugh Fenning OP. **23** Coleman, 'Regestum', p. 211. Fragments of the elaborate late-fourteenth century missal from the Carmelite church in London survive. See M. Rickert, *The reconstructed Carmelite missal* (1952). **24** R. Howlett (ed.), *Monumenta Franciscana* (1882), ii, p. xlviii. **25** Ó Clabaigh, *Franciscans*, pp 160–1.

designed for the private use of individuals, to more formal liturgical, legislative
and hagiographical material designed for public reading. Evidence for more
mundane scribal activity is provided by the lead pencils discovered during
excavations at the medieval Dominican priory in Cork.[26] TCD MS 347 contains
a recipe for the production of inks, and one of the two Franciscan pilgrims to
Jerusalem in 1322 was Friar Hugh the Illuminator, whose name indictates a
proficiency at book decoration. Colophons provide further evidence for
mendicant scribes. The Adare copy of the Observant Franciscan *Liber Ordinis*, was
written by Friar Donal O'Cahalan in 1482. While the text itself is in Latin and
written in a clear gothic bookhand designed for public reading, the second
colophon is in Irish and in heavily abbreviated insular minuscule script. The
Carmelite friar Dermot O'Flanagan transcribed the Kilcormac missal in 1458
from an exemplar in the friary at Loughrea at the behest of Prior Edward
O'Hacayn. Well-lit rooms on the first floor of a number of fifteenth-century
foundations suggest that they functioned as scriptoria. This is particularly obvious
at the Observant Franciscan house at Kilcrea, Co. Cork, where the room above the
sacristy is lit by eleven windows, ten of which contain double-light openings. This
room also had a large fireplace in its east gable.[27] At the Observant Franciscan
houses in Adare and Lislaughtin, the library/scriptorium is a well-lit room
occupying the top storey of the lavatory block and is accessed from the friars'
dormitory in the east range (fig. 8.13).

The friars also employed professional scribes on occasion, and the Observant
Franciscans in particular were warned against incurring excessive debts when
commissioning books. William Mac an Legha, the prolific Munster scribe, wrote
portions of the Rennes manuscript while staying with the Observant Franciscan
friars in Kilcrea in 1473, and the breviary commissioned in 1489 by the Carmelite
community at Kilcormac, Co. Offaly, was written by Malachy O'Lachnayn, a
cleric of the diocese of Killaloe.

As a matter of course, each mendicant house had a book collection or library,
reflecting the pastoral and educational activities of the community, though little
survives to illustrate this aspect of Irish mendicant life. There are references to the
destruction of the library of the Franciscan friary at Castledermot by Edward
Bruce in 1316. The library of the Observant Augustinians at Callan is alleged to
have held copies of all the books available in the nearby Cistercian monastery at
Jerpoint. Only one Irish mendicant library catalogue survives; that from the
Franciscan house in Youghal, now MS theol. lat. fol. 703 of the Staatsbibliothek
Preussicher Kulturbesitz in Berlin. It contains the catalogue of the friary library on
fos 150v–152r. It is one of only three such documents known to survive from the

**26** Hurley & Sheehan, *Excavations at the medieval Dominican priory*, p. 121.   **27** D. Maher, *Kilcrea Friary*

period in Ireland,[28] and gives an important insight on the intellectual interests of the friars and the late medieval Irish church. The Youghal catalogue lists 150 volumes and was compiled by three scribes at various stages between 1491 and 1523. Friar William O'Hurrily compiled the largest and most elaborate section of the catalogue, listing seventy-eight volumes, in 1491. The second section lists twenty-one volumes and includes fifteen designated for the use of Friar Maurice Hanlan. This privilege was usually reserved for the lector in the community, and the books assigned suggest that Friar Maurice was involved in the formation of young friars.[29]

Though relatively small in comparison with English and Continental mendicant libraries, the Youghal collection indicates that the friars had the requisite material to provide a solid grounding in philosophy and theology for younger friars. It also possessed sufficient material to enable the friars to competently fulfil their roles as preachers and confessors. The description in the 1491 section of the catalogue of the commentary of St Bonaventure on the Sentences of Peter Lombard as *impressa in papiro* is the first reference to a printed book in Ireland. The impact of the new technology on the collection is evident in the 1523 addendum, where the majority of the books listed were printed works.

The friars' attitude to study represented a radical departure from the intellectual culture of the older monastic orders. For the monk, study was primarily a personal spiritual exercise, designed to give glory to God and tending towards the sanctification of the individual. The mendicants shared this ideal, but added another apostolic and pastoral dimension: the fruits of the friars' study were not for themselves alone, they were to be shared with others. The Dominican exegete Hugh of St Cher, commenting on Genesis 9:13, remarked 'First the bow is bent in study, then the arrow is released in preaching.'[30] It is to their activities as preachers, confessors and moral authorities in late medieval Ireland that we now turn.

(1999), p. 14.    **28** For the two versions of the catalogue of the earl of Kildare's library, see G. Mac Niocaill (ed.), *Crown surveys of Lands, 1540–41, with the Kildare rental begun in 1518* (1992), pp 312–14, 355–6. A catalogue of 45 manuscripts preserved in the cathedral library in Limerick in 1631 has been published by M. Esposito in *Revue des bibliothèques*, 30 (1921), 147–9. These consist entirely of medieval theological works (including two by John Wyclif). The 1624 catalogue of the printed books in this library is preserved in Bodl. MS Rawlinson B480, fos 69–78 and includes a number of late medieval works.    **29** C. Ó Clabaigh OSB, 'Friar Maurice Hanlan, his books and the Franciscan *studium* in Youghal' (forthcoming, 2012).    **30** Cited in Mulchahey, *First the bow is bent*, p. ix.

# CHAPTER TEN

# The pastoral impact of the friars

*Friar Eoin O'Duffy was a most renowned preacher, and not less distinguished for his austere and saintly life. His fame extended to the most remote parts of the kingdom, and is yet on the tongues of all ... He always travelled barefooted, rejecting even the slight protection which sandals would have afforded him. He preached with such wonderful force and unction that he never seemed tedious to his hearers, although he spoke at great length, sometimes for three hours together.*[1]

The mendicant friars enjoyed a reputation as the pre-eminent pastoral agents in medieval Ireland. The purpose of all the structures discussed heretofore was to support them in exercising their twin ministries as preachers and confessors. Confirmation of their efficacy in these roles comes from a wide range of contemporary sources. The *Liber exemplorum* gives a number of valuable glimpses of Dominican and Franciscan preachers in action in the late thirteenth century.[2] The Dominicans, as the Order of Preachers par excellence, produced such noted homilists as the thirteenth-century vicar provincial Walter Blunt and, in the fifteenth century, Friar Maurice Moralis O'Mocháin, who also served as vicar provincial. The early fourteenth-century Anglo-Irish Augustinian Geoffrey Schale preached a sermon on church unity before the council of Constance and produced a work on homiletics.[3] The fourteenth-century Carmelite friars David O'Buge and Ralph Kelly also enjoyed reputations as skilled preachers. The Friars Minor too were noted for their preachers: of the twenty-six superiors who ruled the Irish Observant Franciscans between 1460 and 1534, five were noted as accomplished preachers.[4] Friar Donal O'Fallon (d. 1500) was described in 1486 as 'the preacher who did most service to Irishmen since Patrick was in Ireland', while his obituary in the Annals of Ulster referred to his 'laborious and successful preaching' throughout the country during the previous thirty years.[5]

---

1 'Brussels MS 3947', pp 49–50. Trans. in *Franciscan Tertiary*, 5 (1894), 196–7.  2 *Lib. ex.*, pp 56, 85–6, 98–9; Jones, *Friars tales*, pp 84, 113–14, 126–7.  3 A.B. Scott, 'Latin learning and literature in Ireland, 1169–1500' (2005), pp 956–7; R. Sharpe, *A handlist of the Latin writers of Great Britain and Ireland before 1540* (1997), p. 128.  4 The Franciscan material summarizes C. Ó Clabaigh, 'Preaching in late-medieval Ireland: the Franciscan contribution' (2001). 'Brevis synopsis', pp 166–9.  5 Franciscan vicar provincial from 1472 to 1475 and later bishop of Derry (1485–1500). *AU*, iii, pp 305, 451. They also record the death

The zeal with which the friars approached this apostolate contrasted sharply with the perceived inadequacies of the secular clergy and lay at the root of much of the conflict between both groups.[6] This view found clear expression in an anonymous report on the condition of Ireland of *c.*1515:

> Some sayeth that the prelates of the churche, and clergye, is much cause of all the mysse order of the land; for ther is no archebysshop, ne bysshop, abbot, ne pryor, parson, ne vycar, ne any other person of the churche, highe or lowe, greate or smalle, Englyshe or Iryshe, that useyth to preach the worde of Godde, saveing the poore fryers beggars; and ther worde of Godde do cesse, ther can be no grace and wythoute the specyall grace of Godde, this lande maye never be reformyd.[7]

### THE FRIARS AS PREACHERS

From their earliest days in Ireland, the friars followed the practice of their *confrères* elsewhere and travelled in pairs on preaching tours. The compiler of the *Liber exemplorum* recorded the tale of a murder in Carrigtohill near Cork that he heard while on such a tour when based as a lector in the Cork friary. He also preserved vivid accounts of preaching tours conducted in Clonfert by Friar Thomas O'Quinn before 1252 and by Friar Duncan and his companion in Ulster.[8] These accounts demonstrated the simple, direct style of vernacular preaching favoured by the friars, a style that was popular and effective and which drew large crowds to hear their sermons.

The widespread expansion of the friars into Gaelic areas in the fifteenth century increased the number of bases from which such preaching missions could be launched. The obituary of the Franciscan Friar Patrick O'Feidhil (d. 1505) described him as a celebrated preacher throughout Ireland and Scotland. The fact that his death was recorded in the Annals of Ulster, but he was buried in Timoleague, Co. Cork, corroborates the extent both of his reputation and his travels.[9] Donatus Mooney's account of the Donegal Franciscan Bernard MacGrath records that he once travelled 150 miles to preach before the earl of Kildare and refers to a prophecy made by him during a sermon preached in Clogher.[10] Likewise, the complaints of the people of Kilkenny in 1537 against the tolls

---

of another noted preacher, Friar Angus MacNulty, in 1492. *AU*, iii, p. 305.   **6** Cotter, *Friars Minor*, pp 74–122; M. Robson, 'The ministry of preachers and confessors' (2000); A.J. Fletcher, 'Preaching in late medieval Ireland: the English and Latin tradition' (2001).   **7** 'State of Ireland and plan for its Reformation' in *State Papers for the reign of Henry VIII*, 11 vols (London, 1830–52), iii, p. 15.   **8** *Lib. ex.*, pp 85–6; 98–9; Jones, *Friars' tales*, pp 113–14; 126–7.   **9** *AU*, iii, p. 477.   **10** 'Brussels MS 3947', pp 46–7. Mooney records his death in 1549, while O'Mahony gives it in 1547, cf 'Brevis synopsis', p. 183.

charged by the constables of Athy, Leighlin and Carlow on those travelling to hear the friars preach provide evidence both for extensive preaching tours throughout Leinster and for their popularity.[11] The carved representations of St Francis preserved in the friaries at Ennis and Dromahair depict him carrying the long preacher's cross-staff borne by a friar while on preaching tours (fig. 5.3). In Dromahair, the saint is depicted preaching to birds from a pulpit formed from the calyx of a flower with the preacher's staff behind his right shoulder.[12]

The regular cycles of sermons in the friars' churches constituted the other main occasion for their ministry as preachers and, as already noted, the hall-like layout of friary churches with their wooden or stone rood lofts reflected their roles as venues for preaching.[13] A marginal illustration in the 1427 copy of Piers Plowman depicts a Dominican preaching from a wooden pulpit (pl. 5).

The seasons of Advent and Lent were the friars' most active time for preaching and hearing confessions, as the universal requirement that all confess and receive communion at Easter provided an ideal opportunity for their ministry.[14] On the Continent, Lenten missions in particular were highly developed affairs, with towns vying to secure the services of noted preachers for the course of daily sermons.[15] The earliest evidence for the practice in Ireland dates from the 1270s and comes from the *Promptuarium morale*, a collection of scriptural quotations suitable for preachers, which contained an extensive selection suitable for daily Lenten homilies.[16] The Youghal Franciscans were also aware of the practice, as their library contained several collections of Lenten sermons by noted fifteenth- and sixteenth-century Continental preachers. Mooney conducted a Lenten mission at Monaincha near Roscrea in 1611, and this probably represents a continuation of the medieval practice.[17]

## PREACHING RESOURCES

Following the Fourth Lateran Council (1215), the friars revolutionized pastoral practice both by their actions and through the writings they produced.[18] This material, known as 'Lateran literature', circulated widely and provided resources for mendicant and secular clergy alike.[19] For preachers, these resources consisted

**11** S.P. Henry VIII, ii, I. Quoted in Bradshaw, *The dissolution of the religious orders*, p. 12.   **12** Another image of the saint preaching to the birds appears on the shrine of the *Cathach*. Ó Clabaigh, 'The other Christ', pp 150–1, 155.   **13** Cotter, *Friars Minor*, p. 79; See above, pp 233–6.   **14** Robson, 'The ministry of preachers', pp 132–3.   **15** For Continental examples, see L. Taylor, *Soldiers of Christ* (1992); A. Thompson, *Revival preachers and politics in thirteenth-century Italy: the great devotion of 1233* (1992).   **16** L. Wadding (ed.), *Promptuarium morale Sacrae Scripturae in tres partes distributum* (1624).   **17** 'Brussels MS 3947', p. 76.   **18** N. Tanner, 'The Middle Ages: pastoral care – the Fourth Lateran Council of 1215'.   **19** D.L. d'Avray, *The preaching of the friars: sermons diffused from Paris before 1300* (1985); J. Longère, *La*

of treatises on the *ars predicandi* – the art of preaching, editions of model sermons and collections of *exempla* or moral tales that were incorporated into sermons to illustrate points and maintain interest.[20] Other resources included encyclopedias, biblical commentaries, concordances and florilegia containing excerpts from the scriptures and patristic and classical authors. Combined, these resources provided the preacher with a wealth of entertaining references and lent an air of erudition to his efforts.[21]

The most representative of all these preaching aids was the *vademecum*, a small-format book compiled by individual friars for their personal use and containing material drawn from all the above sources.[22] These were ideal for use on a preaching tour. Easily carried and frequently tabulated for easy reference, they often included canon law notes, advice for confessors, historical and annalistic material, verses, proverbs and anecdotes that give an indication of the range of their compilers' interests. A number of Irish Franciscan and Dominican examples survive from the thirteenth to fifteenth centuries, and some remained in circulation for several centuries.[23] TCD MS 347, a late thirteenth-century Irish Franciscan manuscript, is a particularly good example of a *vademecum*, containing examples of all the above categories of material, in addition to an extensive series of notes for sermons based on the lectionary readings for Sundays and feastdays.[24]

As noted above, the constitutional, educational and disciplinary connections that the Irish friars had with their English and Continental confrères in the thirteenth and early fourteenth centuries provided channels through which texts and ideas could circulate. The Observant reform in the fifteenth century further strengthened these links as the Irish friars diligently attended their respective general chapters on the Continent and were subject to regular visitation by Scottish, Flemish, French and German visitors. These Continental links provide the context for the preponderance of late fifteenth- and sixteenth-century printed works in the Youghal Franciscan library. The community's contacts with Germany are evident from the number of their books that were first printed in Cologne in the 1470s. These included works by the German-speaking Dominican friars John Herolt (*Discipulus*) and John Nider, as well as a volume entitled *Summa vocabulorum cum expositione in lingua tuetonica*, which may have been a German language concordance or dictionary.[25]

*prédication médiévale* (1983).   **20** J.T. Welter, *L'Exemplum dans la littérature religieuse et didactique du moyen âge* (1927); C. Bremond, J. Le Goff & J.C. Schmitt, *L'Exemplum* (1982).   **21** B. Smalley, *English friars and antiquity in the early fourteenth century* (1960); d'Avray, *The preaching of the friars*, pp 64–89.   **22** D. d'Avray, 'Portable *vademecum* books containing Franciscan and Dominican texts' (1980).   **23** Fletcher, 'The English and Latin tradition', pp 57–71.   **24** Colker, *Latin MSS,* i, pp 710–41, particularly pp 714–27 and pp 731–3.   **25** *YLC*, nos 90, 104, 144, 145.

The 150 works in the library in 1523 included twenty-three collections of sermons in addition to numerous other works containing useful preaching material. The collection of sermons included works by the best-known medieval preachers, including St Bernard of Clairvaux (1090–1153), whose sermons headed the list in the preaching category of the catalogue.[26] Surprisingly, there are no references to collections of homilies by the early Church Fathers, and the only patristic works listed were by Gregory the Great (*c.*540–604). Of these, the Dialogues, with their emphasis on the miracles of Italian saints, would have provided useful preaching material.[27] Sermon collections by mendicant preachers, particularly Dominicans, from the thirteenth to the fifteenth century, predominate. Thirteenth-century works include the sermons of the Dominican friars James of Voragine and William Peraldus.[28] The presence of the Sunday sermons of the Franciscan Luke of Bitonto is noteworthy, as this work did not circulate widely outside Italy.[29] Fourteenth-century works included the Sunday sermons of James of Lausanne and the sermons of Graeculus, an Austrian Franciscan.[30] The library also possessed two copies of 'On the four last things', a collection of sermons on death, judgment, hell and heaven, which, though generally attributed to St Bonaventure, was the work of Gerard of Vliederhoven, a Dutch Teutonic knight.[31]

The majority of the texts dated from the fifteenth century and were presumably printed volumes acquired by friars during trips abroad. The included two works by Jean Gerson, the chancellor of the University of Paris, and a collection of sermons by Richard Fleming.[32] The presence of four works by the Italian preacher Robert Carraciolo of Lecce in an Irish Observant friary was curious. Initially an Observant friar, he abandoned the reformers in 1452 and joined the Conventuals, becoming a harsh critic of his former *confrères*, who regarded him as an apostate.[33] Other works included the *Thesaurus novus* and two volumes by the Dominican preacher Leonard of Udine.[34] Other works included the *De tempore* and *De sanctis* sermons of Master Paul Van, twenty-three sermons for feastdays by Michael Lochmayr and a number of unidentifiable collections.[35]

Apart from these sermon collections, the Youghal library held other material that would have been useful for preachers. Entertaining moral anecdotes were available in the *Gesta Romanorum*, which the friars had acquired by 1523. Another work frequently quarried for *exampla* by preachers was the *Vitae Patrum*, with its accounts of the lives and miracles of the first monks in the Egyptian desert.[36] In addition to a copy of the *Legenda aurea* of James of Voragine, with its accounts of

**26** *YLC*, no. 60.   **27** *YLC*, no. 69.   **28** *YLC*, nos 13, 87, 62.   **29** *YLC*, no. 89.   **30** *YLC*, nos 66, 150; Schneyer, *Reportorium*, ii, pp 206–40.   **31** *YLC*, nos 100[a] & 109; R.F.M. Bryn, 'The Cordiale-Auszug: a study of Gerard van Vliederhoven's *Cordiale de iv novissimis*' (1976), pp ii and 23–38.   **32** *YLC*, nos 28, 103, 149.   **33** *YLC*, nos 65, 88, 119, 138.   **34** *YLC*, no. 61, 114.   **35** *YLC*, nos 63, 111, 112, 113, 115, 121, 129.   **36** *YLC*, no. 11, 146.

the lives of the saints, the Youghal Franciscans possessed three biblical concordances and two encyclopedias: the *Proprietatibus rerum* of the thirteenth-century Franciscan, Bartholomeus Anglicus, and the *Catholicon* of Januensis.[37]

## THE *LIBER EXEMPLORUM* AND THE *PROMPTUARIUM MORALE*

As well as exploiting the work of their Continental *confrères*, the Irish friars also produced their own pastoral literature, as thirteenth-century Franciscan works such as the *Liber exemplorum* and the *Promptuarium morale* demonstrate. The *Liber exemplorum* survives in a single manuscript in Durham Cathedral library and was published by A.G. Little in 1918.[38] The manuscript is incomplete, lacking its prologue and up to one third of its original contents. Although regularly cited in histories of the Franciscan order, it has otherwise attracted little attention, despite containing a wealth of material relating to social and religious conditions in late thirteenth-century Ireland. In literary terms, it is significant as the first Franciscan collection of *exempla* known to survive and as the first such collection to arrange its material alphabetically. The compiler was an otherwise unknown English member of the Irish province, possibly a native of Warwickshire. He had spent some time in the friary in Drogheda and was stationed in Dublin between 1256 and 1258. After this, he was sent to Paris, presumably to pursue the order's lectorate programme, but found time to participate in a séance with Roger Bacon and Peter of Ardenne *c.*1264–5.[39] Sometime after this sojourn, he was appointed lector in the friary in Cork, where he compiled the collection between 1275 and 1279. As noted above, the compilation demonstrates the manner in which the *studia* system facilitated the dissemination of texts and ideas throughout the order's provinces. In addition to material he composed himself or which he received from his *confrères* or other religious, the compiler cites forty-eight different scriptural, patristic, scholastic and mendicant authorities in the course of his work.[40] He also refers to two other collections of *exempla* compiled by members of the Irish province. The *Liber exemplorum* was divided into two sections. The first, 'on superior matters', consists of sixty *exempla* dealing with Christ, the Blessed Virgin and the saints. The second, 'on inferior matters', contains over 350 *exempla* arranged alphabetically and dealing with subjects as diverse as avarice, baptism, fraudulent lawyers, defaulting tithe-payers and those who caused injury to the church.

The *Promptuarium morale* is a thematic or conceptual concordance listing quotations from scriptural, liturgical and patristic sources that could be used by a preacher to enhance the impression of a carefully prepared and well-researched

37 *YLC*, nos 13, 18, 38.   38 Durham Cathedral library MS B.IV19; A.G. Little, *Liber exemplorum*. 39 *Lib. ex.*, p. 22; Jones, *Friars' tales*, pp 48–9.   40 *Lib. ex.,* pp x–xi.

homily.[41] It was published in 1624 by Luke Wadding who discovered the manuscript version in Ara Ceoli, the principal Franciscan friary in Rome. Internal evidence indicates that it was compiled sometime between the canonization of St Clare in 1254 and the suppression of the Friars of the Sack in 1274. The inclusion of sermon notes for a number of Irish saints indicates that the compiler was a member of the Irish Franciscan province, while material for the feast of the translation of St Patrick's arm, a relic preserved in Downpatrick Cathedral, may indicate membership of that town's Franciscan community.

The work is divided into three parts. The first two sections correspond to the traditional *de tempore* and *de sanctis* divisions of the liturgical year, with the *de tempore* section containing material suitable for Sunday sermons, commencing with the first Sunday of Advent. This section concludes with a lengthy set of scriptural and patristic quotations based on the phrases of the Athanasian Creed, indicating that sermons functioned as vehicles for catechesis as well as moral exhortation. The second section of the work consists of material suitable for preaching on saints' feastdays, both those of the church's general calendar and those of the Franciscan order. The final and most interesting portion contains 138 sections arranged alphabetically, with material for *Ad statum* homilies (that is, sermons directed to various groups in society ranging from abbots to married men (*uxoratos*)). Extensive material was provided for homilies to members of other religious orders as well as generic sermon notes for preaching to 'good religious', 'bad religious' and apostates.

Although impressively comprehensive, some of the groups, as Brian Scott has noted, made unlikely candidates for congregational preaching. No matter how talented the preacher, congregations of anchorites, prostitutes and besiegers of a city would have been hard to assemble and would, presumably, have had other things on their minds during the sermon.

## HYMNODY AND POETRY

In addition to their academic resources, the friars had a long tradition of composing songs and carols on religious and moral themes for the instruction of the laity.[42] In Ireland, the earliest surviving example of this is the corpus of twenty-seven poems in Hiberno-English and Latin in BL MS Harley 913.[43] The collection includes poems on the Ten Commandments, the seven deadly sins,

---

**41** L. Wadding (ed.), *Promptuarium morale* (1624); A.B. Scott, 'Latin learning and literature in Ireland, 1169–1500' (2005), pp 973–4.   **42** D.L. Jeffrey, *The early English lyric and Franciscan spirituality* (1975). Cotter, *Friars Minor*, pp 80–4; Ó Clabaigh, *Franciscans*, pp 140–1.   **43** See A.M. Lucas, *Anglo-Irish poems of the Middle Ages* (1995), provides the most recent edition of the Hiberno-English material in the codex.

repentance, the fall and the passion, which would have been used by a friar while preaching. Not all of the poems were devotional, however, and the volume also includes some are highly entertaining, if scurrilous, satires on Cistercian and Benedictine monks.[44] Some sixty hymns in the Red Book of Ossory are attributed to the English-born friar-bishop of Ossory, Richard Ledrede (d.*c.*1361). These were sung to the popular tunes of the day to counteract the lewd ditties being sung by the clergy and people in his cathedral city of Kilkenny. They included hymns to the Virgin Mary and on the name of Jesus.[45]

The expansion of the mendicant orders into Gaelic territories in the late fourteenth and fifteenth centuries attracted members of the hereditary learned families into their ranks.[46] These men, trained in the various forms of *seanchas* and the complex and stylized art of bardic composition, included Friars Minor such as the late fourteenth-century Friar Tadhg Camchosach O'Daly and Friar Philip Bocht O'Higgins (d. 1494). In both their works, a synthesis of two traditions is evident: the conventions of bardic poetry blending with Continental motifs and devotional literature. Friars preaching in Irish also employed bardic poetry in their sermons. Mooney recorded that at the end of each sermon, Friar Eoin O'Duffy was

> in the habit of reciting elegant verses in the Irish language, which contained the pith of what he had said. These verses were so fruitful of good that they appear to have been inspired less by the spirit of poetry than by the unction of the Holy Ghost.[47]

CONTENT AND IMPACT

The preaching concerns of the Irish friars were those that were central to late medieval spirituality. The Eucharist, the life, death and resurrection of Christ, repentance, right living, hope of salvation, dread of damnation, intercession for the dead, and the cult of the saints, particularly that of the Virgin Mary, all find their place in the surviving sermon material. The Irish mendicants, like their Continental *confrères*, were charged with preaching the crusades, a commission first recorded in 1234.[48] The over-enthusiastic promotion of the crusade indulgence by the Irish Observant Franciscans, including the vicar provincial

---

For the Latin material, see N. Cartlidge, 'Festivity, order and community in fourteenth-century Ireland: the compostition and context of BL MS Harley 913' (2003), pp 33–52.   **44** Ibid., pp 46–55.   **45** T. Stemmler (ed.), *The Latin hymns of Richard Ledrede* (1975).   **46** E. Bhreathnach, 'The mendicant orders and vernacular learning in the late medieval period' (2011).   **47** 'Brussels MS 3947', pp 49–50. Trans. in *Franciscan Tertiary*, 5 (1894), 196–7.   **48** Cotter, *Friars Minor*, pp 78–9.

Donal O'Fallon, brought them into conflict with Archbishop Octavian of Armagh in 1482.[49]

Despite their reputation as excellent preachers, no full account or transcription of a medieval Irish friar's sermon survives. Mooney's account of the efficacy of the preaching of Friar Eoin O'Duffy is therefore significant, as it gives a rare glimpse of a medieval preacher in action:

> [O'Duffy] was a most renowned preacher, and not less distinguished for his austere and saintly life. His fame extended to the most remote parts of the kingdom, and is yet on the tongues of all … He always travelled barefooted, rejecting even the slight protection which sandals would have afforded him. He preached with such wonderful force and unction that he never seemed tedious to his hearers, although he spoke at great length, sometimes for three hours together. While delivering his discourses he never looked in the faces of his audience, not even opened his eyes. He rebuked the evildoer with great severity, and his words were seldom without effect. Yet in his sermons he was mild and gentle, rarely giving offence to individuals. When he met seculars in society (which, indeed, was very seldom), he conversed in an agreeable and pleasant manner. He had such an intimate knowledge of the writings of St Augustine, especially of his smaller works on devout subjects, that his whole doctrine seemed sometimes founded upon the doctrine and made up of the sayings of that great saint, as if he had consulted no other author.[50]

Then, as now, it is very difficult to gauge what effect a preacher's words had on his congregation, although Mooney's description of the sermon preached in Clogher by Friar Bernard MacGrath provides a notable exception. While denouncing the vices, the preacher was contradicted by an abbot in the congregation whose imminent death he then correctly foretold.[51]

A Lenten mission or a friar on a preaching tour would have caused great excitement, arousing enthusiasm, fostering devotion and giving the congregation a glimpse of a colourful world beyond their own. For all this, the impact of the friars' preaching can be glimpsed only on rare occasions. One such case relates to a sermon preached by Friar Philip Bennett, a Dominican in Drogheda in 1412:

**49** Lynch, 'Franciscan docs', pp 47–50. **50** 'Brussels MS 3947', pp 49–50. Trans. in *Franciscan Tertiary*, 5 (1894), 196–7. **51** 'Brussels MS 3947', pp 46–7.

> Great dissensions having arisen, and the same being carried on, even to
> bloodshed and murder, between the inhabitants of each side of the river,
> Philip Bennett, a friar of this house, did, on Corpus Christi day, invite the
> insurgents of both sides, first to a sermon in St Peter's Church, and
> afterwards to partake of a repast in the monastery of St Mary Magdalene: his
> discourse, which in the strongest terms, represented to his hearers how good
> it is to dwell together in unity, had the happiest effects; they all amicably
> withdrew, and accepting the preacher's second invitation, accompanied him
> to his monastery, where they were sumptuously and elegantly entertained;
> after which they agreed, jointly, to send supplicatory letters to the king, who
> thereupon united the whole into one city.[52]

A number of the features of mendicant preaching outlined above coalesce in this
account. As illustrated by the *Promptuarium morale*, the friar chose as his topic a
line from scripture around which to construct his sermon. The sermon took place
on the feast of Corpus Christi, when the medieval church was accustomed to
celebrate both the sacramental presence of Christ in the Eucharist and the
community's corporate identity as the body of Christ. As on Easter Sunday, it was
an eminently suitable occasion for a sermon on the necessity of reconciliation and
civic unity.[53] The fact that both factions agreed to seek royal approval for
Drogheda as a united corporation confirms both the efficacy of the preacher and
the moral standing of the town's Dominican community.

Another example of the enduring impact of a friar's preaching occurs in the
account given of the death in 1541 of the Donegal chieftain, Tuathal Balbh
O'Gallagher by the Annals of the Four Masters, which noted that in the course of
his military career he had never killed anyone, preferring to take prisoners instead.
This novel approach was attributed to the fact that, as a young man, he had been
profoundly influenced by a sermon on the sanctity of human life that he had
heard preached by a Franciscan in Donegal.[54]

### THE FRIARS AS CONFESSORS

The decree *Omnis utriusque sexus* of the Fourth Lateran Council in 1215 had a
lasting effect on the penitential practices of the church.[55] Its insistence that every

52 Archdall, *Monasticon Hibernicum*, p. 456.   53 On the unitive function of the Eucharist, see J. Bossy,
'The Mass as a social institution' (1983); M. Rubin, *Corpus Christi: the Eucharist in late medieval culture*
(1991), pp 213–87 and E. Duffy, *The stripping of the altars* (1992), pp 91–130.   54 *AFM*, v, p. 1463. It is
possible that he may have been a secular tertiary.   55 T. Tentler, *Sin and confession on the eve of the
Reformation* (1977); N. Berriou, 'Autour de Latran IV (1215): la naissance de la confession moderne et sa

member of the faithful was to confess and receive communion annually brought with it the need for priests who were 'discerning and prudent, so that like a skilled doctor he may pour wine and oil over the wounds of the injured one'.[56] As with the council's call for preachers, this demand for skilled confessors galvanized the friars, whose activities in this area profoundly influenced the administration of the sacrament until the Reformation.

The friars' activities as confessors were governed by both internal and external legislation. Despite the numerous privileges granted to them by the papacy, they still required a licence from the local bishop before they could operate in his diocese. TCD MS 250 contains a formulary letter in the name of the vicar provincial of the Franciscan Observants, requesting such permission and for faculties to absolve cases normally reserved to the bishop.[57]

The friars also produced numerous confessors' manuals and other aids to assist priests in celebrating the sacrament. A number of examples from Ireland survive as complete texts or are cited in contemporary sources.[58] The Franciscan library in Youghal contained an impressive range of these works, ranging in date from the twelfth to the fifteenth century. Some of the works occur in more than one copy and, after the preaching material, formed the next largest section in the library's holdings. The earliest work was the *Penitentiale* of the English canonist, Bartholomew of Exeter (d. 1184).[59] Of the post-conciliar works in the collection, the *Summa de casibus conscientiae*, compiled between 1222 and 1229 by the Catalan Dominican Friar Raymond of Peñaforte (d. 1275), was particularly important.[60] As the work of a distinguished canon lawyer and master general of the Dominicans, the *Summa* had a high reputation and exercised a great influence on later confessors' manuals. It was divided into four books; the first two dealing with sins against God and one's neighbour, the third dealing with the sacraments, while the fourth dealt with matrimonial issues. Each book was divided into chapters, sections and subsections, an arrangement continued by Raymond's revisers and by compilers of later *Summae*.

The developments in canon law and moral theology that followed the Lateran Council in 1215 meant that the *Summa* had to be revised and updated. Raymond himself revised it in 1234 and Friar William of Rennes carried out a further revision between 1240 and 1245. The most comprehensive revision was undertaken by

diffusion' (1983), pp 73–93 gives a useful account of the effect of the decree.    **56** N. Tanner (ed.), *Decrees of the ecumenical councils* (1990), i, p. 245.    **57** Ó Clabaigh, *Franciscans*, p. 183.    **58** Tentler, *Sin and confession*, pp 28–53. The principal works are identified in P. Michaud-Quantin, *Sommes de casuistique et manuels de confession au moyen âge (XII–XV siècles)* (1962).    **59** *YLC*, no. 55. The work was compiled between 1150 and 1170. See A. Morey, *Bartholomew of Exeter: bishop and canonist* (1937). The text of the *Penitentiale*, with an introduction, is found between pages 163 and 300.    **60** Michaud-Quantin, *Sommes de casuistique*, pp 34–43.

another Dominican, John of Freiburg in 1297–8.[61] This revision significantly expanded the earlier work and enjoyed a much greater circulation, both in manuscript and in early printed editions. The similarities of content and format between the *Summa confessorum* and the *Summa de casibus* meant that the former was frequently attributed to Raymond and, for this reason, it is possible that the two copies of the *Summa Remundi* in the Youghal library were actually copies of John of Freiburg's work.[62]

The circulation of John of Freiburg's confessional works is evidenced by the inclusion of an abbreviated copy of the *Summa confessorum*[63] along with his shorter work, the *Confessionale*, in TCD MS 250, a fifteenth-century Observant Franciscan manuscript.[64] The *Confessionale* was intended for 'simpler and less competent confessors'. In the case of difficulties, they were urged to consult the relevant section of the *Summa confessorum* or to ask their more experienced *confrères*. The *Confessionale* outlined the basic techniques for hearing confession, such as how to put penitents at their ease and instruction on what position they should adopt during the proceedings. A marginal image in the 1427 Dublin copy of *Piers Plowman* depicts a kneeling woman receiving absolution from a hooded Dominican friar (pl. 3). It also gave guidance on when the priest should grant and refuse absolution.

The Youghal friars also had a copy of the enormous *Summa Aestesana* compiled by the Franciscan Aestasanus of Asti *c.*1317.[65] This was by far the most comprehensive of the medieval confessors' manuals, drawing almost entirely on scriptural and patristic sources, canon law texts and contemporary theologians (generally Franciscans).[66]

The French theologian Jean Gerson (d. 1429) was one of the most influential writers on confession.[67] His contributions took the form of treatises on moral issues, instructions on how to hear confessions and general advice for confessors, and earned him the sobriquet of 'the consoling doctor'. The Youghal friars possessed two of his works: a collection of eighty-seven treatises and another entitled *Gerson in parvo volumine*.[68] Whereas neither of these is identified, it is likely that they included at least some of his confessional works.

The writings on penance of the Observant Dominican friar Antoninus of Florence (d. 1459) were well known in medieval Irish mendicant circles. The

---

61 Michaud-Quantin, *Sommes de casuistique,* pp 43–53; L. Boyle, 'The *summa confessorum* of John of Freiburg and the popularization of the moral teaching of St Thomas and some of his contemporaries' (1974), ii, pp 245–68.  62 *YLC,* nos 50, 68.  63 TCD MS 250, fos 1–134. Colker, *Latin MSS,* i, pp 441–2. 64 TCD MS 250, fos 134–148v. Colker, *Latin MSS,* i, p. 442.  65 *YLC,* no. 21.  66 Michaud-Quantin, *Sommes de casuistique,* pp 57–9.  67 Tentler describes him as the 'greatest voice in the cure of souls', *Sin and confession,* p. 46. See particularly D.C. Brown, *Pastor and laity in the theology of John Gerson* (1987), pp 56–72, 116–70.  68 *YLC,* nos 28, 103.

Youghal friars had a copy of his most influential work, the *Confessionale-Defecerunt*, and the library of the earl of Kildare contained another two of his works in 1526.[69] The *Confessionale* provided a succinct summary of all that a priest needed to know to hear confessions properly. Its size and layout and the inclusion of a table of contents meant that it could be consulted while hearing confessions.[70] Its forty-seven chapters included an examination of conscience based on the decalogue and the seven deadly sins. Sixteen chapters were devoted to *ad statum* examinations of penitents that display a remarkable degree of psychological insight and knowledge of everyday life.[71] The most comprehensive *ad statum* sections were the six chapters relating to clergy and religious.[72] These included questions on the exercise of their ministry, their treatment of parishioners and subjects, observance of the vows, devotion to the Divine Office and their conduct towards other members of their communities.

The *Preceptorium divinae legis* of John Nider (d. 1438), the German Observant Dominican, was another useful resource for confessors. This was a very detailed commentary on the decalogue, in which the author drew widely on his own experience as a confessor as well as on scripture, canon law and patristic sources, later medieval theologians, particularly Thomas Aquinas. Its bulk meant that it was consulted as a reference book and not used for ready reference, and the Youghal library possessed two copies of the work.[73]

By 1523, the Youghal friars also had two copies of one of the most popular confessor's *summae*, the *Summa de casibus conscientiae* of Angelus Carletti of Chiavasso (1411–95), better known as the *Summa angelica*.[74] The work is thought to have been compiled *c.*1480 and was first printed in 1486. It enjoyed tremendous success and was printed thirty-three times before 1520. Friar Angelus held doctorates in law and theology from Bologna and had entered the Observant Franciscans there on completing his studies. He was four times vicar general of the Cismontane Observants, and this high profile may have recommended his text to the Observants at Youghal. The Third Order Friars at Slane also owned a copy of the *Summa Angelica*.[75] The degree to which it symbolized the late medieval system of penance was demonstrated in December 1520, when it was one of three works publicly burned by Martin Luther in Wittenburg.[76]

---

**69** *YLC*, no. 92. The catalogue of the earl of Kildare's library is found in G. Mac Niocaill (ed.), *Crown surveys of Lands, 1540–41, with the Kildare rental begun in 1518* (1992), pp 312–14, 355–6. **70** Bodl. Auct. 1Q. mfo. 1.17, a copy of the *Confessionale* printed in Cologne in 1469, is in quarto format and could easily have been held in the hand or carried in a pocket. **71** *Confessionale*, ch. 40 gives a list of questions to be put to an innkeeper. **72** Ibid., chs 41–7. **73** *YLC*, nos 90, 144. **74** *YLC*, nos 86, 128. **75** There is a reference to it on the flyleaf of TCD MS 65. Colker, *Latin MSS*, i, pp 116–18. **76** Michaud-Quantin, *Sommes de casuistique*, pp 99–101; Tentler, *Sin and confession*, pp 34–7.

PREACHING PENANCE

There was an intimate connection between the preaching of the friars and their activities as confessors.[77] As noted above, *vademecum* books, such as the thirteenth-century TCD MS 347, often contained canon law notes and excerpts from confessors' manuals, as well as preaching material. On their preaching tours, the preacher and his companions capitalized on the mood of repentance they had aroused and, after the sermon, heard the confessions of the congregation.

The importance of confession formed the subject of a great many *exempla*, including a number in the *Liber exemplorum*[78] and TCD MS 667. A common motif was of the devil being confounded by a sinner's confession just before death. Frequently, the image employed was of the record of the penitent's sins being wiped clean.[79] In other *exempla*, Satan was portrayed as being unable to identify penitents after confession or as bemoaning the losses that he incurred through people's recourse to the sacrament.[80] One of the most vivid examples occurs in the *Liber exemplorum* and concerned the dangers of not making a full confession:

> A certain woman, who was more devoted than many to prayers, almsgiving and other good practices, always, for shame, concealed one sin which she had committed in the flower of her youth. When it came to pass that she was sick unto death an almost infinite number of demons gathered beside the cell of an anchorite who dwelt in that town. Amongst them, one presided like a judge demanding of each what they were doing. One arose and said that tomorrow he would have the soul of a dying woman who was renowned by men for her holiness. Saying that she had one sin that she had never confessed: 'And I,' he said, 'when she wants to confess, block her mouth so that she may not reveal the sin to the priest.' And he named the sin. Truly, the anchorite heard everything. In the morning, the anchorite sent for the priest and made known to him everything he had seen and heard. On the advice of the anchorite, the priest went to the woman and spoke to her about confession. But she did not want to intimate anything to him about this sin. The priest, however, seeing her so near damnation, could dissimulate no longer and he said to her 'Is there not some sin which you committed in your youth and which you have not revealed to me in confession? Hearing this, the woman confessed her sin and with a continual flow of tears washed away that sin until she gave up her spirit. That very

77 Bériou, 'Autour du Latran IV', pp 84–9. Cotter, *Friars Minor*, p. 106; d'Avray, *The preaching of the friars*, pp 50–1.    78 *Lib. ex.,* pp 51–57; Jones, *Friars tales*, pp 79–85 has six *exempla* under the heading *De confessione.*    79 TCD MS 667, nos 9, 11, 301, 302. Colker, *Latin MSS*, ii, pp 1125, 1157.    80 TCD MS 667, nos 303, 304. Colker, *Latin MSS*, ii, p. 1157.

night, for a second time, other demons congregated in the same place as before and the presiding demon demanded the soul promised him. And in reply the one who made the promise said that she had already been confessed (as they say) and through this her soul was borne off to heaven before God by the angels. Behold how great is the power of penance and confession by which a sinner can be thus snatched from the devil.[81]

The friars also provided their penitents with practical advice on how to approach the sacrament, making use of the vernacular to do so. Two Irish language texts on confession occur in the Kilcrea/Rennes manuscript, the Irish language section of TCD MS 667, and in at least four other late fifteenth- or early sixteenth-century codices. They derive from a Latin original, an incomplete fragment of which is also found in TCD MS 667.[82] Their presence in the *Leabhar Chlainne Suibhne* is particularly interesting. This work was compiled in 1513 or 1514 for Máire O'Malley, wife of MacSweeney Fanad, a devout noblewoman, patron of the Donegal Franciscans and co-founder of the Carmelite friary in Rathmullan in 1516. This association with the friars may provide the context for the inclusion of these and other devotional texts in the work.[83]

The first, and more theologically developed, of the two texts listed the sixteen conditions necessary for a good confession.[84] This took the form of a commentary on a short verse attributed to Thomas Aquinas:

> Let confession be simple, humble, pure and faithful,
> and frequent, unadorned, discreet, willing, ashamed,
> whole, secret, most tearful and prompt,
> strong, and reproachful and showing readiness to obey.[85]

In the commentary, the penitent was urged to be simple and humble in his confession, concealing nothing from the priest and not attempting to lessen the seriousness of sins by reciting his good deeds along with them. He was urged to have confidence in the mercy of God and to trust that his sins would be forgiven, and he was assured that once confessed, neither God nor the priest remembered a sin. Through confession, he reduced his stay in purgatory, but any concealed sin

---

**81** *Lib. ex.*, p. 57.   **82** S.H. O'Grady & R. Flower, *Catalogue of the Irish manuscripts in the British Museum* (1926–53), ii, p. 532. He refers to the Latin text on p. 106 of TCD MS F.5.3. This is now catalogued as MS 667 though the Irish language material is known as MS 1699 in T.K. Abbott and E.J. Gwynn, *Catalogue of the Irish manuscripts in Trinity College, Dublin* (1921), pp 323–5. J. Geary, 'An Irish homily on confession', pp 344–66.   **83** S. Ryan, 'Windows on late medieval devotional practice: Máire Ní Mháille's "Book of Piety"' (1513) (2006).   **84** Geary, 'Irish homily on confession', pp 350–9.   **85** *Sit simplex humilis confessio, pura, fidelis, atque frequens, nuda, discreta, libens, verecunda, integra, secreta, lachrimabilis, accelerata, fortis, et accusans, et sit parerere parata.* Also quoted in Tentler, *Sin and confession*, pp 106–7.

would be laid before him in the next life. He was urged to approach the sacrament freely, frequently and with heartfelt contrition, as 'the devil is wearied by frequent confession'.

The second text consisted of a model confession that provided the penitent with formulae for initiating proceedings and for suitably expressing remorse.[86] The bulk of the text consisted of an examination of conscience in the form of detailed self-accusations made by the penitent. These were systematically arranged following the order of the seven capital sins,[87] offences with the bodily senses (speech, hearing, sight and touch), against the articles of faith, the ten commandments and neglect of the works of mercy. The following extracts convey something of the tenor of the whole:

> Dear Father confessor, I declare my faults to God and to you for my own sins in general, and especially for the sins I have committed since my last confession; and in the first place, that I did not make my confession as completely as I ought, and that I did not fulfil faithfully the penance imposed on me and that I did not guard myself against the same sins as I might have done and ought to do; and for these reasons I declare my fault to God and to you, dear father ...[88]
>
> As to the works of mercy, I declare my fault for I do not help the poor nor him who needs clothing, as I ought, and I do not instruct the ignorant as far as I might have knowledge to give them, and I do not visit the sick and do not help their minds according to my ability as I ought, and I do not strengthen the weak, and I do not bury the dead, and I do not help them with almsgiving nor with prayers nor with Masses; and for those reasons and for every degree of guilt that God sees in my sin, I declare my fault to God and to you.[89]

Such lists of sins and model confessions were common ways of instructing the laity about the sacrament. By 1523, the Youghal friars had at their disposal the *Antidotarius animae* of Nicholas of Saliceto,[90] which included the short tract *Modus confitendi* of the Spanish bishop, Andreas Escobar (d. 1427).[91] This was one of the most influential works on confession in the late Middle Ages.[92] It was printed eighty-six times before the end of the fifteenth century and secured an even wider circulation through its inclusion in the *Antidotarius*. It began with a

---

**86** Geary, 'Irish homily on confession', pp 359–64.   **87** Geary's translation omits the comprehensive section on lust.   **88** Geary, 'Irish homily on confession', pp 356 (text), 359 (trans.).   **89** Geary, 'Irish homily on confession', pp 362, 364 (text), 365 (trans.).   **90** *YLC*, no. 132.   **91** Bodl. Auct. 5Q6.70b, a copy of the *Modus confitendi* printed in Germany in 1474, fits on a single fascicule of six leaves in octavo format. **92** Michaud-Quantin, *Sommes de casuistique*, pp 70–1. Tentler, *Sin and confession*, pp 39–40.

simple instruction to the penitent on how to begin confession, and proceeded to an examination of conscience that detailed the various categories of sin. These included sins in thought and word, the seven capital sins, sins against the ten commandments, those committed through the bodily senses, omission of the seven works of mercy, and those against the twelve articles of the faith, the seven sacraments of the church, the nine theological virtues, the seven gifts of the Holy Spirit and the eight evangelical beatitudes. The treatise concludes with various mnemonic devices to remember the principal points and with the formula for absolution, which indicates that it was also used by the priest while hearing confession, as well as by the penitent in preparing for it.

### THE FRIARS AS MORAL AUTHORITIES

Despite the strictures surrounding the seal of confession, sufficient evidence survives to form an impression of the friars' efficacy as spiritual directors and moral authorities. Mooney recorded the involvement of an Ennis Franciscan, identified elsewhere as Friar Fergal O'Trean,[93] in reconciling the O'Brien chieftain, Conor na Srón, who died in 1496. After an eventful and bloody life, O'Brien had despaired of forgiveness for his sins. Friar Fergal, a noted preacher with a reputation for sanctity, offered to bear the burden of the chieftain's sins and placed at his disposal all the merit that he had gained in the course of his life as a friar. This unusual pastoral stratagem worked, O'Brien confessed and received viaticum and unction and his soul was seen entering heaven supported by the prayers of the holy friar.[94] Michael Haren has uncovered something of what may have troubled O'Brien's conscience in his examination of the Irish entries in the papal penitentiary records. The only case of incest in the list concerned two Killaloe clerics, Cornelius and Tathheus O'Brien in 1482 and 1485 respectively. They had been born of an incestuous relationship between their mother and her father, who was most probably Conor na Srón O'Brien. Her position as abbess of the Augustinian nunnery at Killone near Ennis constituted an additional complicating factor as it appears that she had given birth to both sons after her appointment to the abbacy. In 1502, another one of her sons, also a cleric, was dispensed from illegitimacy. His father was the bishop of the diocese.[95]

An incident in Donegal shows the friars as upholders of orthodox teaching on marriage and sexual mores. In defending his quarrel with his father to the Irish

---

**93** *AM*, iii, 574. **94** 'Brussels MS 3947', pp 61–2. **95** M.J. Haren, 'Social structures of the Irish church: a new source in the papal penitentiary dispensations for illegitimacy' (1995), pp 220–1. I am grateful to Simon Kingston for this reference.

council, Manus O'Donnell, later chieftain of Tír Chonaill, excused himself on the grounds that his father

> kept a woman against God's laws and right, and by the instigation and crafty mean of that wicked woman daily procured my said father to have me out of his favour … because I would she would avoid his company, for the discharge of his conscience … and the church and the friars counselled me to do the same.[96]

Mooney also records how Manus O'Donnell was greatly consoled and counselled by Friar Bernard MacGrath of Donegal on the death of his wife.[97]

## LAY ASSOCIATION WITH THE FRIARS

The pastoral zeal of the friars, particularly of the Observants from the fifteenth century onwards, led to a quickening of devotion among the laity, and all orders attracted a coterie of followers who wished to live more intense Christian lives inspired by mendicant ideals. This lay association took a variety of forms, ranging from membership of confraternities to the radical lifelong commitments undertaken by individuals living as vowesses and anchorites adjacent to friaries. It paralleled other forms of lay piety and confraternalism that emerged in the late medieval Irish church.[98] Of particular importance was the emergence in the early fifteenth century of the Franciscan and Dominican Third Orders. These organizations enabled lay men and women, called tertiaries, to practice a modified form of the religious life, while remaining in their secular occupations, marrying and rearing families, and the tertiary movement became one of the most important and widespread vehicles of lay piety in late medieval Ireland. From the ranks of these lay tertiaries a new form of religious life emerged, the Third Order Regular or Regular Tertiaries. This consisted of members, generally men, living as professed religious in communities.

## LETTERS OF CONFRATERNITY

The practice of cathedral chapters, monastic houses and religious orders granting 'confraternity' or 'affiliation' was widespread in the Middle Ages, enabling religious

---

96 Bradshaw, *The dissolution of the religious orders in Ireland* (1974), p. 13.   97 'Brussels MS 3947', p. 47. Mooney does not give the name of the O'Donnell chieftain, but Manus is the only candidate.   98 C. Lennon, 'The confraternities and cultural duality in Ireland, 1450–1550' (2006); idem, 'The parish

communities to reward their benefactors with the intercessory benefits of their prayers and ascetic exercises in this life and, more importantly, in the next.[99] Grants of confraternity emerged among the mendicant friars in the mid-thirteenth century. At first, authority to grant the privilege was reserved to the major superior or general chapter of each order, but eventually it became more widespread, so that, by the fifteenth century, it was common for local superiors to issue confraternity letters to the community's benefactors.[1] Though the practice was widespread in Ireland, the ephemeral nature of the letters means that very little physical evidence for it remains. The earliest Irish reference dates to 1302, when John Luteby, a benefactor of the Carmelites in Ardee, was described as a *confrater* of the community there.[2] The Franciscan annalist, Friar John Clyn, records the establishment of a confraternity in Kilkenny in 1347 to erect a bell tower and renovate the church, though no further evidence survives as to how this organization operated.[3] In 1480, the Dominican friars, meeting in Limerick, admitted to confraternity all who assisted Archbishop John Cantwell in rebuilding their house in Cashel, which had been destroyed by fire.[4] Luke Wadding refers to the large number of people who held confraternity letters from the Observant Franciscans in Cork from 1501 onwards.[5] The practice was roundly criticized by the friars' critics and the 1427 Dublin copy of *Piers Plowman* has a marginal image of a cleric bearing an indulgence or letter of confraternity (pl. 21).

The surviving examples of confraternity letters include one issued in 1507 by Friar Patrick Culuyn, prior of the Dublin Augustinians, to John Stacpoll.[6] Franciscan examples include an elaborately decorated letter issued in Youghal in 1515 by Friar Philip Ó Maighreáin and now preserved in the Cornwall Record Office in Truro (pl. 22).[7] Its recipients were Sir John Arundell, a Cornish aristocrat, his wife, Katherine Grenville, and two of his sons. The Youghal letter formed part of a dossier of indulgences and letters of confraternity from other religious orders notable for their austere observance, including the Carthusian monks at Hinton in Somerset, and the Observant Franciscans at Richmond in Surrey. Its inclusion in this context is indicative of the respect that the Youghal

fraternities of County Meath' (2008), pp 85–101. I am grateful to Prof. Lennon for his advice on this topic. **99** For Irish examples, see J.C. Crosthwaite & J.H. Todd, *The book of obits and the martyrology of the Cathedral Church of the Most Holy Trinity, commonly called Christ Church, Dublin* (1844), passim; D. Hall, *Women and the church in medieval Ireland, c.1140–1540* (2003), pp 24–5, 171–2; C. Lennon, 'The Book of Obits of Christ Church Cathedral, Dublin' (2006). **1** H. Lippens, 'De litteris confraternitatis apud Fratres Minorum ab Ordinis initio ad annum usque 1517' (1939); R.N. Swanson, 'Letters of confraternity and indulgence in late medieval England' (2000); idem, 'Mendicants and confraternity in late medieval England' (2002); idem, *Indulgences in late medieval England* (2007). **2** P. O'Dwyer, *The Irish Carmelites* (1988), p. 10. **3** Clyn, *Annals*, p. 243. **4** M. Archdall, *Monasticon Hibernicum*, p. 647. **5** L. Wadding, *AM*, ii, p. 311. **6** TCD MS 1477, no. 146. I owe this reference to Peter Crooks. **7** Truro, Cornwall Record Office AR 27/6. Published in J. A. Gribbin & C. Ó Clabaigh, 'Confraternity letters of the Irish Observant Franciscans and their benefactors' (2002), pp 469–70.

Observant community enjoyed and the extent of its influence and reputation. At Multyfarnham in 1521, the Franciscan minister provincial, Friar David O'Herlihy, issued a confraternity letter to the Galway merchant Alexander Lynch and his wife Anastasia.[8]

A formulary letter of confraternity is preserved in the chapter book of the Franciscans in Youghal. Dating to 1491–2 and issued in the name of Friar Donal Thomas, vicar provincial of the Observant friars in Ireland, it provides the text of the letter, leaving a blank space for the recipient's name.[9] The document's inclusion in the chapter book suggests that granting confraternity was an event that took place in the chapter room, presumably in the presence of the community. The Kilcormac breviary gives the formula for admitting individuals to confraternity with the Carmelite order, which clearly indicates that it was a public ceremony conducted in the presence of the assembled friars.[10]

Although few in number, the surviving confraternity letters follow a very similar format regardless of which order of friars granted them. A 1505 letter of Friar Simon Lacy, vicar provincial of the Dominicans in Ireland, admitting John Caddell and Benet Taylor to confraternity with the order serves as a representative example of the genre and clearly demonstrated the benefits thought to accrue from confraternity with the friars.[11]

> Symon Lacy, doctor of the sacred pages and vicar general of the order of Friars Preachers in the land of Ireland to his beloved in Christ John Caddell and Benet Taylor greetings and continual increase in celestial grace. The affectionate devotion, which I have heard that you have for our order, requires that the benefits of our order together with the abundant clemency of your Redeemer, should be more graciously conferred upon you. Accordingly, by these presents I accord to you full participation in all Masses, prayers, sermons, fasts, abstinences and the other benefits which the Lord has granted to be made by the brethren of our order throughout Ireland; and that you may here increase of grace and in future possess the prize of the happiness of eternal life. And I further wish that after your death your souls may be recommended in our general chapter to the prayers of the brethren of all the land. If your death has been reported, Masses and prayer shall be enjoined for you as for our own deceased brethren. In witness of this concession, the seal of our office has been attached.
>
>                                        Given in our convent at Dublin, AD 1505.

8 R. O'Flaherty, *A chorographical description of West or H-Iar Connaught* (1846), p. 226; Gribbin & Ó Clabaigh, 'Confraternity letters', pp 468–9.   9 Staatsbibliotek Preussicher Kulturbesitz, Berlin MS theol. lat. fol. 703, fo. 151v; Gribbin & Ó Clabaigh, 'Confraternity letters', p. 469.   10 TCD MS 86, fo. 133, 'De modo recipiendi aliquos ad beneficia ordinis'.   11 TCD MS 1207a 202 (261).

The Observant Franciscans also promoted the 'Confraternity of the Cord' among their lay followers. This devotion was particularly popular in Continental aristocratic circles and was promoted in the court of Duke Francis II of Brittany in the late fifteenth century. It was introduced to England by King Henry VII.[12] In addition to reciting certain prayers and performing other spiritual exercises, members of the confraternity expressed their devotion by wearing the cord of the Franciscan habit as part of their own clothing. Occasionally, these cords were fashioned from expensive fabrics or precious metal. Irish evidence for the devotion comes from the inventory of gold and silver plate belonging to Gerald Fitzgerald, ninth earl of Kildare, compiled *c.*1518. This included two gold chains ornamented with 'freirs knottes', one of which weighed fifty ounces.[13] Given the close association between the Fitzgeralds and the Franciscans, it is not surprising that the earl and his countess should have chosen to express their devotion to the poor man of Assisi in so public, if slightly incongruous, a fashion.

FRANCISCAN AND DOMINICAN TERTIARIES (fig. 10.1)

The Franciscan and Dominican 'tertiary' or 'Third Order' movement emerged from a pre-existing religious group, the 'order of penitents', in thirteenth-century Italy.[14] This consisted of laymen and women who had freely adopted the penitential lifestyle normally imposed by the church on reconciled public sinners. As the Franciscans and Dominicans spread through Italy and the rest of Europe, their preaching led to a revitalization of this movement. In consequence, some groups of penitents became more markedly 'Franciscan' or 'Dominican' in character and came to acknowledge St Francis or St Dominic as their founders and patrons. This process culminated in the emergence of groups associated with the friars and described as the 'Third Order of St Francis' or the 'Third Order of St Dominic'. In 1284, Friar Munio of Zamora, the master general of the Dominicans, formally gathered the Dominican tertiary groups into a Dominican order of penitents.[15] In 1289, Pope Nicholas IV issued a formal rule for the Franciscan penitents, embodied in the bull *Supra montem*.[16] Although the Carmelite and Augustinian friars also promoted the tertiary vocation among their lay followers elsewhere, no evidence survives of them doing so in medieval Ireland.[17]

---

**12** V.K. Henderson, 'Rethinking Henry VII: the man and his piety in the context of the Observant Franciscans' (2004), pp 320–8.   **13** Mac Niocaill, *Kildare rental*, p. 304.   **14** G.G. Meersseman, *Dossier de l'ordre de la penitence au XIIIe siècle* (1981); R.M. Stewart, *De Illis qui faciunt penitentiam: the rule of the Secular Franciscan Order* (1991); M. D'Alatri, *Aetas Poenitentialis: L'antico Ordine Francescano della Penitenza* (1995).   **15** Hinnebusch, *History of the Dominican order*, i (1965), pp 400–4.   **16** *BF*, iv, pp 94–7. The Franciscan material presented here summarizes Ó Clabaigh, *Franciscans*, pp 80–105.   **17** T. Motta Navarro, *Tertii Carmelitici saecularis ordinis historico-iuridicia evolutio* (1960); D. Guttieriez, *History of the order of St*

306

10.1 Map of
Franciscan and
Dominican tertiary
foundations.

- ● Dominican Regular Tertiaries
- ☐ Franciscan Regular Tertiaries
- ★ Nuns

The surviving evidence suggests that, like their *confrères* in England, the Franciscans and Dominicans in Ireland made little effort to promote the tertiary vocation among their lay followers in the thirteenth and fourteenth centuries.[18] A list of the provinces of the Franciscan order compiled in Ragusa by Friar Peter of Trau in 1385 gave the number of tertiary congregations in Ireland as four, but an examination of the Bodleian Library manuscript cited as the authority for this statement suggests that it represents a guess on the part of the author.[19]

The earliest reliable reference to the Franciscan Third Order in Ireland occurs in 1425, when Pope Martin V granted a copy of the bull *Supra montem* to the Irish tertiaries.[20] In the winter of 1426–7, a copy of the Dominican Third Order rule was issued to the Observant friars in Portumna, indicating that they also promoted the tertiary vocation among their lay followers.[21] Such fostering of the

*Augustine*, vol. i, pt 1 (1984), pp 191–7; vol. i, pt 2 (1983), pp 190–4. **18** D.W. Whitfield, 'The Third Order of St Francis in medieval England' (1953). **19** Bodl. MS Canonici Miscell. 535, fo. 13; *FL*, p. 163. The four Franciscan provinces referred to sequentially on this list are described as having the same numbers of Poor Clare monasteries and Tertiary congregations attached to each. **20** A transcript of this bull is preserved in the Representative Church Body Library, Dublin, C.6.1.6.2., *Registrum novum*, vol. ii, pp 652–8. **21** H. Fenning OP, 'The Dominicans of Kilcorban' (1987), p. 10.

Third Order by the Observants was common elsewhere in Europe: the great Observant preacher, St John Capistran, was a keen promoter and protector of the tertiaries in Italy, and the Scottish tertiaries received much support from the Breton Observant, Friar Olivier Maillard.[22] Raymond of Capua was also a keen promoter of the Third Order as part of his efforts to reform the Dominicans.

Membership of the tertiaries was a serious step and entailed a commitment to an austere, ascetic regime that went far beyond what was expected of other lay Christians. The Franciscan tertiaries wore simple grey habits, while the Dominicans wore a white tunic and black cloak. Female tertiaries in both orders wore veils. After profession of their vows, members could only leave the tertiaries if they were transferring to another religious order. Women were not allowed to join the Third Order without the permission of their husbands and Franciscan male tertiaries were forbidden to bear arms.

Franciscan tertiaries celebrated the Liturgy of the Hours by reading the Divine Office if they were literate, or by multiple recitations of the *Pater noster* and the Apostles' Creed and Psalm 50 at the appropriate times. During Lent, they were expected to attend the morning hours of the Office in their parish churches. Given the nature of parochial structures in late medieval Ireland, it is likely that many secular tertiaries fulfilled this obligation by attending services in a friary church. Where possible, they attended daily Mass and confessed and received communion three times a year. The tertiaries fasted from the feast of St Martin (11 November) until Christmas, and their Lenten fast began on Quinquagesima Sunday. They also fasted on Wednesdays from 1 November until the following Easter. Abstinence from meat was observed on Mondays, Wednesdays and Saturdays, and they were to be content with two meals a day. There were a number of exceptions to this regime: pregnant tertiaries were exempt until after their purification, as were travellers. Those engaged in physical work could take three meals a day and no one was to fast for three days after being bled. The local superiors and the visitators could dispense from these requirements as circumstances demanded.[23]

This austere regime gives some indication of the lifestyle of individuals like Nuala O'Brien (d. 1528), the widow of Red Hugh O'Donnell, who spent the last twenty-one years of her life as a tertiary attached to the Observant friary in Donegal. It also sheds light on her decision to live near the friary, as this enabled her to attend the liturgical offices at the times required by the rule.[24] The reference to her spending her wealth in promoting hospitality and humanity and performing

---

**22** Moorman, *History*, pp 565–6. See also A. Andreozzi, 'San Giovanni da Capestrano e la sua defesa del Terz'Ordine Francescano' (1973); F. Delorme, 'Olivier Maillard et le Tiers-Ordre Régulier en Ecosse' (1915). **23** *BF*, iv, pp 94–7, chs 5, 6, 8, 13, 14. **24** *AFM*, v, p. 1393; *Ann. Conn.*, p. 667.

devotion, clemency and good works on behalf of God and the world also indicates a lifestyle entirely consonant with the spirit of the Third Order.[25]

The earliest references to individual members of the Franciscan Third Order occur in a series of papal privileges granted to tertiaries in the west of Ireland. These included the 1433 indulgences granted to Manus Macultucko and Thomas Mac Duorchan, both from the diocese of Tuam, and the 1442 grant to Donal Connolly, a priest of Annaghdown.[26] In 1464, Margaret de Burgh received an indulgence, as did John Barrett and his wife, tertiaries based in Killala diocese, in 1466.[27] In 1469, a similar indulgence was granted to Manus O'Moran, a Raphoe tertiary, and his wife.[28] In 1486, the chief of Uí Maine, Tadhg Caoch O'Kelly, died in the habit of the Third Order.[29] It is likely that O'Kelly was a member of a secular Third Order fraternity attached to one of the three Franciscan friaries in the diocese, most probably that at Kilconnell, which the family had founded before 1400 and where they had right of sepulture. Mooney records the involvement of two secular tertiaries in the construction of the Observant friary at Adare in 1484: Rory O'Dea built one side of the cloister and presented a silver chalice, while Marinus O'Hickey built the refectory and provided the stalls on the north side of the choir. The latter later entered the Adare community and died with a reputation for holiness.[30] This bears comparison with Mooney's account of the career of Felim MacCarthy, a friar of Kilcrea who died in 1588, but who had spent many years as a secular tertiary, doing penance for the murder of his brother, before becoming an Observant. He too came to have a reputation for holiness.[31]

The Franciscan tertiary rule also provided a vehicle for anchoritic living. In 1512, the baron of Slane, Christopher Fleming, and his wife, Elizabeth Stuckley, restored the cells at St Erc's hermitage on their demesne at Slane, Co. Meath, for the use of Father Malachy O'Byren and Brother Donagh O'Byrne, both anchorites and Franciscan tertiaries.[32] Mooney also records the tradition that one of the early barons of Slane, a Franciscan tertiary, had also been enclosed as a recluse there.[33]

Although the surviving references to Franciscan secular tertiaries are relatively few, they are sufficiently dispersed geographically to indicate that they were a widespread phenomenon and that the Third Order was established wherever an Observant friary was founded in the fifteenth or sixteenth century.

## DOMINICAN REGULAR TERTIARIES

The earliest references to Ireland's only house of Dominican tertiaries occurs in March 1445, when Pope Eugene IV instructed the abbot of Abbeygormican in

25 *ALC*, ii, p. 265.   26 *BFNS*, i, p. 56 , no. 104; p. 269, no. 570; *CPL*, ix, p. 233.   27 *CPL*, xii, pp 422, 521.   28 *CPL*, xii, p. 703.   29 Mooney, *Terminus*, xii (1956), 40.   30 'Brussels MS 3947', pp 63–4. 31 Ibid., pp 70–1.   32 *MRH*, pp 274–5.   33 'Brussels MS 3947', p. 104.

Clonfert to investigate and confirm the grant of the chapel of Kilcorban made by Bishop Thomas of Clonfert to the brothers and sisters of the Third Order of St Dominic.[34] This grant was made sometime before 1445, and the tertiaries were described as already dwelling there. The Dominican tertiaries were not as well organized or widespread as their Franciscan counterparts, and there is no further reference to their presence at Kilcorban. In 1570, the house was listed as a house of Dominican friars, indicating that at some stage in the intervening period it had passed from the Third to the First Order of St Dominic.[35]

### FRANCISCAN REGULAR TERTIARIES

The copy of the bull *Supra Monten* granted to the Irish tertiaries by Martin V in 1426 was probably intended for a community of regular tertiaries as it makes no reference to the superiors of the friars minor.[36] The secular tertiaries were normally attached to a First Order friary and were more dependent on the friars for leadership; it was common for copies of the rule intended for their use to acknowledge this.

The first contemporary reference to a community of Franciscan Regular Tertiaries occurs in February 1426, when a papal bull permitted the foundation of a house in the diocese of Clonfert.[37] The identity of the house is not given, but it was to be built on one of the sites in Clonfert and other western dioceses that had been offered to the tertiaries by William de Burgh, chief of his clan. This is also the first indication of one of the most striking features of the movement: its concentration in the rural dioceses of Gaelic Ireland.[38] In June 1426, the Irish regular tertiaries were granted the right to have Mass and the other Offices celebrated in their own chapels during times of interdict and to choose their own chaplains.[39] Such exemptions indicate a high degree of organization and privilege, and it is likely that the order was already well established by this date.[40]

In March 1428, an indulgence was granted to those who visited and gave alms to the church of the Third Order friary at Killeenbrenan in Tuam diocese.[41] This suggests that the friary had been in existence for some time or that the tertiaries

---

**34** *CPL*, ix, p. 495; *MRH*, pp 225–6 gives 1446 as the date and Thomas de Burgh as the bishop of Clonfert. **35** Fenning, 'Kilcorban', pp 10–14. **36** Representative Church Body Library, C.6.1.6.2., *Registrum Novum*, ii, pp 652–8. **37** C. Ó Clabaigh, 'The mendicant friars in medieval diocese of Clonfert' (2007), pp 29–31. **38** *CPL*, vii, p. 452. **39** *BF*, vii, p. 655; *CPL*, vii, p. 427. **40** A copy of the 1232 bull of Gregory IX granting similar privileges to the Friars Minor is found in the fifteenth-century Observant text TCD MS 250, fo. 150. **41** *CPL*, viii, p. 25.

had taken over an old chapel in need of repair, and it is likely that this was one of the communities for whom the privileges in the June 1426 bull were intended. It may also have been founded on one of the other sites granted by the William de Burgh mentioned in the February 1426 bull, as there is a suggestion that a de Burgh was the founder.[42] In 1457, it was described as the principal house of the order in Ireland and it is possible that it was also the first community of regular tertiaries to be established.[43]

The next foundation for the tertiaries was Clonkeenkerrill, also in Clonfert diocese, where a parish church was given into the care of the tertiaries during the reign of the Dominican bishop, Thomas O'Kelly. Although he ruled the diocese from 1405 until his translation to Tuam in 1438, it seems most probable, given the primacy of Killeenbrenan, that this transfer took place sometime between 1428 and 1438.

## MIXED COMMUNITIES AND COMMUNITIES OF WOMEN

A number of the papal bulls addressed to the Irish regular tertiaries were addressed to the 'brothers and sisters of the order of penance' and this has led previous writers to speculate on whether some of the regular houses, at least in their initial phases, were joint establishments with male and female members.[44] The first bull mentioning the regular tertiaries in February 1426 refers to the recent petition of Patrick Yclinnan and the other friars of the Third Order, but makes no mention of any female members.[45] The strongest evidence for a joint community occurs in the 1454 bull licensing the foundation of the friary at Court in the diocese of Achonry.[46] Here, the references to 'brothers and sisters' do not appear to be just notarial formulae, but suggest that this was a community in which male and female religious actually lived together. The 1457 bull appointing a friar of Killeenbrenan as visitor of the tertiaries states that the order was for men and women dwelling in the religious habit and that the visitor's brief include all the houses of the order and the people of both sexes dwelling therein.[47]

Donatus Mooney, writing in 1618, stated that he had never heard of any female members of the Second or Third Orders, and it seems most likely that these joint communities, which at all times seem to have been in a minority among the Irish tertiaries, had died out long before this time.[48]

There is a single reference to a community of 'Poor nuns of St Francis' in Galway in 1511, when Walter Lynch, twice mayor of the city, granted a house

42 *MRH*, pp 271–2.   43 *CPL*, xi, p. 140; *BFNS*, ii, pp 143–4.   44 Quinn, 'Third Order Regular', pp 254–5.   45 *CPL*, vii, p. 452.   46 *BFNS*, i, pp 882–3; *CPL*, x, p. 713.   47 *BFNS*, ii, pp 143–4; *CPL*, xi p. 149.   48 'Brussels MS 3947', p. 102.

near the church of St Nicholas to his daughter, who was a nun there. Although nothing further is known of them, it may have been a community of regular tertiaries.[49] It has been suggested that a fifteenth-century English translation of the Third Order rule may have been made for a community of sisters in Ireland. If this is the case, the Galway house seems the obvious location, as some of the male members of the other houses would have been literate in Latin and, in any case, these communities would have spoken Irish.[50] Such communities were common on the Continent in the fifteenth century, with perhaps the best known of them being the Grey Sisters, who ran hospitals in Flanders and Burgundy. These followed the Third Order rule but adopted constitutions appropriate to community living and their apostolate.[51] Four communities of these sisters were established in Scotland under the influence of the Observant Friars.[52]

## EXPANSION

Between 1426 and 1539, approximately forty-nine houses of regular tertiaries were established in Ireland (fig. 10.1).[53] In many cases, little is known of the identity of the founders or the dates of foundation or dissolution, and it is difficult to draw a detailed picture of the process of expansion, though enough material remains to sketch broad outlines of the expansion in the province of Tuam and the dioceses of Raphoe and Connor. Most of the houses were concentrated in the west and north of the country, with a smaller cluster of houses in the south-western dioceses of Limerick and Emly. Mention has already been made of the first tertiary foundations in Clonfert and Tuam dioceses. Of these, the house at Clonkeenkerrill in Clonfert is the best documented and the activities of its members were to have major repercussions for the order as a whole. It is first mentioned in 1441, when Donatus Okealy was granted the vicarage of Killoscoba in Tuam diocese, which was vacant because David Omulcori had made his profession as a tertiary friar there.[54] It appears that the community had been in existence for some time before this, because later that year another petition mentions that the church of Clonkeenkerrill had been given into the care of the tertiaries by Bishop Thomas O'Kelly, who ruled the diocese from 1405 to 1438.[55] This petition was granted at the request of David and John O'Mulkerrill, priests and tertiary friars. The

---

**49** C. Mooney in *MRH*, p. 317. **50** W. Seton (ed.), *Two fifteenth-century Franciscan rules* (1914). Whitfield, 'Third Order of St Francis', p. 52, suggests it might have been used by a community of English-speaking tertiaries in Ireland. **51** H. Lemaître, 'Statuts des religieuses du Tiers Ordre Franciscain dites soeurs grises hospitaliers' (1911). **52** F.M. Delorme, 'Olivier Maillard et le Tiers Ordre Régulier en Ecosse (1458–1496)' (1915). **53** For identifications and general notes on these houses, see *MRH*, pp 267–81. **54** *CPL*, iv, p. 199. **55** *BFNS*, i, p. 265; *CPL*, ix, pp 211–12.

similarity of their surname and the place-name suggests that this was a case of members of a hereditary clerical family adopting the Third Order rule. In 1453, David O'Mulkerrill found himself unable in conscience to hold Clonkeenkerrill as a Third Order friary and was granted permission to convert it to 'a better and more useful work' by offering it to the Friars Minor.[56] No reason was given for the change that David claimed had the unanimous support of his chapter. It did not, however, have the support of the other tertiary houses and, as will be shown, the transfer of Clonkeenkerrill was one of the main reasons for the regular tertiaries gaining independence from the Friars Minor in 1457.

The later history of the house is also complex. Despite the transfer to the Friars Minor in 1453, it was still described as a Third Order house in a 1483 bull granting an indulgence to all who contributed its repair.[57] This had been granted at the request of the master of the house, Cornelius O'Mulkerrill, who had travelled to Rome to obtain it. In January 1499, three canons of Tuam were ordered to induct Charles O'Mulkerrill to a vicarage in the diocese. The bull also stated that Charles had been dispensed from illegitimacy as the son of a Third Order priest and of a married woman.[58] Katharine Simms uses Clonkeenkerrill as a clear example of hereditary clerical succession in the late medieval Irish church.[59]

In 1442, papal confirmation was granted for tertiary foundations at Rosserk, Ballymote and Tisaxon at the request of three tertiary friars who appear to have been members of the same family.[60] The distribution of the sites and the fact that permission for them had been secured from the local bishops indicates that the order was well established and widespread in Connacht.

In 1445, three years after the formal confirmation of their own community, the friars in Rosserk spearheaded the expansion of the regular tertiaries into the north-east of Ulster, when a licence was granted to them to found a friary in the diocese of Connor.[61] The location of this foundation has not been satisfactorily identified and there has been much speculation about it. Its first patrons were two MacDonnells and a Semiquinus Machon, whom Canice Mooney tentatively identifies as Sinchin MacQuillan, the lord of the Route,[62] but whom M.A. Costello identifies as a Bissett.[63] An attempt has been made to identify this first foundation with the important tertiary house at Glenarm.[64] Previous accounts of Glenarm have relied on a 1465 papal document cited by Luke Wadding, in which the founder of the friary was named as Robert Bisset, a Scot, who was related to

56 *BFNS*, i, pp 844–5; *CPL*, x, p. 649. 57 *CPL*, xiii, p. 836. 58 *CPL*, xviii:1, pp 72–3. 59 K. Simms, 'Frontiers in the Irish church: regional and cultural' (1995), p. 181. 60 *BFNS*, i, pp 270–1. *CPL*, ix, pp 155–6. These were in the dioceses of Killala, Achonry and Tuam and the petition was granted to Patrick, Philip and Andrew Yclumain. 61 *CPL*, ix, p. 493. 62 C. Mooney, *Terminus*, xiii (1956), pp 90–1. 63 M.A. Costello (ed.), *De Annatis Hiberniae, 1400–1535* (1909), i, p. 139. He also identifies this foundation with the tertiary friary at Glenarm. I am grateful to Simon Kingston for this reference. 64 H. MacDonnell, 'Glenarm

the minister provincial of the Third Order in Ireland, also called Robert Bisset.[65] This raises the possibility of the Bisset family's involvement in tertiary houses in both Ireland and Scotland. In 1488, Johanna Bisset, a member of the tertiary community at Aberdour in Scotland, was among those who signed a petition to the Observant ultramontane vicar general, Olivier Maillard.[66]

It is difficult to give anything other than approximate dates for the foundation of the other Ulster houses, though it appears that Dungannon was founded by the O'Neills *c.*1489,[67] and that the house at Inver was established in 1500.[68] The north-western diocese of Raphoe was the scene of much mendicant activity in the late fifteenth and early sixteenth centuries, with the foundation of nine friaries. As noted in chapter three, an important Observant Franciscan house was established at Donegal in 1474 and a Carmelite foundation at Rathmullan in 1516. The remaining seven houses were of regular tertiaries.[69] There were two centres of activity: three houses in the south of the diocese on the shore of Donegal bay and four more in the north near Lough Swilly and Fanad. A surviving 1471 papal bull instructed the dean of Raphoe to licence the foundation of a houses at Killydonnell by two tertiary friars, Dermot Megillasbuig and Dermot Idurnyn, and granted the community the privileges and rights enjoyed by the friars elsewhere.[70] The houses in the south of the diocese may owe their foundation to colonization from Third Order communities in Killala and Achonry, and it is almost certain that the Maherabeg friary pre-dates the First Order foundation at Donegal.[71]

The three friaries in the dioceses of Limerick and Emly are also difficult to date with certainty. There is a reference to regular tertiaries in the decrees of the provincial synod of Cashel held in Limerick in 1453, warning them to observe the customs of the province of Cashel and not to invoke their papal privileges regarding distribution of the burial offerings of lay people buried in their cemeteries.[72] This indicates that they were sufficiently well established to pose a threat to the incomes of the parochial clergy, though it is not clear with which of the three communities the problem had arisen. In 1488, the friars at Kilshane/Ballingarry were involved in a dispute over tithes with the Limerick Cathedral chapter,[73] but there is no further contemporary reference to Kilshane or either of the other houses.

friary and the Bissets' (1987). **65** *MRH*, p. 271. **66** Delorme, 'Olivier Maillard', pp 355–6. **67** C. Mooney, 'The Franciscan Third Order Friary at Dungannon' (1954–5). **68** *MRH*, p. 271. **69** S. Ó Domhnaill, 'Some notes on the houses of the Third Order of Saint Francis in Tirconaill' (1952). **70** *BFNS*, ii, 845–6; *CPL*, xii, p. 643. **71** Ó Domhnaill, 'Some notes', p. 102; *MRH*, p. 273. **72** J. Begley, *The diocese of Limerick, ancient and medieval* (1906), p. 435. **73** *FL*, p. 169.

It is not entirely clear when the tertiary friars occupied Ballymacadane in the diocese of Cork. Various sources state that it was initially founded in the mid-fifteenth century by Cormac MacCarthy for a community of Augustinian nuns,[74] but Mooney lists it as a house of Franciscan tertiaries.[75] It is possible that the friars took over the foundation sometime after the nuns had died out.

ACTIVITIES

The traditional activities of the tertiary friars were succinctly summarized by Mooney in the early seventeenth century:

> There were a great number of men belonging to the Third Order in Ireland who lived in community and devoted themselves to the religious life. They were principally engaged in assisting the local clergy in their pastoral duties, and in conducting schools for the education of the boys of the district. A portion of their monasteries was invariably set apart for the latter purpose, which continues to the present day to be called the schoolhouse.[76]

As the number of priests among the tertiaries increased, they were inevitably drawn into the pastoral care of the people in their localities. A number of the foundation bulls speak of the tertiaries' role in augmenting divine service, and the earliest reference to the regular tertiaries indicated that the liturgy should be celebrated according to the norms of the papal court.[77] The tertiaries worked chiefly as adjuncts to the local secular clergy, unlike the Friars Minor, who developed their own style of ministry based on the preaching tour and the hearing of confessions. Whereas there are a number of annalistic references to noted Franciscan preachers, none of the tertiary friars enjoyed a similar reputation.

Very little is known about tertiary educational organization. In 1457, Thomas Oruayn was described as learned in law, but there is no indication given of where he received this training.[78] It is possible that some tertiaries may have received a basic theological training in the schools attached to the First Order houses, but there is no evidence that any of them pursued higher studies at a general *studium* or a university. The fact that no tertiary is known to have been promoted to a bishopric is probably a further indication that their theological education was rather basic.[79]

74 *MRH*, p. 268.   75 'Brussels MS 3947', p. 104.   76 'Brussels MS 3947', p. 102. Trans. in *Franciscan Tertiary*, 7 (1896), 35.   77 *CPL*, vii, p. 452.   78 *CPL*, xi, 140; *BFNS*, ii, pp 143–4.   79 P. Quinn, 'Third Order Regular', pp 256–7 suggests that Cornelius Ryan, bishop of Killaloe (1576–1616), was a regular tertiary, but this seems most unlikely, and he is otherwise listed as an Observant Franciscan.

Only one text survives from an Irish Third Order house: a biblical concordance now preserved in Trinity College Dublin.[80] Originally compiled for a community of English Augustinian canons in Dorchester in the thirteenth century, it appears to have been pawned by the Slane friars, raising the question of how much use they actually made of it. It carries a flyleaf inscription referring to their copy of the *Summa Angelica*, the influential confessor's manual of the fifteenth-century Italian Observant friar, Angelo Carletti of Chiavasso, which gives an incidental sidelight on the pastoral activities of the Slane friars.

Canice Mooney has tentatively suggested that the tertiary friars at Rosserk may have provided the original Latin text of the *Meditationes Vitae Christi*, which was translated into Irish in 1443 by Thomas Ó Bruacháin, a canon of Killala. Mooney's argument rests solely on the proximity of Rosserk friary to Killala, but it is not implausible.[81] Andrew Breeze accepts this point and suggests that the tertiaries, along with the Observant Franciscans, were the channels through which many of the devotional texts and ideas common on the Continent came to be known in Ireland.[82]

## CONSTITUTIONAL ARRANGEMENTS

In contrast to the secular tertiaries, who depended heavily on the Friars Minor Order for direction and supervision, the Franciscan regular tertiaries, as religious in their own right, chafed somewhat under their supervision. Depending on their strength, they enjoyed varying degrees of independence at different times. Donatus Mooney, writing from the standpoint of a former provincial of the Friars Minor, had no doubt about the relationship between the two groups:

> They were subject, from their first institution, to the jurisdiction of the superiors of the First Order, and, on many occasions, in my own days, I have known members to have been transferred from one convent to another in the interest of the society, by the prelates of our order. Our provincial made a visitation of their monasteries each year and in his absence they requested the guardian of the convent in whose limits they lived to appoint a visitator, who might examine and correct abuses.[83]

Mooney's account needs to be weighed against that of the tertiary historian, Francis Bordoni, who, writing in 1658, noted the degree of independence that the

---

80 TCD MS 65; Colker, *Latin MSS*, i, p. 117.  81 C. Ó Maonaigh [C. Mooney], *Smaointe Beatha Chríost* (1944), p. 363.  82 A. Breeze, 'The Virgin's tears of blood' (1989), pp 121–2.  83 'Brussels MS 3947', p. 102. Trans. in *Franciscan Tertiary*, 7 (1896), 35–6.

Irish regular tertiaries had enjoyed.[84] Neither position accurately reflects the way in which the relationship ebbed and flowed between the two groups, and later writers have fallen prey to the same partisan bias that afflicted their seventeenth-century *confrères*.

It appears that the tertiaries were initially subject to the Friars Minor for visitation and correction, but that they gained a considerable degree of independence in 1457, when Thomas Ornayn, a priest-friar of Killeenbrenan, was appointed visitator and they were given the right to elect his successors.[85] The tertiaries confirmed that they had hitherto been subject to mendicant friars for visitation, but that because of distance it was more convenient to entrust this task to one of their own members. This would be plausible coming from one of the Ulster houses, which lay at great distances from First Order friaries, but is not convincing in a Connacht context. The real reason for this move for independence seems rather to lie in disquiet among the regular tertiaries over the transfer of their house at Clonkeenkerrill to the Friars Minor four years previously. This interpretation is confirmed by the final clause in the 1457 bull, in which such transfers were forbidden without the permission of the tertiaries.

There is no evidence that this privilege was rescinded, and it is likely that it was in force until at least 1521, when Leo X promulgated the new rule for the regular tertiaries, *Inter coetera*, in which the visitation of the order was entrusted to the Friars Minor. No copy of this bull or any reference to it survives in any contemporary Irish source, and it is possible that it took some time for it to take effect. Bordoni notes that exceptions were granted in areas where the Third Order was very strong and, as the second largest tertiary province, Ireland may have been one of these. Donatus Mooney's description is undoubtedly correct in describing the position in the early seventeenth century and indicates that the provisions of *Inter coetera* did eventually come into force. Unlike some of their Continental *confrères*, the Irish tertiaries managed to maintain their own provincial superiors throughout this period: in 1600, their minister provincial, Friar Donatus Cossaeus, was present at a meeting in Donegal friary.[86]

The Franciscan and Dominican Third Orders, both Regular and Secular, represented one of the most important developments in the church in late medieval Ireland. Springing from the contemporary desire for reform among the Friars Minor and Preachers, they developed in their own fashion and, in the case of the Franciscan regular tertiaries, developed a distinct identity and apostolate. The secular tertiaries gave expression in Gaelic Ireland to that burgeoning lay piety

---

**84** F. Bordoni, *Cronologium Fratrum et Sororum Tertii Ordinis S. Francisci* (1658), pp 522–4, 583–4. His work is almost entirely based on Wadding's *Annales Minorum*.   **85** *BFNS*, ii, pp 143–4; *CPL*, xi, p. 140. **86** J. Hagan (ed.), 'Papers relating to the Nine Years War' (1913), p. 293.

that was such a feature of the period throughout Europe. In a predominantly rural society, they provided a spiritual and devotional focus that in more urbanized areas gave rise to guilds and devotional confraternities. The standard of behaviour demanded of each member was high but, unfortunately, as with so much else regarding the medieval Irish laity, little remains to illustrate their lifestyle and impact on their contemporaries. The regular tertiaries made the largest numbers of new foundations of any of the religious orders in late medieval Ireland. The accidents of history, however, make them the group about whom we are least well informed. Their pastoral and educational activities in large areas of Gaelic Ireland must have been hugely influential, but little or no trace of it remains.

# Epilogue, 1530–40

*They broke down the monasteries so that from Aran of the Saints to the Iccian Sea there was not one monastery that was not shattered with the exception of a few in Ireland of which the English took no notice or heed.*[1]

The first half of the sixteenth century witnessed monumental developments that permanently transformed the face of early modern Europe. In Ireland, the dramatic events of the decade between 1530 and 1540 laid the foundations for a radical restructuring of all aspects of society. The friars were not immune to these changes and functioned as significant agents in many of them.

By 1530, the mendicant orders possessed a combined total of approximately 204 friaries in Ireland, of which over one hundred belonged to the Conventual, Observant or Regular Tertiary branches of the Franciscan order. This extensive network was widely dispersed throughout both Gaelic and Anglo-Irish territories and 'lent an air of ubiquity to the friars' that was much commented on by contemporary observers.[2] Their numerical strength, participation in general chapters and interaction with their Continental *confrères* meant that late medieval Irish friars shared in the cosmopolitan, international *esprit de corps* that had characterized the mendicant movement in its initial phases.[3] In Ireland, their committment to regular chapter meetings and visitations ensured that the structures of religious discipline still functioned and, at local level, individual communities enjoyed widespread lay support. As already demonstrated, there was relatively little popular anti-fraternalism in Ireland. With a few exceptions (like the Carmelite prior denounced for keeping a concubine in 1536),[4] the friars enjoyed a widespread reputation for asceticism, pastoral zeal and moral authority and were regarded as the pre-eminent preachers of the late medieval Irish church.[5] This reputation went further afield than Ireland. In noting the intention of the English Franciscan provincial Friar Francis Faber to undertake a visitation of his Irish *confrères* in 1534, Eustace Chapuys, the imperial ambassador to England, informed his master, Charles V, that among the Gaelic

---

1 *AFM, s.a.* 1537. 2 C. Lennon, 'The dissolution to the foundation of St Anthony's College, Louvain, 1534–1607' (2009), p. 3. 3 Ó Clabaigh, *Franciscans*, pp 73–9. 4 Cited in B. Bradshaw, *The dissolution of the religious orders in Ireland* (1974), p. 22. 5 This was in marked contrast to the late medieval Irish Benedictine and Cistercian monks and the Augustinian canons among whom conventual discipline had largely collapsed and where attempts to restore it proved ineffectual. Bradshaw, *The dissolution of the religious orders,* pp 16–38; C. Ó Clabaigh, 'The Benedictines in medieval and early modern Ireland' (2005);

population the Observants were 'feared, obeyed and almost adored not only by the peasants but by the lords who hold them in such reverence as to endure from them blows from a stick'.[6] As Chapuys correctly surmised, the friars' influence and moral authority were soon deployed in responding to the changes and challenges of the Tudor regime in Ireland.

THE FRIARS AND THE REFORMATION

The mendicant friars were at the forefront of the Reformation controversies that beset the Christian church throughout the sixteenth century and, across Europe, each order produced champions for the various opposing sides. This was particularly true of the Observants whose idealistic commitment to austere religious life sometimes developed into support for more radical ecclesial reform and many influential reformers were former reformed friars.[7] Martin Luther had been a member of the Observant Augustinian friars in Saxony, a group particularly noted for its fervour, while Bernardine Ochino, elected vicar-general of the Capuchins in 1538, became a Calvinist in 1542. In England, the early reformers included a disproportionate number of friar-graduates and superiors of houses.[8] Then, as now, religious communities often housed members with diametrically opposed opinions: the Observant Franciscans at Greenwich, noted for their opposition to the Henrician reforms in the 1530s, included at least two Lutheran sympathizers in the mid-1520s.[9]

The printing press, the university and a medieval tradition of heterodoxy provided the means, venue and context for the spread of reformation ideas among the friars in England. As Bradshaw has noted, there is no evidence of a similarly receptive intellectual culture in Ireland and little to indicate the widespread circulation of reformation literature during the reign of Henry VIII.[10] Although the 1523 addition to the library catalogue of the Youghal Franciscans listed a considerable number of Continental printed books, these were all thoroughly orthodox works concerned with improving the friars' pastoral effectiveness with nothing to indicate an interest in contemporary disputes. Indeed, these acquistions included copies of the *Summa Angelica* by the Italian Observant Franciscan, Friar Angelo Carletti (d. 1495). This popular treatise was so emblematic of the late medieval penitential system that it was one of three works publicly burned by Luther at Wittenberg in 1520.[11]

C. Ó Conbhuidhe OCSO, 'Decline and attempted reform of the Irish Cistercians (1445–1531)' (1998), pp 118–20.   **6** *Calendar of letters, despatches and state papers relating to the negotiations between England and Spain, preserved in the archives at Simancas and elsewhere*, v, no. 70.   **7** R. Rex, 'The friars in the English Reformation' (2002).   **8** Ibid., p. 52.   **9** K. Brown, 'Wolsey and the ecclesiastical order: the case of the Franciscan Observants' (1991).   **10** B. Bradshaw, 'The Reformation in the cities' (1988), p. 448.   **11** *YLC*, nos 90, 144; Ó Clabaigh, *Franciscans*, pp 150–1. The Franciscan tertiary friars at Slane also possessed a copy

An exception to the Irish norm was the Augustinian Observant friar and first reformed bishop of Clonfert, Friar Richard Nangle (d. *c.*1541). Nothing is known of his early years, but his surname indicates west of Ireland roots. As already noted, he came to prominence sometime before 1506, when he collaborated with Margaret Athy and Mayor Stephen FitzDominick Dubh Lynch, to establish an Augustinian friary in Galway.[12] In 1517 he was described as a professor of theology in Galway, while Mayor Lynch's 1536 will referred to him as 'Dr Richard Na[n]gle'.[13] This suggests that he was probably a graduate and, though no university is identified, his reformation sympathies may have developed while studying abroad. Nangle enjoyed a high reputation amongst his *confrères* and in April 1514 the reforming prior general and noted humanist, Giles of Viterbo, appointed him president of the forthcoming Irish chapter.[14] Friar Giles was a keen promoter of the Observant movement and Nangle's appointment indicates the prior general's desire to see the movement prosper in Ireland. In 1518, Nangle was appointed vicar provincial of the order's Irish limit and in 1519 was permitted to remain in office until the next chapter.[15] By 1536, however, he had accepted the royal supremacy and was appointed bishop of Clonfert by Henry VIII. He was ordained bishop on 13 June 1537 by George Browne, the former prior provincial of the Augustinians in England and first reformed archbishop of Dublin. While the precise nature of Nangle's protestantism is unknown, Archbishop Browne esteemed him highly for his learning, loyalty to the king and ability to preach in Irish. Nangle was unable to take possession of Clonfert because the papally appointed incumbent, Roland de Burgh, was a kinsman of the earl of Clanrickard and enjoyed influential local support. He therefore functioned as Browne's suffragan in Dublin. Despite his conversion, Nangle also continued to function as vicar provincial of the Augustinian order in Ireland and was prior of the Dublin community at its dispersal in 1539, when he received one of the convent's chalices from the dissolution commissioners.[16] He was presented to the rectory of Ardrahan, Co. Galway, in May 1542 but died shortly afterwards.[17]

## THE FRIARS AND THE KING'S GREAT MATTER

The Franciscan Observants in England were closely associated with the Tudor royal family and with court circles since the foundation of their first house at Greenwich in 1482.[18] They also received considerable support from Henry VIII's

---

of the work. **12** H.A. Jefferies, 'Nangle, Richard', *DNB*, 40, p. 141; F.X. Martin, 'Irish Augustinian reform' (1961), pp 258, 261–2. **13** Martin, 'Irish Augustinian friaries', pp 377–8. **14** Martin & de Meijer, 'Irish material', pp 109–10, no. 130. **15** Ibid., pp 110–11, no. 133. **16** White, *Extents*, p. 80. **17** A.M. McCormack, 'Nangle, Richard', *DIB*, 6, p. 856. **18** Brown, 'Franciscan Observants', pp 24–32; see above, p. 207.

queen, Catherine of Aragon, whose own family had promoted the Observance in Spain, and who was a Franciscan tertiary herself.[19] The Observants took the queen's part in the divorce proceedings initiated by Henry VIII in 1527, with the minister provincial, Friar William Peto, condemning the king to his face in a sermon preached in the friary church at Greenwich on Easter Sunday 1532.[20] Despite Henry's displeasure, the friars remained loyal to Catherine after the divorce was granted in 1533.[21] Nor were the Franciscans the only mendicant group concerned about the English royal marriage: the Carmelite general chapter, meeting in Padua in 1532, discussed the case of the king's 'odious divorce' at length, condemning a friar who had spoken in favour of it in Paris. Friar John of Ireland, the Irish prior provincial, was present at this gathering.[22] The king's position may initially have found some support among other Irish friars, however: Master David Brown, an Irish Dominican lecturing in Cambridge, participated in a royal embassy to Rome, possibly to secure papal support for the divorce.[23]

The Franciscan Observants were also to the fore in the campaign to oppose recognition of the king as the supreme head of the church in England in 1531. This opposition, coming from some of the most respected religious in the realm, caused great concern to King Henry and Friar Francis Faber, a French friar, was dispatched as commissary to England in 1533 ostensibly to placate him. By April 1533, he was minister provincial of the Observants and attempted to defuse the situation by moving some of the king's more obdurate friar-critics to other houses. He was eventually won round to his *confrères'* position, however, as he saw the direction events were taking.[24] His visitation of the Irish houses in 1534 was of major political and religious significance, as is evident from the report of Eustace Chapuys, the imperial ambassador, to his master Charles V. Before departing, Faber had informed the ambassador that 'he would brew up there all he could for the preservation of the authority of the Holy See'.[25] Donatus Mooney indicated that Faber made two visitations of the Irish province, but it is impossible to determine if the 1534 visit was the first or second of these.[26] Faber's visitation(s) further apprised the Irish Observants (and possibly some of their patrons) of the religious situation in England and demonstrate a clear connection between the opposition of the English Observants to the reformation programme in England in the early 1530s and that of their Irish *confrères* throughout the rest of the sixteenth and seventeenth centuries.[27]

**19** G. Mattingly, *Catherine of Aragon* (1963), pp 134–5. **20** Ibid., p. 244; MacCraith, '*Collegium S. Antonii Louvanii*', pp 237–40. **21** Ibid., p. 244. **22** G. Wessels, *Acta Capitulorum Generalium* (1912), pp 384, 398–9. **23** Flynn, *Irish Dominicans*, p. 9. **24** Brown, 'Franciscan Observants', pp 166–7, 174–82, 257. **25** *Calendar of letters, despatches and state papers relating to the negotiations between England and Spain, preserved in the archives at Simancas and elsewhere*, v, no. 70. **26** 'Brussels MS 3947', p. 105. **27** P. Rogers, 'The Irish Franciscan Observants and the royal supremacy' (1934).

## THE FRIARS AND THE KILDARE REBELLION

Along with some prominent secular clerics, the friars also played an important part in the 1534 revolt against Henry VIII led by Thomas, Lord Offaly, son and heir of Garret Óg Fitzgerald, ninth earl of Kildare. While the traditional image of this revolt as the ill-fated action of an impetuous young man has been largely abandoned, historians continue to differ as to what precipitated it.[28] What is indisputable is that the revolt constituted a major assault on the authority of the crown at the precise moment when opposition to Henry VIII's programme of centralization and ecclesiastical reform was gaining ground in England, Scotland and on the Continent. The revolt's failure in 1535 marked a major turning point in how the English crown managed its affairs in Ireland. Since the time of Thomas, the seventh earl (d. 1479), the Kildare Geraldines had dominated Irish politics and all but monopolized the position of the king's lord deputy in Ireland. Their influence reached its peak during the lifetime of Garret Mór, the eighth earl (d. 1513), who intermittently governed Ireland for over thirty years in his own manner and on the crown's often reluctant behalf. His son, Garret Óg, faced harder taskmasters in Henry VIII and his centralizing ministers and his tenures of office as lord deputy were interspersed with periods of detention in England as the crown struggled to find more amenable ways of governing the troublesome lordship. In each instance, until his definitive fall from grace in 1534, Garret Óg was able to undermine these alternative arrangements, securing his own reappointment and reasserting the Kildare ascendancy. Lord Thomas' resignation of office and repudiation of allegiance before a meeting of the Irish privy council on 11 June 1534 was probably orchestrated by his father and was certainly in keeping with previous Fitzgerald stratagems to retain power. In this instance, it backfired badly and Garret Óg was imprisoned in the Tower of London on 29 June and died there on 2 September. On 28 July, Lord Thomas' followers killed the fleeing archbishop of Dublin and crown loyalist, John Alen, and initiated a siege of the capital. This was abandoned on 4 October and three weeks later Sir William Skeffington arrived in Dublin with troops. The fall of Maynooth Castle, the principal Kildare stronghold, to Skeffington on 23 March 1535 effectively marked the end of the rebellion, but Lord Thomas, now tenth earl of Kildare, held out in hope of imperial aid until his surrender, on promise of his life, to Sir Leonard Grey, on 25 March 1535. He and his five paternal uncles were executed in London in February 1537 in an attempt to permanently remove the Fitzgerald element from Irish politics.

---

**28** M.A. Lyons, 'FitzGerald, Thomas ('Silken Thomas')', *DIB*, 3, p. 912; L. McCorristine, *The revolt of Silken Thomas: a challenge to Henry VIII* (1987).

Although Geraldine resistance to Tudor centralization initially sparked the revolt, it quickly developed a religious character under the influence of Lord Thomas' conservative clerical counsellors. This has generally been interpreted as a stratagem to garner Catholic support throughout Ireland, Britain and the Continent, but Lord Thomas' religious convictions may have run deeper than this. Whereas his father Garret Óg had been a signatory to the 1530 petition of the English nobility to Pope Clement VII requesting the dissolution of Henry VIII's marriage to Catherine of Aragon, he did not have any sympathy for reformation ideas. The religious works listed in the earl's library at Maynooth in February 1526 are noteworthy for their orthodoxy and conservatism. Indeed, the only two works of contemporary relevance, Sir Thomas More's defence of pilgrimage and Henry VIII's treatise against Luther, were hostile responses to elements of the reformation crisis.[29] Along with several high-ranking secular clerics, the friars also played an influential role in promoting the religious dimension of the revolt and encouraged the rebels in their loyalty to papal supremacy.[30] Micheál Ó Siochrú suggests that the 1534 visitation of Friar Francis Faber may have been a factor in precipitating the Kildare rebellion.[31] On the international scene, Lord Thomas' envoys to the Emperor Charles V, James V of Scotland and Pope Paul III presented the rebellion as a Catholic crusade against a schismatic king. Though ultimately nothing came of these embassies other than 'prayers and promises', the flurry of diplomatic activity they created was a cause of concern and embarrassment to Henry VIII.[32]

In addition to moral support, the friars offered some practical assistance to Lord Thomas and his supporters during the revolt. At an early stage in the campaign, he sent some of the silver and gold plate from Maynooth Castle to the Carmelites in Kildare for safekeeping. In the autumn of 1534 a Spanish envoy who arrived in Galway was escorted to his headquarters in the midlands by two friars and he himself narrowly escaped capture during a sortie made by the besieged citizens of Dublin by spending the night in the city's Franciscan friary.[33]

Although the revolt was unsuccessful, the crusading element in its inspiration was to prove of abiding significance, with the friars doing their utmost to foster it. A 1538 report to the council in Dublin alleged that

> The friars and priests of all the Irishry, not only of O'Donnell's country, but
> all others whereas I was, do preach daily that every man ought, for the
> salvation of his soul, fight and make war against our sovereign lord the king's

---

**29** Mac Niocaill, *Kildare rental*, pp 312–14. It is possible that these two works were presentation copies to the earl from their authors.   **30** J. Murray, *Enforcing the English Reformation in Ireland* (2009), pp 82–114.   **31** M. Ó Siochrú, 'Foreign involvement in the revolt of Silken Thomas' (1996), 57.   **32** S. Ellis, 'The Kildare rebellion and the early Henrician reformation' (1976), p. 825.   **33** McCorristine, *Revolt of Silken*

majesty, and his true subjects; and if any of them, which so shall fight against his said majesty, or his subjects, die in the quarrel, his soul, that shall bedead, shall go to heaven, as the soul of St Peter, Paul and others which suffered death and martyrdom for God's sake.[34]

Nor was this attitude confined to the friars in Ireland: in 1537, an Irish Dominican, Friar Ulick de Burgh, was hanged for celebrating Mass for seventy-four participants in the Pilgrimage of Grace who were executed in Westmorland and Cumbria. He was described as an 'incendiary offering prayers for rebels who died without benefit of clergy'.[35]

## THE IRISH DOMINICAN PROVINCE

The parlous state of the religious orders in England and Ireland formed the background to the contemporaneous establishment in 1536 of the Irish Dominican province as an independent entity. As noted above, previous attempts to gain independence had foundered on the opposition of the English province, but the annihilation of the order in England galvanized the Irish friars into action. Their success was largely due to the efforts of the Anglo-Irish friar and Observant reformer, Master David Brown.[36] Brown had entered the order in Tralee and in 1513–14 he became a bachelor of divinity at Cambridge, lecturing there on the sentences of Peter Lombard.[37] In 1515, he accompanied the provincial of England to the order's general chapter in Naples, where he was made a master of theology, the Dominicans' highest academic distinction. He was based in England for much of his career and Sir James Ware asserted that he was employed by Henry VIII on a number of diplomatic missions.[38] He next surfaced in 1536 when his appointment as provincial of the newly erected Irish province was recorded in the register of the master general, John du Feynier.[39] This appointment did not follow normal Dominican constitutional practice but was a direct initiative of Pope Paul III, who appears to have been advised throughout by Brown. Despite this, the master general and the general chapter of the order subsequently ratified the pope's decision to erect an independent Irish province in 1558.[40]

*Thomas*, p. 89; Ellis, 'The Kildare rebellion', p. 816. **34** *State Papers*, Henry VIII, iii, p. 141. Cited in McCorristine, *Revolt of Silken Thomas*, p. 135. **35** Flynn, *Irish Dominicans*, p. 36. **36** For what follows, see Flynn, *Irish Dominicans*, pp 8–11; Fenning, 'Irish material', p. 270, no. 78. **37** J. & J.A. Venn, *Alumni Cantabrigiensis*, 1 (1922), p. 232. **38** Flynn, *Irish Dominicans*, p. 9. **39** Fenning, 'Irish material', p. 270, no. 76. In addition, he was appointed inquisitor for Ireland and he and three companions were granted permission to beg alms on their return journey from Rome. **40** Reichert, *MOPH*, 10, pp 10–11.

### THE FRIARS AND ARCHBISHOP GEORGE BROWNE

The appointment of George Browne as archbishop of Dublin in January 1536 was designed to further the cause of the reformation in Ireland.[41] Before his elevation, Browne had been superior of the Augustinian priory in London and in that capacity came into contact with Thomas Cromwell. As a supporter of both the royal supremacy and Henry VIII's divorce attempt, he proved an effective 'pulpit propagandist' for the new order and was appointed prior provincial of the Augustinian friars in England by the king in April 1534. In this capacity, he collaborated with the English Dominican friar, Dr John Hilsey, in a visitation of the country's mendicant friaries, administering the oath of succession to the inmates. Browne was instrumental in breaking the opposition of the English Observant Franciscans to the royal supremacy by dispersing their communities and assigning the hardliners to houses of their more pliant Conventual brethren. Though Browne's credentials as a reformer seemed impeccable, the poverty of his see, opposition from the conservative clergy of his diocese, conflicts with the Dublin administration, particularly the lord deputy, Sir Leonard Grey, and the strength of Observantism among the Irish friars disheartened him and rendered his early efforts at reform largely ineffectual. In September 1537 his seeming inaction earned him stinging rebukes from both the king and Thomas Cromwell that galvanized him into action, beginning with a visitation of his own diocese. Here again, the opposition of the clerical elite of the diocese and the contempt in which the lord deputy held him undermined his authority and he complained to Cromwell that the lowliest holy water clerk in the diocese was better esteemed than he was. He had more success with the campaign for the dissolution of the religious houses, which began in earnest in the Pale in 1539 and 1540 and in which he served as a commissioner.

### THE FRIARS AND THE ROYAL SUPREMACY

The disruption caused by the Kildare rebellion and its aftermath delayed the implementation of the Tudor reform programme in Ireland and meant that there was a considerable backlog of business to be addressed when the Irish parliament met in May 1536.[42] A number of the eleven statutes enacted at the first parliamentary session had major implications for the church, the friars and other religious orders. These included acts for the attainder of the earl of Kildare and his followers; recognition of the union between the king and Anne Boleyn and the

---

**41** For what follows, see J. Murray, 'Browne, George', *DNB*, 8 (2004), pp 161–2; idem, *Enforcing the English Reformation*, pp 91–158; B. Bradshaw, 'George Browne, first reformation archbishop of Dublin, 1536–1534' (1970).    **42** R.D. Edwards, 'The Irish Reformation parliament of Henry VIII, 1536–7' (1968).

succession rights of their offspring; an act for resumption to the crown of the lands held by English absentees in Ireland, including those of a number of religious houses. Other acts recognized King Henry's title as supreme head of the church in Ireland, forbade appeals to Rome and made it treasonable to deny the king's title, regard him as a heretic or deny the legitimacy of the offspring of his union with Anne Boleyn.[43]

Apart from some muted opposition from the proctors representing the lower clergy and perhaps from some bishops, there was little resistance to any of the ecclesiastical legislation enacted at the first parliamentary session. Promoting the royal supremacy was another matter and, predictably, much of the opposition came from the friars. During his visitations in 1537–8, Archbishop Browne attempted to induce them to accept the royal claims and promote them in their preaching, but with little success.[44] Dr Saul, a Franciscan from Waterford, was imprisoned in Dublin Castle for preaching against the supremacy in March 1538 and in May the archbishop wrote to Cromwell relaying an intercepted correspondence between two friars, which illustrated how they used confession to counsel magnates to resistance. He claimed that 'where they ruyle, Godd and the kyng cannot justyle rule', a sentiment which echoed that of Thomas Agarde who, in April 1538 had asserted that it was hard for any good man to speak out against 'that monsttyr, the byschope of Roome, and his adherenttes … the false and crafty bludsukkers, the Observauntes'.[45] In January 1539 a friar was one of five men hanged in Waterford for denying the royal claims.[46] In frustration, Browne adopted a stratagem that he had successfully used in England and attempted to assume the Observant Franciscans into their seemingly more pliant Conventual brethren, but to no avail. The Observants were too numerous and the device resulted in nothing more than a name change, with the communities remaining intact.[47]

### THE FRIARS AND THE DISSOLUTION OF THE MONASTERIES

Initial attempts to dissolve the monasteries in Ireland suffered a setback when a bill to suppress eight small houses was rejected at the second session of the 1536 reformation parliament.[48] Opposition came from a group of gentry families from

43 P. Connolly (ed.), *Statute rolls of the Irish parliament: Richard III–Henry VIII* (2002), pp 147–88. 44 Lennon, 'The suppression to the foundation of St Anthony's College, Louvain', pp 4–6; Rogers, 'The Irish Franciscan Observants and the royal supremacy' (1934), p. 120. 45 *SP Henry VIII*, ii, p. 570; iii, pp 6–7. 46 *SP Henry VIII*, iii, p. 114. 47 Bradshaw, *Dissolution of the religious orders*, p. 95. 48 Bradshaw, *Dissolution of the religious orders* remains the classic study. Important studies of the impact of the dissolution in local areas include M.A. Lyons, *Church and society in County Kildare, c.1470–1547* (2000), pp 109–81; B. Scott, *Religion and reformation in the Tudor diocese of Meath* (2006), pp 90–113; idem, 'The religious houses of Tudor Dublin: their communities and resistance to the Dissolution, 1537–41' (2006).

the Pale, led by the lawyer Patrick Barnewall (d. 1552). They were motivated by concern for their own interests in the monastic estates and properties that they were already administering as lawyers and lessees. Their opposition ceased in 1537 when it became clear that they stood to materially benefit from the redistribution of monastic lands and many opponents of the initial bill subsequently served as dissolution commissioners.

From late 1537, Archbishop Browne's attempts to enforce royal supremacy increasingly brought him into conflict with the friars.[49] In addition, his lack of support from the lord deputy, Sir Leonard Grey, and doubts about his jurisdiction over the mendicant orders further weakened his position. In England, the visitation of the friars began in sping 1538 had turned into a campaign for wholesale dissolution by the summer. In November 1538, the archbishop wrote to Cromwell complaining about Grey's continued interference, but in terms that suggested that the friars within crown territories had become demoralized and that many were abandoning their friaries, sequestering the properties and establishing themselves elsewhere. Simultaneously, in the winter of 1538–9, the campaign to dismantle shrines in territories loyal to the crown also impacted a number of mendicant communities.[50] In January 1539, the shrine of St Dominic was dismantled in the course of the archbishop's visit to the Dominican priory in Limerick, with the saint's image being despoiled of its ornaments, including its silver shoes, as well as of a large quantity of wax and iron.[51]

In April 1539, the campaign for total suppression of religious houses in Ireland began in earnest when a commission ordering their dissolution was issued in London.[52] The campaign got underway in mid-July and within two years practically every religious house in the Pale and other territories loyal to the crown had been officially dissolved. The commissioners encountered little opposition to the dissolution from monastic communities, many of which had pre-empted their demise by disposing of their assets on terms favourable to themselves. Members of these orders also stood to benefit from pensions granted to them from the incomes of their former properties. The crown refused to grant pensions to members of dissolved mendicant communities, as their economic resources were not sufficient to support this. Although they are not sufficiently detailed to provide a precise chronology of the campaign, the surveys or extents undertaken during the visitations to secure the formal surrenders of the friaries provide a summary account of their economic resources and often give the identity of the superior of the suppressed house.

---

**49** Bradshaw, *Dissolution of the religious orders*, pp 92–7.   **50** Ibid., pp 100–9.   **51** BL Add MSS 19,865, fo. 69.   **52** Bradshaw, *Dissolution of the religious orders*, pp 110–46; Flynn, *The Irish Dominicans*, pp 20–6.

The area covered in the suppression campaign stretched from Carlingford to Dungarvan and by July 1540, when the commissioners appointed in April 1539 had ceased to function, fifty-one mendicant houses at thirty-seven different locations had been dissolved. The returns from these communities were extremely meagre, illustrating both the relative poverty of the friars in comparison with monastic foundations and the fact that many of their goods had been borne away by the friars or their supporters before the commissioners arrived.

## WEATHERING THE STORM

While the dissolution campaign was a major blow to the resources and morale of the friars, the incomplete nature of the Tudor regime in Ireland meant that, unlike their *confrères* in England, the orders did not experience complete and rapid annihilation. From the meagre sources that survive, it is clear that some of the dispossessed friars relocated to foundations in Gaelic territories west of the Shannon and in Ulster, which continued unmolested throughout much of the sixteenth century. Even within the Pale and other crown territories, the communities employed a number of stratagems to ensure their survival. In some cases, the support or connivance of a sympathetic patron ensured this. The Franciscan friary at Multyfarnham, though ostensibly dissolved in October 1540, continued as a fully functioning religious community well into the seventeenth century under the aegis of their patrons, the Nugent barons of Delvin.[53] The Dominican communities at Limerick, Kilmallock, Tralee and Youghal continued in peaceful possession of their properties for much of the sixteenth century under the protecting hand of the Fitzgerald earls of Desmond.[54] Their *confrères* in Sligo and Athenry escaped suppression by undertaking to put off the Dominican habit and reconstitute themselves as colleges of secular priests.

The friars' links with their continental *confrères* also proved an important factor in their survival. While a number of Irish friars found refuge in continental houses in the immediate aftermath of the suppression, the links became even more vital as the Tudor conquest of Ireland made it increasingly difficult to maintain centres in which religious could be formed to the standards of Tridentine catholicism. Between 1578 and the end of the seventeenth century, approximately forty-five secular and religious foundations were established on the Continent to train priests for the Irish mission or to prepare candidates for the religious life. Of these,

53 White, *Extents*, pp 274–5. Lennon, 'The dissolution to the foundation', pp 4–11, gives numerous examples of this phenomenon. 54 Flynn, *The Irish Dominicans*, p. 35.

around 60 per cent were religious houses, with seven Franciscan houses, six Capuchin, four Dominican and one Augustinian foundation being set up.[55]

Despite their difficulties, the friars' morale and zeal for religious observance also remained strong, particularly among the Observant Franciscans. Just as many of their houses were being suppressed in Ireland in 1541, an Irish delegate to the Capuchin general chapter meeting in Rome presented an appeal on behalf of a group of clergy and laity in Ireland calling for the introduction of the even more austere Capuchin reform among the friars in Ireland. Though his request was unsuccessful, it provides an interesting example of the strength of the *esprit de corps* among the Observants at a time of great crisis.[56]

The friars continued to enjoy widespread respect and support among the Catholic population. Writing in the 1570s, the English writer and future Jesuit martyr Edmund Campion expressed astonishment at various aspects of the Gaelic character, but particularly at the reverence shown to the mendicants:

> They honour devoute Fryars and Pilgrimes, suffer them to passe quietly, spare them and their mansions, whatever outrage they shew to the country besides them.[57]

Reflecting on the parlous state of the Irish province in Louvain around 1617, the Franciscan provincial Donatus Mooney listed four reasons for its continued survival in the face of all its vicissitudes. These included the poverty of the friars, the respect their vocation engendered and the support of their patrons. The final reason, which he regarded as the most potent, is the one most difficult for those living in a secularized age to grasp, yet, for those drawn to the countercultural project that is monastic and religious life, it is the only one that matters:

> The fourth reason for the preservation of our order, a cause more powerful than any other is the goodness and providence of our good God ... Nor have we any doubt that God will sustain us, and give us increase from day to day as long as we shall be useful labourers in his vineyard of Ireland, living purely and devoutly according to our state.[58]

55 M.A. Lyons, 'St Anthony's College, Louvain and the Irish Franciscan college network' (2009), p. 28; J.J. Silke, 'The Irish abroad, 1534–1691' (1976), p. 616.  56 F.X. Martin, *Friar Nugent: a study of Francis Lavalin Nugent (1569–1635)* (1962), pp 25–6.  57 J. Ware (ed.), *Campion's historie of Ireland* (1633), p. 19. 58 'Brussels MS 3947', p. 18.

# Bibliography

MANUSCRIPT SOURCES

**Berlin**
*Staatsbibliothek Preussicher Kulturbesitz*
MS theol. lat fol. 703.

**Brussels**
*Bibliothèque Royale*
MS 3947.
MS 3410.

**Cambridge**
*Corpus Christi College*
MS 180.

**Dublin**
*Marsh's Library*
MS Z3.1.5.

*National Library of Ireland*
Deed 2014.
Deed 679.
Lismore papers, MS 41,981/ 2.

*Representative Church Body Library*
C.6.1.6.2., Registrum novum.

*Trinity College Dublin*
MS 65.                MS 347.
MS 82.                MS 552.
MS 86.                MS 576.
MS 109.               MS 667/1699.
MS 175.               MS 1477, no. 146.
MS 194.               MS 1207/85–26.
MS 250.               MS 1207a 202 (261).

**Durham**
*Cathedral library*
MS B. IV 19.

## London
*British Library*

Add. MS 4783.
Add. MS 4789.
Add. MS 4814.
Add. MS 4821.
Add. MS 19,513.
Add. MS 19,865.

Add. MS 23,935.
Add. MS 31,885.
Add. MS 42,130.
Harleian MS 416.
Harleian MS 913.
Harleian MS 3838.

*Lambeth Palace Library*
MS 46.
MS 61 ii.
MS 357.
MS 534.

## Oxford
*Bodleian Library*

Canonici Miscell. MS 535.
Digby MS 98 pt 6.
Douce MS 104.
Rawlinson MS B 480.

Rawlinson MS B 484.
Rawlinson MS B 4789.
Rawlinson MS C 320.

## Truro
*Cornwall Record Office*
AR 27/6.

PRINTED/PUBLISHED SOURCES
*Primary printed sources are indicatd by an asterisk.*

Alban, Kevin (ed.), 'The letters of Thomas Netter of Walden' in Patrick Fitzgerald-Lombard (ed.), *Carmel in Britain: essays on the medieval English Carmelite province. Vol. 2: theology and writing* (Rome, 1992), pp 343–80.*

Alemand, Louis, *Histoire monastique de l'Irlande* (Paris, 1690).*

Andreozzi, A., 'San Giovanni da Capestrano e la sua defesa del Terz'Ordine Francescano', *Analecta Tertii Ordinis Regularis*, 6 (1973), 806–14.

Andrews, Frances, *The other friars: Carmelite, Augustinian, Sack and Pied friars in the Middle Ages* (Woodbridge, 2006).

Anstey, Henry, *Monumenta academica; or, Documents illustrative of academical life and studies at Oxford* (2 vols, London, 1868).

Anonymous, 'Charter of Geoffrey de Turville, bishop of Ossory, to the Friars Preachers of Kilkenny', *Transactions of the Kilkenny Archaeological Society*, 1 (1850), 264–7.*

Antoninus of Florence, St, *Confessionale–Defecerunt* (Cologne, 1469).*

Aramburu Cendoya, Ignacio, OSA, *Las primitivas constituciones de los Augustinos* (Valladolid, 1966).*

Archdall, Mervyn, *Monasticon Hibernicum* (Dublin, 1786).*

Armstrong, Regis, & Ignatius C. Brady, *Francis and Clare: the complete works* (Mahwah, NJ, 1982).*

Aubert, Roger, 'Gesta Romanorum', *Dictionnaire d'histoire et géographie ecclésiastique*, 20 (1984), cols 1111–13.

Barratt, J.K., 'The Franciscan friary of Bymacan', *Journal of the Manx Museum*, 6 (1964), 203–13.

Barry, Terry, Robin Frame & Katharine Simms (eds), *Colony and frontier in medieval Ireland: essays presented to J.F. Lydon* (London, 1995), pp 177–200.

Battersby, William, *A history of all the abbeys, convents, churches, and other religious houses of the orders, particularly of the hermits of St Augustine in Ireland, from the earliest period to the present time* (Dublin, 1856).

Becker, P.J., & T. Brandis, *Die theologischen lateinischen Handschriften in folio der Staatsbibliothek Preussicher Kulturbesitz, Berlin* (2 vols, Wiesbaden, 1985).

Begley, John, *The diocese of Limerick: ancient and medieval* (Dublin, 1906).

Bergström-Allen, Johan, 'The Whitefriars return to Carmel' in Elizabeth Herbert McAvoy & M. Hughes-Edwards (eds), *Anchorites, wombs and tombs* (Cardiff, 2005), pp 77–91.

Bernard of Bessa, *Speculum disciplinae* in S. Bonaventura, *Opera Omnia viii* (Quarrachi, nr Florence, 1898), pp 583–622.*

Berriou, Nicole, 'Autour de Latran IV (1215): la naissance de la confession moderne et sa diffusion' in Groupe de la Bussière (ed.), *Pratiques de la confession: des pères du désert à Vatican II* (Paris, 1983), pp 73–93.

Berry, H.F., *Register of wills and inventories of the diocese of Dublin in the time of Archbishops Tregury and Walton, 1457–1483* (Dublin, 1898).*

Bhreathnach, Edel, 'The friars and vernacular Irish learning', *IHS*, 37:147 (2011), 357–75.

Bhreathnach, Edel, Joseph MacMahon OFM & John McCafferty (eds), *The Irish Franciscans, 1534–1990* (Dublin, 2009).

Bigger, F.J., 'The Franciscan friary of Kilconnell in County Galway and its ruins', *JGAHS*, 1 (1900–1), 145–67; 2 (1902), 3–20; 3 (1903–4), 11–15, 167.

Bihl, Michael, OFM, 'Formulae et documenta e cancellaria Fr Michaelis de Caesena OFM, ministri generalis, 1316–1328 (Disseritur de aliquibus actis eiusdem)', *AFH*, 23 (1930), 106–71.*

Blake, M.J., 'The abbey of Athenry', *JGAHS*, 2 (1902), 65–90.

Blake, M.J., 'The obituary book of the Franciscan monastery at Galway', *JGAHS*, 6 (1909–10), 222–35.*

Blake, M.J., *Blake family records, 1300–1600* (London, 1902).*

Bliss, W.H., *Calendar of the entries in the papal registers relating to Great Britain and Ireland: petitions to the pope, vol. I: AD1342–1419* (London, 1896).*

Boaga, Emmanuele, 'L'abito degli Ordini mendicanti' in Giancarlo Rocca (ed.), *La sostanza dell'effimero: gli abiti degli ordine religiosi in occidente* (Rome, 2000), pp 97–104.

Bodenstedt, M.I., *Praying the life of Christ* (*Analecta Cartusiana*, 15, Salzburg, 1973).

Boece, Hector, *Heir beginnis the history and croniklis of Scotland* (Edinburgh, 1540). *

Bolster, Evelyn, *A history of the diocese of Cork from the earliest times to the Reformation* (Shannon, 1972).

Bonaventure, St, 'Apologia pauperum' in *S. Bonaventura, opera omnia*, viii (Quarrachi, nr Florence, 1898), pp 233–330.*

Bonniwell, William R., OP, *A history of the Dominican liturgy* (New York, 1945).

Bordoni, Franciscus, *Historia Tertii Ordinis S. Francisci* (Parma, 1658).*

Bordua, Louise, & Anne Dunlop (eds), *Art and the Augustinian order in early Renaissance Italy* (Farnham, 2007).

Bossy, John, 'The Mass as a social institution', *Past & Present* (1983), 29–61.

Bougerol, J.G., 'Saint Bonaventure et la défense de la vie évangélique de 1252 au Concile de Lyons' in *S. Bonaventura francescano* (Todi, 1974), pp 109–26.

Bowen, John R., & Conor O'Brien, *A celebration of Limerick's silver* (Limerick, 2007).

Bower, Walter, *Scotichronicon*, ed. D.E.R. Watt (9 vols, Edinburgh, 1987–97).*

Boyce, James, *Praising God in Carmel: studies in Carmelite liturgy* (Washington, DC, 1999).

Boyle, L.E., 'Notes on the education of the *fratres communes* in the Dominican order in the thirteenth century' in idem, *Pastoral care, clerical education and canon law, 1200–1400* (London, 1981), pp 249–67.

Boyle, L.E., OP, Pierre-Marie Gy OP & Pawel Krupa OP (eds), *Aux origines de la liturgie Dominicaine: le manuscrit Santa Sabina XIV L1* (Rome, 2004).

Boyle, L.E., OP, 'The *summa confessorum* of John of Freiburg and the popularisation of the moral teaching of St Thomas and some of his contemporaries' in A.A. Maurer (ed.), *St Thomas Aquinas, 1274–1974: commemorative studies* (2 vols, Toronto, 1974), ii, pp 245–68.

Bradley, John, & Thomas Brett (eds), *Treasures of Kilkenny* (Kilkenny, 2003).

Bradley, John, Andrew Halpin & Heather King, 'Urban archaeology survey xv: County Clare' (Office of Public Works unpublished report, Dublin, 1988).

Bradshaw, Brendan, 'George Browne, first Reformation archbishop of Dublin, 1536–1554', *Journal of Ecclesiastical History*, 21 (1970), 301–26.

Bradshaw, Brendan, 'The Reformation in the cities' in John Bradley (ed.), *Settlement and society in medieval Ireland: studies presented to F.X. Martin OSA* (Kilkenny, 1988), pp 445–76.

Bradshaw, Brendan, *The dissolution of the religious orders in Ireland under Henry VIII* (Cambridge, 1974).

Brady, Ignatius, OFM, 'The history of mental prayer in the Order of Friars Minor', *Franciscan Studies*, 11 (1951), 317–45.

Brand, P.A. 'The licensing of mortmain alienations in the medieval Lordship of Ireland', *Irish Jurist*, 21 (1986), 125–44.

Brand, P.A., 'King, church and property: the enforcement of restrictions on alienations into mortmain in the lordship of Ireland in the later Middle Ages', *Peritia*, 3 (1983), 481–502.

Bray, Gerard (ed.), *Records of Convocation XVI: Ireland, 1101–1690* (Woodbridge, 2006).*

Bremond, C., J. Le Goff & J.C. Schmitt, *L'Exemplum* (Turnhout, 1982).

Brewer, J.S. (ed.), *Monumenta Franciscana* (London, 1882).*

Brooke, R.B., *Early Franciscan government* (Cambridge, 1959).

Brooke, R.B., *The image of St Francis: responses to sainthood in the thirteenth century* (Cambridge, 2006).

Brown, D.C., *Pastor and laity in the theology of John Gerson* (Cambridge, 1987).

Brown, K.D., 'The Franciscan Observants in England, 1482–1559' (DPhil., U Oxford, 1986).

Brown, Keith, 'Wolsey and the ecclesiastical order: the case of the Franciscan Observants' in S.J. Gunn & P.G. Lindley (eds), *Cardinal Wolsey: church, state and art* (Cambridge, 1991), pp 178–218.

Browne, R.L. (trans.), 'History of the Franciscan order in Ireland', *Franciscan Tertiary*, 4 (1894) –9 (1899).*

Bryn, R.F.M., 'The Cordiale-Auszug: a study of Gerard van Vliederhoven's Cordiale de IV novissimis' (PhD, U Leeds, 1976).

Buckley, J.J., *Some Irish altar plate* (Dublin, 1943).

Burr, David, *The spiritual Franciscans: from protest to persecution in the century after Saint Francis* (Philadelphia, PA, 2001).

Burton, Janet, *Monastic and religious orders in Britain, 1000–1300* (Cambridge, 1994).

Butler, R. (ed.), *Annals of Ireland by Friar John Clyn and Thady Dowling, together with the Annals of Ross* (Dublin, 1849).*

Butler, T.C., OSA, *Near restful waters: the Augustinians in New Ross and Clonmines* (Naas, n.d.).

Butler, T.C., OSA, *The Augustinians in Callan, 1467–1977* (Naas, 1977).

Butler, T.C., OSA, *The Augustinians in Cork, 1280–1985* (Cork, 1986).

Butler, T.C., OSA, 'Augustinian foundations in the south-east (Dungarvan, Clonmines, New Ross and Callan)', *Decies: Journal of the Waterford Archaeological and Historical Society*, 8 (1978), 9–11.

Butler, T.C., OSA, *Journey of an abbey: history of the Augustinians in Dungarvan, 1292–1972* (Ballyboden, Dublin, c.1972).

Butler, T.C., OSA, *John's Lane: a history of the Augustinian friars in Dublin, 1280–1980* (Dublin, 1983).

Butler, T.C., OSA, *The Augustinians in Limerick* (Limerick, 1988).

Butler, T.C., OSA, *The Friars of Fethard* (Ballyboden, Dublin, 1976).

Byrne, Niall, *The Irish crusade* (Dublin, 2007).

*Calendar of letters, despatches and state papers relating to the negotiations between England and Spain, preserved in the archives at Simancas and elsewhere*, G.A. Bergenroth et al. (eds) (London, 1862).*

*Calendar of the patent and close rolls of Ireland, Henry VIII–Elizabeth*, i (Dublin, 1861).*

Cannon, Joanna, 'Panorama geografico, cronologico e statistico sulla distribuzione degli Studia degli ordini mendicanti (Inghilterra)' in *Le scuole degli mendicanti* (Todi, 1978), pp 93–126.

Caroline, countess of Dunraven, *Memorials of Adare Manor* (Oxford, 1865).

Carrigan, William, *The history and antiquities of the diocese of Ossory* (4 vols, Dublin, 1905).

Cartlidge, Neil, 'Festivity, order and community in fourteenth-century Ireland: the composition and context of BL MS Harley 913', *Yearbook of English Studies*, 33 (2003), 33–52.

Carville, Geraldine, *The impact of the Cistercians on the landscape of Ireland, 1142–1541* (Ashford, Co. Wicklow, 2002).

Carville, Geraldine, *The occupation of Celtic sites in Ireland by the Canons Regular of St Augustine and the Cistercians* (Kalamazoo, MI, 1982).

Catto, Jeremy, 'The Cistercians in Oxford' in Henry Wansbrough & Anthony Marett-Crosby (eds), *Benedictines in Oxford* (London, 1997), pp 108–15.

Cenci, Caesaris, & R.G. Mailleux, *Constitutiones generales Ordinis Fratrum Minorum I (Saeculum XIII), Analecta Franciscana*, 13 (Grottaferrata, nr Rome, 2007).*

Cendoya, I.A., OSA, *Las primitivas constituciones de los Augustinos* (Valladolid, 1966).*

Ceyssens, L., 'Les ducs de Bourgogne et l'introduction de l'observance à Malines (1447–1469)', *AFH*, 30 (1937), 391–419.

Chart, D.A. (ed.), *The register of John Swayne, archbishop of Armagh and primate of Ireland, 1418–1439* (Belfast, 1935).*

Cicconetti, Carlo, OCarm., *La regola del Carmine: origine, natura, significato* (Rome, 1973).

Cleary, Gregory, OFM, *The Friars Minor in Dublin, 1233–1939* (Dublin, 1939).

Clopper, L.M., *'Songes of rechlesnesse': Langland and the Franciscans* (Ann Arbor, MI, 1997).

Clyne, Miriam, 'Archaeological excavations at Holy Trinity Abbey, Lough Key, Co. Roscommon', *PRIA*, 105 (2005), 2–98.

Coen, Martin, *The wardenship of Galway* (Galway, 1984).

Coleman, Ambrose (ed.), 'Regestum Monasterii Fratrum Praedicatorum de Athenry', *AH*, 1 (1912), 201–21.*

Coleman, Ambrose (ed.), *The Irish Dominicans of the seventeenth century, by Father John O'Heyne OP. First published at Louvain in 1706. Reprinted with an appendix containing historical sketches of all the Dominican foundations in Ireland* (Dundalk, 1902).*

Colker, M.L., *Trinity College Library Dublin: descriptive catalogue of the medieval and Renaissance Latin manuscripts* (2 vols, Aldershot, 1991).

Colledge, Edmund (ed.), *The Latin poems of Richard Ledrede OFM, bishop of Ossory, 1317–1360* (Toronto, 1974).*

Collins, J.T., 'An island friary' in O'Callaghan (ed.), *Franciscan Cork* (1953), pp 48–9.

Collins, J.T., 'The friary at Timoleague' in O'Callaghan (ed.), *Franciscan Cork* (1953), pp 44–7.

Congar, Yves, 'Aspects ecclésiologiques de la querelle Mendiants-Séculiers', *Archives d'histoire doctrinale et littéraire du Moyen Age*, 28 (1961), 35–151.

Conlan, Patrick, OFM, 'Irish Dominican medieval architecture' in M.A. Timoney (ed.), *A celebration of Sligo: first essays for Sligo Field Club* (Sligo, 2002), pp 215–28.

Conlan, Patrick, OFM, 'The Franciscans at Buttevant', *JCHAS*, 107 (2002), 195–8.

Conlan, Patrick, OFM, 'The Franciscans in Carrick-on-Suir', *Tipperary Historical Journal*, 16 (2003), 31–9.

Conlan, Patrick, OFM, 'The Franciscans in Clonmel, 1269–1998', *Tipperary Historical Journal*, 9 (1999), 98–110

Conlan, Patrick, OFM, 'The secular Franciscans' in Bhreathnach et al. (eds), *The Irish Franciscans* (2009), pp 260–70.

Conlan, Patrick, OFM, *Franciscan Ireland* (Mullingar, 1988).

Conlan, Patrick, OFM, *Secular Franciscans down the ages* (Dublin, 1996).

Conlan, Patrick, OFM, *The Franciscan friary, Kilconnell, Co. Galway* (Athlone, 2007).

Conlan, Patrick, OFM, *The Franciscans in Drogheda* (Drogheda, 1987).

Connolly, Philomena (ed.), *Statute rolls of the Irish parliament, Richard III–Henry VIII* (Dublin, 2002).*

Connolly, Philomena, *Irish exchequer payments, 1270–1446* (2 vols, Dublin, 1998).*

Connolly, Philomena, *Medieval record sources* (Dublin, 2002).

Constable, Giles, 'The ideal of the imitation of Christ' in idem, *Three studies in medieval religious and social thought* (Cambridge, 1995), pp 144–248.

Conway, C.A., *The Vita Christi of Ludolph of Saxony and late medieval devotion centred on the incarnation* (*Analecta Cartusiana*, 34, Salzburg, 1976).

Conway, P., & B. Jarrett (eds), *Lives of the brethren of the Order of Preachers, 1206–1259* (London, 1955).*

Copsey, Richard, OCarm., 'Simon Stock and the Carmelite vision' in Copsey (ed.), *Carmel in Britain, 3: the hermits from Mount Carmel* (2004), pp 75–112.

Copsey, Richard, OCarm., 'The Scottish Carmelite province and its provincials' in idem, *Carmel in Britain, 3: the hermits from Mount Carmel* (2004), pp 113–33.

Copsey, Richard, OCarm., *Carmel in Britain, 3: the hermits from Mount Carmel* (York, 2004).

Copsey, Richard, OCarm. (ed. & trans.), *The ten books on the way of life and the great deeds of the Carmelites* (Faversham, 2005).*

Copsey, Richard, OCarm., 'The formation of the medieval English friar: from Dominican model to Carmelite practice' in Anne Duggan, Joan Greatrex & Brenda Bolton (eds), *Omnia disce: medieval studies in memory of Leonard Boyle OP* (Aldershot, 2005), pp 245–62.

Corish, Patrick, *The Catholic community in the seventeenth and eighteenth centuries* (Dublin, 1981).

Costello, M.A. (ed.), *De Annatis Hiberniae, 1400–1535*, vol. 1 (Dundalk, 1909).*

Cotter, Francis, OFM, *The Friars Minor in Ireland from their arrival to 1400* (New York, 1994).

Courtenay, W.J., 'The Augustinian community at Paris in the early 14th century', *Augustiniana*, 51 (2001), 219–29.

Courtenay, W.J., 'The Parisian Franciscan community in 1303', *Franciscan Studies*, 53 (1993), 155–74.

Crooks, Peter, 'Historical introduction', www.irishchancery.net/irish_chancery_rolls.php; accessed 7 July 2011.

Crosthwaite, J.C., & J.H. Todd, *The book of obits and the martyrology of the cathedral church of the Most Holy Trinity, commonly called Christ Church, Dublin* (Dublin, 1844).*

Cunningham, Bernadette, 'Illustrations of the passion of Christ in the *Seanchas Búrcach* manuscript' in Moss et al. (eds), *Art and devotion in late medieval Ireland* (2006), pp 16–32.

Cunningham, Bernadette, 'The Louvain achievement I: the Annals of the Four Masters' in Bhreathnach et al. (eds), *The Irish Franciscans* (2009), pp 177–88.

Cunningham, Bernadette, 'The Poor Clare order in Ireland' in Bhreathnach et al. (eds), *The Irish Franciscans* (2009), pp 159–74.

Curran, A., 'The Dominican order in Carlingford and Dundalk', *CLAHJ*, 16:3 (1968), 143–60.

Curtis, Edmund (ed.), *Calendar of Ormond deeds* (6 vols, Dublin, 1932–43).

D'Alton, E.A., *History of the archdiocese of Tuam* (Dublin, 1928).

D'Alton, John, *History of Drogheda* (Dublin, 1863).

d'Avray, D.L., *The preaching of the friars: sermons diffused from Paris before 1300* (Oxford, 1985).

d'Avray, D.L., 'Portable *vademecum* books containing Franciscan and Dominican texts' in A.C. de la Mare & B.C. Barker-Benfield (eds), *Manuscripts at Oxford* (Oxford, 1980), pp 60–4.

Dahan, Gilbert, 'Les textes bibliques dans le lectionnaire du "prototype" de la liturgie dominicaine' in Boyle et al. (eds), *Aux origines de la liturgie Dominicaine* (2004), pp 159–82.

David of Augsburg [David ab Augusta], *De exterioris et interioris hominis compositione* (Quarrachi, nr Florence, 1899).*

de Barra, Gearóid, 'Buttevant' in O'Callaghan, *Franciscan Cork* (1953), pp 54–7.

de Burgo, Thomas, *Hibernia Dominicana* (Cologne, 1762; repr. 1772).*

de Meyer, Albert, *La congrégation de Hollande ou la réforme dominicaine en territoire Bourguignon, 1465–1515* (Lüttisch, 1946).

Delorme, F.M., 'Olivier Maillard et le Tiers Ordre Régulier en Ecosse (1458–1496)', *AFH*, 8 (1915), 353–7.

Dillon, Myles, Canice Mooney OFM & Pádraig de Brún, *Catalogue of the Irish manuscripts in the Franciscan Library, Killiney* (Dublin, 1969).

Dolan, T.P., 'Richard FitzRalph's *Defensio curatorum* in transmission' in H.B. Clarke & J.R.S. Phillips (eds), *Ireland, England and the Continent in the Middle Ages and beyond* (Dublin, 2006), pp 177–94.

Doran, Linda, & James Lyttleton (eds), *Lordship in medieval Ireland: image and reality* (Dublin, 2007).

Doran, Linda, 'Lords of the river valleys: economic and military lordship in the Carlow corridor, *c.*1200–1350: European model in an Irish context' in Doran & Lyttleton (eds), *Lordship in medieval Ireland* (2007), pp 99–129.

Dottin, G., 'Le manuscrit irlandais de la bibliothèque de Rennes', *Revue Celtique*, 15 (1894), 79–91.

Douie, Decima, *The conflict between the seculars and the mendicants at the University of Paris in the thirteenth century* (London, 1954).

Dryburgh, Paul, & Brendan Smith, *Inquisitions and extents of medieval Ireland*, Lists and Index Society, vol. 320 (London, 2007).*

Duffner, Patrick, *The Low Lane church: the story of the Augustinians in Drogheda, 1300–1979* (Drogheda, 1979).

Duffy, Eamonn, *The stripping of the altars* (New Haven & London, 1992).

Duffy, Seán, & Linzi Simpson, 'The hermits of St Augustine in Medieval Dublin: their history and archaeology' in John Bradley, Alan Fletcher & Anngret Simms (eds), *Dublin in the medieval world: studies in honour of Howard B. Clarke* (Dublin, 2009), pp 202–48.

Duffy, Seán (ed.), *Robert the Bruce's Irish wars* (Stroud, Gloucestershire, 2002).

Duffy, Seán, 'The Bruce invasion of Ireland: a revised itinerary and chronology' in Duffy (ed.), *Robert the Bruce's Irish wars* (2002), pp 9–43.

Dunne, Laurence, 'Murder, pillage and destruction: archaeological finds from medieval Tralee' in Griffin Murray (ed.), *Medieval treasures of County Kerry* (Tralee, 2010), pp 61–72.

Dwyer, J.A., *The Dominicans of Cork city and county* (Cork, 1896).

Eames, E.S., & Tom Fanning, *Medieval Irish tiles* (Dublin, 1988).

Easson, D.E., *Medieval religious houses: Scotland* (London, 1957).

Edwards, Bede, ODC, *The rule of St Albert* (Aylesford & Kensington, 1973).*

Edwards, R.D., 'The Irish Reformation parliament of Henry VIII, 1536–7', *Historical Studies*, 6 (1968), 59–84.

Egan, Bartholomew, OFM, 'The Carmelite cell of Bealaneny', *JGAHS*, 26 (1954–6), 19–25.

Egan, Bartholomew, OFM, *Franciscan Limerick* (Limerick, 1971).

Egan, K.J., 'Dating English Carmelite foundations' in Patrick Fitzgerald-Lombard (ed.), *Carmel in Britain, 1: people and places* (Rome, 1992), pp 120–42.

Egan, P.K., 'Clonfert diocesan museum and its collections', *JGAHS*, 27 (1956–7), 33–76.

Ellis, Steven, 'The Kildare rebellion and the early Henrician reformation', *Historical Journal*, 19 (1976), 807–30.

Elm, Kaspar (ed.), *Reformbemühungen und Observanzbestrebungen im spätmittelalterlichen Ordenswesen* (Berlin, 1989).

Emden, A.B., *A survey of Dominicans in England based on the ordination lists in episcopal registers (1268 to 1538)* (Rome, 1967).

Emery, William, 'A note on the Friars of the Sack', *Speculum*, 35 (1960), 591–5.

Emery, William, 'The Friars of the Sack', *Speculum*, 18 (1943), 323–34.

Empey, Adrian, 'The Augustinian priory of Kells: an historical introduction' in Tom Fanning & Miriam Clyne (eds), *Kells priory, Co. Kilkenny: archaeological excavations* (Dublin, 2007), pp 1–11.

Erickson, C.M., 'The fourteenth-century Franciscans and their critics', *Franciscan Studies*, 13 (1975), 107–35; 14 (1976), 108–47.

Escobar, Andreas, *Modus confitendi* (Germany, 1474).*

Esposito, Mario (ed.), *Itinerarium Symonis Semeonis ab Hibernia ad Terram Sanctam*, Scriptores Latini Hiberniae, iv (Dublin, 1960).*

Esser, Caietanus (ed.), *Opuscula Sancti Patris Francisci Assisiensis* (Grottaferrata, nr Rome, 1978).*

Etzi, Priamo, OFM, *Iuridica Franciscana* (Padua, 2005).

Evans, G.R. (ed.), *A history of pastoral care* (London, 2000).

Fanning, Tom, & Miriam Clyne (eds), *Kells priory, Co. Kilkenny: archaeological investigations* (Dublin, 2007).

Fawcett, Richard, *Scottish architecture from the accession of the Stewarts to the Reformation, 1371–1560* (Edinburgh, 1994).

Fennessy, Ignatius, OFM, 'Castledermot and the Franciscans', *JCKAHS*, 18 (1998–9), 542–64.

Fennessy, Ignatius, OFM, 'The Franciscan friary at Kildare', *JCKAHS*, 18 (1996/7), 322–36.

Fenning, Hugh, OP (ed.), 'Irish material in the registers of the Dominican masters general (1360–1649)', *Archivum Fratrum Praedicatorum*, 39 (1969), 249–336.*

[Fenning, Hugh, OP], *St Magdalen's Church, Drogheda: centenary, 1878–1978* (Drogheda, 1978).

Fenning, Hugh, OP, 'Founders of Irish Dominican friaries, 1647', *Collectanea Hibernica*, 44 & 45 (2002–3), 56–62.*

Fenning, Hugh, OP, 'The Dominicans of Glanworth, 1474–1814' in M. MacNamara & M. O'Neill (eds), *Glanworth millennium, 2000* (Kilworth, 2000), pp 73–7.

Fenning, Hugh, OP, 'The Dominicans of Galway, 1488–1988' in Eustás Ó Héideáin, *The Dominicans in Galway, 1241–1991* (Galway, 1991), pp 22–36.

Fenning, Hugh, OP, 'The Dominicans of Kilcorban' in Cathal Stanley (ed.), *Kilcorban Priory* (Ballinasloe, 1987), pp 7–17.

Fenning, Hugh, OP, *Dominicans of Athy, 1257–2007* (Athy, 2007).

Fenning, Hugh, OP, *The Black Abbey: the Kilkenny Dominicans, 1225–1996* (Kilkenny, 1996).

Fenning, Hugh, OP, *The Dominicans of Sligo* (Enniscrone, 2002).

Fenning, Hugh, OP, 'The Dominicans of Trim, 1263–1682', *Ríocht na Mídhe*, 3:1 (1963), 15–23.

Fenning, Hugh, OP, *The Waterford Dominicans* (Waterford, 1990).

Fenning, Hugh, OP, 'The Dominicans of Mullingar, 1237–1610', *Ríocht na Mídhe*, 3:2 (1964), 105–13.

Field, W.G., *The handbook for Youghal* (Youghal, 1896).

Fitzmaurice, E.B., & A.G. Little, *Materials for the history of the Franciscan province of Ireland* (Manchester, 1920).*

Fitzmaurice, E.B., 'The Franciscans in Armagh', *Ulster Journal of Archaeology*, 6 (1900), 67–77.

FitzPatrick, Elizabeth, & Caimin O'Brien, *The medieval churches of County Offaly* (Dublin, 1998).

Flanagan, J.G., 'The formative development of the Dominican and Franciscan orders in Ireland, with special reference to the Observant reform' (MA, UCC, 1947).

Flanagan, Marie Therese, *Irish royal charters: texts and contexts* (Oxford, 2005).

Flanagan, U.G., OP, 'Our Lady of Graces, Youghal', *JCHAS*, 55 (1950), 1–14; 56 (1951), 1–10.

Fleming, J.V., *Introduction to the Franciscan literature of the Middle Ages* (Chicago, 1977).

Fletcher, A.J., *Late medieval popular preaching in Britain and Ireland* (Turnhout, 2009).

Fletcher, A.J., & Raymond Gillespie (eds), *Irish preaching, 700–1700* (Dublin, 2001).

Fletcher, A.J., 'Preaching in late-medieval Ireland: the English and Latin tradition' in Fletcher & Gillespie, *Irish preaching* (2001), pp 56–80.

Flower, Robin (ed.), 'The Kilkenny chronicle in Cotton MS Vespasian B XI', *Anal. Hib.*, 2 (1931), 330–40.*

Flower, Robin, *The Irish tradition* (Dublin, 1947).

Flynn, T.S., OP, *The Dominicans of Rosbercon (1267–c.1800)* (Freshford, Co. Kilkenny, 1981).

Flynn, T.S., OP, *The Irish Dominicans, 1536–1641* (Dublin, 1993).

Flynn, T.S., OP, *The Dominicans of Aghaboe, c.1382–c.1782* (Freshford, Co. Kilkenny, 1975).

Foggie, J.P., *Renaissance religion in urban Scotland: the Dominican order, 1450–1560* (Leiden, 2003).

Foley, Edward, 'Franciscan liturgical prayer' in T.J. Johnson (ed.), *Franciscans at prayer* (Leiden, 2007), pp 385–412.

Frame, Robin, 'Power and society in the lordship of Ireland', *Past & Present*, 26 (1977), 3–33.

Freed, J.B, 'The friars and the delineation of state boundaries in the thirteenth century' in W.C. Jordan, Bruce McNab & T.F. Ruiz (eds), *Order and innovation in the Middle Ages* (1976), pp 31–40.

Friends of Ballindoon Abbey, *Ballindoon Abbey, 1507–2007* (Sligo, 2007).

Furlong, Senan, OSB, 'Officium S. Patricii: the medieval office of St Patrick' (MLitt., NUIM, 2008).

Galbraith, G.R., *The constitution of the Dominican order, 1216–1360* (Manchester, 1925).

Gallagher, Niav, 'The Irish Franciscan province: from foundation to the aftermath of the Bruce Invasion' in Michael Robson & Jens Röhrkasten, *Franciscan organisation in the mendicant context* (Berlin, 2010), pp 19–41.

Gallagher, Niav, 'The Franciscans and the Scottish wars of independence; an Irish perspective', *Journal of Medieval History*, 32 (2006), 3–17.

Geary, J.A. (ed.), *An Irish version of Innocent III's* De Contemptu Mundi (Washington, DC, 1931).*

Geary, J.A., 'An Irish homily on confession: text and translation', *Catholic University Bulletin*, 18:4 (1912), 344–66.*

Geraghty, Siobhán, 'The plant remains' in Ann Lynch, *Tintern Abbey, Co. Wexford: Cistercians and Colcloughs, excavations, 1982–2007* (2010), p. 233.

Gerson, John, *Opusculum tripartitum* (Cologne, 1469).*

Giblin, Cathaldus, OFM, 'The Franciscan ministry in the diocese of Clogher', *Clogher Record*, 7:2 (1970), 149–203.

Giblin, Cathaldus, OFM, 'The Franciscans in Elphin', *Roscommon Historical and Archaeological Society Journal*, 2 (1988), 23–9.

Gilbert, J.T., *Chartularies of St Mary's Abbey, Dublin: with the register of its house at Dunbrody, and the annals of Ireland Annals* (2 vols, London, 1884).*

Gilchrist, Roberta, & Barney Sloane, *Requiem: the medieval monastic cemetery in Britain* (London, 2005).

Gilchrist, Roberta, *Contemplation and action: the other monasticism* (London, 1995).

Gillespie, Raymond, 'Irish funeral monuments and social change, 1500–1700: perceptions of death' in Raymond Gillespie & B.P. Kennedy, *Ireland: art into history* (Dublin, 1994), pp 155–68, 236.

Gleeson, D.F., 'The annals of Nenagh', *Anal. Hib.*, 12 (1943), 157–64.*

Gleeson, D.F., 'The Franciscan convent at Nenagh', *Molua* (1938), 18–35.

Gomes, E.X., et al. (eds), *The Carmelite rule, 1207–2007* (Rome, 2008).

Gonzaga, Franciscus, *De origine seraphicae religionis Franciscanae* (Rome, 1587).*

Gonzalez Fuente, Antolin, OP, *La vida liturgica en la orden de Predicadores* (Rome, 1981).

Gormanston: *Calendar of the Gormanston register, c.1175–1397*, ed. James Mills & M.J. McEnery (Dublin, 1916).*

Graham, Brian, 'Anglo-Norman colonization and the size and spread of the colonial town in medieval Ireland' in H.B. Clarke & Anngret Simms (eds), *The comparative history of urban origins in non-Roman Europe: Ireland, Wales, Denmark, Germany, Poland and Russia from the ninth to the thirteenth century* (BAR, International ser., 255, 2 vols, Oxford, 1985), 2, pp 355–72.

Grannell, Fergal, OFM, 'Galway', *Dictionnaire d'histoire et géographie ecclésiastiques*, 19 (Paris, 1981), cols 925–53.

Grannell, Fergal, OFM, *The Franciscans in Athlone* (Athlone, 1978).

Grannell, Fergal, OFM, *The Franciscans in Wexford* (Wexford, n.d.).

Grattan Flood, W.H., 'Irish organ builders from the eighth to the close of the eighteenth century', *JRSAI*, 20 (1910), 229–34.

Grattan Flood, W.H., *History of the diocese of Ferns* (Waterford, 1916).

Greene, J.P., *Medieval monasteries* (Leicester, 1992).

Greene, R.L., *The lyrics of the Red Book of Ossory* (Oxford, 1974).*

Gribbin, J.A., & Colmán Ó Clabaigh (eds), 'Confraternity letters of the Irish Observant Franciscans and their benefactors', *Peritia*, 16 (2002), 459–71.*

Guttiériez, David, OSA, *The Augustinians in the Middle Ages*, 1 vol. in 2 pts (Villanova, 1984).

Gwynn, Aubrey, SJ, 'The medieval university of St Patrick's, Dublin', *Studies*, 27 (1938), 199–212, 437–54.

Gwynn, Aubrey, & Dermot Gleeson, *A history of the diocese of Killaloe* (Dublin, 1962).

Gwynn, Aubrey, SJ, 'A breviary from St Mary's Abbey, Trim', *Ríocht na Mídhe*, 3:4 (1966), 290–8.

Gwynn, Aubrey, SJ, 'Anglo-Irish church life: fourteenth and fifteenth centuries' in P.J. Corish (ed.), *A history of Irish Catholicism*, 2:4 (Dublin, 1968).

Gwynn, Aubrey, SJ, *The English Austin friars in the time of Wyclif* (Oxford, 1940).

Hall, Diane, *Women and the church in medieval Ireland, c.1140–1540* (Dublin, 2003).

Haren, M.J., 'Friars as confessors: the canonist background to the fourteenth-century controversy', *Peritia*, 3 (1984), 503–16.

Haren, M.J., 'Social structures of the Irish church: a new source in the papal penitentiary dispensations for illegitimacy' in Béatrice Wiggenhauser (ed.), *Illegitimät in Spätmittelalter* (Oldenburg, 1995), pp 207–26.

Haren, M.J., 'Richard Fitzralph of Dundalk, Oxford and Armagh: scholar, prelate and controversialist' in James McEvoy & Michael Dunne (eds), *The Irish contribution to European scholastic thought* (Dublin, 2009), pp 88–110.

Haren, M.J., 'Vatican archives as a historical source to 1530', *AH*, 39 (1984), 3–12.

Harline, Craig, & Eddy Put, *A bishop's tale: Mathias Hovius among his flock in seventeenth-century Flanders* (New Haven, CT, 2000).

Harris, Walter (ed. & trans.), *The antiquities and history of Ireland by the Right Honourable Sir James Ware, Knt* (Dublin, 1705).*

Harvey, Barbara, *Living and dying in Medieval England, 1100–1540* (Oxford, 1995).

Hawkes, William, 'The liturgy in Dublin, 1200–1500: manuscript sources', *Reportorium Novum*, 2:1 (1957–8), 33–67.

Hay, John, 'Chronicle of the Observantine province of Scotland' in W. Moir Byrce, *The Scottish Grey Friars* (Edinburgh, 1909), vol. ii, pp 173–83 (text); 184–94 (trans.).*

Hayman, Canon, *Memorials of Youghal, ecclesiastical and civil* (Youghal, 1879).

Hazard, Benjamin, *Faith and patronage: the political career of Flaithrí Ó Maolchonaire, c.1560–1629* (Dublin, 2010).

Henderson, V.K., 'Rethinking Henry VII: the man and his piety in the context of the Observant Franciscans' in D.L. Briggs et al. (eds), *Reputation and representation in fifteenth-century Europe* (Leiden, 2004), pp 317–47.

Henry, P.L., 'The Land of Cokayne: cultures in contact in medieval Ireland', *Studia Hibernica*, 12 (1972), 120–41.

Heuser, W. (ed.), *Die Kildare Gedichte* (Bonn, 1904).*

Hewson, R.F., 'The Augustinian priory, Adare', *North Munster Antiquarian Journal*, 1 (1938), 108–12.

Hinnesbusch, W.A., OP, 'Diplomatic activities of the English Dominicans in the thirteenth century', *Catholic Historical Review*, 28 (1942), 309–39.

Hinnesbusch, W.A., OP, *The early English Friars Preachers* (Rome, 1951).

Hinnesbusch, W.A., OP, *The history of the Dominican order* (2 vols, New York, 1965).

Hogan, Arlene, *Kilmallock Dominican priory: an architectural perspective* (Limerick, 1991).

Hogan, Arlene, *The priory of Llanthony Prima and Secunda in Ireland: lands, patronage and politics, 1172–1541* (Dublin, 2008).

Hourihane, Colum, 'Holye crossys: a catalogue of processional, altar, pendant and crucifix figures for medieval Ireland', *PRIA*, 100C (2000), 1–85

Hourihane, Colum, *The mason and his mark: masons' marks in the medieval Irish archbishoprics of Cashel and Dublin* (BAR 294, 2000).

Hourihane, Colum, 'Foreword' in Moss et al. (eds), *Art and devotion in late medieval Ireland* (2006), pp xvii–xxii.

Howlett, Richard (ed.), *Monumenta Franciscana* (2 vols, London, 1882).*

Huber, R.M., *A documented history of the Franciscan order* (Washington, DC, 1944).

Hudson, Anne, 'The legacy of *Piers Plowman*' in J.A. Alford (ed.), *A companion to Piers Plowman* (Berkeley, CA, 1988), pp 251–66.

Huglo, Michel, 'Comparaison du "prototype" du couvent Saint-Jacques de Paris avec l'exemplaire personnel du maître de l'Ordre des Prêcheurs (Londres, BL Add. MS 23935)' in Boyle et al. (eds), *Aux origines de la liturgie Dominicaine* (2004), pp 197–214.

Hugonis de Foliceto, 'De claustro animae', *Patrologia Latina*, 176 (Paris, 1880), cols 1017–1182.*

Humbert of Romans OP, 'Expositio super constitutiones FF Predicatorum' in Joachim Joseph Berthier OP (ed.), *Opera de vita regulari*, ii (Turin, 1956), pp 1–175.*

Humbert of Romans OP, 'Instructiones Magistri Humberti de officiis Ordinis' in J.J. Berthier OP (ed.), *Opera de vita regulari*, ii (Turin, 1956), pp 179–371.*

Humphreys, K.W., *The book provisions of the medieval friars* (Amsterdam, 1974).

Humphreys, K.W., *The friars' libraries* (London, 1990).

Hunt, John, & Peter Harbison, 'Medieval English alabasters in Ireland', *Studies*, 65 (1976), 310–21.

Hunt, John, 'The influence of alabaster carvings on medieval sculpture in Ennis friary', *North Munster Antiquarian Journal*, 17 (1975), 35–41.

Hunt, John, *Irish medieval figure sculpture* (2 vols, Dublin, 1974).

Hüntemann, U., & C. Schmitt (eds), *Bullarium Franciscanum continens constitutiones epistolas diplomata Romanorum pontificum, nova series* (Quarrachi, nr Florence, 1929–).*

Hurley, M.F., & C.M. Sheehan, *Excavations at the Dominican priory, St Mary's of the Isle, Crosse's Green, Cork* (Cork, 1995).

*Il papato duecentesco e gli ordini mendicanti: atti del 25. Convegno internazionale, Assisi, 13–14 febbraio.* Società internazionale di studi francescani (1998).

Jacques, Paul, 'La signification sociale du Franciscanisme' in André Vauchez (ed.), *Mouvements franciscains de société française, XII–XX siècle* (Paris, 1984), pp 9–25.

James, M.R., & Claude Jenkins, *A descriptive catalogue of the manuscripts in the library of Lambeth palace* (Cambridge, 1937).

Jefferies, H.A., 'Nangle, Richard', *ODNB*, 40 (Oxford, 2004), p. 141.

Jefferies, H.A., 'The role of the laity in the parishes of Armagh *inter anglicos*, 1518–1553', *AH*, 52 (1998), 73–84.

Jefferies, H.A., *Priests and prelates of Armagh in the age of reformations* (Dublin, 1997).

Jeffrey, D.L., 'Authors, anthologists and Franciscan spirituality' in Susanna Kein (ed.), *The scribes, contents and social contexts of British Library MS Harley 2253* (Kalamazoo, MI, 2000), pp 261–70.

Jeffrey, D.L., *The early English lyric and Franciscan spirituality* (Lincoln, 1975).

Jennings, Brendan (ed.), 'Brevis Synopsis Provnciae Hiberniae FF Minorum', *Anal. Hib.*, 6 (1934), 139–91.*

Jennings, Brendan (ed.), *Wadding papers, 1614–38* (Dublin, 1953).*

Jennings, Brendan, 'The abbey of St Francis, Galway', *JGAHS*, 22 (1947), 101–19.

Johnson, Dorothy, 'Richard II and the submissions of Gaelic Ireland', *IHS*, 22:85 (1985), 1–20.

Johnson, T.J. (ed.), *Franciscans at prayer* (Leiden, 2007).

Jones, David, *Friars' tales: thirteenth-century exempla from the British Isles* (Manchester, 2011).

Jotischky, Andrew, *The Carmelites and antiquity: mendicants and their pasts in the Middle Ages* (Oxford, 2002).

Kaeppelli, Thomas, OP, *Scriptores Ordinis Praedicatorum medii aevi* (4 vols, Rome, 1980).

Kallenberg, Paschalis, *Fontes liturgiae Carmelitanae* (Rome, 1962).

Kavanagh, M., 'The White Friars and the white castle of Leighlin', *Carloviana*, 43 (1996 for 1995), 24–6.

Kearns, Conleth, 'Medieval Dominicans and the Irish language', *Irish Ecclesiastical Record*, 94 (1960), 17–38.

Kehnel, Annette, 'The narrative tradition of the medieval Franciscan friars in the British Isles: introduction to the sources', *Franciscan Studies*, 63 (2005), 461–530.

Kelly, David, OSA, 'The arrival of the Augustinian canons and the Augustinian friars in Britain', *Canterbury Studies in Franciscan History*, 2 (2009), pp 201–7.

Kelly, David, OSA, 'The Augustinians in Dublin', *DHR*, 58:2 (2005), 166–75.

Kelly, Maria, *A history of the Black Death in Ireland* (Stroud, Gloucestershire, 2001).

Kelly, Maria, *The great dying: the Black Death in Dublin* (Stroud, Gloucestershire, 2003).

Kerby-Fulton, Kathryn, & D. Despres, *Iconography and the professional reader: the politics of book production in the Douce Piers Plowman* (Minneapolis, MN, 1999).

Kerby-Fulton, Kathryn, & Steven Justice, 'Langlandian reading circles and the civil service in London and Dublin, 1380–1427', *New Medieval Literatures*, 1 (1997), 59–83.

Kerby-Fulton, Kathryn, 'Professional readers of Langland at home and abroad: new directions in the political and bureaucratic codicology of *Piers Plowman*' in Derek Pearsall (ed.), *New directions in later medieval manuscript studies* (Woodbridge, 2000), pp 103–29.

Kildare, Marquis of, *The earls of Kildare and their ancestors from 1057 to 1773* (Dublin, 1864).

Knott, Eleanor (ed.), *Tadhg Dall Ó hUiginn* (2 vols, London, 1922).*

Knowles, David, & R.N. Hadcock, *Medieval religious houses: England and Wales* (London, 1971).

Knowles, David, *The religious orders in England*, I (Cambridge, 1948).

Krasnodebska-D'Aughton, Malgorzata, 'Franciscan chalices, 1600–50' in Bhreathnach et al. (eds), *The Irish Franciscans* (2009), pp 287–304.

Lambert, M.D., *Franciscan poverty: the doctrine of the absolute poverty of Christ and the apostles in the Franciscan order, 1210–1323* (St Bonaventure, NY, 1998).

Langland, William, *Piers Plowman: a new annotated edition of the C text*, ed. Derek Pearsall (Exeter, 2008).

Lawlor, H.J., 'The calendar of the Liber Niger and the Liber Albus of Christ Church, Dublin', *PRIA*, 27 (1908/9), 1–93.*

Lawlor, H.J., 'The Kilcormic Missal: a manuscript in the library of Trinity College, Dublin', *Transactions of the Royal Irish Academy*, 31 (Dublin, 1900), 393–430.

Lawrence, C.H., *The friars: the impact of the early mendicant movement on Western society* (London, 1994).

Leask, H.G., 'Donegal Abbey: the buildings' in T. O'Donnell, *Franciscan Donegal* (1952), pp 53–7.

Leask, H.G., *Irish churches and monastic buildings* (3 vols, Dundalk, 1955–60).

Leclercq, Jean, & A. Boni, 'Noviziato i & ii', *Dizionario degli instituti di perfezione*, vi (Rome, 1980), cols 442–60.

Lemaître, H., 'Statuts des religieuses du Tiers Ordre Franciscain dites soeurs grises hospitaliers', *AFH*, 4 (1911), 713–31.*

Lennon, Colm, 'The confraternities and cultural duality in Ireland, 1450–1550' in Christopher Black & Pamela Gravestock (eds), *Early modern confraternities in Europe and the Americas* (Aldershot, 2006), pp 35–52.

Lennon, Colm, 'The dissolution to the foundation of St Anthony's College, Louvain, 1534–1607' in Bhreathnach et al. (eds), *The Irish Franciscans* (2009), pp 3–26.

Lennon, Colm, 'The parish fraternities of County Meath in the late Middle Ages', *Ríocht na Midhe*, 19 (2008), 85–101.

Lennon, Colm, *Archbishop Richard Creagh of Armagh, 1523–1586* (Dublin, 2000).

Lennon, Colm, 'The Book of Obits of Christ Church Cathedral, Dublin' in Raymond Gillespie & Raymond Refaussé (eds), *The medieval manuscripts of Christ Church Cathedral, Dublin* (Dublin, 2006), pp 163–82.

Lerner, R.E., *The powers of prophecy: the cedar of Lebanon vision from the Mongol onslaught to the dawn of the enlightenment* (Ithaca, NY, 1983).

Lippens, Hugolin, OFM, 'De litteris confraternitatis apud Fratres Minorum ab Ordinis initio ad annum usque 1517', *AFH*, 32 (1939), 49–88.*

Lippens, Hugolin, OFM, 'Le droit nouveau des mendiants en conflit avec le droit coutumier du clergé séculier du concile de Vienne à celui de Trente', *AFH*, 47 (1954), 241–92.

Little, A.G. (ed.), 'A letter of Fr Angelus Christophori, minister general, appointing an Irish friar to a studentship at Oxford, c.AD1450', *AFH*, 23 (1930), 267–8.*

Little, A.G. (ed.), *Fratris Thomae (vulgo dicti de Eccleston) tractatus De Adventu Fratrum Minorum in Angliam* (Manchester, 1951).*

Little, A.G., 'Introduction of the Observant friars into England: a bull of Alexander VI', *Proceedings of the British Academy*, 10 (1921–3), 155–66.*

Little, A.G., 'The Franciscans and the Statute of Mortmain', *English Historical Record*, 49 (1934), 673–6.

Little, A.G., *Franciscan history and legend in English medieval art* (Manchester, 1937).

Little, A.G. (ed.), *Liber exemplorum ad usum predicantium saeculo xiii compositus a quodam Fratre Minore Anglico de provincia Hiberniae* (Aberdeen, 1918).*

Little, A.G., *Studies in English Franciscan history* (Manchester, 1917).

Little, L.K., *Religious poverty and the profit economy in medieval Europe* (London, 1978).

Logan, D.F., *Runaway religious in medieval England, c.1240–1540* (Cambridge, 1996).

Longère, J., *La prédication médiévale* (Paris, 1983).

Lucas, A.M. (ed.), *Anglo-Irish poems of the Middle Ages* (Dublin, 1995).

Lydon, J.F., 'The case against Alexander Bicknor, archbishop and peculator' in Brendan Smith (ed.), *Ireland the English world in the Late Middle Ages* (London, 2009), pp 103–11.

Lydon, J.F., 'The impact of the Bruce invasion' in Art Cosgrove (ed.), *A new history of Ireland*, ii: *Medieval Ireland, 1169–1534* (Oxford, 1987), pp 275–302.

Lynch, Anthony (ed.), 'Documents of Franciscan interest from the episcopal archives of Armagh, 1265–1508', *Collectanea Hibernica*, 31/2 (1989/90), 9–102.*

Lyons, Mary Ann, 'FitzGerald, Thomas ('Silken Thomas'), *DIB*, 3 (Cambridge, 2009), pp 912–15.

Lyons, Mary Ann, 'Lay female piety and church patronage in late medieval Ireland' in Brendan Bradshaw & Dáire Keogh (eds), *Christianity in Ireland: revisiting the story* (Dublin, 2002), pp 57–75.

Lyons, Mary Ann, 'St Anthony's College, Louvain, and the Irish Franciscan college network' in Bhreathnach et al. (eds), *The Irish Franciscans* (2009), pp 27–44.

Lyons, Mary Ann, 'The foundation of the Geraldine college of the Blessed Virgin Mary, Maynooth, 1518', *JCKAHS*, 18 (1994–5), 134–50.

Mac Airt, Seán, *The annals of Inisfallen* (Dublin, 1951).*

Macalister, R.A.S., 'The Dominican church at Athenry', *JRSAI*, 43 (1913), 196–222.

McConville, S. (ed.), *The Dominicans in Kerry, 1243–1987* (Tralee, 1987).

McCormack, A.M., 'Nangle, Richard', *DIB*, 6 (Cambridge, 2009), p. 856.

McCorristine, Laurence, *The revolt of Silken Thomas: a challenge to Henry VIII* (Dublin, 1987).

Mac Craith, Mícheál, "'*Collegium S. Antonii Lovanii, quod Collegium est unicum remedium ad conservandum Provinciam*" (Donnchadh Ó Maonaigh, 1617–18)' in Bhreathnach et al. (eds), *The Irish Franciscans* (2009), pp 233–59.

McCutcheon, Clare, 'Pottery' in Hurley & Sheehan, *Excavations at the Dominican priory* (1995), pp 85–96.

McCutcheon, Clare, 'Pottery' in Shee Twohig, 'Excavations at St Saviour's Dominican priory, Limerick, part II' (1996), pp 65–72.

McDermott, Yvonne, 'The Dominican priory of Burrishoole: an "irregular" foundation of the lower MacWilliam Burkes', *Cathair na Mart*, 28 (2010), 4–16.

McDermott, Yvonne, 'Returning to core principles', *History Ireland*, 15:1 (2007), 12–17.

McDermott, Yvonne, 'Strade friary: patronage and development at a medieval mendicant friary, *Cathair na Mart*, 27 (2009), 92–108.

McDermott, Yvonne, 'The priory of the Holy Cross, Cloonshanville: a fourteenth-century Dominican foundation', *County Roscommon Historical and Archaeological Journal*, 11 (2009), 22–5.

Mac Donncha, Frederic, *The abbey of St Francis, Galway* (Galway, n.d. [1971]).

MacDonnell, H., 'Glenarm friary and the Bissets', *The Glynns*, 15 (1987), 34–49.

McEneaney, Eamonn, 'Politics and the art of devotion in late fifteenth-century Waterford' in R. Moss et al. (eds), *Art and devotion* (2006), pp 33–50.

McEneaney, Eamonn, & Rosemary Ryan, *Waterford treasures* (Waterford, 2004), pp 108–9.

McEnery, M.J., & Raymond Refaussé (eds), *Christ Church deeds* (Dublin, 2001).*

McEvoy, James, & Michael Dunne (eds), *The Irish contribution to European scholastic thought* (Dublin, 2009).

McEvoy, James, 'Minor scholastics of Irish origin up to 1500' in McEvoy & Dunne (eds), *The Irish contribution* (2009), pp 111–26.

Mac Fhinn, P.E., *Mílic* (Baile Átha Cliath, 1943).

Mac Firbis, Duald, 'The annals of Ireland, from the year 1443 to 1468' (Dublin, 1846).*

MacGrath, Fergal, *Education in ancient and medieval Ireland* (Dublin, 1979).

MacInerney, M.H., OP, *A history of the Irish Dominicans, vol. 1. Irish Dominican bishops, 1224–1307* (Dublin, 1916).

Mac Íomhair, Diarmuid, 'The Carmelites in Ardee', *CLAHJ*, 20 (1983), 180–9.

McKenna, Lambert, SJ (ed.), 'A Franciscan to St Dominic', *Irish Monthly* (Aug. 1929), 435–9.*

McKenna, Lambert, SJ (ed.), *Philip Bocht O Huiginn* (Dublin, 1931).*

McKenna, Lambert, SJ, *Dán Dé: the poems of Donnchadh Mór Ó Dalaigh, and the religious poems in the duanaire of the Yellow Book of Lecan* (Dublin, 1922).*

McKeon, Jim, 'The Dominican priory of SS Peter and Paul, Athenry: high-medieval history and architecture', *JGAHS*, 61 (2009), 24–56.

McKiernan, F.J., *St Mary's Abbey, Cavan* (Cavan, 2000).

MacLeod, Caitriona, 'Medieval figure sculpture in Ireland: statues in the Holy Ghost Hospital, Waterford', *JRSAI*, 76 (1946), 89–100.

McMahon, Michael, *Portumna priory* (Portumna, 1985).

MacNamee, J.J., *History of the diocese of Ardagh* (Dublin, 1954).

McNeill, Charles (ed.), 'Harris: *Collectanea de rebus Hibernicis*', *Anal. Hib.*, 6 (1934), 248–450.

McNeill, Charles (ed.), *Registrum de Kilmainham, 1326–39* (Dublin, 1932).*

McNeill, Charles (ed.), *Liber primus Kilkenniensis* (Dublin, 1931).*

McNeill, T.E., 'The larger castles of later medieval Limerick' in Stalley (ed.), *Limerick and the south-west of Ireland* (2011), pp 176–88.

Mac Niocaill, Gearóid (ed.), 'The *Registrum cantariae S. Salvatoris Waterfordensis*', *Anal. Hib.*, 23 (1966), 135–222.*

Mac Niocaill, Gearóid (ed.), *Crown surveys of lands, 1540–41, with the Kildare rental begun in 1518* (Dublin 1992).*

Mac Niocaill, Gearóid, 'Uilliam Ó Raghallaigh OFM', *Irisleabhar Maighe Nuadhat* (1961), 47–9.

Mac Niocaill, Gearóid, *The medieval Irish annals* (Dublin, 1975).

MacVicar, Thaddeus, *The Franciscan spirituals and the Capuchin reform* (New York, 1986).

Maher, Denise, *Kilcrea friary: Franciscan heritage in County Cork* (Ballincollig, 1999).

Manning, Conleth, *The history and archaeology of Glanworth Castle, Co. Cork: excavations, 1982–4* (Dublin, 2010).

Mapelli, F.J., *L'amministrazione Francescana di Inghilterra e Francia* (Rome, 2003).

Martin, A.R., *Franciscan architecture in England* (Manchester, 1937).

Martin, F.X., OSA, & Alberic de Meijer OSA (eds), 'Irish material in the Augustinian general archives, Rome, 1354–1624', *AH*, 19 (1956), 61–134.*

Martin, F.X., OSA, 'An Irish Augustinian disputes at Oxford: Adam Payn, 1402' in Cornelius Petrus Mayer & Willigis Eckermann (eds), *Scientia Augustiniana* (Würzburg, 1975), pp 289–322.

Martin, F.X., OSA, 'Murder in a Dublin monastery, 1379' in Gearóid Mac Niocaill & P.F. Wallace (eds), *Keimelia* (Galway, 1988), pp 468–98.

Martin, F.X., OSA, 'The Augustinian friaries in pre-Reformation Ireland (1280–1500)', *Augustiniana*, 6 (1956), 346–84.

Martin, F.X., OSA, 'The Augustinian Observant movement' in Elm (ed.), *Reform-bemühungen* (1989), pp 325–45.

Martin, F.X., OSA, 'The Irish Augustinian reform movement in the fifteenth century' in J.A. Watt, J.B. Morrall & F.X. Martin (eds), *Medieval studies presented to Aubrey Gwynn SJ* (Dublin, 1961), pp 230–64.

Martin, F.X., OSA, 'The Irish friars and the Observant movement in the fifteenth century', *Proceedings of the Irish Catholic Historical Committee*, 6 (1960), 10–16.

Martin, F.X., OSA, *Friar Nugent: a study of Francis Lavalin Nugent (1569–1635)* (Rome, 1962).

Massey, Eithne, *Prior Roger Outlaw of Kilmainham, 1314–1341* (Dublin, 2000).

Mattingly, Garret, *Catherine of Aragon* (London, 1963),

Meehan, C.P., *The rise, increase and exit of the Geraldines, earls of Desmond* (Dublin, 1878).*

Meersseman, G.G., *Dossier de l'ordre de la pénitence au XIIIe siècle* (Fribourg, 1981).*

Merlo, G.G., 'Eremitismo nel francescanesimo medievale', *Eremitismo nel francescanesimo medievale* (1991), 27–50.

Mhág Craith, Cuthbert, *Dán na mBráthar Mionúr* (2 vols, Dublin, 1967; repr. 1980).*

Michaud-Quantin, P. *Sommes de casuistique et manuels de confession au moyen âge (XII–XV siècles)* (Louvain, Lille & Montréal, 1962).

Millett, Benignus, OFM, 'The Franciscans in County Wicklow', *AFH*, 77 (1984), 110–36.

Millett, Benignus, OFM, 'The Irish Franciscans and education in late medieval times and in the early Counter-Reformation', *Seanchas Ardmhacha*, 18 (2001), 1–30.

Millett, Benignus, OFM, 'The translation work of the Irish Franciscans', *Seanchas Ardmhacha*, 17 (1996–7), 1–25.

Mills, James (ed.), *Account roll of the priory of the Holy Trinity, Dublin, 1337–1346* (Dublin, 1891).*

Mills, James (ed.), *Calendar of the justiciary rolls or proceedings in the court of the justiciar of Ireland, 1295–1303* (Dublin, 1905).*

Moir Bryce, William (ed.), *The Scottish Grey Friars* (2 vols, Edinburgh & London, 1909).*

Monsignano, Eliseo, *Bullarium Carmelitanum* (2 vols, Rome, 1715).*

Montague, John, 'The cloister arcade' in Fanning & Clyne, *Kells priory* (2007), pp 187–206.

Mooney, Canice, OFM, 'Franciscan architecture in pre-Reformation Ireland', I, *JRSAI*, 85 (1955), 133–73; II, 86 (1956), 125–69; III, 87 (1957), 1–39; IV, 87 (1957), 103–24.

Mooney, Canice, OFM, 'The founding of the friary of Donegal', *Donegal Annual*, 3 (1954–5), 15–23.

Mooney, Canice, OFM, 'The Franciscan Third Order friary at Dungannon', *Seanchas Ardmhacha*, 1 (1954–5), 12–23.

Mooney, Canice, OFM, 'The Franciscans in Waterford', *JCHAS*, 49 (1964), 73–93.

Mooney, Canice, OFM, 'The friars and friary of Donegal, 1474–1840' in O'Donnell, *Franciscan Donegal* (1952), pp 3–49.

Mooney, Canice, OFM, 'The friary of Ross: foundation and early years', *JGAHS*, 39 (1960–1), 7–14.

Mooney, Canice, OFM, 'The mirror of all Ireland' in O'Callaghan (ed.), *Franciscan Cork* (1953), pp 5–26, 97–100.

Mooney, Canice, OFM, *Devotional writings of the Irish Franciscans, 1224–1950* (Dublin, 1952).

Mooney, Canice, OFM, *Irish Franciscans and France* (Dublin, 1964).

Moorman, J.R.H., *The sources for the life of S. Francis of Assisi* (Manchester, 1940).

Moran, Josephine, 'The shattered image: archaeological evidence for painted and stained glass in medieval Ireland' in Moss et al. (eds), *Art and devotion* (2006), pp 121–41.

Morey, Adrian, *Bartholomew of Exeter: bishop and canonist* (Cambridge, 1937).

Mortier, R.P., *Histoire des maîtres généraux de l'ordre des frères prêcheurs* (7 vols, Paris, 1903–20).

Morton, Karena, 'Iconography and dating of the wall paintings' in Conleth Manning et al. (eds), *New survey of Clare Island, vol. 4: the abbey* (Dublin, 2005), pp 97–122.

Morton, Karena, 'Later medieval Irish wall paintings, *c.*1100–*c.*1600AD' (PhD, UCD, 2007).

Moss, Rachel, 'Dominican order' in *Dictionary of Irish art* (forthcoming).

Moss, Rachel, 'Permanent expression of piety: the secular and the sacred in later medieval stone sculpture' in R. Moss et al. (eds), *Art and devotion* (2006), pp 72–97.

Moss, Rachel, Colmán Ó Clabaigh & Salvador Ryan (eds), *Art and devotion in late medieval Ireland* (Dublin, 2006).

Motta Navarro, Thomas, *Tertii Carmelitici saecularis ordinis historico-iuridicia evolutio* (Rome, 1960).

Mulchahey, M.M., *First the bow is bent in study: Dominican education before 1350* (Toronto, 1998).

Müller, Anne, 'Conflicting loyalties: the Irish Franciscans and the English crown in the High Middle Ages', *PRIA*, 107C (2007), 87–106.

Müller, Anne, 'Managing crises: institutional re-stabilisation of the religious orders in England after the Black Death (1347–1350)', *Revue Mabillon*, n.s. 16 (77) (2005), 205–19.

Müller, Anne, 'Nationale Abgrenzung in universalen Verbänden Zur Entwicklung und Autonomiebestrebung der schottishen Franziskaner im 13. und 14. Jarhundert' (2004) in Reinhardt Butz & Jörg Oberste (eds), *Studia monastica: beiträge zum klösterlichen Leben in Mittelalter*, Vita regularis, 22 (Münster, 2004), pp 261–85.

Murphy, Margaret, & Michael Potterton, *The Dublin region in the Middle Ages: settlement, land-use and economy* (Dublin, 2010).

Murphy, Margaret, & Michael Potterton, 'Investigating living standards in medieval Dublin and its region' in Seán Duffy (ed.), *Medieval Dublin VI* (2005), pp 224–56.

Murphy, Margaret, 'The high cost of dying: an analysis of *pro anima* bequests in medieval Dublin', *Studies in Church History*, 24: *The church and wealth* (Oxford, 1987), pp 111–22.

Murray, James, 'Browne, George', *ODNB*, 8 (Oxford, 2004), pp 161–2.

Murray, James, *Enforcing the English Reformation in Ireland* (Cambridge, 2009).

Murray, L.P., & Aubrey Gwynn, 'Archbishop Cromer's register', *CLAHJ*, 7 (1929–32), 516–24; 8 (1933–6), 38–49, 169–88, 257–74, 322–51; 9 (1937–40), 36–41, 124–30; 10 (1941–4), 116–27, 165–79.*

Neary, Anne, 'Richard Ledrede: English Franciscan bishop of Ossory', *Butler Society Journal*, 2 (1984), 273–82.

Netter, Thomas, *Fasciculi zizaniorum magistri Johannis Wyclif cum tritico*, ed. W.W. Shirley (London, 1858).*

Nicholls, K.W., 'The Lisgoole agreement of 1580', *Clogher Record*, 7:1 (1960), 27–33.*

Nicholson, Helen, 'The trial of the Templars in Ireland' in Jochen Burgtorf, P.F. Crawford & H.J. Nicholson (eds), *The debate on the trial of the Templars (1307–1314)* (Farnham, Surrey, 2010), pp 225–35.

Nicholson, Helen, 'The testimony of Brother Henry Danet and the trial of the Templars in Ireland' in Iris Shagrir, Ronnie Ellenblum & Jonathan Riley-Smith (eds), *In Laudem Hierosolymitani: Studies in Crusades and medieval culture in honour of Benjamin Z. Kedar*, Crusades Subsidia, 1 (Aldershot, 2008), pp 411–23.

Nicholson, Helen, *The Knights Templar on trial: the trial of the Templars in the British Isles, 1308–1311* (Stroud, Gloucestershire, 2009).

Nimmo, Duncan, *Reform and division in the medieval Franciscan order* (Rome, 1987).

Nolan, Myles, OP, *St Saviour's priory, Limerick, 1227–1977* (Limerick, 1977).

O'Callaghan, Jerome, OFM (ed.), *Franciscan Cork* (Cork, 1953).

O'Carroll, Maura, SND, 'The lectionary for the proper of the year in the Dominican and Franciscan rites of the thirteenth century', *Archivum Fratrum Praedicatorum*, 49 (1979), 79–104.

Ó Catháin, Diarmaid (ed.), 'Some Augustinian material in Irish', *Augustiniana*, 48 (1998), 31–9.*

Ó Clabaigh, Colmán, OSB, 'Anchorites in late medieval Ireland' in Elizabeth Herbert-McAvoy, *Anchoritic traditions of medieval Europe* (Woodbridge, 2010), pp 153–77.

Ó Clabaigh, Colmán, OSB, 'Friar Maurice Hanlan, his books and the Franciscan *studium* in Youghal' in Peter Harbison & Valerie Hall (eds), *A carnival of learning': George Cunningham and his fifty medieval conferences in Mt St Joseph Roscrea, 1987–2012* (forthcoming, 2012).

Ó Clabaigh, Colmán, OSB, 'Patronage, politics and prestige: the Observant Franciscans at Adare' in Janet Burton & Karen Stöber (eds), *Monasteries and society in the British Isles in the later Middle Ages* (Woodbridge, 2008), pp 71–82.

Ó Clabaigh, Colmán, OSB, 'Preaching in late medieval Ireland: the Franciscan contribution' in Fletcher & Gillespie, *Irish preaching* (2001), pp 81–93.

Ó Clabaigh, Colmán, OSB, 'The other Christ: the cult of St Francis of Assisi in late medieval Ireland' in Moss et al. (eds), *Art and devotion* (2006), pp 142–62.

Ó Clabaigh, Colmán, OSB, 'The Benedictines in medieval and early modern Ireland' in Martin Browne & Colmán Ó Clabaigh (eds), *The Irish Benedictines: a history* (Dublin, 2005), pp 79–121.

Ó Clabaigh, Colmán, OSB, *The Franciscans in Ireland, 1400–1534* (Dublin, 2002).

Ó Clabaigh, Colmán, OSB, 'The mendicant friars in the medieval diocese of Clonfert', *JGAHS*, 59 (2007), 25–36.

Ó Conbhuidhe, Colmcille, OCSO, 'Decline and attempted reform of the Irish Cistercians (1445–1531)' in idem, *Studies in Irish Cistercian history* (Dublin, 1998), pp 1–47.

O'Connor, John, *The Galway Augustinians* (Ballyboden, nr Dublin, 1979).

O'Conor, Kieran, 'Medieval rural settlement in Munster', *Barryscourt Lectures, 1–10* (Kinsale, 2004), pp 227–56.

O'Conor, Kieran, Mark Keegan & Padraig Tiernan, 'Tulsk Abbey', *County Roscommon Historical and Archaeological Society Journal*, 6 (1996), 67–9.

Ó Dálaigh, Brian, 'Mistress, mother and abbess: Renalda Ní Bhriain (*c*.1447–1510)', *North Munster Antiquarian Journal*, 32 (1990), 50–63.

O'Daly, Dominic de Rosario, OP, *Initium, incrementa, et exitus Familiae Geraldinorum Desmoniae Comitum, Palatinorum Kyrriae in Hybernia* (Lisbon, 1655).*

Ó Domhnaill, Seán, 'Some notes on the Third Order Regular houses in Donegal' in O'Donnell (ed.), *Franciscan Donegal* (1952), pp 97–107.

O'Donnell, Christopher, OCarm., 'Mary and the liturgy' in Kevin Alban (ed.), *Fons et culmen vitae Carmelitanae* (Rome, 2007), pp 167–93.

O'Donnell, Terence, *Franciscan Donegal* (Ros Nuala, Donegal, 1952).

O'Donnell, Terence, *The Franciscan friary at Multyfarnham* (Multyfarnham, Co. Westmeath, 1951).

O'Donoghue, Aisling, 'Mendicant cloisters in Munster' in Stalley (ed.), *Limerick and the south-west of Ireland* (2011), pp 111–31.

O'Donovan, Danielle, 'Building the Butler lordship, 1405–*c*.1552' (PhD, TCD, 2007).

O'Donovan, Danielle, 'Holycross and the language of Irish Late Gothic in Munster' in Stalley (ed.), *Limerick and the south-west of Ireland* (2011), pp 132–57.

O'Dowd, Peadar, 'Holy wells of Galway city', *JGAHS*, 60 (2008), 138–45.

O'Dwyer, Barry, 'The problem of reform in the Irish Cistercian monasteries and the attempted solution of Stephen of Lexington in 1228', *Journal of Ecclesiastical History*, 15 (1964), 186–91.

O'Dwyer, Peter, OCarm., *Mary: a history of devotion in Ireland* (Dublin, 1990).

O'Dwyer, Peter, OCarm., *The Irish Carmelites (of the ancient observance)* (Dublin, 1988).

O'Flaherty, Roderick, *A chorographical description of west or H-Iar Connaught*, rev. ed. James Hardiman (Dublin, 1846).*

Ó Floinn, Raghnall, 'Irish Franciscan church furnishings in the pre-Reformation period' in Raghnall Ó Floinn (ed.), *Franciscan faith: sacred art in Ireland, AD1600–1750* (Dublin, 2011), pp 7–19.

Ó Floinn, Raghnall, 'The Lislaughtin Cross' in Griffin Murray (ed.), *Medieval treasures of County Kerry* (Tralee, 2010), pp 82–96.

Ó Gibealláin, Athanasius, 'The Franciscan friary of Kilcrea' in M. Ó Murchú (ed.), *Kilcrea friary: 1465–1965* (Kilcrea, 1965), pp 9–26.

O'Grady, S.H., & Robin Flower, *Catalogue of the Irish manuscripts in the British Museum* (3 vols, London, 1926–53).

O'Grady, S.H., *Caithréim Thoirdhealbhaigh* (Dublin, 1929).*

Ó Héideáin, Eustás, *The Dominicans in Galway, 1241–1991* (Galway, 1991).

O'Heyne, John, OP, *Epilogus chronologicus* (Louvain, 1706).*

Ó Maonaigh, Cainneach, OFM (ed.), *Smaointe beatha Chríost* (Baile Átha Cliath, 1944).*

Ó Maonaigh, Cainneach, OFM, 'Ciníochas agus náisiúnachas san eaglais in Éirinn, 1169–1534', *Galvia*, 10 (1964–5), 4–17.

Ó Maonaigh, Cainneach, OFM, 'Scríbhneoirí Gaeilge Oird San Fronsias' in Benignus Millett & Anthony Lynch (eds), *Dún Mhure, Killiney, 1945–95* (Dublin, 1995), pp 8–13.

Ombres, Robert, OP, 'L'autorità religiosa nei Frati Predicatori come Ordine Mendicante', *Angelicum*, 85 (2008), 947–63.

O'Neill, Michael, 'Irish Franciscan friary architecture: late medieval and early modern' in Bhreathnach et al. (eds), *The Irish Franciscans* (2009), pp 305–27.

Ó Riain, Diarmuid, OFM, *The Moor Abbey, Galbally: the Franciscans in the parish of Galbally and Aherlow* (1992).

Ó Riain, Pádraig, 'Deascán lámhscríbhinní: a manuscript miscellany', *JCHAS*, 108 (2003), 62–8.

Ó Riain, Pádraig, 'The Louvain achievement II: hagiography' in Bhreathnach et al. (eds), *The Irish Franciscans* (2009), pp 189–200.

Ó Riain, Pádraig, *Feastdays of the saints: a history of Irish martyrologies* (Brussels, 2006).

Ó Siochrú, Micheál, 'Foreign involvement in the revolt of Silken Thomas', *PRIA*, 96 (1996), 49–66.

Ó Súilleabháin, Pádraig (ed.), *Rialachas San Fronsias* (Dublin, 1953).*

O'Sullivan, Benedict, OP, 'The Dominicans in medieval Dublin' in H.B. Clarke (ed.), *Medieval Dublin: the living city* (Dublin, 1990), pp 83–99.

O'Sullivan, Benedict, OP, 'The Dominicans in medieval Dublin', *DHR*, 9:2 (1947), 41–58.

O'Sullivan, Benedict, OP, *Medieval Irish Dominican studies*, ed. Hugh Fenning OP (Dublin, 2009).

O'Sullivan, C.M., *Hospitality in medieval Ireland, 900–1500* (Dublin, 2004).

O'Sullivan, Denis (ed.), 'The testament of John de Wynchedon of Cork anno 1306', *JCHAS*, 61:2 (1956), 75–88.*

O'Sullivan, Denis, 'The Augustinian convent of medieval Cork', *JCHAS*, 46 (1941), 144–5.

O'Sullivan, Denis, 'Youghal, the first house of the Friars Minor in Ireland' in O'Callaghan (ed.), *Franciscan Cork* (Cork, 1953), pp 28–33, 95.

O'Sullivan, Harold, 'The Franciscans in Dundalk', *Seanchas Ard Mhacha*, 4:1 (1960–1), 33–71.

O'Sullivan, Jerry, Julie Roberts & Stuart Halliday, 'Archaeological excavation of medieval, post-medieval and modern burials at Ennis Friary, Co. Clare', *North Munster Antiquarian Journal*, 43 (2003), 21–42.

O'Sullivan, William, 'A finding list of Sir James Ware's manuscripts', *PRIA*, 97C (1997), 2–99.

O'Sullivan, William, 'Ware, Sir James', *DIB*, 9 (Cambridge, 2009), pp 798–9.

Parisciani, Gustavo, OFM Conv. (ed.), *Regesta Ordinis Fratrum Minorum Conventualium*, 1: *1484–1494* (Padua, 1989).*

Parisciani, Gustavo, OFM Conv. (ed.), *Regesta Ordinis Fratrum Minorum Conventualium*, 2: *1504–1506* (Padua, 1998).*

Pazzelli, Raffaele, *St Francis and the Third Order* (Chicago, 1991).

Pearsall, Derek, & Kathleen Scott, *Piers Plowman: a facsimile of Bodleian Library, Oxford, MS Douce 104* (Cambridge, 1992).*

Philips, J.R.S., 'The Remonstrance revisited: England and Ireland in the early fourteenth century' in T.G. Fraser & Keith Jeffrey (eds), *Historical Studies*, 18: *Men, women and war* (Dublin, 1993), pp 13–27.

Pochin-Mould, Daphne, *The Irish Dominicans: the Friars Preachers in the history of Catholic Ireland* (Dublin, 1957).

Potterton, Michael, *Medieval Trim: history and archaeology* (Dublin, 2005).

Power, Gillian, *Anglo-Irish and Gaelic women in Ireland, c.1170–1540* (Dublin, 2007).

Prudlo, Donald, 'The cult of St Peter of Verona in the British Isles' in Rogers (ed.), *The friars in medieval Britain* (2010), pp 194–207.

Prudlo, Donald, *The martyred inquisitor: the life and cult of Peter of Verona (+1252)* (Aldershot, 2008).

Quigley, W.G.H., & E.F.D. Roberts (eds), *Registrum Johannis Mey: the register of John Mey, archbishop of Armagh, 1443–1456* (Belfast, 1972).*

Quinlan, Margaret, *Conservation plan: Athassel Augustinian priory, County Tipperary* (Dublin, *c.*2009).

Quinn, Patrick, 'The Third Order Regular of St Francis in Ireland', *Analecta Tertii Ordinis Regularis*, 26 (1993), 247–63.

Raban, Sandra, *Mortmain legislation and the English Church, 1279–1500* (Cambridge, 1982).

Rae, E.C., 'Architecture and sculpture, 1169–1603' in Art Cosgrove (ed.), *A new history of Ireland*, II: *Medieval Ireland, 1169–1534* (Oxford, 1987), pp 737–80.

Rano, Balbino, 'Agostiniani' in Giancarlo Rocca (ed.), *La sostanza dell'effimero*, pp 378–83.

Reeves, Majorie, *The influence of prophecy in the later Middle Ages: a study of Joachism* (Oxford, 1969).

Reichert, B.M. (ed.), 'Acta capitulorum ordinis Fratrum Praedicatorum', I, 1220–1303 (*MOPH*, 3); II, 1304–78 (*MOPH*, 4); III, 1380–1498 (*MOPH*, 8); 1503–53 (*MOPH*, 9) (Rome, 1898–1901).*

Reichert, B.M. (ed.), 'Acta capitulorum generalium ordinis fratrum praedicatorum, 1220–1844' (8 vols, Rome, 1898–1904).*

Rex, Richard, 'The friars in the English Reformation' in P. Marshall & A.G. Ryrie, *The beginnings of English Protestantism* (Cambridge, 2002), pp 38–59.

Rickert, Margaret, *The reconstructed Carmelite missal* (Chicago, 1952).

Ripoll, T., & A. Bremond (eds), *Bullarium ordinis fratrum Praedicatorum* (8 vols, Rome, 1729–40).*

Robson, Michael, OFM Conv., & Jens Röhrkasten, *Franciscan organisation in the mendicant context: formal and informal structures of the friars' lives and ministry in the Middle Ages* (Berlin, 2010).

Robson, Michael, OFM Conv., 'Benefactors of the Greyfriars in York: alms from testators, 1530–1538', *Northern History*, 38:2 (2001), 221–39.

Robson, Michael, OFM Conv., 'Franciscan bishops of Irish dioceses active in medieval England', *Collectanea Hibernica*, 38 (1997), 7–39.

Robson, Michael, OFM Conv., 'The Franciscan custody of York in the thirteenth century' in Rogers (ed.), *The friars in medieval Britain* (2010), pp 1–24.

Robson, Michael, OFM Conv., 'The Greyfriars itinerant ministry inside their *limitatio*: evidence from the custody of York', *Canterbury Studies in Franciscan History*, 1 (2008), 9–49.

Robson, Michael, OFM Conv., 'The Greyfriars of Lincoln, c.1230–1330: the establishment of the friary and the friars' ministry and life in the city and its environs' in Robson & Röhrkasten, *Franciscan organisation* (2010), pp 113–37.

Robson, Michael, OFM Conv., 'The ministry of preachers and confessors: the pastoral impact of the friars' in Evans (ed.), *A history of pastoral care* (2000), pp 126–47.

Robson, Michael, OFM Conv., *The Franciscans in the Middle Ages* (Woodbridge, 2006).

Rocha, Pedro, SJ, 'Liturgia della Cappella Papale, liturgia dei Frati Minori e liturgia dei Frati Predicatori' in Boyle et al. (eds), *Aux origines de la liturgie Dominicaine* (2004), pp 115–25.

Roest, Bert, 'Franciscan educational perspectives: reworking monastic traditions' in G. Ferzoco & Carolyn Muessig (eds), *Medieval monastic education* (Leicester, 2000), pp 168–81.

Roest, Bert, *Franciscan literature of religious instruction before the Council of Trent* (Leiden, 2004).

Roest, Bert, 'The discipline of the heart: pedagogies of prayer in medieval Franciscan works of religious instruction' in T.J. Johnson (ed.), *Franciscans at prayer* (Leiden, 2007), pp 413–48.

Roest, Bert, *A history of Franciscan education (c.1210–1517)* (Leiden, 2000).

Roest, Bert, *Reading the book of history* (Groningen, 1996).

Rogers, Juliet, & Tony Waldron, 'DISH and the monastic way of life', *International Journal of Osteoarchaeology*, 11:5 (published online 21 Sept. 2001), 357–65; accessed 18 Sept. 2010.

Rogers, Nicholas (ed.), *The friars in medieval Britain* (Donington, 2010).

Rogers, Patrick, 'The Irish Franciscan Observants and the royal supremacy', *Capuchin Annual* (1934), 203–14.

Röhrkasten, Jens, *The mendicant houses of medieval London, 1221–1539* (Münster, 2004).

Ronan, M.V., *The Reformation in Dublin, 1536–58* (London, 1926).

Ronan, M.V., 'The ancient Chapel Royal, Dublin Castle', *Irish Ecclesiastical Record*, 21 (1923), 353–71.

Ross, Anthony, OP, *The dogs of the Lord: the story of the Dominican order in Scotland* (Edinburgh, 1981).

Roth, Francis, 'A history of the English Austin Friars', *Augustiniana*, 11 (1961), 533–63.

Rubin, Miri, *Corpus Christi: the Eucharist in late medieval culture* (Cambridge, 1991).

Russell, George, & George Kane, *Piers Plowman: the C version* (Berkeley, CA, 1997).*

Ryan, Salvador, '"Reign of blood": aspects of devotion to the wounds of Christ in late medieval Gaelic Ireland' in Joost Augusteijn & Mary Ann Lyons (eds), *Irish history: a research yearbook* (Dublin, 2002), pp 137–49.

Ryan, Salvador, 'A wooden key to open Heaven's door: lessons in practical Catholicism from St Anthony's College, Louvain' in Bhreathnach et al., *The Irish Franciscans* (2009), pp 221–32.

Ryan, Salvador, 'Popular religion in Ireland, 1445–1645' (2 vols, PhD, NUIM, 2002).

Ryan, Salvador, 'Windows on late medieval devotional practice: Máire Ní Mháille's "Book of Piety" (1513) and the world behind the texts' in Moss et al. (eds), *Art and devotion* (2006), pp 1–15.

Sayles, G.O., *Documents on the affairs of Ireland before the King's Council* (Dublin, 1979).*

Sbaralea, Hyacynth, et al. (eds), *Bullarium Franciscanum Romanorum Pontificum constitutiones, epistolae, ac diplomata continens tribus ordinibus minorum clarissarum et poenitentium a seraphica sancto Francisco institutis concessa ab illorum exordio ad nostra usque tempora* (7 vols, 1759–1904).*

Schenkluhn, Wolfgang, *Architettura degli ordini mendicanti* (Padua, 2003).

Schlotheuber, Eva, 'Late medieval Franciscan statutes on convent libraries and education', *Canterbury Studies in Franciscan History*, 1 (2008), 153–84.

Schneyer, J.B., *Repertorium der lateinischen sermons des Mittelalters für die Zeit von 1150–1350* (9 vols, Münster, 1969–).

Scott, A.B., 'Latin learning and literature in Ireland, 1169–1500' in Dáibhí Ó Cróinín, *New history of Ireland*, I: *Prehistoric and early Ireland* (Oxford, 2005), pp 934–95.

Scott, K.L., 'The illustrations of Piers Plowman in Bodleian Library MS Douce 104' in J.A. Alford & M.T. Tavormina (eds), *The Yearbook of Langland Studies*, 4 (1990), pp 1–86.

Senocak, Neslihan, 'Book acquisition in the medieval Franciscan order', *Journal of Religious History*, 27 (2003), 14–28.

Senocak, Neslihan, 'Circulation of books in the medieval Franciscan order: attitude, methods and critics', *Journal of Religious History*, 28 (2004), 146–61.

Seton, W.W. (ed.), *Two fifteenth-century Franciscan rules* (London, 1914).*

Sever, John, *The English Franciscans under Henry III* (Oxford, 1915).

Sharpe, Richard, *A handlist of the Latin writers of Great Britain and Ireland before 1540* (Turnhout, 1997).

Sharpe, Richard, *Medieval Irish saints' lives: an introduction to Vitae sanctorum Hiberniae* (Oxford, 1991).

Shee Twohig, Elizabeth, 'Excavations at St Saviour's Dominican priory, Limerick, pt I', *North Munster Antiquarian Journal*, 36 (1995), 104–29.

Shee Twohig, Elizabeth, 'Excavations at St Saviour's Dominican priory, Limerick, pt II', *North Munster Antiquarian Journal*, 37 (1996), 68–87.

Sheehy, M.P. (ed.), *Pontificia Hibernia: medieval papal chancery records relating to Ireland, 640–1261* (2 vols, Dublin, 1962–5).*

Silke, J.J., 'The Irish abroad, 1534–1691' in T.W. Moody, F.X. Martin & F.J. Byrne (eds), *A new History of Ireland*, iii (Oxford, 1976), pp 587–633.

Simms, Katharine, 'Frontiers in the Irish church: regional and cultural' in Barry et al. (eds), *Colony and frontier* (1995), pp 176–200.

Simms, Katherine, *Medieval Gaelic sources* (Dublin, 2009).

Smalley, Beryl, *English friars and antiquity in the early fourteenth century* (Oxford, 1960).

Smet, Joachim, OCarm., 'Pre-Tridentine reform in the Carmelite order' in Elm (ed.), *Reformbemühungen* (1989), pp 293–323.

Smet, Joachim, OCarm., *The Carmelites: a history of the brothers of Our Lady of Mount Carmel*, 1 (Barrington, IL, & Rome, 1975).

Smith, Aquila (ed.), 'Annales de Monte Fernandi', *Tracts relating to Ireland*, ii (Dublin, 1842), 1–26.*

Smith, Brendan (ed.), *The register of Milo Sweetman, archbishop of Armagh, 1361–1380* (Dublin, 1996).*

Smith, Brendan (ed.), *The register of Nicholas Fleming, archbishop of Armagh, 1404–1416* (Dublin, 2003).*

Smith, Brendan, 'Fitzgerald, Maurice (c.1194–1257)', *ODNB*, 19 (Oxford, 2004), pp 832–3.

Smith, Brendan, *Colonisation and conquest in medieval Ireland: the English in Louth, 1170–1330* (Cambridge, 1999, [pbk 2007]).

Smyly, J.G. (ed.), 'Old deeds in the library of Trinity College, 1246–1538', *Hermathena*, 67 (1946), 1–30; 69 (1947), 31–48; 71 (1948), 36–51.*

Somers, M.H., 'Irish scholars at the universities of Paris and Oxford before 1500' (PhD, City University of New York, 1979).

Stalley, Roger, 'The abbey in its later Gothic context' in Conleth Manning et al. (eds), *New survey of Clare Island, volume 4: the Abbey* (Dublin, 2005), pp 135–49.

Stalley, Roger, 'The archbishop's residence at Swords: castle or country retreat?' in Seán Duffy (ed.), *Medieval Dublin VII* (Dublin, 2006), pp 152–76.

Stalley, Roger (ed.), *Limerick and the south-west of Ireland: medieval art and architecture* (Leeds, 2011).

Stalley, Roger, 'Architecture and patronage in fifteenth-century Adare', *Irish Arts Review*, 20:4 (2003), 110–15.

Stalley, Roger, 'Gaelic friars and Gothic design' in E. Fernie & P. Crossley (eds), *Medieval architecture and its intellectual context* (London, 1990), pp 191–202.

Stalley, Roger, 'Irish Gothic and English fashion' in J.F. Lydon (ed.), *The English in medieval Ireland* (Dublin, 1984), pp 65–86.

Stalley, Roger, 'The end of the Middle Ages: Gothic survival in sixteenth-century Connacht', *JRSAI*, 133 (2003), 5–23.

Stalley, Roger, *The Cistercian monasteries of Ireland* (New Haven, CT, 1987).

Staring, Adrian, OCarm., 'Four bulls of Innocent IV: a critical edition', *Carmelus*, 27 (1980), 273–85.*

Staring, Adrian, OCarm., 'The letter of Pierre de Millau to King Edward I of England, 1282' in idem, *Medieval Carmelite heritage* (1989), pp 44–8.*

Staring, Adrian, OCarm., *Medieval Carmelite heritage* (Rome, 1989).*

'State of Ireland and plan for its Reformation' in *State papers for the reign of Henry VIII* (11 vols, London, 1830–52), iii, p. 15.*

Staunton, Michael, & Colmán Ó Clabaigh OSB, 'Thomas Becket and Ireland' in Elizabeth Mullins & Diarmuid Scully (eds), *'Listen, O Isles, unto me': studies in medieval word and image in honour of Jennifer O'Reilly* (Cork, 2011), pp 87–101; 340–3; 464–6.

Stemmler, T. (ed.), *The Latin hymns of Richard Ledrede* (Mannheim, 1975).*

Stevens, John, *Monasticon Hibernicum; or, The monastical history of Ireland* (London, 1722).*

Stewart, R.M., *'De illis qui faciunt penitentiam': the rule of the secular Franciscan order: origins, development, interpretation* (Rome, 1991).

Stöber, Karen, *Late medieval monasteries and their patrons: England and Wales, c.1300–1540* (Woodbridge, 2007).

Stokes, W., 'The Gaelic Maundeville', *Zeitschrift für celtische Philologie*, 2 (1898–9), 1–63, 226–312.*

Stone, M.W.F., 'Punch's riposte: the Irish contribution to early modern Scotism from Maurice O'Fihely OFM Conv. to Anthony Rourke OFM Obs.' in McEvoy & Dunne (eds), *The Irish contribution* (2009), pp 137–91.

Stone, M.W.F., 'The theological and philosophical accomplishments of the Irish Franciscans' in Bhreathnach et al. (eds), *The Irish Franciscans* (2009), pp 201–20.

Strauch, C.A., 'Royal connections: the Scottish Observants and the house of Stewart', *Innes Review*, 58 (2007), 156–72.

Sughi, M.A. (ed.), *Registrum Octaviani* (2 vols, Dublin, 1999).*

Sundt, R.A., 'Mediocres domos et humiles habeant fratres nostri: Dominican legislation on architecture and architectural decoration in the 13th century', *Journal of the Society of Architectural Historians*, 46:4 (1987), 394–407.

Swanson, R.N., 'Letters of confraternity and indulgence in late medieval England', *Archives*, 25 (2000), 40–57.

Swanson, R.N., 'Mendicants and confraternity in late medieval England' in J.G. Clark (ed.), *The religious orders in pre-Reformation England* (Woodbridge, 2002), pp 121–41.

Swanson, R.N., 'The mendicant problem in the later Middle Ages' in Peter Biller & Barrie Dobson (eds), *The medieval church: universities, heresy and the religious life* (Woodbridge, 1999), pp 217–38.

Swanson, R.N., *Indulgences in late medieval England: passports to paradise?* (Cambridge, 2007).

Sweetman, H.S., *Calendar of documents relating to Ireland, 1171–1251* [etc.] (5 vols, London, 1875–86).*

Szittya, Penn R. *The anti-fraternal tradition in medieval literature* (Princeton, NJ, 1986).

Taheny, Luke, *The Dominicans of Roscommon* (Dublin, 1990).

Tait, Clodagh, 'Art and the cult of the Virgin Mary in Ireland, c.1500–1660' in Moss et al. (eds), *Art and devotion* (2006), pp 163–83.

Tait, Clodagh, *Death, burial and commemoration in Ireland, 1550–1650* (Basingstoke, 2002).

Tanner, N.P. (ed.), *Decrees of the ecumenical councils* (2 vols, London, 1990).*

Tanner, N.P., 'The Middle Ages: pastoral care – the Fourth Lateran Council of 1215' in Evans (ed.), *A history of pastoral care* (2000), pp 112–25.

Taylor, Larissa, *Soldiers of Christ* (Oxford, 1992).

Tempest, H.G., 'Tiles from the old Dominican friary, Drogheda', *CLAHJ*, 12:2 (1950), 182–3.

Tentler, Thomas, *Sin and confession on the eve of the Reformation* (Princeton, NJ, 1977).

Theiner, Augustin, *Vetera monumenta hibernorum et scotorum historiam illustrantia* (Rome, 1864).*

Thompson, Augustine, *Revival preachers and politics in thirteenth-century Italy; the great devotion of 1233* (Oxford, 1992).

Thomson, W.R., 'The image of the mendicants in the chronicles of Matthew Paris', *AFH*, 70 (1977), 3–34.

Thomson, W.R., *Friars in the cathedral: the first Franciscan bishops, 1226–1271* (Toronto, 1975).

Threfall-Holmes, Miranda, *Monks and markets: Durham cathedral priory, 1460–1520* (Oxford, 2005).

Tipton, C.L., 'The Irish Hospitallers during the Great Schism', *PRIA*, 69 (1970), 33–43.

Todd, J.H. (ed.), 'Obits of Kilcormick', *Miscellany of the Irish Archaeological Society*, 1 (Dublin, 1846), 99–106.*

Tresham, Edward (ed.), *Rotulorum patentium et clausorum cancellariae Hiberniae calendarium, 1, pars 1: Hen. II–Hen. VII* (Dublin, 1828).*

Tugwell, Simon, *Early Dominicans: selected writings* (Mahwah, NJ, 1982).*

Van Dijk, S.J.P., & J. Hazelden Walker, *The origins of the modern Roman liturgy* (London, 1960).

Van Luijk, B. (ed.), *Bullarium Ordinis Eremitarum S. Augustini periodis formationis, 1187–1256* (Würzburg, 1964).*

Vauchez, André (ed.), *Mouvements franciscains de société française, XII–XX siècle* (Paris, 1984).

Vauchez, André, 'Gli Ordini mendicanti e la reconquista religiosa della società cittadina' in idem, *Francesco d'Assisi e gli Ordini mendicanti* (Assisi, 2005), pp 99–133.

Vauchez, André, 'La papauté du XIIIe siècle et les ordres mendiants' in Vauchez, *Francesco d'Assisi e gli Ordini mendicanti* (2005), pp 181–8.

Vauchez, André, & Cécile Caby, *L'histoire des moines, chanoines et religieux au moyen âge* (Turnhout, 2003).

Vauchez, André, *Francesco d'Assisi e gli Ordini mendicanti* (Assisi, 2005).

Vauchez, André, *Ordini mendicanti societa italiana, xiii–xv secolo* (Milan, 1990).

Vauchez, André, *Sainthood in the later Middle Ages* (Cambridge, 2005).

Venn, J., & J.A. Venn, *Alumni Cantabrigiensis*, 1 (Cambridge, 1922).

Verheijen, Luc (ed.), *La règle de saint Augustin* (Paris, 1961).*

Viallet, Ludovic, 'Le rôle du gardien dans les couvents franciscains au XVe siècle' in Michael Robson & Jens Röhrkasten (eds), *Franciscan organisation in the mendicant context* (Berlin, 2010), pp 225–51.

Volti, Panayota, *Couvents des ordres mendiants et leur environnement à la fin du moyen âge* (Paris, 2003).

Wadding, Luke, OFM (ed.), *Promptuarium morale Sacrae Scripturae in tres partes distributum* (Rome, 1624).*

Wadding, Luke, OFM, et al., *Annales Ordinis Minorum* (32 vols, 1931–64).*

Wagner, Elamar, OFM, *Historia constitutionum generalium Ordinis Fratrum Minorum* (Rome, 1954).

Wallace, P.F., & Raghnall Ó Floinn, *Treasures of the National Museum of Ireland* (Dublin, 2002).

Walsh, D., 'The Dominicans in Arklow (1264–1793)', *Reportorium Novum*, 3:2 (1963–4), 307–23.

Walsh, Katherine, 'Richard FitzRalph of Armagh (d. 1360): professor-prelate-saint', *CLAHJ*, 22:2 (1990), 111–24.

Walsh, Katherine, 'Crumpe, Henry', *ODNB*, 14 (Oxford, 2004).

Walsh, Katherine, 'Fitzralph, Richard', *ODNB*, 19 (Oxford, 2004).

Walsh, Katherine, 'Ireland, the papal curia and the schism: a border case' in Jean Favier et al. (eds), *Genèse et débuts du Grand Schisme d'Occident* (Paris, 1980), pp 561–74.

Walsh, Katherine, 'Norris, Philip', *ODNB*, 41 (Oxford, 2004).

Walsh, Katherine, 'The Observance: sources for a history of the Observant reform movement in the order of Augustinian friars in the fourteenth and fifteenth century', *Revista di storia della Chiesa in Italia*, 31 (1977), 40–67.

Walsh, Katherine, 'Wyclif's legacy in Central Europe in the late fourteenth and early fifteenth century' in Anne Hudson & Michael Wilks (eds), *Studies in Church History, Subsidia 5: From Ockham to Wyclif* (Oxford, 1987), pp 397–417.

Walsh, Katherine, *A fourteenth-century scholar and primate: Richard Fitzralph in Oxford, Avignon and Armagh* (Oxford, 1981).

Walsh, Katherine, 'Franciscan friaries in pre-Reformation Kerry', *Journal of the Kerry Archaeological and Historical Society*, 9 (1976), 18–31.

Walsh, Paul (ed.), *Leabhar Chlainne Suibhne* (Dublin, 1920).*

Walsh, Paul, 'The foundation of the Augustinian friary at Galway: a review of the sources', *JGAHS*, 40 (1985–6), 72–80.

Walton, J.C., 'A list of the early burials in the French Church, Waterford', *JRSAI*, 103 (1973), 70–7.*

Wansbrough, Henry, OSB, & Anthony Maret-Crosby OSB (eds), *The Benedictines in Oxford* (London, 1997).

Ware, James (ed.), *Campion's historie of Ireland* (Dublin, 1633).*

Ware, James, *Archiespiscoporum Casseliensium et Tuamensium vitae duobus expressae …* (Dublin, 1628).*

Ware, James, *De Hibernia et antiquitatibus ejus disquisitiones* (London, 1654).*

Watt, John, *A tender watering: Franciscans in Scotland from the 13th to the 21st century* (Canterbury, 2011).

Watt, J.A., 'Negotiations between Edward II and John XXII concerning Ireland', *IHS*, 10 (1956), 1–20.*

Watt, J.A., 'The church and the two nations in late medieval Armagh' in W.J. Shiels & D. Wood (eds), *Studies in Church History*, 25: *The churches, Ireland and the Irish* (Oxford, 1989), pp 37–54.

Watt, J.A., *The church and the two nations in medieval Ireland* (Cambridge, 1970).

Watt, J.A., *The church in medieval Ireland* (Dublin, 1998).

Welter, J.T., *L'Exemplum dans la littérature religieuse et didactique du moyen âge* (Paris, 1927).

Went, A.E.J., 'Irish monastic fisheries', *JCHAS*, 60 (1955), 47–56.

Wessels, Gabriel, OCarm. (ed.), *Acta capitulorum generalium ordinis Fratrum B.V. Mariae de Monte Carmelo*, vol. 1 (Rome, 1912).*

Westropp, T.J., 'Bells of Askeaton Franciscan friary, Co. Limerick', *JRSAI*, 44 (1914), 166.

Westropp, T.J., 'Notes on Askeaton, County Limerick, part III: the abbey', *JRSAI*, 13 (1903), 239–54.

Westropp, T.J., 'Paintings at Adare "Abbey", Co. Limerick', *JRSAI*, 45 (1916), 151–2.

White, Allan, 'Dominicans and the Scottish university tradition', *New Blackfriars*, 82:968 (October, 2001), 434–49.

White, N.B. (ed.), *Registrum Diocesis Dublinensis: a sixteenth-century precedent book* (Dublin, 1959).*

White, N.B., *Extents of Irish monastic possessions, 1540–1541* (Dublin, 1943).*

White, N.B., *Irish monastic and episcopal deeds, AD1200–1600* (Dublin, 1936).*

Whitehead, Christiana, 'Making a cloister of the soul in medieval religious treatises', *Medium Ævum*, 67:1 (1998), 1–29.

Whitfield, D.W., 'The Third Order of St Francis in medieval England', *Franciscan Studies*, 13 (1953), 50–9.

Wilkins, David, *Concilia Magnae Britaniae et Hiberniae* (London, 1737).*

William of Saint-Amour, *De periculis novissimorum temporum*, ed. G. Geltner, Dallas Medieval Texts and Translations, 8 (Louvain & Paris, 2007).*

Williams, Arnold, 'The "limitour" of Chaucer's time and his "limitacioun"', *Studies in Philology*, 58 (1960), 463–78.

Williams, Bernadette (ed.), *The Annals of Ireland by Friar John Clyn* (Dublin, 2007).*

Williams, Bernadette, 'The "Kilkenny Chronicle"' in Barry et al. (eds), *Colony and frontier* (1995), pp 75–95.

Williams, Bernadette, 'The Dominican annals of Dublin' in Seán Duffy (ed.), *Medieval Dublin II* (Dublin, 2001), pp 142–68.

Wolf, S.P., 'Dominikanische Observanzbestrebungen: Die Congregation Hollandiae (1464–1517)' in Elm (ed.), *Reformbemühungen* (1989), pp 273–92.

Wright, Thomas (ed.), *A contemporary narrative of the proceedings against Dame Alice Kytler* (London, 1843).*

Ximenez, J.A., *Bullarium Carmelitanum* (2 vols, Rome, 1768).*

Ypma, Eelcko, OESA, *La formations des professeurs chez les ermites de Saint-Augustin de 1256 a 1354* (Paris, 1956).

# Index

Butler, James, third earl of Ormond, 90
Butler, James, fourth earl of Ormond, 81, 94
Butler, Piers, earl of Ossory, 105
Butler, Richard, 79
Butler, Sir James MacRichard, 105
Butler, Sir James, 275
Butler, Stephen, 19
Butler, Thomas Theobald FitzWalter, 10
butter, 129–3
Buttevant, Co. Cork, Franciscan friary, 14,
    38–9, 205, 215, 248, 275
Buttiler, William, 249, 253
Bymacan, Isle of Man, Franciscan friary, 44, 66

Caddell, John, 304
Caernarfon, Wales, 36
Cairo, Egypt, 196–8
*Caithreim Thoirdhealbhaigh*, 246
*Calender of papal registers relating to Great
    Britain and Ireland*, xxi
Callan, Co. Kilkenny, Augustinian priory,
    74–6, 79, 105, 207, 209, 228, 233,
    242, 283
Calle, Friar Thomas de, OP, 104–5
Callixtus III, pope, 159, 166
Caltra, Co. Galway, Carmelite priory, 18
Calvinists, 319
Cambridge, England, 25, 51, 272, 274, 278,
    280, 321, 324
Campion, Edmund, 329
candles/candlesticks, 11, 101, 110, 150, 151
Caneton, Friar Gerald, OESA, 47
Canice, St, 59
canon law/canon law texts, xiv, 105, 142,
    163, 273, 282, 288, 295–8
canonical portion, 150, 152
canonization, 179
canopied tombs, 189, 234, 249, 250, 252
Canterbury, 2, 13, 194, 196–8, 249;
    archbishop of, 150, 157, 158; convo-
    cation of, 159; Franciscan friary, 88
*Canterbury Tales, The*, 16
cantors, 241, 255
Cantwell, Archbishop John, OP, 303
Cantwell, Dean John, 71
Cantwell, Oliver, 101

Capistran, St John, OFM, 307
Capuchin friars, OFM Cap., xxiv, 54, 121,
    319, 329
Carew family, 17
Carew, Friar William, OCarm., 82, 83
Carletti, Friar Angelus of Chiavasso, OFM,
    297, 315, 319
Carletti, Friar Angelus, OFM, *Summa
    angelica*, 297
Carlingford, Co. Louth, Dominican priory,
    43, 204, 232, 328
Carlow, 287
Carmarthen, Wales, 109
Carmelite friars, Whitefriars/Order of Friars of
    Our Lady of Mount Carmel (OCarm.),
    xvi, xx, xxv, 1–2, 6–7, 15–18, 21, 23,
    28, 29, 35–6, 42, 44, 54, 77, 80–3, 86,
    88–90, 92, 94, 103, 109, 113, 121,
    125, 127, 130, 135, 142, 152, 156,
    166, 174–5, 177–8, 199, 203, 212–13,
    218, 227, 231, 237, 239, 243, 246,
    265, 270–1, 276–7, 283, 285, 299,
    303–5, 318, 321; constitutional
    arrangements, 28–9; Hiberno-Scottish
    province, 28, 35; liturgy, 174–5; nuns,
    81; Third Order, 81
Carpenter, Bishop John, 56
Carraciolo, Friar Robert, OFM, 289
Carrewe, Friar David, OFM, 71
Carrickbeg (Carrickmagriffin), Co. Waterford,
    Franciscan friary, 14, 90, 205
Carrickfergus, Co. Antrim, Franciscan friary,
    12, 35, 64, 69, 92, 94
Carrigan, Canon William, 79
Carrigtohill, Co. Cork, 286
Carthusian monks, 192, 303
Cartlidge, Neil, 149
Cashel, Co. Tipperary, 71, 199, 216, 233,
    238, 303; archbishop of, 12, 20, 36, 39,
    51, 84, 106, 150, 157, 167, 264;
    archdiocese of, 18; cathedral, 216;
    Dominican priory, 9, 24, 134, 216,
    233, 239, 303; Franciscan friary, 12–13,
    26n, 39, 51, 91, 134, 199, 200, 208;
    school of masons, 216; Cashel, synod of
    (1453), 137, 313